New Testament

with

Psalms and Proverbs

New King James Version

Thomas Nelson Publishers
Nashville • Atlanta • London • Vancouver

⚔ Table of Contents

⚔ The New Testament with Psalms and Proverbs

People Sharing Jesus is a person-centered approach for sharing Christ with individuals at the point of their particular need. It emphasizes sensitive, interactive witnessing and encourages the use of both intentional and relational principles in reaching the lost for Christ. *People Sharing Jesus* is a personal witnessing implementation plan of the Total Church Life evangelism strategy. The *People Sharing Jesus* book and other learning helps for sharing Christ were published in conjunction with the *People Sharing Jesus* New Testament by Thomas Nelson Publishers in 1995. This New Testament contains a summary of the principles of sharing that are fully presented in the book.

The *People Sharing Jesus* New Testament is designed to assist Believers in spiritual growth, in experiencing the indwelling power of the Holy Spirit and in sharing Christ with lost people. It can help any Christian live the life of intimate fellowship with the Savior and share His life and love with others. Sharing Christ is both the natural expression and the obedient lifestyle of a true Believer. It is the *outflow* of the *overflow* of the *inflow* of the Christ-filled life.

Sharing Jesus is the natural expression of a Christian's life. When we experience the reality of "Christ in you, the hope of glory" (Col. 1:27b), we identify with Peter and John when they answered their critics. Those who crucified Jesus commanded them not to speak or teach again in His name. Their honest and open reply was, "Whether it is right in the sight of God to listen to you more than to God, you judge. For we cannot but speak the things which we have seen and heard" (Acts 4:19,20).

Sharing Jesus is also the obedient lifestyle of the Christian. Every Christian is on assignment for Jesus to share Him with others (Acts 1:8). When we live in obedient fellowship with Him, we will consistently witness for Him. We will discipline ourselves to do it. Our human tendency is to drift away from the Christ-centered, Christ-filled life and from sharing His gospel with others. Thus, the discipline of our spiritual lives is essential for continued spiritual victory and effective witnessing.

Motivation for disciplining our lives to intentionally share the gospel and to seek to establish witnessing relationships is twofold: First, we love Jesus and want to exalt Him so everyone may glorify Him. Second, we love people and want every person to experience forgiveness of sin, eternal life and abundant life through our Lord.

The *People Sharing Jesus* New Testament will be a real asset to you, to your church, to the work of the kingdom of God and to lost people. It will help you develop a meaningful and consistent witnessing pattern in your life. When you and other Christians consistently share Christ in your daily life and contacts, it will have four positive results.

1. *It will change your life as a Christian.* Because you are involved in a supernatural work, you cannot depend on your own power. The Holy Spirit will perform it. Consistently sharing Christ will drive you to Bible study and cause you to pray much. It will confront you with your own inconsistencies and sinful habits. You will be concerned about anything in your life that will be a barrier to your effectiveness in sharing your Savior with the lost and will want to change those things. You will continue to grow in Christ and, as you do, you will never be the same again.

2. *It will charge your church with mighty power.* Witnessing is not only the individual assignment of every Christian, it is also the corporate expression of the body of Christ. Teamship is a key New Testament principle for effective witnessing. As you and other members consistently share Jesus, the fire of spiritual revival and awakening will be ignited in your

church. As new Believers are added they will increase the spiritual life and vitality of the church and it will grow in maturity and in number.

3. *It will climatize your community for evangelism.* As Believers consistently share Christ, it will create a God-consciousness and a climate for evangelism in your area. People will become aware of the church and become open to the gospel. Through saturating your area with the seed of the gospel, it will be prepared for a bountiful harvest of people coming to Christ.

4. *It will convert the lost to Christ.* Through the personal witness of Believers, lost people will be reached for Christ daily in the marketplace, through casual contacts and through the organized outreach visitation of the church.

This New Testament will help equip you to be a successful witness. Successful witnessing is sharing Christ in the power of the Holy Spirit and leaving the results to God. You will be liberated from the pressure of feeling responsible for the outcome because that is the role of the Holy Spirit. Our role is to faithfully and intentionally share Christ. His role is to produce the results.

According to Acts 4:31, God brings people to Himself in three ways. He uses His Word, the work of His Spirit and the witness of the Believer. You are on His unbeatable team of three. What confidence for sharing Jesus this gives to Believers. You can simply share the Word of God with lost people and the Holy Spirit will use the Word of God as His instrument to enlighten, convict, and draw them to Christ. As a witnessing Believer, you will need to know how to guide the lost person through the conversion experience as the Holy Spirit gives you opportunity. This New Testament can help you at that point if you will refer to the *Seven Steps for Leading a Person to Christ.*

The greatest barriers to witnessing are not "out there" in the lives of lost people. Their attitude is not the problem. It is "in here" in our own lives. The greatest prob-lems are our own attitudes. The writer of Proverbs 23:7 says, "As [a man] thinks in his heart, so is he." This New Testament will help you overcome fear and intimidation through focusing on Jesus and the power, promises and confidence He gives for witness. It will help you understand the condition of the lost and realize how to break down barriers and share Jesus with them. It will help you develop a sensitivity to lost people so you will recognize the "divine appointments" God gives you to witness.

To be effective in any pursuit requires that a person be equipped with the right resources and tools. A carpenter has a tool kit. A lawyer has law books. The effective witness for Christ, also, must be equipped with resources, tools and techniques. Included in the *People Sharing Jesus* New Testament are the following resources, tools and techniques:

• *Thirty-one Daily Devotionals* designed to help develop a mind-set for sharing Christ, a sensitivity to lost people and a deeper love for the Savior.

• A *summary of the witnessing principles* from the *People Sharing Jesus* book that will help in relating to lost people and sharing Christ with them in a non-threatening way.

• *Sharing the Word in Witness* which gives several techniques of presenting the gospel to a lost person. Included are:

How to Share the Roman Road

How to Use the Lifeline Illustration

How to Use John 3

How to Share the Message of the Cross

• *Practical Help for Hurting People* designed to give guidance in overcoming ten of the leading problem areas in the lives of people through applying Bibilcal principles.

He will reach others through you as you make the definite and deliberate commitment to Christ to be available to Him. God will use the uniqueness of your personality and giftedness in leading people to know and follow Christ as you study the Word, understand lost people, and be-

Introduction

come proficient in using various approaches to sharing Jesus. May God give you maximum effectiveness as one of His people sharing Jesus. May God help us all to "become all things to all men, that [we] might by all means save some" (1 Cor. 9:22).

With appreciation and prayers,
Darrell W. Robinson

The Great Question

There is but one singly important question for all who would follow Me. If you would live each day getting ready for eternity you must know this question and learn the answer, "Why do you call Me Lord and do not the things I say?" Could it be that whirl is too much king in your life? Could it be that you have sped ahead of Grace? Beware hurried one. Like Martha you may be troubled about "many things," and there are not many things that should require your attention. I sense that your busy discipleship is still flawed by seeking answers to unimportant questions. You rarely walk with Me, because you walk too fast. This hurried agenda runs past all those I once stopped for. Read of Me in the Gospels. See how I was moved with compassion on those who hurt. The lepers, the bereaved, the diseased, the demoniacs: they were all around Me. I deliberately walked through life slowly so I could see them all. They are all around you now. Slow down and you too will see them. You will see they have no purpose. They live that way. They die that way.

I require this very simple thing of you: Look around you! You are so often like an irresponsible physician, who walks through a battlefield with medicine and never sees the dying. You are too casual among the intense. You are too prone to celebrate your blessings among the needy. You rest in your own security to the point that you cannot see that the prince of fear has made the world afraid. Please look and you will see that I love all of those you hurry past. They live lives of quiet desperation. They are on the broad road that leads at last to destruction.

It is immoral to discover fire in a crowded theater and not cry "fire!" To use the EXIT merely to save yourself is a safe way to live, but it is also a little way to live. Speak up then! Tell the dying what you know, that they, like you, may live. If you do not, most of them will die never suspecting they were passionately loved. And why? Because your hurried passion was spent on little things. Because you never learned the answer to this one important question: "Why do you call Me Lord and do not the things that I say?"

And behold, a certain lawyer stood up and tested Him, saying, "Teacher, what shall I do to inherit eternal life?" He said to him, "What is written in the law? What is your reading of it?" So he answered and said, "You shall love the LORD your God with all your heart, with all your soul, with all your strength, and with all your mind . . ." (Luke 10:25–27)

"Why do you call me, 'Lord, Lord,' and do not do the things which I say?"
(Luke 6:46)

Lord,
I cannot call You Lord with a capital "L"
While I remain sovereign over all my petty
involvements.
Help me to vacate the throne of my life and
offer You
that empty chair.
"Lord" is but a little word to say,
And yet it holds the very world in sway.
Amen

If I Be Lifted Up

Pride is the vehicle that ego drives into eternity. Pride is the spoiling of My Father's dream for every person. Israel in flight from Egypt became proud and self-willed. She sinned against God and would not celebrate His glorious salvation. Judgment came. Israel awoke to find poisonous snakes within their tents. There were cobras in the camp. Moses made a serpent and put it on the pole. Those marked by the venom of their pride were given a very simple prescription. They had but to look to live. Some remained too proud to do things God's way and died. But most found their desperation sweet. They looked. They lived. God so loved His world as to make salvation easy. Still, it always requires a stepping over pride.

Do you remember when first we met? You discovered that I had dealt with your sins long ago. It was gloriously easy for you to lay them at the high altar of My complete forgiveness. Calvary sufficed. It was My wonderful gift to you. In the cross, My Father, once again, simplified salvation for all of humankind. The brass serpent did not save Israel by some dire, threatening commandment. There was an early antidote. The bitten had but to look to live.

And so it was when you were rescued. I did the hard work of redemption, the bleeding and the dying. You had only to believe. I struggled to breathe, strangling in My pain; you had only to take a short walk to confession, joy, and complete forgiveness. I grieved in nakedness above the men who diced and My own broken-hearted mother. Beyond the nails, the spear, the water and the blood, I died near sundown. Still I redeemed you with no remembrance of the cost. Nothing was laid to your account. After all, what good giver gives a gift and leaves the price tag on it? I have never reminded you of what I paid. I only glory that the price was adequate to purchase you forever. You are My glorious treasure, purchased one awful Friday in April. Your gift was free—not cheap. All gifts are free to those who receive them. But they are always purchased at great expense by the giver.

It is your indestructible, imperishable inheritance that My Father wants to give to the whole world at once. Like you once were, most now are. Those who are dying do not suspect the gift that they might own if only they would look and live. Would you tell them how to own that great wealth that ended your spiritual poverty? Would you tell them there is a serpent on a pole? Would you tell them how you met Me? Tell them how My lavish expense purchased their souls? Please tell them that their only hope lies in those three little words of grace—LOOK AND LIVE!

"And as Moses lifted up the serpent in the wilderness, even so must the Son of Man be lifted up, that whoever believes in Him should not perish but have eternal life." (John 3:14,15)

"And I, if I am lifted up from the earth, will draw all peoples to Myself."
(John 12:32)

Lord,
I remember how I looked upon
Your cross and then found life. Help me
to tell all that they have but
to look upon Your sacrifice and believe.
By such a simple act they reach
out and receive the glory of eternity as
the prize of Calvary.
Help me to warn the lost, "beware your
pride.
The humble look and live, the haughty die."
Amen

Follow Me . . . And Fish

I have called you into life and you are My disciples. Many of My first disciples were fishers. These men made their living by setting out to sea in boats and casting their nets into the dark mysterious waters of Galilee. Sometimes they caught fish. Sometimes they didn't. Sometimes they felt productive and sometimes they didn't. Before they met Me, their whole life was wrapped up in fishing. Whether or not they felt good about their occupations had to do with what came up in their nets. They counted what they caught and the count either denied them good feelings or rewarded them with real occupational pride. Like most working men their feelings of self-worth were pretty much tied to their jobs.

Then I came!

"Come, follow Me," I said, "and I will make you fishers of men." At once they left their nets and followed. They understood that I was not merely inviting them to church. I was inviting them to change their life-styles. I was calling them to be as intensely concerned about catching men for God as they had been about catching fish for a career. They understood what I was saying. They had never been casual about their fishing. They often worked all night, counted their catch, and sold what they had taken to provide for themselves and their families. But they didn't always catch fish. There were many empty periods in their lives. Sometimes they toiled all night and caught nothing. When their nets were empty, they were stalked by a horrible dread. They knew until they found more fish, their empty nets always threatened them with poverty.

These disciples went fishing for the last time in John 21. In fact, the fourth Gospel ends with My meeting them for an early morning fish fry. I found my final meeting with My disciples, after their last fishing trip, somewhat amusing. There they were still counting their catch, just like always. On that final morning, they had caught 153 fish (John 21:11). I understood this universal need to measure all that is produced. Which fishers do not brag about their catch? Long before I had told them that if they were going to follow Me, they must fish (Matthew 4:19). This is My word to you as well. If you do not fish, you are not following. But what of those days when your nets are empty? My Father will never be abusive with His children, but neither is He casual concerning the nets. He does not demand that you always come up with something to be counted. But He has commanded you to fish. He knows that there are days when all your nets will come up empty. But you must beware lest you grow contented with always having empty nets. To cease to grieve the emptiness of the nets is to forget your calling. Such contentment means that you have counted My commandment as nothing. To forsake fishing is to admit you have ceased to care about My dearest passion. To follow is to fish.

And He said to them, "Follow Me, and I will make you fishers of men." Then they immediately left their nets and followed Him. (Matthew 4:19,20)

Lord,
Help me to know the utter thrill
of catching people. To cast my net into the
social sea and draw in human beings must
be the highest glory earth can offer.
I turn my back on my own Galilee
to fish for God and thus to follow Thee.
Amen

♥

The Treasure

I know you are rejoicing that I have come into your life. But let Me ask you, have you numbered your assets? Have you totaled up your riches? I want you to see Me as a treasure hidden in a field. I once told My disciples about a man who was working in someone else's field. It might have come about as he was plowing in the field, that his plowshare suddenly struck a buried box. There the dark and rotted exterior was unearthed in open sunlight. The farmer, stopped by the unusual occurrence, pried the cask open. Its contents glittered gold in the Palestine sun.

The man's good fortune paralyzed him with doubt, but he did a wise thing. He closed the cask and quickly buried the box again. He marked the place where this rich treasure lay. He hurried into town, totaled up all he owned, and sold every asset. Then, still celebrating his good fortune, he took his total life savings—all his worth—and bought the field. Then he returned to the field and claimed the treasure that was his.

His good fortune reminds us of the jeweler who, in the process of buying and selling gems, came across a pearl of rare size and beauty. He too sold every other jewel he owned and with the proceeds he bought this splendid pearl of great worth. The people of your day are intrigued by stories of those who win lotteries, or come at once to immense wealth. These fortunate people are made the celebrated heroes of society.

But never envy them. Such fortune—indeed a greater fortune—has also come to you. You, who live on somewhat smaller means, are now enfranchised with heaven itself. I am the treasure hidden in the field. You discovered Me, claimed Me, and in owning Me, you have become a child of the King. Wisely you confessed to all men that you had come to Me and found heaven. You saw the treasure, and bought the field.

Now, I want you to look around at the poor people who hoard their worthless values. See those whose values are eroded. Their earthly possessions may make them look rich. But in your heart you know that they are desperately in need. Death will be, for them, the grand disinheritance. For in any moment they might die and then they would have to enter eternity owning nothing of real value. Think about your joy. Share your story. Help them to their field of dreams, that weedy earth that holds their treasure. Help them to sell all they have that they might own Me, the only true treasure.

"Again, the kingdom of heaven is like treasure hidden in a field, which a man found and hid; and for joy over it he goes and sells all that he has and buys that field. Again, the kingdom of heaven is like a merchant seeking beautiful pearls, who, when he had found one pearl of great price, went and sold all that he had and bought it."
(Matthew 13:44–46)

Lord,
There exists nothing of value,
unless it has value in heaven. There is
no money that holds any worth
unless it is laid up
in deposit in
Your eternal home.
I'm spending all my life to purchase You.
To own the world and lose my soul won't do.
Amen

Harvest

When I walked in Galilee, I never failed to mark the joy with which the farmers celebrated harvest. It was, as it should be, the joyous conclusion of a year's work. They had plowed the ground and readied the earth to make it tender for the seed. Then the sower had walked in sunlight and sowed the grain, casting forth the seed in golden handfuls. And the grain had lain in wait for showers and sunlight. And the farmers waited too, many even prayed, with faithful expectation. But whether they prayed for their crops or only waited, they all watched. The seeds cracked open and sent down white roots and even as they sent up tendrils of green promise: The sun rose warm and the rain came cool for months. At last the grain was green and forming in its bristled heads. Then came the gold. The anticipation gave way to glory. The farmers' work and watching beckoned them to stand in a vast sea of summer gold. With the scythe in their hands they drew the blade and the grain fell. And they threshed the sheaves and winnowed out the chaff. And when the first loaves came they celebrated the gathering of grain. Harvest!

My Father sent me into the world. His wealth lay in the vast seas of human potential. You see, My Father is in love with humankind. He wants nothing to be lost.

He wants all the precious grain gathered into His coffers. You must gather it in for Him. You are the farmers in His field. Do not wait. The fields are ready for the reapers. They are white even now. If you tarry much of the grain will go down. High winds can whip and destroy a field. Storms can bury a harvest. Hail can destroy. A prairie fire can blaze before an all-consuming wind.

Can My Father count on you? Do you understand how much He loves all men and women? Will you help Him gather in what might be lost? The time is now.

Jesus said to them, "My food is to do the will of Him who sent Me, and to finish His work. Do you not say, 'There are still four months and then comes the harvest'? Behold, I say to you, lift up your eyes and look at the fields, for they are already white for harvest!"
(John 4:34,35)

*Lord,
I will no longer postpone my obligation
to reap. Help me to see that every hour I put
off the harvest, the grain goes down, and
what You
want to save is gone forever.
It's now that I must reach to win the lost.
We reapers race against the holocaust.
Amen*

Trusting God for Our Sharing

I know that a part of your reluctance to witness for Me is born in your fears. You are still very afraid that you will not know exactly what to say. These fears come mostly from your own desire to look successful in every venture. I want to remind you that sharing does not depend upon a successful conclusion to be successful. Evangelizing is defined very simply. It is sharing in the power of the Spirit and leaving the results to God. You are not responsible for making converts, only for sharing My love. So you may lay aside all fear of failure connected with making sales. You are not called to close deals, that is the work of the Father. You are called to stop being silent when the occasion demands that you speak up.

Nonetheless, I want to teach you nineteen words of glory. They are these: "Tell me my friend, wouldn't you like to ask Jesus Christ to become Lord of your life right now!" You should never use these words to force the lost into the kingdom of heaven. I want you to use them, because until you ask people forthrightly to believe, they may stand at the door of the kingdom forever and never enter it. I know what you are thinking. You are thinking, "What if they refuse? What if they reject me?" Please, I beg you, ask them to believe. Some always refuse. But it is not you they refuse. It is not you they reject. Please detach your own pride from the bargaining of God. Get yourself out of the way of His reckoning. I encourage you to be specific not so that you may feel good that you have cinched celestial encounters with your adept techniques. Still your courageous challenge may be just the impetus the Spirit needs to embrace those outside the kingdom in eternal love.

Afraid that you may not have the words? What I promised all the future martyrs, I promise unto you. I will give you in that hour what you must say. Ask them to believe and believe yourself that I will be with you in your asking. You will never share My saving grace, but that you will find My presence plenteous in your courage. The words of your witness are Mine. The willingness to speak them is yours.

"And you will be brought before governors and kings for My sake, as a testimony to them and to the Gentiles. But when they deliver you up, do not worry about how or what you should speak. For it will be given to you in that hour what you should speak; for it is not you who speak, but the Spirit of your Father who speaks in you." (Matthew 10:18–20)

Lord,
I talk all the time; help
me to begin really saying something.
Help me to be a steward of my speech.
Make me a verbal force in the
bland and never ending stream of
human conversation.
I'm furnished well with unimportant speech.
My tongue needs courage only You can teach.
Amen

The Divine Imperative

"You must be born again," I once said to Nicodemus. But it was not just to him. I said it to all who would ever live. When a baby comes into the world a marvelous miracle occurs. And yet it is a very delicate miracle, for all human life is as beautiful as it is fragile. It has been said that all human beings travel a dubious journey between two hospitals, the one where they are born and the one where they die. Birth is the life moment where all begin to live. This definition of first birth lies in the passing of a child from the womb into the world. There in the pain of childbirth a life becomes independent. The umbilical dependency is gone and the infant must live in the world at hand. Yet biological life marks only the beginning of breath and pulse. These weak accouterments cannot take life very far. Life with such tiny definitions as these is over in 70 years or so. But when I told My night visitor, Nicodemus, that he must be born again I meant he must acquire that kind and quality of life that transcends mere breath and pulse. Unlike the first birth we alone choose the time for being born again. Then, upon the choice, we are visited by grace. Then life comes, mysterious, almighty, eternal. This is a new and imperishable life, unthreatenable by death. Its mystery is hidden in a powerful and unseen reality like the wind. We can hear and feel the wind, but we are never able to see it. So is everyone who is born of the Spirit.

Being born again is a real miracle. Here in this storm of saving grace, mere mortals put on immortality. Mere weaklings become strong enough to handle life. Those who have been doing "all right under the circumstances" are able to live on top of their circumstances.

Now that you have tasted this miracle of the new birth, give it to some defeated friend who is living under stress because she has only been born once. Tell her what I told Nicodemus long ago, "You must be born again."

Jesus answered and said to him, "Most assuredly, I say to you, unless one is born again, he cannot see the kingdom of God."

"Do not marvel that I said to you, 'You must be born again.' The wind blows where it wishes, and you hear the sound of it, but cannot tell where it comes from and where it goes. So is everyone who is born of the Spirit." (John 3:3,7,8)

Lord,
I will never cease to praise You
for giving me eternal life. Oh, help me to be
so excited about the new birth,
it drives me to tell everyone
I know about it.
Help me to be gentle but unafraid
in offering it.
There is but one real life which You applaud.
It's life that issues from the womb of God.
Amen

The Great Gift

There are but two gifts you should strive to obtain. They are both My gifts. The first is the gift of eternal life. I gave you this gift because I love you. It is this gift which makes your life unthreatenable. One of the most instinctual human drives is self preservation. When your life comes under judgment or threat, your entire nervous system comes to attention. In an instant all of your reflexive instincts move to keep you alive. Eternal life is My gift which guarantees self preservation. This life was the martyrs' security. They could take dynamic stands, courageously defying an arena full of lions, because they knew that their real lives were always secure. They knew that to be absent from the body was to be present with Me. Neither flame nor sword could change the meaning of the word "life" as I had taught it to them. To be sure, they trembled at the idea of dying, but they were not afraid of death. These martyrs demonstrated the value of My first great gift.

My second gift to all believers is the Holy Spirit. My first gift is to be celebrated for it makes life unending. But my second gift is to be celebrated for it makes life manageable. My first gift is to be cherished, my second gift is to be used. My first gift ornaments the life with unspeakable wealth. My second gift is gloriously functional. Gifts can be like that. Some gifts make you wealthy, other gifts are given to make life work.

The gift of the Holy Spirit I give not merely to be celebrated, I give this gift so that none of My disciples will ever have to live life powerlessly, alone and without counsel. I want you to know My presence when you are afraid or tempted to despair. I want you to have power when you feel powerless. And I want to live inside you, so that My nearness will be your security. I want to direct you when you seek to tell others of My salvation. I want you to be a witness who speaks of Me with certainty, knowing that you do not have to tell others of My love from some isolated position of doubt. I will be there in the person of the Holy Spirit. Witness to Me outwardly and listen to Me inwardly. You will find that I'll be speaking to you even as you speak for Me.

"If a son asks for bread from any father among you, will he give him a stone? Or if he asks for a fish, will he give him a serpent instead of a fish? Or if he asks for an egg, will he offer him a scorpion? If you then, being evil, know how to give good gifts to your children, how much more will your heavenly Father give the Holy Spirit to those who ask Him!" (Luke 11:11–13)

Lord,
Help me to be very careful lest I try to
live in my own strength and witness
in my own power. Help me to walk
in the Spirit so that I may be sure that
I do not run ahead of God.
Give me Your Holy Spirit ev'ry hour
So He may gild my witness with His power.
Amen

Heaven at Joy

I am the Shepherd who carries a double concern for My sheep. First, I own them and they are Mine. I bought them with My blood that long-ago Friday of My crucifixion. Every believer is part of heaven's inventory, a part of God's vast celestial treasury. Not one person for whom I died does My Father consider cheap. They are all precious to Him. They are His sheep, and He is their Shepherd. My father would not part with a one of them for those who are believers comprise the wealth of all He holds dear. "For you are a holy people to the LORD your God; the LORD your God has chosen you to be a people for Himself, a special treasure above all the peoples on the face of the earth" (Deuteronomy 7:6).

But there is a second reason I am concerned about My sheep. I care about their welfare. Why would I readily leave the ninety-nine to search out the missing one? It is not just that the one is absent from the fold. A lone sheep is ever in danger. The predators of the wilderness prey on that sheep which wanders away unprotected. God loves all who stray and need His saving grace. Is not such love too marvelous for human understanding? *Grace* is that glorious idea that if you were the only one who had ever needed it, I would still have died for you. My Father walks the edges of eternity and weeps over all who perish. I pray that you may sense how much My Father loves the straying sheep. Every sheep is His concern. He wants them safe forever within His eternal fold.

And this is why I seek the lost one, even when the ninety-nine are safe. This is why heaven waits till that one is found and music breaks out on the boulevards of gold. Joy is born. My Father rages forth in Spirit fire driven by the wind. And the one who cares enough to rescue His precious sheep gets caught up in heaven's rejoicing. Where there is ecstasy on earth there is dancing at the throne. Joy is always the music of rescue. It spills out of heaven as you seek those whom the Father loves.

So He spoke this parable to them, saying: "What man of you, having a hundred sheep, if he loses one of them, does not leave the ninety-nine in the wilderness, and go after the one which is lost until he finds it? And when he has found it, he lays it on his shoulders, rejoicing. And when he comes home, he calls together his friends and neighbors, saying to them, 'Rejoice with me for I have found my sheep which was lost!' I say to you that likewise there will be more joy in heaven over one sinner who repents than over ninety-nine just persons who need no repentance."
(Luke 15:3–7)

Lord,
There is one out there
which is lost. Help me to leave the
fellowship of the redeemed—the
ninety-nine—and get on with the rescue
work. It is Your holiest work and
so it must be mine.
I praise Your name for seeking out the lost.
I'm found. I'm loved. I can but bless the
cross.
Amen

Security Forever

I give to all my disciples a security that is unthreatenable. Your desire for security was born when you were. Who knows where you first learned your need for it? I suspect that you learned it at your mother's bosom. Snuggled close, your fearful crying dissolved in her strong love and you were nourished in the darkness. Your infantile fears could not exist within the circle of her mighty love.

Only as you grew and became bigger, could you see that she was not as large as you at first supposed. And yet, she had a fierce maternal instinct that roused itself in force if ever you were in danger. You knew that she would lay down her life to spare yours. Somehow in seeing her, you felt that life was possible and nothing could destroy your security while she protected you.

I saw such sacrificial love in My own mother. When I was twelve, I left My parents in the harried madding crowd of a holiday in Jerusalem. I went to the temple to talk with scribes and theologians. When My parents found me, it was easy to see My mother's agitation. I told her I had to be about my Father's business (Luke 2:49). She seemed to understand.

Security is the ground of joy for all children. A child who is protected will play and sing. Such children will spend themselves creating little gifts that they suppose to be the focus of their parents' joy. Further, they will grow and mature in wisdom and stature, and in favor with God and men (Luke 2:52). Everybody wants to be secure. Mothers pray for security.

Children whimper for it. The strongest man asks God to make him ever stronger so his little family will be secure in his presence.

My disciples in every generation grow as I protect them. Consider the nature of My security: I hold them in My hand. While I hold them they know they are secure forever, for My Father who gave them to Me holds Me in His hand. Here then is the double-handed security of all who are redeemed. All who are Mine are in My hand, and My hand is in God's hand. Protected, they are free to grow in the kingdom and become all that they may. Made secure by My love they may confidently share it with others—for no one can ever tear them from My Father's hand.

"My sheep hear My voice, and I know them, and they follow Me. And I give them eternal life, and they shall never perish; neither shall anyone snatch them out of My hand. My Father, who has given them to Me, is greater than all; and no one is able to snatch them out of my Father's hand. I and My Father are one." (John 10:27-30)

Lord,
I realize my security is in You.
Help me to pray the Psalmist's prayer,
God is my refuge and strength. Help me to
willfully place my hand in Yours.
The world was warm and I alone knew cold.
You loved, You searched, You drew me to the
fold.
Amen

The Character of the Witness

Hypocrisy is born the moment that our witness dies. It is born the moment that we dare to think that we can believe Jesus to be the light of the world while we hide every attempt to tell others of His love. To be undivided in your love for Me is to speak as openly about Me in public as you believe in Me in your hearts. As you freely believe in Me, freely speak of Me. Purity of heart is the essence of the witness's power. Therefore, strive to make the person you are, and the one you appear to be, the same person. Do not forget that what you really are roars so loudly all about you, that no one ever hears what you say you are. You should live for Me so completely that your witness will be made without speaking. Let your character speak so eloquently that your voice need not be heard for all to know how much you love Me. But never assume that your character has such volume in its silence it can win the world without your courageous utterance. Live so wholeheartedly for Me that you need not speak actual words of witness; then speak so wholeheartedly for Me as though your all-powerful character was mute.

People do hear lives before they hear words. Words can be cheap. Like pennies in the snow we sometimes see their little worth but will not stoop to pick them up for fear our fingers could be bitten by the frost. Character acts out truth in grandeur. Character demonstrates by example and example is the school where even cynics sit to learn. So witness by example. "Do what I say and you'll receive Christ" always lacks the power of "Be what I am, that you may find the heart of God!"

But if you really want to win the world to Me, garrison your mind with character then speak your witness verbally in power. Your words of witness will be a sign of courage as you demolish "arguments and every high thing that exalts itself against the knowledge of God, bringing every thought into captivity to the obedience of Christ" (2 Corinthians 10:5). So guard your mind as you strive to make every word authentic. Remember the witness of Andrew as a master example. He both spoke and lived his witness. Yet he is proof that it is often better to "listen" people into the kingdom of God than to try to "talk" them into it. The ear and not the mouth is the organ of a gentle witness. If much talking could lead the world to faith, the entire planet would surely be Christians now. Alas, we learn too late that we must be still not only to know that God is God, we must be still so that our words do not get in the way of His words. My simple, lovely "Come unto Me" is often obscured by your loud and mechanical "Go unto Him." Try praying more and listening more. Then speak with courage. Never fear to speak and never speak out of fear. Learn how to put character together with a listening ear and a courageous tongue, and you will witness with power.

"For there is nothing covered that will not be revealed, nor hidden that will not be known. Therefore whatever you have spoken in the dark will be heard in the light, and whatever you have spoken in the ear in inner rooms will be proclaimed on the housetops."
(Luke 12:2,3)

Lord,
Help me to learn this trinity
of values: first let me live
Christ, then let me hear Him
with a "fast" ear, then let me
speak with a steady
tongue.
Guard my tongue lest it should bring You
shame.
May every word I speak exalt Your name.
Amen

The Light

Bear your witness to Me with this understanding. Darkness and blindness are not the same thing but they do keep the same company. Darkness is but the absence of light. Blindness is the hunger for it. It is possible to walk in darkness, but the hazards it conceals—the stones, the pits, the terrors—define existence for so many. Darkness is customary for most who live. It's hard to make real the splendor of the light to those who've only known the night. They are like those creatures in the ocean depths who've lived so long in darkness their eyes are dead. They are like bats which have flown a thousand nights and never seen a single star. You cannot tell such sightless creatures there is such a thing as darkness. For if they could understand the word *darkness*, they would know there was a better state.

If heaven were not so moved by their condition, it would see the lost as comic. For they transact business, hurry off to their engagements, meet, marry, love and die all in darkness. They compete furiously for the preeminence in their dark worlds. They seem to think that to rule in deep shadow is good fortune indeed. If they knew the wholesome light of Christ they would see that their dreams were small. But in poor illumination they believe themselves to be quite important. In their darkness they say they are rich and do not need a thing. They cannot see that they are "wretched, miserable, poor, blind, and naked" (Revelation 3:17).

In such universal and well-accepted darkness, it is hard to make the lost understand the word *lost*. They've no reckoning to imagine their world any other way. I've called you to bear witness to the light, but bring it gently unto them. Don't eulogize the light so radically you seem otherworldly to them. Don't condemn their darkness.

Just let your light shine! Take the candle of my love-power out from under the bowl of your timidity. The best way to tell the lost of the darkness is to show them light. Then some will see. Share the light, then they will finally understand it has never been the darkness that made them captive but their willing blindness. Remember how you felt when first you saw Me? Remember how the scales fell from your eyes? I stood within the golden beam that ended your sinful blindness with light. Now you walk in that light and it is abundant light. Remember how you felt when first you came to light? Now that you have seen all that light can do when it is filtered through your obedience, be ready to sing the prophet's song (Isaiah 9:2): "The people who walked in darkness have seen a great light; those who dwelt in the land of the shadow of death, upon them a light has shined." This song is life's best music for every faithful witness.

"You are the light of the world. A city
that is set on a hill cannot be hidden.
Nor do they light a lamp and put it
under a basket, but on a lampstand, and
it gives light to all who are in the house."
(Matthew 5:14,15)

Lord,
I am so troubled by the
self-imposed darkness in which most people
live. You've given me the light. Help me
to cherish what You've entrusted unto
me. Help me to remember the light
will flicker and fail if I try to keep
it only for myself. Help me to pass it on.
For someone's darkened world, I am the light.
Ignite in me the flame to end their night.
Amen

The Inner Light

I have come to you to reveal My nearness unto you. I am pleased to sense your delight in my indwelling reality. I treasure the intimacy of our relationship. I am your Lord, and that manifestation of the Trinity that became flesh at Bethlehem and succumbed to crucifixion at Calvary. I am human enough to be like you and God enough to redeem you. I am flesh enough to understand your pain and God enough to heal it. I am human enough to understand your fear of dying but God enough to remove the sting of death forever.

I am the Son of God and a part of the Trinity. The Trinity is not so difficult as it may seem. A single man may be described by many names; by his children a man will be called father, by his father he may be called son, and by his wife he may be called husband. Yet he is only one man and not three. Thus, God as He creates is called Father. I am God as He redeems. As I indwell your life I am the Spirit. So, I am the Son of God. My intimacy with you is made possible by the Holy Spirit, the near end of the Trinity. The near end? Yes. He, the Holy Spirit lives within you. He is the inner Counselor who came into your life at conversion. He furnishes you with an inner instruction that was even more than your conscience could ever be. Your conscience could tell you right from wrong. But the Holy Spirit is there to teach you your holy duty. This glorious Indweller was God shaped to the very size of your heart so that you would never have to live a single moment without divine counsel.

Never forget that it is His counsel for you to evangelize. Those who do not know Christ sin against Him by refusing to allow Him into their lives. But you who know Christ sin against the Holy Spirit by refusing to obey His clear command to bear witness to those outside of Christ. Please honor the Spirit. Listen as He directs you to draw all you can to honor Me.

Never ignore the Holy Spirit. Never blaspheme His name. Never speak against His direction. Never ignore His glorious counsel. My Father has created you, and I have redeemed you. We all dwell within you in the blessed Holy Spirit. When you ignore His counsel, you ignore My counsel and you hurt the Father, you grieve the Spirit as Paul has said (Ephesians 4:30). *Grieve* is a love-word. God is like a human parent. A human parent is not as much angered by a disobedient child as he is hurt. So then I beg you, do not grieve the Holy Spirit. He is the Indweller. Listen to His counsel as He leads you to evangelize.

"And anyone who speaks a word against
the Son of Man, it will be forgiven him;
but to him who blasphemes against the
Holy Spirit, it will not be forgiven."
(Luke 12:10)

Lord,
I want to walk in step with the
Spirit of God. I want to be so perfectly
attuned with His glorious counsel, that
I thrill at every opportunity to obey Him.
I want to listen to His every command
to evangelize all who need the Savior.
Help me to yield to all the Spirit asks,
to work and bless the sweetness of His tasks.
Amen

The Seeker's Priority

Bring those beyond the borders of My kingdom unto Me. But to enlarge My realm you must act out your celebration of My reign in your life. Therefore, do not divide your heart with many priorities. You do not need many things. There is but one thing you need, My kingdom. If you want more, you want too much. If you want less, you want too little. I am the King. When I died, they put the *titulus* above My cross that said in Hebrew, Greek and Latin, "Jesus of Nazareth, King of the Jews!" But I can tell you it has been hard to gather subjects because My kingdom is not of this world. Further, the road to it is narrow and difficult, and there is a much wider road that leads to the illusory land of self-importance. Most are going down that road.

As you seek to make disciples you will notice that humanity seems divided between two great alternatives. The basic choice is whether they will have a king or be a king. Most, I am afraid, would rather rule some shoddy empire of their own, than to seek that city whose Builder and Maker is God (Hebrews 11:10). But I alone am King in that eternal city.

Kingdom seeking is the only earthly pursuit that gains esteem in heaven. Because it is the only appetite that sees time for what it is. Notice how those outside the kingdom drive themselves to have a bigger house, a bigger bank account, a bigger car, a bigger pedestal of civic celebration. If you watch them long enough you will see these emblems of their petty success dwindle into the long, long shadows of their headstones. The debris of their personal pursuits and the wreckage of ambition wash up hourly on the shoals of hell. Those who tried to build their own kingdoms perish and their large estates are often swallowed up by greedy heirs in human courts.

Will you walk with Me along such pointless avenues of human dreaming? We will see them wherever people are trying to make their futures more secure by tearing down their barns to build bigger barns. We can find them where we hear people saying, "I have plenty of goods laid up for many years. I'll take life easy: eat, drink and be merry." Will you not search them out and tell them, "You fool! This night your soul will be required of you . . . So is he who lays up treasure for himself, and is not rich toward God" (Luke 12:20,21). You have found the kingdom, and now you must supply the chart and compass to those who have not. My Father weeps to see so many spend their lives pursuing all the wrong things. Will you bear witness to these micromonarchs? Will you tell them there is but one way to know eternal life?

"But seek first the kingdom of God and His righteousness, and all these things shall be added to you." (Matthew 6:33)

Lord,
*Forgive me when
I fail to witness, for this
is the only way we have been
commanded to enlarge Your
kingdom. Help me to sing "all
hail, King Jesus!" and then
build Your kingdom in the hearts
of all those who've never
known excellent
music.
Your kingdom is my one priority.
Your reign, delicious sovereignty.*
Amen

The Longing Savior

While I walked here on the earth I wept several times. So often when I cried, My heart was broken over the faithlessness of those who lived on the thin resources of their willful poverty. I felt that way the night I looked down over Jerusalem. My heart was anguished over the pointless living concerning My frantic countrymen. How busy they were! Their frantic running, their empty pursuits told Me that they were living completely unaware of My Father's love.

I used the metaphor of a mother hen. It was earthy but it did express My longing. My Father made even such lowly creatures as chickens with an instinct that would exhibit love. If a hen is injured unto death she will spread her wings and cluck her little ones underneath them. And they will cheep and draw beneath the broad feathers, holding their fragile lives close enough to her to gather in her dying warmth. And she, in dying, will give them all the warmth she has until she is gone and they must leave her cold, spent body to face their world unprotected.

When I cried, "O Jerusalem!" I saw already the long, long shadow of My cross. It fell across a city made empty by its hurriedness. I stretched My arms above the empty citadel, and bid them draw the final warmth of God. The chill of human busyness went totally unwarmed. And yet My naked dying was but the agony of God calling out His love and longing to warm the world with eternal life.

I still weep above cities. I weep above yours. Do you? If you bend your knee in prayer, fold your hands upon an open Bible, and listen hard, you will hear Me crying "O Chicago, O Tokyo, O Calcutta! How often I have longed to gather your children together as a hen gathers her chicks under her wings!" I know the world. It's cold out there. The sub-zero air of an unfeeling culture is chilled by despair, glitzy prosperity and me-first-ism. My Father drove My gallows into the hill of human hope and begged the world consider how much He loved it. Come to the warm. Cry with the psalmist, ". . . hide me under the shadow of Your wings!" (Psalm 17:8).

"O Jerusalem, Jerusalem, the one who kills the prophets and stones those who are sent to her! How often I wanted to gather your children together, as a hen gathers her brood under her wings, but you were not willing!" (Luke 13:34)

Lord,
You were broken
when You saw the lostness
of Israel.
Teach me that any land is
made a Holy Land by
such concern. It
grieves me that
I am so often
uncaring about a Christless
humanity.
Above Jerusalem You once looked down.
Help me to care as much for my hometown.
Amen

The Healthy and The Sick

The Pharisees were forever asking why I ate with tax collectors and sinners. It was an "us and them" kind of question. The Pharisees were the "us" the sinners were the "them". How frequently we sin the sin of "us and them". It is so natural to congratulate ourselves and to condemn others. How frequently is the game of "us and them" played in church. The sermon is for "them," the high congratulations of godly living are for "us." How soon revival would fall upon "us" if only "they" would repent. "We" do most of the work in this church, but then "they" don't love the church like "we" do.

But nothing is so heartless as the believer who seems sometimes to rebuke the unredeemed just for being lost. Christians so often charge out from the church into the world, condemning its vile pastimes. As a large and holy *us* you condemn the sinful *them*, "How sinful is your gambling, your drunkenness, your sexual license, your corrupt philosophies!" Could I entreat you to turn your judgment into pity? Is it not enough that those who have not called me Lord, are dying with no hope in eternity? Would you walk through a cancer ward, and rebuke the suffering for their malignancies? Would you walk through the AIDS section of the hospital and rebuke the sick for their contagion?

The Pharisees often criticized Me because I hung around a lot with sinners. But I could never define sinners as people who were excessively more vile than others. I liked sinners for their honesty. They rarely pretended a righteousness they didn't have. It is never much trouble for My Father to heal the sick. The problem lies within the sick themselves. All things good start as they admit their diagnosis. The first step to healing always lies in the honest cry of Bartimaeus, "Jesus, Son of David, have mercy on me!" (Luke 18:38). A mass tragedy was obscuring this blind man's victory; there were a dozen blind men in Jericho that day. I would have healed them all. But the rest were too content in their blindness to admit their need.

All the sick need a physician but only the honest sick stand a chance of being cured. Would you help Me win the world? Then you must help Me, as I help them to see they are lost. The problem has never been getting people to "respond" to My love, rather the Spirit labors to "share" it. Heaven's music never comes to those who feel no need of repentance. But the angels balance anthems on the fulcrum of that single human cry, "God be merciful to me a sinner!" (Luke 18:13). My kingdom is born a thousand times each day on the rails of desperate integrity. Help Me love the honest sick. They can be made well. Help Me help them.

And so it was, as Jesus sat at the table in the house, that behold, many tax collectors and sinners came and sat down with Him and His disciples. And when the Pharisees saw it, they said to His disciples, "Why does your Teacher eat with tax collectors and sinners?" But when Jesus heard that, He said to them, "Those who are well have no need of a physician, but those who are sick. But go and learn what this means: 'I desire mercy and not sacrifice.' For I did not come to call the righteous, but sinners, to repentance." (Matthew 9:10–13)

Lord,
I want to bring the
honest needy unto You. Help
me to be honest enough
to confess my
need for Your power
as I help
them confess
their need
for
forgiveness.
Forgive us when we live self-righteously
on bragging, arrogant sufficiency.
Amen

Blessed Are The Poor

Many of the saints of centuries past encouraged those they taught that it is better to have enemies than to be popular. Can you bless their wisdom? They knew that as long as you have even one warm source of counsel you will turn to that friend for affirmation. To be poor in spirit is to find yourself so alone in your circumstances that your loneliness causes you to seek Christ. But you should never despise such needy aloneness. Your need can become that wellspring of brokenness that causes you to look to Me. Seek God therefore and let His joy break forth within you. You will find that your brokenness can heal you. Remember that the sacrifices of God are a broken spirit. Remember that a broken and contrite heart He will never despise (Psalm 51:17). Come to Me in utter poverty of spirit and I will fold you to Myself.

Can you see why I bless all those who are poor in spirit? Their inner poverty makes them disciples of dependency. To be broken in spirit indicates a neediness that hungers for My completion. It is not a natural state, however. From the time you were a little child, you were taught that you should seek to be wealthy if you could be. You have always been taught to be self-sufficient and pride yourself on such sufficiency. But it is so often true that riches become the real impoverishment of life. There are two reasons you should not seek them. First of all, you will never get enough of them to make you feel complete. But even worse, your riches will separate you from the need of real friendship. The rich are always isolated from the world over which they preside. The self-sufficiency which they so treasure builds walls of smug complacency between them and their world. They never reach out. They don't have to; they can take care of

themselves. They can make their own way.

Be not like them! Hunger to be poor in spirit. The poor need each other. So many out there in the world are broken and in need of Me. They will best be won by those who've known brokenness. It is the needy who understand the needy. Do you not know of some couple who met and married in poverty? They were once happy with nothing, because they needed each other. But then their circumstances improved. They moved from rags to riches. Then they began to compete and quarrel over the material things their marriage acquired. Their marriage died. They strove to achieve the very self-sufficiency that at last destroyed their union.

Those who are spiritually impoverished—ground into the dust of their despair—become open to being My disciples. Be broken in this world and you will see that you will be able to find those who are also broken and need My salvation. Bless every human need that says to you, "I am so alone and so poor in spirit, I believe I am ready to hear how your Jesus can make me rich with grace!"

"Blessed are the poor in spirit, for theirs is the kingdom of heaven."
(Matthew 5:3)

Lord,
So often You were moved
with compassion on those
who were broken in spirit. I don't
ask You to spare me
the pain that
wakes my sensitivity to
bring eternal life
to all those who haven't got much going for
them in this life.
Give me so little I have need of thee.
Then I'll be poor and bless my poverty.
Amen

The Way

Why is it important that you seek to bring the world to Me? It is because I am *the* way, not *a* way. Please hear Me say this yet again, "I am *the* way—the only way." I came to Bethlehem and endured the cruel abuse of a crude manger, the feeding trough of beasts. Do you think that I would have done this if there had been some other way? Gethsemane brought huge drops of blood, so great was My burden of knowing that I had come to bear the heaviness of human sin. Would I have anguished there alone, waiting for the betrayer's kiss, if there had been some other way? There in the garden I asked My Father to take the cup from Me and give Me some alternative plan to save humankind if it was His will. But it was not to be. I died the next day, sagging outward, downward from the wood. I tell you I am *the* way. To say there is any other is to make a mockery of My dying.

Secular thinkers often suggest other ways which they believe are adequate to supplant *the way*. These often issue the call to join the cult of deep sincerity. Those who preach sincerity raise a thousand world options against My solitary proposition. They cry to every Christian witness, "Please. Make room for all. Be generous! Allow for other ways! Sincerity is weightier than truth." They cry for the broad belief that alludes that just as there are many roads that lead to Rome, so there are many roads that lead to God.

To dispel this sweet inclusivism, I beg you hear the desperation in My name, "Savior." It is a name that is so singular it cries, "Nor is there salvation in any other, for there is no other name under heaven given among men by which we must be saved" (Acts 4:12). I did not come to earth to provide *a* way. I did not die to provide some set of alternate solutions to human desperation. If there had been any other way, believe Me, I would have stayed safely in heaven and sent a prophet to announce the other options.

So when they tell you God will give them heaven on any other terms than they unflinchingly believe, beware their words. Share with them that I died because I am the only way.

"I am the way, the truth, and the life. No one comes to the Father except through Me." (John 14:6)

Lord,
I know
that salvation
is in no other source than the cross—Your
saving work. Since I
know You are the only hope,
let me tell the world I
touch that nothing
is ever hopeless.
I must point all the lost to You and say,
"Look nowhere else, Christ is the only way!"
Amen

The Confessional Life

Are you not proud of those associations you esteem? Are not most human beings? A child will keep a picture of his mother. A young woman will show everyone a picture of her fiancé even as they admire her engagement ring. Grandparents will stop strangers on the street and compel them to see photos of their children's children. This kind of pride is what My Father would expect of you. If you are in love with Me, say so. It is this confession that keeps My church alive.

Is it easy for you to admit, "I am of Christ"? Does such a simple confession make you feel overly spiritual for being under religious? There have been times in history when confessing Me was not a glib proposition. In the early days of Christianity, those who confessed Christ were severely persecuted. This is why Paul said, " 'For your sake we are killed all day long;' we are accounted as sheep for the slaughter'" (Romans 8:36). The catacombs during the second and third centuries became mass burial fields for those who openly lived the confessing life. I spoke to John, the Revelator, blessing those in Pergamum who had not denied My name. "I know your works, and where you dwell," I said to those whose confession was costing them dearly, "where Satan's throne is. And you hold fast to My name, and did not deny My faith even in the days in which Antipas was My faithful martyr, who was killed among you" (Revelation 2:13). When the Lamb opens the fifth seal, there is revealed all of those who were under the altar—those who had been slain because they maintained the testimony (Revelation 6:9). So you see, the confession of My name can be quite costly at times; if you think of your own confession as an easy matter, it is because you have been blessed to live in a special world of religious freedom, where grace sells cheap because it requires less.

Confession has always been the costly work of the church. Nor did all those confessors who paid with their blood live centuries ago. No century has been more replete with martyrs than the 20th. More have died confessing My name in your century than any other. Deitrich Bonhoeffer, the German martyr, translated Luke 9:23 (Take up your cross and follow Me), "Come with Me and die!"

How expensive can confession be? It can demand the price of family rejection. "Do not think that I came to bring peace on earth. I did not come to bring peace but a sword. For I have come to 'set a man against his father, a daughter against her mother, and a daughter-in-law against her mother-in-law.' And 'a man's foes will be those of his own household'" (Matthew 10:34–36). So you see even within the family it can be very costly to confess My Lordship. So practice your confession while it is easy, for the day may come when it will require utter courage.

"Therefore whoever confesses Me before men, him I will also confess before My Father who is in heaven. But whoever denies Me before men, him I will also deny before My Father who is in heaven." (Matthew 10:32,33)

Lord,
I want to learn to
confess Your name before all.
I want to
confess You as freely as You
saved me.
I want to confess You
as openly as You once
died for me.
I want to confess You without
timidity, in great boldness.
I call the world to this acknowledgment.
That You are mine! O Glorious Testament.
Amen

Water

I will tell you of the power of water. Have you seen how it caresses a seed until the plant—perhaps a tiny blade of grass—will send up a shoot with such force that it will split the very rocks to reach for sunlight? Water will, when driven by the wind, rebuke its earthen levees and crush a city underneath its tides. See it in its full artesian power. It will seep at first, then gurgle up through a small crevasse, then burst the wall, then gush, then rear its roaring fountainhead, until its silvery spray reaches toward sunlight falling back in misty rainbows.

Do you see I am the water of life? Don't you see I want to be a well of water which, if you drink, will never leave you thirsty? Indeed, the water I give will become . . . a spring of water, welling up to eternal life. If you drink Me not, there will be an emptiness, an awful darkness, dry and deep that will suck all hope, all joy, down into the empty center of your life. Like a desert at midnight, the dark sands, still hot from the midday sun, will sap what little moisture you may have, and leave your soul so dry and arid nothing beautiful will ever grow there.

Look around you. Can you see all those whose arid lives are void of hope? Yet they are not hopeless, for you are the water bearer and I am the water. Carry Me to all those who are worn with dry and empty purpose. Tell them of the power in water. Give them to drink and I will become in them a fountain springing up unto eternal life.

Once a thirsty pilgrim came upon a desert well. In his dire thirst he lowered the bucket into the well and pulled it up. It was full of jewels. Emptying the bucket, he lowered it again into the well. This time it came up full of gold. The pilgrim spoke simply to God: "Please Lord, I don't want to be rich, I am merely thirsty." There is a kind of thirst that only pure, cold water can slake. I am that water for that kind of thirst. Drink Me and know joy; give Me to others that they may have eternal life.

A woman of Samaria came to draw water. Jesus said to her, "Give Me a drink."
Jesus answered and said to her, "If you knew the gift of God, and who it is who says to you, 'Give Me a drink,' you would have asked Him, and He would have given you living water."
Jesus answered and said to her, "Whoever drinks of this water will thirst again, but whoever drinks of the water that I shall give him will never thirst. But the water that I shall give him will become in him a fountain of water springing up into everlasting life."
(John 4:7,10,13,14)

Lord,
I have tasted that which is so cold and so
pure, it has made eternity mine. Help me to
give it freely to those who
have never known
this water that
quenches the parched
soul
permanently.
I thirsted for a drink of meaning, when
I drank of grace and thirsted not again.
Amen

Living Bread

I am the Christ who nourishes. There is nothing like knowing that when you are weak with hunger, you may, at any time you wish, sit down and eat at the table which My Father spreads. Once I was with My disciples on the far shore of Galilee in a very rural district. When I saw the multitudes My heart ached in knowing that most of those who followed Me were poor.

I was deeply moved by the plight of My countrymen. They lived life under the heel of Rome, yet never had they been her citizens. Life has always been hard for most of those who have lived in any generation. I suddenly was moved by great compassion. "Where shall we buy bread, that these may eat?" I asked Philip (John 6:5).

The question was not mere conversation. I had already determined what I would do. I loved them. I wanted more than anything to give them at least one good square meal. Andrew had made friends with a boy, who had brought his lunch. He had five small barley loaves and two small fish. Andrew had a way with children, and children have a way of sharing. The story is so familiar I have no need to repeat it. But when the crowd had eaten, I felt the power that was so glorious in My Father's love. He is in love with everyone. He sees their hunger of heart. He sets the table and waits, while most of the starving pass it by.

Most human beings do not die of disease or accident or old age or any of the verifiable causes of death that get scratched on to their death certificates. Most die of hunger—a hunger for meaning and truth. How do meaning-starved people act? How do they behave? They live fast and sample every idea. They taste every pleasure yet starve for hope. Please tell them there is an end to their hunger for meaning. They need to know I am the bread. Do you know someone running from job to job, house to house, husband to husband, all in a desperate attempt to escape from themselves? Tell them they have a hunger only one food can satisfy— the Bread of Heaven. I am that bread. You hold the loaves that redeem. Multiply the bread. Give them to eat, please.

And Jesus said to them, "I am the bread of life. He who comes to Me shall never hunger, and he who believes in Me shall never thirst. But I said to you that you have seen Me and yet do not believe. All that the Father gives Me will come to Me, and the one who comes to Me I will by no means cast out." (John 6:35–37)

Lord,
Bread is the staff of life.
But You are that bread that is the staff
of eternal life.
Help me to be that unselfish beggar,
Who, having tasted this glorious
life, may share it
freely with
the next.
All those without You starve—may they be
fed,
And taught to hunger for the living bread.
Amen

The Cross

I call all who want to be My disciples to take up their cross and follow Me. What is this cross of which I speak? Is it merely one-hundred-fifty pounds of wood? Is it the discipline of learning to carry awfully heavy pain? How differently people define the crosses they must carry. For some it is an aging and requiring parent that they must pacify year after year. For another their cross may be a horribly demanding boss who controls them in a job they'd like to quit but know they can't. For another the cross may be a chronic toothache, arthritis or the chicken pox.

The cross I beg you bear is the very one I carried. It is the knowledge that you must serve My Father, whatever the cost. It is the pain of seeing those you love reject My Father. The cross is caring supremely for someone, and feeling them betray you in your own particular garden of Gethsemane.

The cross I want you to carry will at times feel very heavy, but once you see how much your faithfulness in carrying it pleases My Father, you will be overwhelmed with joy and you will find your burden light. You will hurt when those you try to win to faith in Me reject Me, and at those times your cross will seem unbearably heavy. But when you see the scornful bow their head and give up their reluctance to believe, joy will be born in you. Then the burden will seem light.

How can the heaviness of God's cross result in this lightness of joy? It all lies in the pleasure you feel when you know you are pleasing God. When you have followed this source of joy for a long time you will find other sources of joy insufficient. Only when you are serving His great pleasure, will you discover that nothing is of pleasure unto you that does not please Him alone. "Not My will," I said to Him one awful Thursday night, "Please take away this cup!" But He gave it unto Me. That chalice I so dreaded saved the world and God was pleased. All that pleases Him pleases Me. Someday, when you have sought His pleasure long enough, it will be like that for you. So I say again, come after Me and bear your cross.

Then He said to them all, "If anyone desires to come after Me, let him deny himself, and take up his cross daily, and follow Me." (Luke 9:23)

"Come to Me, all you who labor and are heavy laden, and I will give you rest. Take My yoke upon you and learn from Me, for I am gentle and lowly in heart, and you will find rest for your souls. For My yoke is easy and my burden is light." (Matthew 11:28–30)

Lord,
I want to be like You.
I want to live as You lived.
I want to carry all that You
carried in Your desire
to see all people
bless Your holy name.
I loved You at Your cross. I love You still.
Give me Your cross and point me to the hill.
Amen

The Responsibility for Our Words

I counsel you to remember that a witness is not one who is brought to court to share information. Let us consider a woman who sees a certain crime committed. It is not expected that she be able to speak on a wide range of subjects. A witness is brought to the stand for only one reason: she knows some specific bit of information that might come to bear on the case. A witness is someone who has seen something that is so strategic it may alter the outcome of the case. A witness who refuses to come to court and bear her testimony must risk subpoena. The law makes it clear that if a witness has seen something that bears strategically on the case, she must tell it. Once she is on the stand she must tell the truth, all the truth. If she refuses to communicate what she knows or distorts what she knows, she perjures herself.

I want all to understand that you have come to know Me. I want everyone to know that you understand the way to life. It is imperative that you commit yourself to telling those who do not know, so that they can live. Like a witness, you are under oath. You have taken the stand. Tell what you know. You have all the informa-tion necessary. If you withhold that information, those you could rescue will be lost. If you retract or refuse to witness the cost to someone will be immense. It is time to speak out responsibly. Hurting people are in the dock. God is on the bench. You are on the stand. Do not prat-tle or rattle on about the weather. Do not make small talk. Someone is hanging in the balance and you possess the truth of My salvation. You must witness.

"But I say to you that for every idle word men may speak, they will give account of it in the day of judgment. For by your words you will be justified, and by your words you will be condemned."
(Matthew 12:36,37)

Lord,
Help me to see
how important I
am as
I remain
faithful
to You.
I am strategic to some soul today.
Help me to measure every word I say.
Amen

The Vine

It is the nature of every living plant to reproduce itself. "I am the vine and you are the branch," I am the one who nourishes your spiritual life in order that you may produce fruit. Nourishment is the business of the vine. Vines nourish their branches for only one reason; the branch is designed to do what the vine cannot—it bears fruit. Once My earthly sojourn was over, I came to live at the right hand of My Father. I am not on earth now. I have sent My Comforter, the Holy Spirit, to finish what I began during My earthly sojourn. My Spirit now lives in you to enable and empower you to draw many to eternal life. You have received Him and find great joy in knowing that you will live forever. Now, it is My desire that you reproduce yourself in kind. You must produce the fruit of eternal life in someone else. Then like you, they too will bear fruit in yet another and so on until all the world is drawn to Me.

I must tell you this: I am disappointed when My branches remain barren. When a gardener finds an unproductive plant, he wants to cut it down and replace it with a new plant that will be productive. During the week of My crucifixion, I was walking with My disciples and saw in the distance a fig tree. It was fully leafed. At that stage of foliage it should have been heavy with fruit. But when I got there it had no fruit (Matthew 21:19), and so I cursed it and it withered. Some earthly theologians have criticized Me for this. But let Me tell you why I cursed the tree. The tree was acting contrary to all that I created trees to be. I created trees to bear fruit.

Do you see you are the branch? You take your life from Me. As you draw upon My all-sufficiency it is expected that you will bear fruit. Do not rashly try to disconnect yourself from My nourishing power,

as though you are clever enough or resourceful enough to create fruit on your own. In such a detached state you will feel the sting of living an unproductive life. Remember this: without Me you can do nothing (John 15:5). The moment that any branch is detached from Me it is already dying. You must remain in the vine to bear fruit. The key word is *remain*. Remaining is not clinging to the vine as though you alone must hold desperately to the source of your witnessing power. Remaining is the simple act of being in relationship. It is a relationship of utter trust. You must trust Me to nourish you and hold you. Then I can trust you to bear fruit.

"I am the true vine, and My Father is the vinedresser. Every branch in Me that does not bear fruit He takes away; and every branch that bears fruit He prunes, that it may bear more fruit. You are already clean because of the word which I have spoken to you. Abide in Me, and I in you. As the branch cannot bear fruit of itself, unless it abides in the vine, neither can you, unless you abide in Me. I am the vine, you are the branches. He who abides in Me, and I in him, bears much fruit; for without Me you can do nothing." (John 15:1–5)

Lord,
More than anything I
need Your nourishment in my life.
I want You to feed me
with Your Spirit of life, so that having
eaten of Your empowerment,
I will never be
weak in producing
precious fruit.
I go to tell the world You're mine.
I can bear fruit when nourished by the vine.
Amen

The Nazarene Manifesto

At the beginning of My ministry I stood in the synagogue at Nazareth to announce to all of those in my hometown, who I was. I declared Myself openly to be Messiah, and to remind them that I had come to save humankind. I did not see the declaration as courageous—only honest. I had to tell them who I was and to what end I had come to be among them. They did not believe, but it did not matter. It was the declaration that was all important.

Most who live never know why they are in the world. But in trusting me as your Savior, you entered under the sway of My Lordship. You agreed to take up the work I came to do. Now you must begin living out the truth of My Nazarene Manifesto. Like Myself, you are not responsible for how others receive your declaration. But you are responsible for declaring yourself.

In the nineteenth century, Adoniram Judson went to India to win as many of that state as he possibly could. For seven years he worked without a single convert. His life was beset by many personal problems. He lost his wife and suffered many illnesses. Yet he never ceased to proclaim the truth. I have named his life as beautiful because he declared himself for seven years with no visible results. Do you see that I never hold anyone responsible for a lack of response? Rather, I always bless the faithfulness of those who cannot be discouraged by the difficulty of their calling.

My declaration is yours. Paul cried "For if I preach the gospel, I have nothing to boast of, for necessity is laid upon me; yes, woe is me if I do not preach the gospel . . . I have become all things to all men, that I might by all means save some" (I Corinthians 9:16,22). This apostle knew the glorious compulsion that caused me to declare those words in Nazareth. Are you living your life under the sway of such a glorious compulsion? Are you witnessing under the direction of such a magnificent obsession?

It can be quite an experience to make this declaration. That day in Nazareth they tried to push me over a precipice (Luke 4:29). The apostle Paul too was likely martyred for his declaration. In the centuries of bearing witness to My name, "Still others had trial of mockings and scourgings, yes, and of chains and imprisonment. They were stoned, they were sawn in two, were tempted, were slain with the sword. They wandered about in sheepskins and goatskins, being destitute, afflicted, tormented—of whom the world was not worthy" (Hebrews 11:36–38). Still, in their faithfulness they finally obtained the goal of their unfailing proclamation: they arrived in that city for whose honor their lives were committed. Their faithfulness was not only their declaration, it was their reward. Are you carrying on that work I announced so long ago in Nazareth? Tell someone who you are—who I made you to be. Tell someone why you're on the planet. Perhaps they will believe, perhaps not. But tell them.

"The Spirit of the Lord is upon Me,
because He has anointed Me to preach
the gospel to the poor. He has sent Me
to heal the brokenhearted, to preach
deliverance to the captives and recovery
of sight to the blind, to set at liberty
those who are oppressed, to preach the
acceptable year of the Lord."
(Luke 4:18,19)

Lord,
Make me a
witness. Help me never forget
that the word "martyr" means
"witness." "Martyrs" are
not always those who are persecuted.
But martyrs are those who never
quit telling the
story.
I'll be what You declared Yourself to be:
the inmate's hope, the captive's liberty.
Amen

Legion's Commission

I once came across a poor demoniac among the tombs of Gadarenes. I cast the demons from him, and when he was healed and in his right mind he asked Me if he could be one of those disciples who traveled with Me. "Return to your own house," I told him, "and tell what great things God has done for you" (Luke 8:39). It was not what he wanted to hear but I knew that "home" was where he would be most effective. For years he had raved in madness among the tombs. The populace was afraid of him. Fearing for their very lives, they walked a wide path around the tombs where he dwelt (Matthew 8:28). They had seen his huge and strong body. So strong was he that when the demons stirred within him he broke chains (Mark 5:4). I was asked to leave the poor man's country. When I cast those demons out of him they had entered into a herd of swine, and the demon-crazed pigs rushed over a cliff and perished in the sea (Luke 8:33). The loss of the swine made the people fearful of Me.

But the manner of his healing had wonderful results. While I was not welcome in Gadarenes and could not stay to conduct a wide ministry, the exorcised Legion could. He was a new believer. The outstanding changes that had come over him had made him the center of Gadarene conversation. His home country was the best place for him to share his testimony. Are you thinking, *that's all very well for Legion—it's a very nice story—but to be truthful, he must have had some gifts that I do not? Witnessing to people who know me is a terror all its own.* Legion must have felt that way too. Some of my itinerant disciples, which Legion so wanted to be, would later write Gospels. Peter would write. Mark, Matthew and John would also write Gospels. But their marvelous biographies would not reach everywhere.

Legion's calling was going to be the gospel for Gadarenes. His gospel would be less grand than the apostles' but one equally effective within his community. So before you say you cannot bear witness, ask yourself if there is not someone whom you can lead to faith better than the most effective of Christian communicators. Perhaps it is a father who admires you, a grandmother who dotes on you. Perhaps it is a child who so adores you that your witness to them would be even more effective than that of your pastor's. It may be an employee who would listen to you better than anyone else. It may be your boss, who is impressed with the way you work. But, please, look around you. Ask yourself, who are those people with whom you would have more personal force than anyone else in the world. Now that you've isolated who they are, begin to pray for them. And as you pray, wait for that moment when you are with them and the Holy Spirit is urging you to tell them your own experience of grace.

In such an effective testimony will you write a little gospel that will turn them at last to the grand narratives of those who were My apostles. Then will they hear your personal, effective word that turns them to the Living Word. Thus I say to you what I said to Legion long ago, "Return home and tell!"

"Return to your own house, and tell what great things God has done for you." (Luke 8:39)

Lord,
I know the margins
of my effectiveness. Help me
to win those who are
within my tightest circle
of influence. Help me
to be faithful where
my witness will be
most
fruitful. I know where I can speak effectively.
I'm going home to tell my family.
Amen

Where Are The Thankful

Praise is but the thank-you note you give to God in remembering His gifts. Witnessing speaks with the voice of praise. A witness is one who has received a gift so great that he or she is not able to stop talking with effusive feelings of gratitude. I would caution you who witness against memorizing some scheme which you believe is an adequate "sales program" for the kingdom of God. You will witness more effectively if you stop in prayer to be thankful for the gift of grace you received when first you came to know Me.

R.W. Dale was a well-known pastor of the last century. He lived and ministered during those years when Moody was an evangelist. He said that he was not all that taken with either Moody's popularity or talent. He was a skeptic of the evangelist's motives and the strength of his converts' commitment. Then one day, when Rev. Dale sat on the platform and heard Moody preach, he became convinced of Moody's sincerity. What was it that convinced him? He said that Moody could never speak of the lost without tears in his eyes.

Were Moody's tears shed merely for the fate of the lost? Perhaps. But his contemplation of his own spiritual neediness may also have brought Moody tears of gratitude and praise for all that God had done for him. Do you see how you are to rejoice? It is to be done in a continual spirit of thankfulness. Be thankful as a way of life. Let gratitude become your attitude. "For you were once darkness, but now you are light in the Lord . . . Therefore do not be unwise, but understand what the will of the Lord is. And do not be drunk with wine, in which is dissipation; but be filled with the Spirit, speaking to one another in psalms and hymns and spiritual songs, singing and making melody in your heart to the Lord, giving thanks always for all things to God the Father in the name of our Lord Jesus Christ" (Ephesians 5:8, 17–20).

Thankfulness for all that He has done for you will put an effervescence in your testimony that no "plan of salvation" can ever supply you. I once cleansed ten lepers, only one returned to give Me thanks. It was he whose thankful heart bore radiant witness to his cleansing. Be like that leper and you will bring other lepers to the same wonderful cleansing that is yours.

"Were there not ten cleansed? But where are the nine?" (Luke 17:17)

Lord,
I know that only as I
am most thankful for my
salvation will I remember
my joy enough to want to
reproduce this
joy in the
life of another.
I am grateful I am saved, made whole, and
free—
a thankful leper, free of leprosy.
Amen

The Needle's Eye

All that you will hold in your cold, dead hand will be what you have given away. There are no suitcases allowed through the portals of heaven. There will be no pockets in your shroud. There are no rental trailers that may be pulled behind your hearse. Again and again it is said that you can't take it with you. You will hear the scholars debate about the eye of the needle and all I meant by the term. But I did not speak in hyperbole to create laughter with this ridiculous picture of a literal camel going through a literal needle's eye. Such a maneuver is not merely comical, it is impossible.

Self-denial is the call of the kingdom. This needle's eye which I warned My disciples against was a teaching I gave them after a rich young ruler erroneously claimed his perfect keeping of the Ten Commandments. I have no doubt that he had done well with most of them. But the commandment on covetousness was his nemesis. He did well with those commandments that lead the list, but alas the final commandment challenged his love of riches. He could not manage enough self-denial to pass the needle's eye.

Consider what many of the citizens of my country called the "Needle's eye." There was a tiny gate beside the large gate in many ancient cities. Because of the thickness of the city walls, this little gate really became a long, narrow tunnel protected by a garrison of one or two sentries. It would often happen that when anyone got to the city after the large gates were closed for the night, they might secure permission to enter through the "needle's eye." It would require traversing the tunnel to enter the city. The constricting passage was easy enough for one person. But if the late arriver was leading a donkey or a camel the procedure became more demanding. The camel would often have to be unloaded of its baggage and then forced to kneel and struggle through the low passageway.

It is a picture of this sort that I want you to consider about heaven. You will not be able to squeeze through those narrow portals with all your material treasures. Yet it is hard to give them up, isn't it? As you seek to win the people, see them as individuals who need to replace their heavy affections with the lighter luggage of grace and truth. Only as they abandon what they wrongly cherish, will they learn to treasure what is right. Be a witness who has properly evaluated true riches. Then you will be able to call for that same self-denial in all those you would call to grace.

"How hard it is for those who have riches to enter the kingdom of God! It is easier for a camel to go through the eye of a needle than for a rich man to enter the kingdom of God." (Mark 10:23,25)

Lord,
Help me to lay up true
treasure in heaven. Help me
to conceive of heaven as that
place which will be peopled
by some of those I
have led to Christ.
May the riches of my spiritual
inheritance consist of
those with whom I've
shared Christ.
I give away the rich man's longing sigh,
to pass in joy the narrow needle's eye.
Amen

Who Is My Neighbor?

The word *neighbor* comes from two old Celtic words *neah gebur*, which mean to "dwell beside." But in telling the parable of the hapless traveler who fell among muggers on the ancient Jericho road, I redefined the word. A neighbor is no longer one who lives near you. Your neighbor is one who is in need. There is often an abuse of this word in the church. We often grow to love the warm fellowship of the church, because those who gather there are our friends. They feel like us, look like us, share our value system and our faith in God. It is easy to show ourselves friendly to those who show themselves friendly to us. It is easy to call them neighbors.

But a neighbor is one who needs us. And those who need us define us as their neighbors on the basis of our mercy. If there is any word which is as significant as the word *neighbor* it must sure be the word *mercy.* Mercy is that mystique of caring which is not required. If you are a paid professional, like a doctor or a nurse, medicine may be a saving science for which you are paid and trained—a way of life which is expected of you. But if you go out of your way to staunch the blood or teach someone's failing lungs to breath again, you are saving a life in a way that no one felt you were obligated to do.

In the case of the traveler who was robbed and beaten, both a Levite and a priest passed him by at his hour of awful need (see Luke 10). No one would judge them in a court of law. His need was not their fault and they were not accountable. It was also not the fault of the Good Samaritan. But he, on the contrary, was moved with compassion. He rescued, bandaged and cared for the wounded man. It was his compassion that taught him his obligation. How well did Shakespeare say:

The quality of mercy is not
strain'd,

It droppeth as the gentle rain from
heaven
Upon the place beneath: it is twice
blest;
It blesseth him that gives and him
that takes:
'Tis mightiest in the mightiest: it
becomes
The throned monarch better than
his crown:
(*Merchant of Venice,* Act IV,
Scene I Lines 186–189)

Mercy, in its grandest form, knows only one mandate: the obligation of service. Mercy met you one day when you needed Christ. Had you died in that condition you would never know that peace and joy which are now your constant companions. Then, while you languished, you met your neighbor. It was not someone who lived near you, but someone who helped you when they didn't have to. They bound up your wounds with repentance and grace. Mercy is always the first plea of the needy. It was yours, remember? And since you found mercy just before you found Me, make giving it away the principle of your life.

"Freely you have received, freely give."
(Matthew 10:8)

"So which of these three do you think was neighbor to him who fell among the thieves?" And he said, "He who showed mercy on him." (Luke 10:36,37)

Lord,
Then sometimes it seems that there
are two kinds of
people: Needers and Need-Meeters.
Help me be the latter in a
constant search for the former.
We never cry for justice. Our one plea
is, Jesus, please be merciful to me.
Amen

Last Minute Life

I died between a skeptic and a believer. There is a sense in which dying between these two becomes a picture of the options that flank the Christian witness. All of life must be lived between faith and doubt, between those who believe and those who don't. And occasionally you will run across a dying skeptic like the believing felon who died beside Me. The unbelieving thief illustrates this truth: most skeptics die in the same skepticism in which they have always lived. It is not the unbelieving thief which I find intriguing. In fact, I found him customary. Having insulted faith all his life, his last recorded words were typical. Dying blasphemy is the usual end to which all living blasphemy is directed.

But what was surprising was the believing thief. His last recorded words were "Lord, remember me when You come into Your kingdom" (Luke 23:42). The dying skeptic blasphemed and entered hell. The dying believer blessed My redeeming power and entered heaven. One never knowing eternal life watched as his earthly life ran out. The other, at a moment when all his life signs were in doubt, came to the kingdom. The skeptical thief proves that evangelism at the zero hour is usually futile. The blaspheming thief teaches us we should never presume. The believing thief proves that we should never give up hope.

It is glorious when a dying doubter comes to faith. But I point you to my example of utter glory for your life. Is it not wonderful that the believing thief would bear witness to the dying skeptic? Do not excuse yourself with the notion that there is coming some final hour, when having been faithful to a life of sharing, you can retire from your need of witnessing to others. If I witnessed in My dying hour, do not presume that you can take your final years off. The moment you received Me, you committed yourself to sharing My grace for as long as you live.

Who knows, it could be in your dying moment you will witness on the very threshold of heaven and take someone to glory with you. I entered paradise bringing a repentant thief home with Me. Most of the angels rejoiced to see Me back in heaven, knowing the ordeal of human redemption was over. But when any sinner repents there is "joy in heaven" (Luke 15). And some of the angels rejoiced for the "death-bed conversion" of that thief who entered heaven with Me. Consider this wonderful truth: there are now two in heaven with nail-scarred hands. I who furnished redemption with My scars, and him who hanging beside Me, came with Me into glory. Imagine being executed as a thief and crossing immediately to claim a crown of righteousness. He was destined for the throne but only claimed that destiny at the zero hour.

*But the other, answering, rebuked him,
saying, "Do you not even fear God,
seeing you are under the same
condemnation? And we indeed justly, for
we receive the due reward of our deeds,
but this Man has done nothing wrong."
Then he said to Jesus, "Lord, remember
me when You come into Your kingdom."
And Jesus said to him, "Assuredly, I say
to you, today you will be with me in
Paradise." (Luke 23:40–43)*

*Lord,
I want to be sure that
I make myself the courier
of last hope. I want
to sit with those who
meet their time of death with
little cheer, so I can
tell them
heaven
stands ready to receive them.
You snatched but one from death's cold final
doom,
That all should hope and none dare to
presume.
Amen*

Since You're Going Anyway

Going is the human milieu. Everybody in the current culture is always going somewhere. In a way, it was never necessary for Me to say to my disciples "Go!" "Go" is written in the very psyche of the human spirit. Why then was My last command to My church the word "go"? How was my "go" different from the way they would have gone if I had never spoken to them?

God too is a go-er. Never believe that human beings are always on the run while God sits immobile. The entire Bible is a tale of the goings of God. He moved Abraham to go into a land that He would show him. He led Moses to go into the wilderness. He led all of Israel to go up out of Egypt into the land of Canaan. He led Me to go up to Jerusalem where I would be betrayed into the hands of sinful men and women. God is dynamic, not static; He is the ultimate go-er.

So My command to go is the command to go with this special purpose. It is a command to go into all the world and preach the gospel, tell the story, make converts and baptize. The word "go" stands at the end of My earthly sojourn because it is a most important word. It is My last command to the church.

But hear the word as I speak it. I do not say "Go somewhere else to make disciples!" Nor do I say, "Go somewhere far away . . . cross an ocean to prove how sincere you are." This kind of artificial commandment might allow Christians to excuse themselves from sharing Christ on the basis that they are not called to be career missionaries or pastors. Such a commission would indicate that only some are

to go and witness while others are meant to stay and not share.

What I really say is, "Since you are going into the world anyway, witness while you are going." Out *there* somewhere is not *where* you will go to share. *Here* is where you will share. Witnessing is not something you go somewhere to do. You do it while you're on the way *there*. You do it as you go so that every person between here and there will realize that sharing is not something we do in some particular place. It is something we do in every place. Hear My words and obey Me in the moment, at every moment of the journey of life. That entire journey is your place to share.

Then Jesus came and spoke to them, saying, "All authority has been given to Me in heaven and on earth. Go therefore and make disciples of all the nations, baptizing them in the name of the Father and of the Son and of the Holy Spirit, teaching them to observe all things that I have commanded you; and lo, I am with you always, even to the end of the age." (Matthew 28:18–20)

Lord,
Help me never to see
sharing Christ as having some
final geography. Witnessing
is not done when I get
somewhere, but while
I'm going somewhere.
Witnessing is never a matter
of place, but of the journey.
Forgive my need to go somewhere to say
what I should share while I am on the way.
Amen

1. Guilt. Psalm 32:3–5, page 339.

2. Depression. Philippians 4:8, page 244.

3. Loneliness. Psalm 23:1–6, page 333.

4. Hopelessness. Psalm 55:22, page 358.

5. Failure. Colossians 2:8, page 246.

6. Fear. Philippians 4:6–7, page 244.

7. Purpose. Proverbs 23:4–5, page 457.

8. Anger. Proverbs 16:32, page 449.

9. Broken Relationships. Ephesians 4:31–32, page 239.

10. Self-image. Ephesians 3:17–20, page 237.

People who are hurting face many painful and pressing issues. Ten of the most common have been chain referenced through this book so that you can provide practical help from God's Word for people who are hurting. We all know that forgiveness of sin and eternal life are everyone's greatest needs, but people often need answers to the other real hurts in their lives before they can receive the Gospel.

On the other hand, some people will need to be led through this process after they have trusted Christ. These issues are not listed in any particular order and are certainly not exhaustive. God's answers to these situations are clearly marked by the heart symbol in this New Testament. Read the phrase at the top of the page and then read the shaded portion of scripture. You will find directions to the next verse at the bottom of the page. Please read all the verses.

Using Scripture To Share The Gospel

1. Be sensitive to the seeker and to the leading of the Holy Spirit. A divine appointment happens when the path of a willing witness crosses the path of a seeker. Unbelievers become seekers as the Holy Spirit draws them to Jesus.

2. Hold the New Testament so the seeker can see it clearly. Use a pen to focus on key points.

3. During the conversation you will want to involve the seeker in order to maintain his or her interest and attention. This will also allow you to cooperate with the Spirit as He draws the person to Christ. You might ask the person to read aloud or ask for comments (in a nonthreatening way). For example, ask, "What does this verse mean to you?"

4. If the seeker is ready to receive Christ, be sure to lead that person in prayer, to guide them, to offer assurance, and to help them understand how to grow spiritually. You may use the guide provided for you on page 470 or use a plan of your own.

5. Leave the seeker some way to contact you. If possible, make arrangements for him or her to ride with you to church.

How to Share the Roman Road

The Book of Romans contains an orderly presentation of the power of the gospel. It presents the need of sinful humanity, the remedy for sin, and the way to receive salvation. The following passages have been called "the Roman Road to Salvation":

• Romans 3:23
• Romans 6:23
• Romans 5:8
• Romans 10:9,10,13

These scriptures are chain referenced for you in the Book of Romans.

Witness: "May I share with you from the Bible how you can come to Christ and receive the gift of salvation? The Book of Romans clearly points the way."

Seeker: "Yes, you may."

Witness: "Romans 3:23 is a summary of chapters 1—3. It tells about the condition of every person before God. Please read the verse aloud." (Reading the verse aloud utilizes the senses of sight, speech, and hearing to impress the Scripture more strongly on the mind of the seeker.) "What does this verse mean to you?"

Seeker: "It means that everyone has sinned."

Witness: "What about you yourself? Have you sinned against God?"

Seeker: "Yes, I know I've sinned, too."

Witness: "I could not point my finger at you and condemn you as a sinner. I'm a sinner, too. Notice that verse 22 says that there is no difference. We have all sinned. We are all in the same boat, and it is a sinking ship. We have all fallen short of what God has for us. The word picture is that of an archer shooting an arrow. It falls short and misses the target. This is what sin is. It is missing the target or mark that God has set for our lives.

"Romans 6:23 tells us the result, or 'wages,' of sin. If a person works all week, he expects to be paid. According to this verse, what is the payment—wages—of sin?"

Seeker: "It says that the wages of sin is death."

Witness: "Yes. The payment for sin is death. This death is speaking of eternal death or separation from God. Thank God, the verse does not stop there! He inserted the word *but*. And what an important word it is. It says that the gift of God is eternal life through Jesus Christ, our Lord. You can't buy, merit, nor earn it. The question is 'How do you get a gift?'"

Seeker: "You have to accept a gift."

Witness: "True! As you receive Jesus Christ, you have the gift of eternal life. Romans 5:8 indicates that God provided for your salvation by giving His own Son because He loves you. Romans 10:9–13 tells us how to come to God and receive forgiveness for our sins. Verse 9: Confess Jesus Christ as your Lord. Believe that He died for your sin, was buried, and rose again. Verse 13: Ask Him in prayer to forgive your sin and come into your heart. He promises that He will. I would like to pray with you as you ask Him to forgive your sin and come into your heart as Lord and Savior. Are you ready to do that now?"

(Lead the seeker to pray. Then share God's promises of assurance and give instruction for following Christ. You may use the guide provided on page 470 or use a plan of your own.)

How to Use the Lifeline Illustration

Illustrating what God has done to effect our salvation is a powerful tool in presenting the plan of salvation. It can help people understand by visualizing as well as hearing the gospel. I have used this simple demonstration many times in leading people to Christ.

The illustration may be presented, using a pen or pencil and a piece of paper, napkin, or lightweight card. If these are not available, you may use your hands.

Early one Saturday morning, David was having breakfast in the almost-vacated downtown hotel restaurant before attending a company meeting. The waiter, whose name tag read "Nasir," brought a menu and water to the table.

"Good morning, Nasir. You have an interesting name. Where are you from?" David began, employing the FIRM conversation guide to open the way to share Jesus with him.

Nasir smiled. "Good morning. I am from Bangladesh."

"Bangladesh must be an interesting country, but I've never been there. Tell me about it."

Obviously pleased to find someone with an interest in his homeland, Nasir delightedly shared some details about the country, his family, and himself. He was an engineer who had come to the USA to work and was employed in the restaurant while getting established in his profession. He indicated that he now lived in a suburban area named Sugar Creek.

"Oh, I know where that is," David replied, picking up on this opportunity to establish a common bond with Nasir. "I've visited the Sugar Creek Church. Have you attended there?"

"Oh, no!" Nasir corrected him. "I am Moslem."

"Then I'm sure you know about Jesus. Moslems call Him Esa. Isn't that right?" David probed.

"Yes, it is. We believe that He was a prophet."

"Nasir, the Bible teaches that Jesus is the Son of God. I have come to know Him as my personal Savior. He changed my life. May I share with you how you can know Him, be forgiven of your sins, and know that you have eternal life?" David asked. "I'll use this napkin and my pen to illustrate.

"Romans 3:9 indicates that all humanity is under sin," David went on. "As I hold the napkin here, we will let it represent the barrier of sin that stands between humanity and God. As I place my pen beneath it, the pen represents the human race which is 'under' sin. As I place the pen over the napkin, it represents God who is holy and above sin. All of us have a capacity and a yearning for God, yet we have a prideful sin nature that causes us to resist God and attempt to reach Him through our own efforts." David moved the pen, which was under the napkin, upward illustrating the attempt of humanity to penetrate the sin barrier and try to reach God. "But it is impossible! Sinful humanity cannot make its own way to God. The sin barrier is impenetrable.

"God intervened to do what no human could do. He came in and through the person of Jesus Christ to penetrate the sin barrier. He came into our situation and lived a sinless life." David penetrated the napkin with his pen until it formed the shape of a cross. "Then Jesus was crucified, bearing our sins in his own body on the cross. He became the lifeline from God to us. He is the only way we can have life. He made the way to bring us through the sin barrier by coming to Him and receiving Him. Does this make sense to you?"

Nasir nodded slowly. "Yes . . . but I believe in one god, Allah. You have spoken of *two* gods."

"No, Nasir, I am sharing with you about one God. There is one God who has manifested Himself as three Persons—Father, Son, and Holy Spirit. As an illustration, I am one man, but I am a son to my mother, a husband to my wife, and a father to my daughter. . . ."

David was about to explain further when Nasir interrupted. "Yes, that's it! I understand! It is wonderful!"

It seemed almost too good to be true, but David hurried on, pressing for a decision. "Nasir, are you ready to believe in Jesus as the Son of God who died for your sins?"

"Yes, I am!"

"Will you accept Him as your Savior and Lord? Will you pray with me now and ask Him to forgive you of your sins and be your Savior?" David asked.

Standing there beside the table, Nasir bowed his head and prayed, receiving Christ as his own Savior and Lord. Both Nasir and David praised God together.

When David finished breakfast, he asked for the check. Nasir refused to bring one. "I want to take care of it!" he insisted. "After all you have done for me in helping me know Jesus, I must do something for you."

Presentation:

Ask, "May I share with you about how to come to know Christ as your Savior? I can demonstrate, using my pen and this piece of paper.

"All humanity is 'under sin' (Rom. 3:9 NKJV). As an illustration, the paper will represent sin. If I place my pen *under* the paper, we can easily see that humankind is under sin.

"On the other hand, God is holy. When I place my pen *above* the paper, it represents God's position with regard to sin. God is above sin.

"One who has sinned may attempt to reach God." (Using your pen to represent sinful people, move it up toward God. It will collide with the paper representing the sin barrier.) "Sinful people attempt to reach God in many ways. These may in-

clude good works, reformation, morality, religious performance, and philanthropy. But it is impossible for one who has sinned to reach holy God in these ways."

"The only possibility for sinful people to break through the sin barrier and receive life from God is for God to intervene in the human situation. Under sin, we are spiritually dead. God is the only source of spiritual life. Jesus Christ is the 'way, the truth, and the life' (John 14:6). *He is the only lifeline to God.*

"God did what human beings could never do! In the person of Jesus Christ, His Son, God came into the human situation. He penetrated the sin barrier to live a sinless life on earth. On the cross, He died as He paid the price for our sins. There He 'bore our sins in his own body' (1 Peter 2:24 NKJV), providing the way for sinful people to come to God."

(Penetrate the paper with your pen. It will form a cross, representing Jesus dying for our sins to be "the way, the truth, and the life." Sinful people can now come to God through Him.)

"You can receive the gift of salvation by repenting (turning from your sin and personal efforts) and by faith coming to Christ. You must receive Him as your Savior and Lord. You will be born again as a child of God. You will have a new position of being made right with God. You will have peace with God and begin your new life on your way to heaven.

"You may receive Him now through prayer. Romans 10:13 says 'Whoever calls upon the name of the LORD shall be saved' (NKJV). Will you call on Him now and ask Him to forgive your sins and come into your heart as Lord and Savior?"

(Lead the seeker to pray. Then share God's promises of assurance and give instruction for following Christ. You may use the guide provided on page 470 or use a plan of your own.)

How to Use John 3

John 3:1–18 is one of the most effective and natural passages of the entire Bible to use in witnessing. For several reasons it is highly conducive to leading people to Christ.

• It is a single passage that can be used without skipping through several chapters and books that may give the appearance of using proof texts. By simply reading through it, a person can come to understand how to receive life through trusting Christ.

• It is a direct transcription of Jesus' words. It is Jesus Himself leading a man to conversion. His pattern and plan are the best anyone could follow.

• It is an excellent way to deal with excuses, problems, objections, and concerns before they arise. This is important. When people position themselves with an argument or excuse, they often feel bound to defend it because of human ego. It is better to deal with it scripturally before they position themselves.

Jesus answers numerous concerns, questions, and problems in this passage. They can be shared as you read through it together. Some of these are as follows:

• Jesus loves and is concerned for the individual (vv. 1–2, 16–17).

• Religion cannot save (vv. 1–3).

• Church membership cannot save (verses throughout passage).

• Morality, social, economic, or family position cannot save (vv. 1–5).

• Fear keeps people from Christ (v. 2).

• Conviction of sin opens people to Christ (v. 2).

• A person can receive the gift of salvation without having all the answers to spiritual questions (v. 6).

• Salvation is not by feeling, but by faith (vv. 14–15).

• Every person, regardless of his or her life situation, must experience the spiritual birth to become a child of God and go to heaven (vv. 3–5).

• There is only *one* way of salvation—through Jesus Christ. There are not *many* ways. There are not even *two* ways (v. 13).

• The death of Christ on the cross is necessary for the payment for sin (vv. 14–15).

• Every person has been made for eternity. Each will live forever somewhere—in heaven with Christ, or in hell, separated from Him (v. 16).

• God has proven that He is for every person by giving His Son (v. 17).

• Spiritually there are only two groups of people in the world—believers and unbelievers. There is no middle ground (v. 18).

Conversation Guide Through the Passage

The following is an example of a conversational approach in sharing John 3:1–18 (NKJV) with someone. I have personally used this many times. Responses usually are very natural and spontaneous. During a thirty-minute training period, I went through John 3:1–18 and explained how to use the following conversation guide with a group of Christians. Later, a young adult couple who had participated in the training reported that they had shared John 3 with three adults. All three accepted Christ!

In Kansas, I shared John 3 with a brokenhearted father whose daughter had recently been killed in a tragic accident. Christian friends had been praying for Ed for years, but it took this incident for the Holy Spirit to prepare his heart for the gospel. I went to his home to minister to him and his family. During the course of the visit, I read through John 3 with Ed and asked him to receive Christ. He responded to God's love, and his life was changed as he accepted Christ and followed Him in baptism and church membership.

In presenting the John 3 conversation guide, the one sharing will be designated

Using Scripture to Share the Gospel

as the **witness**. The witness has a divine appointment with an unbeliever who is called the **seeker**. Remember that a divine appointment is when the path of a willing witness crosses the path of a seeker. Unbelievers become seekers as the Holy Spirit draws them to Jesus.

Following is a conversation guide.

Witness: "May I ask you a personal question?"

Seeker: "Yes, you may."

Witness: "Have you come to know Jesus Christ in a personal way, or would you say you are still in the process?"

Seeker: "I guess I am still in the process."

Witness: "Then you have given serious thought to it?"

Seeker: "Yes, I've thought a lot about it lately."

Witness: "May I take a few minutes to share with you from the Bible how you can know for sure you have eternal life?" (Using the seeker's Bible can help in breaking down barriers and in establishing rapport. Comment favorably about his or her Bible. Ask when it was obtained. Usually there are positive memories related to the Bible. If the person is hesitant, of course, use your own.)

"The greatest sermon ever preached, of course, was preached by Jesus. We usually think of great sermons being preached to a multitude of people. But the sermon in John 3 was given by Jesus to just one man in the middle of the night. Does that suggest anything to you?"

Seeker: "Yes. It suggests that Jesus cares for the individual."

Witness: "Let's read verse 1. If you had lived next door to Nicodemus, you would have thought that he had it all. He appears to be an ideal person. Yet, all of Nicodemus's fine qualities did not change the fact that he was a sinner

with a deep need. He was religious, a Pharisee. He was rich. He was respectable, a ruler. But none of these qualities filled the need of his heart. He saw in Jesus what he needed but did not have.

"Verse 2 says that Nicodemus came to Jesus at night. Why do you think he came in the night?"

Seeker: "He was probably afraid that others might see him."

Witness: "I think you're right. He was afraid of what others might say or do. Fear and peer pressure sometimes keep people from coming to Christ. It kept me from coming to Him for some time." (This would be a good time to share your own experience.) "Has that ever happened to you? Have you ever felt like that?"

Seeker: "Yes, I have." (Give the seeker an opportunity to express fear and deal with it.)

Witness: "There may have been another reason he came at night." (The purpose of this thought is to lead the seeker to realize his or her own sin.) "Nicodemus might have chosen this time because of his own conviction for sin. In the stillness of the night, with no distractions, he had to face the loneliness of his spiritual emptiness.

"When he came face to face with himself, he got up and came to Jesus, so as not to expose the superficiality of his spiritual life. He attempted to flatter Jesus by saying, 'Rabbi, we know that You are a teacher come from God; for no one can do these signs that You do unless God is with him.' Jesus brushed aside his compliment and got right to the point. He knew the heart of Nicodemus. John 2:25 says, 'and [He] had no need that anyone should testify of man, for He knew what was in man.'"

(At this point ask the seeker to read v. 3 aloud.) "Here is a verse where Jesus tells Nicodemus what is really important."

Seeker: "Jesus answered and said to him, 'Most assuredly, I say to you, unless one is born again, he cannot see the kingdom of God.'"

Witness: "What does this verse mean to you?" (Do not ask the seeker to interpret or give its meaning. Ask what it means *to him or her.*)

Seeker: "It means to me that you have to be born again."

Witness: "What does being born again mean to you?" (The seeker may explain or hesitate. If there is hesitation, explain it yourself.) "It's perfectly understandable not to know. Nicodemus didn't understand it. Neither did I the first time I heard it."

(Read verse 4.) "In verse 4, Nicodemus revealed his lack of understanding when he asked Jesus, 'How can a man be born when he is old? Can he enter the second time into his mother's womb and be born?' Nicodemus thought Jesus was speaking about the physical birth—reversing the process of nature and being born a second time. But in verses 5 and 6, Jesus corrects Nicodemus and tells him that He is speaking of a spiritual birth. Nicodemus's problem was that he equated his physical birth with salvation. He thought that because he had been born into a Jewish family and was a religious man, he was a child of God. Jesus reveals that to be born physically, one becomes a member of a human family. But to be a part of the family of God, one must be born spiritually."

(Read verse 5.) "In verse 5 Jesus speaks about being born of water. When some read this verse, they immediately think about baptism. Baptism is important, of course. But baptism does not save you from the consequences of your sin. When you commit your life to Christ, you will want to be baptized. However, this verse is not speaking about baptism. The water birth is the physical, or flesh, birth. Before a baby is born, it is encased in a bag of water in its mother's womb. The water breaks and the baby is born. The flesh, or water, birth is necessary for physical life. The spiritual birth is necessary for spiritual life and to be a child of God. You must have the inner change of a spiritual birth to come to know Christ as your Savior." (You may choose to use this opportunity to explain the meaning of baptism.)

"At this point Nicodemus's eyes must have popped out on stems. In verse 7 Jesus said, 'Do not marvel that I said to you, You must be born again.' Then, in verse 8 He used an illustration of the wind. (Ask the seeker to read the verse.) How do we know the wind is blowing? We can't see it. We don't know where it comes from or where it is going."

Seeker: "You know the wind is blowing because you feel it and see the evidence of it."

Witness: "This is like being born of the Spirit. You can't see the Holy Spirit. You can't understand all the Spirit does. But you can feel His presence as He convicts you and draws you to Christ. And you can experience the changing work He does in your heart."

(Read verse 9.) "In verse 9 Nicodemus asked the question you or I would have asked: 'How can these things be?' In other words, 'How can this happen to me?' In verse 10 Jesus gently rebuked him, 'Are you the teacher of Israel, and do not know these things?' Then in verse 13, Jesus answered the question about how it can happen for you and me." (Ask the seeker to read the verse, or read it yourself.) "This verse indicates that the only one who can go to heaven is the One who came from heaven. Who would you say this is talking about?"

Seeker: "I guess it is talking about Jesus."

Using Scripture to Share the Gospel ♥

Witness: "Yes it is. The question is, 'If Jesus is the only One who is qualified to go to heaven, then how can you and I go to heaven?'"

Seeker: "The only way we can go to heaven is through Jesus."

Witness: (Read vv. 14–16.) "Right. The only way we can go to heaven is through the One who is going there, Jesus. In verses 14–16, Jesus explains how this can happen. He draws an illustration from the history of Israel. The people of Israel were in the wilderness. God miraculously provided food and water for them, but they continued to murmur and complain against the Lord. So God disciplined them by sending a plague of snakes into their camp. When the snakes began to bite the people and they died, Moses interceded in prayer. God told him to mold a snake out of brass and raise it up on a pole in the middle of the camp. Then when the people were bitten, they were to look to the brass snake on the pole and God would heal them. There was no magic in the brass snake. God healed as they responded by faith.

"Jesus applied this incident to His being lifted up on the cross. Whoever has been bitten by the serpent bite of sin will die spiritually. But if they will look to Him by faith, they will be forgiven of their sins and have eternal life. Then Jesus gave that beautiful promise, John 3:16: 'For God so loved the world, that He gave His only begotten Son, that whoever believes in Him should not perish but have everlasting life.'" (Ask the seeker to read verse 17.)

Seeker: "For God did not send His Son into the world to condemn the world, but that the world through Him might be saved."

Witness: "Jesus did not come to condemn you. He came to save you. Now let's read verse 18. This verse tells us that there are only two groups of people in the world as far as God is concerned.

Note who they are and what God says about them: 'He who believes in Him is not condemned; but he who does not believe is condemned already, because he has not believed in the name of the only begotten Son of God.' Who are the two groups?"

Seeker: "Those who believe and those who do not believe."

Witness: "What does the verse say about the believer?"

Seeker: "The believer is not condemned."

Witness: "What about the unbeliever?"

Seeker: "The unbeliever is condemned already."

Witness: "Why does it say that the unbeliever is condemned already?"

Seeker: "Because he has not believed in Jesus."

Witness: "May I ask you a very personal question? I don't want to embarrass you. But in which of the two groups would you say you are right now?"
    (The seeker may respond in one of three ways: "I am a believer. I am not a believer. I do believe, but . . .")

Seeker 1: "I am a believer. I am not condemned."

Witness: "That's wonderful! When did you believe on Christ and receive Him?" (Give the seeker an opportunity to share his or her testimony of salvation and rejoice together.)

Seeker 2: "No, I am not a believer."

Witness: "Then may I share with you now about believing on Him? Will you believe now that Jesus is God's Son, that He died for your sins and will save you? Will you receive Him now?"

Seeker 3: "I do believe a lot of things about Jesus, but . . ."

Witness: "I think I understand what you're saying. Then, you do believe in

Jesus intellectually, but you have not received Him personally into your life. Is that true?"

Seeker: "Yes, that is true."

Witness: "Let's read John 1:12. Notice two key words about becoming God's child. 'But as many as received Him, to them He gave the right to become children of God, even to those who believe in His name.' What are the two key words?"

Seeker: "They are *receive* and *believe*." (If the seeker has difficulty, share them with him or her.)

Witness: "If you truly believe on Christ, you will want to turn from your sin and receive Him into your heart. Now, because you believe, will you receive now through prayer? I'll pray with you and for you as you call on Him. But my prayer will not make you a Christian. After I pray, call on Him in prayer yourself. He promised, 'Whoever calls on the name of the LORD shall be saved'

(Rom. 10:13 NKJV)." (Lead the seeker to pray, then share God's promises of assurance and give instruction about following Christ. You may use the guide provided on page 470 of *People Sharing Jesus* or use a plan of your own).

This conversation guide through John 3 is one model for using the passage to share Christ. Of course, the seeker may give different responses and not follow this pattern at all. If so, you may discuss his or her responses and return to John 3 as quickly as possible. If the seeker appears to be going off on a tangent, you may courteously ask, "May we look back to what Jesus said in John 3? I believe it may answer some of your questions."

If the seeker is not open to receive Christ, ask him or her to read John 3 after you leave and consider praying privately to receive Christ. Courteously ask permission for an opportunity to visit at another time. Ask him or her to call you if you can be of help. Ask to have prayer before you go. Leave the door open for a follow-up visit.

How to Share the Message of the Cross

The story of the cross is captivating and convicting. Non-Christians may be turned off by organized religion and by invitations to church, but they will usually listen with interest to the biblical stories about Jesus. The cross is of particular interest. The message of the cross is the power of God to save. "For the message of the cross is foolishness to those who are perishing, but to us who are being saved it is the power of God" (1 Cor. 1:18 NKJV).

The message of the shedding of the blood of Jesus for sin will often pierce hearts like nothing else can. Hearing about His loving and willing sacrifice stirs a person's mind, emotions, and will.

Those who have experienced the sacrificial love and forgiveness of our Lord are God's spokesmen and representatives to take His message to others. No person in the world should be deprived of knowing what Jesus did on the cross. Every Christian should be committed to getting the message of the cross and the resurrection to every person.

The message of the cross can be easily memorized and the story told in your own words. Even hardened, hostile people have become brokenhearted seekers as the story has been told simply by a Christian.

If you will memorize seven events and some of the details surrounding them, you will be able to adequately summarize the "greatest story ever told." These seven events enable us to follow the footsteps of Jesus from the Garden of Gethsemane to the open tomb. The seven key events listed in chronological order are:

1. Jesus in the Garden of Gethsemane (Luke 22:40–50)
2. Jesus Before the High Priest (Matt. 26:57–68)
3. Jesus Before Pilate the First Time (Luke 23:1–6)
4. Jesus Before Herod (Luke 23:7–12)
5. Jesus Scourged by Pilate and Delivered to the Crowd (Matt. 27:11–31; Luke 23:13–23)
6. Jesus Crucified on Calvary (Matt. 27:33–60; Luke 23:32–56)
7. Jesus Rises Again (Luke 24:1–12)

In sharing the message of the cross, begin with each of the seven steps and summarize the main thoughts in your own words. The following is an example:

Jesus in the Garden of Gethsemane (Luke 22:40–50)

On the night before He was crucified, Jesus withdrew with His disciples to a private place of prayer. There He agonized in prayer as he accepted on Himself the sins of the world. "Father, if it is Your will," He prayed, "remove this cup from Me; nevertheless not My will, but Yours, be done" (v. 42 NKJV). As He continued to pray, so intense was His agony that He sweat great drops of blood. This is the blood shed for our sins without which there can be no forgiveness. "And according to the law almost all things are purged with blood, and without shedding of blood there is no remission" (Heb. 9:22 NKJV).

Judas led the temple soldiers to arrest Jesus and take Him from the Garden to the court of the high priest. He would be tried in an illegal trial in the middle of the night. His disciples forsook Him and fled.

Jesus Before the High Priest (Matt. 26:57–68)

The high priest and the council interrogated and condemned Him. "But Jesus remained silent. The high priest said to him, . . . 'Tell us if you are the Christ, the Son of God' (v. 63 NKJV).

"Jesus said to him, 'It is as you said. Nevertheless, I say to you, hereafter you will see the Son of Man sitting at the right hand of the Power, and coming on the clouds of heaven'" (v. 64 NKJV).

The high priest went into a rage and tore his robe. Then the Sanhedrin charged Jesus with blasphemy and illegally sentenced Him to death. "Then they spat in His face and beat Him; and others struck Him with the palms of their hands, saying, 'Prophesy to us, Christ! Who is the one who struck You?'" (vv. 67–68 NKJV).

Since the Sanhedrin had no authority to order the death sentence, they took Jesus to Pilate, the Roman governor, to appeal for execution.

Jesus before Pilate the First Time (Luke 23:1–6)

Jesus was accused of being an insurrectionist, refusing to pay taxes to Caesar, and claiming to be a king. But upon examining Him, Pilate declared that he found no fault in Him. Still, Pilate was afraid to let Jesus go because the crowd was demanding His crucifixion, accusing Him of stirring up the people from Galilee to Jerusalem. When Pilate heard that Jesus was from Galilee, he conceived a way out of his dilemma. He would send Jesus to Herod, the ruler of Galilee, who was in Jerusalem for the feast.

Jesus before Herod (Luke 23:7–12)

Herod was greatly pleased to see Jesus, hoping to see Him perform some miracle. Herod asked Him many questions, but Jesus did not answer. The chief priests and scribes vehemently accused Jesus, after which Herod and the soldiers ridiculed and mocked Him, then dressed Him in one of Herod's old royal robes and sent Him back to Pilate. As a result, Herod and Pilate, who had been enemies, became friends.

Jesus Scourged by Pilate (Matt. 27:11–31; Luke 23:13–23)

Pilate further examined Jesus, while the religious leaders continued to demand His death. Then Pilate conceived the idea of releasing a prisoner to show mercy in recognition of the feast of the Passover, thus hoping to be able to free Jesus. He selected the notable criminal and insurrectionist, Barabbas, to give the crowd a choice.

"The governor answered and said to them, 'Which of the two do you want me to release to you?' They said, 'Barabbas!' Pilate said to them, 'What then shall I do with Jesus who is called Christ?' They all said to him, 'Let Him be crucified!'" (Matt. 27:21–23 NKJV).

At that point Pilate's wife appeared, asking her husband to have nothing to do with this just man. She said that she had had a terrible dream about Him. Pilate took a basin of water and washed his hands saying, "I am innocent of the blood of this just Person. You see to it'" (v. 24 NKJV).

Pilate ordered the soldiers to strip Jesus of His clothing and beat him with a cat-o'-nine-tails whip, tipped with bone, metal, and lead balls. Many men died under the severity of this kind of scourging. Often, the victim's eyes were knocked out, rib bones were bared, and the stomach ripped open. The blood of Jesus ran down to the pavement—the blood without which there is no remission for sin.

They crowned Him with a crown of thorns and beat it down into the flesh of His head with a reed. The blood spurted out and matted His face and beard—the blood without which there is no remission for sin. They put on Him a scarlet robe, placed a reed in His hand, and mocked Him, saying, "Hail, King of the Jews!" (v. 29).

Then Pilate delivered Jesus to the crowd. They placed the beam of the cross on His back and led Him away to be crucified. Exhausted from all that had transpired, Jesus stumbled under the weight of the cross. At that point, they hailed a passerby, Simon of Cyrene, and made him bear the cross. Making their way up the Via Dolorosa to Golgotha, the hill of the skull, they crucified Jesus where common criminals were executed.

Using Scripture to Share the Gospel

Jesus Crucified on Calvary
(Matt. 27:33–60; Luke 23:32–56)

The soldiers threw Jesus to the ground and stretched out His arms on the beam of the cross. One of them pounded spikes through the palms of His hands, then through His feet, fastening Him to the cross. They lifted up the cross and, with a thud, dropped it into the hole, tearing Jesus' soft flesh. "Sitting down, they kept watch over Him there" (Matt. 27:36, NKJV). Like uncivilized savages, these doctors of law and philosophy—religious and political leaders—watched with sadistic glee, even joining the crowd in mocking Him. "If You are the Son of God, come down from the cross." Then again, "He saved others; Himself He cannot save. If He is the King of Israel, let Him now come down from the cross, and we will believe Him" (vv. 40, 42).

Looking down from the cross, His voice breaking with pathos and agony, Jesus cried, "Father, forgive them, for they do not know what they do" (Luke 23:34 NKJV). The words of that prayer ring down through the ages and reaches all the way to you and me. Thank God that He shed His blood for us!

The sun refused to shine on that hideous scene on Calvary. From about nine o'clock in the morning, darkness covered the land. Suddenly at about noon, Jesus' horrifying cry pierced the darkness, "'Eli, Eli, lama sabachthani?' that is 'My God, My God, why have You forsaken me?'" (Matt. 27:46, NKJV).

At that moment God did a miracle. He reached out into all of time to bring together all the sin of all humanity and concentrate all of our guilt into the body of Jesus. On the cross the One who knew no sin became sin for us (2 Cor. 5:21). Jesus, who had never sinned, suddenly felt the combined intensity of all the guilt of all sin of all time. God, who cannot look upon sin, withdrew from His own Son. For the first time in all eternity, the Son was separated from the Father. Our sin killed Him!

Just before He died, Jesus cried out, "It is finished" (John 19:30). This was not the defeated cry of a man facing the dismal end. It was a shout of triumph! He had accomplished that for which He had come into the world. The sin debt was paid in full. He had provided the way for mankind to come to God. And with the words, "Father, into Your hands I commend My spirit" (Luke 23:46 NKJV), Jesus released His spirit to the Father.

After Jesus died, they pierced His side with a spear. Out gushed blood and water. Blood and water in that area of His body indicates that His heart had ruptured. So intense was His spiritual agony that it literally broke His heart.

At the cross Joseph of Arimathea and Nicodemus, who had been secret disciples, received courage for open confession of their commitment. They came forward to ask for the body of Jesus. They took His body down from the cross and prepared it for burial, and afterwards laid it in Joseph's tomb.

Jesus Resurrected from the Dead
(Luke 24:1–12)

On the third day after Jesus' death, the women came to the tomb to find the stone rolled away and His body missing. Jesus appeared to His disciples at least eleven times following His resurrection. By many infallible proofs He showed Himself alive from the dead. He gave instructions and commands. He promised to send the Holy Spirit to enable His followers to take the good news of His death, burial, and resurrection to every person in their world. Then, He ascended to take His place at the right hand of the Father to guarantee access to God through Him (Acts 1:1–11).

Now, by faith, you can come to Him and receive forgiveness for all your sins and be born into the family of God. Like Joseph and Nicodemus, you will have the courage and joy to openly confess Him as your Savior and Lord.

May I ask you now to pray with me?

1

Ask Jesus, who died to pay for your sins and rose again, to forgive your sins and to come into your heart as Lord and Savior. (Lead the seeker to pray. Then, share God's promises of assurance and give instruction for following Christ. You may use the guide provided on page 470 or use a plan of your own.)

Outline

People Sharing Jesus
by Dr. Darrell W. Robinson

THE GOSPEL ACCORDING TO
MATTHEW

THE book of the genealogy of Jesus Christ, the Son of David, the Son of Abraham:

2 Abraham begot Isaac, Isaac begot Jacob, and Jacob begot Judah and his brothers.

3 Judah begot Perez and Zerah by Tamar, Perez begot Hezron, and Hezron begot Ram.

4 Ram begot Amminadab, Amminadab begot Nahshon, and Nahshon begot Salmon.

5 Salmon begot Boaz by Rahab, Boaz begot Obed by Ruth, Obed begot Jesse,

6 and Jesse begot David the king.

David the king begot Solomon by her *who had been the wife* of Uriah.

7 Solomon begot Rehoboam, Rehoboam begot Abijah, and Abijah begot Asa.

8 Asa begot Jehoshaphat, Jehoshaphat begot Joram, and Joram begot Uzziah.

9 Uzziah begot Jotham, Jotham begot Ahaz, and Ahaz begot Hezekiah.

10 Hezekiah begot Manasseh, Manasseh begot Amon, and Amon begot Josiah.

11 Josiah begot Jeconiah and his brothers about the time they were carried away to Babylon.

12 And after they were brought to Babylon, Jeconiah begot Shealtiel, and Shealtiel begot Zerubbabel.

13 Zerubbabel begot Abiud, Abiud begot Eliakim, and Eliakim begot Azor.

14 Azor begot Zadok, Zadok begot Achim, and Achim begot Eliud.

15 Eliud begot Eleazar, Eleazar begot Matthan, and Matthan begot Jacob.

16 And Jacob begot Joseph the husband of Mary, of whom was born Jesus who is called Christ.

17 So all the generations from Abraham to David *are* fourteen generations, from David until the captivity in Babylon *are* fourteen generations, and from the captivity in Babylon until the Christ *are* fourteen generations.

18 Now the birth of Jesus Christ was as follows: After His mother Mary was betrothed to Joseph, before they came together, she was found with child of the Holy Spirit.

19 Then Joseph her husband, being a just *man,* and not wanting to make her a public example, was minded to put her away secretly.

20 But while he thought about these things, behold, an angel of the Lord appeared to him in a dream, saying, "Joseph, son of David, do not be afraid to take to you Mary your wife, for that which is conceived in her is of the Holy Spirit.

21 "And she will bring forth a Son, and you shall call His name JESUS, for He will save His people from their sins."

22 Now all this was done that it might be fulfilled which was spoken by the Lord through the prophet, saying:

23 *"Behold, a virgin shall be with child, and bear a Son, and they shall call His name Immanuel,"* which is translated, "God with us."

24 Then Joseph, being aroused from sleep, did as the angel of the Lord commanded him and took to him his wife,

25 and did not know her till she had brought forth her firstborn Son. And he called His name JESUS.

2 Now after Jesus was born in Bethlehem of Judea in the days of Herod the king, behold, wise men from the East came to Jerusalem,

2 saying, "Where is He who has been born King of the Jews? For

we have seen His star in the East and have come to worship Him."

3 When Herod the king heard *these things,* he was troubled, and all Jerusalem with him.

4 And when he had gathered all the chief priests and scribes of the people together, he inquired of them where the Christ was to be born.

5 So they said to him, "In Bethlehem of Judea, for thus it is written by the prophet:

6   *'But you, Bethlehem, in the*
     land of Judah,
  Are not the least among the
     rulers of Judah;
  For out of you shall come a
     Ruler
  Who will shepherd My people
     Israel.'"

7 Then Herod, when he had secretly called the wise men, determined from them what time the star appeared.

8 And he sent them to Bethlehem and said, "Go and search diligently for the young Child, and when you have found *Him,* bring back word to me, that I may come and worship Him also."

9 When they heard the king, they departed; and behold, the star which they had seen in the East went before them, till it came and stood over where the young Child was.

10 When they saw the star, they rejoiced with exceedingly great joy.

11 And when they had come into the house, they saw the young Child with Mary His mother, and fell down and worshiped Him. And when they had opened their treasures, they presented gifts to Him: gold, frankincense, and myrrh.

12 Then, being divinely warned in a dream that they should not return to Herod, they departed for their own country another way.

13 Now when they had departed, behold, an angel of the Lord appeared to Joseph in a dream, saying, "Arise, take the young Child and His mother, flee to Egypt, and stay there until I bring you word; for Herod will seek the young Child to destroy Him."

14 When he arose, he took the young Child and His mother by night and departed for Egypt,

15 and was there until the death of Herod, that it might be fulfilled which was spoken by the Lord through the prophet, saying, *"Out of Egypt I called My Son."*

16 Then Herod, when he saw that he was deceived by the wise men, was exceedingly angry; and he sent forth and put to death all the male children who were in Bethlehem and in all its districts, from two years old and under, according to the time which he had determined from the wise men.

17 Then was fulfilled what was spoken by Jeremiah the prophet, saying:

18 *"A voice was heard in Ramah,*
  Lamentation, weeping,
    and great mourning,
  Rachel weeping for her
    children,
  Refusing to be comforted,
    because they were no more."

19 But when Herod was dead, behold, an angel of the Lord appeared in a dream to Joseph in Egypt,

20 saying, "Arise, take the young Child and His mother, and go to the land of Israel, for those who sought the young Child's life are dead."

21 Then he arose, took the young Child and His mother, and came into the land of Israel.

22 But when he heard that Archelaus was reigning over Judea instead of his father Herod, he was afraid to go there. And being

warned by God in a dream, he turned aside into the region of Galilee.

23 And he came and dwelt in a city called Nazareth, that it might be fulfilled which was spoken by the prophets, "He shall be called a Nazarene."

3 In those days John the Baptist came preaching in the wilderness of Judea,

2 and saying, "Repent, for the kingdom of heaven is at hand!"

3 For this is he who was spoken of by the prophet Isaiah, saying:

*"The voice of one crying
    in the wilderness:
'Prepare the way of the Lord,
    Make His paths straight.'"*

4 And John himself was clothed in camel's hair, with a leather belt around his waist; and his food was locusts and wild honey.

5 Then Jerusalem, all Judea, and all the region around the Jordan went out to him

6 and were baptized by him in the Jordan, confessing their sins.

7 But when he saw many of the Pharisees and Sadducees coming to his baptism, he said to them, "Brood of vipers! Who has warned you to flee from the wrath to come?

8 "Therefore bear fruits worthy of repentance,

9 "and do not think to say to yourselves, 'We have Abraham as our father.' For I say to you that God is able to raise up children to Abraham from these stones.

10 "And even now the ax is laid to the root of the trees. Therefore every tree which does not bear good fruit is cut down and thrown into the fire.

11 "I indeed baptize you with water unto repentance, but He who is coming after me is mightier than I, whose sandals I am not worthy to carry. He will baptize you with the Holy Spirit and fire.

12 "His winnowing fan *is* in His hand, and He will thoroughly purge His threshing floor, and gather His wheat into the barn; but He will burn up the chaff with unquenchable fire."

13 Then Jesus came from Galilee to John at the Jordan to be baptized by him.

14 And John *tried to* prevent Him, saying, "I have need to be baptized by You, and are You coming to me?"

15 But Jesus answered and said to him, "Permit *it to be so* now, for thus it is fitting for us to fulfill all righteousness." Then he allowed Him.

16 Then Jesus, when He had been baptized, came up immediately from the water; and behold, the heavens were opened to Him, and He saw the Spirit of God descending like a dove and alighting upon Him.

17 And suddenly a voice *came* from heaven, saying, "This is My beloved Son, in whom I am well pleased."

4 Then Jesus was led up by the Spirit into the wilderness to be tempted by the devil.

2 And when He had fasted forty days and forty nights, afterward He was hungry.

3 Now when the tempter came to Him, he said, "If You are the Son of God, command that these stones become bread."

4 But He answered and said, "It is written, *'Man shall not live by bread alone, but by every word that proceeds from the mouth of God.'"*

5 Then the devil took Him up into the holy city, set Him on the pinnacle of the temple,

6 and said to Him, "If You are the Son of God, throw Yourself down. For it is written:

'He shall give His angels charge
   concerning you,'

and,

'In their hands they shall bear
   you up,
Lest you dash your foot
   against a stone.'"

7 Jesus said to him, "It is written again, 'You shall not tempt the LORD your God.'"

8 Again, the devil took Him up on an exceedingly high mountain, and showed Him all the kingdoms of the world and their glory.

9 And he said to Him, "All these things I will give You if You will fall down and worship me."

10 Then Jesus said to him, "Away with you, Satan! For it is written, 'You shall worship the LORD your God, and Him only you shall serve.'"

11 Then the devil left Him, and behold, angels came and ministered to Him.

12 Now when Jesus heard that John had been put in prison, He departed to Galilee.

13 And leaving Nazareth, He came and dwelt in Capernaum, which is by the sea, in the regions of Zebulun and Naphtali,

14 that it might be fulfilled which was spoken by Isaiah the prophet, saying:

15 "The land of Zebulun and the
   land of Naphtali,
The way of the sea, beyond the
   Jordan,
Galilee of the Gentiles:
16 The people who sat in darkness
   saw a great light,
And upon those who sat in the
   region and shadow of death
Light has dawned."

17 From that time Jesus began to preach and to say, "Repent, for the kingdom of heaven is at hand."

18 Now Jesus, walking by the Sea of Galilee, saw two brothers, Simon called Peter, and Andrew his brother, casting a net into the sea; for they were fishermen.

19 And He said to them, "Follow Me, and I will make you fishers of men."

20 Then they immediately left *their* nets and followed Him.

21 And going on from there, He saw two other brothers, James *the son* of Zebedee, and John his brother, in the boat with Zebedee their father, mending their nets. And He called them,

22 and immediately they left the boat and their father, and followed Him.

23 Now Jesus went about all Galilee, teaching in their synagogues, preaching the gospel of the kingdom, and healing all kinds of sickness and all kinds of disease among the people.

24 Then His fame went throughout all Syria; and they brought to Him all sick people who were afflicted with various diseases and torments, and those who were demon-possessed, epileptics, and paralytics; and He healed them.

25 And great multitudes followed Him—from Galilee, and *from* Decapolis, Jerusalem, Judea, and beyond the Jordan.

5 And seeing the multitudes, He went up on a mountain, and when He was seated His disciples came to Him.

2 Then He opened His mouth and taught them, saying:

3 "Blessed *are* the poor in spirit,
   For theirs is the kingdom of
    heaven.
4 Blessed *are* those who mourn,
   For they shall be comforted.
5 Blessed *are* the meek,
   For they shall inherit the
    earth.
6 Blessed *are* those who hunger
   and thirst for righteousness,
   For they shall be filled.

7 Blessed *are* the merciful,
　For they shall obtain mercy.
8 Blessed *are* the pure in heart,
　For they shall see God.
9 Blessed *are* the peacemakers,
　For they shall be called sons
　　of God.
10 Blessed are those who are
　　persecuted for righ-
　　teousness' sake,
　For theirs is the kingdom of
　　heaven.

11 "Blessed are you when they revile and persecute you, and say all
kinds of evil against you falsely for
My sake.
12 "Rejoice and be exceedingly
glad, for great *is* your reward in
heaven, for so they persecuted the
prophets who were before you.
13 "You are the salt of the earth;
but if the salt loses its flavor, how
shall it be seasoned? It is then good
for nothing but to be thrown out
and trampled under foot by men.
14 "You are the light of the world.
A city that is set on a hill cannot
be hidden.
15 "Nor do they light a lamp and
put it under a basket, but on a
lampstand, and it gives light to all
who are in the house.
16 "Let your light so shine before
men, that they may see your good
works and glorify your Father in
heaven.
17 "Do not think that I came to
destroy the Law or the Prophets. I
did not come to destroy but to
fulfill.
18 "For assuredly, I say to you, till
heaven and earth pass away, one
jot or one tittle will by no means
pass from the law till all is fulfilled.
19 "Whoever therefore breaks one
of the least of these commandments, and teaches men so, shall
be called least in the kingdom of
heaven; but whoever does and
teaches *them*, he shall be called
great in the kingdom of heaven.
20 "For I say to you, that unless

your righteousness exceeds *the
righteousness* of the scribes and
Pharisees, you will by no means
enter the kingdom of heaven.
21 "You have heard that it was
said to those of old, *'You shall not
murder,'* and whoever murders
will be in danger of the judgment.
22 "But I say to you that whoever
is angry with his brother without a
cause shall be in danger of the
judgment. And whoever says to his
brother, 'Raca!' shall be in danger
of the council. But whoever says,
'You fool!' shall be in danger of hell
fire.
23 "Therefore if you bring your gift
to the altar, and there remember
that your brother has something
against you,
24 "leave your gift there before the
altar, and go your way. First be
reconciled to your brother, and
then come and offer your gift.
25 "Agree with your adversary
quickly, while you are on the way
with him, lest your adversary deliver you to the judge, the judge
hand you over to the officer, and
you be thrown into prison.
26 "Assuredly, I say to you, you
will by no means get out of there
till you have paid the last penny.
27 "You have heard that it was
said to those of old, *'You shall not
commit adultery.'*
28 "But I say to you that whoever
looks at a woman to lust for her
has already committed adultery
with her in his heart.
29 "And if your right eye causes
you to sin, pluck it out and cast *it*
from you; for it is more profitable
for you that one of your members
perish, than for your whole body
to be cast into hell.
30 "And if your right hand causes
you to sin, cut it off and cast *it*
from you; for it is more profitable
for you that one of your members
perish, than for your whole body
to be cast into hell.
31 "Furthermore it has been said,

'Whoever divorces his wife, let him give her a certificate of divorce.'

32 "But I say to you that whoever divorces his wife for any reason except sexual immorality causes her to commit adultery; and whoever marries a woman who is divorced commits adultery.

33 "Again you have heard that it was said to those of old, 'You shall not swear falsely, but shall perform your oaths to the Lord.'

34 "But I say to you, do not swear at all: neither by heaven, for it is God's throne;

35 "nor by the earth, for it is His footstool; nor by Jerusalem, for it is the city of the great King.

36 "Nor shall you swear by your head, because you cannot make one hair white or black.

37 "But let your 'Yes' be 'Yes,' and your 'No,' 'No.' For whatever is more than these is from the evil one.

38 "You have heard that it was said, *'An eye for an eye and a tooth for a tooth.'*

39 "But I tell you not to resist an evil person. But whoever slaps you on your right cheek, turn the other to him also.

40 "If anyone wants to sue you and take away your tunic, let him have *your* cloak also.

41 "And whoever compels you to go one mile, go with him two.

42 "Give to him who asks you, and from him who wants to borrow from you do not turn away.

43 "You have heard that it was said, 'You shall love your neighbor and hate your enemy.'

44 "But I say to you, love your enemies, bless those who curse you, do good to those who hate you, and pray for those who spitefully use you and persecute you,

45 "that you may be sons of your Father in heaven; for He makes His sun rise on the evil and on the good, and sends rain on the just and on the unjust.

46 "For if you love those who love you, what reward have you? Do not even the tax collectors do the same?

47 "And if you greet your brethren only, what do you do more *than others?* Do not even the tax collectors do so?

48 "Therefore you shall be perfect, just as your Father in heaven is perfect.

6 "Take heed that you do not do your charitable deeds before men, to be seen by them. Otherwise you have no reward from your Father in heaven.

2 "Therefore, when you do a charitable deed, do not sound a trumpet before you as the hypocrites do in the synagogues and in the streets, that they may have glory from men. Assuredly, I say to you, they have their reward.

3 "But when you do a charitable deed, do not let your left hand know what your right hand is doing,

4 "that your charitable deed may be in secret; and your Father who sees in secret will Himself reward you openly.

5 "And when you pray, you shall not be like the hypocrites. For they love to pray standing in the synagogues and on the corners of the streets, that they may be seen by men. Assuredly, I say to you, they have their reward.

6 "But you, when you pray, go into your room, and when you have shut your door, pray to your Father who *is* in the secret *place;* and your Father who sees in secret will reward you openly.

7 "But when you pray, do not use vain repetitions as the heathen *do.* For they think that they will be heard for their many words.

8 "Therefore do not be like them. For your Father knows the things you have need of before you ask Him.

9 "In this manner, therefore, pray:

See Matthew 18:15, page 24   6

Our Father in heaven,
Hallowed be Your name.
10 Your kingdom come.
Your will be done
On earth as *it is* in heaven.
11 Give us this day our daily
bread.
12 And forgive us our debts,
As we forgive our debtors.
13 And do not lead us into
temptation,
But deliver us from the evil
one.
For Yours is the kingdom and
the power and the glory
forever. Amen.
14 "For if you forgive men their
trespasses, your heavenly Father
will also forgive you.
15 "But if you do not forgive men
their trespasses, neither will your
Father forgive your trespasses.
16 "Moreover, when you fast, do
not be like the hypocrites, with a
sad countenance. For they disfig-
ure their faces that they may appear to men to be fasting. Assuredly, I say to you, they have
their reward.
17 "But you, when you fast, anoint
your head and wash your face,
18 "so that you do not appear to
men to be fasting, but to your Father who *is* in the secret *place;* and
your Father who sees in secret will
reward you openly.
19 "Do not lay up for yourselves
treasures on earth, where moth
and rust destroy and where thieves
break in and steal;
20 "but lay up for yourselves treasures in heaven, where neither
moth nor rust destroys and where
thieves do not break in and steal.
21 "For where your treasure is,
there your heart will be also.
22 "The lamp of the body is the
eye. If therefore your eye is good,
your whole body will be full of
light.
23 "But if your eye is bad, your

whole body will be full of darkness.
If therefore the light that is in you
is darkness, how great *is* that darkness!
24 "No one can serve two masters;
for either he will hate the one and
love the other, or else he will be
loyal to the one and despise the
other. You cannot serve God and
mammon.
25 "Therefore I say to you, do not
worry about your life, what you
will eat or what you will drink; nor
about your body, what you will put
on. Is not life more than food and
the body more than clothing?
26 "Look at the birds of the air, for
they neither sow nor reap nor
gather into barns; yet your heavenly Father feeds them. Are you
not of more value than they?
27 "Which of you by worrying can
add one cubit to his stature?
28 "So why do you worry about
clothing? Consider the lilies of the
field, how they grow: they neither
toil nor spin;
29 "and yet I say to you that even
Solomon in all his glory was not
arrayed like one of these.
30 "Now if God so clothes the
grass of the field, which today is,
and tomorrow is thrown into the
oven, *will He* not much more
clothe you, O you of little faith?
31 "Therefore do not worry, saying, 'What shall we eat?' or 'What
shall we drink?' or 'What shall we
wear?'
32 "For after all these things the
Gentiles seek. For your heavenly
Father knows that you need all
these things.
33 "But seek first the kingdom of
God and His righteousness, and all
these things shall be added to you. ❤
34 "Therefore do not worry about
tomorrow, for tomorrow will
worry about its own things. Sufficient for the day *is* its own trouble.
7 "Judge not, that you be not
judged.
2 "For with what judgment you

See Matthew 11:29, page 14

judge, you will be judged; and with the *same* measure you use, it will be measured back to you.

3 "And why do you look at the speck in your brother's eye, but do not consider the plank in your own eye?

4 "Or how can you say to your brother, 'Let me remove the speck out of your eye'; and look, a plank *is* in your own eye?

5 "Hypocrite! First remove the plank from your own eye, and then you will see clearly to remove the speck out of your brother's eye.

6 "Do not give what is holy to the dogs; nor cast your pearls before swine, lest they trample them under their feet, and turn and tear you in pieces.

7 "Ask, and it will be given to you; seek, and you will find; knock, and it will be opened to you.

8 "For everyone who asks receives, and he who seeks finds, and to him who knocks it will be opened.

9 "Or what man is there among you who, if his son asks for bread, will give him a stone?

10 "Or if he asks for a fish, will he give him a serpent?

11 "If you then, being evil, know how to give good gifts to your children, how much more will your Father who is in heaven give good things to those who ask Him!

12 "Therefore, whatever you want men to do to you, do also to them, for this is the Law and the Prophets.

13 "Enter by the narrow gate; for wide *is* the gate and broad *is* the way that leads to destruction, and there are many who go in by it.

14 "Because narrow *is* the gate and difficult *is* the way which leads to life, and there are few who find it.

15 "Beware of false prophets, who come to you in sheep's clothing, but inwardly they are ravenous wolves.

16 "You will know them by their fruits. Do men gather grapes from thornbushes or figs from thistles?

17 "Even so, every good tree bears good fruit, but a bad tree bears bad fruit.

18 "A good tree cannot bear bad fruit, nor *can* a bad tree bear good fruit.

19 "Every tree that does not bear good fruit is cut down and thrown into the fire.

20 "Therefore by their fruits you will know them.

21 "Not everyone who says to Me, 'Lord, Lord,' shall enter the kingdom of heaven, but he who does the will of My Father in heaven.

22 "Many will say to Me in that day, 'Lord, Lord, have we not prophesied in Your name, cast out demons in Your name, and done many wonders in Your name?'

23 "And then I will declare to them, 'I never knew you; depart from Me, you who practice lawlessness!'

24 "Therefore whoever hears these sayings of Mine, and does them, I will liken him to a wise man who built his house on the rock:

25 "and the rain descended, the floods came, and the winds blew and beat on that house; and it did not fall, for it was founded on the rock.

26 "Now everyone who hears these sayings of Mine, and does not do them, will be like a foolish man who built his house on the sand:

27 "and the rain descended, the floods came, and the winds blew and beat on that house; and it fell. And great was its fall."

28 And so it was, when Jesus had ended these sayings, that the people were astonished at His teaching,

29 for He taught them as one having authority, and not as the scribes.

8 When He had come down from the mountain, great multitudes followed Him.

See John 15:7, page 135

2 And behold, a leper came and worshiped Him, saying, "Lord, if You are willing, You can make me clean."

3 Then Jesus put out *His* hand and touched him, saying, "I am willing; be cleansed." And immediately his leprosy was cleansed.

4 And Jesus said to him, "See that you tell no one; but go your way, show yourself to the priest, and offer the gift that Moses commanded, as a testimony to them."

5 Now when Jesus had entered Capernaum, a centurion came to Him, pleading with Him,

6 saying, "Lord, my servant is lying at home paralyzed, dreadfully tormented."

7 And Jesus said to him, "I will come and heal him."

8 The centurion answered and said, "Lord, I am not worthy that You should come under my roof. But only speak a word, and my servant will be healed.

9 "For I also am a man under authority, having soldiers under me. And I say to this *one,* 'Go,' and he goes; and to another, 'Come,' and he comes; and to my servant, 'Do this,' and he does *it.*"

10 When Jesus heard *it,* He marveled, and said to those who followed, "Assuredly, I say to you, I have not found such great faith, not even in Israel!

11 "And I say to you that many will come from east and west, and sit down with Abraham, Isaac, and Jacob in the kingdom of heaven.

12 "But the sons of the kingdom will be cast out into outer darkness. There will be weeping and gnashing of teeth."

13 Then Jesus said to the centurion, "Go your way; and as you have believed, *so* let it be done for you." And his servant was healed that same hour.

14 Now when Jesus had come into Peter's house, He saw his wife's mother lying sick with a fever.

15 And He touched her hand, and the fever left her. Then she arose and served them.

16 When evening had come, they brought to Him many who were demon-possessed. And He cast out the spirits with a word, and healed all who were sick,

17 that it might be fulfilled which was spoken by Isaiah the prophet, saying:

*"He Himself took our infirmities
And bore our sicknesses."*

18 Now when Jesus saw great multitudes about Him, He gave a command to depart to the other side.

19 Then a certain scribe came and said to Him, "Teacher, I will follow You wherever You go."

20 And Jesus said to him, "Foxes have holes and birds of the air *have* nests, but the Son of Man has nowhere to lay *His* head."

21 Then another of His disciples said to Him, "Lord, let me first go and bury my father."

22 But Jesus said to him, "Follow Me, and let the dead bury their own dead."

23 Now when He got into a boat, His disciples followed Him.

24 And suddenly a great tempest arose on the sea, so that the boat was covered with the waves. But He was asleep.

25 Then His disciples came to *Him* and awoke Him, saying, "Lord, save us! We are perishing!"

26 But He said to them, "Why are you fearful, O you of little faith?" Then He arose and rebuked the winds and the sea. And there was a great calm.

27 And the men marveled, saying, "Who can this be, that even the winds and the sea obey Him?"

28 When He had come to the other side, to the country of the Gergesenes, there met Him two demon-possessed *men,* coming out of the tombs, exceedingly fierce, so that no one could pass that way.

29 And suddenly they cried out, saying, "What have we to do with You, Jesus, You Son of God? Have You come here to torment us before the time?"

30 Now a good way off from them there was a herd of many swine feeding.

31 So the demons begged Him, saying, "If You cast us out, permit us to go away into the herd of swine."

32 And He said to them, "Go." So when they had come out, they went into the herd of swine. And suddenly the whole herd of swine ran violently down the steep place into the sea, and perished in the water.

33 Then those who kept *them* fled; and they went away into the city and told everything, including what *had happened* to the demon-possessed *men*.

34 And behold, the whole city came out to meet Jesus. And when they saw Him, they begged *Him* to depart from their region.

9 So He got into a boat, crossed over, and came to His own city.

2 And behold, they brought to Him a paralytic lying on a bed. And Jesus, seeing their faith, said to the paralytic, "Son, be of good cheer; your sins are forgiven you."

3 And at once some of the scribes said within themselves, "This *Man* blasphemes!"

4 But Jesus, knowing their thoughts, said, "Why do you think evil in your hearts?

5 "For which is easier, to say, '*Your* sins are forgiven you,' or to say, 'Arise and walk'?

6 "But that you may know that the Son of Man has power on earth to forgive sins"—then He said to the paralytic, "Arise, take up your bed, and go to your house."

7 And he arose and departed to his house.

8 Now when the multitudes saw *it*, they marveled and glorified God, who had given such power to men.

9 Then as Jesus passed on from there, He saw a man named Matthew sitting at the tax office. And He said to him, "Follow Me." And he arose and followed Him.

10 And so it was, as Jesus sat at the table in the house, *that* behold, many tax collectors and sinners came and sat down with Him and His disciples.

11 And when the Pharisees saw *it*, they said to His disciples, "Why does your Teacher eat with tax collectors and sinners?"

12 But when Jesus heard *that*, He said to them, "Those who are well have no need of a physician, but those who are sick.

13 "But go and learn what *this* means: '*I desire mercy and not sacrifice.*' For I did not come to call the righteous, but sinners, to repentance."

14 Then the disciples of John came to Him, saying, "Why do we and the Pharisees fast often, but Your disciples do not fast?"

15 And Jesus said to them, "Can the friends of the bridegroom mourn as long as the bridegroom is with them? But the days will come when the bridegroom will be taken away from them, and then they will fast.

16 "No one puts a piece of unshrunk cloth on an old garment; for the patch pulls away from the garment, and the tear is made worse.

17 "Nor do *people* put new wine into old wineskins, or else the wineskins break, the wine is spilled, and the wineskins are ruined. But they put new wine into new wineskins, and both are preserved."

18 While He spoke these things to them, behold, a ruler came and worshiped Him, saying, "My daughter has just died, but come

and lay Your hand on her and she will live."

19 So Jesus arose and followed him, and so *did* His disciples.

20 And suddenly, a woman who had a flow of blood for twelve years came from behind and touched the hem of His garment;

21 for she said to herself, "If only I may touch His garment, I shall be made well."

22 But Jesus turned around, and when He saw her He said, "Be of good cheer, daughter; your faith has made you well." And the woman was made well from that hour.

23 And when Jesus came into the ruler's house, and saw the flute players and the noisy crowd wailing,

24 He said to them, "Make room, for the girl is not dead, but sleeping." And they laughed Him to scorn.

25 But when the crowd was put outside, He went in and took her by the hand, and the girl arose.

26 And the report of this went out into all that land.

27 When Jesus departed from there, two blind men followed Him, crying out and saying, "Son of David, have mercy on us!"

28 And when He had come into the house, the blind men came to Him. And Jesus said to them, "Do you believe that I am able to do this?" They said to Him, "Yes, Lord."

29 Then He touched their eyes, saying, "According to your faith let it be to you."

30 And their eyes were opened. And Jesus sternly warned them, saying, "See *that* no one knows *it.*"

31 But when they had departed, they spread the news about Him in all that country.

32 As they went out, behold, they brought to Him a man, mute and demon-possessed.

33 And when the demon was cast out, the mute spoke. And the mul-

titudes marveled, saying, "It was never seen like this in Israel!"

34 But the Pharisees said, "He casts out demons by the ruler of the demons."

35 And Jesus went about all the cities and villages, teaching in their synagogues, preaching the gospel of the kingdom, and healing every sickness and every disease among the people.

36 But when He saw the multitudes, He was moved with compassion for them, because they were weary and scattered, like sheep having no shepherd.

37 Then He said to His disciples, "The harvest truly *is* plentiful, but the laborers *are* few.

38 "Therefore pray the Lord of the harvest to send out laborers into His harvest."

10 And when He had called His twelve disciples to *Him,* He gave them power *over* unclean spirits, to cast them out, and to heal all kinds of sickness and all kinds of disease.

2 Now the names of the twelve apostles are these: first, Simon, who is called Peter, and Andrew his brother; James the *son* of Zebedee, and John his brother;

3 Philip and Bartholomew; Thomas and Matthew the tax collector; James the *son* of Alphaeus, and Lebbaeus, whose surname was Thaddaeus;

4 Simon the Canaanite, and Judas Iscariot, who also betrayed Him.

5 These twelve Jesus sent out and commanded them, saying: "Do not go into the way of the Gentiles, and do not enter a city of the Samaritans.

6 "But go rather to the lost sheep of the house of Israel.

7 "And as you go, preach, saying, 'The kingdom of heaven is at hand.'

8 "Heal the sick, cleanse the lepers, raise the dead, cast out de-

mons. Freely you have received, freely give.

9 "Provide neither gold nor silver nor copper in your moneybelts,

10 "nor bag for *your* journey, nor two tunics, nor sandals, nor staffs; for a worker is worthy of his food.

11 "Now whatever city or town you enter, inquire who in it is worthy, and stay there till you go out.

12 "And when you go into a household, greet it.

13 "If the household is worthy, let your peace come upon it. But if it is not worthy, let your peace return to you.

14 "And whoever will not receive you nor hear your words, when you depart from that house or city, shake off the dust from your feet.

15 "Assuredly, I say to you, it will be more tolerable for the land of Sodom and Gomorrah in the day of judgment than for that city!

16 "Behold, I send you out as sheep in the midst of wolves. Therefore be wise as serpents and harmless as doves.

17 "But beware of men, for they will deliver you up to councils and scourge you in their synagogues.

18 "And you will be brought before governors and kings for My sake, as a testimony to them and to the Gentiles.

19 "But when they deliver you up, do not worry about how or what you should speak. For it will be given to you in that hour what you should speak;

20 "for it is not you who speak, but the Spirit of your Father who speaks in you.

21 "Now brother will deliver up brother to death, and a father *his* child; and children will rise up against parents and cause them to be put to death.

22 "And you will be hated by all for My name's sake. But he who endures to the end will be saved.

23 "But when they persecute you in this city, flee to another. For

assuredly, I say to you, you will not have gone through the cities of Israel before the Son of Man comes.

24 "A disciple is not above *his* teacher, nor a servant above his master.

25 "It is enough for a disciple that he be like his teacher, and a servant like his master. If they have called the master of the house Beelzebub, how much more *will they call* those of his household!

26 "Therefore do not fear them. For there is nothing covered that will not be revealed, and hidden that will not be known.

27 "Whatever I tell you in the dark, speak in the light; and what you hear in the ear, preach on the housetops.

28 "And do not fear those who kill the body but cannot kill the soul. But rather fear Him who is able to destroy both soul and body in hell.

29 "Are not two sparrows sold for a copper coin? And not one of them falls to the ground apart from your Father's will.

30 "But the very hairs of your head are all numbered.

31 "Do not fear therefore; you are of more value than many sparrows.

32 "Therefore whoever confesses Me before men, him I will also confess before My Father who is in heaven.

33 "But whoever denies Me before men, him I will also deny before My Father who is in heaven.

34 "Do not think that I came to bring peace on earth. I did not come to bring peace but a sword.

35 "For I have come to 'set a man *against his father, a daughter against her mother, and a daughter-in-law against her mother-in-law.*'

36 "And '*a man's foes will be those of his own household.*'

37 "He who loves father or mother more than Me is not worthy of Me.

And he who loves son or daughter more than Me is not worthy of Me. 38 "And he who does not take his cross and follow after Me is not worthy of Me.

39 "He who finds his life will lose it, and he who loses his life for My sake will find it.

40 "He who receives you receives Me, and he who receives Me receives Him who sent Me.

41 "He who receives a prophet in the name of a prophet shall receive a prophet's reward. And he who receives a righteous man in the name of a righteous man shall receive a righteous man's reward.

42 "And whoever gives one of these little ones only a cup of cold *water* in the name of a disciple, assuredly, I say to you, he shall by no means lose his reward."

11 Now it came to pass, when Jesus finished commanding His twelve disciples, that He departed from there to teach and to preach in their cities.

2 And when John had heard in prison about the works of Christ, he sent two of his disciples

3 and said to Him, "Are You the Coming One, or do we look for another?"

4 Jesus answered and said to them, "Go and tell John the things which you hear and see:

5 "*The* blind receive their sight and *the* lame walk; *the* lepers are cleansed and *the* deaf hear; *the* dead are raised up and *the* poor have the gospel preached to them.

6 "And blessed is he who is not offended because of Me."

7 As they departed, Jesus began to say to the multitudes concerning John: "What did you go out into the wilderness to see? A reed shaken by the wind?

8 "But what did you go out to see? A man clothed in soft garments? Indeed, those who wear soft *clothing* are in kings' houses.

9 "But what did you go out to see? A prophet? Yes, I say to you, and more than a prophet.

10 "For this is *he* of whom it is written:

'Behold, I send My messenger
    before Your face,
Who will prepare Your way
    before You.'

11 "Assuredly, I say to you, among those born of women there has not risen one greater than John the Baptist; but he who is least in the kingdom of heaven is greater than he.

12 "And from the days of John the Baptist until now the kingdom of heaven suffers violence, and the violent take it by force.

13 "For all the prophets and the law prophesied until John.

14 "And if you are willing to receive *it*, he is Elijah who is to come.

15 "He who has ears to hear, let him hear!

16 "But to what shall I liken this generation? It is like children sitting in the marketplaces and calling to their companions,

17 "and saying:

'We played the flute for you,
    And you did not dance;
We mourned to you,
    And you did not lament.'

18 "For John came neither eating nor drinking, and they say, 'He has a demon.'

19 "The Son of Man came eating and drinking, and they say, 'Look, a gluttonous man and a winebibber, a friend of tax collectors and sinners!' But wisdom is justified by her children."

20 Then He began to upbraid the cities in which most of His mighty works had been done, because they did not repent:

21 "Woe to you, Chorazin! Woe to

13

you, Bethsaida! For if the mighty works which were done in you had been done in Tyre and Sidon, they would have repented long ago in sackcloth and ashes.

22 "But I say to you, it will be more tolerable for Tyre and Sidon in the day of judgment than for you.

23 "And you, Capernaum, who are exalted to heaven, will be brought down to Hades; for if the mighty works which were done in you had been done in Sodom, it would have remained until this day.

24 "But I say to you that it shall be more tolerable for the land of Sodom in the day of judgment than for you."

25 At that time Jesus answered and said, "I thank You, Father, Lord of heaven and earth, because You have hidden these things from the wise and prudent and have revealed them to babes.

26 "Even so, Father, for so it seemed good in Your sight.

27 "All things have been delivered to Me by My Father, and no one knows the Son except the Father. Nor does anyone know the Father except the Son, and *he* to whom the Son wills to reveal *Him.*

28 "Come to Me, all *you* who labor and are heavy laden, and I will give you rest.

❤ 29 "Take My yoke upon you and learn from Me, for I am gentle and lowly in heart, and you will find rest for your souls.

30 "For My yoke *is* easy and My burden is light."

12 At that time Jesus went through the grainfields on the Sabbath. And His disciples were hungry, and began to pluck heads of grain and to eat.

2 But when the Pharisees saw *it,* they said to Him, "Look, Your disciples are doing what is not lawful to do on the Sabbath!"

3 Then He said to them, "Have you not read what David did when

See John 14:27, page 134

he was hungry, he and those who were with him:

4 "how he entered the house of God and ate the showbread which was not lawful for him to eat, nor for those who were with him, but only for the priests?

5 "Or have you not read in the law that on the Sabbath the priests in the temple profane the Sabbath, and are blameless?

6 "But I say to you that in this place there is *One* greater than the temple.

7 "But if you had known what this means, '*I desire mercy and not sacrifice,*' you would not have condemned the guiltless.

8 "For the Son of Man is Lord even of the Sabbath."

9 Now when He had departed from there, He went into their synagogue.

10 And behold, there was a man who had a withered hand. And they asked Him, saying, "Is it lawful to heal on the Sabbath?"—that they might accuse Him.

11 Then He said to them, "What man is there among you who has one sheep, and if it falls into a pit on the Sabbath, will not lay hold of it and lift *it* out?

12 "Of how much more value then is a man than a sheep? Therefore it is lawful to do good on the Sabbath."

13 Then He said to the man, "Stretch out your hand." And he stretched *it* out, and it was restored as whole as the other.

14 Then the Pharisees went out and took counsel against Him, how they might destroy Him.

15 But when Jesus knew *it,* He withdrew from there; and great multitudes followed Him, and He healed them all.

16 And He warned them not to make Him known,

17 that it might be fulfilled which was spoken by Isaiah the prophet, saying:

18 "Behold, My Servant whom I
   have chosen,
My Beloved in whom My soul
   is well pleased;
I will put My Spirit upon Him,
And He will declare justice
   to the Gentiles.
19 He will not quarrel nor cry out,
Nor will anyone hear His voice
   in the streets.
20 A bruised reed He will not
   break,
And smoking flax He will not
   quench,
Till He sends forth justice to
   victory.
21 And in His name Gentiles will
   trust."

22 Then one was brought to Him who was demon-possessed, blind and mute; and He healed him, so that the blind and mute man both spoke and saw.
23 And all the multitudes were amazed and said, "Could this be the Son of David?"
24 But when the Pharisees heard *it* they said, "This *fellow* does not cast out demons except by Beelzebub, the ruler of the demons."
25 But Jesus knew their thoughts, and said to them: "Every kingdom divided against itself is brought to desolation, and every city or house divided against itself will not stand.
26 "And if Satan casts out Satan, he is divided against himself. How then will his kingdom stand?
27 "And if I cast out demons by Beelzebub, by whom do your sons cast *them* out? Therefore they shall be your judges.
28 "But if I cast out demons by the Spirit of God, surely the kingdom of God has come upon you.
29 "Or *else* how can one enter a strong man's house and plunder his goods, unless he first binds the strong man? And then he will plunder his house.
30 "He who is not with Me is against Me, and he who does not gather with Me scatters abroad.
31 "Therefore I say to you, every sin and blasphemy will be forgiven men, but the blasphemy *against* the Spirit will not be forgiven men.
32 "Anyone who speaks a word against the Son of Man, it will be forgiven him; but whoever speaks against the Holy Spirit, it will not be forgiven him, either in this age or in the *age* to come.
33 "Either make the tree good and its fruit good, or else make the tree bad and its fruit bad; for a tree is known by *its* fruit.
34 "Brood of vipers! How can you, being evil, speak good things? For out of the abundance of the heart the mouth speaks.
35 "A good man out of the good treasure of his heart brings forth good things, and an evil man out of the evil treasure brings forth evil things.
36 "But I say to you that for every idle word men may speak, they will give account of it in the day of judgment.
37 "For by your words you will be justified, and by your words you will be condemned."
38 Then some of the scribes and Pharisees answered, saying, "Teacher, we want to see a sign from You."
39 But He answered and said to them, "An evil and adulterous generation seeks after a sign, and no sign will be given to it except the sign of the prophet Jonah.
40 "For as Jonah was three days and three nights in the belly of the great fish, so will the Son of Man be three days and three nights in the heart of the earth.
41 "The men of Nineveh will rise in the judgment with this generation and condemn it, because they repented at the preaching of Jonah; and indeed a greater than Jonah *is* here.
42 "The queen of the South will

rise up in the judgment with this generation and condemn it, for she came from the ends of the earth to hear the wisdom of Solomon; and indeed a greater than Solomon *is* here.

43 "When an unclean spirit goes out of a man, he goes through dry places, seeking rest, and finds none.

44 "Then he says, 'I will return to my house from which I came.' And when he comes, he finds it empty, swept, and put in order.

45 "Then he goes and takes with him seven other spirits more wicked than himself, and they enter and dwell there; and the last *state* of that man is worse than the first. So shall it also be with this wicked generation."

46 While He was still talking to the multitudes, behold, His mother and brothers stood outside, seeking to speak with Him.

47 Then one said to Him, "Look, Your mother and Your brothers are standing outside, seeking to speak with You."

48 But He answered and said to the one who told Him, "Who is My mother and who are My brothers?"

49 And He stretched out His hand toward His disciples and said, "Here are My mother and My brothers!

50 "For whoever does the will of My Father in heaven is My brother and sister and mother."

13 On the same day Jesus went out of the house and sat by the sea.

2 And great multitudes were gathered together to Him, so that He got into a boat and sat; and the whole multitude stood on the shore.

3 Then He spoke many things to them in parables, saying: "Behold, a sower went out to sow.

4 "And as he sowed, some *seed* fell by the wayside; and the birds came and devoured them.

5 "Some fell on stony places, where they did not have much earth; and they immediately sprang up because they had no depth of earth.

6 "But when the sun was up they were scorched, and because they had no root they withered away.

7 "And some fell among thorns, and the thorns sprang up and choked them.

8 "But others fell on good ground and yielded a crop: some a hundredfold, some sixty, some thirty.

9 "He who has ears to hear, let him hear!"

10 And the disciples came and said to Him, "Why do You speak to them in parables?"

11 He answered and said to them, "Because it has been given to you to know the mysteries of the kingdom of heaven, but to them it has not been given.

12 "For whoever has, to him more will be given, and he will have abundance; but whoever does not have, even what he has will be taken away from him.

13 "Therefore I speak to them in parables, because seeing they do not see, and hearing they do not hear, nor do they understand.

14 "And in them the prophecy of Isaiah is fulfilled, which says:

'Hearing you will hear
  and shall not understand,
And seeing you will see
  and not perceive;
15 For the heart of this people
  has grown dull.
Their ears are hard of hearing,
And their eyes they have
  closed,
Lest they should see with their
  eyes and hear with their ears,
Lest they should understand
  with their heart and turn,
So that I should heal them.'

16 "But blessed *are* your eyes for

they see, and your ears for they hear;

17 "for assuredly, I say to you that many prophets and righteous *men* desired to see what you see, and did not see *it*, and to hear what you hear, and did not hear *it*.

18 "Therefore hear the parable of the sower:

19 "When anyone hears the word of the kingdom, and does not understand *it*, then the wicked *one* comes and snatches away what was sown in his heart. This is he who received seed by the wayside.

20 "But he who received the seed on stony places, this is he who hears the word and immediately receives it with joy;

21 "yet he has no root in himself, but endures only for a while. For when tribulation or persecution arises because of the word, immediately he stumbles.

22 "Now he who received seed among the thorns is he who hears the word, and the cares of this world and the deceitfulness of riches choke the word, and he becomes unfruitful.

23 "But he who received seed on the good ground is he who hears the word and understands *it*, who indeed bears fruit and produces: some a hundredfold, some sixty, some thirty."

24 Another parable He put forth to them, saying: "The kingdom of heaven is like a man who sowed good seed in his field;

25 "but while men slept, his enemy came and sowed tares among the wheat and went his way.

26 "But when the grain had sprouted and produced a crop, then the tares also appeared.

27 "So the servants of the owner came and said to him, 'Sir, did you not sow good seed in your field? How then does it have tares?'

28 "He said to them, 'An enemy has done this.' The servants said to him, 'Do you want us then to go and gather them up?'

29 "But he said, 'No, lest while you gather up the tares you also uproot the wheat with them.

30 'Let both grow together until the harvest, and at the time of harvest I will say to the reapers, "First gather together the tares and bind them in bundles to burn them, but gather the wheat into my barn." ' "

31 Another parable He put forth to them, saying: "The kingdom of heaven is like a mustard seed, which a man took and sowed in his field,

32 "which indeed is the least of all the seeds; but when it is grown it is greater than the herbs and becomes a tree, so that the birds of the air come and nest in its branches."

33 Another parable He spoke to them: "The kingdom of heaven is like leaven, which a woman took and hid in three measures of meal till it was all leavened."

34 All these things Jesus spoke to the multitude in parables; and without a parable He did not speak to them,

35 that it might be fulfilled which was spoken by the prophet, saying:

> *"I will open My mouth in*
> *parables;*
> *I will utter things which have*
> *been kept secret from the*
> *foundation of the world."*

36 Then Jesus sent the multitude away and went into the house. And His disciples came to Him, saying, "Explain to us the parable of the tares of the field."

37 He answered and said to them: "He who sows the good seed is the Son of Man.

38 "The field is the world, the good seeds are the sons of the kingdom, but the tares are the sons of the wicked *one*.

39 "The enemy who sowed them is the devil, the harvest is the end of the age, and the reapers are the angels.

40 "Therefore as the tares are gathered and burned in the fire, so it will be at the end of this age.

41 "The Son of Man will send out His angels, and they will gather out of His kingdom all things that offend, and those who practice lawlessness,

42 "and will cast them into the furnace of fire. There will be wailing and gnashing of teeth.

43 "Then the righteous will shine forth as the sun in the kingdom of their Father. He who has ears to hear, let him hear!

44 "Again, the kingdom of heaven is like treasure hidden in a field, which a man found and hid; and for joy over it he goes and sells all that he has and buys that field.

45 "Again, the kingdom of heaven is like a merchant seeking beautiful pearls,

46 "who, when he had found one pearl of great price, went and sold all that he had and bought it.

47 "Again, the kingdom of heaven is like a dragnet that was cast into the sea and gathered some of every kind,

48 "which, when it was full, they drew to shore; and they sat down and gathered the good into vessels, but threw the bad away.

49 "So it will be at the end of the age. The angels will come forth, separate the wicked from among the just,

50 "and cast them into the furnace of fire. There will be wailing and gnashing of teeth."

51 Jesus said to them, "Have you understood all these things?" They said to Him, "Yes, Lord."

52 Then He said to them, "Therefore every scribe instructed concerning the kingdom of heaven is like a householder who brings out of his treasure *things* new and old."

53 Now it came to pass, when Jesus had finished these parables, that He departed from there.

54 And when He had come to His own country, He taught them in their synagogue, so that they were astonished and said, "Where did this *Man* get this wisdom and *these* mighty works?

55 "Is this not the carpenter's son? Is not His mother called Mary? And His brothers James, Joses, Simon, and Judas?

56 "And His sisters, are they not all with us? Where then did this *Man* get all these things?"

57 So they were offended at Him. But Jesus said to them, "A prophet is not without honor except in his own country and in his own house."

58 And He did not do many mighty works there because of their unbelief.

14 At that time Herod the tetrarch heard the report about Jesus

2 and said to his servants, "This is John the Baptist; he is risen from the dead, and therefore these powers are at work in him."

3 For Herod had laid hold of John and bound him, and put *him* in prison for the sake of Herodias, his brother Philip's wife.

4 For John had said to him, "It is not lawful for you to have her."

5 And although he wanted to put him to death, he feared the multitude, because they counted him as a prophet.

6 But when Herod's birthday was celebrated, the daughter of Herodias danced before them and pleased Herod.

7 Therefore he promised with an oath to give her whatever she might ask.

8 So she, having been prompted by her mother, said, "Give me

John the Baptist's head here on a platter."

9 And the king was sorry; nevertheless, because of the oaths and because of those who sat with him at the table, he commanded *it* to be given to *her.*

10 So he sent and had John beheaded in prison.

11 And his head was brought on a platter and given to the girl, and she brought *it* to her mother.

12 Then his disciples came and took away the body and buried it, and went and told Jesus.

13 When Jesus heard *it,* He departed from there by boat to a deserted place by Himself. But when the multitudes heard it, they followed Him on foot from the cities.

14 And when Jesus went out He saw a great multitude; and He was moved with compassion for them, and healed their sick.

15 When it was evening, His disciples came to Him, saying, "This is a deserted place, and the hour is already late. Send the multitudes away, that they may go into the villages and buy themselves food."

16 But Jesus said to them, "They do not need to go away. You give them something to eat."

17 And they said to Him, "We have here only five loaves and two fish."

18 He said, "Bring them here to Me."

19 Then He commanded the multitudes to sit down on the grass. And He took the five loaves and the two fish, and looking up to heaven, He blessed and broke and gave the loaves to the disciples; and the disciples gave to the multitudes.

20 So they all ate and were filled, and they took up twelve baskets full of the fragments that remained.

21 Now those who had eaten were about five thousand men, besides women and children.

22 Immediately Jesus made His disciples get into the boat and go before Him to the other side, while He sent the multitudes away.

23 And when He had sent the multitudes away, He went up on a mountain by Himself to pray. And when evening had come, He was alone there.

24 But the boat was now in the middle of the sea, tossed by the waves, for the wind was contrary.

25 Now in the fourth watch of the night Jesus went to them, walking on the sea.

26 And when the disciples saw Him walking on the sea, they were troubled, saying, "It is a ghost!" And they cried out for fear.

27 But immediately Jesus spoke to them, saying, "Be of good cheer! It is I; do not be afraid."

28 And Peter answered Him and said, "Lord, if it is You, command me to come to You on the water."

29 So He said, "Come." And when Peter had come down out of the boat, he walked on the water to go to Jesus.

30 But when he saw that the wind *was* boisterous, he was afraid; and beginning to sink he cried out, saying, "Lord, save me!"

31 And immediately Jesus stretched out *His* hand and caught him, and said to him, "O you of little faith, why did you doubt?"

32 And when they got into the boat, the wind ceased.

33 Then those who were in the boat came and worshiped Him, saying, "Truly You are the Son of God."

34 When they had crossed over, they came to the land of Gennesaret.

35 And when the men of that place recognized Him, they sent out into all that surrounding region, brought to Him all who were sick,

36 and begged Him that they might only touch the hem of His garment. And as many as touched it were made perfectly well.

15 Then the scribes and Pharisees who were from Jerusalem came to Jesus, saying,

2 "Why do Your disciples transgress the tradition of the elders? For they do not wash their hands when they eat bread."

3 But He answered and said to them, "Why do you also transgress the commandment of God because of your tradition?

4 "For God commanded, saying, *'Honor your father and your mother'*; and, *'He who curses father or mother, let him be put to death.'*

5 "But you say, 'Whoever says to *his* father or mother, "Whatever profit you might have received from me has been dedicated *to the* temple"—

6 *'is released from* honoring his father or mother.' Thus you have made the commandment of God of no effect by your tradition.

7 "Hypocrites! Well did Isaiah prophesy about you, saying:

8 *'These people draw near to Me with their mouth,*
And honor Me with their lips,
But their heart is far from Me.
9 *And in vain they worship Me,*
Teaching as doctrines the commandments of men.'"

10 Then He called the multitude and said to them, "Hear and understand:

11 "Not what goes into the mouth defiles a man; but what comes out of the mouth, this defiles a man."

12 Then His disciples came and said to Him, "Do You know that the Pharisees were offended when they heard this saying?"

13 But He answered and said, "Every plant which My heavenly Father has not planted will be uprooted.

14 "Let them alone. They are blind leaders of the blind. And if the blind leads the blind, both will fall into a ditch."

15 Then Peter answered and said to Him, "Explain this parable to us."

16 So Jesus said, "Are you also still without understanding?

17 "Do you not yet understand that whatever enters the mouth goes into the stomach and is eliminated?

18 "But those things which proceed out of the mouth come from the heart, and they defile a man.

19 "For out of the heart proceed evil thoughts, murders, adulteries, fornications, thefts, false witness, blasphemies.

20 "These are *the things* which defile a man, but to eat with unwashed hands does not defile a man."

21 Then Jesus went out from there and departed to the region of Tyre and Sidon.

22 And behold, a woman of Canaan came from that region and cried out to Him, saying, "Have mercy on me, O Lord, Son of David! My daughter is severely demon-possessed."

23 But He answered her not a word. And His disciples came and urged Him, saying, "Send her away, for she cries out after us."

24 But He answered and said, "I was not sent except to the lost sheep of the house of Israel."

25 Then she came and worshiped Him, saying, "Lord, help me!"

26 But He answered and said, "It is not good to take the children's bread and throw *it* to the little dogs."

27 And she said, "True, Lord, yet even the little dogs eat the crumbs which fall from their masters' table."

28 Then Jesus answered and said to her, "O woman, great *is* your faith! Let it be to you as you desire." And her daughter was healed from that very hour.

29 And Jesus departed from there, skirted the Sea of Galilee, and went up on the mountain and sat down there.

30 Then great multitudes came to Him, having with them *those who were* lame, blind, mute, maimed, and many others; and they laid them down at Jesus' feet, and He healed them.

31 So the multitude marveled when they saw *the* mute speaking, *the* maimed made whole, *the* lame walking, and *the* blind seeing; and they glorified the God of Israel.

32 Then Jesus called His disciples *to Him* and said, "I have compassion on the multitude, because they have now continued with Me three days and have nothing to eat. And I do not want to send them away hungry, lest they faint on the way."

33 Then His disciples said to Him, "Where could we get enough bread in the wilderness to fill such a great multitude?"

34 Jesus said to them, "How many loaves do you have?" And they said, "Seven, and a few little fish."

35 And He commanded the multitude to sit down on the ground.

36 And He took the seven loaves and the fish and gave thanks, broke *them* and gave *them* to His disciples; and the disciples *gave* to the multitude.

37 So they all ate and were filled, and they took up seven large baskets full of the fragments that were left.

38 Now those who ate were four thousand men, besides women and children.

39 And He sent away the multitude, got into the boat, and came to the region of Magdala.

16 Then the Pharisees and Sadducees came, and testing Him asked that He would show them a sign from heaven.

2 He answered and said to them,

"When it is evening you say, '*It will be* fair weather, for the sky is red';

3 "and in the morning, '*It will be* foul weather today, for the sky is red and threatening.' Hypocrites! You know how to discern the face of the sky, but you cannot *discern* the signs of the times.

4 "A wicked and adulterous generation seeks after a sign, and no sign shall be given to it except the sign of the prophet Jonah." And He left them and departed.

5 And when His disciples had come to the other side, they had forgotten to take bread.

6 Then Jesus said to them, "Take heed and beware of the leaven of the Pharisees and the Sadducees."

7 And they reasoned among themselves, saying, "*It is* because we have taken no bread."

8 But when Jesus perceived it, He said to them, "O you of little faith, why do you reason among yourselves because you have brought no bread?

9 "Do you not yet understand, or remember the five loaves of the five thousand and how many baskets you took up?

10 "Nor the seven loaves of the four thousand and how many large baskets you took up?

11 "How is it you do not understand that I did not speak to you concerning bread?—*but you* should beware of the leaven of the Pharisees and Sadducees."

12 Then they understood that He did not tell *them* to beware of the leaven of bread, but of the doctrine of the Pharisees and Sadducees.

13 When Jesus came into the region of Caesarea Philippi, He asked His disciples, saying, "Who do men say that I, the Son of Man, am?"

14 So they said, "Some *say* John the Baptist, some Elijah, and others Jeremiah or one of the prophets."

15 He said to them, "But who do you say that I am?"

16 And Simon Peter answered and said, "You are the Christ, the Son of the living God."

17 Jesus answered and said to him, "Blessed are you, Simon Bar-Jonah, for flesh and blood has not revealed *this* to you, but My Father who is in heaven.

18 "And I also say to you that you are Peter, and on this rock I will build My church, and the gates of Hades shall not prevail against it.

19 "And I will give you the keys of the kingdom of heaven, and whatever you bind on earth will be bound in heaven, and whatever you loose on earth will be loosed in heaven."

20 Then He commanded His disciples that they should tell no one that He was Jesus the Christ.

21 From that time Jesus began to show to His disciples that He must go to Jerusalem, and suffer many things from the elders and chief priests and scribes, and be killed, and be raised again the third day.

22 Then Peter took Him aside and began to rebuke Him, saying, "Far be it from You, Lord; this shall not happen to You!"

23 But He turned and said to Peter, "Get behind Me, Satan! You are an offense to Me, for you are not mindful of the things of God, but the things of men."

24 Then Jesus said to His disciples, "If anyone desires to come after Me, let him deny himself, and take up his cross, and follow Me.

25 "For whoever desires to save his life will lose it, and whoever loses his life for My sake will find it.

26 "For what is a man profited if he gains the whole world, and loses his own soul? Or what will a man give in exchange for his soul?

27 "For the Son of Man will come in the glory of His Father with His angels, and then He will reward each according to his works.

28 "Assuredly, I say to you, there are some standing here who shall not taste death till they see the Son of Man coming in His kingdom."

17 Now after six days Jesus took Peter, James, and John his brother, brought them up on a high mountain by themselves,

2 and was transfigured before them. His face shone like the sun, and His clothes became as white as the light.

3 And behold, Moses and Elijah appeared to them, talking with Him.

4 Then Peter answered and said to Jesus, "Lord, it is good for us to be here; if You wish, let us make here three tabernacles: one for You, one for Moses, and one for Elijah."

5 While he was still speaking, behold, a bright cloud overshadowed them; and suddenly a voice came out of the cloud, saying, "This is My beloved Son, in whom I am well pleased. Hear Him!"

6 And when the disciples heard *it*, they fell on their faces and were greatly afraid.

7 But Jesus came and touched them and said, "Arise, and do not be afraid."

8 And when they had lifted up their eyes, they saw no one but Jesus only.

9 Now as they came down from the mountain, Jesus commanded them, saying, "Tell the vision to no one until the Son of Man is risen from the dead."

10 And His disciples asked Him, saying, "Why then do the scribes say that Elijah must come first?"

11 Then Jesus answered and said to them, "Elijah truly is coming first and will restore all things.

12 "But I say to you that Elijah has come already, and they did not know him but did to him whatever they wished. Likewise the Son of

Man is also about to suffer at their hands."

13 Then the disciples understood that He spoke to them of John the Baptist.

14 And when they had come to the multitude, a man came to Him, kneeling down to Him and saying,

15 "Lord, have mercy on my son, for he is an epileptic and suffers severely; for he often falls into the fire and often into the water.

16 "So I brought him to Your disciples, but they could not cure him."

17 Then Jesus answered and said, "O faithless and perverse generation, how long shall I be with you? How long shall I bear with you? Bring him here to Me."

18 And Jesus rebuked the demon, and he came out of him; and the child was cured from that very hour.

19 Then the disciples came to Jesus privately and said, "Why could we not cast him out?"

20 So Jesus said to them, "Because of your unbelief; for assuredly, I say to you, if you have faith as a mustard seed, you will say to this mountain, 'Move from here to there,' and it will move; and nothing will be impossible for you.

21 "However, this kind does not go out except by prayer and fasting."

22 Now while they were staying in Galilee, Jesus said to them, "The Son of Man is about to be betrayed into the hands of men,

23 "and they will kill Him, and the third day He will be raised up." And they were exceedingly sorrowful.

24 And when they had come to Capernaum, those who received the *temple* tax came to Peter and said, "Does your Teacher not pay the *temple* tax?"

25 He said, "Yes." And when he had come into the house, Jesus anticipated him, saying, "What do you think, Simon? From whom do the kings of the earth take cus-toms or taxes, from their *own* sons or from strangers?"

26 Peter said to Him, "From strangers." Jesus said to him, "Then the sons are free.

27 "Nevertheless, lest we offend them, go to the sea, cast in a hook, and take the fish that comes up first. And when you have opened its mouth, you will find a piece of money; take that and give it to them for Me and you."

18 At that time the disciples came to Jesus, saying, "Who then is greatest in the kingdom of heaven?"

2 And Jesus called a little child to Him, set him in the midst of them,

3 and said, "Assuredly, I say to you, unless you are converted and become as little children, you will by no means enter the kingdom of heaven.

4 "Therefore whoever humbles himself as this little child is the greatest in the kingdom of heaven.

5 "And whoever receives one little child like this in My name receives Me.

6 "But whoever causes one of these little ones who believe in Me to sin, it would be better for him if a millstone were hung around his neck, and he were drowned in the depth of the sea.

7 "Woe to the world because of offenses! For offenses must come, but woe to that man by whom the offense comes!

8 "And if your hand or foot causes you to sin, cut it off and cast *it* from you. It is better for you to enter into life lame or maimed, rather than having two hands or two feet, to be cast into the everlasting fire.

9 "And if your eye causes you to sin, pluck it out and cast *it* from you. It is better for you to enter into life with one eye, rather than having two eyes, to be cast into hell fire.

10 "Take heed that you do not de-

spise one of these little ones, for I say to you that in heaven their angels always see the face of My Father who is in heaven.

11 "For the Son of Man has come to save that which was lost.

12 "What do you think? If a man has a hundred sheep, and one of them goes astray, does he not leave the ninety-nine and go to the mountains to seek the one that is straying?

13 "And if he should find it, assuredly, I say to you, he rejoices more over that *sheep* than over the ninety-nine that did not go astray.

14 "Even so it is not the will of your Father who is in heaven that one of these little ones should perish.

♥ 15 "Moreover if your brother sins against you, go and tell him his fault between you and him alone. If he hears you, you have gained your brother.

16 "But if he will not hear *you*, take with you one or two more, that *'by the mouth of two or three witnesses every word may be established.'*

17 "And if he refuses to hear them, tell *it* to the church. But if he refuses even to hear the church, let him be to you like a heathen and a tax collector.

18 "Assuredly, I say to you, whatever you bind on earth will be bound in heaven, and whatever you loose on earth will be loosed in heaven.

19 "Again I say to you that if two of you agree on earth concerning anything that they ask, it will be done for them by My Father in heaven.

20 "For where two or three are gathered together in My name, I am there in the midst of them."

21 Then Peter came to Him and said, "Lord, how often shall my brother sin against me, and I forgive him? Up to seven times?"

22 Jesus said to him, "I do not say to you, up to seven times, but up to seventy times seven.

23 "Therefore the kingdom of heaven is like a certain king who wanted to settle accounts with his servants.

24 "And when he had begun to settle accounts, one was brought to him who owed him ten thousand talents.

25 "But as he was not able to pay, his master commanded that he be sold, with his wife and children and all that he had, and that payment be made.

26 "The servant therefore fell down before him, saying, 'Master, have patience with me, and I will pay you all.'

27 "Then the master of that servant was moved with compassion, released him, and forgave him the debt.

28 "But that servant went out and found one of his fellow servants who owed him a hundred denarii; and he laid hands on him and took *him* by the throat, saying, 'Pay me what you owe!'

29 "So his fellow servant fell down at his feet and begged him, saying, 'Have patience with me, and I will pay you all.'

30 "And he would not, but went and threw him into prison till he should pay the debt.

31 "So when his fellow servants saw what had been done, they were very grieved, and came and told their master all that had been done.

32 "Then his master, after he had called him, said to him, 'You wicked servant! I forgave you all that debt because you begged me.

33 'Should you not also have had compassion on your fellow servant, just as I had pity on you?'

34 "And his master was angry, and delivered him to the torturers until he should pay all that was due to him.

See 1 John 4:9–11, page 291

35 "So My heavenly Father also will do to you if each of you, from his heart, does not forgive his brother his trespasses."

19 Now it came to pass, when Jesus had finished these sayings, *that* He departed from Galilee and came to the region of Judea beyond the Jordan.

2 And great multitudes followed Him, and He healed them there.

3 The Pharisees also came to Him, testing Him, and saying to Him, "Is it lawful for a man to divorce his wife for *just* any reason?"

4 And He answered and said to them, "Have you not read that He who made *them* at the beginning *'made them male and female,'*

5 "and said, *'For this reason a man shall leave his father and mother and be joined to his wife, and the two shall become one flesh'*?

6 "So then, they are no longer two but one flesh. Therefore what God has joined together, let not man separate."

7 They said to Him, "Why then did Moses command to give a certificate of divorce, and to put her away?"

8 He said to them, "Moses, because of the hardness of your hearts, permitted you to divorce your wives, but from the beginning it was not so.

9 "And I say to you, whoever divorces his wife, except for sexual immorality, and marries another, commits adultery; and whoever marries her who is divorced commits adultery."

10 His disciples said to Him, "If such is the case of the man with *his* wife, it is better not to marry."

11 But He said to them, "All cannot accept this saying, but only *those* to whom it has been given:

12 "For there are eunuchs who were born thus from *their* mother's womb, and there are eunuchs who were made eunuchs by men, and there are eunuchs who have made themselves eunuchs for the kingdom of heaven's sake. He who is able to accept *it,* let him accept *it.*"

13 Then little children were brought to Him that He might put *His* hands on them and pray, but the disciples rebuked them.

14 But Jesus said, "Let the little children come to Me, and do not forbid them; for of such is the kingdom of heaven."

15 And He laid *His* hands on them and departed from there.

16 Now behold, one came and said to Him, "Good Teacher, what good thing shall I do that I may have eternal life?"

17 So He said to him, "Why do you call Me good? No one *is* good but One, *that is,* God. But if you want to enter into life, keep the commandments."

18 He said to Him, "Which ones?" Jesus said, "*'You shall not murder,' 'You shall not commit adultery,' 'You shall not steal,' 'You shall not bear false witness,'*

19 *'Honor your father and your mother,'* and, *'You shall love your neighbor as yourself.'*"

20 The young man said to Him, "All these things I have kept from my youth. What do I still lack?"

21 Jesus said to him, "If you want to be perfect, go, sell what you have and give to the poor, and you will have treasure in heaven; and come, follow Me."

22 But when the young man heard that saying, he went away sorrowful, for he had great possessions.

23 Then Jesus said to His disciples, "Assuredly, I say to you that it is hard for a rich man to enter the kingdom of heaven.

24 "And again I say to you, it is easier for a camel to go through the eye of a needle than for a rich man to enter the kingdom of God."

25 When His disciples heard *it,* they were exceedingly amazed, saying, "Who then can be saved?"

26 But Jesus looked at *them* and said to them, "With men this is impossible, but with God all things are possible."

27 Then Peter answered and said to Him, "See, we have left all and followed You. Therefore what shall we have?"

28 So Jesus said to them, "Assuredly I say to you, that in the regeneration, when the Son of Man sits on the throne of His glory, you who have followed Me will also sit on twelve thrones, judging the twelve tribes of Israel.

29 "And everyone who has left houses or brothers or sisters or father or mother or wife or children or lands, for My name's sake, shall receive a hundredfold, and inherit everlasting life.

30 "But many *who are* first will be last, and the last first.

20 "For the kingdom of heaven is like a landowner who went out early in the morning to hire laborers for his vineyard.

2 "Now when he had agreed with the laborers for a denarius a day, he sent them into his vineyard.

3 "And he went out about the third hour and saw others standing idle in the marketplace,

4 "and said to them, 'You also go into the vineyard, and whatever is right I will give you.' And they went.

5 "Again he went out about the sixth and the ninth hour, and did likewise.

6 "And about the eleventh hour he went out and found others standing idle, and said to them, 'Why have you been standing here idle all day?'

7 "They said to him, 'Because no one hired us.' He said to them, 'You also go into the vineyard, and whatever is right you will receive.'

8 "So when evening had come, the owner of the vineyard said to his steward, 'Call the laborers and give them *their* wages, beginning with the last to the first.'

9 "And when those came who *were hired* about the eleventh hour, they each received a denarius.

10 "But when the first came, they supposed that they would receive more; and they likewise received each a denarius.

11 "And when they had received *it*, they murmured against the landowner,

12 "saying, 'These last *men* have worked *only* one hour, and you made them equal to us who have borne the burden and the heat of the day.'

13 "But he answered one of them and said, 'Friend, I am doing you no wrong. Did you not agree with me for a denarius?

14 'Take *what is* yours and go your way. I wish to give to this last man *the same* as to you.

15 'Is it not lawful for me to do what I wish with my own things? Or is your eye evil because I am good?'

16 "So the last will be first, and the first last. For many are called, but few chosen."

17 Then Jesus, going up to Jerusalem, took the twelve disciples aside on the road and said to them,

18 "Behold, we are going up to Jerusalem, and the Son of Man will be betrayed to the chief priests and to the scribes; and they will condemn Him to death,

19 "and deliver Him to the Gentiles to mock and to scourge and to crucify. And the third day He will rise again."

20 Then the mother of Zebedee's sons came to Him with her sons, kneeling down and asking something from Him.

21 And He said to her, "What do you wish?" She said to Him, "Grant that these two sons of mine may sit, one on Your right hand

and the other on the left, in Your kingdom."

22 But Jesus answered and said, "You do not know what you ask. Are you able to drink the cup that I am about to drink, and be baptized with the baptism that I am baptized with?" They said to Him, "We are able."

23 So He said to them, "You will indeed drink My cup, and be baptized with the baptism that I am baptized with; but to sit on My right hand and on My left is not Mine to give, but *it is for those* for whom it is prepared by My Father."

24 And when the ten heard *it*, they were moved with indignation against the two brothers.

25 But Jesus called them *to Himself* and said, "You know that the rulers of the Gentiles lord it over them, and those who are great exercise authority over them.

26 "Yet it shall not be so among you; but whoever desires to become great among you, let him be your servant.

27 "And whoever desires to be first among you, let him be your slave—

28 "just as the Son of Man did not come to be served, but to serve, and to give His life a ransom for many."

29 Now as they departed from Jericho, a great multitude followed Him.

30 And behold, two blind men sitting by the road, when they heard that Jesus was passing by, cried out, saying, "Have mercy on us, O Lord, Son of David!"

31 Then the multitude warned them that they should be quiet; but they cried out all the more, saying, "Have mercy on us, O Lord, Son of David!"

32 So Jesus stood still and called them, and said, "What do you want Me to do for you?"

33 They said to Him, "Lord, that our eyes may be opened."

34 So Jesus had compassion and touched their eyes. And immediately their eyes received sight, and they followed Him.

21 Now when they drew near to Jerusalem, and came to Bethphage, at the Mount of Olives, then Jesus sent two disciples,

2 saying to them, "Go into the village opposite you, and immediately you will find a donkey tied, and a colt with her. Loose *them* and bring *them* to Me.

3 "And if anyone says anything to you, you shall say, 'The Lord has need of them,' and immediately he will send them."

4 All this was done that it might be fulfilled which was spoken by the prophet, saying:

5 *"Tell the daughter of Zion,*
  'Behold, your King is coming to
    you,
  Lowly, and sitting on a donkey,
  A colt, the foal of a donkey.' "

6 So the disciples went and did as Jesus commanded them.

7 They brought the donkey and the colt, laid their clothes on them, and set *Him* on them.

8 And a very great multitude spread their garments on the road; others cut down branches from the trees and spread *them* on the road.

9 Then the multitudes who went before and those who followed cried out, saying:

  "Hosanna to the Son of David!
  '*Blessed is He who comes*
    in the name of the LORD!'
  Hosanna in the highest!"

10 And when He had come into Jerusalem, all the city was moved, saying, "Who is this?"

11 So the multitudes said, "This is Jesus, the prophet from Nazareth of Galilee."

12 Then Jesus went into the temple of God and drove out all those who bought and sold in the temple, and overturned the tables of the moneychangers and the seats of those who sold doves.

13 And He said to them, "It is written, *'My house shall be called a house of prayer,'* but you have made it a *'den of thieves.'*"

14 Then *the* blind and *the* lame came to Him in the temple, and He healed them.

15 But when the chief priests and scribes saw the wonderful things that He did, and the children crying out in the temple and saying, "Hosanna to the Son of David!" they were indignant

16 and said to Him, "Do You hear what these are saying?" And Jesus said to them, "Yes. Have you never read, *'Out of the mouth of babes and nursing infants You have perfected praise'?* "

17 Then He left them and went out of the city to Bethany, and He lodged there.

18 Now in the morning, as He returned to the city, He was hungry.

19 And seeing a fig tree by the road, He came to it and found nothing on it but leaves, and said to it, "Let no fruit grow on you ever again." And immediately the fig tree withered away.

20 Now when the disciples saw *it,* they marveled, saying, "How did the fig tree wither away so soon?"

21 So Jesus answered and said to them, "Assuredly, I say to you, if you have faith and do not doubt, you will not only do what was done to the fig tree, but also if you say to this mountain, 'Be removed and be cast into the sea,' it will be done.

22 "And all things, whatever you ask in prayer, believing, you will receive."

23 Now when He came into the temple, the chief priests and the elders of the people confronted Him as He was teaching, and said, "By what authority are You doing these things? And who gave You this authority?"

24 But Jesus answered and said to them, "I also will ask you one thing, which if you tell Me, I likewise will tell you by what authority I do these things:

25 "The baptism of John, where was it from? From heaven or from men?" And they reasoned among themselves, saying, "If we say, 'From heaven,' He will say to us, 'Why then did you not believe him?'

26 "But if we say, 'From men,' we fear the multitude, for all count John as a prophet."

27 So they answered Jesus and said, "We do not know." And He said to them, "Neither will I tell you by what authority I do these things.

28 "But what do you think? A man had two sons, and he came to the first and said, 'Son, go, work today in my vineyard.'

29 "He answered and said, 'I will not,' but afterward he regretted it and went.

30 "Then he came to the second and said likewise. And he answered and said, 'I go, sir,' but he did not go.

31 "Which of the two did the will of *his* father?" They said to Him, "The first." Jesus said to them, "Assuredly, I say to you that tax collectors and harlots enter the kingdom of God before you.

32 "For John came to you in the way of righteousness, and you did not believe him; but tax collectors and harlots believed him; and when you saw *it,* you did not afterward relent and believe him.

33 "Hear another parable: There was a certain landowner who planted a vineyard and set a hedge around it, dug a winepress in it and built a tower. And he leased it to vinedressers and went into a far country.

34 "Now when vintage-time drew near, he sent his servants to the vinedressers, that they might receive its fruit.

35 "And the vinedressers took his servants, beat one, killed one, and stoned another.

36 "Again he sent other servants, more than the first, and they did likewise to them.

37 "Then last of all he sent his son to them, saying, 'They will respect my son.'

38 "But when the vinedressers saw the son, they said among themselves, 'This is the heir. Come, let us kill him and seize his inheritance.'

39 "And they caught him, and cast *him* out of the vineyard, and killed *him.*

40 "Therefore, when the owner of the vineyard comes, what will he do to those vinedressers?"

41 They said to Him, "He will destroy those wicked men miserably, and lease *his* vineyard to other vinedressers who will render to him the fruits in their seasons."

42 Jesus said to them, "Did you never read in the Scriptures:

'The stone which the builders rejected
Has become the chief cornerstone.
This was the Lord's *doing,*
And it is marvelous in our eyes'?

43 "Therefore I say to you, the kingdom of God will be taken from you and given to a nation bearing the fruits of it.

44 "And whoever falls on this stone will be broken; but on whomever it falls, it will grind him to powder."

45 Now when the chief priests and Pharisees heard His parables, they perceived that He was speaking of them.

46 But when they sought to lay hands on Him, they feared the multitudes, because they took Him for a prophet.

22 And Jesus answered and spoke to them again by parables and said:

2 "The kingdom of heaven is like a certain king who arranged a marriage for his son,

3 "and sent out his servants to call those who were invited to the wedding; and they were not willing to come.

4 "Again, he sent out other servants, saying, 'Tell those who are invited, "See, I have prepared my dinner; my oxen and fatted cattle *are* killed, and all things *are* ready. Come to the wedding." '

5 "But they made light of it and went their ways, one to his own farm, another to his business.

6 "And the rest seized his servants, treated *them* spitefully, and killed *them.*

7 "But when the king heard *about it,* he was furious. And he sent out his armies, destroyed those murderers, and burned up their city.

8 "Then he said to his servants, 'The wedding is ready, but those who were invited were not worthy.

9 'Therefore go into the highways, and as many as you find, invite to the wedding.'

10 "So those servants went out into the highways and gathered together all whom they found, both bad and good. And the wedding *hall* was filled with guests.

11 "But when the king came in to see the guests, he saw a man there who did not have on a wedding garment.

12 "So he said to him, 'Friend, how did you come in here without a wedding garment?' And he was speechless.

13 "Then the king said to the servants, 'Bind him hand and foot,

take him away, and cast *him* into outer darkness; there will be weeping and gnashing of teeth.'

14 "For many are called, but few *are* chosen."

15 Then the Pharisees went and plotted how they might entangle Him in *His* talk.

16 And they sent to Him their disciples with the Herodians, saying, "Teacher, we know that You are true, and teach the way of God in truth; nor do You care about anyone, for You do not regard the person of men.

17 "Tell us, therefore, what do You think? Is it lawful to pay taxes to Caesar, or not?"

18 But Jesus perceived their wickedness, and said, "Why do you test Me, *you* hypocrites?

19 "Show Me the tax money." So they brought Him a denarius.

20 And He said to them, "Whose image and inscription *is* this?"

21 They said to Him, "Caesar's." And He said to them, "Render therefore to Caesar the things that are Caesar's, and to God the things that are God's."

22 When they had heard *these words*, they marveled, and left Him and went their way.

23 The same day the Sadducees, who say there is no resurrection, came to Him and asked Him,

24 saying: "Teacher, Moses said that if a man dies, having no children, his brother shall marry his wife and raise up offspring for his brother.

25 "Now there were with us seven brothers. The first died after he had married, and having no offspring, left his wife to his brother.

26 "Likewise the second also, and the third, even to the seventh.

27 "And last of all the woman died also.

28 "Therefore, in the resurrection, whose wife of the seven will she be? For they all had her."

29 Jesus answered and said to them, "You are mistaken, not knowing the Scriptures nor the power of God.

30 "For in the resurrection they neither marry nor are given in marriage, but are like angels of God in heaven.

31 "But concerning the resurrection of the dead, have you not read what was spoken to you by God, saying,

32 *'I am the God of Abraham, the God of Isaac, and the God of Jacob'*? God is not the God of the dead, but of the living."

33 And when the multitudes heard *this*, they were astonished at His teaching.

34 But when the Pharisees heard that He had silenced the Sadducees, they gathered together.

35 Then one of them, a lawyer, asked *Him a question*, testing Him, and saying,

36 "Teacher, which *is* the great commandment in the law?"

37 Jesus said to him, "*'You shall love the LORD your God with all your heart, with all your soul, and with all your mind.'*

38 "This is *the* first and great commandment.

39 "And *the* second *is* like it: *'You shall love your neighbor as yourself.'*

40 "On these two commandments hang all the Law and the Prophets."

41 While the Pharisees were gathered together, Jesus asked them,

42 saying, "What do you think about the Christ? Whose Son is He?" They said to Him, *"The Son* of David."

43 He said to them, "How then does David in the Spirit call Him *'Lord'*, saying:

44 *'The LORD said to my Lord,*
  "Sit at My right hand,
  Till I make Your enemies
    Your footstool" '?

45 "If David then calls Him *'Lord'*, how is He is Son?"

46 And no one was able to answer Him a word, nor from that day on did anyone dare question Him anymore.

23 Then Jesus spoke to the multitudes and to His disciples,

2 saying: "The scribes and the Pharisees sit in Moses' seat.

3 "Therefore whatever they tell you to observe, *that* observe and do, but do not do according to their works; for they say, and do not do.

4 "For they bind heavy burdens, hard to bear, and lay *them* on men's shoulders; but they *themselves* will not move them with one of their fingers.

5 "But all their works they do to be seen by men. They make their phylacteries broad and enlarge the borders of their garments.

6 "They love the best places at feasts, the best seats in the synagogues,

7 "greetings in the marketplaces, and to be called by men, 'Rabbi, Rabbi.'

8 "But you, do not be called 'Rabbi'; for One is your Teacher, the Christ, and you are all brethren.

9 "Do not call anyone on earth your father; for One is your Father, He who is in heaven.

10 "And do not be called teachers; for One is your Teacher, the Christ.

11 "But he who is greatest among you shall be your servant.

12 "And whoever exalts himself will be abased, and he who humbles himself will be exalted.

13 "But woe to you, scribes and Pharisees, hypocrites! For you shut up the kingdom of heaven against men; for you neither go in *yourselves*, nor do you allow those who are entering to go in.

14 "Woe to you, scribes and Pharisees, hypocrites! For you devour widows' houses, and for a pretense make long prayers. Therefore you will receive greater condemnation.

15 "Woe to you, scribes and Pharisees, hypocrites! For you travel land and sea to win one proselyte, and when he is won, you make him twice as much a son of hell as yourselves.

16 "Woe to you, blind guides, who say, 'Whoever swears by the temple, it is nothing; but whoever swears by the gold of the temple, he is obliged *to perform it.*'

17 "Fools and blind! For which is greater, the gold or the temple that sanctifies the gold?

18 "And, 'Whoever swears by the altar, it is nothing; but whoever swears by the gift that is on it, he is obliged *to perform it.*'

19 "Fools and blind! For which is greater, the gift or the altar that sanctifies the gift?

20 "Therefore he who swears by the altar, swears by it and by all things on it.

21 "He who swears by the temple, swears by it and by Him who dwells in it.

22 "And he who swears by heaven, swears by the throne of God and by Him who sits on it.

23 "Woe to you, scribes and Pharisees, hypocrites! For you pay tithe of mint and anise and cummin, and have neglected the weightier *matters* of the law: justice and mercy and faith. These you ought to have done, without leaving the others undone.

24 "Blind guides, who strain out a gnat and swallow a camel!

25 "Woe to you, scribes and Pharisees, hypocrites! For you cleanse the outside of the cup and dish, but inside they are full of extortion and self-indulgence.

26 "Blind Pharisee, first cleanse the inside of the cup and dish, that the outside of them may be clean also.

27 "Woe to you, scribes and Pharisees, hypocrites! For you are like

whitewashed tombs which indeed appear beautiful outwardly, but inside are full of dead *men's* bones and all uncleanness.

28 "Even so you also outwardly appear righteous to men, but inside you are full of hypocrisy and lawlessness.

29 "Woe to you, scribes and Pharisees, hypocrites! Because you build the tombs of the prophets and adorn the monuments of the righteous,

30 "and say, 'If we had lived in the days of our fathers, we would not have been partakers with them in the blood of the prophets.'

31 "Therefore you are witnesses against yourselves that you are sons of those who murdered the prophets.

32 "Fill up, then, the measure of your fathers' *guilt.*

33 "Serpents, brood of vipers! How can you escape the condemnation of hell?

34 "Therefore, indeed, I send you prophets, wise men, and scribes: *some* of them you will kill and crucify, and *some* of them you will scourge in your synagogues and persecute from city to city,

35 "that on you may come all the righteous blood shed on the earth, from the blood of righteous Abel to the blood of Zechariah, son of Berechiah, whom you murdered between the temple and the altar.

36 "Assuredly, I say to you, all these things will come upon this generation.

37 "O Jerusalem, Jerusalem, the one who kills the prophets and stones those who are sent to her! How often I wanted to gather your children together, as a hen gathers her chicks under *her* wings, but you were not willing!

38 "See! Your house is left to you desolate;

39 "for I say to you, you shall see Me no more till you say, '*Blessed is*

He who comes in the name of the LORD!'"

24 Then Jesus went out and departed from the temple, and His disciples came to *Him* to show Him the buildings of the temple.

2 And Jesus said to them, "Do you not see all these things? Assuredly, I say to you, not one stone shall be left here upon another, that shall not be thrown down."

3 Now as He sat on the Mount of Olives, the disciples came to Him privately, saying, "Tell us, when will these things be? And what *will be* the sign of Your coming, and of the end of the age?"

4 And Jesus answered and said to them: "Take heed that no one deceives you.

5 "For many will come in My name, saying, 'I am the Christ,' and will deceive many.

6 "And you will hear of wars and rumors of wars. See that you are not troubled; for all *these things* must come to pass, but the end is not yet.

7 "For nation will rise against nation, and kingdom against kingdom. And there will be famines, pestilences, and earthquakes in various places.

8 "All these *are* the beginning of sorrows.

9 "Then they will deliver you up to tribulation and kill you, and you will be hated by all nations for My name's sake.

10 "And then many will be offended, will betray one another, and will hate one another.

11 "Then many false prophets will rise up and deceive many.

12 "And because lawlessness will abound, the love of many will grow cold.

13 "But he who endures to the end shall be saved.

14 "And this gospel of the kingdom will be preached in all the world as a witness to all the nations, and then the end will come.

15 "Therefore when you see the *'abomination of desolation,'* spoken of by Daniel the prophet, standing in the holy place" (whoever reads, let him understand),

16 "then let those who are in Judea flee to the mountains.

17 "Let him who is on the housetop not come down to take anything out of his house.

18 "And let him who is in the field not go back to get his clothes.

19 "But woe to those who are pregnant and to those with nursing babies in those days!

20 "And pray that your flight may not be in winter or on the Sabbath.

21 "For then there will be great tribulation, such as has not been since the beginning of the world until this time, no, nor ever shall be.

22 "And unless those days were shortened, no flesh would be saved; but for the elect's sake those days will be shortened.

23 "Then if anyone says to you, 'Look, here *is* the Christ!' or 'There!' do not believe *it*.

24 "For false christs and false prophets will arise and show great signs and wonders, so as to deceive, if possible, even the elect.

25 "See, I have told you beforehand.

26 "Therefore if they say to you, 'Look, He is in the desert!' do not go out; *or* 'Look, *He is* in the inner rooms!' do not believe *it*.

27 "For as the lightning comes from the east and flashes to the west, so also will the coming of the Son of Man be.

28 "For wherever the carcass is, there the eagles will be gathered together.

29 "Immediately after the tribulation of those days the sun will be darkened, and the moon will not give its light; the stars will fall from heaven, and the powers of the heavens will be shaken.

30 "Then the sign of the Son of Man will appear in heaven, and then all the tribes of the earth will mourn, and they will see the Son of Man coming on the clouds of heaven with power and great glory.

31 "And He will send His angels with a great sound of a trumpet, and they will gather together His elect from the four winds, from one end of heaven to the other.

32 "Now learn this parable from the fig tree: When its branch has already become tender and puts forth leaves, you know that summer *is* near.

33 "So you also, when you see all these things, know that it is near, at the *very* doors.

34 "Assuredly, I say to you, this generation will by no means pass away till all these things are fulfilled.

35 "Heaven and earth will pass away, but My words will by no means pass away.

36 "But of that day and hour no one knows, no, not even the angels of heaven, but My Father only.

37 "But as the days of Noah *were*, so also will the coming of the Son of Man be.

38 "For as in the days before the flood, they were eating and drinking, marrying and giving in marriage, until the day that Noah entered the ark,

39 "and did not know until the flood came and took them all away, so also will the coming of the Son of Man be.

40 "Then two *men* will be in the field: one will be taken and the other left.

41 "Two *women will be* grinding at the mill: one will be taken and the other left.

42 "Watch therefore, for you do not know what hour your Lord is coming.

43 "But know this, that if the master of the house had known what hour the thief would come, he would have watched and not allowed his house to be broken into.

44 "Therefore you also be ready, for the Son of Man is coming at an hour when you do not expect *Him.*

45 "Who then is a faithful and wise servant, whom his master made ruler over his household, to give them food in due season?

46 "Blessed *is* that servant whom his master, when he comes, will find so doing.

47 "Assuredly, I say to you that he will make him ruler over all his goods.

48 "But if that evil servant says in his heart, 'My master is delaying his coming,'

49 "and begins to beat *his* fellow servants, and to eat and drink with the drunkards,

50 "the master of that servant will come on a day when he is not looking for *him* and at an hour that he is not aware of,

51 "and will cut him in two and appoint *him* his portion with the hypocrites. There shall be weeping and gnashing of teeth.

25 "Then the kingdom of heaven shall be likened to ten virgins who took their lamps and went out to meet the bridegroom.

2 "Now five of them were wise, and five *were* foolish.

3 "Those who *were* foolish took their lamps and took no oil with them,

4 "but the wise took oil in their vessels with their lamps.

5 "But while the bridegroom was delayed, they all slumbered and slept.

6 "And at midnight a cry was *heard:* 'Behold, the bridegroom is coming; go out to meet him!'

7 "Then all those virgins arose and trimmed their lamps.

8 "And the foolish said to the wise, 'Give us *some* of your oil, for our lamps are going out.'

9 "But the wise answered, saying,

'*No,* lest there should not be enough for us and you; but go rather to those who sell, and buy for yourselves.'

10 "And while they went to buy, the bridegroom came, and those who were ready went in with him to the wedding; and the door was shut.

11 "Afterward the other virgins came also, saying, 'Lord, Lord, open to us!'

12 "But he answered and said, 'Assuredly, I say to you, I do not know you.'

13 "Watch therefore, for you know neither the day nor the hour in which the Son of Man is coming.

14 "For *the kingdom of heaven* is like a man traveling to a far country, *who* called his own servants and delivered his goods to them.

15 "And to one he gave five talents, to another two, and to another one, to each according to his own ability; and immediately he went on a journey.

16 "Then he who had received the five talents went and traded with them, and made another five talents.

17 "And likewise he who *had received* two gained two more also.

18 "But he who had received one went and dug in the ground, and hid his lord's money.

19 "After a long time the lord of those servants came and settled accounts with them.

20 "So he who had received five talents came and brought five other talents, saying, 'Lord, you delivered to me five talents; look, I have gained five more talents besides them.'

21 "His lord said to him, 'Well *done,* good and faithful servant; you were faithful over a few things, I will make you ruler over many things. Enter into the joy of your lord.'

22 "He also who had received two talents came and said, 'Lord, you

delivered to me two talents; look, I have gained two more talents besides them.'

23 "His lord said to him, 'Well *done*, good and faithful servant; you have been faithful over a few things, I will make you ruler over many things. Enter into the joy of your lord.'

24 "Then he who had received the one talent came and said, 'Lord, I knew you to be a hard man, reaping where you have not sown, and gathering where you have not scattered seed.

25 'And I was afraid, and went and hid your talent in the ground. Look, *there* you have *what is* yours.'

26 "But his lord answered and said to him, 'You wicked and lazy servant, you knew that I reap where I have not sown, and gather where I have not scattered seed.

27 'Therefore you ought to have deposited my money with the bankers, and at my coming I would have received back my own with interest.

28 'Therefore take the talent from him, and give *it* to him who has ten talents.

29 'For to everyone who has, more will be given, and he will have abundance; but from him who does not have, even what he has will be taken away.

30 'And cast the unprofitable servant into the outer darkness. There will be weeping and gnashing of teeth.'

31 "When the Son of Man comes in His glory, and all the holy angels with Him, then He will sit on the throne of His glory.

32 "All the nations will be gathered before Him, and He will separate them one from another, as a shepherd divides *his* sheep from the goats.

33 "And He will set the sheep on His right hand, but the goats on the left.

34 "Then the King will say to those on His right hand, 'Come, you blessed of My Father, inherit the kingdom prepared for you from the foundation of the world:

35 'for I was hungry and you gave Me food; I was thirsty and you gave Me drink; I was a stranger and you took Me in;

36 'I *was* naked and you clothed Me; I was sick and you visited Me; I was in prison and you came to Me.'

37 "Then the righteous will answer Him, saying, 'Lord, when did we see You hungry and feed *You*, or thirsty and give *You* drink?

38 'When did we see You a stranger and take *You* in, or naked and clothe *You*?

39 'Or when did we see You sick, or in prison, and come to You?'

40 "And the King will answer and say to them, 'Assuredly, I say to you, inasmuch as you did *it* to one of the least of these My brethren, you did *it* to Me.'

41 "Then He will also say to those on the left hand, 'Depart from Me, you cursed, into the everlasting fire prepared for the devil and his angels:

42 'for I was hungry and you gave Me no food; I was thirsty and you gave Me no drink;

43 'I was a stranger and you did not take Me in, naked and you did not clothe Me, sick and in prison and you did not visit Me.'

44 "Then they also will answer Him, saying, 'Lord, when did we see You hungry or thirsty or a stranger or naked or sick or in prison, and did not minister to You?'

45 "Then He will answer them, saying, 'Assuredly, I say to you, inasmuch as you did not do *it* to one of the least of these, you did not do *it* to Me.'

46 "And these will go away into everlasting punishment, but the righteous into eternal life."

26 Now it came to pass, when Jesus had finished all these sayings, *that* He said to His disciples,

2 "You know that after two days is the Passover, and the Son of Man will be delivered up to be crucified."

3 Then the chief priests, the scribes, and the elders of the people assembled at the palace of the high priest, who was called Caiaphas,

4 and plotted to take Jesus by trickery and kill *Him*.

5 But they said, "Not during the feast, lest there be an uproar among the people."

6 And when Jesus was in Bethany at the house of Simon the leper,

7 a woman came to Him having an alabaster flask of very costly fragrant oil, and she poured it on His head as He sat *at the table*.

8 But when His disciples saw *it*, they were indignant, saying, "To what purpose *is* this waste?

9 "For this fragrant oil might have been sold for much and given to *the* poor."

10 But when Jesus was aware of *it*, He said to them, "Why do you trouble the woman? For she has done a good work for Me.

11 "For you have the poor with you always, but Me you do not have always.

12 "For in pouring this fragrant oil on My body, she did *it* for My burial.

13 "Assuredly, I say to you, wherever this gospel is preached in the whole world, what this woman has done will also be told as a memorial to her."

14 Then one of the twelve, called Judas Iscariot, went to the chief priests

15 and said, "What are you willing to give me if I deliver Him to you?" And they counted out to him thirty pieces of silver.

16 So from that time he sought opportunity to betray Him.

17 Now on the first *day* of the *Feast of* the Unleavened Bread the disciples came to Jesus, saying to Him, "Where do You want us to prepare for You to eat the Passover?"

18 And He said, "Go into the city to a certain man, and say to him, 'The Teacher says, "My time is at hand; I will keep the Passover at your house with My disciples." ' "

19 So the disciples did as Jesus had directed them; and they prepared the Passover.

20 Now when evening had come, He sat down with the twelve.

21 Now as they were eating, He said, "Assuredly, I say to you, one of you will betray Me."

22 And they were exceedingly sorrowful, and each of them began to say to Him, "Lord, is it I?"

23 Then He answered and said, "He who dipped *his* hand with Me in the dish will betray Me.

24 "The Son of Man goes as it is written of Him, but woe to that man by whom the Son of Man is betrayed! It would have been good for that man if he had not been born."

25 Then Judas, who was betraying Him, answered and said, "Rabbi, is it I?" He said to him, "You have said it."

26 And as they were eating, Jesus took bread, blessed *it* and broke *it*, and gave *it* to the disciples and said, "Take, eat; this is My body."

27 Then He took the cup, and gave thanks, and gave *it* to them, saying, "Drink from it, all of you.

28 "For this is My blood of the new covenant, which is shed for many for the remission of sins.

29 "But I say to you, I will not drink of this fruit of the vine from now on until that day when I drink it new with you in My Father's kingdom."

30 And when they had sung a

hymn, they went out to the Mount of Olives.

31 Then Jesus said to them, "All of you will be made to stumble because of Me this night, for it is written:

'I will strike the Shepherd,
And the sheep of the flock
    will be scattered.'

32 "But after I have been raised, I will go before you to Galilee."

33 Peter answered and said to Him, "Even if all are made to stumble because of You, I will never be made to stumble."

34 Jesus said to him, "Assuredly, I say to you that this night, before the rooster crows, you will deny Me three times."

35 Peter said to Him, "Even if I have to die with You, I will not deny You!" And so said all the disciples.

36 Then Jesus came with them to a place called Gethsemane, and said to the disciples, "Sit here while I go and pray over there."

37 And He took with Him Peter and the two sons of Zebedee, and He began to be sorrowful and deeply distressed.

38 Then He said to them, "My soul is exceedingly sorrowful, even to death. Stay here and watch with Me."

39 He went a little farther and fell on His face, and prayed, saying, "O My Father, if it is possible, let this cup pass from Me; nevertheless, not as I will, but as You *will.*"

40 Then He came to the disciples and found them asleep, and said to Peter, "What, could you not watch with Me one hour?

41 "Watch and pray, lest you enter into temptation. The spirit indeed *is* willing, but the flesh *is* weak."

42 He went away again a second time and prayed, saying, "O My Father, if this cup cannot pass away from Me unless I drink it, Your will be done."

43 And He came and found them asleep again, for their eyes were heavy.

44 So He left them, went away again, and prayed the third time, saying the same words.

45 Then He came to His disciples and said to them, "Are *you* still sleeping and resting? Behold, the hour is at hand, and the Son of Man is being betrayed into the hands of sinners.

46 "Rise, let us be going. See, he who betrays Me is at hand."

47 And while He was still speaking, behold, Judas, one of the twelve, with a great multitude with swords and clubs, came from the chief priests and elders of the people.

48 Now His betrayer had given them a sign, saying, "Whomever I kiss, He is the One; seize Him."

49 Then immediately he went up to Jesus and said, "Greetings, Rabbi!" and kissed Him.

50 And Jesus said to him, "Friend, why have you come?" Then they came and laid hands on Jesus and took Him.

51 And suddenly, one of those *who were* with Jesus stretched out *his* hand and drew his sword, struck the servant of the high priest, and cut off his ear.

52 Then Jesus said to him, "Put your sword in its place, for all who take the sword will perish by the sword.

53 "Or do you think that I cannot now pray to My Father, and He will provide Me with more than twelve legions of angels?

54 "How then could the Scriptures be fulfilled, that it must happen thus?"

55 In that hour Jesus said to the multitudes, "Have you come out, as against a robber, with swords and clubs to take Me? I sat daily with you, teaching in the temple, and you did not seize Me.

56 "But all this was done that the Scriptures of the prophets might be fulfilled." Then all the disciples forsook Him and fled.

57 And those who had laid hold of Jesus led *Him* away to Caiaphas the high priest, where the scribes and the elders were assembled.

58 But Peter followed Him at a distance to the high priest's courtyard. And he went in and sat with the servants to see the end.

59 Now the chief priests, the elders, and all the council sought false testimony against Jesus to put Him to death,

60 but found none. Even though many false witnesses came forward, they found none. But at last two false witnesses came forward

61 and said, "This *fellow* said, 'I am able to destroy the temple of God and to build it in three days.' "

62 And the high priest arose and said to Him, "Do You answer nothing? What *is it that* these men testify against You?"

63 But Jesus kept silent. And the high priest answered and said to Him, "I adjure You by the living God that You tell us if You are the Christ, the Son of God."

64 Jesus said to him, "*It is as* you said. Nevertheless, I say to you, hereafter you will see the Son of Man sitting at the right hand of the Power, and coming on the clouds of heaven."

65 Then the high priest tore his clothes, saying, "He has spoken blasphemy! What further need do we have of witnesses? Look, now you have heard His blasphemy!

66 "What do you think?" They answered and said, "He is deserving of death."

67 Then they spat in His face and beat Him; and others struck *Him* with the palms of their hands,

68 saying, "Prophesy to us, Christ! Who is the one who struck You?"

69 Now Peter sat outside in the courtyard. And a servant girl came to him, saying, "You also were with Jesus of Galilee."

70 But he denied it before *them* all, saying, "I do not know what you are saying."

71 And when he had gone out to the gateway, another *girl* saw him and said to those *who were* there, "This *fellow* also was with Jesus of Nazareth."

72 But again he denied with an oath, "I do not know the Man!"

73 And after a while those who stood by came to *him* and said to Peter, "Surely you also are *one* of them, because your speech betrays you."

74 Then he began to curse and swear, *saying,* "I do not know the Man!" And immediately a rooster crowed.

75 And Peter remembered the word of Jesus who had said to him, "Before the rooster crows, you will deny Me three times." Then he went out and wept bitterly.

27 When morning came, all the chief priests and elders of the people took counsel against Jesus to put Him to death.

2 And when they had bound Him, they led Him away and delivered Him to Pontius Pilate the governor.

3 Then Judas, His betrayer, seeing that He had been condemned, was remorseful and brought back the thirty pieces of silver to the chief priests and elders,

4 saying, "I have sinned by betraying innocent blood." And they said, "What *is that* to us? You see *to it!*"

5 Then he threw down the pieces of silver in the temple and departed, and went and hanged himself.

6 But the chief priests took the silver pieces and said, "It is not lawful to put them into the treasury, because they are the price of blood."

7 And they took counsel and

bought with them the potter's field, to bury strangers in.

8 Therefore that field has been called the Field of Blood to this day.

9 Then was fulfilled what was spoken by Jeremiah the prophet, saying, *"And they took the thirty pieces of silver, the value of Him who was priced,* whom they of the children of Israel priced,

10 *"and gave them for the potter's field, as the* LORD *directed me."*

11 Now Jesus stood before the governor. And the governor asked Him, saying, "Are You the King of the Jews?" So Jesus said to him, *"It is as* you say."

12 And while He was being accused by the chief priests and elders, He answered nothing.

13 Then Pilate said to Him, "Do You not hear how many things they testify against You?"

14 And He answered him not one word, so that the governor marveled greatly.

15 Now at the feast the governor was accustomed to releasing to the multitude one prisoner whom they wished.

16 And they had then a notorious prisoner called Barabbas.

17 Therefore, when they had gathered together, Pilate said to them, "Whom do you want me to release to you? Barabbas, or Jesus who is called Christ?"

18 For he knew that because of envy they had delivered Him.

19 While he was sitting on the judgment seat, his wife sent to him, saying, "Have nothing to do with that just Man, for I have suffered many things today in a dream because of Him."

20 But the chief priests and elders persuaded the multitudes that they should ask for Barabbas and destroy Jesus.

21 The governor answered and said to them, "Which of the two do

you want me to release to you?" They said, "Barabbas!"

22 Pilate said to them, "What then shall I do with Jesus who is called Christ?" *They* all said to him, "Let Him be crucified!"

23 Then the governor said, "Why, what evil has He done?" But they cried out all the more, saying, "Let Him be crucified!"

24 When Pilate saw that he could not prevail at all, but rather that a tumult was rising, he took water and washed *his* hands before the multitude, saying, "I am innocent of the blood of this just Person. You see *to it.*"

25 And all the people answered and said, "His blood *be* on us and on our children."

26 Then he released Barabbas to them; and when he had scourged Jesus, he delivered *Him* to be crucified.

27 Then the soldiers of the governor took Jesus into the Praetorium and gathered the whole garrison around Him.

28 And they stripped Him and put a scarlet robe on Him.

29 When they had twisted a crown of thorns, they put *it* on His head, and a reed in His right hand. And they bowed the knee before Him and mocked Him, saying, "Hail, King of the Jews!"

30 Then they spat on Him, and took the reed and struck Him on the head.

31 Then when they had mocked Him, they took the robe off Him, put His *own* clothes on Him, and led Him away to be crucified.

32 Now as they came out, they found a man of Cyrene, Simon by name. Him they compelled to bear His cross.

33 And when they had come to a place called Golgotha, that is to say, Place of a Skull,

34 they gave Him sour wine mingled with gall to drink. But when

Jesus Dies on the Cross

He had tasted *it*, He would not drink.

35 Then they crucified Him, and divided His garments, casting lots, that it might be fulfilled which was spoken by the prophet:

> "They divided My garments
> among them,
> And for My clothing they cast
> lots."

36 Sitting down, they kept watch over Him there.

37 And they put up over His head the accusation written against Him:

THIS IS JESUS
THE KING OF THE JEWS.

38 Then two robbers were crucified with Him, one on the right and another on the left.

39 And those who passed by blasphemed Him, wagging their heads 40 and saying, "You who destroy the temple and build *it* in three days, save Yourself! If You are the Son of God, come down from the cross."

41 Likewise the chief priests, also mocking with the scribes and elders, said,

42 "He saved others; Himself He cannot save. If He is the King of Israel, let Him now come down from the cross, and we will believe Him.

43 "He trusted in God; let Him deliver Him now if He will have Him; for He said, 'I am the Son of God.'"

44 Even the robbers who were crucified with Him reviled Him with the same thing.

45 Now from the sixth hour until the ninth hour there was darkness over all the land.

46 And about the ninth hour Jesus cried out with a loud voice, saying, "Eli, Eli, lama sabachthani?" that is, *"My God, My God, why have You forsaken Me?"*

47 Some of those who stood there, when they heard *that*, said, "This *Man* is calling for Elijah!"

48 Immediately one of them ran and took a sponge, filled *it* with sour wine and put *it* on a reed, and gave it to Him to drink.

49 The rest said, "Let Him alone; let us see if Elijah will come to save Him."

50 Jesus, when He had cried out again with a loud voice, yielded up His spirit.

51 And behold, the veil of the temple was torn in two from top to bottom; and the earth quaked, and the rocks were split,

52 and the graves were opened; and many bodies of the saints who had fallen asleep were raised;

53 and coming out of the graves after His resurrection, they went into the holy city and appeared to many.

54 Now when the centurion and those with him, who were guarding Jesus, saw the earthquake and the things that had happened, they feared greatly, saying, "Truly this was the Son of God!"

55 And many women who followed Jesus from Galilee, ministering to Him, were there looking on from afar,

56 among whom were Mary Magdalene, Mary the mother of James and Joses, and the mother of Zebedee's sons.

57 Now when evening had come, there came a rich man from Arimathea, named Joseph, who himself had also become a disciple of Jesus.

58 This man went to Pilate and asked for the body of Jesus. Then Pilate commanded the body to be given to him.

59 And when Joseph had taken the body, he wrapped it in a clean linen cloth,

60 and laid it in his new tomb which he had hewn out of the

rock; and he rolled a large stone against the door of the tomb, and departed.

61 And Mary Magdalene was there, and the other Mary, sitting opposite the tomb.

62 On the next day, which followed the Day of Preparation, the chief priests and Pharisees gathered together to Pilate,

63 saying, "Sir, we remember, while He was still alive, how that deceiver said, 'After three days I will rise.'

64 "Therefore command that the tomb be made secure until the third day, lest His disciples come by night and steal Him away, and say to the people, 'He has risen from the dead.' So the last deception will be worse than the first."

65 Pilate said to them, "You have a guard; go your way, make it as secure as you know how."

66 So they went and made the tomb secure, sealing the stone and setting the guard.

28 Now after the Sabbath, as the first day of the week began to dawn, Mary Magdalene and the other Mary came to see the tomb.

2 And behold, there was a great earthquake; for an angel of the Lord descended from heaven, and came and rolled back the stone from the door, and sat on it.

3 His countenance was like lightning, and his clothing as white as snow.

4 And the guards shook for fear of him, and became like dead men.

5 But the angel answered and said to the women, "Do not be afraid, for I know that you seek Jesus who was crucified.

6 "He is not here; for He is risen, as He said. Come, see the place where the Lord lay.

7 "And go quickly and tell His disciples that He is risen from the dead, and indeed He is going before you into Galilee; there you

will see Him. Behold, I have told you."

8 So they departed quickly from the tomb with fear and great joy, and ran to bring His disciples word.

9 And as they went to tell His disciples, behold, Jesus met them, saying, "Rejoice!" And they came and held Him by the feet and worshiped Him.

10 Then Jesus said to them, "Do not be afraid. Go and tell My brethren to go to Galilee, and there they will see Me."

11 Now while they were going, behold, some of the guard came into the city and reported to the chief priests all the things that had happened.

12 When they had assembled with the elders and taken counsel, they gave a large sum of money to the soldiers,

13 saying, "Tell them, 'His disciples came at night and stole Him away while we slept.'

14 "And if this comes to the governor's ears, we will appease him and make you secure."

15 So they took the money and did as they were instructed; and this saying is commonly reported among the Jews until this day.

16 Then the eleven disciples went away into Galilee, to the mountain which Jesus had appointed for them.

17 And when they saw Him, they worshiped Him; but some doubted.

18 Then Jesus came and spoke to ♥ them, saying, "All authority has been given to Me in heaven and on earth.

19 "Go therefore and make disciples of all the nations, baptizing them in the name of the Father and of the Son and of the Holy Spirit,

20 "teaching them to observe all things that I have commanded you; and lo, I am with you always, even to the end of the age." Amen.

THE GOSPEL ACCORDING TO

MARK

T HE beginning of the gospel of
Jesus Christ, the Son of God.
2 As it is written in the Prophets:

> "Behold, I send My messenger
> before Your face,
> Who will prepare Your way
> before You."
3 "The voice of one crying in the
> wilderness:
> 'Prepare the way of the LORD,
> Make His paths straight.' "

4 John came baptizing in the wilderness and preaching a baptism of repentance for the remission of sins.

5 And all the land of Judea, and those from Jerusalem, went out to him and were all baptized by him in the Jordan River, confessing their sins.

6 Now John was clothed with camel's hair and with a leather belt around his waist, and he ate locusts and wild honey.

7 And he preached, saying, "There comes One after me who is mightier than I, whose sandal strap I am not worthy to stoop down and loose.

8 "I indeed baptized you with water, but He will baptize you with the Holy Spirit."

9 It came to pass in those days that Jesus came from Nazareth of Galilee, and was baptized by John in the Jordan.

10 And immediately, coming up from the water, He saw the heavens parting and the Spirit descending upon Him like a dove.

11 Then a voice came from heaven, "You are My beloved Son, in whom I am well pleased."

12 And immediately the Spirit drove Him into the wilderness.

13 And He was there in the wilderness forty days, tempted by Satan,

and was with the wild beasts; and the angels ministered to Him.

14 Now after John was put in prison, Jesus came to Galilee, preaching the gospel of the kingdom of God,

15 and saying, "The time is fulfilled, and the kingdom of God is at hand. Repent, and believe in the gospel."

16 And as He walked by the Sea of Galilee, He saw Simon and Andrew his brother casting a net into the sea; for they were fishermen.

17 Then Jesus said to them, "Come after Me, and I will make you become fishers of men."

18 And immediately they left their nets and followed Him.

19 When He had gone a little farther from there, He saw James the son of Zebedee, and John his brother, who also were in the boat mending their nets.

20 And immediately He called them, and they left their father Zebedee in the boat with the hired servants, and went after Him.

21 Then they went into Capernaum, and immediately on the Sabbath He entered the synagogue and taught.

22 And they were astonished at His teaching, for He taught them as one having authority, and not as the scribes.

23 Now there was a man in their synagogue with an unclean spirit. And he cried out,

24 saying, "Let us alone! What have we to do with You, Jesus of Nazareth? Did You come to destroy us? I know who You are—the Holy One of God!"

25 But Jesus rebuked him, saying, "Be quiet, and come out of him!"

26 And when the unclean spirit had convulsed him and cried out with a loud voice, he came out of him.

27 Then they were all amazed, so that they questioned among themselves, saying, "What is this? What new doctrine *is* this? For with authority He commands even the unclean spirits, and they obey Him."

28 And immediately His fame spread throughout all the region around Galilee.

29 Now as soon as they had come out of the synagogue, they entered the house of Simon and Andrew, with James and John.

30 But Simon's wife's mother lay sick with a fever, and they told Him about her at once.

31 So He came and took her by the hand and lifted her up, and immediately the fever left her. And she served them.

32 Now at evening, when the sun had set, they brought to Him all who were sick and those who were demon-possessed.

33 And the whole city was gathered together at the door.

34 Then He healed many who were sick with various diseases, and cast out many demons; and He did not allow the demons to speak, because they knew Him.

35 Now in the morning, having risen a long while before daylight, He went out and departed to a solitary place; and there He prayed.

36 And Simon and those *who were* with Him searched for Him.

37 When they found Him, they said to Him, "Everyone is looking for You."

38 But He said to them, "Let us go into the next towns, that I may preach there also, because for this purpose I have come forth."

39 And He was preaching in their synagogues throughout all Galilee, and casting out demons.

40 Then a leper came to Him, imploring Him, kneeling down to Him and saying to Him, "If You are willing, You can make me clean."

41 And Jesus, moved with compassion, put out *His* hand and touched him, and said to him, "I am willing; be cleansed."

42 As soon as He had spoken, immediately the leprosy left him, and he was cleansed.

43 And He strictly warned him and sent him away at once.

44 And He said to him, "See that you say nothing to anyone; but go your way, show yourself to the priest, and offer for your cleansing those things which Moses commanded, as a testimony to them."

45 But he went out and began to proclaim *it* freely, and to spread the matter, so that Jesus could no longer openly enter the city, but was outside in deserted places; and they came to Him from every quarter.

2 And again He entered Capernaum after *some* days, and it was heard that He was in the house.

2 Immediately many gathered together, so that there was no longer room to receive *them*, not even near the door. And He preached the word to them.

3 Then they came to Him, bringing a paralytic who was carried by four *men.*

4 And when they could not come near Him because of the crowd, they uncovered the roof where He was. And when they had broken through, they let down the bed on which the paralytic was lying.

5 When Jesus saw their faith, He said to the paralytic, "Son, your sins are forgiven you."

6 But some of the scribes were sitting there and reasoning in their hearts,

7 "Why does this *Man* speak blasphemies like this? Who can forgive sins but God alone?"

8 And immediately, when Jesus perceived in His spirit that they

reasoned thus within themselves, He said to them, "Why do you reason about these things in your hearts?

9 "Which is easier, to say to the paralytic, '*Your* sins are forgiven you,' or to say, 'Arise, take up your bed and walk'?

10 "But that you may know that the Son of Man has power on earth to forgive sins"—He said to the paralytic,

11 "I say to you, arise, take up your bed, and go your way to your house."

12 And immediately he arose, took up the bed, and went out in the presence of them all, so that all were amazed and glorified God, saying, "We never saw *anything* like this!"

13 Then He went out again by the sea; and all the multitude came to Him, and He taught them.

14 And as He passed by, He saw Levi the *son* of Alphaeus sitting at the tax office, and said to him, "Follow Me." And he arose and followed Him.

15 Now it happened, as He was dining in *Levi's* house, that many tax collectors and sinners also sat together with Jesus and His disciples; for there were many, and they followed Him.

16 And when the scribes and Pharisees saw Him eating with the tax collectors and sinners, they said to His disciples, "How *is it* that He eats and drinks with tax collectors and sinners?"

17 When Jesus heard *it,* He said to them, "Those who are well have no need of a physician, but those who are sick. I did not come to call *the* righteous, but sinners, to repentance."

18 And the disciples of John and of the Pharisees were fasting. And they came and said to Him, "Why do the disciples of John and of the Pharisees fast, but Your disciples do not fast?"

19 So Jesus said to them, "Can the friends of the bridegroom fast while the bridegroom is with them? As long as they have the bridegroom with them they cannot fast.

20 "But the days will come when the bridegroom will be taken away from them, and then they will fast in those days.

21 "No one sews a piece of unshrunk cloth on an old garment; or else the new piece pulls away from the old, and the tear is made worse.

22 "And no one puts new wine into old wineskins; or else the new wine bursts the wineskins, the wine is spilled, and the wineskins are ruined. But new wine must be put into new wineskins."

23 Now it happened that He went through the grainfields on the Sabbath; and as they went His disciples began to pluck the heads of grain.

24 And the Pharisees said to Him, "Look, why do they do what is not lawful on the Sabbath?"

25 But He said to them, "Have you never read what David did when he was in need and hungry, he and those with him:

26 "how he went into the house of God *in the days* of Abiathar the high priest, and ate the showbread, which is not lawful to eat, except for the priests, and also gave some to those who were with him?"

27 And He said to them, "The Sabbath was made for man, and not man for the Sabbath.

28 "Therefore the Son of Man is also Lord of the Sabbath."

3 And He entered the synagogue again, and a man was there who had a withered hand.

2 And they watched Him closely, whether He would heal him on the Sabbath, so that they might accuse Him.

3 Then He said to the man who

had the withered hand, "Step forward."

4 And He said to them, "Is it lawful on the Sabbath to do good or to do evil, to save life or to kill?" But they kept silent.

5 So when He had looked around at them with anger, being grieved by the hardness of their hearts, He said to the man, "Stretch out your hand." And he stretched *it* out, and his hand was restored as whole as the other.

6 Then the Pharisees went out and immediately plotted with the Herodians against Him, how they might destroy Him.

7 But Jesus withdrew with His disciples to the sea. And a great multitude from Galilee followed Him, and from Judea

8 and Jerusalem and Idumea and beyond the Jordan; and those from Tyre and Sidon, a great multitude, when they heard how many things He was doing, came to Him.

9 And He told His disciples that a small boat should be kept ready for Him because of the multitude, lest they should crush Him.

10 For He healed many, so that as many as had afflictions pressed about Him to touch Him.

11 And the unclean spirits, whenever they saw Him, fell down before Him and cried out, saying, "You are the Son of God."

12 But He sternly warned them that they should not make Him known.

13 And He went up on the mountain and called *to Him* those He Himself wanted. And they came to Him.

14 Then He appointed twelve, that they might be with Him and that He might send them out to preach,

15 and to have power to heal sicknesses and to cast out demons:

16 Simon, to whom He gave the name Peter;

17 James the *son* of Zebedee and John the brother of James, to whom He gave the name Boanerges, that is, "Sons of Thunder";

18 Andrew, Philip, Bartholomew, Matthew, Thomas, James the *son* of Alphaeus, Thaddaeus, Simon the Canaanite,

19 and Judas Iscariot, who also betrayed Him. And they went into a house.

20 And the multitude came together again, so that they could not so much as eat bread.

21 But when His own people heard *about this*, they went out to lay hold of Him, for they said, "He is out of His mind."

22 And the scribes who came down from Jerusalem said, "He has Beelzebub," and, "By the ruler of the demons He casts out demons."

23 So He called them *to Him* and said to them in parables: "How can Satan cast out Satan?

24 "If a kingdom is divided against itself, that kingdom cannot stand.

25 "And if a house is divided against itself, that house cannot stand.

26 "And if Satan has risen up against himself, and is divided, he cannot stand, but has an end.

27 "No one can enter a strong man's house and plunder his goods, unless he first binds the strong man, and then he will plunder his house.

28 "Assuredly, I say to you, all sins will be forgiven the sons of men, and whatever blasphemies they may utter;

29 "but he who blasphemes against the Holy Spirit never has forgiveness, but is subject to eternal condemnation"—

30 because they said, "He has an unclean spirit."

31 Then His brothers and His mother came, and standing outside they sent to Him, calling Him.

32 And a multitude was sitting around Him; and they said to Him, "Look, Your mother and Your brothers are outside seeking You."

33 But He answered them, saying, "Who is My mother, or My brothers?"

34 And He looked around in a circle at those who sat about Him, and said, "Here are My mother and My brothers!

35 "For whoever does the will of God is My brother and My sister and mother."

4 And again He began to teach by the sea. And a great multitude was gathered to Him, so that He got into a boat and sat *in it* on the sea; and the whole multitude was on the land facing the sea.

2 Then He taught them many things by parables, and said to them in His teaching:

3 "Listen! Behold, a sower went out to sow.

4 "And it happened, as he sowed, *that* some *seed* fell by the wayside; and the birds of the air came and devoured it.

5 "Some fell on stony ground, where it did not have much earth; and immediately it sprang up because it had no depth of earth.

6 "But when the sun was up it was scorched, and because it had no root it withered away.

7 "And some *seed* fell among thorns; and the thorns grew up and choked it, and it yielded no crop.

8 "But other *seed* fell on good ground and yielded a crop that sprang up, increased and produced: some thirtyfold, some sixty, and some a hundred."

9 And He said to them, "He who has ears to hear, let him hear!"

10 But when He was alone, those around Him with the twelve asked Him about the parable.

11 And He said to them, "To you it has been given to know the mystery of the kingdom of God; but to those who are outside, all things come in parables,

12 "so that

'Seeing they may see and not
    perceive,
And hearing they may hear
    and not understand;
Lest they should turn,
    And their sins be forgiven
    them.' "

13 And He said to them, "Do you not understand this parable? How then will you understand all the parables?

14 "The sower sows the word.

15 "And these are the ones by the wayside where the word is sown. And when they hear, Satan comes immediately and takes away the word that was sown in their hearts.

16 "These likewise are the ones sown on stony ground who, when they hear the word, immediately receive it with gladness;

17 "and they have no root in themselves, and so endure only for a time. Afterward, when tribulation or persecution arises for the word's sake, immediately they stumble.

18 "Now these are the ones sown among thorns; *they are* the ones who hear the word,

19 "and the cares of this world, the deceitfulness of riches, and the desires for other things entering in choke the word, and it becomes unfruitful.

20 "But these are the ones sown on good ground, those who hear the word, accept *it*, and bear fruit: some thirtyfold, some sixty, and some a hundred."

21 And He said to them, "Is a lamp brought to be put under a basket or under a bed? Is it not to be set on a lampstand?

22 "For there is nothing hidden which will not be revealed, nor has anything been kept secret but that it should come to light.

23 "If anyone has ears to hear, let him hear."

24 And He said to them, "Take heed what you hear. With the same measure you use, it will be measured to you; and to you who hear, more will be given.

25 "For whoever has, to him more will be given; but whoever does not have, even what he has will be taken away from him."

26 And He said, "The kingdom of God is as if a man should scatter seed on the ground,

27 "and should sleep by night and rise by day, and the seed should sprout and grow, he himself does not know how.

28 "For the earth yields crops by itself: first the blade, then the head, after that the full grain in the head.

29 "But when the grain ripens, immediately he puts in the sickle, because the harvest has come."

30 And He said, "To what shall we liken the kingdom of God? Or with what parable shall we picture it?

31 "*It is* like a mustard seed which, when it is sown on the ground, is smaller than all the seeds on earth;

32 "but when it is sown, it grows up and becomes greater than all herbs, and shoots out large branches, so that the birds of the air may nest under its shade."

33 And with many such parables He spoke the word to them as they were able to hear *it*.

34 But without a parable He did not speak to them. And when they were alone, He explained all things to His disciples.

35 On the same day, when evening had come, He said to them, "Let us cross over to the other side."

36 Now when they had left the multitude, they took Him along in the boat as He was. And other little boats were also with Him.

37 And a great windstorm arose, and the waves beat into the boat, so that it was already filling.

38 But He was in the stern, asleep on a pillow. And they awoke Him and said to Him, "Teacher, do You not care that we are perishing?"

39 Then He arose and rebuked the wind, and said to the sea, "Peace, be still!" And the wind ceased and there was a great calm.

40 But He said to them, "Why are you so fearful? How *is it* that you have no faith?"

41 And they feared exceedingly, and said to one another, "Who can this be, that even the wind and the sea obey Him!"

5 Then they came to the other side of the sea, to the country of the Gadarenes.

2 And when He had come out of the boat, immediately there met Him out of the tombs a man with an unclean spirit,

3 who had *his* dwelling among the tombs; and no one could bind him, not even with chains,

4 because he had often been bound with shackles and chains. And the chains had been pulled apart by him, and the shackles broken in pieces; neither could anyone tame him.

5 And always, night and day, he was in the mountains and in the tombs, crying out and cutting himself with stones.

6 But when he saw Jesus from afar, he ran and worshiped Him.

7 And he cried out with a loud voice and said, "What have I to do with You, Jesus, Son of the Most High God? I implore You by God that You do not torment me."

8 For He said to him, "Come out of the man, unclean spirit!"

9 Then He asked him, "What *is* your name?" And he answered, saying, "My name *is* Legion; for we are many."

10 And he begged Him earnestly that He would not send them out of the country.

11 Now a large herd of swine was feeding there near the mountains.

12 And all the demons begged Him, saying, "Send us to the swine, that we may enter them."

13 And at once Jesus gave them permission. Then the unclean spir-

its went out and entered the swine (there were about two thousand); and the herd ran violently down the steep place into the sea, and drowned in the sea.

14 Now those who fed the swine fled, and they told *it* in the city and in the country. And they went out to see what it was that had happened.

15 Then they came to Jesus, and saw the one *who had been* demon-possessed and had the legion, sitting and clothed and in his right mind. And they were afraid.

16 And those who saw it told them how it happened to him *who had been* demon-possessed, and about the swine.

17 Then they began to plead with Him to depart from their region.

18 And when He got into the boat, he who had been demon-possessed begged Him that he might be with Him.

19 However, Jesus did not permit him, but said to him, "Go home to your friends, and tell them what great things the Lord has done for you, and how He has had compassion on you."

20 And he departed and began to proclaim in Decapolis all that Jesus had done for him; and all marveled.

21 Now when Jesus had crossed over again by boat to the other side, a great multitude gathered to Him; and He was by the sea.

22 And behold, one of the rulers of the synagogue came, Jairus by name. And when he saw Him, he fell at His feet

23 and begged Him earnestly, saying, "My little daughter lies at the point of death. Come and lay Your hands on her, that she may be healed, and she will live."

24 So *Jesus* went with him, and a great multitude followed Him and thronged Him.

25 Now a certain woman had a flow of blood for twelve years,

26 and had suffered many things from many physicians. She had spent all that she had and was no better, but rather grew worse.

27 When she heard about Jesus, she came behind *Him* in the crowd and touched His garment;

28 for she said, "If only I may touch His clothes, I shall be made well."

29 Immediately the fountain of her blood was dried up, and she felt in *her* body that she was healed of the affliction.

30 And Jesus, immediately knowing in Himself that power had gone out of Him, turned around in the crowd and said, "Who touched My clothes?"

31 But His disciples said to Him, "You see the multitude thronging You, and You say, 'Who touched Me?' "

32 And He looked around to see her who had done this thing.

33 But the woman, fearing and trembling, knowing what had happened to her, came and fell down before Him and told Him the whole truth.

34 And He said to her, "Daughter, your faith has made you well. Go in peace, and be healed of your affliction."

35 While He was still speaking, *some* came from the ruler of the synagogue's *house* who said, "Your daughter is dead. Why trouble the Teacher any further?"

36 As soon as Jesus heard the word that was spoken, He said to the ruler of the synagogue, "Do not be afraid; only believe."

37 And He permitted no one to follow Him except Peter, James, and John the brother of James.

38 Then He came to the house of the ruler of the synagogue, and saw a tumult and those who wept and wailed loudly.

39 When He came in, He said to them, "Why make this commotion

and weep? The child is not dead, but sleeping."

40 And they laughed Him to scorn. But when He had put them all out, He took the father and the mother of the child, and those *who were* with Him, and entered where the child was lying.

41 Then He took the child by the hand, and said to her, "Talitha, cumi," which is translated, "Little girl, I say to you, arise."

42 Immediately the girl arose and walked, for she was twelve years *of age.* And they were overcome with great amazement.

43 But He commanded them strictly that no one should know it, and said that *something* should be given her to eat.

6 Then He went out from there and came to His own country, and His disciples followed Him.

2 And when the Sabbath had come, He began to teach in the synagogue. And many hearing *Him* were astonished, saying, "Where *did* this *Man get* these things? And what wisdom *is* this which is given to Him, that such mighty works are performed by His hands!

3 "Is this not the carpenter, the Son of Mary, and brother of James, Joses, Judas, and Simon? And are not His sisters here with us?" And they were offended at Him.

4 But Jesus said to them, "A prophet is not without honor except in his own country, among his own relatives, and in his own house."

5 Now He could do no mighty work there, except that He laid His hands on a few sick people and healed *them.*

6 And He marveled because of their unbelief. Then He went about the villages in a circuit, teaching.

7 And He called the twelve *to* Him, and began to send them out two *by* two, and gave them power over unclean spirits.

8 He commanded them to take nothing for the journey except a staff—no bag, no bread, no copper in *their* money belts—

9 but to wear sandals, and not to put on two tunics.

10 Also He said to them, "In whatever place you enter a house, stay there till you depart from that place.

11 "And whoever will not receive you nor hear you, when you depart from there, shake off the dust under your feet as a testimony against them. Assuredly, I say to you, it will be more tolerable for Sodom and Gomorrah in the day of judgment than for that city!"

12 So they went out and preached that *people* should repent.

13 And they cast out many demons, and anointed with oil many who were sick, and healed *them.*

14 Now King Herod heard *of Him,* for His name had become well known. And he said, "John the Baptist is risen from the dead, and therefore these powers are at work in him."

15 Others said, "It is Elijah." And others said, "It is the Prophet, or like one of the prophets."

16 But when Herod heard, he said, "This is John, whom I beheaded; he has been raised from the dead!"

17 For Herod himself had sent and laid hold of John, and bound him in prison for the sake of Herodias, his brother Philip's wife; for he had married her.

18 For John had said to Herod, "It is not lawful for you to have your brother's wife."

19 Therefore Herodias held it against him and wanted to kill him, but she could not;

20 for Herod feared John, knowing that he *was* a just and holy man, and he protected him. And when he heard him, he did many things, and heard him gladly.

21 Then an opportune day came when Herod on his birthday gave a

feast for his nobles, the high officers, and the chief *men* of Galilee.
22 And when Herodias' daughter herself came in and danced, and pleased Herod and those who sat with him, the king said to the girl, "Ask me whatever you want, and I will give *it* to you."
23 He also swore to her, "Whatever you ask me, I will give you, up to half of my kingdom."
24 So she went out and said to her mother, "What shall I ask?" And she said, "The head of John the Baptist!"
25 Immediately she came in with haste to the king and asked, saying, "I want you to give me at once the head of John the Baptist on a platter."
26 And the king was exceedingly sorry; *yet*, because of the oaths and because of those who sat with him, he did not want to refuse her.
27 And immediately the king sent an executioner and commanded his head to be brought. And he went and beheaded him in prison,
28 brought his head on a platter, and gave it to the girl; and the girl gave it to her mother.
29 And when his disciples heard *of it*, they came and took away his corpse and laid it in a tomb.
30 Then the apostles gathered to Jesus and told Him all things, both what they had done and what they had taught.
31 And He said to them, "Come aside by yourselves to a deserted place and rest a while." For there were many coming and going, and they did not even have time to eat.
32 So they departed to a deserted place in the boat by themselves.
33 But the multitudes saw them departing, and many knew Him and ran there on foot from all the cities. They arrived before them and came together to Him.
34 And Jesus, when He came out, saw a great multitude and was moved with compassion for them,

because they were like sheep not having a shepherd. So He began to teach them many things.
35 And when the day was now far spent, His disciples came to Him and said, "This is a deserted place, and already the hour *is* late.
36 "Send them away, that they may go into the surrounding country and villages and buy themselves bread; for they have nothing to eat."
37 But He answered and said to them, "You give them something to eat." And they said to Him, "Shall we go and buy two hundred denarii worth of bread and give them *something* to eat?"
38 But He said to them, "How many loaves do you have? Go and see." And when they found out they said, "Five, and two fish."
39 Then He commanded them to make them all sit down in groups on the green grass.
40 So they sat down in ranks, in hundreds and in fifties.
41 And when He had taken the five loaves and the two fish, He looked up to heaven, blessed and broke the loaves, and gave *them* to His disciples to set before them; and the two fish He divided among *them* all.
42 So they all ate and were filled.
43 And they took up twelve baskets full of fragments and of the fish.
44 Now those who had eaten the loaves were about five thousand men.
45 Immediately He made His disciples get into the boat and go before Him to the other side, to Bethsaida, while He sent the multitude away.
46 And when He had sent them away, He departed to the mountain to pray.
47 Now when evening came, the boat was in the middle of the sea; and He *was* alone on the land.
48 Then He saw them straining at rowing, for the wind was against

them. And about the fourth watch of the night He came to them, walking on the sea, and would have passed them by.

49 But when they saw Him walking on the sea, they supposed it was a ghost, and cried out;

50 for they all saw Him and were troubled. And immediately He talked with them and said to them, "Be of good cheer! It is I; do not be afraid."

51 Then He went up into the boat to them, and the wind ceased. And they were greatly amazed in themselves beyond measure, and marveled.

52 For they had not understood about the loaves, because their heart was hardened.

53 When they had crossed over, they came to the land of Gennesaret and anchored there.

54 And when they came out of the boat, immediately the people recognized Him,

55 ran through that whole surrounding region, and began to carry about on beds those who were sick to wherever they heard He was.

56 Wherever He entered, into villages, cities, or the country, they laid the sick in the marketplaces, and begged Him that they might just touch the border of His garment. And as many as touched Him were made well.

7 Then the Pharisees and some of the scribes came together to Him, having come from Jerusalem.

2 Now when they saw some of His disciples eat bread with defiled, that is, with unwashed hands, they found fault.

3 For the Pharisees and all the Jews do not eat unless they wash *their* hands in a special way, holding the tradition of the elders.

4 *When they come* from the marketplace, they do not eat unless they wash. And there are many other things which they have re-

ceived and hold, *like* the washing of cups, pitchers, copper vessels, and couches.

5 Then the Pharisees and scribes asked Him, "Why do Your disciples not walk according to the tradition of the elders, but eat bread with unwashed hands?"

6 He answered and said to them, "Well did Isaiah prophesy of you hypocrites, as it is written:

'This people honors Me with
    their lips,
But their heart is far from Me.
7 And in vain they worship Me,
Teaching as doctrines the
    commandments of men.'

8 "For laying aside the commandment of God, you hold the tradition of men—the washing of pitchers and cups, and many other such things you do."

9 And He said to them, "*All too* well you reject the commandment of God, that you may keep your tradition.

10 "For Moses said, '*Honor your father and your mother*'; and, '*He who curses father or mother, let him be put to death.*'

11 "But you say, 'If a man says to his father or mother, "Whatever profit you might have received from me *is* Corban"—' " (that is, dedicated *to the temple*);

12 "and you no longer let him do anything for his father or his mother,

13 "making the word of God of no effect through your tradition which you have handed down. And many such things you do."

14 And when He had called all the multitude *to Him*, He said to them, "Hear Me, everyone, and understand:

15 "There is nothing that enters a man from outside which can defile him; but the things which come out of him, those are the things that defile a man.

Jesus Heals a Deaf-Mute

16 "If anyone has ears to hear, let him hear!"

17 And when He had entered a house away from the crowd, His disciples asked Him concerning the parable.

18 So He said to them, "Are you thus without understanding also? Do you not perceive that whatever enters a man from outside cannot defile him,

19 "because it does not enter his heart but his stomach, and is eliminated, *thus* purifying all foods?"

20 And He said, "What comes out of a man, that defiles a man.

21 "For from within, out of the heart of men, proceed evil thoughts, adulteries, fornications, murders,

22 "thefts, covetousness, wickedness, deceit, licentiousness, an evil eye, blasphemy, pride, foolishness.

23 "All these evil things come from within and defile a man."

24 And from there He arose and went to the region of Tyre and Sidon. And He entered a house and wanted no one to know *it*, but He could not be hidden.

25 For a woman whose young daughter had an unclean spirit heard about Him, and she came and fell at His feet.

26 The woman was a Greek, a Syro-Phoenician by birth, and she kept asking Him to cast the demon out of her daughter.

27 But Jesus said to her, "Let the children be filled first, for it is not good to take the children's bread and throw *it* to the little dogs."

28 And she answered and said to Him, "Yes, Lord, yet even the little dogs under the table eat from the children's crumbs."

29 Then He said to her, "For this saying go your way; the demon has gone out of your daughter."

30 And when she had come to her house, she found the demon gone out, and her daughter lying on the bed.

31 And again, departing from the region of Tyre and Sidon, He came through the midst of the region of Decapolis to the Sea of Galilee.

32 Then they brought to Him one who was deaf and had an impediment in his speech, and they begged Him to put His hand on him.

33 And He took him aside from the multitude, and put His fingers in his ears, and He spat and touched his tongue.

34 Then, looking up to heaven, He sighed, and said to him, "Ephphatha," that is, "Be opened."

35 Immediately his ears were opened, and the impediment of his tongue was loosed, and he spoke plainly.

36 Then He commanded them that they should tell no one; but the more He commanded them, the more widely they proclaimed *it*.

37 And they were astonished beyond measure, saying, "He has done all things well. He makes both the deaf to hear and the mute to speak."

8 In those days, the multitude being very great and having nothing to eat, Jesus called His disciples *to Him* and said to them,

2 "I have compassion on the multitude, because they have now been with Me three days and have nothing to eat.

3 "And if I send them away hungry to their own houses, they will faint on the way; for some of them have come from afar."

4 Then His disciples answered Him, "How can one satisfy these people with bread here in the wilderness?"

5 He asked them, "How many loaves do you have?" And they said, "Seven."

6 And He commanded the multitude to sit down on the ground. And He took the seven loaves and gave thanks, broke *them* and gave *them* to His disciples to set before

them; and they set *them* before the multitude.

7 And they had a few small fish; and having blessed them, He said to set them also before *them.*

8 So they ate and were filled, and they took up seven large baskets of leftover fragments.

9 Now those who had eaten were about four thousand. And He sent them away.

10 And immediately He got into the boat with His disciples and came to the region of Dalmanutha.

11 And the Pharisees came out and began to dispute with Him, seeking from Him a sign from heaven, testing Him.

12 But He sighed deeply in His spirit, and said, "Why does this generation seek a sign? Assuredly, I say to you, no sign shall be given to this generation."

13 And He left them, and getting into the boat again, departed to the other side.

14 Now the disciples had forgotten to take bread, and they did not have more than one loaf with them in the boat.

15 Then He charged them, saying, "Take heed, beware of the leaven of the Pharisees and the leaven of Herod."

16 So they reasoned among themselves, saying, "*It is* because we have no bread."

17 And Jesus, being aware of *it,* said to them, "Why do you reason because you have no bread? Do you not yet perceive nor understand? Is your heart still hardened?

18 "Having eyes, do you not see? And having ears, do you not hear? And do you not remember?

19 "When I broke the five loaves for the five thousand, how many baskets full of fragments did you take up?" They said to Him, "Twelve."

20 "And when I broke the seven for the four thousand, how many large baskets full of fragments did

you take up?" And they said, "Seven."

21 So He said to them, "How *is it* you do not understand?"

22 Then He came to Bethsaida; and they brought a blind man to Him, and begged Him to touch him.

23 So He took the blind man by the hand and led him out of the town. And when He had spit on his eyes and put His hands on him, He asked him if he saw anything.

24 And he looked up and said, "I see men like trees, walking."

25 Then He put *His* hands on his eyes again and made him look up. And he was restored and saw everyone clearly.

26 And He sent him away to his house, saying, "Neither go into the town, nor tell anyone in the town."

27 Now Jesus and His disciples went out to the towns of Caesarea Philippi; and on the road He asked His disciples, saying to them, "Who do men say that I am?"

28 And they answered, "John the Baptist; but some *say,* Elijah; and others, one of the prophets."

29 He said to them, "But who do you say that I am?" And Peter answered and said to Him, "You are the Christ."

30 Then He charged them that they should tell no one about Him.

31 And He began to teach them that the Son of Man must suffer many things, and be rejected by the elders and chief priests and scribes, and be killed, and after three days rise again.

32 He spoke this word openly. And Peter took Him aside and began to rebuke Him.

33 But when He had turned around and looked at His disciples, He rebuked Peter, saying, "Get behind Me, Satan! For you are not mindful of the things of God, but the things of men."

34 And when He had called the people *to Him,* with His disciples

also, He said to them, "Whoever desires to come after Me, let him deny himself, and take up his cross, and follow Me.

35 "For whoever desires to save his life will lose it, but whoever loses his life for My sake and the gospel's will save it.

36 "For what will it profit a man if he gains the whole world, and loses his own soul?

37 "Or what will a man give in exchange for his soul?

38 "For whoever is ashamed of Me and My words in this adulterous and sinful generation, of him the Son of Man also will be ashamed when He comes in the glory of His Father with the holy angels."

9 And He said to them, "Assuredly, I say to you that there are some standing here who will not taste death till they see the kingdom of God present with power."

2 Now after six days Jesus took Peter, James, and John, and led them up on a high mountain apart by themselves; and He was transfigured before them.

3 His clothes became shining, exceedingly white, like snow, such as no launderer on earth can whiten them.

4 And Elijah appeared to them with Moses, and they were talking with Jesus.

5 Then Peter answered and said to Jesus, "Rabbi, it is good for us to be here; and let us make three tabernacles: one for You, one for Moses, and one for Elijah"—

6 because he did not know what to say, for they were greatly afraid.

7 And a cloud came and overshadowed them; and a voice came out of the cloud, saying, "This is My beloved Son. Hear Him!"

8 Suddenly, when they had looked around, they saw no one anymore, but only Jesus with themselves.

9 Now as they came down from the mountain, He commanded them that they should tell no one the things they had seen, till the Son of Man had risen from the dead.

10 So they kept this word to themselves, questioning what the rising from the dead meant.

11 And they asked Him, saying, "Why do the scribes say that Elijah must come first?"

12 Then He answered and told them, "Elijah does come first, and restores all things. And how is it written concerning the Son of Man, that He must suffer many things and be treated with contempt?

13 "But I say to you that Elijah has also come, and they did to him whatever they wished, as it is written of him."

14 And when He came to the disciples, He saw a great multitude around them, and scribes disputing with them.

15 Immediately, when they saw Him, all the people were greatly amazed, and running to *Him,* greeted Him.

16 And He asked the scribes, "What are you discussing with them?"

17 Then one from the multitude answered and said, "Teacher, I brought You my son, who has a mute spirit.

18 "And wherever he seizes him, he throws him down; he foams at the mouth, gnashes his teeth, and becomes rigid. So I spoke to Your disciples, that they should cast him out, but they could not."

19 He answered him and said, "O faithless generation, how long shall I be with you? How long shall I bear with you? Bring him to Me."

20 Then they brought him to Him. And when he saw Him, immediately the spirit convulsed him, and he fell on the ground and wallowed, foaming at the mouth.

21 So He asked his father, "How

long has this been happening to him?" And he said, "From childhood.

22 "And often he has thrown him both into the fire and into the water to destroy him. But if You can do anything, have compassion on us and help us."

23 Jesus said to him, "If you can believe, all things *are* possible to him who believes."

24 Immediately the father of the child cried out and said with tears, "Lord, I believe; help my unbelief!"

25 When Jesus saw that the people came running together, He rebuked the unclean spirit, saying to him, "*You* deaf and dumb spirit, I command you, come out of him, and enter him no more!"

26 Then *the spirit* cried out, convulsed him greatly, and came out of him. And he became as one dead, so that many said, "He is dead."

27 But Jesus took him by the hand and lifted him up, and he arose.

28 And when He had come into the house, His disciples asked Him privately, "Why could we not cast him out?"

29 So He said to them, "This kind can come out by nothing but prayer and fasting."

30 Then they departed from there and passed through Galilee, and He did not want anyone to know it.

31 For He taught His disciples and said to them, "The Son of Man is being delivered into the hands of men, and they will kill Him. And after He is killed, He will rise the third day."

32 But they did not understand this saying, and were afraid to ask Him.

33 Then He came to Capernaum. And when He was in the house He asked them, "What was it you disputed among yourselves on the road?"

34 But they kept silent, for on the road they had disputed among themselves who *would be the* greatest.

35 And He sat down, called the twelve, and said to them, "If anyone desires to be first, he shall be last of all and servant of all."

36 Then He took a little child and set him in the midst of them. And when He had taken him in His arms, He said to them,

37 "Whoever receives one of these little children in My name receives Me; and whoever receives Me, receives not Me but Him who sent Me."

38 Now John answered Him, saying, "Teacher, we saw someone who does not follow us casting out demons in Your name, and we forbade him because he does not follow us."

39 But Jesus said, "Do not forbid him, for no one who works a miracle in My name can soon afterward speak evil of Me.

40 "For he who is not against us is on our side.

41 "For whoever gives you a cup of water to drink in My name, because you belong to Christ, assuredly, I say to you, he will by no means lose his reward.

42 "And whoever causes one of these little ones who believe in Me to stumble, it would be better for him if a millstone were hung around his neck, and he were thrown into the sea.

43 "And if your hand makes you sin, cut it off. It is better for you to enter into life maimed, than having two hands, to go to hell, into the fire that shall never be quenched—

44 "where *their worm does not die and the fire is not quenched.*'

45 "And if your foot makes you sin, cut it off. It is better for you to enter life lame, than having two feet, to be cast into hell, into the fire that shall never be quenched—

46 "where *'their worm does not die and the fire is not quenched.'*

47 "And if your eye makes you sin, pluck it out. It is better for you to enter the kingdom of God with one eye, than having two eyes, to be cast into hell fire—

48 "where *'their worm does not die and the fire is not quenched.'*

49 "For everyone will be seasoned with fire, and every sacrifice will be seasoned with salt.

50 "Salt *is* good, but if the salt loses its flavor, how will you season it? Have salt in yourselves, and have peace with one another."

10 Then He arose from there and came to the region of Judea by the other side of the Jordan. And the people gathered to Him again, and as He was accustomed, He taught them again.

2 The Pharisees came and asked Him, "Is it lawful for a man to divorce *his* wife?" testing Him.

3 And He answered and said to them, "What did Moses command you?"

4 They said, "Moses permitted *a man* to write a certificate of divorce, and to dismiss *her.*"

5 And Jesus answered and said to them, "Because of the hardness of your heart he wrote you this precept.

6 "But from the beginning of the creation, God *'made them male and female.'*

7 *'For this reason a man shall leave his father and mother and be joined to his wife,*

8 *'and the two shall become one flesh'*; so then they are no longer two, but one flesh.

9 "Therefore what God has joined together, let not man separate."

10 And in the house His disciples asked Him again about the same *matter.*

11 So He said to them, "Whoever divorces his wife and marries another commits adultery against her.

12 "And if a woman divorces her husband and marries another, she commits adultery."

13 Then they brought young children to Him, that He might touch them; but the disciples rebuked those who brought *them.*

14 But when Jesus saw *it,* He was greatly displeased and said to them, "Let the little children come to Me, and do not forbid them; for of such is the kingdom of God.

15 "Assuredly, I say to you, whoever does not receive the kingdom of God as a little child will by no means enter it."

16 And He took them up in His arms, put *His* hands on them, and blessed them.

17 Now as He was going out on the road, one came running, knelt before Him, and asked Him, "Good Teacher, what shall I do that I may inherit eternal life?"

18 So Jesus said to him, "Why do you call Me good? No one *is* good but One, *that is,* God.

19 "You know the commandments: *'Do not commit adultery,' 'Do not murder,' 'Do not steal,' 'Do not bear false witness,'* 'Do not defraud,' *'Honor your father and your mother.'*"

20 And he answered and said to Him, "Teacher, all these I have observed from my youth."

21 Then Jesus, looking at him, loved him, and said to him, "One thing you lack: Go your way, sell whatever you have and give to the poor, and you will have treasure in heaven; and come, take up the cross, and follow Me."

22 But he was sad at this word, and went away grieved, for he had great possessions.

23 Then Jesus looked around and said to His disciples, "How hard it is for those who have riches to enter the kingdom of God!"

24 And the disciples were astonished at His words. But Jesus answered again and said to them,

"Children, how hard it is for those who trust in riches to enter the kingdom of God!

25 "It is easier for a camel to go through the eye of a needle than for a rich man to enter the kingdom of God."

26 And they were astonished beyond measure, saying among themselves, "Who then can be saved?"

27 But looking at them, Jesus said, "With men *it is* impossible, but not with God; for with God all things are possible."

28 Then Peter began to say to Him, "See, we have left all and followed You."

29 So Jesus answered and said, "Assuredly, I say to you, there is no one who has left house or brothers or sisters or father or mother or wife or children or lands, for My sake and the gospel's,

30 "who shall not receive a hundredfold now in this time—houses and brothers and sisters and mothers and children and lands, with persecutions—and in the age to come, eternal life.

31 "But many *who are* first will be last, and the last first."

32 Now they were on the road, going up to Jerusalem, and Jesus was going before them; and they were amazed. And as they followed they were afraid. Then He took the twelve aside again and began to tell them the things that would happen to Him:

33 "Behold, we are going up to Jerusalem, and the Son of Man will be delivered to the chief priests and to the scribes, and they will condemn Him to death and deliver Him to the Gentiles;

34 "and they will mock Him, and scourge Him, and spit on Him, and kill Him. And the third day He will rise again."

35 Then James and John, the sons of Zebedee, came to Him, saying,

"Teacher, we want You to do for us whatever we ask."

36 And He said to them, "What do you want Me to do for you?"

37 They said to Him, "Grant us that we may sit, one on Your right hand and the other on Your left, in Your glory."

38 But Jesus said to them, "You do not know what you ask. Can you drink the cup that I drink, and be baptized with the baptism that I am baptized with?"

39 And they said to Him, "We can." And Jesus said to them, "You will indeed drink the cup that I drink, and with the baptism I am baptized with you will be baptized;

40 "but to sit on My right hand and on My left is not Mine to give, but *it is for those* for whom it is prepared."

41 And when the ten heard *it*, they began to be greatly displeased with James and John.

42 But Jesus called them to *Himself* and said to them, "You know that those who are considered rulers over the Gentiles lord it over them, and their great ones exercise authority over them.

43 "Yet it shall not be so among you; but whoever desires to become great among you shall be your servant.

44 "And whoever of you desires to be first shall be slave of all.

45 "For even the Son of Man did not come to be served, but to serve, and to give His life a ransom for many."

46 Then they came to Jericho. And as He went out of Jericho with His disciples and a great multitude, blind Bartimaeus, the son of Timaeus, sat by the road begging.

47 And when he heard that it was Jesus of Nazareth, he began to cry out and say, "Jesus, Son of David, have mercy on me!"

48 Then many warned him to be quiet; but he cried out all the more,

"Son of David, have mercy on me!"

49 So Jesus stood still and commanded him to be called. Then they called the blind man, saying to him, "Be of good cheer. Rise, He is calling you."

50 And throwing aside his garment, he rose and came to Jesus.

51 And Jesus answered and said to him, "What do you want Me to do for you?" The blind man said to Him, "Rabboni, that I may receive my sight."

52 Then Jesus said to him, "Go your way; your faith has made you well." And immediately he received his sight and followed Jesus on the road.

11 Now when they came near Jerusalem, to Bethphage and Bethany, at the Mount of Olives, He sent out two of His disciples;

2 and He said to them, "Go into the village opposite you; and as soon as you have entered it you will find a colt tied, on which no one has sat. Loose it and bring *it*.

3 "And if anyone says to you, 'Why are you doing this?' say, 'The Lord has need of it,' and immediately he will send it here."

4 So they went their way, and found the colt tied by the door outside on the street, and they loosed it.

5 And some of those who stood there said to them, "What are you doing, loosing the colt?"

6 So they spoke to them just as Jesus had commanded. And they let them go.

7 Then they brought the colt to Jesus and threw their garments on it, and He sat on it.

8 And many spread their garments on the road, and others cut down leafy branches from the trees and spread *them* on the road.

9 Then those who went before and those who followed cried out, saying:

"Hosanna!
'Blessed is He who comes in the name of the LORD!'

10 Blessed is the kingdom of our father David
That comes in the name of the Lord!
Hosanna in the highest!"

11 And Jesus went into Jerusalem and into the temple. So when He had looked around at all things, as the hour was already late, He went out to Bethany with the twelve.

12 Now the next day, when they had come out from Bethany, He was hungry.

13 And seeing from afar a fig tree having leaves, He went to see if perhaps He would find something on it. And when He came to it, He found nothing but leaves, for it was not the season for figs.

14 In response Jesus said to it, "Let no one eat fruit from you ever again." And His disciples heard *it*.

15 So they came to Jerusalem. And Jesus went into the temple and began to drive out those who bought and sold in the temple, and overturned the tables of the moneychangers and the seats of those who sold doves.

16 And He would not allow anyone to carry wares through the temple.

17 Then He taught, saying to them, "Is it not written, 'My house shall be called a house of prayer for all nations'? But you have made it a 'den of thieves.'"

18 And the scribes and chief priests heard it and sought how they might destroy Him; for they feared Him, because all the people were astonished at His teaching.

19 And when evening had come, He went out of the city.

20 Now in the morning, as they passed by, they saw the fig tree dried up from the roots.

21 And Peter, remembering, said to Him, "Rabbi, look! The fig tree

which You cursed has withered away."

22 So Jesus answered and said to them, "Have faith in God.

23 "For assuredly, I say to you, whoever says to this mountain, 'Be removed and be cast into the sea,' and does not doubt in his heart, but believes that those things he says will come to pass, he will have whatever he says.

24 "Therefore I say to you, whatever things you ask when you pray, believe that you receive *them*, and you will have *them*.

25 "And whenever you stand praying, if you have anything against anyone, forgive him, that your Father in heaven may also forgive you your trespasses.

26 "But if you do not forgive, neither will your Father in heaven forgive your trespasses."

27 Then they came again to Jerusalem. And as He was walking in the temple, the chief priests, the scribes, and the elders came to Him.

28 And they said to Him, "By what authority are You doing these things? And who gave You this authority to do these things?"

29 But Jesus answered and said to them, "I will also ask you one question; then answer Me, and I will tell you by what authority I do these things:

30 "The baptism of John—was it from heaven or from men? Answer Me."

31 And they reasoned among themselves, saying, "If we say, 'From heaven,' He will say, 'Why then did you not believe him?'

32 "But if we say, 'From men' "— they feared the people, for all counted John to have been a prophet indeed.

33 So they answered and said to Jesus, "We do not know." And Jesus answered and said to them, "Neither will I tell you by what authority I do these things."

12 Then He began to speak to them in parables: "A man planted a vineyard and set a hedge around *it*, dug *a place for* the wine vat and built a tower. And he leased it to vinedressers and went into a far country.

2 "Now at vintage-time he sent a servant to the vinedressers, that he might receive some of the fruit of the vineyard from the vinedressers.

3 "And they took *him* and beat him and sent *him* away empty-handed.

4 "Again he sent them another servant, and at him they threw stones, wounded *him* in the head, and sent *him* away shamefully treated.

5 "And again he sent another, and him they killed; and many others, beating some and killing some.

6 "Therefore still having one son, his beloved, he also sent him to them last, saying, 'They will respect my son.'

7 "But those vinedressers said among themselves, 'This is the heir. Come, let us kill him, and the inheritance will be ours.'

8 "And they took him and killed *him* and cast *him* out of the vineyard.

9 "Therefore what will the owner of the vineyard do? He will come and destroy the vinedressers, and give the vineyard to others.

10 "Have you not read this Scripture:

*'The stone which the builders rejected
Has become the chief cornerstone.*
11 *This was the LORD's doing,
And it is marvelous in our eyes'?"*

12 And they sought to lay hold of Him, but feared the multitude, for they knew He had spoken the parable against them. So they left Him and went away.

The Greatest Commandment

13 Then they sent to Him some of the Pharisees and the Herodians, to catch Him in *His* words.

14 When they had come, they said to Him, "Teacher, we know that You are true, and care about no one; for You do not regard the person of men, but teach the way of God in truth. Is it lawful to pay taxes to Caesar, or not?

15 "Shall we pay, or shall we not pay?" But He, knowing their hypocrisy, said to them, "Why do you test Me? Bring Me a denarius that I may see *it.*"

16 So they brought *it.* And He said to them, "Whose image and inscription *is* this?" And they said to Him, "Caesar's."

17 Then Jesus answered and said to them, "Render to Caesar the things that are Caesar's, and to God the things that are God's." And they marveled at Him.

18 Then *some* Sadducees, who say there is no resurrection, came to Him; and they asked Him, saying:

19 "Teacher, Moses wrote to us that if a man's brother dies, and leaves *his* wife behind, and leaves no children, his brother should take his wife and raise up offspring for his brother.

20 "Now there were seven brothers. The first took a wife; and dying, he left no offspring.

21 "And the second took her, and he died; nor did he leave any offspring. And the third likewise.

22 "So the seven had her and left no offspring. Last of all the woman died also.

23 "Therefore, in the resurrection, when they rise, whose wife will she be? For all seven had her as wife."

24 Jesus answered and said to them, "Are you not therefore mistaken, because you do not know the Scriptures nor the power of God?

25 "For when they rise from the dead, they neither marry nor are given in marriage, but are like angels in heaven.

26 "But concerning the dead, that they rise, have you not read in the book of Moses, in the *burning bush passage,* how God spoke to him, saying, *'I am the God of Abraham, the God of Isaac, and the God of Jacob'?*

27 "He is not the God of the dead, but the God of the living. You are therefore greatly mistaken."

28 Then one of the scribes came, and having heard them reasoning together, perceiving that He had answered them well, asked Him, "Which is the first commandment of all?"

29 Jesus answered him, "The first of all the commandments *is: 'Hear, O Israel, the* LORD *our God, the* LORD *is one.*

30 *'And you shall love the* LORD *your God with all your heart, with all your soul, with all your mind, and with all your strength.'* This *is* the first commandment.

31 "And the second, like *it, is* this: *'You shall love your neighbor as yourself.'* There is no other commandment greater than these."

32 So the scribe said to Him, "Well *said,* Teacher. You have spoken the truth, for there is one God, and there is no other but He.

33 "And to love Him with all the heart, with all the understanding, with all the soul, and with all the strength, and to love one's neighbor as oneself, is more than all the whole burnt offerings and sacrifices."

34 So when Jesus saw that he answered wisely, He said to him, "You are not far from the kingdom of God." And after that no one dared question Him.

35 Then Jesus answered and said, while He taught in the temple, "How *is it* that the scribes say that the Christ is the Son of David?

36 "For David himself said by the Holy Spirit:

    'The LORD said to my Lord,
    "Sit at My right hand,
    Till I make Your enemies
      Your footstool." '

37 "Therefore David himself calls Him *'Lord'*; how is He *then* his Son?" And the common people heard Him gladly.

38 Then He said to them in His teaching, "Beware of the scribes, who desire to go around in long robes, *love* greetings in the marketplaces,

39 "the best seats in the synagogues, and the best places at feasts,

40 "who devour widows' houses, and for a pretense make long prayers. These will receive greater condemnation."

41 Now Jesus sat opposite the treasury and saw how the people put money into the treasury. And many *who were* rich put in much.

42 Then one poor widow came and threw in two mites, which make a quadrans.

43 So He called His disciples *to Him* and said to them, "Assuredly, I say to you that this poor widow has put in more than all those who have given to the treasury;

44 "for they all put in out of their abundance, but she out of her poverty put in all that she had, her whole livelihood."

13 Then as He went out of the temple, one of His disciples said to Him, "Teacher, see what manner of stones and what buildings *are here!*"

2 And Jesus answered and said to him, "Do you see these great buildings? Not *one* stone shall be left upon another, that shall not be thrown down."

3 Now as He sat on the Mount of Olives opposite the temple, Peter, James, John, and Andrew asked Him privately,

4 "Tell us, when will these things be? And what *will be* the sign

when all these things will be fulfilled?"

5 And Jesus, answering them, began to say: "Take heed that no one deceives you.

6 "For many will come in My name, saying, 'I am *He*,' and will deceive many.

7 "And when you hear of wars and rumors of wars, do not be troubled; for *such things* must happen, but the end *is* not yet.

8 "For nation will rise against nation, and kingdom against kingdom. And there will be earthquakes in various places, and there will be famines and troubles. These *are* the beginnings of sorrows.

9 "But watch out for yourselves, for they will deliver you up to councils, and you will be beaten in the synagogues. And you will be brought before rulers and kings for My sake, for a testimony to them.

10 "And the gospel must first be preached to all the nations.

11 "But when they arrest *you* and deliver you up, do not worry beforehand, or premeditate what you will speak. But whatever is given you in that hour, speak that; for it is not you who speak, but the Holy Spirit.

12 "Now brother will betray brother to death, and a father *his* child; and children will rise up against parents and cause them to be put to death.

13 "And you will be hated by all *men* for My name's sake. But he who endures to the end shall be saved.

14 "But when you see the *'abomination of desolation,'* spoken of by Daniel the prophet, standing where it ought not" (let the reader understand), "then let those who are in Judea flee to the mountains.

15 "And let him who is on the housetop not go down into the house, nor enter to take anything out of his house.

16 "And let him who is in the field not go back to get his garment.

17 "But woe to those who are pregnant and to those with nursing babies in those days!

18 "And pray that your flight may not be in winter.

19 "For *in* those days there will be tribulation, such as has not been from the beginning of creation which God created until this time, nor ever shall be.

20 "And unless the Lord had shortened those days, no flesh would be saved; but for the elect's sake, whom He chose, He shortened the days.

21 "Then if anyone says to you, 'Look, here *is* the Christ!' or, 'Look, *He is* there!' do not believe it.

22 "For false christs and false prophets will rise and show signs and wonders to deceive, if possible, even the elect.

23 "But take heed; see, I have told you all things beforehand.

24 "But in those days, after that tribulation, the sun will be darkened, and the moon will not give its light;

25 "the stars of heaven will fall, and the powers in heaven will be shaken.

26 "Then they will see the Son of Man coming in the clouds with great power and glory.

27 "And then He will send His angels, and gather together His elect from the four winds, from the farthest part of earth to the farthest part of heaven.

28 "Now learn this parable from the fig tree: When its branch has already become tender, and puts forth leaves, you know that summer is near.

29 "So you also, when you see these things happening, know that it is near, at the very doors.

30 "Assuredly, I say to you, this generation will by no means pass away till all these things take place.

31 "Heaven and earth will pass away, but My words will by no means pass away.

32 "But of that day and hour no one knows, neither the angels in heaven, nor the Son, but only the Father.

33 "Take heed, watch and pray; for you do not know when the time is.

34 "*It is* like a man going to a far country, who left his house and gave authority to his servants, and to each his work, and commanded the doorkeeper to watch.

35 "Watch therefore, for you do not know when the master of the house is coming—in the evening, at midnight, at the crowing of the rooster, or in the morning—

36 "lest, coming suddenly, he find you sleeping.

37 "And what I say to you, I say to all: Watch!"

14 After two days it was the Passover and *the Feast* of Unleavened Bread. And the chief priests and the scribes sought how they might take Him by trickery and put *Him* to death.

2 But they said, "Not during the feast, lest there be an uproar of the people."

3 And being in Bethany at the house of Simon the leper, as He sat at the table, a woman came having an alabaster flask of very costly oil of spikenard. And she broke the flask and poured *it* on His head.

4 But there were some who were indignant among themselves, and said, "Why was this fragrant oil wasted?

5 "For it might have been sold for more than three hundred denarii and given to the poor." And they criticized her sharply.

6 But Jesus said, "Let her alone. Why do you trouble her? She has done a good work for Me.

7 "For you have the poor with you always, and whenever you wish you may do them good; but Me you do not have always.

8 "She has done what she could. She has come beforehand to anoint My body for burial.

9 "Assuredly, I say to you, wherever this gospel is preached throughout the whole world, what this woman did will also be spoken of as a memorial to her."

10 Then Judas Iscariot, one of the twelve, went to the chief priests to betray Him to them.

11 So when they heard *it,* they were glad, and promised to give him money. So he sought how he might conveniently betray Him.

12 Now on the first day of Unleavened Bread, when they killed the Passover *lamb,* His disciples said to Him, "Where do You want us to go and prepare, that You may eat the Passover?"

13 So He sent out two of His disciples and said to them, "Go into the city, and a man will meet you carrying a pitcher of water; follow him.

14 "And wherever he goes in, say to the master of the house, 'The Teacher says, "Where is the guest room in which I may eat the Passover with My disciples?"'

15 "Then he will show you a large upper room, furnished *and* prepared; there make ready for us."

16 And His disciples went out, and came into the city, and found it just as He had said to them; and they prepared the Passover.

17 In the evening He came with the twelve.

18 Now as they sat and ate, Jesus said, "Assuredly, I say to you, one of you who eats with Me will betray Me."

19 And they began to be sorrowful, and to say to Him one by one, "Is it I?" And another *said,* "Is it I?"

20 Then He answered and said to them, "*It is* one of the twelve, who dips with Me in the dish.

21 "The Son of Man indeed goes just as it is written of Him, but woe to that man by whom the Son of Man is betrayed! It would have been good for that man if he had never been born."

22 And as they were eating, Jesus took bread, blessed *it* and broke *it,* and gave *it* to them and said, "Take, eat; this is My body."

23 Then He took the cup, and when He had given thanks He gave *it* to them, and they all drank from it.

24 And He said to them, "This is My blood of the new covenant, which is shed for many.

25 "Assuredly, I say to you, I will no longer drink of the fruit of the vine until that day when I drink it new in the kingdom of God."

26 And when they had sung a hymn, they went out to the Mount of Olives.

27 Then Jesus said to them, "All of you will be made to stumble because of Me this night, for it is written:

'I will strike the Shepherd,
And the sheep will be
*   scattered.'*

28 "But after I have been raised, I will go before you to Galilee."

29 But Peter said to Him, "Even if all are made to stumble, yet I *will* not *be.*"

30 And Jesus said to him, "Assuredly, I say to you that today, *even* this night, before the rooster crows twice, you will deny Me three times."

31 But he spoke more vehemently, "If I have to die with You, I will not deny You!" And they all said likewise.

32 Then they came to a place which was named Gethsemane; and He said to His disciples, "Sit here while I pray."

33 And He took Peter, James, and John with Him, and He began to be troubled and deeply distressed.

34 Then He said to them, "My soul is exceedingly sorrowful, *even* to death. Stay here and watch."

35 He went a little farther, and fell on the ground, and prayed that if it were possible, the hour might pass from Him.

36 And He said, "Abba, Father, all things *are* possible for You. Take this cup away from Me; nevertheless, not what I will, but what You *will*."

37 Then He came and found them sleeping, and said to Peter, "Simon, are you sleeping? Could you not watch one hour?

38 "Watch and pray, lest you enter into temptation. The spirit truly *is* ready, but the flesh *is* weak."

39 Again He went away and prayed, and spoke the same words.

40 And when He returned, He found them asleep again, for their eyes were heavy; and they did not know what to answer Him.

41 Then He came the third time and said to them, "Are you still sleeping and resting? It is enough! The hour has come; behold, the Son of Man is being betrayed into the hands of sinners.

42 "Rise up, let us go. See, My betrayer is at hand."

43 And immediately, while He was still speaking, Judas, one of the twelve, with a great multitude with swords and clubs, came from the chief priests and the scribes and the elders.

44 Now His betrayer had given them a signal, saying, "Whomever I kiss, He is the One; take Him and lead *Him* away safely."

45 And as soon as He had come, immediately he went up to Him and said to Him, "Rabbi, Rabbi!" and kissed Him.

46 Then they laid their hands on Him and took Him.

47 And one of those who stood by drew his sword and struck the servant of the high priest, and cut off his ear.

48 Then Jesus answered and said to them, "Have you come out, as against a robber, with swords and clubs to take Me?

49 "I was daily with you in the temple teaching, and you did not take Me. But the Scriptures must be fulfilled."

50 Then they all forsook Him and fled.

51 Now a certain young man followed Him, having a linen cloth thrown around *his* naked *body*. And the young men laid hold of him,

52 and he left the linen cloth and fled from them naked.

53 And they led Jesus away to the high priest; and with him were assembled all the chief priests, the elders, and the scribes.

54 But Peter followed Him at a distance, right into the courtyard of the high priest. And he sat with the servants and warmed himself at the fire.

55 And the chief priests and all the council sought testimony against Jesus to put Him to death, and found none.

56 For many bore false witness against Him, but their testimonies did not agree.

57 And some rose up and bore false witness against Him, saying,

58 "We heard Him say, 'I will destroy this temple that *is* made with hands, and within three days I will build another made without hands.' "

59 But not even then did their testimony agree.

60 And the high priest stood up in the midst and asked Jesus, saying, "Do You answer nothing? What *is it* these men testify against You?"

61 But He kept silent and answered nothing. Again the high priest asked Him, saying to Him, "Are You the Christ, the Son of the Blessed?"

62 And Jesus said, "I am. And you will see the Son of Man sitting at the right hand of the Power, and coming with the clouds of heaven."

63 Then the high priest tore his

clothes and said, "What further need do we have of witnesses?

64 "You have heard the blasphemy! What do you think?" And they all condemned Him to be worthy of death.

65 Then some began to spit on Him, and to blindfold Him, and to beat Him, and to say to Him, "Prophesy!" And the officers struck Him with the palms of their hands.

66 Now as Peter was below in the courtyard, one of the servant girls of the high priest came.

67 And when she saw Peter warming himself, she looked at him and said, "You also were with Jesus of Nazareth."

68 But he denied it, saying, "I neither know nor understand what you are saying." And he went out on the porch, and a rooster crowed.

69 And the servant girl saw him again, and began to say to those who stood by, "This is one of them."

70 But he denied it again. And a little later those who stood by said to Peter again, "Surely you are *one* of them; for you are a Galilean, and your speech shows *it*."

71 But he began to curse and swear, "I do not know this Man of whom you speak!"

72 And a second time *the* rooster crowed. And Peter called to mind the word that Jesus had said to him, "Before the rooster crows twice, you will deny Me three times." And when he thought about it, he wept.

15 Immediately, in the morning, the chief priests held a consultation with the elders and scribes and the whole council; and they bound Jesus, led *Him* away, and delivered *Him* to Pilate.

2 Then Pilate asked Him, "Are You the King of the Jews?" And He answered and said to him, "*It is as* you say."

3 And the chief priests accused Him of many things, but He answered nothing.

4 Then Pilate asked Him again, saying, "Do You answer nothing? See how many things they testify against You!"

5 But Jesus still answered nothing, so that Pilate marveled.

6 Now at the feast he was accustomed to releasing one prisoner to them, whomever they requested.

7 And there was one named Barabbas, *who was* chained with his fellow insurrectionists; they had committed murder in the insurrection.

8 Then the multitude, crying aloud, began to ask *him to do* just as he had always done for them.

9 But Pilate answered them, saying, "Do you want me to release to you the King of the Jews?"

10 For he knew that the chief priests had handed Him over because of envy.

11 But the chief priests stirred up the crowd, so that he should rather release Barabbas to them.

12 And Pilate answered and said to them again, "What then do you want me to do *with Him* whom you call the King of the Jews?"

13 So they cried out again, "Crucify Him!"

14 Then Pilate said to them, "Why, what evil has He done?" And they cried out more exceedingly, "Crucify Him!"

15 So Pilate, wanting to gratify the crowd, released Barabbas to them; and he delivered Jesus, after he had scourged *Him*, to be crucified.

16 Then the soldiers led Him away into the hall called Praetorium, and they called together the whole garrison.

17 And they clothed Him with purple; and they twisted a crown of thorns, put it on His *head*,

18 and began to salute Him, "Hail, King of the Jews!"

19 Then they struck Him on the head with a reed and spat on Him;

and bowing the knee, they worshiped Him.

20 And when they had mocked Him, they took the purple off Him, put His own clothes on Him, and led Him out to crucify Him.

21 Now they compelled a certain man, Simon a Cyrenian, the father of Alexander and Rufus, as he was coming out of the country and passing by, to bear His cross.

22 And they brought Him to the place Golgotha, which is translated, Place of a Skull.

23 Then they gave Him wine mingled with myrrh to drink, but He did not take *it.*

24 And when they crucified Him, they divided His garments, casting lots for them to determine what every man should take.

25 Now it was the third hour, and they crucified Him.

26 And the inscription of His accusation was written above:

THE KING OF THE JEWS.

27 With Him they also crucified two robbers, one on His right and the other on His left.

28 So the Scripture was fulfilled which says, *"And He was numbered with the transgressors."*

29 And those who passed by blasphemed Him, wagging their heads and saying, "Aha! *You* who destroy the temple and build *it* in three days,

30 "save Yourself, and come down from the cross!"

31 Likewise the chief priests also, together with the scribes, mocked and said among themselves, "He saved others; Himself He cannot save.

32 "Let the Christ, the King of Israel, descend now from the cross, that we may see and believe." And those who were crucified with Him reviled Him.

33 Now when the sixth hour had come, there was darkness over the whole land until the ninth hour.

34 And at the ninth hour Jesus cried out with a loud voice, saying, "Eloi, Eloi, lama sabachthani?" which is translated, *"My God, My God, why have You forsaken Me?"*

35 Some of those who stood by, when they heard *it,* said, "Look, He is calling for Elijah!"

36 Then someone ran and filled a sponge full of sour wine, put *it* on a reed, and offered *it* to Him to drink, saying, "Let Him alone; let us see if Elijah will come to take Him down."

37 And Jesus cried out with a loud voice, and breathed His last.

38 Then the veil of the temple was torn in two from top to bottom.

39 Now when the centurion, who stood opposite Him, saw that He cried out like this and breathed His last, he said, "Truly this Man was the Son of God!"

40 There were also women looking on from afar, among whom were Mary Magdalene, Mary the mother of James the Less and of Joses, and Salome,

41 who also followed Him and ministered to Him when He was in Galilee; and many other women who came up with Him to Jerusalem.

42 Now when evening had come, because it was the Preparation Day, that is, the day before the Sabbath,

43 Joseph of Arimathea, a prominent council member, who was himself waiting for the kingdom of God, coming and taking courage, went in to Pilate and asked for the body of Jesus.

44 Pilate marveled that He was already dead; and summoning the centurion, he asked him if He had been dead for some time.

45 And when he found out from the centurion, he granted the body to Joseph.

46 Then he bought fine linen, took Him down, and wrapped Him in the linen. And he laid Him in a

tomb which had been hewn out of the rock, and rolled a stone against the door of the tomb.

47 And Mary Magdalene and Mary *the mother* of Joses observed where He was laid.

16 Now when the Sabbath was past, Mary Magdalene, Mary *the mother* of James, and Salome bought spices, that they might come and anoint Him.

2 Very early in the morning, on the first *day* of the week, they came to the tomb when the sun had risen.

3 And they said among themselves, "Who will roll away the stone from the door of the tomb for us?"

4 But when they looked up, they saw that the stone had been rolled away—for it was very large.

5 And entering the tomb, they saw a young man clothed in a long white robe sitting on the right side; and they were alarmed.

6 But he said to them, "Do not be alarmed. You seek Jesus of Nazareth, who was crucified. He is risen! He is not here. See the place where they laid Him.

7 "But go *and* tell His disciples—and Peter—that He is going before you into Galilee; there you will see Him, as He said to you."

8 And they went out quickly and fled from the tomb, for they trembled and were amazed. And they said nothing to anyone, for they were afraid.

9 Now when *He* rose early on the first *day* of the week, He appeared first to Mary Magdalene, out of whom He had cast seven demons.

10 She went and told those who had been with Him, as they mourned and wept.

11 And when they heard that He was alive and had been seen by her, they did not believe.

12 After that, He appeared in another form to two of them as they walked and went into the country.

13 And they went and told *it* to the rest, *but* they did not believe them either.

14 Afterward He appeared to the eleven as they sat at the table; and He rebuked their unbelief and hardness of heart, because they did not believe those who had seen Him after He had risen.

15 And He said to them, "Go into all the world and preach the gospel to every creature.

16 "He who believes and is baptized will be saved; but he who does not believe will be condemned.

17 "And these signs will follow those who believe: In My name they will cast out demons; they will speak with new tongues;

18 "they will take up serpents; and if they drink anything deadly, it will by no means hurt them; they will lay hands on the sick, and they will recover."

19 So then, after the Lord had spoken to them, He was received up into heaven, and sat down at the right hand of God.

20 And they went out and preached everywhere, the Lord working with *them* and confirming the word through the accompanying signs. Amen.

THE GOSPEL ACCORDING TO
LUKE

INASMUCH as many have taken in hand to set in order a narrative of those things which are most surely believed among us,

2 just as those who from the beginning were eyewitnesses and ministers of the word delivered them to us,

3 it seemed good to me also, having had perfect understanding of all things from the very first, to write to you an orderly account, most excellent Theophilus,

4 that you may know the certainty of those things in which you were instructed.

5 There was in the days of Herod, the king of Judea, a certain priest named Zacharias, of the division of Abijah. His wife *was* of the daughters of Aaron, and her name *was* Elizabeth.

6 And they were both righteous before God, walking in all the commandments and ordinances of the Lord blameless.

7 But they had no child, because Elizabeth was barren, and they were both well advanced in years.

8 So it was, that while he was serving as priest before God in the order of his division,

9 according to the custom of the priesthood, his lot fell to burn incense when he went into the temple of the Lord.

10 And the whole multitude of the people was praying outside at the hour of incense.

11 Then an angel of the Lord appeared to him, standing on the right side of the altar of incense.

12 And when Zacharias saw *him*, he was troubled, and fear fell upon him.

13 But the angel said to him, "Do not be afraid, Zacharias, for your prayer is heard; and your wife Elizabeth will bear you a son, and you shall call his name John.

14 "And you will have joy and gladness, and many will rejoice at his birth.

15 "For he will be great in the sight of the Lord, and shall drink neither wine nor strong drink. He will also be filled with the Holy Spirit, even from his mother's womb.

16 "And he will turn many of the children of Israel to the Lord their God.

17 "He will also go before Him in the spirit and power of Elijah, *'to turn the hearts of the fathers to the children,'* and the disobedient to the wisdom of the just, to make ready a people prepared for the Lord."

18 And Zacharias said to the angel, "How shall I know this? For I am an old man, and my wife is well advanced in years."

19 And the angel answered and said to him, "I am Gabriel, who stands in the presence of God, and was sent to speak to you and bring you these glad tidings.

20 "But behold, you will be mute and not able to speak until the day these things take place, because you did not believe my words which will be fulfilled in their own time."

21 And the people waited for Zacharias, and marveled that he lingered so long in the temple.

22 But when he came out, he could not speak to them; and they perceived that he had seen a vision in the temple, for he beckoned to them and remained speechless.

23 And so it was, as soon as the days of his service were completed, that he departed to his own house.

24 Now after those days his wife Elizabeth conceived; and she hid herself five months, saying,

25 "Thus the Lord has dealt with me, in the days when He looked on

me, to take away my reproach among men."

26 Now in the sixth month the angel Gabriel was sent by God to a city of Galilee named Nazareth,

27 to a virgin betrothed to a man whose name was Joseph, of the house of David. The virgin's name *was* Mary.

28 And having come in, the angel said to her, "Rejoice, highly favored *one*, the Lord *is* with you; blessed *are* you among women!"

29 But when she saw *him*, she was troubled at his saying, and considered what manner of greeting this was.

30 Then the angel said to her, "Do not be afraid, Mary, for you have found favor with God.

31 "And behold, you will conceive in your womb and bring forth a Son, and shall call His name Jesus.

32 "He will be great, and will be called the Son of the Highest; and the Lord God will give Him the throne of His father David.

33 "And He will reign over the house of Jacob forever, and of His kingdom there will be no end."

34 Then Mary said to the angel, "How can this be, since I do not know a man?"

35 And the angel answered and said to her, "*The* Holy Spirit will come upon you, and the power of the Highest will overshadow you; therefore, also, that Holy One who is to be born will be called the Son of God.

36 "Now indeed, Elizabeth your relative has also conceived a son in her old age; and this is now the sixth month for her who was called barren.

37 "For with God nothing will be impossible."

38 Then Mary said, "Behold the maidservant of the Lord! Let it be to me according to your word." And the angel departed from her.

39 Now Mary arose in those days and went into the hill country with haste, to a city of Judah,

40 and entered the house of Zacharias and greeted Elizabeth.

41 And it happened, when Elizabeth heard the greeting of Mary, that the babe leaped in her womb; and Elizabeth was filled with the Holy Spirit.

42 Then she spoke out with a loud voice and said, "Blessed *are* you among women, and blessed *is* the fruit of your womb!

43 "But why *is* this *granted* to me, that the mother of my Lord should come to me?

44 "For indeed, as soon as the voice of your greeting sounded in my ears, the babe leaped in my womb for joy.

45 "Blessed *is* she who believed, for there will be a fulfillment of those things which were told her from the Lord."

46 And Mary said:

"My soul magnifies the Lord,
47 And my spirit has rejoiced
   in God my Savior.
48 For He has regarded the lowly
   state of His maidservant;
For behold, henceforth all
   generations will call me
   blessed.
49 For He who is mighty has done
   great things for me,
And holy *is* His name.
50 And His mercy *is* on those
   who fear Him
From generation to generation.
51 He has shown strength with
   His arm;
He has scattered *the* proud in
   the imagination of their
   hearts.
52 He has put down the mighty
   from *their* thrones,
And exalted the lowly.
53 He has filled *the* hungry
   with good things,
And *the* rich He has sent away
   empty.

54 He has helped His servant
Israel,
In remembrance of *His* mercy,
55 As He spoke to our fathers,
To Abraham and to his seed
forever."

56 And Mary remained with her about three months, and returned to her house.

57 Now Elizabeth's full time came for her to be delivered, and she brought forth a son.

58 When her neighbors and relatives heard how the Lord had shown great mercy to her, they rejoiced with her.

59 Now so it was, on the eighth day, that they came to circumcise the child; and they would have called him by the name of his father, Zacharias.

60 And his mother answered and said, "No; he shall be called John."

61 But they said to her, "There is no one among your relatives who is called by this name."

62 So they made signs to his father—what he would have him called.

63 And he asked for a writing tablet, and wrote, saying, "His name is John." And they all marveled.

64 Immediately his mouth was opened and his tongue *loosed*, and he spoke, praising God.

65 Then fear came on all who dwelt around them; and all these sayings were discussed throughout all the hill country of Judea.

66 And all those who heard *them* kept *them* in their hearts, saying, "What kind of child will this be?" And the hand of the Lord was with him.

67 Now his father Zacharias was filled with the Holy Spirit, and prophesied, saying:

68 "Blessed *is* the Lord God of Israel,
For He has visited and redeemed His people,

69 And has raised up a horn of salvation for us
In the house of His servant David,

70 As He spoke by the mouth of His holy prophets,
Who *have been* since the world began,

71 That we should be saved from our enemies
And from the hand of all who hate us,

72 To perform the mercy *promised* to our fathers
And to remember His holy covenant,

73 The oath which He swore to our father Abraham:

74 To grant us that we,
Being delivered from the hand of our enemies,
Might serve Him without fear,

75 In holiness and righteousness before Him all the days of our life.

76 And you, child, will be called the prophet of the Highest;
For you will go before the face of the Lord to prepare His ways,

77 To give knowledge of salvation to His people
By the remission of their sins,

78 Through the tender mercy of our God,
With which the Dayspring from on high has visited us;

79 To give light to those who sit in darkness and the shadow of death,
To guide our feet into the way of peace."

80 So the child grew and became strong in spirit, and was in the deserts till the day of his manifestation to Israel.

2 And it came to pass in those days *that* a decree went out from Caesar Augustus that all the world should be registered.

2 This census first took place while Quirinius was governing Syria.

3 So all went to be registered, everyone to his own city.

4 And Joseph also went up from Galilee, out of the city of Nazareth, into Judea, to the city of David, which is called Bethlehem, because he was of the house and lineage of David,

5 to be registered with Mary, his betrothed wife, who was with child.

6 So it was, that while they were there, the days were completed for her to be delivered.

7 And she brought forth her first-born Son, and wrapped Him in swaddling cloths, and laid Him in a manger, because there was no room for them in the inn.

8 Now there were in the same country shepherds living out in the fields, keeping watch over their flock by night.

9 And behold, an angel of the Lord stood before them, and the glory of the Lord shone around them, and they were greatly afraid.

10 Then the angel said to them, "Do not be afraid, for behold, I bring you good tidings of great joy which will be to all people.

11 "For there is born to you this day in the city of David a Savior, who is Christ the Lord.

12 "And this *will be* the sign to you: You will find a Babe wrapped in swaddling cloths, lying in a manger."

13 And suddenly there was with the angel a multitude of the heavenly host praising God and saying:

14"Glory to God in the highest,
 And on earth peace,
  good will toward men!"

15 So it was, when the angels had gone away from them into heaven, that the shepherds said to one another, "Let us now go to Bethlehem and see this thing that has come to pass, which the Lord has made known to us."

16 And they came with haste and found Mary and Joseph, and the Babe lying in a manger.

17 Now when they had seen *Him*, they made widely known the saying which was told them concerning this Child.

18 And all those who heard *it* marveled at those things which were told them by the shepherds.

19 But Mary kept all these things and pondered *them* in her heart.

20 Then the shepherds returned, glorifying and praising God for all the things that they had heard and seen, as it was told them.

21 And when eight days were completed for the circumcision of the Child, His name was called JESUS, the name given by the angel before He was conceived in the womb.

22 Now when the days of her purification according to the law of Moses were completed, they brought Him to Jerusalem to present *Him* to the Lord

23 (as it is written in the law of the Lord, *"Every male who opens the womb shall be called holy to the LORD"*),

24 and to offer a sacrifice according to what is said in the law of the Lord, *"A pair of turtledoves or two young pigeons."*

25 And behold, there was a man in Jerusalem whose name was Simeon, and this man was just and devout, waiting for the Consolation of Israel, and the Holy Spirit was upon him.

26 And it had been revealed to him by the Holy Spirit that he would not see death before he had seen the Lord's Christ.

27 So he came by the Spirit into the temple. And when the parents brought in the Child Jesus, to do for Him according to the custom of the law,

28 he took Him up in his arms and blessed God and said:

29"Lord, now You are letting Your
  servant depart in peace,
  According to Your word;

30 For my eyes have seen Your salvation

31 Which You have prepared before the face of all peoples,

32 A light to *bring* revelation to the Gentiles,
And the glory of Your people Israel."

33 And Joseph and His mother marveled at those things which were spoken of Him.

34 Then Simeon blessed them, and said to Mary His mother, "Behold, this *Child* is destined for the fall and rising of many in Israel, and for a sign which will be spoken against

35 (yes, a sword will pierce through your own soul also), that the thoughts of many hearts may be revealed."

36 Now there was one, Anna, a prophetess, the daughter of Phanuel, of the tribe of Asher. She was of a great age, and had lived with a husband seven years from her virginity;

37 and this woman *was* a widow of about eighty-four years, who did not depart from the temple, but served God with fastings and prayers night and day.

38 And coming in that instant she gave thanks to the Lord, and spoke of Him to all those who looked for redemption in Jerusalem.

39 So when they had performed all things according to the law of the Lord, they returned to Galilee, to their *own* city, Nazareth.

40 And the Child grew and became strong in spirit, filled with wisdom; and the grace of God was upon Him.

41 His parents went to Jerusalem every year at the Feast of the Passover.

42 And when He was twelve years old, they went up to Jerusalem according to the custom of the feast.

43 When they had finished the days, as they returned, the Boy Jesus lingered behind in Jerusalem. And Joseph and His mother did not know *it;*

44 but supposing Him to have been in the company, they went a day's journey, and sought Him among *their* relatives and acquaintances.

45 So when they did not find Him, they returned to Jerusalem, seeking Him.

46 Now so it was that after three days they found Him in the temple, sitting in the midst of the teachers, both listening to them and asking them questions.

47 And all who heard Him were astonished at His understanding and answers.

48 So when they saw Him, they were amazed; and His mother said to Him, "Son, why have You done this to us? Look, Your father and I have sought You anxiously."

49 And He said to them, "Why *is it* that you sought Me? Did you not know that I must be about My Father's business?"

50 But they did not understand the statement which He spoke to them.

51 Then He went down with them and came to Nazareth, and was subject to them, but His mother kept all these things in her heart.

52 And Jesus increased in wisdom and stature, and in favor with God and men.

3 Now in the fifteenth year of the reign of Tiberius Caesar, Pontius Pilate being governor of Judea, Herod being tetrarch of Galilee, his brother Philip tetrarch of Iturea and the region of Trachonitis, and Lysanias tetrarch of Abilene,

2 Annas and Caiaphas being high priests, the word of God came to John the son of Zacharias in the wilderness.

3 And he went into all the region around the Jordan, preaching a baptism of repentance for the remission of sins,

4 as it is written in the book of the words of Isaiah the prophet, saying:

> "The voice of one crying in the wilderness:
> 'Prepare the way of the LORD,
> Make His paths straight.
5 Every valley shall be filled
> And every mountain and hill brought low;
> And the crooked places shall be made straight
> And the rough ways made smooth;
6 And all flesh shall see the salvation of God.'"

7 Then he said to the multitudes that came out to be baptized by him, "Brood of vipers! Who warned you to flee from the wrath to come?
8 "Therefore bear fruits worthy of repentance, and do not begin to say to yourselves, 'We have Abraham as our father.' For I say to you that God is able to raise up children to Abraham from these stones.
9 "And even now the ax is laid to the root of the trees. Therefore every tree which does not bear good fruit is cut down and thrown into the fire."

10 So the people asked him, saying, "What shall we do then?"
11 He answered and said to them, "He who has two tunics, let him give to him who has none; and he who has food, let him do likewise."
12 Then tax collectors also came to be baptized, and said to him, "Teacher, what shall we do?"
13 And he said to them, "Collect no more than what is appointed for you."
14 Likewise the soldiers asked him, saying, "And what shall we do?" So he said to them, "Do not intimidate anyone or accuse falsely, and be content with your wages."
15 Now as the people were in ex-

pectation, and all reasoned in their hearts about John, whether he was the Christ or not,
16 John answered, saying to them all, "I indeed baptize you with water; but One mightier than I is coming, whose sandal strap I am not worthy to loose. He will baptize you with the Holy Spirit and with fire.
17 "His winnowing fan is in His hand, and He will thoroughly purge His threshing floor, and gather the wheat into His barn; but the chaff He will burn with unquenchable fire."
18 And with many other exhortations he preached to the people.
19 But Herod the tetrarch, being rebuked by him concerning Herodias, his brother Philip's wife, and for all the evils which Herod had done,
20 also added this, above all, that he shut John up in prison.
21 Now when all the people were baptized, it came to pass that Jesus also was baptized; and while He prayed, the heaven was opened.
22 And the Holy Spirit descended in bodily form like a dove upon Him, and a voice came from heaven which said, "You are My beloved Son; in You I am well pleased."
23 Now Jesus Himself began His ministry at about thirty years of age, being (as was supposed) the son of Joseph, the son of Heli,
24 the son of Matthat, the son of Levi, the son of Melchi, the son of Janna, the son of Joseph,
25 the son of Mattathiah, the son of Amos, the son of Nahum, the son of Esli, the son of Naggai,
26 the son of Maath, the son of Mattathiah, the son of Semei, the son of Joseph, the son of Judah,
27 the son of Joannas, the son of Rhesa, the son of Zerubbabel, the son of Shealtiel, the son of Neri,
28 the son of Melchi, the son of Addi, the son of Cosam, the son of Elmodam, the son of Er,

29 *the son* of Jose, *the son* of Eliezer, *the son* of Jorim, *the son* of Matthat, *the son of* Levi,
30 *the son* of Simeon, *the son* of Judah, *the son* of Joseph, *the son* of Jonan, *the son* of Eliakim,
31 *the son* of Melea, *the son* of Menan, *the son* of Mattathah, *the son* of Nathan, *the son* of David,
32 *the son* of Jesse, *the son* of Obed, *the son* of Boaz, *the son* of Salmon, *the son* of Nahshon,
33 *the son* of Amminadab, *the son* of Ram, *the son* of Hezron, *the son* of Perez, *the son* of Judah,
34 *the son* of Jacob, *the son* of Isaac, *the son* of Abraham, *the son* of Terah, *the son* of Nahor,
35 *the son* of Serug, *the son of* Reu, *the son* of Peleg, *the son* of Eber, *the son* of Shelah,
36 *the son* of Cainan, *the son* of Arphaxad, *the son* of Shem, *the son* of Noah, *the son* of Lamech,
37 *the son* of Methuselah, *the son* of Enoch, *the son* of Jared, *the son* of Mahalalel, *the son* of Cainan,
38 *the son* of Enos, *the son* of Seth, *the son* of Adam, *the son* of God.

4 Then Jesus, being filled with the Holy Spirit, returned from the Jordan and was led by the Spirit into the wilderness,
2 being tempted for forty days by the devil. And in those days He ate nothing, and afterward, when they had ended, He was hungry.
3 And the devil said to Him, "If You are the Son of God, command this stone to become bread."
4 But Jesus answered him, saying, "It is written, *'Man shall not live by bread alone, but by every word of God.'"*
5 Then the devil, taking Him up on a high mountain, showed Him all the kingdoms of the world in a moment of time.
6 And the devil said to Him, "All this authority I will give You, and their glory; for *this* has been delivered to me, and I give it to whomever I wish.
7 "Therefore, if You will worship before me, all will be Yours."
8 And Jesus answered and said to him, "Get behind Me, Satan! For it is written, *'You shall worship the* LORD *your God, and Him only you shall serve.'"*
9 Then he brought Him to Jerusalem, set Him on the pinnacle of the temple, and said to Him, "If You are the Son of God, throw Yourself down from here.
10 "For it is written:

'He shall give His angels charge
  over you,
To keep you,'

11 "and,

'In their hands they shall bear
  you up,
Lest you dash your foot
  against a stone.'"

12 And Jesus answered and said to him, "It has been said, *'You shall not tempt the* LORD *your God.'"*
13 Now when the devil had ended every temptation, he departed from Him until an opportune time.
14 Then Jesus returned in the power of the Spirit to Galilee, and news of Him went out through all the surrounding region.
15 And He taught in their synagogues, being glorified by all.
16 So He came to Nazareth, where He had been brought up. And as His custom was, He went into the synagogue on the Sabbath day, and stood up to read.
17 And He was handed the book of the prophet Isaiah. And when He had opened the book, He found the place where it was written:

18 "The Spirit of the LORD is upon
  Me,
Because He has anointed Me to
  preach the gospel to the poor.
He has sent Me to heal the
  brokenhearted,

　　*To preach deliverance to the
　　　captives
　　And recovery of sight to the
　　　blind,
　　To set at liberty those who are
　　　oppressed,*
19 *To preach the acceptable year
　　of the LORD."*

20 Then He closed the book, and gave *it* back to the attendant and sat down. And the eyes of all who were in the synagogue were fixed on Him.

21 And He began to say to them, "Today this Scripture is fulfilled in your hearing."

22 So all bore witness to Him, and marveled at the gracious words which proceeded out of His mouth. And they said, "Is this not Joseph's son?"

23 And He said to them, "You will surely say this proverb to Me, 'Physician, heal yourself! Whatever we have heard done in Capernaum, do also here in Your country.'"

24 Then He said, "Assuredly, I say to you, no prophet is accepted in his own country.

25 "But I tell you truly, many widows were in Israel in the days of Elijah, when the heaven was shut up three years and six months, and there was a great famine throughout all the land;

26 "but to none of them was Elijah sent except to Zarephath, *in the region* of Sidon, to a woman *who was* a widow.

27 "And many lepers were in Israel in the time of Elisha the prophet, and none of them was cleansed except Naaman the Syrian."

28 Then all those in the synagogue, when they heard these things, were filled with wrath,

29 and rose up and thrust Him out of the city; and they led Him to the brow of the hill on which their city was built, that they might throw Him down over the cliff.

30 Then passing through the midst of them, He went His way.

31 Then He went down to Capernaum, a city of Galilee, and was teaching them on the Sabbaths.

32 And they were astonished at His teaching, for His word was with authority.

33 Now in the synagogue there was a man who had a spirit of an unclean demon. And he cried out with a loud voice,

34 saying, "Let *us* alone! What have we to do with You, Jesus of Nazareth? Did You come to destroy us? I know You, who You are—the Holy One of God!"

35 But Jesus rebuked him, saying, "Be quiet, and come out of him!" And when the demon had thrown him in *their* midst, it came out of him and did not hurt him.

36 So they were all amazed and spoke among themselves, saying, "What a word this *is!* For with authority and power He commands the unclean spirits, and they come out."

37 And the report about Him went out into every place in the surrounding region.

38 Now He arose from the synagogue and entered Simon's house. But Simon's wife's mother was sick with a high fever, and they made request of Him concerning her.

39 So He stood over her and rebuked the fever, and it left her. And immediately she arose and served them.

40 Now when the sun was setting, all those who had anyone sick with various diseases brought them to Him; and He laid His hands on every one of them and healed them.

41 And demons also came out of many, crying out and saying, "You are the Christ, the Son of God!" And He, rebuking *them,* did not allow them to speak, for they knew that He was the Christ.

42 Now when it was day, He departed and went into a deserted place. And the crowd sought Him and came to Him, and tried to keep Him from leaving them;

43 but He said to them, "I must preach the kingdom of God to the other cities also, because for this purpose I have been sent."

44 And He was preaching in the synagogues of Galilee.

5 Now so it was, as the multitude pressed about Him to hear the word of God, that He stood by the Lake of Gennesaret,

2 and saw two boats standing by the lake; but the fishermen had gone from them and were washing *their* nets.

3 Then He got into one of the boats, which was Simon's, and asked him to put out a little from the land. And He sat down and taught the multitudes from the boat.

4 Now when He had stopped speaking, He said to Simon, "Launch out into the deep and let down your nets for a catch."

5 But Simon answered and said to Him, "Master, we have toiled all night and caught nothing; nevertheless at Your word I will let down the net."

6 And when they had done this, they caught a great number of fish, and their net was breaking.

7 So they signaled to *their* partners in the other boat to come and help them. And they came and filled both the boats, so that they began to sink.

8 When Simon Peter saw *it,* he fell down at Jesus' knees, saying, "Depart from me, for I am a sinful man, O Lord!"

9 For he and all who were with him were astonished at the catch of fish which they had taken;

10 and so also *were* James and John, the sons of Zebedee, who were partners with Simon. And Jesus said to Simon, "Do not be afraid. From now on you will catch men."

11 So when they had brought their boats to land, they forsook all and followed Him.

12 And it happened when He was in a certain city, that behold, a man who was full of leprosy saw Jesus; and he fell on *his* face and implored Him, saying, "Lord, if You are willing, You can make me clean."

13 Then He put out *His* hand and touched him, saying, "I am willing; be cleansed." And immediately the leprosy left him.

14 And He charged him to tell no one, "But go and show yourself to the priest, and make an offering for your cleansing, as a testimony to them, just as Moses commanded."

15 Then the report went around concerning Him all the more; and great multitudes came together to hear, and to be healed by Him of their infirmities.

16 So He Himself *often* withdrew into the wilderness and prayed.

17 Now it happened on a certain day, as He was teaching, that there were Pharisees and teachers of the law sitting by, who had come out of every town of Galilee, Judea, and Jerusalem. And the power of the Lord was *present* to heal them.

18 Then behold, men brought on a bed a man who was paralyzed. And they sought to bring him in and lay *him* before Him.

19 And when they could not find how they might bring him in, because of the crowd, they went up on the housetop and let him down with *his* bed through the tiling into the midst before Jesus.

20 So when He saw their faith, He said to him, "Man, your sins are forgiven you."

21 And the scribes and the Pharisees began to reason, saying, "Who is this who speaks blasphemies? Who can forgive sins but God alone?"

22 But when Jesus perceived their thoughts, He answered and said to them, "Why are you reasoning in your hearts?

23 "Which is easier, to say, 'Your sins are forgiven you,' or to say, 'Rise up and walk'?

24 "But that you may know that the Son of Man has power on earth to forgive sins"—He said to the man who was paralyzed, "I say to you, arise, take up your bed, and go to your house."

25 Immediately he rose up before them, took up what he had been lying on, and departed to his own house, glorifying God.

26 And they were all amazed, and they glorified God and were filled with fear, saying, "We have seen strange things today!"

27 After these things He went out and saw a tax collector named Levi, sitting at the tax office. And He said to him, "Follow Me."

28 And he left all, rose up, and followed Him.

29 Then Levi gave Him a great feast in his own house. And there were a great number of tax collectors and others who sat down with them.

30 But their scribes and the Pharisees murmured against His disciples, saying, "Why do You eat and drink with tax collectors and sinners?"

31 And Jesus answered and said to them, "Those who are well do not need a physician, but those who are sick.

32 "I have not come to call *the* righteous, but sinners, to repentance."

33 Then they said to Him, "Why do the disciples of John fast often and make prayers, and likewise those of the Pharisees, but Yours eat and drink?"

34 And He said to them, "Can you make the friends of the bride-groom fast while the bridegroom is with them?

35 "But the days will come when the bridegroom will be taken away from them; then they will fast in those days."

36 Then He spoke a parable to them: "No one puts a piece from a new garment on an old one; otherwise the new makes a tear, and also the piece that was *taken* out of the new does not match the old.

37 "And no one puts new wine into old wineskins; or else the new wine will burst the wineskins and be spilled, and the wineskins will be ruined.

38 "But new wine must be put into new wineskins, and both are preserved.

39 "And no one, having drunk old *wine*, immediately desires new; for he says, 'The old is better.' "

6 Now it happened on the second Sabbath after the first that He went through the grainfields. And His disciples plucked the heads of grain and ate *them*, rubbing *them* in *their* hands.

2 And some of the Pharisees said to them, "Why are you doing what is not lawful to do on the Sabbath?"

3 But Jesus answering them said, "Have you not even read this, what David did when he was hungry, he and those who were with him:

4 "how he went into the house of God, took and ate the showbread, and also gave some to those *who were* with him, which is not lawful for any but the priests to eat?"

5 And He said to them, "The Son of Man is also Lord of the Sabbath."

6 Now it happened on another Sabbath, also, that He entered the synagogue and taught. And a man was there whose right hand was withered.

7 And the scribes and Pharisees watched Him closely, whether He

would heal on the Sabbath, that they might find an accusation against Him.

8 But He knew their thoughts, and said to the man who had the withered hand, "Arise and stand here." And he arose and stood.

9 Then Jesus said to them, "I will ask you one thing: Is it lawful on the Sabbath to do good or to do evil, to save life or to destroy *it?*"

10 And looking around at them all, He said to the man, "Stretch out your hand." And he did so, and his hand was restored as whole as the other.

11 But they were filled with rage, and discussed with one another what they might do to Jesus.

12 Now it came to pass in those days that He went out to the mountain to pray, and continued all night in prayer to God.

13 And when it was day, He called His disciples *to Him;* and from them He chose twelve whom He also named apostles:

14 Simon, whom He also named Peter, and Andrew his brother; James and John; Philip and Bartholomew;

15 Matthew and Thomas; James the *son* of Alphaeus, and Simon called the Zealot;

16 Judas *the son* of James, and Judas Iscariot who also became a traitor.

17 And He came down with them and stood on a level place with a crowd of His disciples and a great multitude of people from all Judea and Jerusalem, and from the seacoast of Tyre and Sidon, who came to hear Him and be healed of their diseases,

18 as well as those who were tormented with unclean spirits. And they were healed.

19 And the whole multitude sought to touch Him, for power went out from Him and healed *them* all.

20 Then He lifted up His eyes toward His disciples, and said:

"Blessed *are you* poor,
　For yours is the kingdom of God.
21 Blessed *are you* who hunger now,
　For you shall be filled.
Blessed *are you* who weep now,
　For you shall laugh.
22 Blessed are you when men hate you,
　And when they exclude you,
　And revile *you,* and cast out your name as evil,
　For the Son of Man's sake.
23 Rejoice in that day and leap for joy!
　For indeed your reward *is* great in heaven,
　For in like manner their fathers did to the prophets.
24 "But woe to you who are rich,
　For you have received your consolation.
25 Woe to you who are full,
　For you shall hunger.
Woe to you who laugh now,
　For you shall mourn and weep.
26 Woe to you when all men speak well of you,
　For so did their fathers to the false prophets.

27 "But I say to you who hear: Love your enemies, do good to those who hate you,

28 "bless those who curse you, and pray for those who spitefully use you.

29 "To him who strikes you on the *one* cheek, offer the other also. And from him who takes away your cloak, do not withhold *your* tunic either.

30 "Give to everyone who asks of you. And from him who takes away your goods do not ask *them* back.

31 "And just as you want men to

do to you, you also do to them likewise.

32 "But if you love those who love you, what credit is that to you? For even sinners love those who love them.

33 "And if you do good to those who do good to you, what credit is that to you? For even sinners do the same.

34 "And if you lend *to those* from whom you hope to receive back, what credit is that to you? For even sinners lend to sinners to receive as much back.

35 "But love your enemies, do good, and lend, hoping for nothing in return; and your reward will be great, and you will be sons of the Highest. For He is kind to the unthankful and evil.

36 "Therefore be merciful, just as your Father also is merciful.

37 "Judge not, and you shall not be judged. Condemn not, and you shall not be condemned. Forgive, and you will be forgiven.

38 "Give, and it will be given to you: good measure, pressed down, shaken together, and running over will be put into your bosom. For with the same measure that you use, it will be measured back to you."

39 And He spoke a parable to them: "Can the blind lead the blind? Will they not both fall into the ditch?

40 "A disciple is not above his teacher, but everyone who is perfectly trained will be like his teacher.

41 "And why do you look at the speck in your brother's eye, but do not perceive the plank in your own eye?

42 "Or how can you say to your brother, 'Brother, let me remove the speck that *is* in your eye,' when you yourself do not see the plank that *is* in your own eye? Hypocrite! First remove the plank from your own eye, and then you will see clearly to remove the speck that is in your brother's eye.

43 "For a good tree does not bear bad fruit, nor does a bad tree bear good fruit.

44 "For every tree is known by its own fruit. For *men* do not gather figs from thorns, nor do they gather grapes from a bramble bush.

45 "A good man out of the good treasure of his heart brings forth good; and an evil man out of the evil treasure of his heart brings forth evil. For out of the abundance of the heart his mouth speaks.

46 "But why do you call Me 'Lord, Lord,' and do not do the things which I say?

47 "Whoever comes to Me, and hears My sayings and does them, I will show you whom he is like:

48 "He is like a man building a house, who dug deep and laid the foundation on the rock. And when the flood arose, the stream beat vehemently against that house, and could not shake it, for it was founded on the rock.

49 "But he who heard and did nothing is like a man who built a house on the earth without a foundation, against which the stream beat vehemently; and immediately it fell. And the ruin of that house was great."

7 Now when He concluded all His sayings in the hearing of the people, He entered Capernaum.

2 And a certain centurion's servant, who was dear to him, was sick and ready to die.

3 So when he heard about Jesus, he sent elders of the Jews to Him, pleading with Him to come and heal his servant.

4 And when they came to Jesus, they begged Him earnestly, saying that the one for whom He should do this was worthy,

5 "for he loves our nation, and has built us a synagogue."

79

Jesus and John the Baptist

6 Then Jesus went with them. And when He was already not far from the house, the centurion sent friends to Him, saying to Him, "Lord, do not trouble Yourself, for I am not worthy that You should enter under my roof.

7 "Therefore I did not even think myself worthy to come to You. But say the word, and my servant will be healed.

8 "For I also am a man placed under authority, having soldiers under me. And I say to one, 'Go,' and he goes; and to another, 'Come,' and he comes; and to my servant, 'Do this,' and he does *it*."

9 When Jesus heard these things, He marveled at him, and turned around and said to the crowd that followed Him, "I say to you, I have not found such great faith, not even in Israel!"

10 And those who were sent, returning to the house, found the servant well who had been sick.

11 Now it happened, the day after, *that* He went into a city called Nain; and many of His disciples went with Him, and a large crowd.

12 And when He came near the gate of the city, behold, a dead man was being carried out, the only son of his mother; and she was a widow. And a large crowd from the city was with her.

13 When the Lord saw her, He had compassion on her and said to her, "Do not weep."

14 Then He came and touched the open coffin, and those who carried *him* stood still. And He said, "Young man, I say to you, arise."

15 And he who was dead sat up and began to speak. And He presented him to his mother.

16 Then fear came upon all, and they glorified God, saying, "A great prophet has risen up among us"; and, "God has visited His people."

17 And this report about Him went throughout all Judea and all the surrounding region.

18 Then the disciples of John reported to him concerning all these things.

19 And John, calling two of his disciples to *him*, sent *them* to Jesus, saying, "Are You the Coming One, or do we look for another?"

20 When the men had come to Him, they said, "John the Baptist has sent us to You, saying, 'Are You the Coming One, or do we look for another?'"

21 And that very hour He cured many *people* of *their* infirmities, afflictions, and evil spirits; and to many *who were* blind He gave sight.

22 Then Jesus answered and said to them, "Go and tell John the things you have seen and heard: that *the* blind see, *the* lame walk, *the* lepers are cleansed, *the* deaf hear, *the* dead are raised, *the* poor have the gospel preached to them.

23 "And blessed is *he* who is not offended because of Me."

24 When the messengers of John had departed, He began to speak to the multitudes concerning John: "What did you go out into the wilderness to see? A reed shaken by the wind?

25 "But what did you go out to see? A man clothed in soft garments? Indeed those who are gorgeously appareled and live in luxury are in kings' courts.

26 "But what did you go out to see? A prophet? Yes, I say to you, and more than a prophet.

27 "This is *he* of whom it is written:

*'Behold, I send My messenger
    before Your face,
Who will prepare Your way
    before You.'*

28 "For I say to you, among those born of women there is not a

greater prophet than John the Baptist; but he who is least in the kingdom of God is greater than he."

29 And when all the people heard *Him*, even the tax collectors justified God, having been baptized with the baptism of John.

30 But the Pharisees and lawyers rejected the counsel of God for themselves, not having been baptized by him.

31 And the Lord said, "To what then shall I liken the men of this generation, and what are they like?

32 "They are like children sitting in the marketplace and calling to one another, saying:

'We played the flute for you,
    And you did not dance;
We mourned to you,
    And you did not weep.'

33 "For John the Baptist came neither eating bread nor drinking wine, and you say, 'He has a demon.'

34 "The Son of Man has come eating and drinking, and you say, 'Look, a glutton and a winebibber, a friend of tax collectors and sinners!'

35 "But wisdom is justified by all her children."

36 Then one of the Pharisees asked Him to eat with him. And He went to the Pharisee's house, and sat down to eat.

37 And behold, a woman in the city who was a sinner, when she knew that *Jesus* sat at the table in the Pharisee's house, brought an alabaster flask of fragrant oil,

38 and stood at His feet behind *Him* weeping; and she began to wash His feet with her tears, and wiped *them* with the hair of her head; and she kissed His feet and anointed *them* with the fragrant oil.

39 Now when the Pharisee who had invited Him saw *this*, he spoke to himself, saying, "This man, if He were a prophet, would know who and what manner of woman *this is* who is touching Him, for she is a sinner."

40 And Jesus answered and said to him, "Simon, I have something to say to you." And he said, "Teacher, say it."

41 "There was a certain creditor who had two debtors. One owed five hundred denarii, and the other fifty.

42 "And when they had nothing with which to repay, he freely forgave them both. Tell Me, therefore, which of them will love him more?"

43 Simon answered and said, "I suppose the *one* whom he forgave more." And He said to him, "You have rightly judged."

44 Then He turned to the woman and said to Simon, "Do you see this woman? I entered your house; you gave Me no water for My feet, but she has washed My feet with her tears and wiped *them* with the hair of her head.

45 "You gave Me no kiss, but this woman has not ceased to kiss My feet since the time I came in.

46 "You did not anoint My head with oil, but this woman has anointed My feet with fragrant oil.

47 "Therefore I say to you, her sins, *which are* many, are forgiven, for she loved much. But to whom little is forgiven, *the same* loves little."

48 And He said to her, "Your sins are forgiven."

49 And those who sat at the table with Him began to say to themselves, "Who is this who even forgives sins?"

50 Then He said to the woman, "Your faith has saved you. Go in peace."

8 Now it came to pass, afterward, that He went through every city and village, preaching and

bringing the glad tidings of the kingdom of God. And the twelve *were* with Him,

2 and certain women who had been healed of evil spirits and infirmities—Mary called Magdalene, out of whom had come seven demons,

3 and Joanna the wife of Chuza, Herod's steward, and Susanna, and many others who provided for Him from their substance.

4 And when a great multitude had gathered, and *others* had come to Him from every city, He spoke by a parable:

5 "A sower went out to sow his seed. And as he sowed, some fell by the wayside; and it was trampled down, and the birds of the air devoured it.

6 "Some fell on rock; and as soon as it sprang up, it withered away because it lacked moisture.

7 "And some fell among thorns, and the thorns sprang up with it and choked it.

8 "But others fell on good ground, sprang up, and yielded a crop a hundredfold." When He had said these things He cried, "He who has ears to hear, let him hear!"

9 Then His disciples asked Him, saying, "What does this parable mean?"

10 And He said, "To you it has been given to know the mysteries of the kingdom of God, but to the rest *it is given* in parables, that

'Seeing they may not see,
  And hearing they may not
    understand.'

11 "Now the parable is this: The seed is the word of God.

12 "Those by the wayside are the ones who hear; then the devil comes and takes away the word out of their hearts, lest they should believe and be saved.

13 "But the ones on the rock *are* those who, when they hear, re-

ceive the word with joy; and these have no root, who believe for a while and in time of temptation fall away.

14 "And the ones *that* fell among thorns are those who, when they have heard, go out and are choked with cares, riches, and pleasures of life, and bring no fruit to maturity.

15 "But the ones *that* fell on the good ground are those who, having heard the word with a noble and good heart, keep *it* and bear fruit with patience.

16 "No one, when he has lit a lamp, covers it with a vessel or puts *it* under a bed, but sets *it* on a lampstand, that those who enter may see the light.

17 "For nothing is secret that will not be revealed, nor *anything* hidden that will not be known and come to light.

18 "Therefore take heed how you hear. For whoever has, to him *more* will be given; and whoever does not have, even what he seems to have will be taken from him."

19 Then His mother and brothers came to Him, and could not approach Him because of the crowd.

20 And it was told Him *by some,* who said, "Your mother and Your brothers are standing outside, desiring to see You."

21 But He answered and said to them, "My mother and My brothers are these who hear the word of God and do it."

22 Now it happened, on a certain day, that He got into a boat with His disciples. And He said to them, "Let us go over to the other side of the lake." And they launched out.

23 But as they sailed He fell asleep. And a windstorm came down on the lake, and they were filling *with water,* and were in jeopardy.

24 And they came to Him and awoke Him, saying, "Master, Master, we are perishing!" Then He arose and rebuked the wind and

the raging of the water. And they ceased, and there was a calm.

25 But He said to them, "Where is your faith?" And they were afraid, and marveled, saying to one another, "Who can this be? For He commands even the winds and water, and they obey Him!"

26 Then they sailed to the country of the Gadarenes, which is opposite Galilee.

27 And when He stepped out on the land, there met Him a certain man from the city who had demons for a long time. And he wore no clothes, nor did he live in a house but in the tombs.

28 When he saw Jesus, he cried out, fell down before Him, and with a loud voice said, "What have I to do with You, Jesus, Son of the Most High God? I beg You, do not torment me!"

29 For He had commanded the unclean spirit to come out of the man. For it had often seized him, and he was kept under guard, bound with chains and shackles; and he broke the bonds and was driven by the demon into the wilderness.

30 Jesus asked him, saying, "What is your name?" And he said, "Legion," because many demons had entered him.

31 And they begged Him that He would not command them to go out into the abyss.

32 Now a herd of many swine was feeding there on the mountain. And they begged Him that He would permit them to enter them. And He permitted them.

33 Then the demons went out of the man and entered the swine, and the herd ran violently down the steep place into the lake and drowned.

34 When those who fed *them* saw what had happened, they fled and told *it* in the city and in the country.

35 Then they went out to see what had happened, and came to Jesus, and found the man from whom the demons had departed, sitting at the feet of Jesus, clothed and in his right mind. And they were afraid.

36 They also who had seen *it* told them by what means he who had been demon-possessed was healed.

37 Then the whole multitude of the surrounding region of the Gadarenes asked Him to depart from them, for they were seized with great fear. And He got into the boat and returned.

38 Now the man from whom the demons had departed begged Him that he might be with Him. But Jesus sent him away, saying,

39 "Return to your own house, and tell what great things God has done for you." And he went his way and proclaimed throughout the whole city what great things Jesus had done for him.

40 So it was, when Jesus returned, that the multitude welcomed Him, for they were all waiting for Him.

41 And behold, there came a man named Jairus, and he was a ruler of the synagogue. And he fell down at Jesus' feet and begged Him to come to his house,

42 for he had an only daughter about twelve years of age, and she was dying. But as He went, the multitudes thronged Him.

43 Now a woman, having a flow of blood for twelve years, who had spent all her livelihood on physicians and could not be healed by any,

44 came from behind and touched the border of His garment. And immediately her flow of blood stopped.

45 And Jesus said, "Who touched Me?" When all denied it, Peter and those with him said, "Master, the multitudes throng You and press *You*, and You say, 'Who touched Me?' "

46 But Jesus said, "Somebody

touched Me, for I perceived power going out from Me."

47 Now when the woman saw that she was not hidden, she came trembling; and falling down before Him, she declared to Him in the presence of all the people the reason she had touched Him and how she was healed immediately.

48 And He said to her, "Daughter, be of good cheer; your faith has made you well. Go in peace."

49 While He was still speaking, someone came from the ruler of the synagogue's *house*, saying to him, "Your daughter is dead. Do not trouble the Teacher."

50 But when Jesus heard *it*, He answered him, saying, "Do not be afraid; only believe, and she will be made well."

51 When He came into the house, He permitted no one to go in except Peter, James, and John, and the father and mother of the girl.

52 Now all wept and mourned for her; but He said, "Do not weep; she is not dead, but sleeping."

53 And they laughed Him to scorn, knowing that she was dead.

54 But He put them all out, took her by the hand and called, saying, "Little girl, arise."

55 Then her spirit returned, and she arose immediately. And He commanded that she be given *something* to eat.

56 And her parents were astonished, but He charged them to tell no one what had happened.

9 Then He called His twelve disciples together and gave them power and authority over all demons, and to cure diseases.

2 He sent them to preach the kingdom of God and to heal the sick.

3 And He said to them, "Take nothing for the journey, neither staffs nor bag nor bread nor money; and do not have two tunics apiece.

4 "Whatever house you enter, stay there, and from there depart.

5 "And whoever will not receive you, when you go out of that city, shake off the very dust from your feet as a testimony against them."

6 So they departed and went through the towns, preaching the gospel and healing everywhere.

7 Now Herod the tetrarch heard of all that was done by Him; and he was perplexed, because it was said by some that John had risen from the dead,

8 and by some that Elijah had appeared, and by others that one of the old prophets had risen again.

9 And Herod said, "John I have beheaded, but who is this of whom I hear such things?" And he sought to see Him.

10 And the apostles, when they had returned, told Him all that they had done. And He took them and went aside privately into a deserted place belonging to the city called Bethsaida.

11 But when the multitudes knew *it*, they followed Him; and He received them and spoke to them about the kingdom of God, and healed those who had need of healing.

12 When the day began to wear away, the twelve came and said to Him, "Send the multitude away, that they may go into the surrounding towns and country, and lodge and get provisions; for we are in a deserted place here."

13 But He said to them, "You give them something to eat." And they said, "We have no more than five loaves and two fish, unless we go and buy food for all these people."

14 For there were about five thousand men. And He said to His disciples, "Make them sit down in groups of fifty."

15 And they did so, and made them all sit down.

16 Then He took the five loaves and the two fish, and looking up to heaven, He blessed and broke

them, and gave *them* to the disciples to set before the multitude.

17 So they all ate and were filled, and twelve baskets of the leftover fragments were taken up by them.

18 And it happened, as He was alone praying, *that* His disciples joined Him, and He asked them, saying, "Who do the crowds say that I am?"

19 So they answered and said, "John the Baptist, but some *say* Elijah; and others *say* that one of the old prophets has risen again."

20 He said to them, "But who do you say that I am?" Peter answered and said, "The Christ of God."

21 And He strictly warned and commanded them to tell this to no one,

22 saying, "The Son of Man must suffer many things, and be rejected by the elders and chief priests and scribes, and be killed, and be raised the third day."

23 Then He said to *them* all, "If anyone desires to come after Me, let him deny himself, and take up his cross daily, and follow Me.

24 "For whoever desires to save his life will lose it, but whoever loses his life for My sake will save it.

25 "For what advantage is it to a man if he gains the whole world, and is himself destroyed or lost?

26 "For whoever is ashamed of Me and My words, of him the Son of Man will be ashamed when He comes in His *own* glory, and in *His* Father's, and of the holy angels.

27 "But I tell you truly, there are some standing here who shall not taste death till they see the kingdom of God."

28 And it came to pass, about eight days after these sayings, that He took Peter, John, and James and went up on the mountain to pray.

29 And as He prayed, the appearance of His face was altered, and His robe *became* white *and* glistening.

30 Then behold, two men talked with Him, who were Moses and Elijah,

31 who appeared in glory and spoke of His decease which He was about to accomplish at Jerusalem.

32 But Peter and those with him were heavy with sleep; and when they were fully awake, they saw His glory and the two men who stood with Him.

33 And it happened, as they were parting from Him, *that* Peter said to Jesus, "Master, it is good for us to be here; and let us make three tabernacles: one for You, one for Moses, and one for Elijah"—not knowing what he said.

34 While he was saying this, a cloud came and overshadowed them; and they were fearful as they entered the cloud.

35 Then a voice came out of the cloud, saying, "This is My beloved Son. Hear Him!"

36 And when the voice had ceased, Jesus was found alone. But they kept quiet, and told no one in those days any of the things they had seen.

37 Now it happened on the next day, when they had come down from the mountain, that a great multitude met Him.

38 Suddenly a man from the multitude cried out, saying, "Teacher, I implore You, look on my son, for he is my only child.

39 "And behold, a spirit seizes him, and he suddenly cries out; it convulses him so that he foams *at the mouth,* and bruising him, it departs from him with great difficulty.

40 "So I implored Your disciples to cast it out, but they could not."

41 Then Jesus answered and said, "O faithless and perverse generation, how long shall I be with you and bear with you? Bring your son here."

42 And as he was still coming, the demon threw him down and convulsed *him.* Then Jesus rebuked

the unclean spirit, healed the child, and gave him back to his father.

43 And they were all amazed at the majesty of God. But while everyone marveled at all the things which Jesus did, He said to His disciples,

44 "Let these words sink down into your ears, for the Son of Man is about to be delivered into the hands of men."

45 But they did not understand this saying, and it was hidden from them so that they did not perceive it; and they were afraid to ask Him about this saying.

46 Then a dispute arose among them as to which of them would be greatest.

47 And Jesus, perceiving the thought of their heart, took a little child and set him by Him,

48 and said to them, "Whoever receives this little child in My name receives Me; and whoever receives Me receives Him who sent Me. For he who is least among you all will be great."

49 Then John answered and said, "Master, we saw someone casting out demons in Your name, and we forbade him because he does not follow with us."

50 But Jesus said to him, "Do not forbid *him*, for he who is not against us is for us."

51 Now it came to pass, when the time had come for Him to be received up, that He steadfastly set His face to go to Jerusalem,

52 and sent messengers before His face. And as they went, they entered a village of the Samaritans, to prepare for Him.

53 But they did not receive Him, because His face was *set* for the journey to Jerusalem.

54 And when His disciples James and John saw *this,* they said, "Lord, do You want us to command fire to come down from heaven and consume them, just as Elijah did?"

55 But He turned and rebuked them, and said, "You do not know what manner of spirit you are of.

56 "For the Son of Man did not come to destroy men's lives but to save *them.*" And they went to another village.

57 Now it happened as they journeyed on the road, *that* someone said to Him, "Lord, I will follow You wherever You go."

58 And Jesus said to him, "Foxes have holes and birds of the air *have* nests, but the Son of Man has nowhere to lay *His* head."

59 Then He said to another, "Follow Me." But he said, "Lord, let me first go and bury my father."

60 Jesus said to him, "Let the dead bury their own dead, but you go and preach the kingdom of God."

61 And another also said, "Lord, I will follow You, but let me first go *and* bid them farewell who are at my house."

62 But Jesus said to him, "No one, having put his hand to the plow, and looking back, is fit for the kingdom of God."

10 After these things the Lord appointed seventy others also, and sent them two by two before His face into every city and place where He Himself was about to go.

2 Then He said to them, "The harvest truly *is* great, but the laborers *are* few; therefore pray the Lord of the harvest to send out laborers into His harvest.

3 "Go your way; behold, I send you out as lambs among wolves.

4 "Carry neither money bag, sack, nor sandals; and greet no one along the road.

5 "But whatever house you enter, first say, 'Peace to this house.'

6 "And if a son of peace is there, your peace will rest on it; if not, it will return to you.

7 "And remain in the same house, eating and drinking such things as they give, for the laborer is worthy

of his wages. Do not go from house to house.

8 "Whatever city you enter, and they receive you, eat such things as are set before you.

9 "And heal the sick *who are* there, and say to them, 'The kingdom of God has come near to you.'

10 "But whatever city you enter, and they do not receive you, go out into its streets and say,

11 'The very dust of your city which clings to us we wipe off against you. Nevertheless know this, that the kingdom of God has come near you.'

12 "But I say to you that it will be more tolerable in that Day for Sodom than for that city.

13 "Woe to you, Chorazin! Woe to you, Bethsaida! For if the mighty works which were done in you had been done in Tyre and Sidon, they would have repented a great while ago, sitting in sackcloth and ashes.

14 "But it will be more tolerable for Tyre and Sidon at the judgment than for you.

15 "And you, Capernaum, who are exalted to heaven, will be thrust down to Hades.

16 "He who hears you hears Me, he who rejects you rejects Me, and he who rejects Me rejects Him who sent Me."

17 Then the seventy returned with joy, saying, "Lord, even the demons are subject to us in Your name."

18 And He said to them, "I saw Satan fall like lightning from heaven.

19 "Behold, I give you the authority to trample on serpents and scorpions, and over all the power of the enemy, and nothing shall by any means hurt you.

20 "Nevertheless do not rejoice in this, that the spirits are subject to you, but rather rejoice because your names are written in heaven."

21 In that hour Jesus rejoiced in the Spirit and said, "I praise You, Father, Lord of heaven and earth, that You have hidden these things from *the* wise and prudent and revealed them to babes. Even so, Father, for so it seemed good in Your sight.

22 "All things have been delivered to Me by My Father, and no one knows who the Son is but the Father, and who the Father is but the Son, and *the one* to whom the Son wills to reveal *Him*."

23 And He turned to *His* disciples and said privately, "Blessed *are* the eyes which see the things you see;

24 "for I tell you that many prophets and kings have desired to see what you see, and have not seen *it*, and to hear what you hear, and have not heard *it*."

25 And behold, a certain lawyer stood up and tested Him, saying, "Teacher, what shall I do to inherit eternal life?"

26 He said to him, "What is written in the law? What is your reading *of it*?"

27 So he answered and said, " '*You shall love the* LORD *your God with all your heart, with all your soul, with all your strength, and with all your mind,*' and '*your neighbor as yourself.*' "

28 And He said to him, "You have answered rightly; do this and you will live."

29 But he, wanting to justify himself, said to Jesus, "And who is my neighbor?"

30 Then Jesus answered and said: "A certain *man* went down from Jerusalem to Jericho, and fell among thieves, who stripped him of his clothing, wounded *him*, and departed, leaving *him* half dead.

31 "Now by chance a certain priest came down that road. And when he saw him, he passed by on the other side.

32 "Likewise a Levite, when he arrived at the place, came and

looked, and passed by on the other side.

33 "But a certain Samaritan, as he journeyed, came where he was. And when he saw him, he had compassion *on him,*

34 "and went to *him* and bandaged his wounds, pouring on oil and wine; and he set him on his own animal, brought him to an inn, and took care of him.

35 "On the next day, when he departed, he took out two denarii, gave *them* to the innkeeper, and said to him, 'Take care of him; and whatever more you spend, when I come again, I will repay you.'

36 "So which of these three do you think was neighbor to him who fell among the thieves?"

37 And he said, "He who showed mercy on him." Then Jesus said to him, "Go and do likewise."

38 Now it happened as they went that He entered a certain village; and a certain woman named Martha welcomed Him into her house.

39 And she had a sister called Mary, who also sat at Jesus' feet and heard His word.

40 But Martha was distracted with much serving, and she approached Him and said, "Lord, do You not care that my sister has left me to serve alone? Therefore tell her to help me."

41 And Jesus answered and said to her, "Martha, Martha, you are worried and troubled about many things.

42 "But one thing is needed, and Mary has chosen that good part, which will not be taken away from her."

11 And it came to pass, as He was praying in a certain place, when He ceased, *that* one of His disciples said to Him, "Lord, teach us to pray, as John also taught his disciples."

2 So He said to them, "When you pray, say:

Our Father in heaven,
Hallowed be Your name.
Your kingdom come.
Your will be done
On earth as *it is* in heaven.
3 Give us day by day our daily
    bread.
4 And forgive us our sins,
For we also forgive everyone
    who is indebted to us.
And do not lead us into
    temptation,
But deliver us from the evil
    one."

5 And He said to them, "Which of you shall have a friend, and go to him at midnight and say to him, 'Friend, lend me three loaves;

6 'for a friend of mine has come to me on his journey, and I have nothing to set before him';

7 "and he will answer from within and say, 'Do not trouble me; the door is now shut, and my children are with me in bed; I cannot rise and give to you'?

8 "I say to you, though he will not rise and give to him because he is his friend, yet because of his persistence he will rise and give him as many as he needs.

9 "And I say to you, ask, and it will be given to you; seek, and you will find; knock, and it will be opened to you.

10 "For everyone who asks receives, and he who seeks finds, and to him who knocks it will be opened.

11 "If a son asks for bread from any father among you, will he give him a stone? Or if *he asks* for a fish, will he give him a serpent instead of a fish?

12 "Or if he asks for an egg, will he offer him a scorpion?

13 "If you then, being evil, know how to give good gifts to your children, how much more will *your*

heavenly Father give the Holy Spirit to those who ask Him!"

14 And He was casting out a demon, and it was mute. So it was, when the demon had gone out, that the mute spoke; and the multitudes marveled.

15 But some of them said, "He casts out demons by Beelzebub, the ruler of the demons."

16 And others, testing *Him*, sought from Him a sign from heaven.

17 But He, knowing their thoughts, said to them: "Every kingdom divided against itself is brought to desolation, and a house *divided* against a house falls.

18 "If Satan also is divided against himself, how will his kingdom stand? Because you say I cast out demons by Beelzebub.

19 "And if I cast out demons by Beelzebub, by whom do your sons cast *them* out? Therefore they will be your judges.

20 "But if I cast out demons with the finger of God, surely the kingdom of God has come upon you.

21 "When a strong man, fully armed, guards his own palace, his goods are in peace.

22 "But when a stronger than he comes upon him and overcomes him, he takes from him all his armor in which he trusted, and divides his spoils.

23 "He who is not with Me is against Me, and he who does not gather with Me scatters.

24 "When an unclean spirit goes out of a man, he goes through dry places, seeking rest; and finding none, he says, 'I will return to my house from which I came.'

25 "And when he comes, he finds *it* swept and put in order.

26 "Then he goes and takes with *him* seven other spirits more wicked than himself, and they enter and dwell there; and the last *state* of that man is worse than the first."

27 And it happened, as He spoke these things, that a certain woman from the crowd raised her voice and said to Him, "Blessed *is* the womb that bore You, and *the* breasts which nursed You!"

28 But He said, "More than that, blessed *are* those who hear the word of God and keep it!"

29 And while the crowds were thickly gathered together, He began to say, "This is an evil generation. It seeks a sign, and no sign will be given to it except the sign of Jonah the prophet.

30 "For as Jonah became a sign to the Ninevites, so also the Son of Man will be to this generation.

31 "The queen of the South will rise up in the judgment with the men of this generation and condemn them, for she came from the ends of the earth to hear the wisdom of Solomon; and indeed a greater than Solomon *is* here.

32 "The men of Nineveh will rise up in the judgment with this generation and condemn it, for they repented at the preaching of Jonah; and indeed a greater than Jonah *is* here.

33 "No one, when he has lit a lamp, puts *it* in a secret place or under a basket, but on a lampstand, that those who come in may see the light.

34 "The lamp of the body is the eye. Therefore, when your eye is good, your whole body also is full of light. But when *your eye* is bad, your body also *is* full of darkness.

35 "Therefore take heed that the light which is in you is not darkness.

36 "If then your whole body *is* full of light, having no part dark, *the* whole *body* will be full of light, as when the bright shining of a lamp gives you light."

37 And as He spoke, a certain Pharisee asked Him to dine with him. So He went in and sat down to eat.

38 And when the Pharisee saw *it*,

Beware of Hypocrisy

he marveled that He had not first washed before dinner.

39 But the Lord said to him, "Now you Pharisees make the outside of the cup and dish clean, but your inward part is full of greed and wickedness.

40 "Foolish ones! Did not He who made the outside make the inside also?

41 "But rather give alms of such things as you have; then indeed all things are clean to you.

42 "But woe to you Pharisees! For you tithe mint and rue and all manner of herbs, and pass by justice and the love of God. These you ought to have done, without leaving the others undone.

43 "Woe to you Pharisees! For you love the best seats in the synagogues and greetings in the marketplaces.

44 "Woe to you, scribes and Pharisees, hypocrites! For you are like graves which are not seen, and the men who walk over *them* are not aware *of them*."

45 Then one of the lawyers answered and said to Him, "Teacher, by saying these things You reproach us also."

46 And He said, "Woe to you also, *you* lawyers! For you load men with burdens hard to bear, and you yourselves do not touch the burdens with one of your fingers.

47 "Woe to you! For you build the tombs of the prophets, and your fathers killed them.

48 "In fact, you bear witness that you approve the deeds of your fathers; for they indeed killed them, and you build their tombs.

49 "Therefore the wisdom of God also said, 'I will send them prophets and apostles, and *some* of them they will kill and persecute,'

50 "that the blood of all the prophets which was shed from the foundation of the world may be required of this generation,

51 "from the blood of Abel to the blood of Zechariah who perished between the altar and the temple. Yes, I say to you, it shall be required of this generation.

52 "Woe to you lawyers! For you have taken away the key of knowledge. You did not enter in yourselves, and those who were entering in you hindered."

53 And as He said these things to them, the scribes and the Pharisees began to assail *Him* vehemently, and to cross-examine Him about many things,

54 lying in wait for Him, and seeking to catch Him in something He might say, that they might accuse Him.

12 In the meantime, when an innumerable multitude of people had gathered together, so that they trampled one another, He began to say to His disciples first *of all*, "Beware of the leaven of the Pharisees, which is hypocrisy.

2 "For there is nothing covered that will not be revealed, nor hidden that will not be known.

3 "Therefore whatever you have spoken in the dark will be heard in the light, and what you have spoken in the ear in inner rooms will be proclaimed on the housetops.

4 "And I say to you, My friends, do not be afraid of those who kill the body, and after that have no more that they can do.

5 "But I will show you whom you should fear: Fear Him who, after He has killed, has power to cast into hell; yes, I say to you, fear Him!

6 "Are not five sparrows sold for two copper coins? And not one of them is forgotten before God.

7 "But the very hairs of your head are all numbered. Do not fear therefore; you are of more value than many sparrows.

8 "Also I say to you, whoever confesses Me before men, him the Son of Man also will confess before the angels of God.

9 "But he who denies Me before men will be denied before the angels of God.

10 "And anyone who speaks a word against the Son of Man, it will be forgiven him; but to him who blasphemes against the Holy Spirit, it will not be forgiven.

11 "Now when they bring you to the synagogues and magistrates and authorities, do not worry about how or what you should answer, or what you should say.

12 "For the Holy Spirit will teach you in that very hour what you ought to say."

13 Then one from the crowd said to Him, "Teacher, tell my brother to divide the inheritance with me."

14 But He said to him, "Man, who made Me a judge or an arbitrator over you?"

15 And He said to them, "Take heed and beware of covetousness, for one's life does not consist in the abundance of the things he possesses."

16 Then He spoke a parable to them, saying: "The ground of a certain rich man yielded plentifully.

17 "And he thought within himself, saying, 'What shall I do, since I have no room to store my crops?'

18 "So he said, 'I will do this: I will pull down my barns and build greater, and there I will store all my crops and my goods.

19 'And I will say to my soul, "Soul, you have many goods laid up for many years; take your ease; eat, drink, *and* be merry." '

20 "But God said to him, '*You* fool! This night your soul will be required of you; then whose will those things be which you have provided?'

21 "So *is* he who lays up treasure for himself, and is not rich toward God."

22 And He said to His disciples, "Therefore I say to you, do not worry about your life, what you will eat; nor about the body, what you will put on.

23 "Life is more than food, and the body *is more* than clothing.

24 "Consider the ravens, for they neither sow nor reap, which have neither storehouse nor barn; and God feeds them. Of how much more value are you than the birds?

25 "And which of you by worrying can add one cubit to his stature?

26 "If you then are not able to do *the* least, why are you anxious for the rest?

27 "Consider the lilies, how they grow: they neither toil nor spin; and yet I say to you, even Solomon in all his glory was not arrayed like one of these.

28 "If then God so clothes the grass, which today is in the field and tomorrow is thrown into the oven, how much more *will He clothe* you, O *you* of little faith?

29 "And do not seek what you should eat or what you should drink, nor have an anxious mind.

30 "For all these things the nations of the world seek after, and your Father knows that you need these things.

31 "But seek the kingdom of God, and all these things shall be added to you.

32 "Do not fear, little flock, for it is your Father's good pleasure to give you the kingdom.

33 "Sell what you have and give alms; provide yourselves money bags which do not grow old, a treasure in the heavens that does not fail, where no thief approaches nor moth destroys.

34 "For where your treasure is, there your heart will be also.

35 "Let your waist be girded and *your* lamps burning;

36 "and you yourselves be like men who wait for their master, when he will return from the wedding, that when he comes and knocks they may open to him immediately.

37 "Blessed *are* those servants

whom the master, when he comes, will find watching. Assuredly, I say to you that he will gird himself and have them sit down *to eat,* and will come and serve them.

38 "And if he should come in the second watch, or come in the third watch, and find *them* so, blessed are those servants.

39 "But know this, that if the master of the house had known what hour the thief would come, he would have watched and not allowed his house to be broken into.

40 "Therefore you also be ready, for the Son of Man is coming at an hour you do not expect."

41 Then Peter said to Him, "Lord, do You speak this parable *only* to us, or to all *people?*"

42 And the Lord said, "Who then is that faithful and wise steward, whom *his* master will make ruler over his household, to give *them their* portion of food in due season?

43 "Blessed *is* that servant whom his master will find so doing when he comes.

44 "Truly, I say to you that he will make him ruler over all that he has.

45 "But if that servant says in his heart, 'My master is delaying his coming,' and begins to beat the menservants and maidservants, and to eat and drink and be drunk,

46 "the master of that servant will come on a day when he is not looking for *him,* and at an hour when he is not aware, and will cut him in two and appoint *him* his portion with the unbelievers.

47 "And that servant who knew his master's will, and did not prepare *himself* or do according to his will, shall be beaten with many *stripes.*

48 "But he who did not know, yet committed things worthy of stripes, shall be beaten with few. For everyone to whom much is given, from him much will be required; and to whom much has been committed, of him they will ask the more.

49 "I came to send fire on the earth, and how I wish it were already kindled!

50 "But I have a baptism to be baptized with, and how distressed I am till it is accomplished!

51 "Do *you* suppose that I came to give peace on earth? I tell you, not at all, but rather division.

52 "For from now on five in one house will be divided: three against two, and two against three.

53 "Father will be divided against son and son against father, mother against daughter and daughter against mother, mother-in-law against her daughter-in-law and daughter-in-law against her mother-in-law."

54 Then He also said to the multitudes, "When *you see* a cloud rising out of the west, immediately you say, 'A shower is coming'; and so it is.

55 "And when you see the south wind blow, you say, 'There will be hot weather'; and there is.

56 "Hypocrites! You can discern the face of the sky and of the earth, but how *is it* you do not discern this time?

57 "Yes, and why, even of yourselves, do you not judge what is right?

58 "When you go with your adversary to the magistrate, make every effort along the way to settle with him, lest he drag you to the judge, the judge deliver you to the officer, and the officer throw you into prison.

59 "I tell you, you shall not depart from there till you have paid the very last mite."

13 There were present at that season some who told Him about the Galileans whose blood Pilate had mingled with their sacrifices.

2 And Jesus answered and said to them, "Do you suppose that these

Galileans were worse sinners than all *other* Galileans, because they suffered such things?

3 "I tell you, no; but unless you repent you will all likewise perish.

4 "Or those eighteen on whom the tower in Siloam fell and killed them, do you think that they were worse sinners than all *other* men who dwelt in Jerusalem?

5 "I tell you, no; but unless you repent you will all likewise perish."

6 He also spoke this parable: "A certain *man* had a fig tree planted in his vineyard, and he came seeking fruit on it and found none.

7 "Then he said to the keeper of his vineyard, 'Look, for three years I have come seeking fruit on this fig tree and find none. Cut it down; why does it use up the ground?'

8 "But he answered and said to him, 'Sir, let it alone this year also, until I dig around it and fertilize *it*.

9 'And if it bears fruit, *well.* But if not, after that you can cut it down.'"

10 Now He was teaching in one of the synagogues on the Sabbath.

11 And behold, there was a woman who had a spirit of infirmity eighteen years, and was bent over and could in no way raise *herself* up.

12 But when Jesus saw her, He called *her* to *Him* and said to her, "Woman, you are loosed from your infirmity."

13 And He laid *His* hands on her, and immediately she was made straight, and glorified God.

14 But the ruler of the synagogue answered with indignation, because Jesus had healed on the Sabbath; and he said to the crowd, "There are six days on which men ought to work; therefore come and be healed on them, and not on the Sabbath day."

15 The Lord then answered him and said, "Hypocrite! Does not each one of you on the Sabbath loose his ox or *his* donkey from the stall, and lead *it* away to water it?

16 "So ought not this woman, being a daughter of Abraham, whom Satan has bound—think of it—for eighteen years, be loosed from this bond on the Sabbath?"

17 And when He said these things, all His adversaries were put to shame; and all the multitude rejoiced for all the glorious things that were done by Him.

18 Then He said, "What is the kingdom of God like? And to what shall I compare it?

19 "It is like a mustard seed, which a man took and put in his garden; and it grew and became a large tree, and the birds of the air nested in its branches."

20 And again He said, "To what shall I liken the kingdom of God?

21 "It is like leaven, which a woman took and hid in three measures of meal till it was all leavened."

22 And He went through the cities and villages, teaching, and journeying toward Jerusalem.

23 Then one said to Him, "Lord, are there few who are saved?" And He said to them,

24 "Strive to enter through the narrow gate, for many, I say to you, will seek to enter and will not be able.

25 "When once the Master of the house has risen up and shut the door, and you begin to stand outside and knock at the door, saying, 'Lord, Lord, open for us,' and He will answer and say to you, 'I do not know you, where you are from,'

26 "then you will begin to say, 'We ate and drank in Your presence, and You taught in our streets.'

27 "But He will say, 'I tell you I do not know you, where you are from. Depart from Me, all you workers of iniquity.'

28 "There will be weeping and gnashing of teeth, when you see Abraham and Isaac and Jacob and all the prophets in the kingdom of God, and yourselves thrust out.

29 "They will come from the east and the west, from the north and the south, and sit down in the kingdom of God.

30 "And indeed there are last who will be first, and there are first who will be last."

31 On that very day some Pharisees came, saying to Him, "Get out and depart from here, for Herod wants to kill You."

32 And He said to them, "Go, tell that fox, 'Behold, I cast out demons and perform cures today and tomorrow, and the third *day* I shall be perfected.'

33 "Nevertheless I must journey today, tomorrow, and the *day* following; for it cannot be that a prophet should perish outside of Jerusalem.

34 "O Jerusalem, Jerusalem, the one who kills the prophets and stones those who are sent to her! How often I wanted to gather your children together, as a hen *gathers* her brood under *her* wings, but you were not willing!

35 "See! Your house is left to you desolate; and assuredly, I say to you, you shall not see Me until *the time* comes when you say, '*Blessed is He who comes in the name of the* LORD!'"

14 Now it happened, as He went into the house of one of the rulers of the Pharisees to eat bread on the Sabbath, that they watched Him closely.

2 And behold, there was a certain man before Him who had dropsy.

3 And Jesus, answering, spoke to the lawyers and Pharisees, saying, "Is it lawful to heal on the Sabbath?"

4 But they kept silent. And He took *him* and healed him, and let him go.

5 Then He answered them, saying, "Which of you, having a donkey or an ox that has fallen into a pit, will not immediately pull him out on the Sabbath day?"

6 And they could not answer Him regarding these things.

7 So He told a parable to those who were invited, when He noted how they chose the best places, saying to them:

8 "When you are invited by anyone to a wedding feast, do not sit down in the best place, lest one more honorable than you be invited by him;

9 "and he who invited you and him come and say to you, 'Give place to this man,' and then you begin with shame to take the lowest place.

10 "But when you are invited, go and sit down in the lowest place, so that when he who invited you comes he may say to you, 'Friend, go up higher.' Then you will have glory in the presence of those who sit at the table with you.

11 "For whoever exalts himself will be abased, and he who humbles himself will be exalted."

12 Then He also said to him who invited Him, "When you give a dinner or a supper, do not ask your friends, your brothers, your relatives, nor *your* rich neighbors, lest they also invite you back, and you be repaid.

13 "But when you give a feast, invite *the* poor, *the* maimed, *the* lame, *the* blind.

14 "And you will be blessed, because they cannot repay you; for you shall be repaid at the resurrection of the just."

15 Now when one of those who sat at the table with Him heard these things, he said to Him, "Blessed *is* he who shall eat bread in the kingdom of God!"

16 Then He said to him, "A certain man gave a great supper and invited many,

17 "and sent his servant at supper time to say to those who were invited, 'Come, for all things are now ready.'

18 "But they all with one *accord*

began to make excuses. The first said to him, 'I have bought a piece of ground, and I must go and see it. I ask you to have me excused.'

19 "And another said, 'I have bought five yoke of oxen, and I am going to test them. I ask you to have me excused.'

20 "Still another said, 'I have married a wife, and therefore I cannot come.'

21 "So that servant came and reported these things to his master. Then the master of the house, being angry, said to his servant, 'Go out quickly into the streets and lanes of the city, and bring in here *the* poor and *the* maimed and *the* lame and *the* blind.'

22 "And the servant said, 'Master, it is done as you commanded, and still there is room.'

23 "Then the master said to the servant, 'Go out into the highways and hedges, and compel *them* to come in, that my house may be filled.

24 'For I say to you that none of those men who were invited shall taste my supper.' "

25 And great multitudes went with Him. And He turned and said to them,

26 "If anyone comes to Me and does not hate his father and mother, wife and children, brothers and sisters, yes, and his own life also, he cannot be My disciple.

27 "And whoever does not bear his cross and come after Me cannot be My disciple.

28 "For which of you, intending to build a tower, does not sit down first and count the cost, whether he has *enough* to finish *it*—

29 "lest, after he has laid the foundation, and is not able to finish *it*, all who see *it* begin to mock him,

30 "saying, 'This man began to build and was not able to finish.'

31 "Or what king, going to make war against another king, does not sit down first and consider whether he is able with ten thousand to meet him who comes against him with twenty thousand?

32 "Or else, while the other is still a great way off, he sends a delegation and asks conditions of peace.

33 "So likewise, whoever of you does not forsake all that he has cannot be My disciple.

34 "Salt *is* good; but if the salt has lost its flavor, how shall it be seasoned?

35 "It is neither fit for the land nor for the dunghill, *but* men throw it out. He who has ears to hear, let him hear!"

15 Then all the tax collectors and the sinners drew near to Him to hear Him.

2 And the Pharisees and scribes murmured, saying, "This man receives sinners and eats with them."

3 So He spoke this parable to them, saying:

4 "What man of you, having a hundred sheep, if he loses one of them, does not leave the ninety-nine in the wilderness, and go after the one which is lost until he finds it?

5 "And when he has found *it*, he lays *it* on his shoulders, rejoicing.

6 "And when he comes home, he calls together *his* friends and neighbors, saying to them, 'Rejoice with me, for I have found my sheep which was lost!'

7 "I say to you that likewise there will be more joy in heaven over one sinner who repents than over ninety-nine just persons who need no repentance.

8 "Or what woman, having ten silver coins, if she loses one coin, does not light a lamp, sweep the house, and seek diligently until she finds *it*?

9 "And when she has found *it*, she calls *her* friends and neighbors together, saying, 'Rejoice with me,

for I have found the piece which I lost!'

10 "Likewise, I say to you, there is joy in the presence of the angels of God over one sinner who repents."

11 Then He said: "A certain man had two sons.

12 "And the younger of them said to *his* father, 'Father, give me the portion of goods that falls *to me.*' So he divided to them *his* livelihood.

13 "And not many days after, the younger son gathered all together, journeyed to a far country, and there wasted his possessions with prodigal living.

14 "But when he had spent all, there arose a severe famine in that land, and he began to be in want.

15 "Then he went and joined himself to a citizen of that country, and he sent him into his fields to feed swine.

16 "And he would gladly have filled his stomach with the pods that the swine ate, and no one gave him *anything.*

17 "But when he came to himself, he said, 'How many of my father's hired servants have bread enough and to spare, and I perish with hunger!

18 'I will arise and go to my father, and will say to him, "Father, I have sinned against heaven and before you,

19 and I am no longer worthy to be called your son. Make me like one of your hired servants." '

20 "And he arose and came to his father. But when he was still a great way off, his father saw him and had compassion, and ran and fell on his neck and kissed him.

21 "And the son said to him, 'Father, I have sinned against heaven and in your sight, and am no longer worthy to be called your son.'

22 "But the father said to his servants, 'Bring out the best robe and put *it* on him, and put a ring on his hand and sandals on *his* feet.

23 'And bring the fatted calf here and kill *it,* and let us eat and be merry;

24 'for this my son was dead and is alive again; he was lost and is found.' And they began to be merry.

25 "Now his older son was in the field. And as he came and drew near to the house, he heard music and dancing.

26 "So he called one of the servants and asked what these things meant.

27 "And he said to him, 'Your brother has come, and because he has received him safe and sound, your father has killed the fatted calf.'

28 "But he was angry and would not go in. Therefore his father came out and pleaded with him.

29 "So he answered and said to *his* father, 'Lo, these many years I have been serving you; I never transgressed your commandment at any time; and yet you never gave me a young goat, that I might make merry with my friends.

30 'But as soon as this son of yours came, who has devoured your livelihood with harlots, you killed the fatted calf for him.'

31 "And he said to him, 'Son, you are always with me, and all that I have is yours.

32 'It was right that we should make merry and be glad, for your brother was dead and is alive again, and was lost and is found.' "

16 And He also said to His disciples: "There was a certain rich man who had a steward, and an accusation was brought to him that this man was wasting his goods.

2 "So he called him and said to him, 'What is this I hear about you? Give an account of your stewardship, for you can no longer be steward.'

3 "Then the steward said within himself, 'What shall I do? For my

master is taking the stewardship away from me. I cannot dig; I am ashamed to beg.

4 'I have resolved what to do, that when I am put out of the stewardship, they may receive me into their houses.'

5 "So he called every one of his master's debtors to *him*, and said to the first, 'How much do you owe my master?'

6 "And he said, 'A hundred measures of oil.' So he said to him, 'Take your bill, and sit down quickly and write fifty.'

7 "Then he said to another, 'And how much do you owe?' So he said, 'A hundred measures of wheat.' And he said to him, 'Take your bill, and write eighty.'

8 "So the master commended the unjust steward because he had dealt shrewdly. For the sons of this world are more shrewd in their generation than the sons of light.

9 "And I say to you, make friends for yourselves by unrighteous mammon, that when you fail, they may receive you into everlasting habitations.

10 "He who *is* faithful in *what is* least is faithful also in much; and he who is unjust in *what is* least is unjust also in much.

11 "Therefore if you have not been faithful in the unrighteous mammon, who will commit to your trust the true *riches*?

12 "And if you have not been faithful in what is another man's, who will give you what is your own?

13 "No servant can serve two masters; for either he will hate the one and love the other, or else he will be loyal to the one and despise the other. You cannot serve God and mammon."

14 Now the Pharisees, who were lovers of money, also heard all these things, and they derided Him.

15 And He said to them, "You are those who justify yourselves be-fore men, but God knows your hearts. For what is highly esteemed among men is an abomination in the sight of God.

16 "The law and the prophets *were* until John. Since that time the kingdom of God has been preached, and everyone is pressing into it.

17 "And it is easier for heaven and earth to pass away than for one tittle of the law to fail.

18 "Whoever divorces his wife and marries another commits adultery; and whoever marries her who is divorced from *her* husband commits adultery.

19 "There was a certain rich man who was clothed in purple and fine linen and fared sumptuously every day.

20 "But there was a certain beggar named Lazarus, full of sores, who was laid at his gate,

21 "desiring to be fed with the crumbs which fell from the rich man's table. Moreover the dogs came and licked his sores.

22 "So it was that the beggar died, and was carried by the angels to Abraham's bosom. The rich man also died and was buried.

23 "And being in torments in Hades, he lifted up his eyes and saw Abraham afar off, and Lazarus in his bosom.

24 "Then he cried and said, 'Father Abraham, have mercy on me, and send Lazarus that he may dip the tip of his finger in water and cool my tongue; for I am tormented in this flame.'

25 "But Abraham said, 'Son, remember that in your lifetime you received your good things, and likewise Lazarus evil things; but now he is comforted and you are tormented.

26 'And besides all this, between us and you there is a great gulf fixed, so that those who want to pass from here to you cannot, nor can those from there pass to us.'

27 "Then he said, 'I beg you therefore, father, that you would send him to my father's house,

28 'for I have five brothers, that he may testify to them, lest they also come to this place of torment.'

29 "Abraham said to him, 'They have Moses and the prophets; let them hear them.'

30 "And he said, 'No, father Abraham; but if one goes to them from the dead, they will repent.'

31 "But he said to him, 'If they do not hear Moses and the prophets, neither will they be persuaded though one rise from the dead.' "

17 Then He said to the disciples, "It is impossible that no offenses should come, but woe *to him* through whom they do come!

2 "It would be better for him if a millstone were hung around his neck, and he were thrown into the sea, than that he should offend one of these little ones.

3 "Take heed to yourselves. If your brother sins against you, rebuke him; and if he repents, forgive him.

4 "And if he sins against you seven times in a day, and seven times in a day returns to you, saying, 'I repent,' you shall forgive him."

5 And the apostles said to the Lord, "Increase our faith."

6 So the Lord said, "If you have faith as a mustard seed, you can say to this mulberry tree, 'Be pulled up by the roots and be planted in the sea,' and it would obey you.

7 "And which of you, having a servant plowing or tending sheep, will say to him when he has come in from the field, 'Come at once and sit down to eat'?

8 "But will he not rather say to him, 'Prepare something for my supper, and gird yourself and serve me till I have eaten and drunk, and afterward you will eat and drink'?

9 "Does he thank that servant because he did the things that were commanded him? I think not.

10 "So likewise you, when you have done all those things which you are commanded, say, 'We are unprofitable servants. We have done what was our duty to do.' "

11 Now it happened as He went to Jerusalem that He passed through the midst of Samaria and Galilee.

12 Then as He entered a certain village, there met Him ten men who were lepers, who stood afar off.

13 And they lifted up *their* voices and said, "Jesus, Master, have mercy on us!"

14 So when He saw *them*, He said to them, "Go, show yourselves to the priests." And so it was that as they went, they were cleansed.

15 Now one of them, when he saw that he was healed, returned, and with a loud voice glorified God,

16 and fell down on *his* face at His feet, giving Him thanks. And he was a Samaritan.

17 So Jesus answered and said, "Were there not ten cleansed? But where *are* the nine?

18 "Were there not any found who returned to give glory to God except this foreigner?"

19 And He said to him, "Arise, go your way. Your faith has made you well."

20 Now when He was asked by the Pharisees when the kingdom of God would come, He answered them and said, "The kingdom of God does not come with observation;

21 "nor will they say, 'See here!' or 'See there!' For indeed, the kingdom of God is within you."

22 Then He said to the disciples, "The days will come when you will desire to see one of the days of the Son of Man, and you will not see *it*.

23 "And they will say to you, 'Look here!' or 'Look there!' Do not go after *them* or follow *them*.

24 "For as the lightning that

flashes out of one *part* under heaven shines to the other *part* under heaven, so also the Son of Man will be in His day.

25 "But first He must suffer many things and be rejected by this generation.

26 "And as it was in the days of Noah, so it will be also in the days of the Son of Man:

27 "They ate, they drank, they married wives, they were given in marriage, until the day that Noah entered the ark, and the flood came and destroyed them all.

28 "Likewise as it was also in the days of Lot: They ate, they drank, they bought, they sold, they planted, they built;

29 "but on the day that Lot went out of Sodom it rained fire and brimstone from heaven and destroyed *them* all.

30 "Even so will it be in the day when the Son of Man is revealed.

31 "In that day, he who is on the housetop, and his goods *are* in the house, let him not come down to take them away. And likewise the one who is in the field, let him not turn back.

32 "Remember Lot's wife.

33 "Whoever seeks to save his life will lose it, and whoever loses his life will preserve it.

34 "I tell you, in that night there will be two *men* in one bed: the one will be taken and the other will be left.

35 "Two *women* will be grinding together: the one will be taken and the other left.

36 "Two *men* will be in the field: the one will be taken and the other left."

37 And they answered and said to Him, "Where, Lord?" So He said to them, "Wherever the body is, there the eagles will be gathered together."

18 Then He spoke a parable to them, that men always ought to pray and not lose heart,

2 saying: "There was in a certain city a judge who did not fear God nor regard man.

3 "Now there was a widow in that city; and she came to him, saying, 'Avenge me of my adversary.'

4 "And he would not for a while; but afterward he said within himself, 'Though I do not fear God nor regard man,

5 'yet because this widow troubles me I will avenge her, lest by her continual coming she weary me.' "

6 Then the Lord said, "Hear what the unjust judge said.

7 "And shall God not avenge His own elect who cry out day and night to Him, though He bears long with them?

8 "I tell you that He will avenge them speedily. Nevertheless, when the Son of Man comes, will He really find faith on the earth?"

9 Also He spoke this parable to some who trusted in themselves that they were righteous, and despised others:

10 "Two men went up to the temple to pray, one a Pharisee and the other a tax collector.

11 "The Pharisee stood and prayed thus with himself, 'God, I thank You that I am not like other men—extortioners, unjust, adulterers, or even as this tax collector.

12 'I fast twice a week; I give tithes of all that I possess.'

13 "And the tax collector, standing afar off, would not so much as raise *his* eyes to heaven, but beat his breast, saying, 'God be merciful to me a sinner!'

14 "I tell you, this man went down to his house justified *rather* than the other; for everyone who exalts himself will be abased, and he who humbles himself will be exalted."

15 Then they also brought infants to Him that He might touch them; but when *His* disciples saw *it*, they rebuked them.

16 But Jesus called them to *Him*

and said, "Let the little children come to Me, and do not forbid them; for of such is the kingdom of God.

17 "Assuredly, I say to you, whoever does not receive the kingdom of God as a little child will by no means enter it."

18 Now a certain ruler asked Him, saying, "Good Teacher, what shall I do to inherit eternal life?"

19 So Jesus said to him, "Why do you call Me good? No one *is* good but One, *that is,* God.

20 "You know the commandments: *'Do not commit adultery,' 'Do not murder,' 'Do not steal,' 'Do not bear false witness,' 'Honor your father and your mother.'*"

21 And he said, "All these I have kept from my youth."

22 So when Jesus heard these things, He said to him, "You still lack one thing. Sell all that you have and distribute to the poor, and you will have treasure in heaven; and come, follow Me."

23 But when he heard this, he became very sorrowful, for he was very rich.

24 And when Jesus saw that he became very sorrowful, He said, "How hard it is for those who have riches to enter the kingdom of God!

25 "For it is easier for a camel to go through a needle's eye than for a rich man to enter the kingdom of God."

26 And those who heard it said, "Who then can be saved?"

27 But He said, "The things which are impossible with men are possible with God."

28 Then Peter said, "See, we have left all and followed You."

29 So He said to them, "Assuredly, I say to you, there is no one who has left house or parents or brothers or wife or children, for the sake of the kingdom of God,

30 "who shall not receive many times more in this present time,

and in the age to come everlasting life."

31 Then He took the twelve aside and said to them, "Behold, we are going up to Jerusalem, and all things that are written by the prophets concerning the Son of Man will be accomplished.

32 "For He will be delivered to the Gentiles and will be mocked and insulted and spit upon.

33 "And they will scourge *Him* and put Him to death. And the third day He will rise again."

34 But they understood none of these things; this saying was hidden from them, and they did not know the things which were spoken.

35 Then it happened, that as He was coming near Jericho, that a certain blind man sat by the road begging.

36 And hearing a multitude passing by, he asked what it meant.

37 So they told him that Jesus of Nazareth was passing by.

38 And he cried out, saying, "Jesus, Son of David, have mercy on me!"

39 Then those who went before warned him that he should be quiet; but he cried out all the more, "Son of David, have mercy on me!"

40 So Jesus stood still and commanded him to be brought to Him. And when he had come near, He asked him,

41 saying, "What do you want Me to do for you?" And he said, "Lord, that I may receive my sight."

42 Then Jesus said to him, "Receive your sight; your faith has saved you."

43 And immediately he received his sight, and followed Him, glorifying God. And all the people, when they saw *it,* gave praise to God.

19 Then *Jesus* entered and passed through Jericho.

2 Now behold, *there was* a man

named Zacchaeus who was a chief tax collector, and he was rich.

3 And he sought to see who Jesus was, but could not because of the crowd, for he was of short stature.

4 So he ran ahead and climbed up into a sycamore tree to see Him, for He was going to pass that *way*.

5 And when Jesus came to the place, He looked up and saw him, and said to him, "Zacchaeus, make haste and come down, for today I must stay at your house."

6 So he made haste and came down, and received Him joyfully.

7 But when they saw *it*, they all murmured, saying, "He has gone to be a guest with a man who is a sinner."

8 Then Zacchaeus stood and said to the Lord, "Look, Lord, I give half of my goods to the poor; and if I have taken anything from anyone by false accusation, I restore fourfold."

9 And Jesus said to him, "Today salvation has come to this house, because he also is a son of Abraham;

10 "for the Son of Man has come to seek and to save that which was lost."

11 Now as they heard these things, He spoke another parable, because He was near Jerusalem and because they thought the kingdom of God would appear immediately.

12 Therefore He said: "A certain nobleman went into a far country to receive for himself a kingdom and to return.

13 "So he called ten of his servants, delivered to them ten minas, and said to them, 'Do business till I come.'

14 "But his citizens hated him, and sent a delegation after him, saying, 'We will not have this *man* to reign over us.'

15 "And so it was that when he returned, having received the kingdom, he then commanded these servants, to whom he had given the money, to be called to him, that he might know how much every man had gained by trading.

16 "Then came the first, saying, 'Master, your mina has earned ten minas.'

17 "And he said to him, 'Well *done*, good servant; because you were faithful in a very little, have authority over ten cities.'

18 "And the second came, saying, 'Master, your mina has earned five minas.'

19 "Likewise he said to him, 'You also be over five cities.'

20 "And another came, saying, 'Master, here is your mina, which I have kept put away in a handkerchief.

21 'For I feared you, because you are an austere man. You collect what you did not deposit, and reap what you did not sow.'

22 "And he said to him, 'Out of your own mouth I will judge you, *you* wicked servant. You knew that I was an austere man, collecting what I did not deposit and reaping what I did not sow.

23 'Why then did you not put my money in the bank, that at my coming I might have collected it with interest?'

24 "And he said to those who stood by, 'Take the mina from him, and give *it* to him who has ten minas.'

25 ("But they said to him, 'Master, he has ten minas.')

26 'For I say to you, that to everyone who has will be given; and from him who does not have, even what he has will be taken away from him.

27 'But bring here those enemies of mine, who did not want me to reign over them, and slay *them* before me.'"

28 When He had said this, He went on ahead, going up to Jerusalem.

29 And it came to pass, when He came near to Bethphage and Bethany, at the mountain called Olivet, *that* He sent two of His disciples,

30 saying, "Go into the village op-

posite *you,* where as you enter you will find a colt tied, on which no one has ever sat. Loose him and bring *him here.*

31 "And if anyone asks you, 'Why are you loosing *him?*' thus you shall say to him, 'Because the Lord has need of him.' "

32 So those who were sent departed and found *it* just as He had said to them.

33 But as they were loosing the colt, the owners of it said to them, "Why are you loosing the colt?"

34 And they said, "The Lord has need of him."

35 Then they brought him to Jesus. And they threw their own garments on the colt, and they set Jesus on him.

36 And as He went, they spread their clothes on the road.

37 Then, as He was now drawing near the descent of the Mount of Olives, the whole multitude of the disciples began to rejoice and praise God with a loud voice for all the mighty works they had seen,

38 saying:

" *'Blessed is the King who comes in the name of the LORD!'*
Peace in heaven and glory in the highest!"

39 And some of the Pharisees called to Him from the crowd, "Teacher, rebuke Your disciples."

40 But He answered and said to them, "I tell you that if these should keep silent, the stones would immediately cry out."

41 Now as He drew near, He saw the city and wept over it,

42 saying, "If you had known, even you, especially in this your day, the things *that make* for your peace! But now they are hidden from your eyes.

43 "For *the* days will come upon you when your enemies will build an embankment around you, sur-

round you and close you in on every side,

44 "and level you, and your children within you, to the ground; and they will not leave in you one stone upon another, because you did not know the time of your visitation."

45 Then He went into the temple and began to drive out those who bought and sold in it,

46 saying to them, "It is written, *'My house is a house of prayer,'* but you have made it a *'den of thieves.'* "

47 And He was teaching daily in the temple. But the chief priests, the scribes, and the leaders of the people sought to destroy Him,

48 and were unable to do anything; for all the people were very attentive to hear Him.

20 Now it happened on one of those days, as He taught the people in the temple and preached the gospel, *that* the chief priests and the scribes, together with the elders, confronted *Him*

2 and spoke to Him, saying, "Tell us, by what authority are You doing these things? Or who is he who gave You this authority?"

3 But He answered and said to them, "I will also ask you one thing, and answer Me:

4 "The baptism of John—was it from heaven or from men?"

5 And they reasoned among themselves, saying, "If we say, 'From heaven,' He will say, 'Why then did you not believe him?'

6 "But if we say, 'From men,' all the people will stone us, for they are persuaded that John was a prophet."

7 So they answered that they did not know where *it was* from.

8 And Jesus said to them, "Neither will I tell you by what authority I do these things."

9 Then He began to tell the people this parable: "A certain man planted a vineyard, leased it to

vinedressers, and went into a far country for a long time.

10 "Now at vintage time he sent a servant to the vinedressers, that they might give him some of the fruit of the vineyard. But the vinedressers beat him and sent *him* away empty-handed.

11 "Again he sent another servant; and they beat him also, treated *him* shamefully, and sent *him* away empty-handed.

12 "And again he sent a third; and they wounded him also and cast *him* out.

13 "Then the owner of the vineyard said, 'What shall I do? I will send my beloved son. Probably they will respect *him* when they see him.'

14 "But when the vinedressers saw him, they reasoned among themselves, saying, 'This is the heir. Come, let us kill him, that the inheritance may be ours.'

15 "So they cast him out of the vineyard and killed *him*. Therefore what will the owner of the vineyard do to them?

16 "He will come and destroy those vinedressers and give the vineyard to others." And when they heard *it* they said, "Certainly not!"

17 And He looked at them and said, "What then is this that is written:

'The stone which the builders rejected
Has become the chief cornerstone'?

18 "Whoever falls on that stone will be broken; but on whomever it falls, it will grind him to powder."

19 And the chief priests and the scribes that very hour sought to lay hands on Him, but they feared the people—for they knew that He had spoken this parable against them.

20 So they watched *Him*, and sent spies who pretended to be righteous, that they might seize on His words, in order to deliver Him to the power and the authority of the governor.

21 And they asked Him, saying, "Teacher, we know that You say and teach rightly, and You do not show personal favoritism, but teach the way of God truly:

22 "Is it lawful for us to pay taxes to Caesar or not?"

23 But He perceived their craftiness, and said to them, "Why do you test Me?

24 "Show Me a denarius. Whose image and inscription does it have?" They answered and said, "Caesar's."

25 And He said to them, "Render therefore to Caesar the things that are Caesar's, and to God the things that are God's."

26 But they could not catch Him in His words in the presence of the people. And they marveled at His answer and kept silent.

27 Then some of the Sadducees, who deny that there is a resurrection, came to *Him* and asked Him,

28 saying: "Teacher, Moses wrote to us *that* if a man's brother dies, having a wife, and he dies without children, his brother should take his wife and raise up offspring for his brother.

29 "Now there were seven brothers. And the first took a wife, and died without children.

30 "And the second took her as wife, and he died childless.

31 "Then the third took her, and in like manner the seven also; and they left no children, and died.

32 "Last of all the woman died also.

33 "Therefore, in the resurrection, whose wife does she become? For all seven had her as wife."

34 And Jesus answered and said to them, "The sons of this age marry and are given in marriage.

35 "But those who are counted worthy to attain that age, and the

resurrection from the dead, neither marry nor are given in marriage; 36 "nor can they die anymore, for they are equal to the angels and are sons of God, being sons of the resurrection.

37 "Now even Moses showed in the *burning* bush *passage* that the dead are raised, when he called the Lord *'the God of Abraham, the God of Isaac, and the God of Jacob.'*

38 "For He is not the God of the dead but of the living, for all live to Him."

39 Then some of the scribes answered and said, "Teacher, You have spoken well."

40 But after that they dared not question Him anymore.

41 And He said to them, "How can they say that the Christ is David's Son?

42 "Now David himself said in the Book of Psalms,

   'The LORD said to my Lord,
    "Sit at My right hand,
43 *Till I make Your enemies*
    Your footstool." '

44 "David therefore calls Him *'Lord'*; how is He then his Son?"

45 Then, in the hearing of all the people, He said to His disciples,

46 "Beware of the scribes, who desire to walk in long robes, love greetings in the marketplaces, the best seats in the synagogues, and the best places at feasts,

47 "who devour widows' houses, and for a pretense make long prayers. These will receive greater condemnation."

21 Then He looked up and saw the rich putting their gifts into the treasury,

2 and he saw also a certain poor widow putting in two mites.

3 So He said, "Truly I say to you that this poor widow has put in more than all;

4 "for all these out of their abun-

dance have put in offerings for God, but she out of her poverty has put in all the livelihood that she had."

5 Then, as some spoke of the temple, how it was adorned with beautiful stones and donations, He said,

6 "As for these things which you see, the days will come in which not one stone shall be left upon another that shall not be thrown down."

7 And they asked Him, saying, "Teacher, but when will these things be? And what sign *will there be* when these things are about to take place?"

8 And He said: "Take heed that you not be deceived. For many will come in My name, saying, 'I am He,' and, 'The time has drawn near.' Therefore do not go after them.

9 "But when you hear of wars and commotions, do not be terrified; for these things must come to pass first, but the end *will not come* immediately."

10 Then He said to them, "Nation will rise against nation, and kingdom against kingdom.

11 "And there will be great earthquakes in various places, and famines and pestilences; and there will be fearful sights and great signs from heaven.

12 "But before all these things, they will lay their hands on *you* and persecute *you,* delivering *you* up to the synagogues and prisons, and you will be brought before kings and rulers for My name's sake.

13 "But it will turn out for you as an occasion for testimony.

14 "Therefore settle *it* in your hearts not to meditate beforehand on what you will answer;

15 "for I will give you a mouth and wisdom which all your adversaries will not be able to contradict or resist.

16 "You will be betrayed even by parents and brothers, relatives and friends; and they will send *some* of you to *your* death.

17 "And you will be hated by all for My name's sake.

18 "But not a hair of your head shall be lost.

19 "In your patience possess your souls.

20 "But when you see Jerusalem surrounded by armies, then know that its desolation is near.

21 "Then let those in Judea flee to the mountains, let those who are in the midst of her depart, and let not those who are in the country enter her.

22 "For these are the days of vengeance, that all things which are written may be fulfilled.

23 "But woe to those who are pregnant and to those who are nursing babies in those days! For there will be great distress in the land and wrath upon this people.

24 "And they will fall by the edge of the sword, and be led away captive into all nations. And Jerusalem will be trampled by Gentiles until the times of the Gentiles are fulfilled.

25 "And there will be signs in the sun, in the moon, and in the stars; and on the earth distress of nations, with perplexity, the sea and the waves roaring;

26 "men's hearts failing them from fear and the expectation of those things which are coming on the earth, for the powers of heaven will be shaken.

27 "Then they will see the Son of Man coming in a cloud with power and great glory.

28 "Now when these things begin to happen, look up and lift up your heads, because your redemption draws near."

29 And He spoke to them a parable: "Look at the fig tree, and all the trees.

30 "When they are already budding, you see and know for yourselves that summer is now near.

31 "So you, likewise, when you see these things happening, know that the kingdom of God is near.

32 "Assuredly, I say to you, this generation will by no means pass away till all things are fulfilled.

33 "Heaven and earth will pass away, but My words will by no means pass away.

34 "But take heed to yourselves, lest your hearts be weighed down with carousing, drunkenness, and cares of this life, and that Day come on you unexpectedly.

35 "For it will come as a snare on all those who dwell on the face of the whole earth.

36 "Watch therefore, and pray always that you may be counted worthy to escape all these things that will come to pass, and to stand before the Son of Man."

37 And in the daytime He was teaching in the temple, but at night He went out and stayed on the mountain called Olivet.

38 Then early in the morning all the people came to Him in the temple to hear Him.

22 Now the Feast of Unleavened Bread drew near, which is called Passover.

2 And the chief priests and the scribes sought how they might kill Him, for they feared the people.

3 Then Satan entered Judas, surnamed Iscariot, who was numbered among the twelve.

4 So he went his way and conferred with the chief priests and captains, how he might betray Him to them.

5 And they were glad, and agreed to give him money.

6 Then he promised and sought opportunity to betray Him to them in the absence of the multitude.

7 Then came the Day of Unleavened Bread, when the Passover must be killed.

8 And He sent Peter and John,

saying, "Go and prepare the Passover for us, that we may eat."

9 So they said to Him, "Where do You want us to prepare?"

10 And He said to them, "Behold, when you have entered the city, a man will meet you carrying a pitcher of water; follow him into the house which he enters.

11 "Then you shall say to the master of the house, 'The Teacher says to you, "Where is the guest room in which I may eat the Passover with My disciples?"'

12 "Then he will show you a large, furnished upper room; there make ready."

13 So they went and found it as He had said to them, and they prepared the Passover.

14 And when the hour had come, He sat down, and the twelve apostles with Him.

15 Then He said to them, "With *fervent* desire I have desired to eat this Passover with you before I suffer;

16 "for I say to you, I will no longer eat of it until it is fulfilled in the kingdom of God."

17 Then He took the cup, and gave thanks, and said, "Take this and divide *it* among yourselves;

18 "for I say to you, I will not drink of the fruit of the vine until the kingdom of God comes."

19 And He took bread, gave thanks and broke *it*, and gave *it* to them, saying, "This is My body which is given for you; do this in remembrance of Me."

20 Likewise He also *took* the cup after supper, saying, "This cup *is* the new covenant in My blood, which is shed for you.

21 "But behold, the hand of My betrayer *is* with Me on the table.

22 "And truly the Son of Man goes as it has been determined, but woe to that man by whom He is betrayed!"

23 Then they began to question among themselves, which of them it was who would do this thing.

24 But there was also rivalry among them, as to which of them should be considered the greatest.

25 And He said to them, "The kings of the Gentiles exercise lordship over them, and those who exercise authority over them are called 'benefactors.'

26 "But not so *among* you; on the contrary, he who is greatest among you, let him be as the younger, and he who governs as he who serves.

27 "For who *is* greater, he who sits at the table, or he who serves? *Is* it not he who sits at the table? Yet I am among you as the One who serves.

28 "But you are those who have continued with Me in My trials.

29 "And I bestow upon you a kingdom, just as My Father bestowed *one* upon Me,

30 "that you may eat and drink at My table in My kingdom, and sit on thrones judging the twelve tribes of Israel."

31 And the Lord said, "Simon, Simon! Indeed, Satan has asked for you, that he may sift *you* as wheat.

32 "But I have prayed for you, that your faith should not fail; and when you have returned to *Me*, strengthen your brethren."

33 But he said to Him, "Lord, I am ready to go with You, both to prison and to death."

34 Then He said, "I tell you, Peter, the rooster will not crow this day before you will deny three times that you know Me."

35 And He said to them, "When I sent you without money bag, sack, and sandals, did you lack anything?" So they said, "Nothing."

36 Then He said to them, "But now, he who has a money bag, let him take *it*, and likewise a sack; and he who has no sword, let him sell his garment and buy one.

37 "For I say to you that this

which is written must still be accomplished in Me: *'And He was numbered with the transgressors.'* For the things concerning Me have an end."

38 Then they said, "Lord, look, here *are* two swords." And He said to them, "It is enough."

39 And coming out, He went to the Mount of Olives, as He was accustomed, and His disciples also followed Him.

40 When He came to the place, He said to them, "Pray that you may not enter into temptation."

41 And He was withdrawn from them about a stone's throw, and He knelt down and prayed,

42 saying, "Father, if it is Your will, remove this cup from Me; nevertheless not My will, but Yours, be done."

43 Then an angel appeared to Him from heaven, strengthening Him.

44 And being in agony, He prayed more earnestly. And His sweat became like great drops of blood falling down to the ground.

45 When He rose up from prayer, and had come to His disciples, He found them sleeping from sorrow.

46 Then He said to them, "Why do you sleep? Rise and pray, lest you enter into temptation."

47 And while He was still speaking, behold, a multitude; and he who was called Judas, one of the twelve, went before them and drew near to Jesus to kiss Him.

48 But Jesus said to him, "Judas, are you betraying the Son of Man with a kiss?"

49 When those around Him saw what was going to happen, they said to Him, "Lord, shall we strike with the sword?"

50 And one of them struck the servant of the high priest and cut off his right ear.

51 But Jesus answered and said, "Permit even this." And He touched his ear and healed him.

52 Then Jesus said to the chief priests, captains of the temple, and the elders who had come to Him, "Have you come out, as against a robber, with swords and clubs?

53 "When I was with you daily in the temple, you did not try to seize Me. But this is your hour, and the power of darkness."

54 Then, having arrested Him, they led *Him* and brought Him into the high priest's house. And Peter followed at a distance.

55 Now when they had kindled a fire in the midst of the courtyard and sat down together, Peter sat among them.

56 And a certain servant girl, seeing him as he sat by the fire, looked intently at him and said, "This man was also with Him."

57 But he denied Him, saying, "Woman, I do not know Him."

58 And after a little while another saw him and said, "You also are of them." But Peter said, "Man, I am not!"

59 Then after about an hour had passed, another confidently affirmed, saying, "Surely this *fellow* also was with Him, for he is a Galilean."

60 But Peter said, "Man, I do not know what you are saying!" And immediately, while he was still speaking, the rooster crowed.

61 And the Lord turned and looked at Peter. And Peter remembered the word of the Lord, how He had said to him, "Before the rooster crows, you will deny Me three times."

62 Then Peter went out and wept bitterly.

63 Now the men who held Jesus mocked Him and beat Him.

64 And having blindfolded Him, they struck Him on the face and asked Him, saying, "Prophesy! Who is it that struck You?"

65 And many other things they blasphemously spoke against Him.

66 As soon as it was day, the elders of the people, both chief priests and scribes, came together and led Him into their council, saying,

67 "If You are the Christ, tell us." But He said to them, "If I tell you, you will by no means believe.

68 "And if I also ask *you*, you will by no means answer Me or let *Me* go.

69 "Hereafter the Son of Man will sit on the right hand of the power of God."

70 Then they all said, "Are You then the Son of God?" And He said to them, "You *rightly* say that I am."

71 And they said, "What further testimony do we need? For we have heard it ourselves from His own mouth."

23 Then the whole multitude of them arose and led Him to Pilate.

2 And they began to accuse Him, saying, "We found this *fellow* perverting the nation, and forbidding to pay taxes to Caesar, saying that He Himself is Christ, a King."

3 So Pilate asked Him, saying, "Are You the King of the Jews?" And He answered him and said, "*It is as* you say."

4 Then Pilate said to the chief priests and the crowd, "I find no fault in this Man."

5 But they were the more fierce, saying, "He stirs up the people, teaching throughout all Judea, beginning from Galilee to this place."

6 When Pilate heard of Galilee, he asked if the Man were a Galilean.

7 And as soon as he knew that He belonged to Herod's jurisdiction, he sent Him to Herod, who was also in Jerusalem at that time.

8 Now when Herod saw Jesus, he was exceedingly glad; for he had desired for a long *time* to see Him, because he had heard many things about Him, and he hoped to see some miracle done by Him.

9 Then he questioned Him with many words, but He answered him nothing.

10 And the chief priests and scribes stood and vehemently accused Him.

11 Then Herod, with his men of war, treated Him with contempt and mocked Him, arrayed Him in a gorgeous robe, and sent Him back to Pilate.

12 That very day Pilate and Herod became friends with each other, for before *that* they had been at enmity with each other.

13 Then Pilate, when he had called together the chief priests, the rulers, and the people,

14 said to them, "You have brought this Man to me, as one who misleads the people. And indeed, having examined *Him* in your presence, I have found no fault in this Man concerning those things of which you accuse Him;

15 "no, neither did Herod, for I sent you back to him; and indeed nothing worthy of death has been done by Him.

16 "I will therefore chastise Him and release *Him*"

17 (for it was necessary for him to release one to them at the feast).

18 And they all cried out at once, saying, "Away with this *Man*, and release to us Barabbas"—

19 who had been thrown into prison for a certain insurrection made in the city, and for murder.

20 Pilate, therefore, wishing to release Jesus, again called out to them.

21 But they shouted, saying, "Crucify *Him*, crucify Him!"

22 And he said to them the third time, "Why, what evil has He done? I have found no reason for death in Him. I will therefore chastise Him and let *Him* go."

23 But they were insistent, demanding with loud voices that He be crucified. And the voices of these men and of the chief priests prevailed.

24 So Pilate gave sentence that it should be as they requested.

25 And he released to them the one they requested, who for insurrection and murder had been thrown into prison; but he delivered Jesus to their will.

26 Now as they led Him away, they laid hold of a certain man, Simon a Cyrenian, who was coming from the country, and on him they laid the cross that he might bear *it* after Jesus.

27 And a great multitude of the people followed Him, and women who also mourned and lamented Him.

28 But Jesus, turning to them, said, "Daughters of Jerusalem, do not weep for Me, but weep for yourselves and for your children.

29 "For indeed the days are coming in which they will say, 'Blessed *are* the barren, *the* wombs which never bore, and *the* breasts which never nursed!'

30 "Then they will begin *'to say to the mountains, "Fall on us!" and to the hills, "Cover us!" '*

31 "For if they do these things in the green wood, what will be done in the dry?"

32 There were also two others, criminals, led with Him to be put to death.

33 And when they had come to the place called Calvary, there they crucified Him, and the criminals, one on the right hand and the other on the left.

34 Then Jesus said, "Father, forgive them, for they do not know what they do." And they divided His garments and cast lots.

35 And the people stood looking on. But even the rulers with them sneered, saying, "He saved others; let Him save Himself if He is the Christ, the chosen of God."

36 And the soldiers also mocked Him, coming and offering Him sour wine,

37 and saying, "If You are the King of the Jews, save Yourself."

38 And an inscription also was written over Him in letters of Greek, Latin, and Hebrew:

THIS IS
THE KING OF THE JEWS.

39 Then one of the criminals who were hanged blasphemed Him, saying, "If You are the Christ, save Yourself and us."

40 But the other, answering, rebuked him, saying, "Do you not even fear God, seeing you are under the same condemnation?

41 "And we indeed justly, for we receive the due reward of our deeds; but this Man has done nothing wrong."

42 Then he said to Jesus, "Lord, remember me when You come into Your kingdom."

43 And Jesus said to him, "Assuredly, I say to you, today you will be with Me in Paradise."

44 And it was about the sixth hour, and there was darkness over all the earth until the ninth hour.

45 Then the sun was darkened, and the veil of the temple was torn in two.

46 And when Jesus had cried out with a loud voice, He said, "Father, *'into Your hands I commend My spirit.'*" And having said this, He breathed His last.

47 Now when the centurion saw what had happened, he glorified God, saying, "Certainly this was a righteous Man!"

48 And the whole crowd who came together to that sight, seeing what had been done, beat their breasts and returned.

49 But all His acquaintances, and the women who followed Him from Galilee, stood at a distance, watching these things.

50 And behold, *there was* a man named Joseph, a council member, a good and just man.

51 He had not consented to their counsel and deed. *He was* from Arimathea, a city of the Jews, who himself was also waiting for the kingdom of God.

52 This *man* went to Pilate and asked for the body of Jesus.

53 Then he took it down, wrapped it in linen, and laid it in a tomb *that was* hewn out of the rock, where no one had ever lain before.

54 That day was the Preparation, and the Sabbath drew near.

55 And the women who had come with Him from Galilee followed after, and they observed the tomb and how His body was laid.

56 Then they returned and prepared spices and fragrant oils. And they rested on the Sabbath according to the commandment.

24 Now on the first *day* of the week, very early in the morning, they, and certain *other women* with them, came to the tomb bringing the spices which they had prepared.

2 But they found the stone rolled away from the tomb.

3 Then they went in and did not find the body of the Lord Jesus.

4 And it happened, as they were greatly perplexed about this, that behold, two men stood by them in shining garments.

5 Then, as they were afraid and bowed *their* faces to the earth, they said to them, "Why do you seek the living among the dead?

6 "He is not here, but is risen! Remember how He spoke to you when He was still in Galilee,

7 "saying, 'The Son of Man must be delivered into the hands of sinful men, and be crucified, and the third day rise again.'"

8 And they remembered His words.

9 Then they returned from the tomb and told all these things to the eleven and to all the rest.

10 It was Mary Magdalene, Joanna, Mary *the mother* of James, and the other *women* with them, who told these things to the apostles.

11 And their words seemed to them like idle tales, and they did not believe them.

12 But Peter arose and ran to the tomb; and stooping down, he saw the linen cloths lying by themselves; and he departed, marveling to himself at what had happened.

13 Now behold, two of them were traveling that same day to a village called Emmaus, which was *about* seven miles from Jerusalem.

14 And they talked together of all these things which had happened.

15 So it was, while they conversed and reasoned, that Jesus Himself drew near and went with them.

16 But their eyes were restrained, so that they did not know Him.

17 And He said to them, "What kind of conversation *is* this that you have with one another as you walk and are sad?"

18 Then the one whose name was Cleopas answered and said to Him, "Are You the only stranger in Jerusalem, and have You not known the things which happened there in these days?"

19 And He said to them, "What things?" And they said to Him, "The things concerning Jesus of Nazareth, who was a Prophet mighty in deed and word before God and all the people,

20 "and how the chief priests and our rulers delivered Him to be condemned to death, and crucified Him.

21 "But we were hoping that it was He who was going to redeem Israel. Indeed, besides all this, today is the third day since these things happened.

22 "Yes, and certain women of our company, who arrived at the tomb early, astonished us.

23 "When they did not find His body, they came saying that they had also seen a vision of angels who said He was alive.

24 "And certain of those *who were* with us went to the tomb and found *it* just as the women had said; but Him they did not see."

25 Then He said to them, "O fool-

ish ones, and slow of heart to believe in all that the prophets have spoken!

26 "Ought not the Christ to have suffered these things and to enter into His glory?"

27 And beginning at Moses and all the Prophets, He expounded to them in all the Scriptures the things concerning Himself.

28 Then they drew near to the village where they were going, and He indicated that He would have gone farther.

29 But they constrained Him, saying, "Abide with us, for it is toward evening, and the day is far spent." And He went in to stay with them.

30 Now it came to pass, as He sat at the table with them, that He took bread, blessed and broke *it*, and gave it to them.

31 Then their eyes were opened and they knew Him; and He vanished from their sight.

32 And they said to one another, "Did not our heart burn within us while He talked with us on the road, and while He opened the Scriptures to us?"

33 So they rose up that very hour and returned to Jerusalem, and found the eleven and those *who were* with them gathered together,

34 saying, "The Lord is risen indeed, and has appeared to Simon!"

35 And they told about the things *that had happened* on the road, and how He was known to them in the breaking of bread.

36 Now as they said these things, Jesus Himself stood in the midst of them, and said to them, "Peace to you."

37 But they were terrified and frightened, and supposed they had seen a spirit.

38 And He said to them, "Why are you troubled? And why do doubts arise in your hearts?

39 "Behold My hands and My feet, that it is I Myself. Handle Me and see, for a spirit does not have flesh and bones as you see I have."

40 When He had said this, He showed them His hands and His feet.

41 But while they still did not believe for joy, and marveled, He said to them, "Have you any food here?"

42 So they gave Him a piece of a broiled fish and some honeycomb.

43 And He took *it* and ate in their presence.

44 Then He said to them, "These *are* the words which I spoke to you while I was still with you, that all things must be fulfilled which were written in the Law of Moses and *the* Prophets and *the* Psalms concerning Me."

45 And He opened their understanding, that they might comprehend the Scriptures.

46 Then He said to them, "Thus it is written, and thus it was necessary for the Christ to suffer and to rise from the dead the third day,

47 "and that repentance and remission of sins should be preached in His name to all nations, beginning at Jerusalem.

48 "And you are witnesses of these things.

49 "Behold, I send the Promise of My Father upon you; but tarry in the city of Jerusalem until you are endued with power from on high."

50 And He led them out as far as Bethany, and He lifted up His hands and blessed them.

51 Now it came to pass, while He blessed them, that He was parted from them and carried up into heaven.

52 And they worshiped Him, and returned to Jerusalem with great joy,

53 and were continually in the temple praising and blessing God. Amen.

THE GOSPEL ACCORDING TO

JOHN

IN the beginning was the Word, and the Word was with God, and the Word was God.

2 He was in the beginning with God.

3 All things were made through Him, and without Him nothing was made that was made.

4 In Him was life, and the life was the light of men.

5 And the light shines in the darkness, and the darkness did not comprehend it.

6 There was a man sent from God, whose name was John.

7 This man came for a witness, to bear witness of the Light, that all through him might believe.

8 He was not that Light, but *was sent* to bear witness of that Light.

9 *That was* the true Light which gives light to every man who comes into the world.

10 He was in the world, and the world was made through Him, and the world did not know Him.

11 He came to His own, and His own did not receive Him.

12 But as many as received Him, to them He gave the right to become children of God, *even* to those who believe in His name:

13 who were born, not of blood, nor of the will of the flesh, nor of the will of man, but of God.

14 And the Word became flesh and dwelt among us, and we beheld His glory, the glory as of the only begotten of the Father, full of grace and truth.

15 John bore witness of Him and cried out, saying, "This was He of whom I said, 'He who comes after me is preferred before me, for He was before me.' "

16 And of His fullness we have all received, and grace for grace.

17 For the law was given through Moses, *but* grace and truth came through Jesus Christ.

18 No one has seen God at any time. The only begotten Son, who is in the bosom of the Father, He has declared *Him.*

19 Now this is the testimony of John, when the Jews sent priests and Levites from Jerusalem to ask him, "Who are you?"

20 He confessed, and did not deny, but confessed, "I am not the Christ."

21 And they asked him, "What then? Are you Elijah?" He said, "I am not." "Are you the Prophet?" And he answered, "No."

22 Then they said to him, "Who are you, that we may give an answer to those who sent us? What do you say about yourself?"

23 He said: "I am

'The voice of one crying in the
    wilderness:
"Make straight the way of the
    Lord," '

as the prophet Isaiah said."

24 Now those who were sent were from the Pharisees.

25 And they asked him, saying, "Why then do you baptize if you are not the Christ, nor Elijah, nor the Prophet?"

26 John answered them, saying, "I baptize with water, but there stands One among you whom you do not know.

27 "It is He who, coming after me, is preferred before me, whose sandal strap I am not worthy to loose."

28 These things were done in Bethabara beyond the Jordan, where John was baptizing.

29 The next day John saw Jesus coming toward him, and said, "Behold! The Lamb of God who takes away the sin of the world!

30 "This is He of whom I said, 'After me comes a Man who is pre-

ferred before me, for He was before me.'

31 "I did not know Him; but that He should be revealed to Israel, therefore I came baptizing with water."

32 And John bore witness, saying, "I saw the Spirit descending from heaven like a dove, and He remained upon Him.

33 "I did not know Him, but He who sent me to baptize with water said to me, 'Upon whom you see the Spirit descending, and remaining on Him, this is He who baptizes with the Holy Spirit.'

34 "And I have seen and testified that this is the Son of God."

35 Again, the next day, John stood with two of his disciples.

36 And looking at Jesus as He walked, he said, "Behold the Lamb of God!"

37 The two disciples heard him speak, and they followed Jesus.

38 Then Jesus turned, and seeing them following, said to them, "What do you seek?" They said to Him, "Rabbi" (which is to say, when translated, Teacher), "where are You staying?"

39 He said to them, "Come and see." They came and saw where He was staying, and remained with Him that day (now it was about the tenth hour).

40 One of the two who heard John *speak*, and followed Him, was Andrew, Simon Peter's brother.

41 He first found his own brother Simon, and said to him, "We have found the Messiah" (which is translated, the Christ).

42 And he brought him to Jesus. Now when Jesus looked at him, He said, "You are Simon the son of Jonah. You shall be called Cephas" (which is translated, A Stone).

43 The following day Jesus wanted to go to Galilee, and He found Philip and said to him, "Follow Me."

44 Now Philip was from Bethsaida, the city of Andrew and Peter.

45 Philip found Nathanael and said to him, "We have found Him of whom Moses in the law, and also the prophets, wrote—Jesus of Nazareth, the son of Joseph."

46 And Nathanael said to him, "Can anything good come out of Nazareth?" Philip said to him, "Come and see."

47 Jesus saw Nathanael coming toward Him, and said of him, "Behold, an Israelite indeed, in whom is no guile!"

48 Nathanael said to Him, "How do You know me?" Jesus answered and said to him, "Before Philip called you, when you were under the fig tree, I saw you."

49 Nathanael answered and said to Him, "Rabbi, You are the Son of God! You are the King of Israel!"

50 Jesus answered and said to him, "Because I said to you, 'I saw you under the fig tree,' do you believe? You will see greater things than these."

51 And He said to him, "Most assuredly, I say to you, hereafter you shall see heaven open, and the angels of God ascending and descending upon the Son of Man."

2 On the third day there was a wedding in Cana of Galilee, and the mother of Jesus was there.

2 Now both Jesus and His disciples were invited to the wedding.

3 And when they ran out of wine, the mother of Jesus said to Him, "They have no wine."

4 Jesus said to her, "Woman, what does your concern have to do with Me? My hour has not yet come."

5 His mother said to the servants, "Whatever He says to you, do *it*."

6 Now there were set there six waterpots of stone, according to the manner of purification of the Jews, containing twenty or thirty gallons apiece.

7 Jesus said to them, "Fill the waterpots with water." And they filled them up to the brim.

8 And He said to them, "Draw

some out now, and take *it* to the master of the feast." And they took *it*.

9 When the master of the feast had tasted the water that was made wine, and did not know where it came from (but the servants who had drawn the water knew), the master of the feast called the bridegroom.

10 And he said to him, "Every man at the beginning sets out the good wine, and when the *guests* have well drunk, then that *which is* inferior; *but* you have kept the good wine until now."

11 This beginning of signs Jesus did in Cana of Galilee, and manifested His glory; and His disciples believed in Him.

12 After this He went down to Capernaum, He, His mother, His brothers, and His disciples; and they did not stay there many days.

13 Now the Passover of the Jews was at hand, and Jesus went up to Jerusalem.

14 And He found in the temple those who sold oxen and sheep and doves, and the moneychangers doing business.

15 When He had made a whip of cords, He drove them all out of the temple, with the sheep and the oxen, and poured out the changers' money and overturned the tables.

16 And He said to those who sold doves, "Take these things away! Do not make My Father's house a house of merchandise!"

17 Then His disciples remembered that it was written, *"Zeal for Your house has eaten Me up."*

18 So the Jews answered and said to Him, "What sign do You show to us, since You do these things?"

19 Jesus answered and said to them, "Destroy this temple, and in three days I will raise it up."

20 Then the Jews said, "It has taken forty-six years to build this temple, and will You raise it up in three days?"

21 But He was speaking of the temple of His body.

22 Therefore, when He had risen from the dead, His disciples remembered that He had said this to them; and they believed the Scripture and the word which Jesus had said.

23 Now when He was in Jerusalem at the Passover, during the feast, many believed in His name when they saw the signs which He did.

24 But Jesus did not commit Himself to them, because He knew all *men,*

25 and had no need that anyone should testify of man, for He knew what was in man.

3 There was a man of the Pharisees named Nicodemus, a ruler of the Jews.

2 This man came to Jesus by night and said to Him, "Rabbi, we know that You are a teacher come from God; for no one can do these signs that You do unless God is with him."

3 Jesus answered and said to him, "Most assuredly, I say to you, unless one is born again, he cannot see the kingdom of God."

4 Nicodemus said to Him, "How can a man be born when he is old? Can he enter a second time into his mother's womb and be born?"

5 Jesus answered, "Most assuredly, I say to you, unless one is born of water and the Spirit, he cannot enter the kingdom of God.

6 "That which is born of the flesh is flesh, and that which is born of the Spirit is spirit.

7 "Do not marvel that I said to you, 'You must be born again.'

8 "The wind blows where it wishes, and you hear the sound of it, but cannot tell where it comes from and where it goes. So is everyone who is born of the Spirit."

9 Nicodemus answered and said to Him, "How can these things be?"

10 Jesus answered and said to him,

Using John 3 to Share the Gospel

- Jesus loves and is concerned for the individual (vv. 1–2, 16–17).

- Religion cannot save (vv. 1–3).

- Church membership cannot save (verses throughout passage).

- Morality, social, economic, or family position cannot save (vv. 1–5).

- Fear keeps people from Christ (v. 2).

- Conviction of sin opens people to Christ (v. 2).

- A person can receive the gift of salvation without having all the answers to spiritual questions (v. 6).

- Salvation is not by feeling, but by faith (vv. 14–15).

- Every person, regardless of his or her life situation, must experience the spiritual birth to become a child of God and go to heaven (vv. 3–5).

- There is only *one* way of salvation—through Jesus Christ. There are not *many* ways. There are not even *two* ways (v. 13).

- The death of Christ on the cross is necessary for the payment for sin (vv. 14–15).

- Every person has been made for eternity. Each will live forever somewhere—in heaven with Christ, or in hell, separated from Him (v. 16).

- God has proven that He is for every person by giving His Son (v. 17).

- Spiritually there are only two groups of people in the world—believers and unbelievers. There is no middle ground (v. 18).

"Are you the teacher of Israel, and do not know these things?

11 "Most assuredly, I say to you, We speak what We know and testify what We have seen, and you do not receive Our witness.

12 "If I have told you earthly things and you do not believe, how will you believe if I tell you heavenly things?

13 "No one has ascended to heaven but He who came down from heaven, *that is,* the Son of Man who is in heaven.

14 "And as Moses lifted up the serpent in the wilderness, even so must the Son of Man be lifted up,

15 "that whoever believes in Him should not perish but have eternal life.

16 "For God so loved the world that He gave His only begotten Son, that whoever believes in Him should not perish but have everlasting life.

17 "For God did not send His Son into the world to condemn the world, but that the world through Him might be saved.

18 "He who believes in Him is not condemned; but he who does not believe is condemned already, because he has not believed in the name of the only begotten Son of God.

19 "And this is the condemnation, that the light has come into the world, and men loved darkness rather than light, because their deeds were evil.

20 "For everyone practicing evil hates the light and does not come to the light, lest his deeds should be exposed.

21 "But he who does the truth comes to the light, that his deeds may be clearly seen, that they have been done in God."

22 After these things Jesus and His disciples came into the land of Judea, and there He remained with them and baptized.

23 Now John also was baptizing in Aenon near Salim, because there was much water there. And they came and were baptized.

24 For John had not yet been thrown into prison.

25 Then there arose a dispute between *some* of John's disciples and the Jews about purification.

26 And they came to John and said to him, "Rabbi, He who was with you beyond the Jordan, to whom you have testified—behold, He is baptizing, and all are coming to Him!"

27 John answered and said, "A man can receive nothing unless it has been given to him from heaven.

28 "You yourselves bear me witness, that I said, 'I am not the Christ,' but, 'I have been sent before Him.'

29 "He who has the bride is the bridegroom; but the friend of the bridegroom, who stands and hears him, rejoices greatly because of the bridegroom's voice. Therefore this joy of mine is fulfilled.

30 "He must increase, but I *must* decrease.

31 "He who comes from above is above all; he who is of the earth is earthly and speaks of the earth. He who comes from heaven is above all.

32 "And what He has seen and heard, that He testifies; and no one receives His testimony.

33 "He who has received His testimony has certified that God is true.

34 "For He whom God has sent speaks the words of God, for God does not give the Spirit by measure.

35 "The Father loves the Son, and has given all things into His hand.

36 "He who believes in the Son has everlasting life; and he who does not believe the Son shall not see life, but the wrath of God abides on him."

4 Therefore, when the Lord knew that the Pharisees had heard that Jesus made and baptized more disciples than John

2 (though Jesus Himself did not baptize, but His disciples),

3 He left Judea and departed again to Galilee.

4 But He needed to go through Samaria.

5 So He came to a city of Samaria which is called Sychar, near the plot of ground that Jacob gave to his son Joseph.

6 Now Jacob's well was there. Jesus therefore, being wearied from *His* journey, sat thus by the well. It was about the sixth hour.

7 A woman of Samaria came to draw water. Jesus said to her, "Give Me a drink."

8 For His disciples had gone away into the city to buy food.

9 Then the woman of Samaria said to Him, "How is it that You, being a Jew, ask a drink from me, a Samaritan woman?" For Jews have no dealings with Samaritans.

10 Jesus answered and said to her, "If you knew the gift of God, and who it is who says to you, 'Give Me a drink,' you would have asked Him, and He would have given you living water."

11 The woman said to Him, "Sir, You have nothing to draw with, and the well is deep. Where then do You get that living water?

12 "Are You greater than our father Jacob, who gave us the well, and drank from it himself, as well as his sons and his livestock?"

13 Jesus answered and said to her, "Whoever drinks of this water will thirst again,

14 "but whoever drinks of the water that I shall give him will never thirst. But the water that I shall give him will become in him a fountain of water springing up into everlasting life."

15 The woman said to Him, "Sir, give me this water, that I may not thirst, nor come here to draw."

16 Jesus said to her, "Go, call your husband, and come here."

17 The woman answered and said, "I have no husband." Jesus said to her, "You have well said, 'I have no husband,'

18 "for you have had five husbands, and the one whom you now have is not your husband; in that you spoke truly."

19 The woman said to Him, "Sir, I perceive that You are a prophet.

20 "Our fathers worshiped on this mountain, and you *Jews* say that in Jerusalem is the place where one ought to worship."

21 Jesus said to her, "Woman, believe Me, the hour is coming when you will neither on this mountain, nor in Jerusalem, worship the Father.

22 "You worship what you do not know; we know what we worship, for salvation is of the Jews.

23 "But the hour is coming, and now is, when the true worshipers will worship the Father in spirit and truth; for the Father is seeking such to worship Him.

24 "God *is* Spirit, and those who worship Him must worship in spirit and truth."

25 The woman said to Him, "I know that Messiah is coming" (who is called Christ). "When He comes, He will tell us all things."

26 Jesus said to her, "I who speak to you am *He*."

27 And at this *point* His disciples came, and they marveled that He talked with a woman; yet no one said, "What do You seek?" or, "Why are You talking with her?"

28 The woman then left her waterpot, went her way into the city, and said to the men,

29 "Come, see a Man who told me all things that I ever did. Could this be the Christ?"

30 Then they went out of the city and came to Him.

31 In the meantime His disciples urged Him, saying, "Rabbi, eat."

32 But He said to them, "I have

food to eat of which you do not know."

33 Therefore the disciples said to one another, "Has anyone brought Him *anything* to eat?"

34 Jesus said to them, "My food is to do the will of Him who sent Me, and to finish His work.

35 "Do you not say, 'There are still four months and *then* comes the harvest'? Behold, I say to you, lift up your eyes and look at the fields, for they are already white for harvest!

36 "And he who reaps receives wages, and gathers fruit for eternal life, that both he who sows and he who reaps may rejoice together.

37 "For in this the saying is true: 'One sows and another reaps.'

38 "I sent you to reap that for which you have not labored; others have labored, and you have entered into their labors."

39 And many of the Samaritans of that city believed in Him because of the word of the woman who testified, "He told me all that I *ever* did."

40 So when the Samaritans had come to Him, they urged Him to stay with them; and He stayed there two days.

41 And many more believed because of His own word.

42 Then they said to the woman, "Now we believe, not because of what you said, for we have heard for ourselves and know that this is indeed the Christ, the Savior of the world."

43 Now after the two days He departed from there and went to Galilee.

44 For Jesus Himself testified that a prophet has no honor in his own country.

45 So when He came to Galilee, the Galileans received Him, having seen all the things He did in Jerusalem at the feast; for they also had gone to the feast.

46 So Jesus came again to Cana of Galilee where He had made the water wine. And there was a certain nobleman whose son was sick at Capernaum.

47 When he heard that Jesus had come out of Judea into Galilee, he went to Him and implored Him to come down and heal his son, for he was at the point of death.

48 Then Jesus said to him, "Unless you *people* see signs and wonders, you will by no means believe."

49 The nobleman said to Him, "Sir, come down before my child dies!"

50 Jesus said to him, "Go your way; your son lives." So the man believed the word that Jesus spoke to him, and he went his way.

51 And as he was now going down, his servants met him and told *him*, saying, "Your son lives!"

52 Then he inquired of them the hour when he got better. And they said to him, "Yesterday at the seventh hour the fever left him."

53 So the father knew that *it was* at the same hour in which Jesus said to him, "Your son lives." And he himself believed, and his whole household.

54 This again *is* the second sign *that* Jesus did when He had come out of Judea into Galilee.

5 After this there was a feast of the Jews, and Jesus went up to Jerusalem.

2 Now there is in Jerusalem by the Sheep *Gate* a pool, which is called in Hebrew, Bethesda, having five porches.

3 In these lay a great multitude of sick people, blind, lame, paralyzed, waiting for the moving of the water.

4 For an angel went down at a certain time into the pool and stirred up the water; then whoever stepped in first, after the stirring of the water, was made well of whatever disease he had.

5 Now a certain man was there who had an infirmity thirty-eight years.

6 When Jesus saw him lying there, and knew that he already had been *in that condition* a long time, He said to him, "Do you want to be made well?"

7 The sick man answered Him, "Sir, I have no man to put me into the pool when the water is stirred up; but while I am coming, another steps down before me."

8 Jesus said to him, "Rise, take up your bed and walk."

9 And immediately the man was made well, took up his bed, and walked. And that day was the Sabbath.

10 The Jews therefore said to him who was cured, "It is the Sabbath; it is not lawful for you to carry *your* bed."

11 He answered them, "He who made me well said to me, 'Take up your bed and walk.' "

12 Then they asked him, "Who is the Man who said to you, 'Take up your bed and walk'?"

13 But the one who was healed did not know who it was, for Jesus had withdrawn, a multitude being in *that* place.

14 Afterward Jesus found him in the temple, and said to him, "See, you have been made well. Sin no more, lest a worse thing come upon you."

15 The man departed and told the Jews that it was Jesus who had made him well.

16 For this reason the Jews persecuted Jesus, and sought to kill Him, because He had done these things on the Sabbath.

17 But Jesus answered them, "My Father has been working until now, and I have been working."

18 Therefore the Jews sought all the more to kill Him, because He not only broke the Sabbath, but also said that God was His Father, making Himself equal with God.

19 Then Jesus answered and said to them, "Most assuredly, I say to you, the Son can do nothing of Himself, but what He sees the Father do; for whatever He does, the Son also does in like manner.

20 "For the Father loves the Son, and shows Him all things that He Himself does; and He will show Him greater works than these, that you may marvel.

21 "For as the Father raises the dead and gives life to *them,* even so the Son gives life to whom He will.

22 "For the Father judges no one, but has committed all judgment to the Son,

23 "that all should honor the Son just as they honor the Father. He who does not honor the Son does not honor the Father who sent Him.

24 "Most assuredly, I say to you, he who hears My word and believes in Him who sent Me has everlasting life, and shall not come into judgment, but has passed from death into life.

25 "Most assuredly, I say to you, the hour is coming, and now is, when the dead will hear the voice of the Son of God; and those who hear will live.

26 "For as the Father has life in Himself, so He has granted the Son to have life in Himself,

27 "and has given Him authority to execute judgment also, because He is the Son of Man.

28 "Do not marvel at this; for the hour is coming in which all who are in the graves will hear His voice

29 "and come forth—those who have done good, to the resurrection of life, and those who have done evil, to the resurrection of condemnation.

30 "I can of Myself do nothing. As I hear, I judge; and My judgment is righteous, because I do not seek My own will but the will of the Father who sent Me.

31 "If I bear witness of Myself, My witness is not true.

32 "There is another who bears witness of Me, and I know that the witness which He witnesses of Me is true.

33 "You have sent to John, and he has borne witness to the truth.

34 "Yet I do not receive testimony from man, but I say these things that you may be saved.

35 "He was the burning and shining lamp, and you were willing for a time to rejoice in his light.

36 "But I have a greater witness than John's; for the works which the Father has given Me to finish—the very works that I do—bear witness of Me, that the Father has sent Me.

37 "And the Father Himself, who sent Me, has testified of Me. You have neither heard His voice at any time, nor seen His form.

38 "But you do not have His word abiding in you, because whom He sent, Him you do not believe.

39 "You search the Scriptures, for in them you think you have eternal life; and these are they which testify of Me.

40 "But you are not willing to come to Me that you may have life.

41 "I do not receive honor from men.

42 "But I know you, that you do not have the love of God in you.

43 "I have come in My Father's name, and you do not receive Me; if another comes in his own name, him you will receive.

44 "How can you believe, who receive honor from one another, and do not seek the honor that *comes* from the only God?

45 "Do not think that I shall accuse you to the Father; there is *one* who accuses you—Moses, in whom you trust.

46 "For if you believed Moses, you would believe Me; for he wrote about Me.

47 "But if you do not believe his writings, how will you believe My words?"

6 After these things Jesus went over the Sea of Galilee, which is *the Sea* of Tiberias.

2 Then a great multitude followed Him, because they saw His signs which He performed on those who were diseased.

3 And Jesus went up on a mountain, and there He sat with His disciples.

4 Now the Passover, a feast of the Jews, was near.

5 Then Jesus lifted up *His* eyes, and seeing a great multitude coming toward Him, He said to Philip, "Where shall we buy bread, that these may eat?"

6 But this He said to test him, for He Himself knew what He would do.

7 Philip answered Him, "Two hundred denarii worth of bread is not sufficient for them, that every one of them may have a little."

8 One of His disciples, Andrew, Simon Peter's brother, said to Him,

9 "There is a lad here who has five barley loaves and two small fish, but what are they among so many?"

10 Then Jesus said, "Make the people sit down." Now there was much grass in the place. So the men sat down, in number about five thousand.

11 And Jesus took the loaves, and when He had given thanks He distributed *them* to the disciples, and the disciples to those sitting down; and likewise of the fish, as much as they wanted.

12 So when they were filled, He said to His disciples, "Gather up the fragments that remain, so that nothing is lost."

13 Therefore they gathered *them* up, and filled twelve baskets with the fragments of the five barley loaves which were left over by those who had eaten.

14 Then those men, when they had seen the sign that Jesus did, said, "This is truly the Prophet who is to come into the world."

15 Therefore when Jesus perceived that they were about to come and take Him by force to make Him king, He departed again to a mountain by Himself alone.

16 And when evening came, His disciples went down to the sea,

17 got into the boat, and went over the sea toward Capernaum. And it was now dark, and Jesus had not come to them.

18 Then the sea arose because a great wind was blowing.

19 So when they had rowed about three or four miles, they saw Jesus walking on the sea and drawing near the boat; and they were afraid.

20 But He said to them, "It is I; do not be afraid."

21 Then they willingly received Him into the boat, and immediately the boat was at the land where they were going.

22 On the following day, when the people who were standing on the other side of the sea saw that there was no other boat there, except that one which His disciples had entered, and that Jesus had not entered the boat with His disciples, but His disciples had gone away alone—

23 however, other boats came from Tiberias, near the place where they ate bread after the Lord had given thanks—

24 when the people therefore saw that Jesus was not there, nor His disciples, they also got into boats and came to Capernaum, seeking Jesus.

25 And when they found Him on the other side of the sea, they said to Him, "Rabbi, when did You come here?"

26 Jesus answered them and said, "Most assuredly, I say to you, you seek Me, not because you saw the signs, but because you ate of the loaves and were filled.

27 "Do not labor for the food which perishes, but for the food which endures to everlasting life, which the Son of Man will give you, because God the Father has set His seal on Him."

28 Then they said to Him, "What shall we do, that we may work the works of God?"

29 Jesus answered and said to them, "This is the work of God, that you believe in Him whom He sent."

30 Therefore they said to Him, "What sign will You perform then, that we may see it and believe You? What work will You do?

31 "Our fathers ate the manna in the desert; as it is written, *'He gave them bread from heaven to eat.'*"

32 Then Jesus said to them, "Most assuredly, I say to you, Moses did not give you the bread from heaven, but My Father gives you the true bread from heaven.

33 "For the bread of God is He who comes down from heaven and gives life to the world."

34 Then they said to Him, "Lord, give us this bread always."

35 And Jesus said to them, "I am the bread of life. He who comes to Me shall never hunger, and he who believes in Me shall never thirst.

36 "But I said to you that you have seen Me and yet do not believe.

37 "All that the Father gives Me will come to Me, and the one who comes to Me I will by no means cast out.

38 "For I have come down from heaven, not to do My own will, but the will of Him who sent Me.

39 "This is the will of the Father who sent Me, that of all He has given Me I should lose nothing, but should raise it up at the last day.

40 "And this is the will of Him who sent Me, that everyone who sees the Son and believes in Him may have everlasting life; and I will raise him up at the last day."

41 The Jews then murmured against Him, because He said, "I

120

am the bread which came down from heaven."

42 And they said, "Is not this Jesus, the son of Joseph, whose father and mother we know? How is it then that He says, 'I have come down from heaven'?"

43 Jesus therefore answered and said to them, "Do not murmur among yourselves.

44 "No one can come to Me unless the Father who sent Me draws him; and I will raise him up at the last day.

45 "It is written in the prophets, *'And they shall all be taught by God.'* Therefore everyone who has heard and learned from the Father comes to Me.

46 "Not that anyone has seen the Father, except He who is from God; He has seen the Father.

47 "Most assuredly, I say to you, he who believes in Me has everlasting life.

48 "I am the bread of life.

49 "Your fathers ate the manna in the wilderness, and are dead.

50 "This is the bread which comes down from heaven, that one may eat of it and not die.

51 "I am the living bread which came down from heaven. If anyone eats of this bread, he will live forever; and the bread that I shall give is My flesh, which I shall give for the life of the world."

52 The Jews therefore quarreled among themselves, saying, "How can this *Man* give us *His* flesh to eat?"

53 Then Jesus said to them, "Most assuredly, I say to you, unless you eat the flesh of the Son of Man and drink His blood, you have no life in you.

54 "Whoever eats My flesh and drinks My blood has eternal life, and I will raise him up at the last day.

55 "For My flesh is food indeed, and My blood is drink indeed.

56 "He who eats My flesh and drinks My blood abides in Me, and I in him.

57 "As the living Father sent Me, and I live because of the Father, so he who feeds on Me will live because of Me.

58 "This is the bread which came down from heaven—not as your fathers ate the manna, and are dead. He who eats this bread will live forever."

59 These things He said in the synagogue as He taught in Capernaum.

60 Therefore many of His disciples, when they heard *this*, said, "This is a hard saying; who can understand it?"

61 When Jesus knew in Himself that His disciples murmured about this, He said to them, "Does this offend you?

62 "*What* then if you should see the Son of Man ascend where He was before?

63 "It is the Spirit who gives life; the flesh profits nothing. The words that I speak to you are spirit, and *they* are life.

64 "But there are some of you who do not believe." For Jesus knew from the beginning who they were who did not believe, and who would betray Him.

65 And He said, "Therefore I have said to you that no one can come to Me unless it has been granted to him by My Father."

66 From that *time* many of His disciples went back and walked with Him no more.

67 Then Jesus said to the twelve, "Do you also want to go away?"

68 Then Simon Peter answered Him, "Lord, to whom shall we go? You have the words of eternal life.

69 "Also we have come to believe and know that You are the Christ, the Son of the living God."

70 Jesus answered them, "Did I not choose you, the twelve, and one of you is a devil?"

71 He spoke of Judas Iscariot, *the*

son of Simon, for it was he who would betray Him, being one of the twelve.

7 After these things Jesus walked in Galilee; for He did not want to walk in Judea, because the Jews sought to kill Him.

2 Now the Jews' Feast of Tabernacles was at hand.

3 His brothers therefore said to Him, "Depart from here and go into Judea, that Your disciples also may see the works that You are doing.

4 "For no one does anything in secret while he himself seeks to be known openly. If You do these things, show Yourself to the world."

5 For even His brothers did not believe in Him.

6 Then Jesus said to them, "My time has not yet come, but your time is always ready.

7 "The world cannot hate you, but it hates Me because I testify of it that its works are evil.

8 "You go up to this feast. I am not yet going up to this feast, for My time has not yet fully come."

9 When He had said these things to them, He remained in Galilee.

10 But when His brothers had gone up, then He also went up to the feast, not openly, but as it were in secret.

11 Then the Jews sought Him at the feast, and said, "Where is He?"

12 And there was much murmuring among the people concerning Him. Some said, "He is good"; others said, "No, on the contrary, He deceives the people."

13 However, no one spoke openly of Him for fear of the Jews.

14 Now about the middle of the feast Jesus went up into the temple and taught.

15 And the Jews marveled, saying, "How does this Man know letters, having never studied?"

16 Jesus answered them and said, "My doctrine is not Mine, but His who sent Me.

17 "If anyone wants to do His will, he shall know concerning the doctrine, whether it is from God or *whether* I speak on My own *authority*.

18 "He who speaks from himself seeks his own glory; but He who seeks the glory of the One who sent Him is true, and no unrighteousness is in Him.

19 "Did not Moses give you the law, and *yet* none of you keeps the law? Why do you seek to kill Me?"

20 The people answered and said, "You have a demon. Who is seeking to kill You?"

21 Jesus answered and said to them, "I did one work, and you all marvel.

22 "Moses therefore gave you circumcision (not that it is from Moses, but from the fathers), and you circumcise a man on the Sabbath.

23 "If a man receives circumcision on the Sabbath, so that the law of Moses should not be broken, are you angry with Me because I made a man completely well on the Sabbath?

24 "Do not judge according to appearance, but judge with righteous judgment."

25 Then some of them from Jerusalem said, "Is this not He whom they seek to kill?

26 "But look! He speaks boldly, and they say nothing to Him. Do the rulers know indeed that this is truly the Christ?

27 "However, we know where this Man is from; but when the Christ comes, no one knows where He is from."

28 Then Jesus cried out, as He taught in the temple, saying, "You both know Me, and you know where I am from; and I have not come of Myself, but He who sent Me is true, whom you do not know.

29 "But I know Him, for I am from Him, and He sent Me."

30 Then they sought to take Him; but no one laid a hand on Him,

because His hour had not yet come.

31 And many of the people believed in Him, and said, "When the Christ comes, will He do more signs than these which this *Man* has done?"

32 The Pharisees heard the crowd murmuring these things concerning Him, and the Pharisees and the chief priests sent officers to take Him.

33 Then Jesus said to them, "I shall be with you a little while longer, and *then* I go to Him who sent Me.

34 "You will seek Me and not find *Me*, and where I am you cannot come."

35 Then the Jews said among themselves, "Where does He intend to go that we shall not find Him? Does He intend to go to the Dispersion among the Greeks and teach the Greeks?

36 "What is this thing that He said, 'You will seek Me and not find Me, and where I am you cannot come'?"

37 On the last day, that great *day* of the feast, Jesus stood and cried out, saying, "If anyone thirsts, let him come to Me and drink.

38 "He who believes in Me, as the Scripture has said, out of his heart will flow rivers of living water."

39 But this He spoke concerning the Spirit, whom those believing in Him would receive; for the Holy Spirit was not yet *given*, because Jesus was not yet glorified.

40 Therefore many from the crowd, when they heard this saying, said, "Truly this is the Prophet."

41 Others said, "This is the Christ," but some said, "Will the Christ come out of Galilee?

42 "Has not the Scripture said that the Christ comes from the seed of David and from the town of Bethlehem, where David was?"

43 So there was a division among the people because of Him.

44 Now some of them wanted to take Him, but no one laid hands on Him.

45 Then the officers came to the chief priests and Pharisees, who said to them, "Why have you not brought Him?"

46 The officers answered, "No man ever spoke like this Man!"

47 Then the Pharisees answered them, "Are you also deceived?

48 "Have any of the rulers or the Pharisees believed in Him?

49 "But this crowd that does not know the law is accursed."

50 Nicodemus (he who came to Jesus by night, being one of them) said to them,

51 "Does our law judge a man before it hears him and knows what he is doing?"

52 They answered and said to him, "Are you also from Galilee? Search and look, for no prophet has arisen out of Galilee."

53 And everyone went to his *own* house.

8 But Jesus went to the Mount of Olives.

2 But early in the morning He came again into the temple, and all the people came to Him; and He sat down and taught them.

3 Then the scribes and Pharisees brought to Him a woman caught in adultery. And when they had set her in the midst,

4 they said to Him, "Teacher, this woman was caught in adultery, in the very act.

5 "Now Moses, in the law, commanded us that such should be stoned. But what do You say?"

6 This they said, testing Him, that they might have *something* of which to accuse Him. But Jesus stooped down and wrote on the ground with *His* finger, as though He did not hear.

7 So when they continued asking Him, He raised Himself up and said to them, "He who is without sin among you, let him throw a stone at her first."

8 And again He stooped down and wrote on the ground.

9 Then those who heard *it*, being convicted by *their* conscience, went out one by one, beginning with the oldest *even* to the last. And Jesus was left alone, and the woman standing in the midst.

10 When Jesus had raised Himself up and saw no one but the woman, He said to her, "Woman, where are those accusers of yours? Has no one condemned you?"

11 She said, "No one, Lord." And Jesus said to her, "Neither do I condemn you; go and sin no more."

12 Then Jesus spoke to them again, saying, "I am the light of the world. He who follows Me shall not walk in darkness, but have the light of life."

13 The Pharisees therefore said to Him, "You bear witness of Yourself; Your witness is not true."

14 Jesus answered and said to them, "Even if I bear witness of Myself, My witness is true, for I know where I came from and where I am going; but you do not know where I come from and where I am going.

15 "You judge according to the flesh; I judge no one.

16 "And yet if I do judge, My judgment is true; for I am not alone, but I *am* with the Father who sent Me.

17 "It is also written in your law that the testimony of two men is true.

18 "I am One who bears witness of Myself, and the Father who sent Me bears witness of Me."

19 Then they said to Him, "Where is Your Father?" Jesus answered, "You know neither Me nor My Father. If you had known Me, you would have known My Father also."

20 These words Jesus spoke in the treasury, as He taught in the temple; and no one laid hands on Him, for His hour had not yet come.

21 Then Jesus said to them again, "I am going away, and you will seek Me, and will die in your sin. Where I go you cannot come."

22 So the Jews said, "Will He kill Himself, because He says, 'Where I go you cannot come'?"

23 And He said to them, "You are from beneath; I am from above. You are of this world; I am not of this world.

24 "Therefore I said to you that you will die in your sins; for if you do not believe that I am *He*, you will die in your sins."

25 Then they said to Him, "Who are You?" And Jesus said to them, "Just what I have been saying to you from the beginning.

26 "I have many things to say and to judge concerning you, but He who sent Me is true; and I speak to the world those things which I heard from Him."

27 They did not understand that He spoke to them of the Father.

28 Then Jesus said to them, "When you lift up the Son of Man, then you will know that I am *He*, and *that* I do nothing of Myself; but as My Father taught Me, I speak these things.

29 "And He who sent Me is with Me. The Father has not left Me alone, for I always do those things that please Him."

30 As He spoke these words, many believed in Him.

31 Then Jesus said to those Jews who believed Him, "If you abide in My word, you are My disciples indeed.

32 "And you shall know the truth, and the truth shall make you free."

33 They answered Him, "We are Abraham's descendants, and have never been in bondage to anyone. How *can* you say, 'You will be made free'?"

34 Jesus answered them, "Most assuredly, I say to you, whoever commits sin is a slave of sin.

35 "And a slave does not abide in

the house forever, *but* a son abides forever.

36 "Therefore if the Son makes you free, you shall be free indeed.

37 "I know that you are Abraham's descendants, but you seek to kill Me, because My word has no place in you.

38 "I speak what I have seen with My Father, and you do what you have seen with your father."

39 They answered and said to Him, "Abraham is our father." Jesus said to them, "If you were Abraham's children, you would do the works of Abraham.

40 "But now you seek to kill Me, a Man who has told you the truth which I heard from God. Abraham did not do this.

41 "You do the deeds of your father." Then they said to Him, "We were not born of fornication; we have one Father—God."

42 Jesus said to them, "If God were your Father, you would love Me, for I proceeded forth and came from God; nor have I come of Myself, but He sent Me.

43 "Why do you not understand My speech? Because you are not able to listen to My word.

44 "You are of *your* father the devil, and the desires of your father you want to do. He was a murderer from the beginning, and *does not* stand in the truth, because there is no truth in him. When he speaks a lie, he speaks from his own *resources*, for he is a liar and the father of it.

45 "But because I tell the truth, you do not believe Me.

46 "Which of you convicts Me of sin? And if I tell the truth, why do you not believe Me?

47 "He who is of God hears God's words; therefore you do not hear, because you are not of God."

48 Then the Jews answered and said to Him, "Do we not say rightly that You are a Samaritan and have a demon?"

49 Jesus answered, "I do not have a demon; but I honor My Father, and you dishonor Me.

50 "And I do not seek My *own* glory; there is One who seeks and judges.

51 "Most assuredly, I say to you, if anyone keeps My word he shall never see death."

52 Then the Jews said to Him, "Now we know that You have a demon! Abraham is dead, and the prophets; and You say, 'If anyone keeps My word he shall never taste death.'

53 "Are You greater than our father Abraham, who is dead? And the prophets are dead. Who do You make Yourself out to be?"

54 Jesus answered, "If I honor Myself, My honor is nothing. It is My Father who honors Me, of whom you say that He is your God.

55 "Yet you have not known Him, but I know Him. And if I say, 'I do not know Him,' I shall be a liar like you; but I do know Him and keep His word.

56 "Your father Abraham rejoiced to see My day, and he saw *it* and was glad."

57 Then the Jews said to Him, "You are not yet fifty years old, and have You seen Abraham?"

58 Jesus said to them, "Most assuredly, I say to you, before Abraham was, I AM."

59 Then they took up stones to throw at Him; but Jesus hid Himself and went out of the temple, going through the midst of them, and so passed by.

9 Now as *Jesus* passed by, He saw a man who was blind from birth.

2 And His disciples asked Him, saying, "Rabbi, who sinned, this man or his parents, that he was born blind?"

3 Jesus answered, "Neither this man nor his parents sinned, but that the works of God should be revealed in him.

4 "I must work the works of Him who sent Me while it is day; *the* night is coming when no one can work.

5 "As long as I am in the world, I am the light of the world."

6 When He had said these things, He spat on the ground and made clay with the saliva; and He anointed the eyes of the blind man with the clay.

7 And He said to him, "Go, wash in the pool of Siloam" (which is translated, Sent). So he went and washed, and came back seeing.

8 Therefore the neighbors and those who previously had seen that he was blind said, "Is not this he who sat and begged?"

9 Some said, "This is he." Others *said,* "He is like him." He said, "I am *he.*"

10 Therefore they said to him, "How were your eyes opened?"

11 He answered and said, "A Man called Jesus made clay and anointed my eyes and said to me, 'Go to the pool of Siloam and wash.' So I went and washed, and I received sight."

12 Then they said to him, "Where is He?" He said, "I do not know."

13 They brought him who formerly was blind to the Pharisees.

14 Now it was a Sabbath when Jesus made the clay and opened his eyes.

15 Then the Pharisees also asked him again how he had received his sight. He said to them, "He put clay on my eyes, and I washed, and I see."

16 Therefore some of the Pharisees said, "This Man is not from God, because He does not keep the Sabbath." Others said, "How can a man who is a sinner do such signs?" And there was a division among them.

17 They said to the blind man again, "What do you say about Him because He opened your eyes?" He said, "He is a prophet."

18 But the Jews did not believe concerning him, that he had been blind and received his sight, until they called the parents of him who had received his sight.

19 And they asked them, saying, "Is this your son, who you say was born blind? How then does he now see?"

20 His parents answered them and said, "We know that this is our son, and that he was born blind;

21 "but by what means he now sees we do not know, or who opened his eyes we do not know. He is of age; ask him. He will speak for himself."

22 His parents said these *things* because they feared the Jews, for the Jews had agreed already that if anyone confessed *that* He *was* Christ, he would be put out of the synagogue.

23 Therefore his parents said, "He is of age; ask him."

24 So they again called the man who was blind, and said to him, "Give God the glory! We know that this Man is a sinner."

25 He answered and said, "Whether He is a sinner *or not* I do not know. One thing I know: that though I was blind, now I see."

26 Then they said to him again, "What did He do to you? How did He open your eyes?"

27 He answered them, "I told you already, and you did not listen. Why do you want to hear *it* again? Do you also want to become His disciples?"

28 Then they reviled him and said, "You are His disciple, but we are Moses' disciples.

29 "We know that God spoke to Moses; *as for* this *fellow,* we do not know where He is from."

30 The man answered and said to them, "Why, this is a marvelous thing, that you do not know where He is from, and *yet* He has opened my eyes!

31 "Now we know that God does

not hear sinners; but if anyone is a worshiper of God and does His will, He hears him.

32 "Since the world began it has been unheard of that anyone opened the eyes of one who was born blind.

33 "If this Man were not from God, He could do nothing."

34 They answered and said to him, "You were completely born in sins, and are you teaching us?" And they cast him out.

35 Jesus heard that they had cast him out; and when He had found him, He said to him, "Do you believe in the Son of God?"

36 He answered and said, "Who is He, Lord, that I may believe in Him?"

37 And Jesus said to him, "You have both seen Him and it is He who is talking with you."

38 Then he said, "Lord, I believe!" And he worshiped Him.

39 And Jesus said, "For judgment I have come into this world, that those who do not see may see, and that those who see may be made blind."

40 Then *some* of the Pharisees who were with Him heard these words, and said to Him, "Are we blind also?"

41 Jesus said to them, "If you were blind, you would have no sin; but now you say, 'We see.' Therefore your sin remains.

10 "Most assuredly, I say to you, he who does not enter the sheepfold by the door, but climbs up some other way, the same is a thief and a robber.

2 "But he who enters by the door is the shepherd of the sheep.

3 "To him the doorkeeper opens, and the sheep hear his voice; and he calls his own sheep by name and leads them out.

4 "And when he brings out his own sheep, he goes before them; and the sheep follow him, for they know his voice.

5 "Yet they will by no means follow a stranger, but will flee from him, for they do not know the voice of strangers."

6 Jesus used this illustration, but they did not understand the things which He spoke to them.

7 Then Jesus said to them again, "Most assuredly, I say to you, I am the door of the sheep.

8 "All who *ever* came before Me are thieves and robbers, but the sheep did not hear them.

9 "I am the door. If anyone enters by Me, he will be saved, and will go in and out and find pasture.

10 "The thief does not come except to steal, and to kill, and to destroy. I have come that they may have life, and that they may have *it* more abundantly.

11 "I am the good shepherd. The good shepherd gives His life for the sheep.

12 "But *he who is* a hireling and not the shepherd, one who does not own the sheep, sees the wolf coming and leaves the sheep and flees; and the wolf catches the sheep and scatters them.

13 "The hireling flees because he is a hireling and does not care about the sheep.

14 "I am the good shepherd; and I know My *sheep*, and am known by My own.

15 "As the Father knows Me, even so I know the Father; and I lay down My life for the sheep.

16 "And other sheep I have which are not of this fold; them also I must bring, and they will hear My voice; and there will be one flock *and* one shepherd.

17 "Therefore My Father loves Me, because I lay down My life that I may take it again.

18 "No one takes it from Me, but I lay it down of Myself. I have power to lay it down, and I have power to take it again. This command I have received from My Father."

19 Therefore there was a division

127

again among the Jews because of these sayings.

20 And many of them said, "He has a demon and is mad. Why do you listen to Him?"

21 Others said, "These are not the words of one who has a demon. Can a demon open the eyes of the blind?"

22 Now it was the Feast of Dedication in Jerusalem, and it was winter.

23 And Jesus walked in the temple, in Solomon's porch.

24 Then the Jews surrounded Him and said to Him, "How long do You keep us in doubt? If You are the Christ, tell us plainly."

25 Jesus answered them, "I told you, and you do not believe. The works that I do in My Father's name, they bear witness of Me.

26 "But you do not believe, because you are not of My sheep, as I said to you.

27 "My sheep hear My voice, and I know them, and they follow Me.

28 "And I give them eternal life, and they shall never perish; neither shall anyone snatch them out of My hand.

29 "My Father, who has given *them* to Me, is greater than all; and no one is able to snatch *them* out of My Father's hand.

30 "I and *My* Father are one."

31 Then the Jews took up stones again to stone Him.

32 Jesus answered them, "Many good works I have shown you from My Father. For which of those works do you stone Me?"

33 The Jews answered Him, saying, "For a good work we do not stone You, but for blasphemy, and because You, being a Man, make Yourself God."

34 Jesus answered them, "Is it not written in your law, *'I said, "You are gods"* '?

35 "If He called them gods, to whom the word of God came (and the Scripture cannot be broken),

36 "do you say of Him whom the Father sanctified and sent into the world, 'You are blaspheming,' because I said, 'I am the Son of God'?

37 "If I do not do the works of My Father, do not believe Me;

38 "but if I do, though you do not believe Me, believe the works, that you may know and believe that the Father *is* in Me, and I in Him."

39 Therefore they sought again to seize Him, but He escaped out of their hand.

40 And He went away again beyond the Jordan to the place where John was baptizing at first, and there He stayed.

41 Then many came to Him and said, "John performed no sign, but all the things that John spoke about this Man were true."

42 And many believed in Him there.

11 Now a certain *man* was sick, Lazarus of Bethany, the town of Mary and her sister Martha.

2 It was *that* Mary who anointed the Lord with fragrant oil and wiped His feet with her hair, whose brother Lazarus was sick.

3 Therefore the sisters sent to Him, saying, "Lord, behold, he whom You love is sick."

4 When Jesus heard *that*, He said, "This sickness is not unto death, but for the glory of God, that the Son of God may be glorified through it."

5 Now Jesus loved Martha and her sister and Lazarus.

6 So, when He heard that he was sick, He stayed two more days in the place where He was.

7 Then after this He said to *the* disciples, "Let us go to Judea again."

8 *The* disciples said to Him, "Rabbi, lately the Jews sought to stone You, and are You going there again?"

9 Jesus answered, "Are there not twelve hours in the day? If anyone

walks in the day, he does not stumble, because he sees the light of this world.

10 "But if one walks in the night, he stumbles, because the light is not in him."

11 These things He said, and after that He said to them, "Our friend Lazarus sleeps, but I go that I may wake him up."

12 Then His disciples said, "Lord, if he sleeps he will get well."

13 However, Jesus spoke of his death, but they thought that He was speaking about taking rest in sleep.

14 Then Jesus said to them plainly, "Lazarus is dead.

15 "And I am glad for your sakes that I was not there, that you may believe. Nevertheless let us go to him."

16 Then Thomas, who is called Didymus, said to his fellow disciples, "Let us also go, that we may die with Him."

17 So when Jesus came, He found that he had already been in the tomb four days.

18 Now Bethany was near Jerusalem, about two miles away.

19 And many of the Jews had joined the women around Martha and Mary, to comfort them concerning their brother.

20 Then Martha, as soon as she heard that Jesus was coming, went and met Him, but Mary was sitting in the house.

21 Then Martha said to Jesus, "Lord, if You had been here, my brother would not have died.

22 "But even now I know that whatever You ask of God, God will give You."

23 Jesus said to her, "Your brother will rise again."

24 Martha said to Him, "I know that he will rise again in the resurrection at the last day."

25 Jesus said to her, "I am the resurrection and the life. He who believes in Me, though he may die, he shall live.

26 "And whoever lives and believes in Me shall never die. Do you believe this?"

27 She said to Him, "Yes, Lord, I believe that You are the Christ, the Son of God, who is to come into the world."

28 And when she had said these things, she went her way and secretly called Mary her sister, saying, "The Teacher has come and is calling for you."

29 As soon as she heard *that*, she arose quickly and came to Him.

30 Now Jesus had not yet come into the town, but was in the place where Martha met Him.

31 Then the Jews who were with her in the house, and comforting her, when they saw that Mary rose up quickly and went out, followed her, saying, "She is going to the tomb to weep there."

32 Then, when Mary came where Jesus was, and saw Him, she fell down at His feet, saying to Him, "Lord, if You had been here, my brother would not have died."

33 Therefore, when Jesus saw her weeping, and the Jews who came with her weeping, He groaned in the spirit and was troubled.

34 And He said, "Where have you laid him?" They said to Him, "Lord, come and see."

35 Jesus wept.

36 Then the Jews said, "See how He loved him!"

37 And some of them said, "Could not this Man, who opened the eyes of the blind, also have kept this man from dying?"

38 Then Jesus, again groaning in Himself, came to the tomb. It was a cave, and a stone lay against it.

39 Jesus said, "Take away the stone." Martha, the sister of him who was dead, said to Him, "Lord, by this time there is a stench, for he has been *dead* four days."

40 Jesus said to her, "Did I not say to you that if you would believe you would see the glory of God?"

41 Then they took away the stone

from the place where the dead man was lying. And Jesus lifted up *His* eyes and said, "Father, I thank You that You have heard Me.

42 "And I know that You always hear Me, but because of the people who are standing by I said *this*, that they may believe that You sent Me."

43 Now when He had said these things, He cried with a loud voice, "Lazarus, come forth!"

44 And he who had died came out bound hand and foot with grave-clothes, and his face was wrapped with a cloth. Jesus said to them, "Loose him, and let him go."

45 Then many of the Jews who had come to Mary, and had seen the things Jesus did, believed in Him.

46 But some of them went away to the Pharisees and told them the things Jesus did.

47 Then the chief priests and the Pharisees gathered a council and said, "What shall we do? For this Man works many signs.

48 "If we let Him alone like this, everyone will believe in Him, and the Romans will come and take away both our place and nation."

49 And one of them, Caiaphas, being high priest that year, said to them, "You know nothing at all,

50 "nor do you consider that it is expedient for us that one man should die for the people, and not that the whole nation should perish."

51 Now this he did not say on his own *authority*; but being high priest that year he prophesied that Jesus would die for the nation,

52 and not for that nation only, but also that He would gather together in one the children of God who were scattered abroad.

53 Then from that day on they plotted to put Him to death.

54 Therefore Jesus no longer walked openly among the Jews, but went from there into the country near the wilderness, to a city called Ephraim, and there remained with His disciples.

55 And the Passover of the Jews was near, and many went from the country up to Jerusalem before the Passover, to purify themselves.

56 Then they sought Jesus, and spoke among themselves as they stood in the temple, "What do you think—that He will not come to the feast?"

57 Now both the chief priests and the Pharisees had given a command, that if anyone knew where He was, he should report *it*, that they might seize Him.

12 Then, six days before the Passover, Jesus came to Bethany, where Lazarus was who had been dead, whom He had raised from the dead.

2 There they made Him a supper; and Martha served, but Lazarus was one of those who sat at the table with Him.

3 Then Mary took a pound of very costly oil of spikenard, anointed the feet of Jesus, and wiped His feet with her hair. And the house was filled with the fragrance of the oil.

4 Then one of His disciples, Judas Iscariot, Simon's *son*, who would betray Him, said,

5 "Why was this fragrant oil not sold for three hundred denarii and given to the poor?"

6 This he said, not that he cared for the poor, but because he was a thief, and had the money box; and he used to take what was put in it.

7 Then Jesus said, "Let her alone; she has kept this for the day of My burial.

8 "For the poor you have with you always, but Me you do not have always."

9 Then a great many of the Jews knew that He was there; and they came, not for Jesus' sake only, but that they might also see Lazarus, whom He had raised from the dead.

10 But the chief priests took counsel that they might also put Lazarus to death,

11 because on account of him many of the Jews went away and believed in Jesus.

12 The next day a great multitude that had come to the feast, when they heard that Jesus was coming to Jerusalem,

13 took branches of palm trees and went out to meet Him, and cried out:

"Hosanna!
  'Blessed is He who comes
    in the name of the LORD!'
  The King of Israel!"

14 Then Jesus, when He had found a young donkey, sat on it; as it is written:

15 *"Fear not, daughter of Zion;
  Behold, your King is coming,
  Sitting on a donkey's colt."*

16 His disciples did not understand these things at first; but when Jesus was glorified, then they remembered that these things were written about Him and *that* they had done these things to Him.

17 Therefore the people, who were with Him when He called Lazarus out of his tomb and raised him from the dead, bore witness.

18 For this reason the people also met Him, because they heard that He had done this sign.

19 The Pharisees therefore said among themselves, "You see that you are accomplishing nothing. Look, the world has gone after Him!"

20 Now there were certain Greeks among those who came up to worship at the feast.

21 Then they came to Philip, who was from Bethsaida of Galilee, and asked him, saying, "Sir, we wish to see Jesus."

22 Philip came and told Andrew, and in turn Andrew and Philip told Jesus.

23 But Jesus answered them, saying, "The hour has come that the Son of Man should be glorified.

24 "Most assuredly, I say to you, unless a grain of wheat falls into the ground and dies, it remains alone; but if it dies, it produces much grain.

25 "He who loves his life will lose it, and he who hates his life in this world will keep it for eternal life.

26 "If anyone serves Me, let him follow Me; and where I am, there My servant will be also. If anyone serves Me, him *My* Father will honor.

27 "Now My soul is troubled, and what shall I say? 'Father, save Me from this hour'? But for this purpose I came to this hour.

28 "Father, glorify Your name." Then a voice came from heaven, *saying,* "I have both glorified *it* and will glorify *it* again."

29 Therefore the people who stood by and heard *it* said that it had thundered. Others said, "An angel has spoken to Him."

30 Jesus answered and said, "This voice did not come because of Me, but for your sake.

31 "Now is the judgment of this world; now the ruler of this world will be cast out.

32 "And I, if I am lifted up from the earth, will draw all *peoples* to Myself."

33 This He said, signifying by what death He would die.

34 The people answered Him, "We have heard from the law that the Christ remains forever; and how *can* You say, 'The Son of Man must be lifted up'? Who is this Son of Man?"

35 Then Jesus said to them, "A little while longer the light is with you. Walk while you have the light, lest darkness overtake you; he who walks in darkness does not know where he is going.

36 "While you have the light, believe in the light, that you may become sons of light." These things Jesus spoke, and departed, and was hidden from them.

37 But although He had done so many signs before them, they did not believe in Him,

38 that the word of Isaiah the prophet might be fulfilled, which he spoke:

> *"Lord, who has believed our*
> *report?*
> *And to whom has the arm*
> *of the LORD been revealed?"*

39 Therefore they could not believe, because Isaiah said again:

> 40 *"He has blinded their eyes and*
> *hardened their heart,*
> *Lest they should see with*
> *their eyes*
> *And understand with their*
> *heart,*
> *Lest they should turn,*
> *so that I should heal them."*

41 These things Isaiah said when he saw His glory and spoke of Him.

42 Nevertheless even among the rulers many believed in Him, but because of the Pharisees they did not confess *Him*, lest they should be put out of the synagogue;

43 for they loved the praise of men more than the praise of God.

44 Then Jesus cried out and said, "He who believes in Me, believes not in Me but in Him who sent Me.

45 "And he who sees Me sees Him who sent Me.

46 "I have come *as* a light into the world, that whoever believes in Me should not abide in darkness.

47 "And if anyone hears My words and does not believe, I do not judge him; for I did not come to judge the world but to save the world.

48 "He who rejects Me, and does not receive My words, has that which judges him—the word that I have spoken will judge him in the last day.

49 "For I have not spoken on My own *authority;* but the Father who sent Me gave Me a command, what I should say and what I should speak.

50 "And I know that His command is everlasting life. Therefore, whatever I speak, just as the Father has told Me, so I speak."

13 Now before the feast of the Passover, when Jesus knew that His hour had come that He should depart from this world to the Father, having loved His own who were in the world, He loved them to the end.

2 And supper being ended, the devil having already put it into the heart of Judas Iscariot, Simon's *son,* to betray Him,

3 Jesus, knowing that the Father had given all things into His hands, and that He had come from God and was going to God,

4 rose from supper and laid aside His garments, took a towel and girded Himself.

5 After that, He poured water into a basin and began to wash the disciples' feet, and to wipe *them* with the towel with which He was girded.

6 Then He came to Simon Peter. And *Peter* said to Him, "Lord, are You washing my feet?"

7 Jesus answered and said to him, "What I am doing you do not understand now, but you will know after this."

8 Peter said to Him, "You shall never wash my feet!" Jesus answered him, "If I do not wash you, you have no part with Me."

9 Simon Peter said to Him, "Lord, not my feet only, but also *my* hands and *my* head!"

10 Jesus said to him, "He who is bathed needs only to wash *his* feet, but is completely clean; and you are clean, but not all of you."

11 For He knew who would betray Him; therefore He said, "You are not all clean."

12 So when He had washed their feet, taken His garments, and sat down again, He said to them, "Do you know what I have done to you?

13 "You call Me Teacher and Lord, and you say well, for so I am.

14 "If I then, your Lord and Teacher, have washed your feet, you also ought to wash one another's feet.

15 "For I have given you an example, that you should do as I have done to you.

16 "Most assuredly, I say to you, a servant is not greater than his master; nor is he who is sent greater than he who sent him.

17 "If you know these things, happy are you if you do them.

18 "I do not speak concerning all of you. I know whom I have chosen; but that the Scripture may be fulfilled, 'He who eats bread with Me has lifted up his heel against Me.'

19 "Now I tell you before it comes, that when it does come to pass, you may believe that I am He.

20 "Most assuredly, I say to you, he who receives whomever I send receives Me; and he who receives Me receives Him who sent Me."

21 When Jesus had said these things, He was troubled in spirit, and testified and said, "Most assuredly, I say to you, one of you will betray Me."

22 Then the disciples looked at one another, perplexed about whom He spoke.

23 Now there was leaning on Jesus' bosom one of His disciples, whom Jesus loved.

24 Simon Peter therefore motioned to him to ask who it was of whom He spoke.

25 Then, leaning back on Jesus' breast, he said to Him, "Lord, who is it?"

26 Jesus answered, "It is he to whom I shall give a piece of bread when I have dipped it." And having dipped the bread, He gave it to Judas Iscariot, the son of Simon.

27 Now after the piece of bread, Satan entered him. Then Jesus said to him, "What you do, do quickly."

28 But no one at the table knew for what reason He said this to him.

29 For some thought, because Judas had the money box, that Jesus had said to him, "Buy those things we need for the feast," or that he should give something to the poor.

30 Having received the piece of bread, he then went out immediately. And it was night.

31 So, when he had gone out, Jesus said, "Now the Son of Man is glorified, and God is glorified in Him.

32 "If God is glorified in Him, God will also glorify Him in Himself, and glorify Him immediately.

33 "Little children, I shall be with you a little while longer. You will seek Me; and as I said to the Jews, 'Where I am going, you cannot come,' so now I say to you.

34 "A new commandment I give to you, that you love one another; as I have loved you, that you also love one another. ❤

35 "By this all will know that you are My disciples, if you have love for one another."

36 Simon Peter said to Him, "Lord, where are You going?" Jesus answered him, "Where I am going you cannot follow Me now, but you shall follow Me afterward."

37 Peter said to Him, "Lord, why can I not follow You now? I will lay down my life for Your sake."

38 Jesus answered him, "Will you lay down your life for My sake? Most assuredly, I say to you, the rooster shall not crow till you have denied Me three times.

14 "Let not your heart be troubled; you believe in God, believe also in Me.

2 "In My Father's house are many

mansions; if *it were* not *so*, I would have told you. I go to prepare a place for you.

3 "And if I go and prepare a place for you, I will come again and receive you to Myself; that where I am, *there* you may be also.

4 "And where I go you know, and the way you know."

5 Thomas said to Him, "Lord, we do not know where You are going, and how can we know the way?"

6 Jesus said to him, "I am the way, the truth, and the life. No one comes to the Father except through Me.

7 "If you had known Me, you would have known My Father also; and from now on you know Him and have seen Him."

8 Philip said to Him, "Lord, show us the Father, and it is sufficient for us."

9 Jesus said to him, "Have I been with you so long, and yet you have not known Me, Philip? He who has seen Me has seen the Father; so how can you say, 'Show us the Father'?

10 "Do you not believe that I am in the Father, and the Father in Me? The words that I speak to you I do not speak on My own *authority;* but the Father who dwells in Me does the works.

11 "Believe Me that I *am* in the Father and the Father in Me, or else believe Me for the sake of the works themselves.

12 "Most assuredly, I say to you, he who believes in Me, the works that I do he will do also; and greater *works* than these he will do, because I go to My Father.

13 "And whatever you ask in My name, that I will do, that the Father may be glorified in the Son.

14 "If you ask anything in My name, I will do *it.*

15 "If you love Me, keep My commandments.

16 "And I will pray the Father, and He will give you another Helper,

that He may abide with you forever,

17 *"even* the Spirit of truth, whom the world cannot receive, because it neither sees Him nor knows Him; but you know Him, for He dwells with you and will be in you.

18 "I will not leave you orphans; I will come to you.

19 "A little while longer and the world will see Me no more, but you will see Me. Because I live, you will live also.

20 "At that day you will know that I *am* in My Father, and you in Me, and I in you.

21 "He who has My commandments and keeps them, it is he who loves Me. And he who loves Me will be loved by My Father, and I will love him and manifest Myself to him."

22 Judas (not Iscariot) said to Him, "Lord, how is it that You will manifest Yourself to us, and not to the world?"

23 Jesus answered and said to him, "If anyone loves Me, he will keep My word; and My Father will love him, and We will come to him and make Our home with him.

24 "He who does not love Me does not keep My words; and the word which you hear is not Mine but the Father's who sent Me.

25 "These things I have spoken to you while being present with you.

26 "But the Helper, the Holy Spirit, whom the Father will send in My name, He will teach you all things, and bring to your remembrance all things that I said to you.

27 "Peace I leave with you, My peace I give to you; not as the world gives do I give to you. Let not your heart be troubled, neither let it be afraid.

28 "You have heard Me say to you, 'I am going away and coming *back* to you.' If you loved Me, you would rejoice because I said, 'I am going to the Father,' for My Father is greater than I.

29 "And now I have told you before it comes, that when it does come to pass, you may believe.

30 "I will no longer talk much with you, for the ruler of this world is coming, and he has nothing in Me.

31 "But that the world may know that I love the Father, and as the Father gave Me commandment, so I do. Arise, let us go from here.

15 "I am the true vine, and My Father is the vinedresser.

2 "Every branch in Me that does not bear fruit He takes away; and every *branch* that bears fruit He prunes, that it may bear more fruit.

3 "You are already clean because of the word which I have spoken to you.

4 "Abide in Me, and I in you. As the branch cannot bear fruit of itself, unless it abides in the vine, neither can you, unless you abide in Me.

5 "I am the vine, you *are* the branches. He who abides in Me, and I in him, bears much fruit; for without Me you can do nothing.

6 "If anyone does not abide in Me, he is cast out as a branch and is withered; and they gather them and throw *them* into the fire, and they are burned.

7 "If you abide in Me, and My words abide in you, you will ask what you desire, and it shall be done for you.

8 "By this My Father is glorified, that you bear much fruit; so you will be My disciples.

9 "As the Father loved Me, I also have loved you; abide in My love.

10 "If you keep My commandments, you will abide in My love, just as I have kept My Father's commandments and abide in His love.

11 "These things I have spoken to you, that My joy may remain in you, and *that* your joy may be full.

12 "This is My commandment, that you love one another as I have loved you.

13 "Greater love has no one than this, than to lay down one's life for his friends.

14 "You are My friends if you do whatever I command you.

15 "No longer do I call you servants, for a servant does not know what his master is doing; but I have called you friends, for all things that I heard from My Father I have made known to you.

16 "You did not choose Me, but I chose you and appointed you that you should go and bear fruit, and *that* your fruit should remain, that whatever you ask the Father in My name He may give you.

17 "These things I command you, that you love one another.

18 "If the world hates you, you know that it hated Me before *it hated* you.

19 "If you were of the world, the world would love its own. Yet because you are not of the world, but I chose you out of the world, therefore the world hates you.

20 "Remember the word that I said to you, 'A servant is not greater than his master.' If they persecuted Me, they will also persecute you. If they kept My word, they will keep yours also.

21 "But all these things they will do to you for My name's sake, because they do not know Him who sent Me.

22 "If I had not come and spoken to them, they would have no sin, but now they have no excuse for their sin.

23 "He who hates Me hates My Father also.

24 "If I had not done among them the works which no one else did, they would have no sin; but now they have seen and also hated both Me and My Father.

25 "But *this happened* that the word might be fulfilled which is written in their law, *'They hated Me without a cause.'*

26 "But when the Helper comes,

135   *See Proverbs 27:17, page 463*

whom I shall send to you from the Father, the Spirit of truth who proceeds from the Father, He will testify of Me.

27 "And you also will bear witness, because you have been with Me from the beginning.

16 "These things I have spoken to you, that you should not be made to stumble.

2 "They will put you out of the synagogues; yes, the time is coming that whoever kills you will think that he offers God service.

3 "And these things they will do to you because they have not known the Father nor Me.

4 "But these things I have told you, that when the time comes, you may remember that I told you of them. And these things I did not say to you at the beginning, because I was with you.

5 "But now I go away to Him who sent Me, and none of you asks Me, 'Where are You going?'

6 "But because I have said these things to you, sorrow has filled your heart.

7 "Nevertheless I tell you the truth. It is to your advantage that I go away; for if I do not go away, the Helper will not come to you; but if I depart, I will send Him to you.

8 "And when He has come, He will convict the world of sin, and of righteousness, and of judgment:

9 "of sin, because they do not believe in Me;

10 "of righteousness, because I go to My Father and you see Me no more;

11 "of judgment, because the ruler of this world is judged.

12 "I still have many things to say to you, but you cannot bear *them* now.

13 "However, when He, the Spirit of truth, has come, He will guide you into all truth; for He will not speak on His own *authority*, but whatever He hears He will speak;

and He will tell you things to come.

14 "He will glorify Me, for He will take of what is Mine and declare *it* to you.

15 "All things that the Father has are Mine. Therefore I said that He will take of Mine and declare *it* to you.

16 "A little while, and you will not see Me; and again a little while, and you will see Me, because I go to the Father."

17 Then *some* of His disciples said among themselves, "What is this that He says to us, 'A little while, and you will not see Me; and again a little while, and you will see Me'; and, 'because I go to the Father'?"

18 They said therefore, "What is this that He says, 'A little while'? We do not know what He is saying."

19 Now Jesus knew that they desired to ask Him, and He said to them, "Are you inquiring among yourselves about what I said, 'A little while, and you will not see Me; and again a little while, and you will see Me'?

20 "Most assuredly, I say to you that you will weep and lament, but the world will rejoice; and you will be sorrowful, but your sorrow will be turned into joy.

21 "A woman, when she is in labor, has sorrow because her hour has come; but as soon as she has given birth to the child, she no longer remembers the anguish, for joy that a human being has been born into the world.

22 "Therefore you now have sorrow; but I will see you again and your heart will rejoice, and your joy no one will take from you.

23 "And in that day you will ask Me nothing. Most assuredly, I say to you, whatever you ask the Father in My name He will give you.

24 "Until now you have asked nothing in My name. Ask, and you

will receive, that your joy may be full.

25 "These things I have spoken to you in figurative language; but the time is coming when I will no longer speak to you in figurative language, but I will tell you plainly about the Father.

26 "In that day you will ask in My name, and I do not say to you that I shall pray the Father for you;

27 "for the Father Himself loves you, because you have loved Me, and have believed that I came forth from God.

28 "I came forth from the Father and have come into the world. Again, I leave the world and go to the Father."

29 His disciples said to Him, "See, now You are speaking plainly, and using no figure of speech!

30 "Now we are sure that You know all things, and have no need that anyone should question You. By this we believe that You came forth from God."

31 Jesus answered them, "Do you now believe?

32 "Indeed the hour is coming, yes, has now come, that you will be scattered, each to his own, and will leave Me alone. And yet I am not alone, because the Father is with Me.

33 "These things I have spoken to you, that in Me you may have peace. In the world you will have tribulation; but be of good cheer, I have overcome the world."

17 Jesus spoke these words, lifted up His eyes to heaven, and said: "Father, the hour has come. Glorify Your Son, that Your Son also may glorify You,

2 "as You have given Him authority over all flesh, that He should give eternal life to as many as You have given Him.

3 "And this is eternal life, that they may know You, the only true God, and Jesus Christ whom You have sent.

4 "I have glorified You on the earth. I have finished the work which You have given Me to do.

5 "And now, O Father, glorify Me together with Yourself, with the glory which I had with You before the world was.

6 "I have manifested Your name to the men whom You have given Me out of the world. They were Yours, You gave them to Me, and they have kept Your word.

7 "Now they have known that all things which You have given Me are from You.

8 "For I have given to them the words which You have given Me; and they have received *them*, and have known surely that I came forth from You; and they have believed that You sent Me.

9 "I pray for them. I do not pray for the world but for those whom You have given Me, for they are Yours.

10 "And all Mine are Yours, and Yours are Mine, and I am glorified in them.

11 "Now I am no longer in the world, but these are in the world, and I come to You. Holy Father, keep through Your name those whom You have given Me, that they may be one as We *are*.

12 "While I was with them in the world, I kept them in Your name. Those whom You gave Me I have kept; and none of them is lost except the son of perdition, that the Scripture might be fulfilled.

13 "But now I come to You, and these things I speak in the world, that they may have My joy fulfilled in themselves.

14 "I have given them Your word; and the world has hated them because they are not of the world, just as I am not of the world.

15 "I do not pray that You should take them out of the world, but that You should keep them from the evil *one*.

16 "They are not of the world, just as I am not of the world.

17 "Sanctify them by Your truth. Your word is truth.

18 "As You sent Me into the world, I also have sent them into the world.

19 "And for their sakes I sanctify Myself, that they also may be sanctified by the truth.

20 "I do not pray for these alone, but also for those who will believe in Me through their word;

21 "that they all may be one, as You, Father, *are* in Me, and I in You; that they also may be one in Us, that the world may believe that You sent Me.

22 "And the glory which You gave Me I have given them, that they may be one just as We are one:

23 "I in them, and You in Me; that they may be made perfect in one, and that the world may know that You have sent Me, and have loved them as You have loved Me.

24 "Father, I desire that they also whom You gave Me may be with Me where I am, that they may behold My glory which You have given Me; for You loved Me before the foundation of the world.

25 "O righteous Father! The world has not known You, but I have known You; and these have known that You sent Me.

26 "And I have declared to them Your name, and will declare *it*, that the love with which You loved Me may be in them, and I in them."

18 When Jesus had spoken these words, He went out with His disciples over the Brook Kidron, where there was a garden, which He and His disciples entered.

2 And Judas, who betrayed Him, also knew the place; for Jesus often met there with His disciples.

3 Then Judas, having received a detachment *of troops*, and officers from the chief priests and Pharisees, came there with lanterns, torches, and weapons.

4 Jesus therefore, knowing all things that would come upon Him, went forward and said to them, "Whom are you seeking?"

5 They answered Him, "Jesus of Nazareth." Jesus said to them, "I am *He*." And Judas, who betrayed Him, also stood with them.

6 Then—when He said to them, "I am *He*,"—they drew back and fell to the ground.

7 Then He asked them again, "Whom are you seeking?" And they said, "Jesus of Nazareth."

8 Jesus answered, "I have told you that I am *He*. Therefore, if you seek Me, let these go their way,"

9 that the saying might be fulfilled which He spoke, "Of those whom You gave Me I have lost none."

10 Then Simon Peter, having a sword, drew it and struck the high priest's servant, and cut off his right ear. The servant's name was Malchus.

11 Then Jesus said to Peter, "Put your sword into the sheath. Shall I not drink the cup which My Father has given Me?"

12 Then the detachment *of troops* and the captain and the officers of the Jews arrested Jesus and bound Him.

13 And they led Him away to Annas first, for he was the father-in-law of Caiaphas who was high priest that year.

14 Now it was Caiaphas who gave counsel to the Jews that it was expedient that one man should die for the people.

15 And Simon Peter followed Jesus, and so *did* another disciple. Now that disciple was known to the high priest, and went with Jesus into the courtyard of the high priest.

16 But Peter stood at the door outside. Then the other disciple, who was known to the high priest, went out and spoke to her who kept the door, and brought Peter in.

17 Then the servant girl who kept the door said to Peter, "You are not also *one* of this Man's disciples, are you?" He said, "I am not."

18 And the servants and officers who had made a fire of coals stood there, for it was cold, and they warmed themselves. And Peter stood with them and warmed himself.

19 The high priest then asked Jesus about His disciples and His doctrine.

20 Jesus answered him, "I spoke openly to the world. I always taught in synagogues and in the temple, where the Jews always meet, and in secret I have said nothing.

21 "Why do you ask Me? Ask those who have heard Me what I said to them. Indeed they know what I said."

22 And when He had said these things, one of the officers who stood by struck Jesus with the palm of his hand, saying, "Do You answer the high priest like that?"

23 Jesus answered him, "If I have spoken evil, bear witness of the evil; but if well, why do you strike Me?"

24 Then Annas sent Him bound to Caiaphas the high priest.

25 Now Simon Peter stood and warmed himself. Therefore they said to him, "You are not also *one* of His disciples, are you?" He denied *it* and said, "I am not!"

26 One of the servants of the high priest, a relative *of him* whose ear Peter cut off, said, "Did I not see you in the garden with Him?"

27 Peter then denied again; and immediately a rooster crowed.

28 Then they led Jesus from Caiaphas to the Praetorium, and it was early morning. But they themselves did not go into the Praetorium, lest they should be defiled, but that they might eat the Passover.

29 Pilate then went out to them and said, "What accusation do you bring against this Man?"

30 They answered and said to him, "If He were not an evildoer, we would not have delivered Him up to you."

31 Then Pilate said to them, "You take Him and judge Him according to your law." Therefore the Jews said to him, "It is not lawful for us to put anyone to death,"

32 that the saying of Jesus might be fulfilled which He spoke, signifying by what death He would die.

33 Then Pilate entered the Praetorium again, called Jesus, and said to Him, "Are You the King of the Jews?"

34 Jesus answered him, "Are you speaking for yourself on this, or did others tell you this about Me?"

35 Pilate answered, "Am I a Jew? Your own nation and the chief priests have delivered You to me. What have You done?"

36 Jesus answered, "My kingdom is not of this world. If My kingdom were of this world, My servants would fight, so that I should not be delivered to the Jews; but now My kingdom is not from here."

37 Pilate therefore said to Him, "Are You a king then?" Jesus answered, "You say *rightly* that I am a king. For this cause I was born, and for this cause I have come into the world, that I should bear witness to the truth. Everyone who is of the truth hears My voice."

38 Pilate said to Him, "What is truth?" And when he had said this, he went out again to the Jews, and said to them, "I find no fault in Him *at all*.

39 "But you have a custom that I should release someone to you at the Passover. Do you therefore want me to release to you the King of the Jews?"

40 Then they all cried again, saying, "Not this Man, but Barabbas!" Now Barabbas was a robber.

19 So then Pilate took Jesus and scourged *Him*.

2 And the soldiers twisted a crown of thorns and put *it* on His head, and they put on Him a purple robe.

3 Then they said, "Hail, King of the Jews!" And they struck Him with their hands.

4 Pilate then went out again, and said to them, "Behold, I am bringing Him out to you, that you may know that I find no fault in Him."

5 Then Jesus came out, wearing the crown of thorns and the purple robe. And *Pilate* said to them, "Behold the Man!"

6 Therefore, when the chief priests and officers saw Him, they cried out, saying, "Crucify *Him*, crucify *Him!*" Pilate said to them, "You take Him and crucify *Him*, for I find no fault in Him."

7 The Jews answered him, "We have a law, and according to our law He ought to die, because He made Himself the Son of God."

8 Therefore, when Pilate heard that saying, he was the more afraid,

9 and went again into the Praetorium, and said to Jesus, "Where are You from?" But Jesus gave him no answer.

10 Then Pilate said to Him, "Are You not speaking to me? Do You not know that I have power to crucify You, and power to release You?"

11 Jesus answered, "You could have no power *at all* against Me unless it had been given you from above. Therefore the one who delivered Me to you has the greater sin."

12 From then on Pilate sought to release Him, but the Jews cried out, saying, "If you let this Man go, you are not Caesar's friend. Whoever makes himself a king speaks against Caesar."

13 When Pilate therefore heard that saying, he brought Jesus out

and sat down in the judgment seat in a place that is called *The* Pavement, but in Hebrew, Gabbatha.

14 Now it was the Preparation Day of the Passover, and about the sixth hour. And he said to the Jews, "Behold your King!"

15 But they cried out, "Away with *Him*, away with *Him!* Crucify Him!" Pilate said to them, "Shall I crucify your King?" The chief priests answered, "We have no king but Caesar!"

16 So he delivered Him to them to be crucified. So they took Jesus and led *Him* away.

17 And He, bearing His cross, went out to a place called *the Place* of a Skull, which is called in Hebrew, Golgotha,

18 where they crucified Him, and two others with Him, one on either side, and Jesus in the center.

19 Now Pilate wrote a title and put *it* on the cross. And the writing was:

JESUS OF NAZARETH,
THE KING OF THE JEWS.

20 Then many of the Jews read this title, for the place where Jesus was crucified was near the city; and it was written in Hebrew, Greek, *and* Latin.

21 Then the chief priests of the Jews said to Pilate, "Do not write, 'The King of the Jews,' but, 'He said, "I am the King of the Jews." '"

22 Pilate answered, "What I have written, I have written."

23 Then the soldiers, when they had crucified Jesus, took His garments and made four parts, to each soldier a part, and also the tunic. Now the tunic was without seam, woven from the top in one piece.

24 They said therefore among themselves, "Let us not tear it, but cast lots for it, whose it shall be," that the Scripture might be fulfilled which says:

"They divided My garments
  among them,
And for My clothing they cast
  lots."

Therefore the soldiers did these
things.

25 Now there stood by the cross of
Jesus His mother, and His mother's
sister, Mary the *wife* of Clopas,
and Mary Magdalene.

26 When Jesus therefore saw His
mother, and the disciple whom He
loved standing by, He said to His
mother, "Woman, behold your
son!"

27 Then He said to the disciple,
"Behold your mother!" And from
that hour that disciple took her to
his own *home.*

28 After this, Jesus, knowing that
all things were now accomplished,
that the Scripture might be fulfilled, said, "I thirst!"

29 Now a vessel full of sour wine
was sitting there; and they filled a
sponge with sour wine, put *it* on
hyssop, and put *it* to His mouth.

30 So when Jesus had received the
sour wine, He said, "It is finished!"
And bowing His head, He gave up
His spirit.

31 Therefore, because it was the
Preparation *Day,* that the bodies
should not remain on the cross on
the Sabbath (for that Sabbath was
a high day), the Jews asked Pilate
that their legs might be broken,
and *that* they might be taken
away.

32 Then the soldiers came and
broke the legs of the first and of
the other who was crucified with
Him.

33 But when they came to Jesus
and saw that He was already dead,
they did not break His legs.

34 But one of the soldiers pierced
His side with a spear, and immediately blood and water came out.

35 And he who has seen has testified, and his testimony is true; and
he knows that he is telling the
truth, so that you may believe.

36 For these things were done that
the Scripture should be fulfilled,
"Not one of His bones shall be
broken."

37 And again another Scripture
says, "They shall look on Him
whom they pierced."

38 After this, Joseph of Arimathea,
being a disciple of Jesus, but secretly, for fear of the Jews, asked
Pilate that he might take away the
body of Jesus; and Pilate gave *him*
permission. So he came and took
the body of Jesus.

39 And Nicodemus, who at first
came to Jesus by night, also came,
bringing a mixture of myrrh and
aloes, about a hundred pounds.

40 Then they took the body of
Jesus, and bound it in strips of
linen with the spices, as the custom of the Jews is to bury.

41 Now in the place where He was
crucified there was a garden, and
in the garden a new tomb in which
no one had yet been laid.

42 So there they laid Jesus, because of the Jews' Preparation
Day, for the tomb was nearby.

20 On the first *day* of the week
Mary Magdalene came to the
tomb early, while it was still dark,
and saw *that* the stone had been
taken away from the tomb.

2 Then she ran and came to Simon Peter, and to the other disciple, whom Jesus loved, and said to
them, "They have taken away the
Lord out of the tomb, and we do
not know where they have laid
Him."

3 Peter therefore went out, and
the other disciple, and were going
to the tomb.

4 So they both ran together, and
the other disciple outran Peter and
came to the tomb first.

5 And he, stooping down and
looking in, saw the linen cloths
lying *there;* yet he did not go in.

6 Then Simon Peter came, following him, and went into the tomb;
and he saw the linen cloths lying
there,

7 and the handkerchief that had been around His head, not lying with the linen cloths, but folded together in a place by itself.

8 Then the other disciple, who came to the tomb first, went in also; and he saw and believed.

9 For as yet they did not know the Scripture, that He must rise again from the dead.

10 Then the disciples went away again to their own homes.

11 But Mary stood outside by the tomb weeping, and as she wept she stooped down *and looked* into the tomb.

12 And she saw two angels in white sitting, one at the head and the other at the feet, where the body of Jesus had lain.

13 Then they said to her, "Woman, why are you weeping?" She said to them, "Because they have taken away my Lord, and I do not know where they have laid Him."

14 Now when she had said this, she turned around and saw Jesus standing *there,* and did not know that it was Jesus.

15 Jesus said to her, "Woman, why are you weeping? Whom are you seeking?" She, supposing Him to be the gardener, said to Him, "Sir, if You have carried Him away, tell me where You have laid Him, and I will take Him away."

16 Jesus said to her, "Mary!" She turned and said to Him, "Rabboni!" (which is to say, Teacher).

17 Jesus said to her, "Do not cling to Me, for I have not yet ascended to My Father; but go to My brethren and say to them, 'I am ascending to My Father and your Father, and *to* My God and your God.'"

18 Mary Magdalene came and told the disciples that she had seen the Lord, and *that* He had spoken these things to her.

19 Then, the same day at evening, being the first *day* of the week, when the doors were shut where the disciples were assembled, for fear of the Jews, Jesus came and stood in the midst, and said to them, "Peace *be* with you."

20 Now when He had said this, He showed them *His* hands and His side. Then the disciples were glad when they saw the Lord.

21 Then Jesus said to them again, "Peace to you! As the Father has sent Me, I also send you."

22 And when He had said this, He breathed on *them,* and said to them, "Receive the Holy Spirit.

23 "If you forgive the sins of any, they are forgiven them; if you retain the *sins* of any, they are retained."

24 But Thomas, called Didymus, one of the twelve, was not with them when Jesus came.

25 The other disciples therefore said to him, "We have seen the Lord." But he said to them, "Unless I see in His hands the print of the nails, and put my finger into the print of the nails, and put my hand into His side, I will not believe."

26 And after eight days His disciples were again inside, and Thomas with them. Jesus came, the doors being shut, and stood in the midst, and said, "Peace to you!"

27 Then He said to Thomas, "Reach your finger here, and look at My hands; and reach your hand *here,* and put *it* into My side. Do not be unbelieving, but believing."

28 And Thomas answered and said to Him, "My Lord and my God!"

29 Jesus said to him, "Thomas, because you have seen Me, you have believed. Blessed *are* those who have not seen and *yet* have believed."

30 And truly Jesus did many other signs in the presence of His disciples, which are not written in this book;

31 but these are written that you may believe that Jesus is the Christ, the Son of God, and that

believing you may have life in His name.

21 After these things Jesus showed Himself again to the disciples at the Sea of Tiberias, and in this way He showed *Himself:*

2 Simon Peter, Thomas called Didymus, Nathanael of Cana in Galilee, the *sons* of Zebedee, and two others of His disciples were together.

3 Simon Peter said to them, "I am going fishing." They said to him, "We are going with you also." They went out and immediately got into the boat, and that night they caught nothing.

4 But when the morning had now come, Jesus stood on the shore; yet the disciples did not know that it was Jesus.

5 Then Jesus said to them, "Children, have you any food?" They answered Him, "No."

6 And He said to them, "Cast the net on the right side of the boat, and you will find *some.*" So they cast, and now they were not able to draw it in because of the multitude of fish.

7 Therefore that disciple whom Jesus loved said to Peter, "It is the Lord!" Now when Simon Peter heard that it was the Lord, he put on *his* outer garment (for he had removed it), and plunged into the sea.

8 But the other disciples came in the little boat (for they were not far from land, but about two hundred cubits), dragging the net with fish.

9 Then, as soon as they had come to land, they saw a fire of coals there, and fish laid on it, and bread.

10 Jesus said to them, "Bring some of the fish which you have just caught."

11 Simon Peter went up and dragged the net to land, full of large fish, one hundred and fifty-three; and although there were so many, the net was not broken.

12 Jesus said to them, "Come *and* eat breakfast." Yet none of the disciples dared ask Him, "Who are You?"—knowing that it was the Lord.

13 Jesus then came and took the bread and gave it to them, and likewise the fish.

14 This *is* now the third time Jesus showed Himself to His disciples after He was raised from the dead.

15 So when they had eaten breakfast, Jesus said to Simon Peter, "Simon, *son* of Jonah, do you love Me more than these?" He said to Him, "Yes, Lord; You know that I love You." He said to him, "Feed My lambs."

16 He said to him again a second time, "Simon, *son* of Jonah, do you love Me?" He said to Him, "Yes, Lord; You know that I love You." He said to him, "Tend My sheep."

17 He said to him the third time, "Simon, *son* of Jonah, do you love Me?" Peter was grieved because He said to him the third time, "Do you love Me?" And he said to Him, "Lord, You know all things; You know that I love You." Jesus said to him, "Feed My sheep.

18 "Most assuredly, I say to you, when you were younger, you girded yourself and walked where you wished; but when you are old, you will stretch out your hands, and another will gird you and carry *you* where you do not wish."

19 This He spoke, signifying by what death he would glorify God. And when He had spoken this, He said to him, "Follow Me."

20 Then Peter, turning around, saw the disciple whom Jesus loved following, who also had leaned on His breast at the supper, and said, "Lord, who is the one who betrays You?"

21 Peter, seeing him, said to Jesus, "But Lord, what *about* this man?"

22 Jesus said to him, "If I will that he remain till I come, what *is that* to you? You follow Me."

23 Then this saying went out among the brethren that this disciple would not die. Yet Jesus did not say to him that he would not die, but, "If I will that he remain till I come, what *is that* to you?" 24 This is the disciple who testifies of these things, and wrote these things; and we know that his testimony is true.

25 And there are also many other things that Jesus did, which if they were written one by one, I suppose that even the world itself could not contain the books that would be written. Amen.

THE ACTS

OF THE APOSTLES

THE former account I made, O Theophilus, of all that Jesus began both to do and teach,

2 until the day in which He was taken up, after He through the Holy Spirit had given commandments to the apostles whom He had chosen,

3 to whom He also presented Himself alive after His suffering by many infallible proofs, being seen by them during forty days and speaking of the things pertaining to the kingdom of God.

4 And being assembled together with *them*, He commanded them not to depart from Jerusalem, but to wait for the Promise of the Father, "which," *He said*, "you have heard from Me;

5 "for John truly baptized with water, but you shall be baptized with the Holy Spirit not many days from now."

6 Therefore, when they had come together, they asked Him, saying, "Lord, will You at this time restore the kingdom to Israel?"

7 And He said to them, "It is not for you to know times or seasons which the Father has put in His own authority.

8 "But you shall receive power when the Holy Spirit has come upon you; and you shall be witnesses to Me in Jerusalem, and in all Judea and Samaria, and to the end of the earth."

9 Now when He had spoken these things, while they watched, He was taken up, and a cloud received Him out of their sight.

10 And while they looked steadfastly toward heaven as He went up, behold, two men stood by them in white apparel,

11 who also said, "Men of Galilee, why do you stand gazing up into heaven? This *same* Jesus, who was taken up from you into heaven, will so come in like manner as you saw Him go into heaven."

12 Then they returned to Jerusalem from the Mount called Olivet, which is near Jerusalem, a Sabbath day's journey.

13 And when they had entered, they went up into the upper room where they were staying: Peter, James, John, and Andrew; Philip and Thomas; Bartholomew and Matthew; James *the son* of Alphaeus and Simon the Zealot; and Judas *the son* of James.

14 These all continued with one accord in prayer and supplication, with the women and Mary the mother of Jesus, and with His brothers.

15 And in those days Peter stood up in the midst of the disciples (altogether the number of names

was about a hundred and twenty), and said,

16 "Men *and* brethren, this Scripture had to be fulfilled, which the Holy Spirit spoke before by the mouth of David concerning Judas, who became a guide to those who arrested Jesus;

17 "for he was numbered with us and obtained a part in this ministry."

18 (Now this man purchased a field with the wages of iniquity; and falling headlong, he burst open in the middle and all his entrails gushed out.

19 And it became known to all those dwelling in Jerusalem; so that field is called in their own language, Akel Dama, that is, Field of Blood.)

20 "For it is written in the book of Psalms:

'Let his habitation be desolate,
   And let no one live in it';

and,

'Let another take his office.'

21 "Therefore, of these men who have accompanied us all the time that the Lord Jesus went in and out among us,

22 "beginning from the baptism of John to that day when He was taken up from us, one of these must become a witness with us of His resurrection."

23 And they proposed two: Joseph called Barsabas, who was surnamed Justus, and Matthias.

24 And they prayed and said, "You, O Lord, who know the hearts of all, show which of these two You have chosen

25 "to take part in this ministry and apostleship from which Judas by transgression fell, that he might go to his own place."

26 And they cast their lots, and the lot fell on Matthias. And he was numbered with the eleven apostles.

2 Now when the Day of Pentecost had fully come, they were all with one accord in one place.

2 And suddenly there came a sound from heaven, as of a rushing mighty wind, and it filled the whole house where they were sitting.

3 Then there appeared to them divided tongues, as of fire, and *one* sat upon each of them.

4 And they were all filled with the Holy Spirit and began to speak with other tongues, as the Spirit gave them utterance.

5 Now there were dwelling in Jerusalem Jews, devout men, from every nation under heaven.

6 And when this sound occurred, the multitude came together, and were confused, because everyone heard them speak in his own language.

7 Then they were all amazed and marveled, saying to one another, "Look, are not all these who speak Galileans?

8 "And how *is it that* we hear, each in our own language in which we were born?

9 "Parthians and Medes and Elamites, those dwelling in Mesopotamia, Judea and Cappadocia, Pontus and Asia,

10 "Phrygia and Pamphylia, Egypt and the parts of Libya adjoining Cyrene, visitors from Rome, both Jews and proselytes,

11 "Cretans and Arabs—we hear them speaking in our own tongues the wonderful works of God."

12 So they were all amazed and perplexed, saying to one another, "Whatever could this mean?"

13 Others mocking said, "They are full of new wine."

14 But Peter, standing up with the eleven, raised his voice and said to them, "Men of Judea and all who dwell in Jerusalem, let this be known to you, and heed my words.

15 "For these are not drunk, as you

suppose, since it is *only* the third hour of the day.

16 "But this is what was spoken by the prophet Joel:

17 'And it shall come to pass in
    the last days, says God,
   That I will pour out of My
    Spirit on all flesh;
   Your sons and your daughters
    shall prophesy,
   Your young men shall see
    visions,
   Your old men shall dream
    dreams.
18 And on My menservants and
    on My maidservants
   I will pour out My Spirit in
    those days;
   And they shall prophesy.
19 I will show wonders in heaven
    above
   And signs in the earth beneath:
   Blood and fire and vapor of
    smoke.
20 The sun shall be turned into
    darkness,
   And the moon into blood,
   Before the coming of the great
    and notable day of the LORD.
21 And it shall come to pass that
    whoever calls on the name of
    the LORD shall be saved.'

22 "Men of Israel, hear these words: Jesus of Nazareth, a Man attested by God to you by miracles, wonders, and signs which God did through Him in your midst, as you yourselves also know—

23 "Him, being delivered by the determined counsel and foreknowledge of God, you have taken by lawless hands, have crucified, and put to death;

24 "whom God raised up, having loosed the pains of death, because it was not possible that He should be held by it.

25 "For David says concerning Him:

'I foresaw the LORD always
    before my face,
 For He is at my right hand,
    that I may not be shaken;
26 Therefore my heart rejoiced,
    and my tongue was glad;
   Moreover my flesh will also
    rest in hope,
27 Because You will not leave
    my soul in Hades,
   Nor will You allow Your Holy
    One to see corruption.
28 You have made known to me
    the ways of life;
   You will make me full of joy
    in Your presence.'

29 "Men *and* brethren, let *me* speak freely to you of the patriarch David, that he is both dead and buried, and his tomb is with us to this day.

30 "Therefore, being a prophet, and knowing that God had sworn with an oath to him that of the fruit of his body, according to the flesh, He would raise up the Christ to sit on his throne,

31 "he, foreseeing this, spoke concerning the resurrection of the Christ, that His soul was not left in Hades, nor did His flesh see corruption.

32 "This Jesus God has raised up, of which we are all witnesses.

33 "Therefore being exalted to the right hand of God, and having received from the Father the promise of the Holy Spirit, He poured out this which you now see and hear.

34 "For David did not ascend into the heavens, but he says himself:

'The LORD said to my Lord,
    "Sit at My right hand,
35 Till I make Your enemies Your
    footstool." '

36 "Therefore let all the house of Israel know assuredly that God has made this Jesus, whom you crucified, both Lord and Christ."

37 Now when they heard *this*, they were cut to the heart, and said to Peter and the rest of the apostles, "Men *and* brethren, what shall we do?"

38 Then Peter said to them, "Repent, and let every one of you be baptized in the name of Jesus Christ for the remission of sins; and you shall receive the gift of the Holy Spirit.

39 "For the promise is to you and to your children, and to all who are afar off, as many as the Lord our God will call."

40 And with many other words he testified and exhorted them, saying, "Be saved from this perverse generation."

41 Then those who gladly received his word were baptized; and that day about three thousand souls were added *to them*.

42 And they continued steadfastly in the apostles' doctrine and fellowship, in the breaking of bread, and in prayers.

43 Then fear came upon every soul, and many wonders and signs were done through the apostles.

44 Now all who believed were together, and had all things in common,

45 and sold their possessions and goods, and divided them among all, as anyone had need.

46 So continuing daily with one accord in the temple, and breaking bread from house to house, they ate their food with gladness and simplicity of heart,

47 praising God and having favor with all the people. And the Lord added to the church daily those who were being saved.

3 Now Peter and John went up together to the temple at the hour of prayer, the ninth *hour*.

2 And a certain man lame from his mother's womb was carried, whom they laid daily at the gate of the temple which is called Beautiful, to ask alms from those who entered the temple;

3 who, seeing Peter and John about to go into the temple, asked for alms.

4 And fixing his eyes on him, with John, Peter said, "Look at us."

5 So he gave them his attention, expecting to receive something from them.

6 Then Peter said, "Silver and gold I do not have, but what I do have I give you: In the name of Jesus Christ of Nazareth, rise up and walk."

7 And he took him by the right hand and lifted *him* up, and immediately his feet and ankle bones received strength.

8 So he, leaping up, stood and walked and entered the temple with them—walking, leaping, and praising God.

9 And all the people saw him walking and praising God.

10 Then they knew that it was he who sat begging alms at the Beautiful Gate of the temple; and they were filled with wonder and amazement at what had happened to him.

11 Now as the lame man who was healed held on to Peter and John, all the people ran together to them in the porch which is called Solomon's, greatly amazed.

12 So when Peter saw *it*, he responded to the people: "Men of Israel, why do you marvel at this? Or why look so intently at us, as though by our own power or godliness we had made this man walk?

13 "The God of Abraham, Isaac, and Jacob, the God of our fathers, glorified His Servant Jesus, whom you delivered up and denied in the presence of Pilate, when he was determined to let *Him* go.

14 "But you denied the Holy One and the Just, and asked for a murderer to be granted to you,

15 "and killed the Prince of life, whom God raised from the dead, of which we are witnesses.

16 "And His name, through faith in

147 *See Hebrews 10:23–25, page 272*

His name, has made this man strong, whom you see and know. Yes, the faith which *comes* through Him has given him this perfect soundness in the presence of you all.

17 "Yet now, brethren, I know that you did *it* in ignorance, as *did* also your rulers.

18 "But those things which God foretold by the mouth of all His prophets, that the Christ would suffer, He has thus fulfilled.

19 "Repent therefore and be converted, that your sins may be blotted out, so that times of refreshing may come from the presence of the Lord,

20 "and that He may send Jesus Christ, who was preached to you before,

21 "whom heaven must receive until the times of restoration of all things, which God has spoken by the mouth of all His holy prophets since the world began.

22 "For Moses truly said to the fathers, *'The Lord your God will raise up for you a Prophet like me from your brethren. Him you shall hear in all things, whatever He says to you.*

23 *'And it shall come to pass that every soul who will not hear that Prophet shall be utterly destroyed from among the people.'*

24 "Yes, and all the prophets, from Samuel and those who follow, as many as have spoken, have also foretold these days.

25 "You are sons of the prophets, and of the covenant which God made with our fathers, saying to Abraham, *'And in your seed all the families of the earth shall be blessed.'*

26 "To you first, God, having raised up His Servant Jesus, sent Him to bless you, in turning away every one *of you* from your iniquities."

4 Now as they spoke to the people, the priests, the captain of the temple, and the Sadducees came upon them,

2 being greatly disturbed that they taught the people and preached in Jesus the resurrection from the dead.

3 And they laid hands on them, and put *them* in custody until the next day, for it was already evening.

4 However, many of those who heard the word believed; and the number of the men came to be about five thousand.

5 And it came to pass, on the next day, that their rulers, elders, and scribes,

6 as well as Annas the high priest, Caiaphas, John, and Alexander, and as many as were of the family of the high priest, were gathered together at Jerusalem.

7 And when they had set them in the midst, they asked, "By what power or by what name have you done this?"

8 Then Peter, filled with the Holy Spirit, said to them, "Rulers of the people and elders of Israel:

9 "If we this day are judged for a good deed *done to the* helpless man, by what means he has been made well,

10 "let it be known to you all, and to all the people of Israel, that by the name of Jesus Christ of Nazareth, whom you crucified, whom God raised from the dead, by Him this man stands here before you whole.

11 "This is the *'stone which was rejected by you builders, which has become the chief cornerstone.'*

12 "Nor is there salvation in any other, for there is no other name under heaven given among men by which we must be saved."

13 Now when they saw the boldness of Peter and John, and perceived that they were uneducated and untrained men, they marveled. And they realized that they had been with Jesus.

148

14 And seeing the man who had been healed standing with them, they could say nothing against it. 15 But when they had commanded them to go aside out of the council, they conferred among themselves, 16 saying, "What shall we do to these men? For, indeed, that a notable miracle has been done through them *is* evident to all who dwell in Jerusalem, and we cannot deny *it*. 17 "But so that it spreads no further among the people, let us severely threaten them, that from now on they speak to no man in this name." 18 And they called them and commanded them not to speak at all nor teach in the name of Jesus. 19 But Peter and John answered and said to them, "Whether it is right in the sight of God to listen to you more than to God, you judge. 20 "For we cannot but speak the things which we have seen and heard." 21 So when they had further threatened them, they let them go, finding no way of punishing them, because of the people, since they all glorified God for what had been done. 22 For the man was over forty years old on whom this miracle of healing had been performed. 23 And being let go, they went to their own *companions* and reported all that the chief priests and elders had said to them. 24 So when they heard that, they raised their voice to God with one accord and said: "Lord, You *are* God, who made heaven and earth and the sea, and all that is in them, 25 "who by the mouth of Your servant David have said:

'Why did the nations rage,
　And the people plot vain
　　things?
26 The kings of the earth took
　their stand,

*And the rulers were gathered
　together
Against the LORD and against
　His Christ.'*

27 "For truly against Your holy Servant Jesus, whom You anointed, both Herod and Pontius Pilate, with the Gentiles and the people of Israel, were gathered together 28 "to do whatever Your hand and Your purpose determined before to be done. 29 "Now, Lord, look on their threats, and grant to Your servants that with all boldness they may speak Your word, 30 "by stretching out Your hand to heal, and that signs and wonders may be done through the name of Your holy Servant Jesus." 31 And when they had prayed, the place where they were assembled together was shaken; and they were all filled with the Holy Spirit, and they spoke the word of God with boldness. 32 Now the multitude of those who believed were of one heart and one soul; neither did anyone say that any of the things he possessed was his own, but they had all things in common. 33 And with great power the apostles gave witness to the resurrection of the Lord Jesus. And great grace was upon them all. 34 Nor was there anyone among them who lacked; for all who were possessors of lands or houses sold them, and brought the proceeds of the things that were sold, 35 and laid *them* at the apostles' feet; and they distributed to each as anyone had need. 36 And Joses, who was also named Barnabas by the apostles (which is translated Son of Encouragement), a Levite of the country of Cyprus, 37 having land, sold *it*, and brought the money and laid *it* at the apostles' feet.

5 But a certain man named Ananias, with Sapphira his wife, sold a possession.

2 And he kept back *part* of the proceeds, his wife also being aware of *it*, and brought a certain part and laid *it* at the apostles' feet.

3 But Peter said, "Ananias, why has Satan filled your heart to lie to the Holy Spirit and keep back *part* of the price of the land for yourself?

4 "While it remained, was it not your own? And after it was sold, was it not in your own control? Why have you conceived this thing in your heart? You have not lied to men but to God."

5 Then Ananias, hearing these words, fell down and breathed his last. So great fear came upon all those who heard these things.

6 And the young men arose and wrapped him up, carried *him* out, and buried *him*.

7 Now it was about three hours later when his wife came in, not knowing what had happened.

8 And Peter answered her, "Tell me whether you sold the land for so much?" And she said, "Yes, for so much."

9 Then Peter said to her, "How is it that you have agreed together to test the Spirit of the Lord? Look, the feet of those who have buried your husband *are* at the door, and they will carry you out."

10 Then immediately she fell down at his feet and breathed her last. And the young men came in and found her dead, and carrying *her* out, buried *her* by her husband.

11 So great fear came upon all the church and upon all who heard these things.

12 And through the hands of the apostles many signs and wonders were done among the people. And they were all with one accord in Solomon's Porch.

13 Yet none of the rest dared join them, but the people esteemed them highly.

14 And believers were increasingly added to the Lord, multitudes of both men and women,

15 so that they brought the sick out into the streets and laid *them* on beds and couches, that at least the shadow of Peter passing by might fall on some of them.

16 Also a multitude gathered from the surrounding cities to Jerusalem, bringing sick people and those who were tormented by unclean spirits, and they were all healed.

17 Then the high priest rose up, and all those who *were* with him (which is the sect of the Sadducees), and they were filled with indignation,

18 and laid their hands on the apostles and put them in the common prison.

19 But at night an angel of the Lord opened the prison doors and brought them out, and said,

20 "Go, stand in the temple and speak to the people all the words of this life."

21 And when they heard *that*, they entered the temple early in the morning and taught. But the high priest and those with him came and called the council together, with all the elders of the children of Israel, and sent to the prison to have them brought.

22 But when the officers came and did not find them in the prison, they returned and reported,

23 saying, "Indeed we found the prison shut securely, and the guards standing outside before the doors; but when we opened them, we found no one inside!"

24 Now when the high priest, the captain of the temple, and the chief priests heard these things, they wondered what the outcome would be.

25 Then one came and told them, saying, "Look, the men whom you put in prison are standing in the temple and teaching the people!"

26 Then the captain went with the officers and brought them without

violence, for they feared the people, lest they should be stoned.

27 And when they had brought them, they set *them* before the council. And the high priest asked them,

28 saying, "Did we not strictly command you not to teach in this name? And look, you have filled Jerusalem with your doctrine, and intend to bring this Man's blood on us!"

29 Then Peter and the *other* apostles answered and said: "We ought to obey God rather than men.

30 "The God of our fathers raised up Jesus whom you murdered by hanging on a tree.

31 "Him God has exalted to His right hand *to be* Prince and Savior, to give repentance to Israel and forgiveness of sins.

32 "And we are His witnesses to these things, and *so* also *is* the Holy Spirit whom God has given to those who obey Him."

33 When they heard *this*, they were furious and took counsel to kill them.

34 Then one in the council stood up, a Pharisee named Gamaliel, a teacher of the law held in respect by all the people, and commanded them to put the apostles outside for a little while.

35 And he said to them: "Men of Israel, take heed to yourselves what you intend to do regarding these men.

36 "For some time ago Theudas rose up, claiming to be somebody. A number of men, about four hundred, joined him. He was slain, and all who obeyed him were scattered and came to nothing.

37 "After this man, Judas of Galilee rose up in the days of the census, and drew away many people after him. He also perished, and all who obeyed him were dispersed.

38 "And now I say to you, keep away from these men and let them alone; for if this plan or this work is of men, it will come to nothing;

39 "but if it is of God, you cannot overthrow it—lest you even be found to fight against God."

40 And they agreed with him, and when they had called for the apostles and beaten *them*, they commanded that they should not speak in the name of Jesus, and let them go.

41 So they departed from the presence of the council, rejoicing that they were counted worthy to suffer shame for His name.

42 And daily in the temple, and in every house, they did not cease teaching and preaching Jesus *as* the Christ.

6 Now in those days, when *the number of* the disciples was multiplying, there arose a murmuring against the Hebrews by the Hellenists, because their widows were neglected in the daily distribution.

2 Then the twelve summoned the multitude of the disciples and said, "It is not desirable that we should leave the word of God and serve tables.

3 "Therefore, brethren, seek out from among you seven men of *good* reputation, full of the Holy Spirit and wisdom, whom we may appoint over this business;

4 "but we will give ourselves continually to prayer and to the ministry of the word."

5 And the saying pleased the whole multitude. And they chose Stephen, a man full of faith and the Holy Spirit, and Philip, Prochorus, Nicanor, Timon, Parmenas, and Nicolas, a proselyte from Antioch,

6 whom they set before the apostles; and when they had prayed, they laid hands on them.

7 And the word of God spread, and the number of the disciples multiplied greatly in Jerusalem, and a great many of the priests were obedient to the faith.

8 And Stephen, full of faith and

power, did great wonders and signs among the people.

9 Then there arose some from what is called the Synagogue of the Freedmen (Cyrenians, Alexandrians, and those from Cilicia and Asia), disputing with Stephen.

10 And they were not able to resist the wisdom and the Spirit by which he spoke.

11 Then they secretly induced men to say, "We have heard him speak blasphemous words against Moses and God."

12 And they stirred up the people, the elders, and the scribes; and they came upon *him*, seized him, and brought *him* to the council.

13 They also set up false witnesses who said, "This man does not cease to speak blasphemous words against this holy place and the law;

14 "for we have heard him say that this Jesus of Nazareth will destroy this place and change the customs which Moses delivered to us."

15 And all who sat in the council, looking steadfastly at him, saw his face as the face of an angel.

7 Then the high priest said, "Are these things so?"

2 And he said, "Men and brethren and fathers, listen: The God of glory appeared to our father Abraham when he was in Mesopotamia, before he dwelt in Haran,

3 "and said to him, *'Get out of your country and from your relatives, and come to a land that I will show you.'*

4 "Then he came out of the land of the Chaldeans and dwelt in Haran. And from there, when his father was dead, He moved him to this land in which you now dwell.

5 "And *God* gave him no inheritance in it, not even *enough* to set his foot on. But even when *Abraham* had no child, He promised to give it to him for a possession, and to his descendants after him.

6 "But God spoke in this way: that his descendants would sojourn in a foreign land, and that

they would bring them into bondage and oppress *them* four hundred years.

7 *'And the nation to whom they will be in bondage I will judge,'* said God, *'and after that they shall come out and serve Me in this place.'*

8 "Then He gave him the covenant of circumcision; and so *Abraham* begot Isaac and circumcised him on the eighth day; and Isaac *begot* Jacob, and Jacob *begot* the twelve patriarchs.

9 "And the patriarchs, becoming envious, sold Joseph into Egypt. But God was with him

10 "and delivered him out of all his troubles, and gave him favor and wisdom in the presence of Pharaoh, king of Egypt; and he made him governor over Egypt and all his house.

11 "Now a famine and great trouble came over all the land of Egypt and Canaan, and our fathers found no sustenance.

12 "But when Jacob heard that there was grain in Egypt, he sent out our fathers first.

13 "And the second *time* Joseph was made known to his brothers, and Joseph's family became known to the Pharaoh.

14 "Then Joseph sent and called his father Jacob and all his relatives to *him*, seventy-five people.

15 "So Jacob went down to Egypt; and he died, he and our fathers.

16 "And they were carried back to Shechem and laid in the tomb that Abraham bought for a sum of money from the sons of Hamor, *the father* of Shechem.

17 "But when the time of the promise drew near which God had sworn to Abraham, the people grew and multiplied in Egypt

18 "till another king arose who did not know Joseph.

19 "This man dealt treacherously with our people, and oppressed our forefathers, making them expose

their babies, so that they might not live.

20 "At this time Moses was born, and was well pleasing to God; and he was brought up in his father's house for three months.

21 "But when he was set out, Pharaoh's daughter took him away and brought him up as her own son.

22 "And Moses was learned in all the wisdom of the Egyptians, and was mighty in words and deeds.

23 "But when he was forty years old, it came into his heart to visit his brethren, the children of Israel.

24 "And seeing one of *them* suffer wrong, he defended and avenged him who was oppressed, and struck down the Egyptian.

25 "For he supposed that his brethren would have understood that God would deliver them by his hand, but they did not understand.

26 "And the next day he appeared to two of them as they were fighting, and *tried* to reconcile them, saying, 'Men, you are brethren; why do you wrong one another?'

27 "But he who did his neighbor wrong pushed him away, saying, 'Who made you a ruler and a judge over us?

28 'Do you want to kill me as you did the Egyptian yesterday?'

29 "Then, at this saying, Moses fled and became a sojourner in the land of Midian, where he had two sons.

30 "And when forty years had passed, an Angel of the Lord appeared to him in a flame of fire in a bush, in the wilderness of Mount Sinai.

31 "When Moses saw *it,* he marveled at the sight; and as he drew near to observe, the voice of the Lord came to him,

32 "saying, 'I am the God of your fathers—the God of Abraham, the God of Isaac, and the God of Jacob.' And Moses trembled and dared not look.

33 'Then the LORD said to him, "Take your sandals off your feet, for the place where you stand is holy ground.

34 "I have certainly seen the oppression of My people who are in Egypt; I have heard their groaning and have come down to deliver them. And now come, I will send you to Egypt." '

35 "This Moses whom they rejected, saying, 'Who made you a ruler and a judge?' is the one God sent *to be* a ruler and a deliverer by the hand of the Angel who appeared to him in the bush.

36 "He brought them out, after he had shown wonders and signs in the land of Egypt, and in the Red Sea, and in the wilderness forty years.

37 "This is that Moses who said to the children of Israel, 'The LORD your God will raise up for you a Prophet like me from your brethren. Him you shall hear.'

38 "This is he who was in the congregation in the wilderness with the Angel who spoke to him on Mount Sinai, and *with* our fathers, the one who received the living oracles to give to us,

39 "whom our fathers would not obey, but rejected. And in their hearts they turned back to Egypt,

40 "saying to Aaron, 'Make us gods to go before us; as for this Moses who brought us out of the land of Egypt, we do not know what has become of him.'

41 "And they made a calf in those days, offered sacrifices to the idol, and rejoiced in the works of their own hands.

42 "Then God turned and gave them up to worship the host of heaven, as it is written in the book of the Prophets:

'Did you offer Me slaughtered
    animals and sacrifices during
    forty years in the wilderness,
O house of Israel?
43 Yes, you took up the
    tabernacle of Moloch,

And the star of your god
    Remphan,
Images which you made to
    worship;
And I will carry you away
    beyond Babylon.'

44 "Our fathers had the tabernacle of witness in the wilderness, as He appointed, instructing Moses to make it according to the pattern that he had seen,

45 "which our fathers, having received it in turn, also brought with Joshua into the land possessed by the Gentiles, whom God drove out before the face of our fathers until the days of David,

46 "who found favor before God and asked to find a dwelling for the God of Jacob.

47 "But Solomon built Him a house.

48 "However, the Most High does not dwell in temples made with hands, as the prophet says:

49 'Heaven is My throne,
    And earth is My footstool.
What house will you build for
    Me? says the LORD,
Or what is the place of My
    rest?

50 Has My hand not made all
    these things?'

51 "You stiff-necked and uncircumcised in heart and ears! You always resist the Holy Spirit; as your fathers did, so do you.

52 "Which of the prophets did your fathers not persecute? And they killed those who foretold the coming of the Just One, of whom you now have become the betrayers and murderers,

53 "who have received the law by the direction of angels and have not kept it."

54 When they heard these things they were cut to the heart, and they gnashed at him with their teeth.

55 But he, being full of the Holy Spirit, gazed into heaven and saw the glory of God, and Jesus standing at the right hand of God,

56 and said, "Look! I see the heavens opened and the Son of Man standing at the right hand of God!"

57 Then they cried out with a loud voice, stopped their ears, and ran at him with one accord;

58 and they cast him out of the city and stoned him. And the witnesses laid down their clothes at the feet of a young man named Saul.

59 And they stoned Stephen as he was calling on God and saying, "Lord Jesus, receive my spirit."

60 Then he knelt down and cried out with a loud voice, "Lord, do not charge them with this sin." And when he had said this, he fell asleep.

8 Now Saul was consenting to his death. At that time a great persecution arose against the church which was at Jerusalem; and they were all scattered throughout the regions of Judea and Samaria, except the apostles.

2 And devout men carried Stephen to his burial, and made great lamentation over him.

3 As for Saul, he made havoc of the church, entering every house, and dragging off men and women, committing them to prison.

4 Therefore those who were scattered went everywhere preaching the word.

5 Then Philip went down to the city of Samaria and preached Christ to them.

6 And the multitudes with one accord heeded the things spoken by Philip, hearing and seeing the miracles which he did.

7 For unclean spirits, crying with a loud voice, came out of many who were possessed; and many who were paralyzed and lame were healed.

8 And there was great joy in that city.

9 But there was a certain man called Simon, who previously practiced sorcery in the city and astonished the people of Samaria, claiming that he was someone great,

10 to whom they all gave heed, from the least to the greatest, saying, "This man is the great power of God."

11 And they heeded him because he had astonished them with his sorceries for a long time.

12 But when they believed Philip as he preached the things concerning the kingdom of God and the name of Jesus Christ, both men and women were baptized.

13 Then Simon himself also believed; and when he was baptized he continued with Philip, and was amazed, seeing the miracles and signs which were done.

14 Now when the apostles who were at Jerusalem heard that Samaria had received the word of God, they sent Peter and John to them,

15 who, when they had come down, prayed for them that they might receive the Holy Spirit.

16 For as yet He had fallen upon none of them. They had only been baptized in the name of the Lord Jesus.

17 Then they laid hands on them, and they received the Holy Spirit.

18 Now when Simon saw that through the laying on of the apostles' hands the Holy Spirit was given, he offered them money,

19 saying, "Give me this power also, that anyone on whom I lay hands may receive the Holy Spirit."

20 But Peter said to him, "Your money perish with you, because you thought that the gift of God could be purchased with money!

21 "You have neither part nor portion in this matter, for your heart is not right in the sight of God.

22 "Repent therefore of this your wickedness, and pray God if perhaps the thought of your heart may be forgiven you.

23 "For I see that you are poisoned by bitterness and bound by iniquity."

24 Then Simon answered and said, "Pray to the Lord for me, that none of the things which you have spoken may come upon me."

25 So when they had testified and preached the word of the Lord, they returned to Jerusalem, preaching the gospel in many villages of the Samaritans.

26 Now an angel of the Lord spoke to Philip, saying, "Arise and go toward the south along the road which goes down from Jerusalem to Gaza." This is desert.

27 So he arose and went. And behold, a man of Ethiopia, a eunuch of great authority under Candace the queen of the Ethiopians, who had charge of all her treasury, and had come to Jerusalem to worship,

28 was returning. And sitting in his chariot, he was reading Isaiah the prophet.

29 Then the Spirit said to Philip, "Go near and overtake this chariot."

30 So Philip ran to him, and heard him reading the prophet Isaiah, and said, "Do you understand what you are reading?"

31 And he said, "How can I, unless someone guides me?" And he asked Philip to come up and sit with him.

32 The place in the Scripture which he read was this:

> "He was led as a sheep to the
>   slaughter;
> And like a lamb silent before
>   its shearer,
> So He opened not His mouth.
> 33 In His humiliation His justice
>   was taken away.
> And who will declare His
>   generation?
> For His life is taken from the
>   earth."

34 So the eunuch answered Philip and said, "I ask you, of whom does the prophet say this, of himself or of some other man?"

35 Then Philip opened his mouth, and beginning at this Scripture, preached Jesus to him.

36 Now as they went down the road, they came to some water. And the eunuch said, "See, *here is* water. What hinders me from being baptized?"

37 Then Philip said, "If you believe with all your heart, you may." And he answered and said, "I believe that Jesus Christ is the Son of God."

38 So he commanded the chariot to stand still. And both Philip and the eunuch went down into the water, and he baptized him.

39 Now when they came up out of the water, the Spirit of the Lord caught Philip away, so that the eunuch saw him no more; and he went on his way rejoicing.

40 But Philip was found at Azotus. And passing through, he preached in all the cities till he came to Caesarea.

9 Then Saul, still breathing threats and murder against the disciples of the Lord, went to the high priest

2 and asked letters from him to the synagogues of Damascus, so that if he found any who were of the Way, whether men or women, he might bring them bound to Jerusalem.

3 And as he journeyed he came near Damascus, and suddenly a light shone around him from heaven.

4 Then he fell to the ground, and heard a voice saying to him, "Saul, Saul, why are you persecuting Me?"

5 And he said, "Who are You, Lord?" And the Lord said, "I am Jesus, whom you are persecuting. *It is* hard for you to kick against the goads."

6 So he, trembling and astonished, said, "Lord, what do You want me to do?" And the Lord *said* to him, "Arise and go into the city, and you will be told what you must do."

7 And the men who journeyed with him stood speechless, hearing a voice but seeing no one.

8 Then Saul arose from the ground, and when his eyes were opened he saw no one. But they led him by the hand and brought *him* into Damascus.

9 And he was three days without sight, and neither ate nor drank.

10 Now there was a certain disciple at Damascus named Ananias; and to him the Lord said in a vision, "Ananias." And he said, "Here I am, Lord."

11 So the Lord *said* to him, "Arise and go to the street called Straight, and inquire at the house of Judas for *one* called Saul of Tarsus, for behold, he is praying.

12 "And in a vision he has seen a man named Ananias coming in and putting *his* hand on him, so that he might receive his sight."

13 Then Ananias answered, "Lord, I have heard from many about this man, how much harm he has done to Your saints in Jerusalem.

14 "And here he has authority from the chief priests to bind all who call on Your name."

15 But the Lord said to him, "Go, for he is a chosen vessel of Mine to bear My name before Gentiles, kings, and the children of Israel.

16 "For I will show him how many things he must suffer for My name's sake."

17 And Ananias went his way and entered the house; and laying his hands on him he said, "Brother Saul, the Lord Jesus, who appeared to you on the road as you came, has sent me that you may receive your sight and be filled with the Holy Spirit."

18 Immediately there fell from his eyes *something* like scales, and he

received his sight at once; and he arose and was baptized.

19 And when he had received food, he was strengthened. Then Saul spent some days with the disciples at Damascus.

20 Immediately he preached the Christ in the synagogues, that He is the Son of God.

21 Then all who heard were amazed, and said, "Is this not he who destroyed those who called on this name in Jerusalem, and has come here for that purpose, so that he might bring them bound to the chief priests?"

22 But Saul increased all the more in strength, and confounded the Jews who dwelt in Damascus, proving that this *Jesus* is the Christ.

23 Now after many days were past, the Jews plotted to kill him.

24 But their plot became known to Saul. And they watched the gates day and night, to kill him.

25 Then the disciples took him by night and let *him* down through the wall in a large basket.

26 And when Saul had come to Jerusalem, he tried to join the disciples; but they were all afraid of him, and did not believe that he was a disciple.

27 But Barnabas took him and brought *him* to the apostles. And he declared to them how he had seen the Lord on the road, and that He had spoken to him, and how he had preached boldly at Damascus in the name of Jesus.

28 So he was with them at Jerusalem, coming in and going out.

29 And he spoke boldly in the name of the Lord Jesus and disputed against the Hellenists, but they attempted to kill him.

30 When the brethren found out, they brought him down to Caesarea and sent him out to Tarsus.

31 Then the churches throughout all Judea, Galilee, and Samaria had peace and were edified. And walking in the fear of the Lord and in the comfort of the Holy Spirit, they were multiplied.

32 Now it came to pass, as Peter went through all *parts of the country,* that he also came down to the saints who dwelt in Lydda.

33 There he found a certain man named Aeneas, who had been bedridden eight years and was paralyzed.

34 And Peter said to him, "Aeneas, Jesus the Christ heals you. Arise and make your bed." Then he arose immediately.

35 So all who dwelt at Lydda and Sharon saw him and turned to the Lord.

36 At Joppa there was a certain disciple named Tabitha, which is translated Dorcas. This woman was full of good works and charitable deeds which she did.

37 But it happened in those days that she became sick and died. When they had washed her, they laid *her* in an upper room.

38 And since Lydda was near Joppa, and the disciples had heard that Peter was there, they sent two men to him, imploring *him* not to delay in coming to them.

39 Then Peter arose and went with them. When he had come, they brought *him* to the upper room. And all the widows stood by him weeping, showing the tunics and garments which Dorcas had made while she was with them.

40 But Peter put them all out, and knelt down and prayed. And turning to the body he said, "Tabitha, arise." And she opened her eyes, and when she saw Peter she sat up.

41 Then he gave her *his* hand and lifted her up; and when he had called the saints and widows, he presented her alive.

42 And it became known throughout all Joppa, and many believed on the Lord.

43 So it was that he stayed many days in Joppa with Simon, a tanner.

10 There was a certain man in Caesarea called Cornelius, a centurion of what was called the Italian Regiment,

2 a devout *man* and one who feared God with all his household, who gave alms generously to the people, and prayed to God always.

3 About the ninth hour of the day he saw clearly in a vision an angel of God coming in and saying to him, "Cornelius!"

4 And when he observed him, he was afraid, and said, "What is it, lord?" So he said to him, "Your prayers and your alms have come up for a memorial before God.

5 "Now send men to Joppa, and send for Simon whose surname is Peter.

6 "He is lodging with Simon, a tanner, whose house is by the sea. He will tell you what you must do."

7 And when the angel who spoke to him had departed, Cornelius called two of his household servants and a devout soldier from among those who waited on him continually.

8 So when he had explained *these* things to them, he sent them to Joppa.

9 The next day, as they went on their journey and drew near the city, Peter went up on the housetop to pray, about the sixth hour.

10 Then he became very hungry and wanted to eat; but while they made ready, he fell into a trance

11 and saw heaven opened and an object like a great sheet bound at the four corners, descending to him and let down to the earth.

12 In it were all kinds of fourfooted animals of the earth, wild beasts, creeping things, and birds of the air.

13 And a voice came to him, "Rise, Peter; kill and eat."

14 But Peter said, "Not so, Lord! For I have never eaten anything common or unclean."

15 And a voice *spoke* to him again the second time, "What God has cleansed you must not call common."

16 This was done three times. And the object was taken up into heaven again.

17 Now while Peter wondered within himself what this vision which he had seen meant, behold, the men who had been sent from Cornelius had made inquiry for Simon's house, and stood before the gate.

18 And they called and asked whether Simon, whose surname was Peter, was lodging there.

19 While Peter thought about the vision, the Spirit said to him, "Behold, three men are seeking you.

20 "Arise therefore, go down and go with them, doubting nothing; for I have sent them."

21 Then Peter went down to the men who had been sent to him from Cornelius, and said, "Yes, I am he whom you seek. For what reason have you come?"

22 And they said, "Cornelius *the* centurion, a just man, one who fears God and has a good reputation among all the nation of the Jews, was divinely instructed by a holy angel to summon you to his house, and to hear words from you."

23 Then he invited them in and lodged *them*. On the next day Peter went away with them, and some brethren from Joppa accompanied him.

24 And the following day they entered Caesarea. Now Cornelius was waiting for them, and had called together his relatives and close friends.

25 As Peter was coming in, Cornelius met him and fell down at his feet and worshiped *him*.

26 But Peter lifted him up, saying, "Stand up; I myself am also a man."

27 And as he talked with him, he

went in and found many who had come together.

28 Then he said to them, "You know how unlawful it is for a Jewish man to keep company with or go to one of another nation. But God has shown me that I should not call any man common or unclean.

29 "Therefore I came without objection as soon as I was sent for. I ask, then, for what reason have you sent for me?"

30 And Cornelius said, "Four days ago I was fasting until this hour; and at the ninth hour I prayed in my house, and behold, a man stood before me in bright clothing,

31 "and said, 'Cornelius, your prayer has been heard, and your alms are remembered in the sight of God.

32 'Send therefore to Joppa and call Simon here, whose surname is Peter. He is lodging in the house of Simon, a tanner, by the sea. When he comes, he will speak to you.'

33 "So I sent to you immediately, and you have done well to come. Now therefore, we are all present before God, to hear all the things commanded you by God."

34 Then Peter opened *his* mouth and said: "In truth I perceive that God shows no partiality.

35 "But in every nation whoever fears Him and works righteousness is accepted by Him.

36 "The word which *God* sent to the children of Israel, preaching peace through Jesus Christ—He is Lord of all—

37 "that word you know, which was proclaimed throughout all Judea, and began from Galilee after the baptism which John preached:

38 "how God anointed Jesus of Nazareth with the Holy Spirit and with power, who went about doing good and healing all who were oppressed by the devil, for God was with Him.

39 "And we are witnesses of all things which He did both in the land of the Jews and in Jerusalem, whom they killed by hanging on a tree.

40 "Him God raised up on the third day, and showed Him openly,

41 "not to all the people, but to witnesses chosen before by God, *even* to us who ate and drank with Him after He arose from the dead.

42 "And He commanded us to preach to the people, and to testify that it is He who was ordained by God *to be* Judge of the living and the dead.

43 "To Him all the prophets witness that, through His name, whoever believes in Him will receive remission of sins."

44 While Peter was still speaking these words, the Holy Spirit fell upon all those who heard the word.

45 And those of the circumcision who believed were astonished, as many as came with Peter, because the gift of the Holy Spirit had been poured out on the Gentiles also.

46 For they heard them speak with tongues and magnify God. Then Peter answered,

47 "Can anyone forbid water, that these should not be baptized who have received the Holy Spirit just as we *have?*"

48 And he commanded them to be baptized in the name of the Lord. Then they asked him to stay a few days.

11 Now the apostles and brethren who were in Judea heard that the Gentiles had also received the word of God.

2 And when Peter came up to Jerusalem, those of the circumcision contended with him,

3 saying, "You went in to uncircumcised men and ate with them!"

4 But Peter explained *it* to them in order from the beginning, saying:

5 "I was in the city of Joppa praying; and in a trance I saw a vision, an object descending like a great

159

sheet, let down from heaven by four corners; and it came to me.

6 "When I observed it intently and considered, I saw four-footed animals of the earth, wild beasts, creeping things, and birds of the air.

7 "And I heard a voice saying to me, 'Rise, Peter; kill and eat.'

8 "But I said, 'Not so, Lord! For nothing common or unclean has at any time entered my mouth.'

9 "But the voice answered me again from heaven, 'What God has cleansed you must not call common.'

10 "Now this was done three times, and all were drawn up again into heaven.

11 "At that very moment, three men stood before the house where I was, having been sent to me from Caesarea.

12 "Then the Spirit told me to go with them, doubting nothing. Moreover these six brethren accompanied me, and we entered the man's house.

13 "And he told us how he had seen an angel standing in his house, who said to him, 'Send men to Joppa, and call for Simon whose surname is Peter,

14 'who will tell you words by which you and all your household will be saved.'

15 "And as I began to speak, the Holy Spirit fell upon them, as upon us at the beginning.

16 "Then I remembered the word of the Lord, how He said, 'John indeed baptized with water, but you shall be baptized with the Holy Spirit.'

17 "If therefore God gave them the same gift as *He gave* us when we believed on the Lord Jesus Christ, who was I that I could withstand God?"

18 When they heard these things they became silent; and they glorified God, saying, "Then God has also granted to the Gentiles repentance to life."

19 Now those who were scattered after the persecution that arose over Stephen traveled as far as Phoenicia, Cyprus, and Antioch, preaching the word to no one but the Jews only.

20 But some of them were men from Cyprus and Cyrene, who, when they had come to Antioch, spoke to the Hellenists, preaching the Lord Jesus.

21 And the hand of the Lord was with them, and a great number believed and turned to the Lord.

22 Then news of these things came to the ears of the church in Jerusalem, and they sent out Barnabas to go as far as Antioch.

23 When he came and had seen the grace of God, he was glad, and encouraged them all that with purpose of heart they should continue with the Lord.

24 For he was a good man, full of the Holy Spirit and of faith. And a great many people were added to the Lord.

25 Then Barnabas departed for Tarsus to seek Saul.

26 And when he had found him, he brought him to Antioch. So it was that for a whole year they assembled with the church and taught a great many people. And the disciples were first called Christians in Antioch.

27 And in these days prophets came from Jerusalem to Antioch.

28 Then one of them, named Agabus, stood up and showed by the Spirit that there was going to be a great famine throughout all the world, which also happened in the days of Claudius Caesar.

29 Then the disciples, each according to his ability, determined to send relief to the brethren dwelling in Judea.

30 This they also did, and sent it to the elders by the hands of Barnabas and Saul.

12 Now about that time Herod the king stretched out *his*

hand to harass some from the church.

2 Then he killed James the brother of John with the sword.

3 And because he saw that it pleased the Jews, he proceeded further to seize Peter also. Now it was *during* the Days of Unleavened Bread.

4 So when he had apprehended him, he put *him* in prison, and delivered *him* to four squads of soldiers to keep him, intending to bring him before the people after Passover.

5 Peter was therefore kept in prison, but constant prayer was offered to God for him by the church.

6 And when Herod was about to bring him out, that night Peter was sleeping, bound with two chains between two soldiers; and the guards before the door were keeping the prison.

7 Now behold, an angel of the Lord stood by *him*, and a light shone in the prison; and he struck Peter on the side and raised him up, saying, "Arise quickly!" And his chains fell off *his* hands.

8 Then the angel said to him, "Gird yourself and tie on your sandals"; and so he did. And he said to him, "Put on your garment and follow me."

9 So he went out and followed him, and did not know that what was done by the angel was real, but thought he was seeing a vision.

10 When they were past the first and the second guard posts, they came to the iron gate that leads to the city, which opened to them of its own accord; and they went out and went down one street, and immediately the angel departed from him.

11 And when Peter had come to himself, he said, "Now I know for certain that the Lord has sent His angel, and has delivered me from the hand of Herod and *from* all the expectation of the Jewish people."

12 So, when he had considered *this*, he came to the house of Mary, the mother of John whose surname was Mark, where many were gathered together praying.

13 And as Peter knocked at the door of the gate, a girl named Rhoda came to answer.

14 When she recognized Peter's voice, because of *her* gladness she did not open the gate, but ran in and announced that Peter stood before the gate.

15 But they said to her, "You are beside yourself!" Yet she kept insisting that it was so. So they said, "It is his angel."

16 Now Peter continued knocking; and when they opened *the door* and saw him, they were astonished.

17 But motioning to them with his hand to keep silent, he declared to them how the Lord had brought him out of the prison. And he said, "Go, tell these things to James and to the brethren." And he departed and went to another place.

18 Then, as soon as it was day, there was no small stir among the soldiers about what had become of Peter.

19 But when Herod had searched for him and not found him, he examined the guards and commanded that *they* should be put to death. And he went down from Judea to Caesarea, and stayed *there*.

20 Now Herod had been very angry with the people of Tyre and Sidon; but they came to him with one accord, and having made Blastus the king's chamberlain their friend, they asked for peace, because their country was supplied with food by the king's *country*.

21 So on a set day Herod, arrayed in royal apparel, sat on his throne and gave an oration to them.

22 And the people kept shouting, "The voice of a god and not of a man!"

23 Then immediately an angel of the Lord struck him, because he did not give glory to God. And he was eaten by worms and died.

24 But the word of God grew and multiplied.

25 And Barnabas and Saul returned from Jerusalem when they had fulfilled *their* ministry, and they also took with them John whose surname was Mark.

13 Now in the church that was at Antioch there were certain prophets and teachers: Barnabas, Simeon who was called Niger, Lucius of Cyrene, Manaen who had been brought up with Herod the tetrarch, and Saul.

2 As they ministered to the Lord and fasted, the Holy Spirit said, "Now separate to Me Barnabas and Saul for the work to which I have called them."

3 Then, having fasted and prayed, and laid hands on them, they sent *them* away.

4 So, being sent out by the Holy Spirit, they went down to Seleucia, and from there they sailed to Cyprus.

5 And when they arrived in Salamis, they preached the word of God in the synagogues of the Jews. They also had John as *their* assistant.

6 Now when they had gone through the island to Paphos, they found a certain sorcerer, a false prophet, a Jew whose name *was* Bar-Jesus,

7 who was with the proconsul, Sergius Paulus, an intelligent man. This man called for Barnabas and Saul and sought to hear the word of God.

8 But Elymas the sorcerer (for so his name is translated) withstood them, seeking to turn the proconsul away from the faith.

9 Then Saul, who also *is called* Paul, filled with the Holy Spirit, looked intently at him

10 and said, "O full of all deceit and all fraud, *you* son of the devil, *you*

enemy of all righteousness, will you not cease perverting the straight ways of the Lord?

11 "And now, indeed, the hand of the Lord *is* upon you, and you shall be blind, not seeing the sun for a time." And immediately a dark mist fell on him, and he went around seeking someone to lead him by the hand.

12 Then the proconsul believed, when he saw what had been done, being astonished at the teaching of the Lord.

13 Now when Paul and his party set sail from Paphos, they came to Perga in Pamphylia; and John, departing from them, returned to Jerusalem.

14 But when they departed from Perga, they came to Antioch in Pisidia, and went into the synagogue on the Sabbath day and sat down.

15 And after the reading of the Law and the Prophets, the rulers of the synagogue sent to them, saying, "Men *and* brethren, if you have any word of exhortation for the people, say on."

16 Then Paul stood up, and motioning with *his* hand said, "Men of Israel, and you who fear God, listen:

17 "The God of this people Israel chose our fathers, and exalted the people when they dwelt as strangers in the land of Egypt, and with an uplifted arm He brought them out of it.

18 "Now for a time of about forty years He put up with their ways in the wilderness.

19 "And when He had destroyed seven nations in the land of Canaan, He distributed their land to them by allotment.

20 "After that He gave *them* judges for about four hundred and fifty years, until Samuel the prophet.

21 "And afterward they asked for a king; so God gave them Saul the

son of Kish, a man of the tribe of Benjamin, for forty years.

22 "And when He had removed him, He raised up for them David as king, to whom also He gave testimony and said, *I have found David the son of Jesse, a man after My own heart,* who will do all My will.'

23 "From this man's seed, according to *the* promise, God raised up for Israel a Savior—Jesus—

24 "after John had first preached, before His coming, the baptism of repentance to all the people of Israel.

25 "And as John was finishing his course, he said, 'Who do you think I am? I am not *He.* But behold, there comes One after me, the sandals of whose feet I am not worthy to loose.'

26 "Men *and* brethren, sons of the family of Abraham, and those among you who fear God, to you the word of this salvation has been sent.

27 "For those who dwell in Jerusalem, and their rulers, because they did not know Him, nor even the voices of the Prophets which are read every Sabbath, have fulfilled *them* in condemning *Him.*

28 "And though they found no cause for death *in Him,* they asked Pilate that He should be put to death.

29 "Now when they had fulfilled all that was written concerning Him, they took *Him* down from the tree and laid *Him* in a tomb.

30 "But God raised Him from the dead.

31 "He was seen for many days by those who came up with Him from Galilee to Jerusalem, who are His witnesses to the people.

32 "And we declare to you glad tidings—that promise which was made to the fathers,

33 "God has fulfilled this for us their children, in that He has raised up Jesus. As it is also written in the second Psalm:

'You are My Son,
   Today I have begotten You.'

34 "And that He raised Him from the dead, no more to return to corruption, He has spoken thus:

'I will give you the sure mercies of David.'

35 "Therefore He also says in another *Psalm:*

'You will not allow Your Holy One to see corruption.'

36 "For David, after he had served his own generation by the will of God, fell asleep, was buried with his fathers, and saw corruption;

37 "but He whom God raised up saw no corruption.

38 "Therefore let it be known to you, brethren, that through this Man is preached to you the forgiveness of sins; ♥

39 "and by Him everyone who believes is justified from all things from which you could not be justified by the law of Moses.

40 "Beware therefore, lest what has been spoken in the prophets come upon you:

41 'Behold, you despisers,
   Marvel and perish;
   For I work a work in your days,
   A work which you will by no means believe,
   Though one were to declare it to you.'"

42 And when the Jews went out of the synagogue, the Gentiles begged that these words might be preached to them the next Sabbath.

43 Now when the congregation had broken up, many of the Jews and devout proselytes followed Paul and Barnabas, who, speaking to them, persuaded them to continue in the grace of God.

44 And the next Sabbath almost the whole city came together to hear the word of God.

45 But when the Jews saw the multitudes, they were filled with envy; and contradicting and blaspheming, they opposed the things spoken by Paul.

46 Then Paul and Barnabas grew bold and said, "It was necessary that the word of God should be spoken to you first; but since you reject it, and judge yourselves unworthy of everlasting life, behold, we turn to the Gentiles.

47 "For so the Lord has commanded us:

*'I have set you to be a light
to the Gentiles,
That you should be for
salvation to the ends of the
earth.'"*

48 Now when the Gentiles heard this, they were glad and glorified the word of the Lord. And as many as had been appointed to eternal life believed.

49 And the word of the Lord was being spread throughout all the region.

50 But the Jews stirred up the devout and prominent women and the chief men of the city, raised up persecution against Paul and Barnabas, and expelled them from their region.

51 But they shook off the dust from their feet against them, and came to Iconium.

52 And the disciples were filled with joy and with the Holy Spirit.

14 Now it happened in Iconium that they went together to the synagogue of the Jews, and so spoke that a great multitude both of the Jews and of the Greeks believed.

2 But the unbelieving Jews stirred up the Gentiles and poisoned their minds against the brethren.

3 Therefore they stayed there a long time, speaking boldly in the Lord, who was bearing witness to the word of His grace, granting signs and wonders to be done by their hands.

4 But the multitude of the city was divided: part sided with the Jews, and part with the apostles.

5 And when a violent attempt was made by both the Gentiles and Jews, with their rulers, to abuse and stone them,

6 they became aware of it and fled to Lystra and Derbe, cities of Lycaonia, and to the surrounding region.

7 And they were preaching the gospel there.

8 And in Lystra a certain man without strength in his feet was sitting, a cripple from his mother's womb, who had never walked.

9 *This* man heard Paul speaking. Paul, observing him intently and seeing that he had faith to be healed,

10 said with a loud voice, "Stand up straight on your feet!" And he leaped and walked.

11 Now when the people saw what Paul had done, they raised their voices, saying in the Lycaonian *language,* "The gods have come down to us in the likeness of men!"

12 And Barnabas they called Zeus, and Paul, Hermes, because he was the chief speaker.

13 Then the priest of Zeus, whose temple was in front of their city, brought oxen and garlands to the gates, intending to sacrifice with the multitudes.

14 But when the apostles Barnabas and Paul heard this, they tore their clothes and ran in among the multitude, crying out

15 and saying, "Men, why are you doing these things? We also are men with the same nature as you, and preach to you that you should turn from these vain things to the living God, who made the heaven,

the earth, the sea, and all things that are in them,

16 "who in bygone generations allowed all nations to walk in their own ways.

17 "Nevertheless He did not leave Himself without witness, in that He did good, gave us rain from heaven and fruitful seasons, filling our hearts with food and gladness."

18 And with these sayings they could scarcely restrain the multitudes from sacrificing to them.

19 Then Jews from Antioch and Iconium came there; and having persuaded the multitudes, they stoned Paul *and* dragged *him* out of the city, supposing him to be dead.

20 However, when the disciples gathered around him, he rose up and went into the city. And the next day he departed with Barnabas to Derbe.

21 And when they had preached the gospel to that city and made many disciples, they returned to Lystra, Iconium, and Antioch,

22 strengthening the souls of the disciples, exhorting *them* to continue in the faith, and *saying,* "We must through many tribulations enter the kingdom of God."

23 So when they had appointed elders in every church, and prayed with fasting, they commended them to the Lord in whom they had believed.

24 And after they had passed through Pisidia, they came to Pamphylia.

25 Now when they had preached the word in Perga, they went down to Attalia.

26 From there they sailed to Antioch, where they had been commended to the grace of God for the work which they had completed.

27 And when they had come and gathered the church together, they reported all that God had done with them, and that He had opened the door of faith to the Gentiles.

28 So they stayed there a long time with the disciples.

15 And certain *men* came down from Judea and taught the brethren, "Unless you are circumcised according to the custom of Moses, you cannot be saved."

2 Therefore, when Paul and Barnabas had no small dissension and dispute with them, they determined that Paul and Barnabas and certain others of them should go up to Jerusalem, to the apostles and elders, about this question.

3 So, being sent on their way by the church, they passed through Phoenicia and Samaria, describing the conversion of the Gentiles; and they caused great joy to all the brethren.

4 And when they had come to Jerusalem, they were received by the church and the apostles and the elders; and they reported all things that God had done with them.

5 But some of the sect of the Pharisees who believed rose up, saying, "It is necessary to circumcise them, and to command *them* to keep the law of Moses."

6 So the apostles and elders came together to consider this matter.

7 And when there had been much dispute, Peter rose up and said to them: "Men and brethren, you know that a good while ago God chose among us, that by my mouth the Gentiles should hear the word of the gospel and believe.

8 "So God, who knows the heart, acknowledged them, by giving them the Holy Spirit just as *He did* to us,

9 "and made no distinction between us and them, purifying their hearts by faith.

10 "Now therefore, why do you test God by putting a yoke on the neck of the disciples which neither our fathers nor we were able to bear?

165

11 "But we believe that through the grace of the Lord Jesus Christ we shall be saved in the same manner as they."

12 Then all the multitude kept silent and listened to Barnabas and Paul declaring how many miracles and wonders God had worked through them among the Gentiles.

13 And after they had become silent, James answered, saying, "Men *and* brethren, listen to me:

14 "Simon has declared how God at the first visited the Gentiles to take out of them a people for His name.

15 "And with this the words of the prophets agree, just as it is written:

16 'After this I will return
And will rebuild the tabernacle
    of David which has fallen
    down.
I will rebuild its ruins,
And I will set it up,
17 So that the rest of mankind
    may seek the LORD,
Even all the Gentiles who are
    called by My name,
Says the LORD who does all
    these things.'

18 "Known to God from eternity are all His works.

19 "Therefore I judge that we should not trouble those from among the Gentiles who are turning to God,

20 "but that we write to them to abstain from things polluted by idols, *from* sexual immorality, *from* things strangled, and *from* blood.

21 "For Moses has had throughout many generations those who preach him in every city, being read in the synagogues every Sabbath."

22 Then it pleased the apostles and elders, with the whole church, to send chosen men of their own company to Antioch with Paul and Barnabas, *namely,* Judas who was also named Barsabas, and Silas, leading men among the brethren.

23 They wrote this *letter* by them:

The apostles, the elders, and
    the brethren,
To the brethren who are of the
    Gentiles in Antioch, Syria, and
    Cilicia:
Greetings.

24 Since we have heard that some who went out from us have troubled you with words, unsettling your souls, saying, '*You must* be circumcised and keep the law'—to whom we gave no *such* commandment—

25 it seemed good to us, being assembled with one accord, to send chosen men to you with our beloved Barnabas and Paul,

26 men who have risked their lives for the name of our Lord Jesus Christ.

27 We have therefore sent Judas and Silas, who will also report the same things by word of mouth.

28 For it seemed good to the Holy Spirit, and to us, to lay upon you no greater burden than these necessary things:

29 that you abstain from things offered to idols, from blood, from things strangled, and from sexual immorality. If you keep yourselves from these, you will do well.
Farewell.

30 So when they were sent off, they came to Antioch; and when they had gathered the multitude together, they delivered the letter.

31 When they had read it, they rejoiced over its encouragement.

32 Now Judas and Silas, themselves being prophets also, exhorted the brethren with many words and strengthened *them*.

33 And after they had stayed *there* for a time, they were sent back with greetings from the brethren to the apostles.

34 However, it seemed good to Silas to remain there.

35 Paul and Barnabas also remained in Antioch, teaching and preaching the word of the Lord, with many others also.

36 Then after some days Paul said to Barnabas, "Let us now go back and visit our brethren in every city where we have preached the word of the Lord, *and see* how they are doing."

37 Now Barnabas was determined to take with them John called Mark.

38 But Paul insisted that they should not take with them the one who had departed from them in Pamphylia, and had not gone with them to the work.

39 Then the contention became so sharp that they parted from one another. And so Barnabas took Mark and sailed to Cyprus;

40 but Paul chose Silas and departed, being commended by the brethren to the grace of God.

41 And he went through Syria and Cilicia, strengthening the churches.

16 Then he came to Derbe and Lystra. And behold, a certain disciple was there, named Timothy, *the* son of a certain Jewish woman who believed, but his father *was* Greek.

2 He was well spoken of by the brethren who were at Lystra and Iconium.

3 Paul wanted to have him go on with him. And he took *him* and circumcised him because of the Jews who were in that region, for they all knew that his father was Greek.

4 And as they went through the cities, they delivered to them the decrees to keep, which were determined by the apostles and elders at Jerusalem.

5 So the churches were strengthened in the faith, and increased in number daily.

6 Now when they had gone through Phrygia and the region of Galatia, they were forbidden by the Holy Spirit to preach the word in Asia.

7 After they had come to Mysia, they tried to go into Bithynia, but the Spirit did not permit them.

8 So passing by Mysia, they came down to Troas.

9 And a vision appeared to Paul in the night. A man of Macedonia stood and pleaded with him, saying, "Come over to Macedonia and help us."

10 Now after he had seen the vision, immediately we sought to go to Macedonia, concluding that the Lord had called us to preach the gospel to them.

11 Therefore, sailing from Troas, we ran a straight course to Samothrace, and the next *day* came to Neapolis,

12 and from there to Philippi, which is the foremost city of that part of Macedonia, a colony. And we were staying in that city for some days.

13 And on the Sabbath day we went out of the city to the riverside, where prayer was customarily made; and we sat down and spoke to the women who met *there.*

14 Now a certain woman named Lydia heard *us.* She was a seller of purple from the city of Thyatira, who worshiped God. The Lord opened her heart to heed the things spoken by Paul.

15 And when she and her household were baptized, she begged *us,* saying, "If you have judged me to be faithful to the Lord, come to my house and stay." And she constrained us.

16 Now it happened, as we went to prayer, that a certain slave girl possessed with a spirit of divination met us, who brought her masters much profit by fortune-telling.

17 This girl followed Paul and us, and cried out, saying, "These men are the servants of the Most High God, who proclaim to us the way of salvation."

18 And this she did for many days. But Paul, greatly annoyed, turned and said to the spirit, "I command you in the name of Jesus Christ to come out of her." And he came out that very hour.

19 But when her masters saw that their hope of profit was gone, they seized Paul and Silas and dragged *them* into the marketplace to the authorities.

20 And they brought them to the magistrates, and said, "These men, being Jews, exceedingly trouble our city;

21 "and they teach customs which are not lawful for us, being Romans, to receive or observe."

22 Then the multitude rose up together against them; and the magistrates tore off their clothes and commanded *them* to be beaten with rods.

23 And when they had laid many stripes on them, they threw *them* into prison, commanding the jailer to keep them securely.

24 Having received such a charge, he put them into the inner prison and fastened their feet in the stocks.

25 But at midnight Paul and Silas were praying and singing hymns to God, and the prisoners were listening to them.

26 Suddenly there was a great earthquake, so that the foundations of the prison were shaken; and immediately all the doors were opened and everyone's chains were loosed.

27 And the keeper of the prison, awaking from sleep and seeing the prison doors open, supposing the prisoners had fled, drew his sword and was about to kill himself.

28 But Paul called with a loud voice, saying, "Do yourself no harm, for we are all here."

29 Then he called for a light, ran in, and fell down trembling before Paul and Silas.

30 And he brought them out and said, "Sirs, what must I do to be saved?"

31 So they said, "Believe on the Lord Jesus Christ, and you will be saved, you and your household."

32 Then they spoke the word of the Lord to him and to all who were in his house.

33 And he took them the same hour of the night and washed *their* stripes. And immediately he and all his family were baptized.

34 Now when he had brought them into his house, he set food before them; and he rejoiced, having believed in God with all his household.

35 And when it was day, the magistrates sent the officers, saying, "Let those men go."

36 So the keeper of the prison reported these words to Paul, saying, "The magistrates have sent to let you go. Now therefore depart, and go in peace."

37 But Paul said to them, "They have beaten us openly, uncondemned Romans, *and* have thrown *us* into prison. And now do they put us out secretly? No indeed! Let them come themselves and get us out."

38 And the officers told these words to the magistrates, and they were afraid when they heard that they were Romans.

39 Then they came and pleaded with them and brought *them* out, and asked *them* to depart from the city.

40 So they went out of the prison and entered *the house of* Lydia; and when they had seen the brethren, they encouraged them and departed.

17 Now when they had passed through Amphipolis and Apollonia, they came to Thessalonica, where there was a synagogue of the Jews.

2 Then Paul, as his custom was, went in to them, and for three Sabbaths reasoned with them from the Scriptures,

3 explaining and demonstrating that the Christ had to suffer and rise again from the dead, and *saying*, "This Jesus whom I preach to you is the Christ."

4 And some of them were persuaded; and a great multitude of the devout Greeks, and not a few of the leading women, joined Paul and Silas.

5 But the Jews who were not persuaded, becoming envious, took some of the evil men from the marketplace, and gathering a mob, set all the city in an uproar and attacked the house of Jason, and sought to bring them out to the people.

6 But when they did not find them, they dragged Jason and some brethren to the rulers of the city, crying out, "These who have turned the world upside down have come here too.

7 "Jason has harbored them, and these are all acting contrary to the decrees of Caesar, saying there is another king—Jesus."

8 And they troubled the crowd and the rulers of the city when they heard these things.

9 So when they had taken security from Jason and the rest, they let them go.

10 Then the brethren immediately sent Paul and Silas away by night to Berea. When they arrived, they went into the synagogue of the Jews.

11 These were more fair-minded than those in Thessalonica, in that they received the word with all readiness, and searched the Scriptures daily *to find out* whether these things were so.

12 Therefore many of them believed, and also not a few of the Greeks, prominent women as well as men.

13 But when the Jews from Thessalonica learned that the word of God was preached by Paul at Berea, they came there also and stirred up the crowds.

14 Then immediately the brethren sent Paul away, to go to the sea; but both Silas and Timothy remained there.

15 So those who conducted Paul brought him to Athens; and receiving a command for Silas and Timothy to come to him with all speed, they departed.

16 Now while Paul waited for them at Athens, his spirit was provoked within him when he saw that the city was given over to idols.

17 Therefore he reasoned in the synagogue with the Jews and with the *Gentile* worshipers, and in the marketplace daily with those who happened to be there.

18 Then certain Epicurean and Stoic philosophers encountered him. And some said, "What does this babbler want to say?" Others said, "He seems to be a proclaimer of foreign gods," because he preached to them Jesus and the resurrection.

19 And they took him and brought him to the Areopagus, saying, "May we know what this new doctrine *is* of which you speak?

20 "For you are bringing some strange things to our ears. Therefore we want to know what these things mean."

21 For all the Athenians and the foreigners who were there spent their time in nothing else but either to tell or to hear some new thing.

22 Then Paul stood in the midst of the Areopagus and said, "Men of Athens, I perceive that in all things you are very religious;

23 "for as I was passing through and considering the objects of your worship, I even found an altar with this inscription:

TO THE UNKNOWN GOD.

Therefore, the One whom you worship without knowing, Him I proclaim to you:

24 "God, who made the world and everything in it, since He is Lord of

heaven and earth, does not dwell in temples made with hands.

25 "Nor is He worshiped with men's hands, as though He needed anything, since He gives to all life, breath, and all things.

26 "And He has made from one blood every nation of men to dwell on all the face of the earth, and has determined their preappointed times and the boundaries of their habitation,

27 "so that they should seek the Lord, in the hope that they might grope for Him and find Him, though He is not far from each one of us;

28 "for in Him we live and move and have our being, as also some of your own poets have said, 'For we are also His offspring.'

29 "Therefore, since we are the offspring of God, we ought not to think that the Divine Nature is like gold or silver or stone, something shaped by art and man's devising.

30 "Truly, these times of ignorance God overlooked, but now commands all men everywhere to repent,

31 "because He has appointed a day on which He will judge the world in righteousness by the Man whom He has ordained. He has given assurance of this to all by raising Him from the dead."

32 And when they heard of the resurrection of the dead, some mocked, while others said, "We will hear you again on this *matter*."

33 So Paul departed from among them.

34 However, some men joined him and believed, among them Dionysius the Areopagite, a woman named Damaris, and others with them.

18 After these things Paul departed from Athens and went to Corinth.

2 And he found a certain Jew named Aquila, born in Pontus,

who had recently come from Italy with his wife Priscilla (because Claudius had commanded all the Jews to depart from Rome); and he came to them.

3 So, because he was of the same trade, he stayed with them and worked; for by occupation they were tentmakers.

4 And he reasoned in the synagogue every Sabbath, and persuaded both Jews and Greeks.

5 When Silas and Timothy had come from Macedonia, Paul was constrained by the Spirit, and testified to the Jews *that* Jesus *is* the Christ.

6 But when they opposed him and blasphemed, he shook *his* garments and said to them, "Your blood *be* upon your *own* heads; I *am* clean. From now on I will go to the Gentiles."

7 And he departed from there and entered the house of a certain *man* named Justus, *one* who worshiped God, whose house was next door to the synagogue.

8 Then Crispus, the ruler of the synagogue, believed on the Lord with all his household. And many of the Corinthians, hearing, believed and were baptized.

9 Now the Lord spoke to Paul in the night by a vision, "Do not be afraid, but speak, and do not keep silent;

10 "for I am with you, and no one will attack you to hurt you; for I have many people in this city."

11 And he continued *there* a year and six months, teaching the word of God among them.

12 Now when Gallio was proconsul of Achaia, the Jews with one accord rose up against Paul and brought him to the judgment seat,

13 saying, "This *fellow* persuades men to worship God contrary to the law."

14 And when Paul was about to open *his* mouth, Gallio said to the Jews, "If it were a matter of

wrongdoing or wicked crimes, O Jews, there would be reason why I should bear with you.

15 "But if it is a question of words and names and your own law, look *to it* yourselves; for I do not want to be a judge of such *matters*."

16 And he drove them from the judgment seat.

17 Then all the Greeks took Sosthenes, the ruler of the synagogue, and beat *him* before the judgment seat. But Gallio took no notice of these things.

18 So Paul still remained a good while. Then he took leave of the brethren and sailed for Syria, and Priscilla and Aquila *were* with him. He had *his* hair cut off at Cenchrea, for he had taken a vow.

19 And he came to Ephesus, and left them there; but he himself entered the synagogue and reasoned with the Jews.

20 When they asked *him* to stay a longer time with them, he did not consent,

21 but took leave of them, saying, "I must by all means keep this coming feast in Jerusalem; but I will return again to you, God willing." And he sailed from Ephesus.

22 And when he had landed at Caesarea, and gone up and greeted the church, he went down to Antioch.

23 After he had spent some time *there*, he departed and went over *all* the region of Galatia and Phrygia in order, strengthening all the disciples.

24 Now a certain Jew named Apollos, born at Alexandria, an eloquent man *and* mighty in the Scriptures, came to Ephesus.

25 This man had been instructed in the way of the Lord; and being fervent in spirit, he spoke and taught accurately the things of the Lord, though he knew only the baptism of John.

26 So he began to speak boldly in the synagogue. When Aquila and Priscilla heard him, they took him

aside and explained to him the way of God more accurately.

27 And when he desired to cross to Achaia, the brethren wrote, exhorting the disciples to receive him; and when he arrived, he greatly helped those who had believed through grace;

28 for he vigorously refuted the Jews publicly, showing from the Scriptures that Jesus is the Christ.

19 And it happened, while Apollos was at Corinth, that Paul, having passed through the upper regions, came to Ephesus. And finding some disciples

2 he said to them, "Did you receive the Holy Spirit when you believed?" And they said to him, "We have not so much as heard whether there is a Holy Spirit."

3 And he said to them, "Into what then were you baptized?" So they said, "Into John's baptism."

4 Then Paul said, "John indeed baptized with a baptism of repentance, saying to the people that they should believe on Him who would come after him, that is, on Christ Jesus."

5 When they heard *this*, they were baptized in the name of the Lord Jesus.

6 And when Paul had laid hands on them, the Holy Spirit came upon them, and they spoke with tongues and prophesied.

7 Now the men were about twelve in all.

8 And he went into the synagogue and spoke boldly for three months, reasoning and persuading concerning the things of the kingdom of God.

9 But when some were hardened and did not believe, but spoke evil of the Way before the multitude, he departed from them and withdrew the disciples, reasoning daily in the school of Tyrannus.

10 And this continued for two years, so that all who dwelt in Asia heard the word of the Lord Jesus, both Jews and Greeks.

11 Now God worked unusual miracles by the hands of Paul,

12 so that even handkerchiefs or aprons were brought from his body to the sick, and the diseases left them and the evil spirits went out of them.

13 Then some of the itinerant Jewish exorcists took it upon themselves to call the name of the Lord Jesus over those who had evil spirits, saying, "We adjure you by the Jesus whom Paul preaches."

14 Also there were seven sons of Sceva, a Jewish chief priest, who did so.

15 And the evil spirit answered and said, "Jesus I know, and Paul I know; but who are you?"

16 Then the man in whom the evil spirit was leaped on them, overpowered them, and prevailed against them, so that they fled out of that house naked and wounded.

17 This became known both to all Jews and Greeks dwelling in Ephesus; and fear fell on them all, and the name of the Lord Jesus was magnified.

18 And many who had believed came confessing and telling their deeds.

19 Also, many of those who had practiced magic brought their books together and burned *them* in the sight of all. And they counted up the value of them, and *it* totaled fifty thousand *pieces* of silver.

20 So the word of the Lord grew mightily and prevailed.

21 When these things were accomplished, Paul purposed in the Spirit, when he had passed through Macedonia and Achaia, to go to Jerusalem, saying, "After I have been there, I must also see Rome."

22 So he sent into Macedonia two of those who ministered to him, Timothy and Erastus, but he himself stayed in Asia for a time.

23 And about that time there arose a great commotion about the Way.

24 For a certain man named Demetrius, a silversmith, who made silver shrines of Diana, brought no small profit to the craftsmen.

25 He called them together with the workers of similar occupation, and said: "Men, you know that we have our prosperity by this trade.

26 "Moreover you see and hear that not only at Ephesus, but throughout almost all Asia, this Paul has persuaded and turned away many people, saying that they are not gods which are made with hands.

27 "So not only is this trade of ours in danger of falling into disrepute, but also the temple of the great goddess Diana may be despised and her magnificence destroyed, whom all Asia and the world worship."

28 And when they heard *this*, they were full of wrath and cried out, saying, "Great *is* Diana of the Ephesians!"

29 So the whole city was filled with confusion, and rushed into the theater with one accord, having seized Gaius and Aristarchus, Macedonians, Paul's travel companions.

30 And when Paul wanted to go in to the people, the disciples would not allow him.

31 Then some of the officials of Asia, who were his friends, sent to him pleading that he would not venture into the theater.

32 Some therefore cried one thing and some another, for the assembly was confused, and most of them did not know why they had come together.

33 And they drew Alexander out of the multitude, the Jews putting him forward. And Alexander motioned with his hand, and wanted to make his defense to the people.

34 But when they found out that he was a Jew, all with one voice cried out for about two hours, "Great *is* Diana of the Ephesians!"

35 And when the city clerk had quieted the crowd, he said: "Men of Ephesus, what man is there who does not know that the city of the Ephesians is temple guardian of the great goddess Diana, and of the *image* which fell down from Zeus?

36 "Therefore, since these things cannot be denied, you ought to be quiet and do nothing rashly.

37 "For you have brought these men here who are neither robbers of temples nor blasphemers of your goddess.

38 "Therefore, if Demetrius and his fellow craftsmen have a case against anyone, the courts are open and there are proconsuls. Let them bring charges against one another.

39 "But if you have any other inquiry to make, it shall be determined in the lawful assembly.

40 "For we are in danger of being called in question for today's uproar, there being no reason which we may give to account for this disorderly gathering."

41 And when he had said these things, he dismissed the assembly.

20 After the uproar had ceased, Paul called the disciples to *him*, embraced *them*, and departed to go to Macedonia.

2 Now when he had gone over that region and encouraged them with many words, he came to Greece

3 and stayed three months. And when the Jews plotted against him as he was about to sail to Syria, he decided to return through Macedonia.

4 And Sopater of Berea accompanied him to Asia—also Aristarchus and Secundus of the Thessalonians, and Gaius of Derbe, and Timothy, and Tychicus and Trophimus of Asia.

5 These men, going ahead, waited for us at Troas.

6 But we sailed away from Phi-lippi after the Days of Unleavened Bread, and in five days joined them at Troas, where we stayed seven days.

7 Now on the first *day* of the week, when the disciples came together to break bread, Paul, ready to depart the next day, spoke to them and continued his message until midnight.

8 There were many lamps in the upper room where they were gathered together.

9 And in a window sat a certain young man named Eutychus, who was sinking into a deep sleep; and as Paul continued speaking, he fell down from the third story and was taken up dead.

10 But Paul went down, fell on him, and embracing *him* said, "Do not trouble yourselves, for his life is in him."

11 Now when he had come up, had broken bread and eaten, and talked a long while, even till daybreak, he departed.

12 And they brought the young man in alive, and they were not a little comforted.

13 Then we went ahead to the ship and sailed to Assos, there intending to take Paul on board; for so he had given orders, intending himself to go on foot.

14 And when he met us at Assos, we took him on board and came to Mitylene.

15 We sailed from there, and the next *day* came opposite Chios; the following *day* we arrived at Samos and stayed at Trogyllium; the next *day* we came to Miletus.

16 For Paul had decided to sail past Ephesus, so that he would not have to spend time in Asia; for he was hurrying to be at Jerusalem, if possible, on the Day of Pentecost.

17 From Miletus he sent to Ephesus and called for the elders of the church.

18 And when they had come to

him, he said to them: "You know, from the first day that I came to Asia, in what manner I always lived among you,

19 "serving the Lord with all humility, with many tears and trials which happened to me by the plotting of the Jews;

20 "*and* how I kept back nothing that was helpful, but proclaimed it to you, and taught you publicly and from house to house,

21 "testifying to Jews, and also to Greeks, repentance toward God and faith toward our Lord Jesus Christ.

22 "And see, now I go bound in the spirit to Jerusalem, not knowing the things that will happen to me there,

23 "except that the Holy Spirit testifies in every city, saying that chains and tribulations await me.

24 "But none of these things move me; nor do I count my life dear to myself, so that I may finish my race with joy, and the ministry which I received from the Lord Jesus, to testify to the gospel of the grace of God.

25 "And indeed, now I know that you all, among whom I have gone preaching the kingdom of God, will see my face no more.

26 "Therefore I testify to you this day that I *am* innocent of the blood of all *men.*

27 "For I have not shunned to declare to you the whole counsel of God.

28 "Therefore take heed to yourselves and to all the flock, among which the Holy Spirit has made you overseers, to shepherd the church of God which He purchased with His own blood.

29 "For I know this, that after my departure savage wolves will come in among you, not sparing the flock.

30 "Also from among yourselves men will rise up, speaking perverse things, to draw away the disciples after themselves.

31 "Therefore watch, and remember that for three years I did not cease to warn everyone night and day with tears.

32 "And now, brethren, I commend you to God and to the word of His grace, which is able to build you up and give you an inheritance among all those who are sanctified.

33 "I have coveted no one's silver or gold or apparel.

34 "Yes, you yourselves know that these hands have provided for my necessities, and for those who were with me.

35 "I have shown you in every way, by laboring like this, that you must support the weak. And remember the words of the Lord Jesus, that He said, 'It is more blessed to give than to receive.' "

36 And when he had said these things, he knelt down and prayed with them all.

37 Then they all wept freely, and fell on Paul's neck and kissed him,

38 sorrowing most of all for the words which he spoke, that they would see his face no more. And they accompanied him to the ship.

21 Now it came to pass, that when we had departed from them and set sail, running a straight course we came to Cos, the following *day* to Rhodes, and from there to Patara.

2 And finding a ship sailing over to Phoenicia, we went aboard and set sail.

3 When we had sighted Cyprus, we passed it on the left, sailed to Syria, and landed at Tyre; for there the ship was to unload her cargo.

4 And finding disciples, we stayed there seven days. They told Paul through the Spirit not to go up to Jerusalem.

5 When we had come to the end of those days, we departed and went on our way; and they all ac-

companied us, with wives and children, till *we were* out of the city. And we knelt down on the shore and prayed.

6 When we had taken our leave of one another, we boarded the ship, and they returned home.

7 And when we had finished *our* voyage from Tyre, we came to Ptolemais, greeted the brethren, and stayed with them one day.

8 On the next *day* we who were Paul's companions departed and came to Caesarea, and entered the house of Philip the evangelist, who was *one* of the seven, and stayed with him.

9 Now this man had four virgin daughters who prophesied.

10 And as we stayed many days, a certain prophet named Agabus came down from Judea.

11 When he had come to us, he took Paul's belt, bound his *own* hands and feet, and said, "Thus says the Holy Spirit, 'So shall the Jews at Jerusalem bind the man who owns this belt, and deliver *him* into the hands of the Gentiles.' "

12 And when we heard these things, both we and those from that place pleaded with him not to go up to Jerusalem.

13 Then Paul answered, "What do you mean by weeping and breaking my heart? For I am ready not only to be bound, but also to die at Jerusalem for the name of the Lord Jesus."

14 So when he would not be persuaded, we ceased, saying, "The will of the Lord be done."

15 And after those days we packed and went up to Jerusalem.

16 Also some of the disciples from Caesarea went with us and brought with them one, Mnason of Cyprus, an early disciple, with whom we were to lodge.

17 And when we had come to Jerusalem, the brethren received us gladly.

18 On the following *day* Paul went in with us to James, and all the elders were present.

19 When he had greeted them, he told in detail those things which God had done among the Gentiles through his ministry.

20 And when they heard *it,* they glorified the Lord. And they said to him, "You see, brother, how many myriads of Jews there are who have believed, and they are all zealous for the law;

21 "but they have been informed about you that you teach all the Jews who are among the Gentiles to forsake Moses, saying that they ought not to circumcise *their* children nor to walk according to the customs.

22 "What then? The assembly must certainly meet, for they will hear that you have come.

23 "Therefore do what we tell you: We have four men who have taken a vow.

24 "Take them and be purified with them, and pay their expenses so that they may shave *their* heads, and that all may know that those things of which they were informed concerning you are nothing, but *that* you yourself also walk orderly and keep the law.

25 "But concerning the Gentiles who believe, we have written *and* decided that they should observe no such thing, except that they should keep themselves from *things* offered to idols, from blood, from things strangled, and from sexual immorality."

26 Then Paul took the men, and the next day, having been purified with them, entered the temple to announce the expiration of the days of purification, at which time an offering should be made for each one of them.

27 And when the seven days were almost ended, the Jews from Asia, seeing him in the temple, stirred up the whole crowd and laid hands on him,

28 crying out, "Men of Israel, help! This is the man who teaches all *men* everywhere against the people, the law, and this place; and furthermore he also brought Greeks into the temple and has defiled this holy place."

29 (For they had previously seen Trophimus the Ephesian with him in the city, whom they supposed that Paul had brought into the temple.)

30 And all the city was disturbed; and the people ran together, seized Paul, and dragged him out of the temple; and immediately the doors were shut.

31 Now as they were seeking to kill him, news came to the commander of the garrison that all Jerusalem was in an uproar.

32 He immediately took soldiers and centurions, and ran down to them. And when they saw the commander and the soldiers, they stopped beating Paul.

33 Then the commander came near and took him, and commanded *him* to be bound with two chains; and he asked who he was and what he had done.

34 And some among the multitude cried one thing and some another. And when he could not ascertain the truth because of the tumult, he commanded him to be taken into the barracks.

35 And when he reached the stairs, he had to be carried by the soldiers because of the violence of the mob.

36 For the multitude of the people followed after, crying out, "Away with him!"

37 And as Paul was about to be led into the barracks, he said to the commander, "May I speak to you?" He replied, "Can you speak Greek?

38 "Are you not the Egyptian who some time ago raised an insurrection and led the four thousand assassins out into the wilderness?"

39 But Paul said, "I am a Jew from Tarsus, in Cilicia, a citizen of no mean city; and I implore you, permit me to speak to the people."

40 So when he had given him permission, Paul stood on the stairs and motioned with his hand to the people. And when there was a great silence, he spoke to *them* in the Hebrew language, saying,

22 "Men, brethren, and fathers, hear my defense before you now."

2 And when they heard that he spoke to them in the Hebrew language, they kept all the more silent. Then he said:

3 "I am indeed a Jew, born in Tarsus of Cilicia, but brought up in this city at the feet of Gamaliel, taught according to the strictness of our fathers' law, and was zealous toward God as you all are today.

4 "I persecuted this Way to the death, binding and delivering into prisons both men and women,

5 "as also the high priest bears me witness, and all the council of the elders, from whom I also received letters to the brethren, and went to Damascus to bring in chains even those who were there to Jerusalem to be punished.

6 "Now it happened, as I journeyed and came near Damascus at about noon, suddenly a great light from heaven shone around me.

7 "And I fell to the ground and heard a voice saying to me, 'Saul, Saul, why are you persecuting Me?'

8 "So I answered, 'Who are You, Lord?' And He said to me, 'I am Jesus of Nazareth, whom you are persecuting.'

9 "Now those who were with me indeed saw the light and were afraid, but they did not hear the voice of Him who spoke to me.

10 "So I said, 'What shall I do, Lord?' And the Lord said to me, 'Arise and go into Damascus, and there you will be told all things which are appointed for you to do.'

11 "And since I could not see for

the glory of that light, being led by the hand of those who were with me, I came into Damascus.

12 "Then one, Ananias, a devout man according to the law, having a good testimony with all the Jews who dwelt *there,*

13 "came to me; and he stood and said to me, 'Brother Saul, receive your sight.' And at that same hour I looked up at him.

14 "Then he said, 'The God of our fathers has chosen you that you should know His will, and see the Just One, and hear the voice of His mouth.

15 'For you will be His witness to all men of what you have seen and heard.

16 'And now why are you waiting? Arise and be baptized, and wash away your sins, calling on the name of the Lord.'

17 "Then it happened, when I returned to Jerusalem and was praying in the temple, that I was in a trance

18 "and saw Him saying to me, 'Make haste and get out of Jerusalem quickly, for they will not receive your testimony concerning Me.'

19 "So I said, 'Lord, they know that in every synagogue I imprisoned and beat those who believe on You.

20 'And when the blood of Your martyr Stephen was shed, I also was standing by consenting to his death, and guarding the clothes of those who were killing him.'

21 "Then He said to me, 'Depart, for I will send you far from here to the Gentiles.' "

22 And they listened to him until this word, and *then* they raised their voices and said, "Away with such a *fellow* from the earth, for he is not fit to live!"

23 Then, as they cried out and tore off *their* clothes and threw dust into the air,

24 the commander ordered him to be brought into the barracks, and said that he should be examined under scourging, so that he might know why they shouted so against him.

25 And as they bound him with thongs, Paul said to the centurion who stood by, "Is it lawful for you to scourge a man who is a Roman, and uncondemned?"

26 When the centurion heard *that,* he went and told the commander, saying, "Take care what you do, for this man is a Roman."

27 Then the commander came and said to him, "Tell me, are you a Roman?" He said, "Yes."

28 And the commander answered, "With a large sum I obtained this citizenship." And Paul said, "But I was born *a citizen.*"

29 Then immediately those who were about to examine him withdrew from him; and the commander was also afraid after he found out that he was a Roman, and because he had bound him.

30 The next day, because he wanted to know for certain why he was accused by the Jews, he released him from *his* bonds, and commanded the chief priests and all their council to appear, and brought Paul down and set him before them.

23 Then Paul, looking earnestly at the council, said, "Men *and* brethren, I have lived in all good conscience before God until this day."

2 And the high priest Ananias commanded those who stood by him to strike him on the mouth.

3 Then Paul said to him, "God will strike you, *you* whitewashed wall! For you sit to judge me according to the law, and do you command me to be struck contrary to the law?"

4 And those who stood by said, "Do you revile God's high priest?"

5 Then Paul said, "I did not know, brethren, that he was the high

177

priest; for it is written, *'You shall not speak evil of the ruler of your people.'"*

6 But when Paul perceived that one part were Sadducees and the other Pharisees, he cried out in the council, "Men *and* brethren, I am a Pharisee, the son of a Pharisee; concerning the hope and resurrection of the dead I am being judged!"

7 And when he had said this, a dissension arose between the Pharisees and the Sadducees; and the assembly was divided.

8 For *the* Sadducees say that there is no resurrection—and no angel or spirit; but the Pharisees confess both.

9 Then there arose a loud outcry. And the scribes *who were* of the Pharisees' party arose and protested, saying, "We find no evil in this man; but if a spirit or an angel has spoken to him, let us not fight against God."

10 And when there arose a great dissension, the commander, fearing lest Paul might be pulled to pieces by them, commanded the soldiers to go down and take him by force from among them, and bring *him* into the barracks.

11 But the following night the Lord stood by him and said, "Be of good cheer, Paul; for as you have testified for Me in Jerusalem, so you must also bear witness at Rome."

12 And when it was day, some of the Jews banded together and bound themselves under an oath, saying that they would neither eat nor drink till they had killed Paul.

13 Now there were more than forty who had formed this conspiracy.

14 They came to the chief priests and elders, and said, "We have bound ourselves under a great oath that we will eat nothing until we have killed Paul.

15 "Now you, therefore, together with the council, suggest to the commander that he be brought down to you tomorrow, as though you were going to make further inquiries concerning him; but we are ready to kill him before he comes near."

16 And when Paul's sister's son heard of their ambush, he went and entered the barracks and told Paul.

17 Then Paul called one of the centurions to *him* and said, "Take this young man to the commander, for he has something to tell him."

18 So he took him and brought *him* to the commander and said, "Paul the prisoner called me to *him* and asked *me* to bring this young man to you. He has something to say to you."

19 Then the commander took him by the hand, went aside and asked *him* privately, "What is it that you have to tell me?"

20 And he said, "The Jews have agreed to ask that you bring Paul down to the council tomorrow, as though they were going to inquire more fully about him.

21 "But do not yield to them, for more than forty of them lie in wait for him, men who have bound themselves by an oath that they will neither eat nor drink till they have killed him; and now they are ready, waiting for the promise from you."

22 So the commander let the young man depart, and commanded *him*, "Tell no one that you have revealed these things to me."

23 And he called for two centurions, saying, "Prepare two hundred soldiers, seventy horsemen, and two hundred spearmen to go to Caesarea at the third hour of the night;

24 "and provide mounts to set Paul on, and bring *him* safely to Felix the governor."

25 He wrote a letter in the following manner:

26 Claudius Lysias,
To the most excellent governor Felix:
Greetings.

27 This man was seized by the Jews and was about to be killed by them. Coming with the troops I rescued him, having learned that he was a Roman.

28 And when I wanted to know the reason they accused him, I brought him before their council.

29 I found out that he was accused concerning questions of their law, but had nothing charged against him worthy of death or chains.

30 And when it was told me that the Jews lay in wait for the man, I sent him immediately to you, and also commanded his accusers to state before you the charges against him.
Farewell.

31 Then the soldiers, as they were commanded, took Paul and brought *him* by night to Antipatris.

32 The next day they left the horsemen to go on with him, and returned to the barracks.

33 When they came to Caesarea and had delivered the letter to the governor, they also presented Paul to him.

34 And when the governor had read *it*, he asked what province he was from. And when he understood that *he was* from Cilicia,

35 he said, "I will hear you when your accusers also have come." And he commanded him to be kept in Herod's Praetorium.

24 Now after five days Ananias the high priest came down with the elders and a certain orator *named* Tertullus. These gave evidence to the governor against Paul.

2 And when he was called upon, Tertullus began his accusation, saying: "Seeing that through you

we enjoy great peace, and prosperity is being brought to this nation by your foresight,

3 "we accept *it* always and in all places, most noble Felix, with all thankfulness.

4 "Nevertheless, not to be tedious to you any further, I beg you to hear, by your courtesy, a few words from us.

5 "For we have found this man *a* plague, a creator of dissension among all the Jews throughout the world, and a ringleader of the sect of the Nazarenes.

6 "He even tried to profane the temple, and we seized him, and wanted to judge him according to our law.

7 "But the commander Lysias came by and with great violence took *him* out of our hands,

8 "commanding his accusers to come to you. By examining him yourself you may ascertain all these things of which we accuse him."

9 And the Jews also assented, maintaining that these things were so.

10 Then Paul, after the governor had nodded to him to speak, answered: "Inasmuch as I know that you have been for many years a judge of this nation, I do the more cheerfully answer for myself,

11 "because you may ascertain that it is no more than twelve days since I went up to Jerusalem to worship.

12 "And they neither found me in the temple disputing with anyone nor inciting the crowd, either in the synagogues or in the city.

13 "Nor can they prove the things of which they now accuse me.

14 "But this I confess to you, that according to the Way which they call a sect, so I worship the God of my fathers, believing all things which are written in the Law and in the Prophets.

15 "I have hope in God, which they themselves also accept, that there

will be a resurrection of *the* dead, both of *the* just and *the* unjust.

16 "This *being* so, I myself always strive to have a conscience without offense toward God and men.

17 "Now after many years I came to bring alms and offerings to my nation,

18 "in the midst of which some Jews from Asia found me purified in the temple, neither with a multitude nor with tumult.

19 "They ought to have been here before you to object if they had anything against me.

20 "Or else let those who are *here* themselves say if they found any wrongdoing in me while I stood before the council,

21 "unless *it is* for this one statement which I cried out, standing among them, 'Concerning the resurrection of the dead I am being judged by you this day.' "

22 But when Felix heard these things, having more accurate knowledge of *the* Way, he adjourned the proceedings and said, "When Lysias the commander comes down, I will make a decision on your case."

23 So he commanded the centurion to keep Paul and to let *him* have liberty, and told him not to forbid any of his friends to provide for or visit him. .

24 And after some days, when Felix came with his wife Drusilla, who was Jewish, he sent for Paul and heard him concerning the faith in Christ.

25 Now as he reasoned about righteousness, self-control, and the judgment to come, Felix was afraid and answered, "Go away for now; when I have a convenient time I will call for you."

26 Meanwhile he also hoped that money would be given him by Paul, that he might release him. Therefore he sent for him more often and conversed with him.

27 But after two years Porcius Festus succeeded Felix; and Felix,

wanting to do the Jews a favor, left Paul bound.

25 Now when Festus had come to the province, after three days he went up from Caesarea to Jerusalem.

2 Then the high priest and the chief men of the Jews informed him against Paul; and they petitioned him,

3 asking a favor against him, that he would summon him to Jerusalem—while *they* lay in ambush along the road to kill him.

4 But Festus answered that Paul should be kept at Caesarea, and that he himself was going *there* shortly.

5 "Therefore," he said, "let those who have authority among you go down with *me* and accuse this man, to see if there is any fault in him."

6 And when he had remained among them more than ten days, he went down to Caesarea. And the next day, sitting on the judgment seat, he commanded Paul to be brought.

7 When he had come, the Jews who had come down from Jerusalem stood about and laid many serious complaints against Paul, which they could not prove,

8 while he answered for himself, "Neither against the law of the Jews, nor against the temple, nor against Caesar have I offended in anything at all."

9 But Festus, wanting to do the Jews a favor, answered Paul and said, "Are you willing to go up to Jerusalem and there be judged before me concerning these things?"

10 Then Paul said, "I stand at Caesar's judgment seat, where I ought to be judged. To the Jews I have done no wrong, as you very well know.

11 "For if I am an offender, or have committed anything worthy of death, I do not object to dying; but if there is nothing in these things of which these men accuse me, no

one can deliver me to them. I appeal to Caesar."

12 Then Festus, when he had conferred with the council, answered, "You have appealed to Caesar? To Caesar you shall go!"

13 And after some days King Agrippa and Bernice came to Caesarea to greet Festus.

14 When they had been there many days, Festus laid Paul's case before the king, saying: "There is a certain man left a prisoner by Felix,

15 "about whom the chief priests and the elders of the Jews informed *me*, when I was in Jerusalem, asking for a judgment against him.

16 "To them I answered, 'It is not the custom of the Romans to deliver any man to destruction before the accused meets the accusers face to face, and has opportunity to answer for himself concerning the charge against him.'

17 "Therefore when they had come together, without any delay, the next day I sat on the judgment seat and commanded the man to be brought in.

18 "When the accusers stood up, they brought no accusation against him of such things as I supposed,

19 "but had some questions against him about their own religion and about one, Jesus, who had died, whom Paul affirmed to be alive.

20 "And because I was uncertain of such questions, I asked whether he was willing to go to Jerusalem and there be judged concerning these matters.

21 "But when Paul appealed to be reserved for the decision of Augustus, I commanded him to be kept till I could send him to Caesar."

22 Then Agrippa said to Festus, "I also would like to hear the man myself." "Tomorrow," he said, "you shall hear him."

23 So the next day, when Agrippa and Bernice had come with great pomp, and had entered the auditorium with the commanders and the prominent men of the city, at Festus' command Paul was brought in.

24 And Festus said: "King Agrippa and all the men who are here present with us, you see this man about whom the whole assembly of the Jews petitioned me, both at Jerusalem and here, crying out that he was not fit to live any longer.

25 "But when I found that he had committed nothing worthy of death, and that he himself had appealed to Augustus, I decided to send him.

26 "I have nothing certain to write to my lord concerning him. Therefore I have brought him out before you, and especially before you, King Agrippa, so that after the examination has taken place I may have something to write.

27 "For it seems to me unreasonable to send a prisoner and not to specify the charges against him."

26 Then Agrippa said to Paul, "You are permitted to speak for yourself." So Paul stretched out his hand and answered for himself:

2 "I think myself happy, King Agrippa, because today I shall answer for myself before you concerning all the things of which I am accused by the Jews,

3 "especially because you are expert in all customs and questions which have to do with the Jews. Therefore I beg you to hear me patiently.

4 "My manner of life from my youth, which was spent from the beginning among my own nation at Jerusalem, all the Jews know.

5 "They knew me from the first, if they were willing to testify, that according to the strictest sect of our religion I lived a Pharisee.

6 "And now I stand and am

judged for the hope of the promise made by God to our fathers.

7 "To this *promise* our twelve tribes, earnestly serving *God* night and day, hope to attain. For this hope's sake, King Agrippa, I am accused by the Jews.

8 "Why should it be thought incredible by you that God raises the dead?

9 "Indeed, I myself thought I must do many things contrary to the name of Jesus of Nazareth.

10 "This I also did in Jerusalem, and many of the saints I shut up in prison, having received authority from the chief priests; and when they were put to death, I cast my vote against *them*.

11 "And I punished them often in every synagogue and compelled *them* to blaspheme; and being exceedingly enraged against them, I persecuted *them* even to foreign cities.

12 "While thus occupied, as I journeyed to Damascus with authority and commission from the chief priests,

13 "at midday, O king, along the road I saw a light from heaven, brighter than the sun, shining around me and those who journeyed with me.

14 "And when we all had fallen to the ground, I heard a voice speaking to me and saying in the Hebrew language, 'Saul, Saul, why are you persecuting Me? *It is* hard for you to kick against the goads.'

15 "So I said, 'Who are You, Lord?' And He said, 'I am Jesus, whom you are persecuting.

16 "But rise and stand on your feet; for I have appeared to you for this purpose, to make you a minister and a witness both of the things which you have seen and of the things which I will yet reveal to you.

17 'I will deliver you from the *Jewish* people, as well as *from* the Gentiles, to whom I now send you,

18 'to open their eyes *and* to turn them from darkness to light, and *from* the power of Satan to God, that they may receive forgiveness of sins and an inheritance among those who are sanctified by faith in Me.'

19 "Therefore, King Agrippa, I was not disobedient to the heavenly vision,

20 "but declared first to those in Damascus and in Jerusalem, and throughout all the region of Judea, and *then* to the Gentiles, that they should repent, turn to God, and do works befitting repentance.

21 "For these reasons the Jews seized me in the temple and tried to kill *me*.

22 "Therefore, having obtained help from God, to this day I stand, witnessing both to small and great, saying no other things than those which the prophets and Moses said would come—

23 "that the Christ would suffer, that He would be the first to rise from the dead, and would proclaim light to the *Jewish* people and to the Gentiles."

24 Now as he thus made his defense, Festus said with a loud voice, "Paul, you are beside yourself! Much learning is driving you mad!"

25 But he said, "I am not mad, most noble Festus, but speak the words of truth and reason.

26 "For the king, before whom I also speak freely, knows these things; for I am convinced that none of these things escapes his attention, since this thing was not done in a corner.

27 "King Agrippa, do you believe the prophets? I know that you do believe."

28 Then Agrippa said to Paul, "You almost persuade me to become a Christian."

29 And Paul said, "I would to God that not only you, but also all who hear me today, might become both almost and altogether such as I am, except for these chains."

30 When he had said these things, the king stood up, as well as the governor and Bernice and those who sat with them;

31 and when they had gone aside, they talked among themselves, saying, "This man is doing nothing worthy of death or chains."

32 Then Agrippa said to Festus, "This man might have been set free if he had not appealed to Caesar."

27 And when it was decided that we should sail to Italy, they delivered Paul and some other prisoners to *one* named Julius, a centurion of the Augustan Regiment.

2 So, entering a ship of Adramyttium, we put to sea, meaning to sail along the coasts of Asia. Aristarchus, a Macedonian of Thessalonica, was with us.

3 And the next *day* we landed at Sidon. And Julius treated Paul kindly and gave *him* liberty to go to his friends and receive care.

4 When we had put to sea from there, we sailed under *the shelter of* Cyprus, because the winds were contrary.

5 And when we had sailed over the sea which is off Cilicia and Pamphylia, we came to Myra, *a city of* Lycia.

6 There the centurion found an Alexandrian ship sailing to Italy, and he put us on board.

7 And when we had sailed slowly many days, and arrived with difficulty off Cnidus, the wind not permitting us to proceed, we sailed under *the* shelter of Crete off Salmone.

8 Passing it with difficulty, we came to a place called Fair Havens, near the city *of* Lasea.

9 Now when much time had been spent, and sailing was now dangerous because the Fast was already over, Paul advised them,

10 saying, "Men, I perceive that this voyage will end with disaster and much loss, not only of the cargo and ship, but also our lives."

11 Nevertheless the centurion was more persuaded by the helmsman and the owner of the ship than by the things spoken by Paul.

12 And because the harbor was not suitable to winter in, the majority advised to set sail from there also, if by any means they could reach Phoenix, a harbor of Crete opening toward the southwest and northwest, *and* winter *there*.

13 When the south wind blew softly, supposing that they had obtained *their* purpose, putting out to sea, they sailed close by Crete.

14 But not long after, a tempestuous head wind arose, called Euroclydon.

15 So when the ship was caught, and could not head into the wind, we let *her* drive.

16 And running under *the shelter of* an island called Clauda, we secured the skiff with difficulty.

17 When they had taken it on board, they used cables to undergird the ship; and fearing lest they should run aground on the Syrtis *Sands*, they struck sail and so were driven.

18 And because we were exceedingly tempest-tossed, the next *day* they lightened the ship.

19 On the third *day* we threw the ship's tackle overboard with our own hands.

20 Now when neither sun nor stars appeared for many days, and no small tempest beat on *us*, all hope that we would be saved was finally given up.

21 But after long abstinence from food, then Paul stood in the midst of them and said, "Men, you should have listened to me, and not have sailed from Crete and incurred this disaster and loss.

22 "And now I urge you to take heart, for there will be no loss of life among you, but only of the ship.

23 "For there stood by me this night an angel of the God to whom I belong and whom I serve,

24 "saying, 'Do not be afraid, Paul; you must be brought before Caesar; and indeed God has granted you all those who sail with you.'

25 "Therefore take heart, men, for I believe God that it will be just as it was told me.

26 "However, we must run aground on a certain island."

27 But when the fourteenth night had come, as we were driven up and down in the Adriatic *Sea*, about midnight the sailors sensed that they were drawing near some land.

28 And they took soundings and found *it* to be twenty fathoms; and when they had gone a little farther, they took soundings again and found *it* to be fifteen fathoms.

29 Then, fearing lest we should run aground on the rocks, they dropped four anchors from the stern, and prayed for day to come.

30 And as the sailors were seeking to escape from the ship, when they had let down the skiff into the sea, under pretense of putting out anchors from the prow,

31 Paul said to the centurion and the soldiers, "Unless these men stay in the ship, you cannot be saved."

32 Then the soldiers cut away the ropes of the skiff and let it fall off.

33 And as day was about to dawn, Paul implored *them* all to take food, saying, "Today is the fourteenth day you have waited and continued without food, and eaten nothing.

34 "Therefore I urge you to take nourishment, for this is for your survival, since not a hair will fall from the head of any of you."

35 And when he had said these things, he took bread and gave thanks to God in the presence of them all; and when he had broken *it* he began to eat.

36 Then they were all encouraged, and also took food themselves.

37 And in all we were two hundred and seventy-six persons on the ship.

38 So when they had eaten enough, they lightened the ship and threw out the wheat into the sea.

39 Now when it was day, they did not recognize the land; but they observed a bay with a beach, onto which they planned to run the ship if possible.

40 And they let go the anchors and left *them* in the sea, meanwhile loosing the rudder ropes; and they hoisted the mainsail to the wind and made for shore.

41 But striking a place where two seas met, they ran the ship aground; and the prow stuck fast and remained immovable, but the stern was being broken up by the violence of the waves.

42 Now the soldiers' plan was to kill the prisoners, lest any of them should swim away and escape.

43 But the centurion, wanting to save Paul, kept them from *their* purpose, and commanded that those who could swim should jump *overboard* first and get to land,

44 and the rest, some on boards and some on *broken pieces* of the ship. And so it was that they all escaped safely to land.

28 Now when they had escaped, they then found out that the island was called Malta.

2 And the natives showed us unusual kindness; for they kindled a fire and made us all welcome, because of the rain that was falling and because of the cold.

3 But when Paul had gathered a bundle of sticks and laid *them* on the fire, a viper came out because of the heat, and fastened on his hand.

4 So when the natives saw the creature hanging from his hand, they said to one another, "No

doubt this man is a murderer, whom, though he has escaped the sea, yet justice does not allow to live."

5 But he shook off the creature into the fire and suffered no harm.

6 However, they were expecting that he would swell up or suddenly fall down dead; but after they had looked for a long time and saw no harm come to him, they changed their minds and said that he was a god.

7 Now in that region there was an estate of the leading citizen of the island, whose name was Publius, who received us and entertained us courteously for three days.

8 And it happened that the father of Publius lay sick of a fever and dysentery. Paul went in to him and prayed, and he laid his hands on him and healed him.

9 So when this was done, the rest of those on the island who had diseases also came and were healed.

10 They also honored us in many ways; and when we departed, they provided such things as were necessary.

11 After three months we sailed in an Alexandrian ship whose figurehead was the Twin Brothers, which had wintered at the island.

12 And landing at Syracuse, we stayed three days.

13 From there we circled round and reached Rhegium. And after one day the south wind blew; and the next day we came to Puteoli,

14 where we found brethren, and were invited to stay with them seven days. And so we went toward Rome.

15 And from there, when the brethren heard about us, they came to meet us as far as Appii Forum and Three Inns. When Paul saw them, he thanked God and took courage.

16 Now when we came to Rome, the centurion delivered the prisoners to the captain of the guard; but Paul was permitted to dwell by himself with the soldier who guarded him.

17 And it came to pass after three days that Paul called the leaders of the Jews together. So when they had come together, he said to them: "Men *and* brethren, though I have done nothing against our people or the customs of our fathers, yet I was delivered as a prisoner from Jerusalem into the hands of the Romans.

18 "who, when they had examined me, wanted to let *me* go, because there was no cause for putting me to death.

19 "But when the Jews spoke against *it*, I was compelled to appeal to Caesar, not that I had anything of which to accuse my nation.

20 "For this reason therefore I have called for you, to see *you* and speak with *you*, because for the hope of Israel I am bound with this chain."

21 And they said to him, "We neither received letters from Judea concerning you, nor have any of the brethren who came reported or spoken any evil of you.

22 "But we desire to hear from you what you think; for concerning this sect, we know that it is spoken against everywhere."

23 So when they had appointed him a day, many came to him at *his* lodging, to whom he explained and solemnly testified of the kingdom of God, persuading them concerning Jesus from both the Law of Moses and the Prophets, from morning till evening.

24 And some were persuaded by the things which were spoken, and some disbelieved.

25 So when they did not agree among themselves, they departed after Paul had said one word: "The Holy Spirit spoke rightly through Isaiah the prophet to our fathers,

26 "saying,

'Go to this people and say:
"Hearing you will hear,
　and shall not understand;
And seeing you will see,
　and not perceive;
27 For the heart of this people
　has grown dull.
Their ears are hard of hearing,
And their eyes they have
　closed,
Lest they should see with their
　eyes and hear with their ears,
Lest they should understand
　with their heart and turn,
So that I should heal them." '

28 "Therefore let it be known to you that the salvation of God has been sent to the Gentiles, and they will hear it!"

29 And when he had said these words, the Jews departed and had a great dispute among themselves.

30 Then Paul dwelt two whole years in his own rented house, and received all who came to him,

31 preaching the kingdom of God and teaching the things which concern the Lord Jesus Christ with all confidence, no one forbidding him.

THE EPISTLE OF PAUL THE APOSTLE TO THE

ROMANS

PAUL, a servant of Jesus Christ, called *to be* an apostle, separated to the gospel of God

2 which He promised before through His prophets in the Holy Scriptures,

3 concerning His Son Jesus Christ our Lord, who was born of the seed of David according to the flesh,

4 and declared *to be* the Son of God with power, according to the Spirit of holiness, by the resurrection from the dead,

5 through whom we have received grace and apostleship for obedience to the faith among all nations for His name,

6 among whom you also are the called of Jesus Christ;

7 To all who are in Rome, beloved of God, called *to be* saints:

Grace to you and peace from God our Father and the Lord Jesus Christ.

8 First, I thank my God through Jesus Christ for you all, that your faith is spoken of throughout the whole world.

9 For God is my witness, whom I serve with my spirit in the gospel of His Son, that without ceasing I make mention of you always in my prayers,

10 making request if, by some means, now at last I may find a way in the will of God to come to you.

11 For I long to see you, that I may impart to you some spiritual gift, so that you may be established—

12 that is, that I may be encouraged together with you by the mutual faith both of you and me.

13 Now I do not want you to be unaware, brethren, that I often planned to come to you (but was hindered until now), that I might have some fruit among you also, just as among the other Gentiles.

14 I am a debtor both to Greeks and to barbarians, both to wise and to unwise.

15 So, as much as is in me, *I am* ready to preach the gospel to you who are in Rome also.

16 For I am not ashamed of the gospel of Christ, for it is the power of God to salvation for everyone

186

who believes, for the Jew first and also for the Greek.

17 For in it the righteousness of God is revealed from faith to faith; as it is written, *"The just shall live by faith."*

18 For the wrath of God is revealed from heaven against all ungodliness and unrighteousness of men, who suppress the truth in unrighteousness,

19 because what may be known of God is manifest in them, for God has shown *it* to them.

20 For since the creation of the world His invisible *attributes* are clearly seen, being understood by the things that are made, *even* His eternal power and Godhead, so that they are without excuse,

21 because, although they knew God, they did not glorify *Him* as God, nor were thankful, but became futile in their thoughts, and their foolish hearts were darkened.

22 Professing to be wise, they became fools,

23 and changed the glory of the incorruptible God into an image made like corruptible man—and birds and four-footed beasts and creeping things.

24 Therefore God also gave them up to uncleanness, in the lusts of their hearts, to dishonor their bodies among themselves,

25 who exchanged the truth of God for the lie, and worshiped and served the creature rather than the Creator, who is blessed forever. Amen.

26 For this reason God gave them up to vile passions. For even their women exchanged the natural use for what is against nature.

27 Likewise also the men, leaving the natural use of the woman, burned in their lust for one another, men with men committing what is shameful, and receiving in themselves the penalty of their error which was due.

28 And even as they did not like to retain God in *their* knowledge, God gave them over to a debased mind, to do those things which are not fitting;

29 being filled with all unrighteousness, sexual immorality, wickedness, covetousness, maliciousness; full of envy, murder, strife, deceit, evil-mindedness; *they are* whisperers,

30 backbiters, haters of God, violent, proud, boasters, inventors of evil things, disobedient to parents,

31 undiscerning, untrustworthy, unloving, unforgiving, unmerciful;

32 who, knowing the righteous judgment of God, that those who practice such things are worthy of death, not only do the same but also approve of those who practice them.

2 Therefore you are inexcusable, O man, whoever you are who judge, for in whatever you judge another you condemn yourself; for you who judge practice the same things.

2 But we know that the judgment of God is according to truth against those who practice such things.

3 And do you think this, O man, you who judge those practicing such things, and doing the same, that you will escape the judgment of God?

4 Or do you despise the riches of His goodness, forbearance, and longsuffering, not knowing that the goodness of God leads you to repentance?

5 But in accordance with your hardness and your impenitent heart you are treasuring up for yourself wrath in the day of wrath and revelation of the righteous judgment of God,

6 who *"will render to each one according to his deeds":*

7 eternal life to those who by patient continuance in doing good seek for glory, honor, and immortality;

8 but to those who are self-seeking and do not obey the truth, but

obey unrighteousness—indignation and wrath,

9 tribulation and anguish, on every soul of man who does evil, of the Jew first and also of the Greek;

10 but glory, honor, and peace to everyone who works what is good, to the Jew first and also to the Greek.

11 For there is no partiality with God.

12 For as many as have sinned without law will also perish without law, and as many as have sinned in the law will be judged by the law

13 (for not the hearers of the law *are* just in the sight of God, but the doers of the law will be justified;

14 for when Gentiles, who do not have the law, by nature do the things *contained* in the law, these, although not having the law, are a law to themselves,

15 who show the work of the law written in their hearts, their conscience also bearing witness, and between themselves *their* thoughts accusing or else excusing *them*)

16 in the day when God will judge the secrets of men by Jesus Christ, according to my gospel.

17 Indeed you are called a Jew, and rest on the law, and make your boast in God,

18 and know *His* will, and approve the things that are excellent, being instructed out of the law,

19 and are confident that you yourself are a guide to the blind, a light to those who are in darkness,

20 an instructor of the foolish, a teacher of babes, having the form of knowledge and truth in the law.

21 You, therefore, who teach another, do you not teach yourself? You who preach that a man should not steal, do you steal?

22 You who say, "Do not commit adultery," do you commit adultery? You who abhor idols, do you rob temples?

23 You who make your boast in the law, do you dishonor God through breaking the law?

24 For *"The name of God is blasphemed among the Gentiles because of you,"* as it is written.

25 For circumcision is indeed profitable if you keep the law; but if you are a breaker of the law, your circumcision has become uncircumcision.

26 Therefore, if an uncircumcised man keeps the righteous requirements of the law, will not his uncircumcision be counted as circumcision?

27 And will not the physically uncircumcised, if he fulfills the law, judge you who, *even* with *your* written *code* and circumcision, *are* a transgressor of the law?

28 For he is not a Jew who *is one* outwardly, nor *is* that circumcision *which is* outward in the flesh;

29 but *he is* a Jew who *is one* inwardly; and circumcision *is that* of the heart, in the Spirit, *and* not in the letter; whose praise *is* not from men but from God.

3 What advantage then has the Jew, or what *is* the profit of circumcision?

2 Much in every way! Chiefly because to them were committed the oracles of God.

3 For what if some did not believe? Will their unbelief make the faithfulness of God without effect?

4 Certainly not! Indeed, let God be true but every man a liar. As it is written:

> "That You may be justified
> in Your words,
> And may overcome when
> You are judged."

5 But if our unrighteousness demonstrates the righteousness of God, what shall we say? *Is* God unjust who inflicts wrath? (I speak as a man.)

6 Certainly not! For then how will God judge the world?

7 For if the truth of God has in-

creased through my lie to His glory, why am I also still judged as a sinner?

8 And *why* not *say,* "Let us do evil that good may come"?—as we are slanderously reported and as some affirm that we say. Their condemnation is just.

9 What then? Are we better *than they?* Not at all. For we have previously charged both Jews and Greeks that they are all under sin.

10 As it is written:

"There is none righteous, no,
   not one;

11 There is none who
   understands;
   There is none who seeks after
   God.

12 They have all gone out of the
   way;
   They have together become
   unprofitable;
   There is none who does good,
   no, not one."

13 "Their throat is an open tomb;
   With their tongues they have
   practiced deceit";
   "The poison of asps is under
   their lips";

14 "Whose mouth is full of cursing
   and bitterness."

15 "Their feet are swift to shed
   blood;

16 Destruction and misery are in
   their ways;

17 And the way of peace they
   have not known."

18 "There is no fear of God before
   their eyes."

19 Now we know that whatever the law says, it says to those who are under the law, that every mouth may be stopped, and all the world may become guilty before God.

20 Therefore by the deeds of the law no flesh will be justified in His sight, for by the law *is* the knowledge of sin.

21 But now the righteousness of God apart from the law is revealed,

being witnessed by the Law and the Prophets,

22 even the righteousness of God *which is* through faith in Jesus Christ to all and on all who believe. For there is no difference;

23 for all have sinned and fall short of the glory of God,

24 being justified freely by His grace through the redemption that is in Christ Jesus,

25 whom God set forth *to be* a propitiation by His blood, through faith, to demonstrate His righteousness, because in His forbearance God had passed over the sins that were previously committed,

26 to demonstrate at the present time His righteousness, that He might be just and the justifier of the one who has faith in Jesus.

27 Where *is* boasting then? It is excluded. By what law? Of works? No, but by the law of faith.

28 Therefore we conclude that a man is justified by faith apart from the deeds of the law.

29 Or *is* He the God of the Jews only? *Is* He not also the God of the Gentiles? Yes, of the Gentiles also,

30 since *there is* one God who will justify the circumcision by faith and the uncircumcised through faith.

31 Do we then make void the law through faith? Certainly not! On the contrary, we establish the law.

4 What then shall we say that Abraham our father has found according to the flesh?

2 For if Abraham was justified by works, he has *something of which* to boast, but not before God.

3 For what does the Scripture say? *"Abraham believed God, and it was accounted to him for righteousness."*

4 Now to him who works, the wages are not counted as grace but as debt.

5 But to him who does not work but believes on Him who justifies the ungodly, his faith is accounted for righteousness,

6 just as David also describes the blessedness of the man to whom God imputes righteousness apart from works:

7 *"Blessed are those whose
     lawless deeds are forgiven,
And whose sins are covered;*
8 *Blessed is the man to whom
     the* LORD *shall not impute
     sin."*

9 *Does* this blessedness then *come* upon the circumcised *only,* or upon the uncircumcised also? For we say that faith was accounted to Abraham for righteousness.
10 How then was it accounted? While he was circumcised, or uncircumcised? Not while circumcised, but while uncircumcised.
11 And he received the sign of circumcision, a seal of the righteousness of the faith which *he had while still* uncircumcised, that he might be the father of all those who believe, though they are uncircumcised, that righteousness might be imputed to them also,
12 and the father of circumcision to those who not only *are* of the circumcision, but who also walk in the steps of the faith which our father Abraham *had while still* uncircumcised.
13 For the promise that he would be the heir of the world *was* not to Abraham or to his seed through the law, but through the righteousness of faith.
14 For if those who are of the law *are* heirs, faith is made void and the promise made of no effect,
15 because the law brings about wrath; for where there is no law *there is* no transgression.
16 Therefore *it is* of faith that *it might be* according to grace, so that the promise might be sure to all the seed, not only to those who are of the law, but also to those who are of the faith of Abraham, who is the father of us all

17 (as it is written, *"I have made you a father of many nations"*) in the presence of Him whom he believed, *even* God, who gives life to the dead and calls those things which do not exist as though they did;
18 who, contrary to hope, in hope believed, so that he became the father of many nations, according to what was spoken, *"So shall your descendants be."*
19 And not being weak in faith, he did not consider his own body, already dead (since he was about a hundred years old), and the deadness of Sarah's womb.
20 He did not waver at the promise of God through unbelief, but was strengthened in faith, giving glory to God,
21 and being fully convinced that what He had promised He was also able to perform.
22 And therefore *"it was accounted to him for righteousness."*
23 Now it was not written for his sake alone that it was imputed to him,
24 but also for us. It shall be imputed to us who believe in Him who raised up Jesus our Lord from the dead,
25 who was delivered up because of our offenses, and was raised because of our justification.

5 Therefore, having been justified by faith, we have peace with God through our Lord Jesus Christ,
2 through whom also we have access by faith into this grace in which we stand, and rejoice in hope of the glory of God.
3 And not only *that,* but we also glory in tribulations, knowing that tribulation produces perseverance;
4 and perseverance, character; and character, hope.
5 Now hope does not disappoint, because the love of God has been poured out in our hearts by the Holy Spirit who was given to us.
6 For when we were still without

strength, in due time Christ died for the ungodly.

7 For scarcely for a righteous man will one die; yet perhaps for a good man someone would even dare to die.

8 But God demonstrates His own love toward us, in that while we were still sinners, Christ died for us.

9 Much more then, having now been justified by His blood, we shall be saved from wrath through Him.

10 For if when we were enemies we were reconciled to God through the death of His Son, much more, having been reconciled, we shall be saved by His life.

11 And not only *that*, but we also rejoice in God through our Lord Jesus Christ, through whom we have now received the reconciliation.

12 Therefore, just as through one man sin entered the world, and death through sin, and thus death spread to all men, because all sinned—

13 (For until the law sin was in the world, but sin is not imputed when there is no law.

14 Nevertheless death reigned from Adam to Moses, even over those who had not sinned according to the likeness of the transgression of Adam, who is a type of Him who was to come.

15 But the free gift *is* not like the offense. For if by the one man's offense many died, much more the grace of God and the gift by the grace of the one Man, Jesus Christ, abounded to many.

16 And the gift *is* not like *that which came* through the one who sinned. For the judgment *which came* from one *offense resulted* in condemnation, but the free gift *which came* from many offenses *resulted* in justification.

17 For if by the one man's offense death reigned through the one,

much more those who receive abundance of grace and of the gift of righteousness will reign in life through the One, Jesus Christ.)

18 Therefore, as through one man's offense *judgment* came to all men, resulting in condemnation, even so through one Man's righteous act *the free gift came* to all men, resulting in justification of life.

19 For as by one man's disobedience many were made sinners, so also by one Man's obedience many will be made righteous.

20 Moreover the law entered that the offense might abound. But where sin abounded, grace abounded much more,

21 so that as sin reigned in death, even so grace might reign through righteousness to eternal life through Jesus Christ our Lord.

6 What shall we say then? Shall we continue in sin that grace may abound?

2 Certainly not! How shall we who died to sin live any longer in it?

3 Or do you not know that as many of us as were baptized into Christ Jesus were baptized into His death?

4 Therefore we were buried with Him through baptism into death, that just as Christ was raised from the dead by the glory of the Father, even so we also should walk in newness of life.

5 For if we have been united together in the likeness of His death, certainly we also shall be *in the likeness* of *His* resurrection,

6 knowing this, that our old man was crucified with *Him*, that the body of sin might be done away with, that we should no longer be slaves of sin.

7 For he who has died has been freed from sin.

8 Now if we died with Christ, we believe that we shall also live with Him,

9 knowing that Christ, having

191   *See Romans 10:9, 10, 13, page 196*

been raised from the dead, dies no more. Death no longer has dominion over Him.

10 For *the death* that He died, He died to sin once for all; but *the life* that He lives, He lives to God.

11 Likewise you also, reckon yourselves to be dead indeed to sin, but alive to God in Christ Jesus our Lord.

12 Therefore do not let sin reign in your mortal body, that you should obey it in its lusts.

13 And do not present your members *as* instruments of unrighteousness to sin, but present yourselves to God as being alive from the dead, and your members *as* instruments of righteousness to God.

14 For sin shall not have dominion over you, for you are not under law but under grace.

15 What then? Shall we sin because we are not under law but under grace? Certainly not!

16 Do you not know that to whom you present yourselves slaves to obey, you are that one's slaves whom you obey, whether of sin to death, or of obedience to righteousness?

17 But God be thanked that *though* you were slaves of sin, yet you obeyed from the heart that form of doctrine to which you were delivered.

18 And having been set free from sin, you became slaves of righteousness.

19 I speak in human *terms* because of the weakness of your flesh. For just as you presented your members *as* slaves of uncleanness, and of lawlessness *leading* to *more* lawlessness, so now present your members *as* slaves *of* righteousness for holiness.

20 For when you were slaves of sin, you were free in regard to righteousness.

21 What fruit did you have then in the things of which you are now ashamed? For the end of those things *is* death.

22 But now having been set free from sin, and having become slaves of God, you have your fruit to holiness, and the end, everlasting life.

23 For the wages of sin *is* death, but the gift of God *is* eternal life in Christ Jesus our Lord.

7 Or do you not know, brethren (for I speak to those who know the law), that the law has dominion over a man as long as he lives?

2 For the woman who has a husband is bound by the law to *her* husband as long as he lives. But if the husband dies, she is released from the law of *her* husband.

3 So then if, while *her* husband lives, she marries another man, she will be called an adulteress; but if her husband dies, she is free from that law, so that she is no adulteress, though she has married another man.

4 Therefore, my brethren, you also have become dead to the law through the body of Christ, that you may be married to another, *even* to Him who was raised from the dead, that we should bear fruit to God.

5 For when we were in the flesh, the passions of sins which were aroused by the law were at work in our members to bear fruit to death.

6 But now we have been delivered from the law, having died to what we were held by, so that we should serve in the newness of the Spirit and not *in* the oldness of the letter.

7 What shall we say then? *Is* the law sin? Certainly not! On the contrary, I would not have known sin except through the law. For I would not have known covetousness unless the law had said, *"You shall not covet."*

8 But sin, taking opportunity by the commandment, produced in me all *manner of evil* desire. For apart from the law sin *was* dead.

See Romans 5:8, page 191

9 I was alive once without the law, but when the commandment came, sin revived and I died.

10 And the commandment, which *was* to *bring* life, I found to *bring* death.

11 For sin, taking occasion by the commandment, deceived me, and by it killed *me*.

12 Therefore the law *is* holy, and the commandment holy and just and good.

13 Has then what is good become death to me? Certainly not! But sin, that it might appear sin, was producing death in me through what is good, so that sin through the commandment might become exceedingly sinful.

14 For we know that the law is spiritual, but I am carnal, sold under sin.

15 For what I am doing, I do not understand. For what I will to do, that I do not practice; but what I hate, that I do.

16 If, then, I do what I will not to do, I agree with the law that *it is* good.

17 But now, *it is* no longer I who do it, but sin that dwells in me.

18 For I know that in me (that is, in my flesh) nothing good dwells; for to will is present with me, but *how* to perform what is good I do not find.

19 For the good that I will *to do*, I do not do; but the evil I will not *to do*, that I practice.

20 Now if I do what I will not *to do*, it is no longer I who do it, but sin that dwells in me.

21 I find then a law, that evil is present with me, the one who wills to do good.

22 For I delight in the law of God according to the inward man.

23 But I see another law in my members, warring against the law of my mind, and bringing me into captivity to the law of sin which is in my members.

24 O wretched man that I am! Who will deliver me from this body of death?

25 I thank God—through Jesus Christ our Lord! So then, with the mind I myself serve the law of God, but with the flesh the law of sin.

8 *There is* therefore now no condemnation to those who are in Christ Jesus, who do not walk according to the flesh, but according to the Spirit. ❤

2 For the law of the Spirit of life in Christ Jesus has made me free from the law of sin and death.

3 For what the law could not do in that it was weak through the flesh, God *did* by sending His own Son in the likeness of sinful flesh, on account of sin: He condemned sin in the flesh,

4 that the righteous requirement of the law might be fulfilled in us who do not walk according to the flesh but according to the Spirit.

5 For those who live according to the flesh set their minds on the things of the flesh, but those *who live* according to the Spirit, the things of the Spirit.

6 For to be carnally minded *is* death, but to be spiritually minded *is* life and peace.

7 Because the carnal mind *is* enmity against God; for it is not subject to the law of God, nor indeed can be.

8 So then, those who are in the flesh cannot please God.

9 But you are not in the flesh but in the Spirit, if indeed the Spirit of God dwells in you. Now if anyone does not have the Spirit of Christ, he is not His.

10 And if Christ *is* in you, the body *is* dead because of sin, but the Spirit *is* life because of righteousness.

11 But if the Spirit of Him who raised Jesus from the dead dwells in you, He who raised Christ from the dead will also give life to your

From Suffering to Glory

mortal bodies through His Spirit who dwells in you.

12 Therefore, brethren, we are debtors—not to the flesh, to live according to the flesh.

13 For if you live according to the flesh you will die; but if by the Spirit you put to death the deeds of the body, you will live.

14 For as many as are led by the Spirit of God, these are sons of God.

15 For you did not receive the spirit of bondage again to fear, but you received the Spirit of adoption by whom we cry out, "Abba, Father."

16 The Spirit Himself bears witness with our spirit that we are children of God,

17 and if children, then heirs—heirs of God and joint heirs with Christ, if indeed we suffer with *Him*, that we may also be glorified together.

18 For I consider that the sufferings of this present time are not worthy *to be compared* with the glory which shall be revealed in us.

19 For the earnest expectation of the creation eagerly waits for the revealing of the sons of God.

20 For the creation was subjected to futility, not willingly, but because of Him who subjected *it* in hope;

21 because the creation itself also will be delivered from the bondage of corruption into the glorious liberty of the children of God.

22 For we know that the whole creation groans and labors with birth pangs together until now.

23 And not only *they*, but we also who have the firstfruits of the Spirit, even we ourselves groan within ourselves, eagerly waiting for the adoption, the redemption of our body.

24 For we were saved in this hope, but hope that is seen is not hope; for why does one still hope for what he sees?

25 But if we hope for what we do not see, *then* we eagerly wait for *it* with perseverance.

26 Likewise the Spirit also helps in our weaknesses. For we do not know what we should pray for as we ought, but the Spirit Himself makes intercession for us with groanings which cannot be uttered.

27 Now He who searches the hearts knows what the mind of the Spirit *is*, because He makes intercession for the saints according to *the will of* God.

28 And we know that all things work together for good to those who love God, to those who are the called according to *His* purpose.

29 For whom He foreknew, He also predestined *to be* conformed to the image of His Son, that He might be the firstborn among many brethren.

30 Moreover whom He predestined, these He also called; whom He called, these He also justified; and whom He justified, these He also glorified.

31 What then shall we say to these things? If God *is* for us, who *can be* against us?

32 He who did not spare His own Son, but delivered Him up for us all, how shall He not with Him also freely give us all things?

33 Who shall bring a charge against God's elect? *It is* God who justifies.

34 Who *is* he who condemns? *It is* Christ who died, and furthermore is also risen, who is even at the right hand of God, who also makes intercession for us.

35 Who shall separate us from the love of Christ? *Shall* tribulation, or distress, or persecution, or famine, or nakedness, or peril, or sword?

36 As it is written:

"For Your sake we are killed
all day long;
We are accounted as sheep
for the slaughter."

37 Yet in all these things we are more than conquerors through Him who loved us.

38 For I am persuaded that neither death nor life, nor angels nor principalities nor powers, nor things present nor things to come,

39 nor height nor depth, nor any other created thing, shall be able to separate us from the love of God which is in Christ Jesus our Lord.

9 I tell the truth in Christ, I am not lying, my conscience also bearing me witness in the Holy Spirit,

2 that I have great sorrow and continual grief in my heart.

3 For I could wish that I myself were accursed from Christ for my brethren, my kinsmen according to the flesh,

4 who are Israelites, to whom *pertain* the adoption, the glory, the covenants, the giving of the law, the service *of God*, and the promises;

5 of whom *are* the fathers and from whom, according to the flesh, Christ *came*, who is over all, *the* eternally blessed God. Amen.

6 But it is not that the word of God has taken no effect. For they *are* not all Israel who *are* of Israel,

7 nor *are they* all children because they are the seed of Abraham; but, *"In Isaac your seed shall be called."*

8 That is, those who *are* the children of the flesh, these *are* not the children of God; but the children of the promise are counted as the seed.

9 For this *is* the word of promise: *"At this time I will come and Sarah shall have a son."*

10 And not only *this*, but when Rebecca also had conceived by one man, *even* by our father Isaac

11 (for *the children* not yet being born, nor having done any good or evil, that the purpose of God according to election might stand, not of works but of Him who calls),

12 it was said to her, *"The older shall serve the younger."*

13 As it is written, *"Jacob I have loved, but Esau I have hated."*

14 What shall we say then? *Is there* unrighteousness with God? Certainly not!

15 For He says to Moses, *"I will have mercy on whomever I will have mercy, and I will have compassion on whomever I will have compassion."*

16 So then *it is* not of him who wills, nor of him who runs, but of God who shows mercy.

17 For the Scripture says to Pharaoh, *"Even for this same purpose I have raised you up, that I might show My power in you, and that My name might be declared in all the earth."*

18 Therefore He has mercy on whom He wills, and whom He wills He hardens.

19 You will say to me then, "Why does He still find fault? For who has resisted His will?"

20 But indeed, O man, who are you to reply against God? Will the thing formed say to him who formed *it*, "Why have you made me like this?"

21 Does not the potter have power over the clay, from the same lump to make one vessel for honor and another for dishonor?

22 *What* if God, wanting to show *His* wrath and to make His power known, endured with much longsuffering the vessels of wrath prepared for destruction,

23 and that He might make known the riches of His glory on the vessels of mercy, which He had prepared beforehand for glory,

24 *even* us whom He called, not of the Jews only, but also of the Gentiles?

25 As He says also in Hosea:

> *"I will call them My people,*
> *who were not My people,*
> *And her beloved,*
> *who was not beloved."*

195

See Philippians 1:6, page 241

26 "And it shall come to pass in the place where it was said to them,

'You are not My people,'
There they will be called sons of the living God.'"

27 Isaiah also cries out concerning Israel:

"Though the number of the children of Israel be as the sand of the sea,
The remnant will be saved.
28 For He will finish the work and cut it short in righteousness,
Because the LORD will make a short work upon the earth."

29 And as Isaiah said before:

"Unless the LORD of Sabaoth had left us a seed,
We would have become like Sodom,
And we would have been made like Gomorrah."

30 What shall we say then? That Gentiles, who did not pursue righteousness, have attained to righteousness, even the righteousness of faith;
31 but Israel, pursuing the law of righteousness, has not attained to the law of righteousness.
32 Why? Because they did not seek it by faith, but as it were, by the works of the law. For they stumbled at that stumbling stone.
33 As it is written:

"Behold, I lay in Zion a stumbling stone and rock of offense,
And whoever believes on Him will not be put to shame."

10 Brethren, my heart's desire and prayer to God for Israel is that they may be saved.
2 For I bear them witness that

they have a zeal for God, but not according to knowledge.
3 For they being ignorant of God's righteousness, and seeking to establish their own righteousness, have not submitted to the righteousness of God.
4 For Christ is the end of the law for righteousness to everyone who believes.
5 For Moses writes about the righteousness which is of the law, "The man who does those things shall live by them."
6 But the righteousness of faith speaks in this way, "Do not say in your heart, 'Who will ascend into heaven?' " (that is, to bring Christ down from above)
7 or, " 'Who will descend into the abyss?' " (that is, to bring Christ up from the dead).
8 But what does it say? "The word is near you, even in your mouth and in your heart" (that is, the word of faith which we preach):
9 that if you confess with your mouth the Lord Jesus and believe in your heart that God has raised Him from the dead, you will be saved.
10 For with the heart one believes to righteousness, and with the mouth confession is made to salvation.
11 For the Scripture says, "Whoever believes on Him will not be put to shame."
12 For there is no distinction between Jew and Greek, for the same Lord over all is rich to all who call upon Him.
13 For "whoever calls upon the name of the LORD shall be saved."
14 How then shall they call on Him in whom they have not believed? And how shall they believe in Him of whom they have not heard? And how shall they hear without a preacher?
15 And how shall they preach unless they are sent? As it is written:

> "How beautiful are the feet of
>   those who preach the gospel
>   of peace,
> Who bring glad tidings of good
>   things!"

16 But they have not all obeyed
the gospel. For Isaiah says, *"Lord,
who has believed our report?"*
17 So then faith *comes* by hearing,
and hearing by the word of God.
18 But I say, have they not heard?
Yes indeed:

> "Their sound has gone out
>   to all the earth,
> And their words to the ends
>   of the world."

19 But I say, did Israel not know?
First Moses says:

> "I will provoke you to jealousy
>   by those who are not a
>   nation,
> I will anger you by a foolish
>   nation."

20 But Isaiah is very bold and says:

> "I was found by those
>   who did not seek Me;
> I was made manifest to those
>   who did not ask for Me."

21 But to Israel he says:

> "All day long I have stretched
>   out My hands
> To a disobedient and contrary
>   people."

11 I say then, has God cast
away His people? Certainly
not! For I also am an Israelite, of
the seed of Abraham, *of* the tribe
of Benjamin.
2 God has not cast away His people whom He foreknew. Or do you
not know what the Scripture says
of Elijah, how he pleads with God
against Israel, saying,
3 *"Lord, they have killed Your*

prophets and torn down Your altars, and I alone am left, and they
seek my life"*?
4 But what does the divine response say to him? *"I have reserved for Myself seven thousand
men who have not bowed the knee
to Baal."*
5 Even so then, at this present
time there is a remnant according
to the election of grace.
6 And if by grace, then *it is* no
longer of works; otherwise grace is
no longer grace. But if *it is* of
works, it is no longer grace; otherwise work is no longer work.
7 What then? Israel has not obtained what it seeks; but the elect
have obtained it, and the rest were
hardened.
8 Just as it is written:

> "God has given them a spirit of
>   stupor,
> Eyes that they should not see
> And ears that they should not
>   hear,
> To this very day."

9 And David says:

> "Let their table become a snare
>   and a trap,
> A stumbling block and
>   a recompense to them;
10 Let their eyes be darkened,
>   that they may not see,
> And bow down their back
>   always."

11 I say then, have they stumbled
that they should fall? Certainly
not! But through their fall, to provoke them to jealousy, salvation
has come to the Gentiles.
12 Now if their fall *is* riches for the
world, and their failure riches for
the Gentiles, how much more their
fullness!
13 For I speak to you Gentiles;
inasmuch as I am an apostle to the
Gentiles, I magnify my ministry,
14 if by any means I may provoke

to jealousy *those who are* my flesh and save some of them.

15 For if their being cast away *is* the reconciling of the world, what *will* their acceptance *be* but life from the dead?

16 For if the firstfruit *is* holy, the lump *is* also *holy*; and if the root *is* holy, so *are* the branches.

17 And if some of the branches were broken off, and you, being a wild olive tree, were grafted in among them, and with them became a partaker of the root and fatness of the olive tree,

18 do not boast against the branches. But if you boast, *remember that* you do not support the root, but the root supports you.

19 You will say then, "Branches were broken off that I might be grafted in."

20 Well *said*. Because of unbelief they were broken off, and you stand by faith. Do not be haughty, but fear.

21 For if God did not spare the natural branches, He may not spare you either.

22 Therefore consider the goodness and severity of God: on those who fell, severity; but toward you, goodness, if you continue in *His* goodness. Otherwise you also will be cut off.

23 And they also, if they do not continue in unbelief, will be grafted in, for God is able to graft them in again.

24 For if you were cut out of the olive tree which is wild by nature, and were grafted contrary to nature into a good olive tree, how much more will these, who *are the* natural *branches*, be grafted into their own olive tree?

25 For I do not desire, brethren, that you should be ignorant of this mystery, lest you should be wise in your own opinion, that hardening in part has happened to Israel until the fullness of the Gentiles has come in.

26 And so all Israel will be saved, as it is written:

"The Deliverer will come out of Zion,
And He will turn away ungodliness from Jacob;
27 For this is My covenant with them,
When I take away their sins."

28 Concerning the gospel *they are* enemies for your sake, but concerning the election *they are* beloved for the sake of the fathers.

29 For the gifts and the calling of God *are* irrevocable.

30 For as you were once disobedient to God, yet have now obtained mercy through their disobedience,

31 even so these also have now been disobedient, that through the mercy shown you they also may obtain mercy.

32 For God has committed them all to disobedience, that He might have mercy on all.

33 Oh, the depth of the riches both of the wisdom and knowledge of God! How unsearchable *are* His judgments and His ways past finding out!

34 "For who has known the mind of the LORD?
Or who has become His counselor?"
35 "Or who has first given to Him And it shall be repaid to him?"

36 For of Him and through Him and to Him *are* all things, to whom *be* glory forever. Amen.

12 I beseech you therefore, brethren, by the mercies of God, that you present your bodies a living sacrifice, holy, acceptable to God, *which is* your reasonable service.

2 And do not be conformed to this world, but be transformed by the renewing of your mind, that you may prove what *is* that good and acceptable and perfect will of God.

See Philippians 2:1–4, page 242

3 For I say, through the grace given to me, to everyone who is among you, not to think *of himself* more highly than he ought to think, but to think soberly, as God has dealt to each one a measure of faith.

4 For as we have many members in one body, but all the members do not have the same function,

5 so we, *being* many, are one body in Christ, and individually members of one another.

6 Having then gifts differing according to the grace that is given to us, *let us use them:* if prophecy, *let us prophesy* in proportion to our faith;

7 or ministry, *let us use it* in *our* ministering; he who teaches, in teaching;

8 he who exhorts, in exhortation; he who gives, with liberality; he who leads, with diligence; he who shows mercy, with cheerfulness.

9 *Let* love *be* without hypocrisy. Abhor what is evil. Cling to what is good.

10 *Be* kindly affectionate to one another with brotherly love, in honor giving preference to one another;

11 not lagging in diligence, fervent in spirit, serving the Lord;

12 rejoicing in hope, patient in tribulation, continuing steadfastly in prayer;

13 distributing to the needs of the saints, given to hospitality.

14 Bless those who persecute you; bless and do not curse.

15 Rejoice with those who rejoice, and weep with those who weep.

16 Be of the same mind toward one another. Do not set your mind on high things, but associate with the humble. Do not be wise in your own opinion.

17 Repay no one evil for evil. Have regard for good things in the sight of all men.

18 If it is possible, as much as depends on you, live peaceably with all men.

19 Beloved, do not avenge yourselves, but *rather* give place to wrath; for it is written, *"Vengeance is Mine, I will repay,"* says the Lord.

20 *"Therefore if your enemy
    hungers, feed him;
If he thirsts, give him a drink;
For in so doing you will heap
    coals of fire on his head."*

21 Do not be overcome by evil, but overcome evil with good.

13 Let every soul be subject to the governing authorities. For there is no authority except from God, and the authorities that exist are appointed by God.

2 Therefore whoever resists the authority resists the ordinance of God, and those who resist will bring judgment on themselves.

3 For rulers are not a terror to good works, but to evil. Do you want to be unafraid of the authority? Do what is good, and you will have praise from the same.

4 For he is God's minister to you for good. But if you do evil, be afraid; for he does not bear the sword in vain; for he is God's minister, an avenger to *execute* wrath on him who practices evil.

5 Therefore *you* must be subject, not only because of wrath but also for conscience' sake.

6 For because of this you also pay taxes, for they are God's ministers attending continually to this very thing.

7 Render therefore to all their due: taxes to whom taxes *are* due, customs to whom customs, fear to whom fear, honor to whom honor.

8 Owe no one anything except to love one another, for he who loves another has fulfilled the law.

9 For the commandments, *"You shall not commit adultery," "You shall not murder," "You shall not steal," "You shall not bear false witness," "You shall not covet,"* and if *there is* any other command-

199

ment, are *all* summed up in this saying, namely, *"You shall love your neighbor as yourself."*

10 Love does no harm to a neighbor; therefore love *is* the fulfillment of the law.

11 And *do* this, knowing the time, that now *it is* high time to awake out of sleep; for now our salvation *is* nearer than when we *first* believed.

12 The night is far spent, the day is at hand. Therefore let us cast off the works of darkness, and let us put on the armor of light.

13 Let us walk properly, as in the day, not in revelry and drunkenness, not in licentiousness and lewdness, not in strife and envy.

14 But put on the Lord Jesus Christ, and make no provision for the flesh, to *fulfill its* lusts.

14 Receive one who is weak in the faith, *but* not to disputes over doubtful things.

2 For one believes he may eat all things, but he who is weak eats *only* vegetables.

3 Let not him who eats despise him who does not eat, and let not him who does not eat judge him who eats; for God has received him.

4 Who are you to judge another's servant? To his own master he stands or falls. Indeed, he will be made to stand, for God is able to make him stand.

5 One person esteems *one* day above another; another esteems every day *alike*. Let each be fully convinced in his own mind.

6 He who observes the day, observes *it* to the Lord; and he who does not observe the day, to the Lord he does not observe *it*. He who eats, eats to the Lord, for he gives God thanks; and he who does not éat, to the Lord he does not eat, and gives God thanks.

7 For none of us lives to himself, and no one dies to himself.

8 For if we live, we live to the Lord; and if we die, we die to the Lord. Therefore, whether we live or die, we are the Lord's.

9 For to this end Christ died and rose and lived again, that He might be Lord of both the dead and the living.

10 But why do you judge your brother? Or why do you show contempt for your brother? For we shall all stand before the judgment seat of Christ.

11 For it is written:

> *"As I live, says the LORD,*
> *Every knee shall bow to Me,*
> *And every tongue shall confess*
> *to God."*

12 So then each of us shall give account of himself to God.

13 Therefore let us not judge one another anymore, but rather resolve this, not to put a stumbling block or a cause to fall in *our* brother's way.

14 I know and am convinced by the Lord Jesus that *there is* nothing unclean of itself; but to him who considers anything to be unclean, to him *it is* unclean.

15 Yet if your brother is grieved because of *your* food, you are no longer walking in love. Do not destroy with your food the one for whom Christ died.

16 Therefore do not let your good be spoken of as evil;

17 for the kingdom of God is not food and drink, but righteousness and peace and joy in the Holy Spirit.

18 For he who serves Christ in these things *is* acceptable to God and approved by men.

19 Therefore let us pursue the things *which make* for peace and the things by which one may edify another.

20 Do not destroy the work of God for the sake of food. All things indeed *are* pure, but *it is* evil for the man who eats with offense.

21 *It is* good neither to eat meat

nor drink wine nor *do anything* by which your brother stumbles or is offended or is made weak.

22 Do you have faith? Have *it* to yourself before God. Happy *is* he who does not condemn himself in what he approves.

23 But he who doubts is condemned if he eats, because *he does* not *eat* from faith; for whatever *is* not from faith is sin.

15 We then who are strong ought to bear with the scruples of the weak, and not to please ourselves.

2 Let each of us please *his* neighbor for *his* good, leading to edification.

3 For even Christ did not please Himself; but as it is written, *"The reproaches of those who reproached You fell on Me."*

4 For whatever things were written before were written for our learning, that we through the patience and comfort of the Scriptures might have hope.

5 Now may the God of patience and comfort grant you to be likeminded toward one another, according to Christ Jesus,

6 that you may with one mind *and* one mouth glorify the God and Father of our Lord Jesus Christ.

7 Therefore receive one another, just as Christ also received us, to the glory of God.

8 Now I say that Jesus Christ has become a servant to the circumcision for the truth of God, to confirm the promises *made* to the fathers,

9 and that the Gentiles might glorify God for *His* mercy, as it is written:

> *"For this reason I will confess*
> *to You among the Gentiles,*
> *And sing to Your name."*

10 And again he says:

> *"Rejoice, O Gentiles, with His*
> *people!"*

11 And again:

> *"Praise the LORD, all you*
> *Gentiles!*
> *Laud Him, all you peoples!"*

12 And again, Isaiah says:

> *"There shall be a root of Jesse;*
> *And He who shall rise to reign*
> *over the Gentiles,*
> *In Him the Gentiles shall*
> *hope."*

13 Now may the God of hope fill you with all joy and peace in believing, that you may abound in hope by the power of the Holy Spirit.

14 Now I myself am confident concerning you, my brethren, that you also are full of goodness, filled with all knowledge, able also to admonish one another.

15 Nevertheless, brethren, I have written more boldly to you on *some* points, as reminding you, because of the grace given to me by God,

16 that I might be a minister of Jesus Christ to the Gentiles, ministering the gospel of God, that the offering of the Gentiles might be acceptable, sanctified by the Holy Spirit.

17 Therefore I have reason to glory in Christ Jesus in the things *which pertain* to God.

18 For I will not dare to speak of any of those things which Christ has not accomplished through me, in word and deed, to make the Gentiles obedient—

19 in mighty signs and wonders, by the power of the Spirit of God, so that from Jerusalem and round about to Illyricum I have fully preached the gospel of Christ.

20 And so I have made it my aim to preach the gospel, not where Christ was named, lest I should build on another man's foundation,

21 but as it is written:

*"To whom He was not
announced, they shall see;
And those who have not heard
shall understand."*

22 For this reason I also have been much hindered from coming to you.

23 But now no longer having a place in these parts, and having a great desire these many years to come to you,

24 whenever I journey to Spain, I shall come to you. For I hope to see you on my journey, and to be helped on my way there by you, if first I may enjoy your *company* for a while.

25 But now I am going to Jerusalem to minister to the saints.

26 For it pleased those from Macedonia and Achaia to make a certain contribution for the poor among the saints who are in Jerusalem.

27 It pleased them indeed, and they are their debtors. For if the Gentiles have been partakers of their spiritual things, their duty is also to minister to them in material things.

28 Therefore, when I have performed this and have sealed to them this fruit, I shall go by way of you to Spain.

29 But I know that when I come to you, I shall come in the fullness of the blessing of the gospel of Christ.

30 Now I beg you, brethren, through the Lord Jesus Christ, and through the love of the Spirit, that you strive together with me in *your* prayers to God for me,

31 that I may be delivered from those in Judea who do not believe, and that my service for Jerusalem may be acceptable to the saints,

32 that I may come to you with joy by the will of God, and may be refreshed together with you.

33 Now the God of peace *be* with you all. Amen.

16 I commend to you Phoebe our sister, who is a servant of the church in Cenchrea,

2 that you may receive her in the Lord in a manner worthy of the saints, and assist her in whatever business she has need of you; for indeed she has been a helper of many and of myself also.

3 Greet Priscilla and Aquila, my fellow workers in Christ Jesus,

4 who risked their own necks for my life, to whom not only I give thanks, but also all the churches of the Gentiles.

5 Likewise *greet* the church that is in their house. Greet my beloved Epaenetus, who is the firstfruits of Achaia to Christ.

6 Greet Mary, who labored much for us.

7 Greet Andronicus and Junia, my kinsmen and my fellow prisoners, who are of note among the apostles, who also were in Christ before me.

8 Greet Amplias, my beloved in the Lord.

9 Greet Urbanus, our fellow worker in Christ, and Stachys, my beloved.

10 Greet Apelles, approved in Christ. Greet those who are of the *household* of Aristobulus.

11 Greet Herodion, my kinsman. Greet those who are of the *household* of Narcissus who are in the Lord.

12 Greet Tryphena and Tryphosa, who have labored in the Lord. Greet the beloved Persis, who labored much in the Lord.

13 Greet Rufus, chosen in the Lord, and his mother and mine.

14 Greet Asyncritus, Phlegon, Hermas, Patrobas, Hermes, and the brethren who are with them.

15 Greet Philologus and Julia, Nereus and his sister, and Olympas, and all the saints who are with them.

16 Greet one another with a holy kiss. The churches of Christ greet you.

17 Now I urge you, brethren, note those who cause divisions and offenses, contrary to the doctrine which you learned, and avoid them.

18 For those who are such do not serve our Lord Jesus Christ, but their own belly, and by smooth words and flattering speech deceive the hearts of the simple.

19 For your obedience has become known to all. Therefore I am glad on your behalf; but I want you to be wise in what is good, and simple concerning evil.

20 And the God of peace will crush Satan under your feet shortly. The grace of our Lord Jesus Christ *be* with you. Amen.

21 Timothy, my fellow worker, and Lucius, Jason, and Sosipater, my kinsmen, greet you.

22 I, Tertius, who wrote *this* epistle, greet you in the Lord.

23 Gaius, my host and *the host of* the whole church, greets you. Erastus, the treasurer of the city, greets you, and Quartus, a brother.

24 The grace of our Lord Jesus Christ *be* with you all. Amen.

25 Now to Him who is able to establish you according to my gospel and the preaching of Jesus Christ, according to the revelation of the mystery *which was* kept secret since the world began

26 but now has been made manifest, and by the prophetic Scriptures has been made known to all nations, according to the commandment of the everlasting God, for obedience to the faith—

27 to God, alone wise, *be* glory through Jesus Christ forever. Amen.

THE FIRST EPISTLE OF PAUL THE APOSTLE TO THE

CORINTHIANS

PAUL, called *to be* an apostle of Jesus Christ through the will of God, and Sosthenes *our* brother,

2 To the church of God which is at Corinth, to those who are sanctified in Christ Jesus, called *to be* saints, with all who in every place call on the name of Jesus Christ our Lord, both theirs and ours:

3 Grace to you and peace from God our Father and the Lord Jesus Christ.

4 I thank my God always concerning you for the grace of God which was given to you by Christ Jesus,

5 that you were enriched in everything by Him in all utterance and all knowledge,

6 even as the testimony of Christ was confirmed in you,

7 so that you come short in no gift, eagerly waiting for the revelation of our Lord Jesus Christ,

8 who will also confirm you to the end, *that you may be* blameless in the day of our Lord Jesus Christ.

9 God *is* faithful, by whom you were called into the fellowship of His Son, Jesus Christ our Lord.

10 Now I plead with you, brethren, by the name of our Lord Jesus Christ, that you all speak the same thing, and *that* there be no divisions among you, but *that* you be perfectly joined together in the same mind and in the same judgment.

11 For it has been declared to me concerning you, my brethren, by those of Chloe's *household*, that there are contentions among you.

12 Now I say this, that each of you says, "I am of Paul," or "I am of Apollos," or "I am of Cephas," or "I am of Christ."

13 Is Christ divided? Was Paul crucified for you? Or were you baptized in the name of Paul?

14 I thank God that I baptized none of you except Crispus and Gaius,

15 lest anyone should say that I had baptized in my own name.

16 Yes, I also baptized the household of Stephanas. Besides, I do not know whether I baptized any other.

17 For Christ did not send me to baptize, but to preach the gospel, not with wisdom of words, lest the cross of Christ should be made of no effect.

18 For the message of the cross is foolishness to those who are perishing, but to us who are being saved it is the power of God.

19 For it is written:

> "I will destroy the wisdom of
>   the wise,
> And bring to nothing the
>   understanding of the
>   prudent."

20 Where is the wise? Where is the scribe? Where is the disputer of this age? Has not God made foolish the wisdom of this world?

21 For since, in the wisdom of God, the world through wisdom did not know God, it pleased God through the foolishness of the message preached to save those who believe.

22 For Jews request a sign, and Greeks seek after wisdom;

23 but we preach Christ crucified, to the Jews a stumbling block and to the Greeks foolishness,

24 but to those who are called, both Jews and Greeks, Christ the power of God and the wisdom of God.

25 Because the foolishness of God is wiser than men, and the weakness of God is stronger than men.

26 For you see your calling, brethren, that not many wise according to the flesh, not many mighty, not many noble, *are called.*

27 But God has chosen the foolish things of the world to put to shame the wise, and God has chosen the weak things of the world to put to shame the things which are mighty;

28 and the base things of the world and the things which are despised God has chosen, and the things which are not, to bring to nothing the things that are,

29 that no flesh should glory in His presence.

30 But of Him you are in Christ Jesus, who became for us wisdom from God—and righteousness and sanctification and redemption—

31 that, as it is written, *"He who glories, let him glory in the* LORD."

2 And I, brethren, when I came to you, did not come with excellence of speech or of wisdom declaring to you the testimony of God.

2 For I determined not to know anything among you except Jesus Christ and Him crucified.

3 I was with you in weakness, in fear, and in much trembling.

4 And my speech and my preaching *were* not with persuasive words of human wisdom, but in demonstration of the Spirit and of power,

5 that your faith should not be in the wisdom of men but in the power of God.

6 However, we speak wisdom among those who are mature, yet not the wisdom of this age, nor of the rulers of this age, who are coming to nothing.

7 But we speak the wisdom of God in a mystery, the hidden *wisdom* which God ordained before the ages for our glory,

8 which none of the rulers of this

204

age knew; for had they known, they would not have crucified the Lord of glory.

9 But as it is written:

> *"Eye has not seen, nor ear heard,*
> *Nor have entered into the heart of man*
> *The things which God has prepared for those who love Him."*

10 But God has revealed *them* to us through His Spirit. For the Spirit searches all things, yes, the deep things of God.

11 For what man knows the things of a man except the spirit of the man which is in him? Even so no one knows the things of God except the Spirit of God.

12 Now we have received, not the spirit of the world, but the Spirit who is from God, that we might know the things that have been freely given to us by God.

13 These things we also speak, not in words which man's wisdom teaches but which the Holy Spirit teaches, comparing spiritual things with spiritual.

14 But the natural man does not receive the things of the Spirit of God, for they are foolishness to him; nor can he know *them,* because they are spiritually discerned.

15 But he who is spiritual judges all things, yet he himself is *rightly* judged by no one.

16 For *"Who has known the mind of the* LORD *that he may instruct Him?"* But we have the mind of Christ.

3 And I, brethren, could not speak to you as to spiritual *people* but as to carnal, as to babes in Christ.

2 I fed you with milk and not with solid food; for until now you were not able *to receive it,* and even now you are still not able;

3 for you are still carnal. For

where *there are* envy, strife, and divisions among you, are you not carnal and behaving like *mere* men?

4 For when one says, "I am of Paul," and another, "I *am* of Apollos," are you not carnal?

5 Who then is Paul, and who *is* Apollos, but ministers through whom you believed, as the Lord gave to each one?

6 I planted, Apollos watered, but God gave the increase.

7 So then neither he who plants is anything, nor he who waters, but God who gives the increase.

8 Now he who plants and he who waters are one, and each one will receive his own reward according to his own labor.

9 For we are God's fellow workers; you are God's field, *you are* God's building.

10 According to the grace of God which was given to me, as a wise master builder I have laid the foundation, and another builds on it. But let each one take heed how he builds on it.

11 For no other foundation can anyone lay than that which is laid, which is Jesus Christ.

12 Now if anyone builds on this foundation *with* gold, silver, precious stones, wood, hay, straw,

13 each one's work will become manifest; for the Day will declare it, because it will be revealed by fire; and the fire will test each one's work, of what sort it is.

14 If anyone's work which he has built on *it* endures, he will receive a reward.

15 If anyone's work is burned, he will suffer loss; but he himself will be saved, yet so as through fire.

16 Do you not know that you are the temple of God and *that* the Spirit of God dwells in you?

17 If anyone defiles the temple of God, God will destroy him. For the temple of God is holy, which *temple* you are.

18 Let no one deceive himself. If

anyone among you seems to be wise in this age, let him become a fool that he may become wise.

19 For the wisdom of this world is foolishness with God. For it is written, *"He catches the wise in their own craftiness";*

20 and again, *"The LORD knows the thoughts of the wise, that they are futile."*

21 Therefore let no one glory in men. For all things are yours:

22 whether Paul or Apollos or Cephas, or the world or life or death, or things present or things to come—all are yours.

23 And you *are* Christ's, and Christ *is* God's.

4 Let a man so consider us, as servants of Christ and stewards of the mysteries of God.

2 Moreover it is required in stewards that one be found faithful.

3 But with me it is a very small thing that I should be judged by you or by a human court. In fact, I do not even judge myself.

4 For I know nothing against myself, yet I am not justified by this; but He who judges me is the Lord.

5 Therefore judge nothing before the time, until the Lord comes, who will both bring to light the hidden things of darkness and reveal the counsels of the hearts; and then each one's praise will come from God.

6 Now these things, brethren, I have figuratively transferred to myself and Apollos for your sakes, that you may learn in us not to think beyond what is written, that none of you may be puffed up on behalf of one against the other.

7 For who makes you differ *from another?* And what do you have that you did not receive? Now if you did indeed receive *it,* why do you glory as if you had not received *it?*

8 You are already full! You are already rich! You have reigned as kings without us—and indeed I could wish you did reign, that we also might reign with you!

9 For I think that God has displayed us, the apostles, last, as men condemned to death; for we have been made a spectacle to the world, both to angels and to men.

10 We *are* fools for Christ's sake, but you *are* wise in Christ! We *are* weak, but you *are* strong! You *are* distinguished, but we *are* dishonored!

11 *Even* to the present hour we both hunger and thirst, and we are poorly clothed, and beaten, and homeless.

12 And we labor, working with our own hands. Being reviled, we bless; being persecuted, we endure *it;*

13 being defamed, we entreat. We have been made as the filth of the world, the offscouring of all things until now.

14 I do not write these things to shame you, but as my beloved children I warn *you.*

15 For though you might have ten thousand instructors in Christ, yet *you do* not *have* many fathers; for in Christ Jesus I have begotten you through the gospel.

16 Therefore I urge you, imitate me.

17 For this reason I have sent Timothy to you, who is my beloved and faithful son in the Lord, who will remind you of my ways in Christ, as I teach everywhere in every church.

18 Now some are puffed up, as though I were not coming to you.

19 But I will come to you shortly, if the Lord wills, and I will know, not the word of those who are puffed up, but the power.

20 For the kingdom of God *is* not in word but in power.

21 What do you want? Shall I come to you with a rod, or in love and a spirit of gentleness?

5 It is actually reported *that there is* sexual immorality among you, and such sexual im-

morality as is not even named among the Gentiles—that a man has his father's wife!

2 And you are puffed up, and have not rather mourned, that he who has done this deed might be taken away from among you.

3 For I indeed, as absent in body but present in spirit, have already judged, as though I were present, *concerning* him who has so done this deed.

4 In the name of our Lord Jesus Christ, when you are gathered together, along with my spirit, with the power of our Lord Jesus Christ,

5 deliver such a one to Satan for the destruction of the flesh, that his spirit may be saved in the day of the Lord Jesus.

6 Your glorying *is* not good. Do you not know that a little leaven leavens the whole lump?

7 Therefore purge out the old leaven, that you may be a new lump, since you truly are unleavened. For indeed Christ, our Passover, was sacrificed for us.

8 Therefore let us keep the feast, not with old leaven, nor with the leaven of malice and wickedness, but with the unleavened *bread* of sincerity and truth.

9 I wrote to you in my epistle not to keep company with sexually immoral people.

10 Yet *I* certainly *did* not *mean* with the sexually immoral people of this world, or with the covetous, or extortioners, or idolaters, since then you would need to go out of the world.

11 But now I have written to you not to keep company with anyone named a brother, who is a fornicator, or covetous, or an idolater, or a reviler, or a drunkard, or an extortioner—not even to eat with such a person.

12 For what *have* I *to do* with judging those also who are outside? Do you not judge those who are inside?

13 But those who are outside God judges. Therefore *"put away from yourselves that wicked person."*

6 Dare any of you, having a matter against another, go to law before the unrighteous, and not before the saints?

2 Do you not know that the saints will judge the world? And if the world will be judged by you, are you unworthy to judge the smallest matters?

3 Do you not know that we shall judge angels? How much more, things that pertain to this life?

4 If then you have judgments concerning things pertaining to this life, do you appoint those who are least esteemed by the church to judge?

5 I say this to your shame. Is it so, that there is not a wise man among you, not even one, who will be able to judge between his brethren?

6 But brother goes to law against brother, and that before unbelievers!

7 Now therefore, it is already an utter failure for you that you go to law against one another. Why do you not rather accept wrong? Why do you not rather *let yourselves* be defrauded?

8 No, you yourselves do wrong and defraud, and *you do* these things *to your* brethren!

9 Do you not know that the unrighteous will not inherit the kingdom of God? Do not be deceived. Neither fornicators, nor idolaters, nor adulterers, nor homosexuals, nor sodomites,

10 nor thieves, nor covetous, nor drunkards, nor revilers, nor extortioners will inherit the kingdom of God.

11 And such were some of you. But you were washed, but you were sanctified, but you were justified in the name of the Lord Jesus and by the Spirit of our God.

12 All things are lawful for me, but all things are not helpful. All things are lawful for me, but I will

not be brought under the power of any.

13 Foods for the stomach and the stomach for foods, but God will destroy both it and them. Now the body *is* not for sexual immorality but for the Lord, and the Lord for the body.

14 And God both raised up the Lord and will also raise us up by His power.

15 Do you not know that your bodies are members of Christ? Shall I then take the members of Christ and make *them* members of a harlot? Certainly not!

16 Or do you not know that he who is joined to a harlot is one body *with her*? For *"The two,"* He says, *"shall become one flesh."*

17 But he who is joined to the Lord is one spirit *with Him.*

18 Flee sexual immorality. Every sin that a man does is outside the body, but he who commits sexual immorality sins against his own body.

19 Or do you not know that your body is the temple of the Holy Spirit *who is* in you, whom you have from God, and you are not your own?

20 For you were bought at a price; therefore glorify God in your body and in your spirit, which are God's.

7 Now concerning the things of which you wrote to me: *It is* good for a man not to touch a woman.

2 Nevertheless, because of sexual immorality, let each man have his own wife, and let each woman have her own husband.

3 Let the husband render to his wife the affection due her, and likewise also the wife to her husband.

4 The wife does not have authority over her own body, but the husband *does.* And likewise the husband does not have authority over his own body, but the wife *does.*

5 Do not deprive one another ex-

cept with consent for a time, that you may give yourselves to fasting and prayer; and come together again so that Satan does not tempt you because of your lack of self-control.

6 But I say this as a concession, not as a commandment.

7 For I wish that all men were even as I myself. But each one has his own gift from God, one in this manner and another in that.

8 But I say to the unmarried and to the widows: It is good for them if they remain even as I am;

9 but if they cannot exercise self-control, let them marry. For it is better to marry than to burn *with* passion.

10 Now to the married I command, *yet* not I but the Lord: A wife is not to depart from *her* husband.

11 But even if she does depart, let her remain unmarried or be reconciled to *her* husband. And a husband is not to divorce *his* wife.

12 But to the rest I, not the Lord, say: If any brother has a wife who does not believe, and she is willing to live with him, let him not divorce her.

13 And a woman who has a husband who does not believe, if he is willing to live with her, let her not divorce him.

14 For the unbelieving husband is sanctified by the wife, and the unbelieving wife is sanctified by the husband; otherwise your children would be unclean, but now they are holy.

15 But if the unbeliever departs, let him depart; a brother or a sister is not under bondage in such *cases.* But God has called us to peace.

16 For how do you know, O wife, whether you will save *your* husband? Or how do you know, O husband, whether you will save *your* wife?

17 But as God has distributed to each one, as the Lord has called each one, so let him walk. And so I ordain in all the churches.

18 Was anyone called while circumcised? Let him not become uncircumcised. Was anyone called while uncircumcised? Let him not be circumcised.

19 Circumcision is nothing and uncircumcision is nothing, but keeping the commandments of God *is* what matters.

20 Let each one remain in the same calling in which he was called.

21 Were you called *while* a slave? Do not be concerned about it; but if you can be made free, rather use it.

22 For he who is called in the Lord *while* a slave is the Lord's freedman. Likewise he who is called *while* free is Christ's slave.

23 You were bought at a price; do not become slaves of men.

24 Brethren, let each one remain with God in that *calling* in which he was called.

25 Now concerning virgins: I have no commandment from the Lord; yet I give judgment as one whom the Lord in His mercy *has made* trustworthy.

26 I suppose therefore that this is good because of the present distress—that *it is* good for a man to remain as he is:

27 Are you bound to a wife? Do not seek to be loosed. Are you loosed from a wife? Do not seek a wife.

28 But even if you do marry, you have not sinned; and if a virgin marries, she has not sinned. Nevertheless such will have trouble in the flesh, but I would spare you.

29 But this I say, brethren, the time *is* short, so that from now on even those who have wives should be as though they had none,

30 those who weep as though they did not weep, those who rejoice as though they did not rejoice, those who buy as though they did not possess,

31 and those who use this world as not misusing *it.* For the form of this world is passing away.

32 But I want you to be without care. He who is unmarried cares for the things *that belong* to the Lord—how he may please the Lord.

33 But he who is married cares about the things of the world—how he may please *his* wife.

34 There is a difference between a wife and a virgin. The unmarried woman cares about the things of the Lord, that she may be holy both in body and in spirit. But she who is married cares about the things of the world—how she may please *her* husband.

35 And this I say for your own profit, not that I may put a leash on you, but for what is proper, and that you may serve the Lord without distraction.

36 But if any man thinks he is behaving improperly toward his virgin, if she is past the flower of *her* youth, and thus it must be, let him do what he wishes; he does not sin; let them marry.

37 Nevertheless he who stands steadfast in his heart, having no necessity, but has power over his own will, and has so determined in his heart that he will keep his virgin, does well.

38 So then he who gives *her* in marriage does well, but he who does not give *her* in marriage does better.

39 A wife is bound by law as long as her husband lives; but if her husband dies, she is at liberty to be married to whom she wishes, only in the Lord.

40 But she is happier if she remains as she is, according to my judgment—and I think I also have the Spirit of God.

8 Now concerning things offered to idols: We know that we all have knowledge. Knowledge puffs up, but love edifies.

2 And if anyone thinks that he

209

knows anything, he knows nothing yet as he ought to know.

3 But if anyone loves God, this one is known by Him.

4 Therefore concerning the eating of things offered to idols, we know that an idol *is* nothing in the world, and that *there is* no other God but one.

5 For even if there are so-called gods, whether in heaven or on earth (as there are many gods and many lords),

6 yet for us *there is only* one God, the Father, of whom *are* all things, and we for Him; and one Lord Jesus Christ, through whom *are* all things, and through whom we *live.*

7 However, *there is* not in everyone that knowledge; for some, with consciousness of the idol, until now eat *it* as a thing offered to an idol; and their conscience, being weak, is defiled.

8 But food does not commend us to God; for neither if we eat are we the better, nor if we do not eat are we the worse.

9 But beware lest somehow this liberty of yours become a stumbling block to those who are weak.

10 For if anyone sees you who have knowledge eating in an idol's temple, will not the conscience of him who is weak be emboldened to eat those things offered to idols?

11 And because of your knowledge shall the weak brother perish, for whom Christ died?

12 But when you thus sin against the brethren, and wound their weak conscience, you sin against Christ.

13 Therefore, if food makes my brother stumble, I will never again eat meat, lest I make my brother stumble.

9 Am I not an apostle? Am I not free? Have I not seen Jesus Christ our Lord? Are you not my work in the Lord?

2 If I am not an apostle to others, yet doubtless I am to you. For you are the seal of my apostleship in the Lord.

3 My defense to those who examine me is this:

4 Do we have no right to eat and drink?

5 Do we have no right to take along a believing wife, as *do* also the other apostles, the brothers of the Lord, and Cephas?

6 Or *is it* only Barnabas and I *who* have no right to refrain from working?

7 Who ever goes to war at his own expense? Who plants a vineyard and does not eat of its fruit? Or who tends a flock and does not drink of the milk of the flock?

8 Do I say these things as a *mere* man? Or does not the law say the same also?

9 For it is written in the law of Moses, *"You shall not muzzle an ox while it treads out the grain."* Is it oxen God is concerned about?

10 Or does He say *it* altogether for our sakes? For our sakes, no doubt, *this* is written, that he who plows should plow in hope, and he who threshes in hope should be partaker of his hope.

11 If we have sown spiritual things for you, *is it* a great thing if we reap your material things?

12 If others are partakers of *this* right over you, *are* we not even more? Nevertheless we have not used this right, but endure all things lest we hinder the gospel of Christ.

13 Do you not know that those who minister the holy things eat *of the things* of the temple, and those who serve at the altar partake *of the offerings of* the altar?

14 Even so the Lord has commanded that those who preach the gospel should live from the gospel.

15 But I have used none of these things, nor have I written these things that it should be done so to me; for it *would be* better for me to die than that anyone should make my boasting void.

16 For if I preach the gospel, I have nothing to boast of, for necessity is laid upon me; yes, woe is me if I do not preach the gospel! 17 For if I do this willingly, I have a reward; but if against my will, I have been entrusted with a stewardship. 18 What is my reward then? That when I preach the gospel, I may present the gospel of Christ without charge, that I may not abuse my authority in the gospel.

19 For though I am free from all *men*, I have made myself a servant to all, that I might win the more; 20 and to the Jews I became as a Jew, that I might win Jews; to those *who are* under the law, as under the law, that I might win those *who are* under the law; 21 to those *who are* without law, as without law (not being without law toward God, but under law toward Christ), that I might win those *who are* without law; 22 to the weak I became as weak, that I might win the weak. I have become all things to all *men*, that I might by all means save some. 23 Now this I do for the gospel's sake, that I may be partaker of it with *you*.

24 Do you not know that those who run in a race all run, but one receives the prize? Run in such a way that you may obtain *it*. 25 And everyone who competes *for the prize* is temperate in all things. Now they *do it* to obtain a perishable crown, but we *for* an imperishable *crown*. 26 Therefore I run thus: not with uncertainty. Thus I fight: not as *one who* beats the air. 27 But I discipline my body and bring *it* into subjection, lest, when I have preached to others, I myself should become disqualified.

10 Moreover, brethren, I do not want you to be unaware that all our fathers were under the cloud, all passed through the sea, 2 all were baptized into Moses in the cloud and in the sea, 3 all ate the same spiritual food, 4 and all drank the same spiritual drink. For they drank of that spiritual Rock that followed them, and that Rock was Christ.

5 But with most of them God was not well pleased, for *their bodies* were scattered in the wilderness. 6 Now these things became our examples, to the intent that we should not lust after evil things as they also lusted. 7 And do not become idolaters as *were* some of them. As it is written, *"The people sat down to eat and drink, and rose up to play."* 8 Nor let us commit sexual immorality, as some of them did, and in one day twenty-three thousand fell; 9 nor let us tempt Christ, as some of them also tempted, and were destroyed by serpents; 10 nor murmur, as some of them also murmured, and were destroyed by the destroyer. 11 Now all these things happened to them as examples, and they were written for our admonition, on whom the ends of the ages have come.

12 Therefore let him who thinks he stands take heed lest he fall. 13 No temptation has overtaken you except such as is common to man; but God *is* faithful, who will not allow you to be tempted beyond what you are able, but with the temptation will also make the way of escape, that you may be able to bear *it*.

14 Therefore, my beloved, flee from idolatry. 15 I speak as to wise men; judge for yourselves what I say. 16 The cup of blessing which we bless, is it not the communion of the blood of Christ? The bread which we break, is it not the communion of the body of Christ? 17 For we, *being* many, are one

bread *and* one body; for we all partake of that one bread.

18 Observe Israel after the flesh: Are not those who eat of the sacrifices partakers of the altar?

19 What am I saying then? That an idol is anything, or what is offered to idols is anything?

20 But *I* say that the things which the Gentiles sacrifice they sacrifice to demons and not to God, and I do not want you to have fellowship with demons.

21 You cannot drink the cup of the Lord and the cup of demons; you cannot partake of the Lord's table and of the table of demons.

22 Or do we provoke the Lord to jealousy? Are we stronger than He?

23 All things are lawful for me, but all things are not helpful; all things are lawful for me, but all things do not edify.

24 Let no one seek his own, but each one the other's *well-being.*

25 Eat whatever is sold in the meat market, asking no questions for conscience' sake;

26 for *"The earth is the LORD's, and all its fullness."*

27 If any of those who do not believe invites you *to dinner,* and you desire to go, eat whatever is set before you, asking no question for conscience' sake.

28 But if anyone says to you, "This was offered to idols," do not eat it for the sake of the one who told you, and for conscience' sake; for *"The earth is the LORD's, and all its fullness."*

29 Conscience, I say, not your own, but that of the other. For why is my liberty judged by another *man's* conscience?

30 But if I partake with thanks, why am I evil spoken of for *the food* over which I give thanks?

31 Therefore, whether you eat or drink, or whatever you do, do all to the glory of God.

32 Give no offense, either to the Jews or to the Greeks or to the church of God,

33 just as I also please all *men* in all *things,* not seeking my own profit, but the *profit* of many, that they may be saved.

11 Imitate me, just as I also *imitate* Christ.

2 Now I praise you, brethren, that you remember me in all things and keep the traditions as I delivered *them* to you.

3 But I want you to know that the head of every man is Christ, the head of woman *is* man, and the head of Christ *is* God.

4 Every man praying or prophesying, having *his* head covered, dishonors his head.

5 But every woman who prays or prophesies with *her* head uncovered dishonors her head, for that is one and the same as if her head were shaved.

6 For if a woman is not covered, let her also be shorn. But if it is shameful for a woman to be shorn or shaved, let her be covered.

7 For a man indeed ought not to cover *his* head, since he is the image and glory of God; but woman is the glory of man.

8 For man is not from woman, but woman from man.

9 Nor was man created for the woman, but woman for the man.

10 For this reason the woman ought to have *a symbol of* authority on *her* head, because of the angels.

11 Nevertheless, neither *is* man independent of woman, nor woman independent of man, in the Lord.

12 For as the woman *was* from the man, even so the man also *is* through the woman; but all things are from God.

13 Judge among yourselves. Is it proper for a woman to pray to God with her head uncovered?

14 Does not even nature itself teach you that if a man has long hair, it is a dishonor to him?

15 But if a woman has long hair, it is a glory to her; for *her* hair is given to her for a covering.

16 But if anyone seems to be contentious, we have no such custom, nor *do* the churches of God.

17 Now in giving these instructions I do not praise *you*, since you come together not for the better but for the worse.

18 For first of all, when you come together as a church, I hear that there are divisions among you, and in part I believe it.

19 For there must also be factions among you, that those who are approved may be recognized among you.

20 Therefore when you come together in one place, it is not to eat the Lord's Supper.

21 For in eating, each one takes his own supper ahead of *others;* and one is hungry and another is drunk.

22 What! Do you not have houses to eat and drink in? Or do you despise the church of God and shame those who have nothing? What shall I say to you? Shall I praise you in this? I do not praise *you.*

23 For I received from the Lord that which I also delivered to you: that the Lord Jesus on the *same* night in which He was betrayed took bread;

24 and when He had given thanks, He broke *it* and said, "Take, eat; this is My body which is broken for you; do this in remembrance of Me."

25 In the same manner *He* also *took* the cup after supper, saying, "This cup is the new covenant in My blood. This do, as often as you drink *it*, in remembrance of Me."

26 For as often as you eat this bread and drink this cup, you proclaim the Lord's death till He comes.

27 Therefore whoever eats this bread or drinks *this* cup of the Lord in an unworthy manner will be guilty of the body and blood of the Lord.

28 But let a man examine himself, and so let him eat of *that* bread and drink of *that* cup.

29 For he who eats and drinks in an unworthy manner eats and drinks judgment to himself, not discerning the Lord's body.

30 For this reason many *are* weak and sick among you, and many sleep.

31 For if we would judge ourselves, we would not be judged.

32 But when we are judged, we are chastened by the Lord, that we may not be condemned with the world.

33 Therefore, my brethren, when you come together to eat, wait for one another.

34 But if anyone is hungry, let him eat at home, lest you come together for judgment. And the rest I will set in order when I come.

12 Now concerning spiritual *gifts*, brethren, I do not want you to be ignorant:

2 You know that you were Gentiles, carried away to these dumb idols, however you were led.

3 Therefore I make known to you that no one speaking by the Spirit of God calls Jesus accursed, and no one can say that Jesus is Lord except by the Holy Spirit.

4 Now there are diversities of gifts, but the same Spirit.

5 There are differences of ministries, but the same Lord.

6 And there are diversities of activities, but it is the same God who works all in all.

7 But the manifestation of the Spirit is given to each one for the profit *of all:*

8 for to one is given the word of wisdom through the Spirit, to another the word of knowledge through the same Spirit,

9 to another faith by the same

213

Spirit, to another gifts of healings by the same Spirit,

10 to another the working of miracles, to another prophecy, to another discerning of spirits, to another *different* kinds of tongues, to another the interpretation of tongues.

11 But one and the same Spirit works all these things, distributing to each one individually as He wills.

12 For as the body is one and has many members, but all the members of that one body, being many, are one body, so also *is* Christ.

13 For by one Spirit we were all baptized into one body—whether Jews or Greeks, whether slaves or free—and have all been made to drink into one Spirit.

14 For in fact the body is not one member but many.

15 If the foot should say, "Because I am not a hand, I am not of the body," is it therefore not of the body?

16 And if the ear should say, "Because I am not an eye, I am not of the body," is it therefore not of the body?

17 If the whole body *were* an eye, where *would be* the hearing? If the whole *were* hearing, where *would be* the smelling?

18 But now God has set the members, each one of them, in the body just as He pleased.

19 And if they *were* all one member, where *would* the body *be?*

20 But now indeed *there are* many members, yet one body.

21 And the eye cannot say to the hand, "I have no need of you"; nor again the head to the feet, "I have no need of you."

22 No, much rather, those members of the body which seem to be weaker are necessary.

23 And those *members* of the body which we think to be less honorable, on these we bestow greater honor; and our unpresentable *parts* have greater modesty,

24 but our presentable *parts* have no need. But God composed the body, having given greater honor to that *part* which lacks it,

25 that there should be no schism in the body, but *that* the members should have the same care for one another.

26 And if one member suffers, all the members suffer with *it;* or if one member is honored, all the members rejoice with *it.*

27 Now you are the body of Christ, and members individually.

28 And God has appointed these in the church: first apostles, second prophets, third teachers, after that miracles, then gifts of healings, helps, administrations, varieties of tongues.

29 *Are* all apostles? *Are* all prophets? *Are* all teachers? *Are* all workers of miracles?

30 Do all have gifts of healings? Do all speak with tongues? Do all interpret?

31 But earnestly desire the best gifts. And yet I show you a more excellent way.

13 Though I speak with the tongues of men and of angels, but have not love, I have become *as* sounding brass or a clanging cymbal.

2 And though I have *the gift of* prophecy, and understand all mysteries and all knowledge, and though I have all faith, so that I could remove mountains, but have not love, I am nothing.

3 And though I bestow all my goods to feed *the poor,* and though I give my body to be burned, but have not love, it profits me nothing.

4 Love suffers long *and* is kind; love does not envy; love does not parade itself, is not puffed up;

5 does not behave rudely, does not seek its own, is not provoked, thinks no evil;

6 does not rejoice in iniquity, but rejoices in the truth;

7 bears all things, believes all

things, hopes all things, endures all things.

8 Love never fails. But whether *there are* prophecies, they will fail; whether *there are* tongues, they will cease; whether *there is* knowledge, it will vanish away.

9 For we know in part and we prophesy in part.

10 But when that which is perfect has come, then that which is in part will be done away.

11 When I was a child, I spoke as a child, I understood as a child, I thought as a child; but when I became a man, I put away childish things.

12 For now we see in a mirror, dimly, but then face to face. Now I know in part, but then I shall know just as I also am known.

13 And now abide faith, hope, love, these three; but the greatest of these *is* love.

14 Pursue love, and desire spiritual *gifts*, but especially that you may prophesy.

2 For he who speaks in a tongue does not speak to men but to God, for no one understands *him;* however, in the spirit he speaks mysteries.

3 But he who prophesies speaks edification and exhortation and comfort to men.

4 He who speaks in a tongue edifies himself, but he who prophesies edifies the church.

5 I wish you all spoke with tongues, but even more that you prophesied; for he who prophesies *is* greater than he who speaks with tongues, unless indeed he interprets, that the church may receive edification.

6 But now, brethren, if I come to you speaking with tongues, what shall I profit you unless I speak to you either by revelation, by knowledge, by prophesying, or by teaching?

7 Even things without life, whether flute or harp, when they make a sound, unless they make a distinction in the sounds, how will it be known what is piped or played?

8 For if the trumpet makes an uncertain sound, who will prepare himself for battle?

9 So likewise you, unless you utter by the tongue words easy to understand, how will it be known what is spoken? For you will be speaking into the air.

10 There are, it may be, so many kinds of languages in the world, and none of them *is* without significance.

11 Therefore, if I do not know the meaning of the language, I shall be a foreigner to him who speaks, and he who speaks *will be* a foreigner to me.

12 Even so you, since you are zealous for spiritual *gifts, let it be* for the edification of the church *that* you seek to excel.

13 Therefore let him who speaks in a tongue pray that he may interpret.

14 For if I pray in a tongue, my spirit prays, but my understanding is unfruitful.

15 What is *the result* then? I will pray with the spirit, and I will also pray with the understanding. I will sing with the spirit, and I will also sing with the understanding.

16 Otherwise, if you bless with the spirit, how will he who occupies the place of the uninformed say "Amen" at your giving of thanks, since he does not understand what you say?

17 For you indeed give thanks well, but the other is not edified.

18 I thank my God I speak with tongues more than you all;

19 yet in the church I would rather speak five words with my understanding, that I may teach others also, than ten thousand words in a tongue.

20 Brethren, do not be children in understanding; however, in malice be babes, but in understanding be mature.

21 In the law it is written:

> *"With men of other tongues*
>   *and other lips*
> *I will speak to this people;*
> *And yet, for all that,*
>   *they will not hear Me,"*

says the Lord.
22 Therefore tongues are for a sign, not to those who believe but to unbelievers; but prophesying is not for unbelievers but for those who believe.
23 Therefore if the whole church comes together in one place, and all speak with tongues, and there come in *those who are* uninformed or unbelievers, will they not say that you are out of your mind?
24 But if all prophesy, and an unbeliever or an uninformed person comes in, he is convinced by all, he is judged by all.
25 And thus the secrets of his heart are revealed; and so, falling down on *his* face, he will worship God and report that God is truly among you.
26 How is it then, brethren? Whenever you come together, each of you has a psalm, has a teaching, has a tongue, has a revelation, has an interpretation. Let all things be done for edification.
27 If anyone speaks in a tongue, *let there be* two or at the most three, *each* in turn, and let one interpret.
28 But if there is no interpreter, let him keep silent in church, and let him speak to himself and to God.
29 Let two or three prophets speak, and let the others judge.
30 But if *anything* is revealed to another who sits by, let the first keep silent.
31 For you can all prophesy one by one, that all may learn and all may be encouraged.
32 And the spirits of the prophets are subject to the prophets.
33 For God is not *the author* of confusion but of peace, as in all the churches of the saints.

34 Let your women keep silent in the churches, for they are not permitted to speak; but *they are* to be submissive, as the law also says.
35 And if they want to learn something, let them ask their own husbands at home; for it is shameful for women to speak in church.
36 Or did the word of God come *originally* from you? Or *was it* you only that it reached?
37 If anyone thinks himself to be a prophet or spiritual, let him acknowledge that the things which I write to you are the commandments of the Lord.
38 But if anyone is ignorant, let him be ignorant.
39 Therefore, brethren, desire earnestly to prophesy, and do not forbid to speak with tongues.
40 Let all things be done decently and in order.

15 Moreover, brethren, I declare to you the gospel which I preached to you, which also you received and in which you stand,
2 by which also you are saved, if you hold fast that word which I preached to you—unless you believed in vain.
3 For I delivered to you first of all that which I also received: that Christ died for our sins according to the Scriptures,
4 and that He was buried, and that He rose again the third day according to the Scriptures,
5 and that He was seen by Cephas, then by the twelve.
6 After that He was seen by over five hundred brethren at once, of whom the greater part remain to the present, but some have fallen asleep.
7 After that He was seen by James, then by all the apostles.
8 Then last of all He was seen by me also, as by one born out of due time.
9 For I am the least of the apostles, who am not worthy to be called an apostle, because I persecuted the church of God.

10 But by the grace of God I am what I am, and His grace toward me was not in vain; but I labored more abundantly than they all, yet not I, but the grace of God *which was* with me.

11 Therefore, whether *it was* I or they, so we preach and so you believed.

12 Now if Christ is preached that He has been raised from the dead, how do some among you say that there is no resurrection of the dead?

13 But if there is no resurrection of the dead, then Christ is not risen.

14 And if Christ is not risen, then our preaching *is* vain and your faith *is* also vain.

15 Yes, and we are found false witnesses of God, because we have testified of God that He raised up Christ, whom He did not raise up— if in fact the dead do not rise.

16 For if *the* dead do not rise, then Christ is not risen.

17 And if Christ is not risen, your faith *is* futile; you are still in your sins!

18 Then also those who have fallen asleep in Christ have perished.

19 If in this life only we have hope in Christ, we are of all men the most pitiable.

20 But now Christ is risen from the dead, *and* has become the first-fruits of those who have fallen asleep.

21 For since by man *came* death, by Man also *came* the resurrection of the dead.

22 For as in Adam all die, even so in Christ all shall be made alive.

23 But each one in his own order: Christ the firstfruits, afterward those *who are* Christ's at His coming.

24 Then *comes* the end, when He delivers the kingdom to God the Father, when He puts an end to all rule and all authority and power.

25 For He must reign till He has put all enemies under His feet.

26 The last enemy *that* will be destroyed *is* death.

27 For *"He has put all things under His feet."* But when He says "all things are put under *Him,"* it is evident that He who put all things under Him is excepted.

28 Now when all things are made subject to Him, then the Son Himself will also be subject to Him who put all things under Him, that God may be all in all.

29 Otherwise, what will they do who are baptized for the dead, if the dead do not rise at all? Why then are they baptized for the dead?

30 And why do we stand in jeopardy every hour?

31 I affirm, by the boasting in you which I have in Christ Jesus our Lord, I die daily.

32 If, in the manner of men, I have fought with beasts at Ephesus, what advantage *is it* to me? If *the* dead do not rise, *"Let us eat and drink, for tomorrow we die."*

33 Do not be deceived: "Evil company corrupts good habits."

34 Awake to righteousness, and do not sin; for some do not have the knowledge of God. I speak *this* to your shame.

35 But someone will say, "How are the dead raised up? And with what body do they come?"

36 Foolish one, what you sow is not made alive unless it dies.

37 And what you sow, you do not sow that body that shall be, but mere grain—perhaps wheat or some other *grain.*

38 But God gives it a body as He pleases, and to each seed its own body.

39 All flesh *is* not the same flesh, but *there is* one *kind of* flesh of men, another flesh of beasts, another of fish, *and* another of birds.

40 *There are* also celestial bodies and terrestrial bodies; but the glory of the celestial *is* one, and the *glory* of the terrestrial *is* another.

41 *There is* one glory of the sun,

another glory of the moon, and another glory of the stars; for *one* star differs from *another* star in glory.

42 So also *is* the resurrection of the dead. *The body* is sown in corruption, it is raised in incorruption.

43 It is sown in dishonor, it is raised in glory. It is sown in weakness, it is raised in power.

44 It is sown a natural body, it is raised a spiritual body. There is a natural body, and there is a spiritual body.

45 And so it is written, *"The first man Adam became a living being."* The last Adam *became* a life-giving spirit.

46 However, the spiritual is not first, but the natural, and afterward the spiritual.

47 The first man *was* of the earth, *made* of dust; the second Man *is* the Lord from heaven.

48 As *was* the *man* of dust, so also *are* those *who are made* of dust; and as *is* the heavenly *Man*, so also *are* those *who are* heavenly.

49 And as we have borne the image of the *man* of dust, we shall also bear the image of the heavenly *Man.*

50 Now this I say, brethren, that flesh and blood cannot inherit the kingdom of God; nor does corruption inherit incorruption.

51 Behold, I tell you a mystery: We shall not all sleep, but we shall all be changed—

52 in a moment, in the twinkling of an eye, at the last trumpet. For the trumpet will sound, and the dead will be raised incorruptible, and we shall be changed.

53 For this corruptible must put on incorruption, and this mortal *must* put on immortality.

54 So when this corruptible has put on incorruption, and this mortal has put on immortality, then shall be brought to pass the saying that is written: *"Death is swallowed up in victory."*

55 *"O Death, where is your sting?
O Hades, where is your
victory?"*

56 The sting of death *is* sin, and the strength of sin *is* the law.

57 But thanks *be* to God, who gives us the victory through our Lord Jesus Christ.

58 Therefore, my beloved brethren, be steadfast, immovable, always abounding in the work of the Lord, knowing that your labor is not in vain in the Lord.

16 Now concerning the collection for the saints, as I have given orders to the churches of Galatia, so you must do also:

2 On the first *day* of the week let each one of you lay something aside, storing up as he may prosper, that there be no collections when I come.

3 And when I come, whomever you approve by *your* letters I will send to bear your gift to Jerusalem.

4 But if it is fitting that I go also, they will go with me.

5 Now I will come to you when I pass through Macedonia (for I am passing through Macedonia).

6 But it may be that I will remain, or even spend the winter with you, that you may send me on my journey, wherever I go.

7 For I do not wish to see you now on the way; but I hope to stay a while with you, if the Lord permits.

8 But I will tarry in Ephesus until Pentecost.

9 For a great and effective door has opened to me, and *there are* many adversaries.

10 Now if Timothy comes, see that he may be with you without fear; for he does the work of the Lord, as I also *do.*

11 Therefore let no one despise him. But send him on his journey in peace, that he may come to me; for I am waiting for him with the brethren.

12 Now concerning *our* brother Apollos, I strongly urged him to come to you with the brethren, but he was quite unwilling to come at this time; however, he will come when he has a convenient time.

13 Watch, stand fast in the faith, be brave, be strong.

14 Let all *that* you *do* be done with love.

15 I urge you, brethren—you know the household of Stephanas, that it is the firstfruits of Achaia, and *that* they have devoted themselves to the ministry of the saints—

16 that you also submit to such, and to everyone who works and labors with *us*.

17 I am glad about the coming of Stephanas, Fortunatus, and Achai-cus, for what was lacking on your part they supplied.

18 For they refreshed my spirit and yours; therefore acknowledge such men.

19 The churches of Asia greet you. Aquila and Priscilla greet you heartily in the Lord, with the church that is in their house.

20 All the brethren greet you. Greet one another with a holy kiss.

21 The salutation with my own hand—Paul.

22 If anyone does not love the Lord Jesus Christ, let him be accursed. O Lord, come!

23 The grace of our Lord Jesus Christ *be* with you.

24 My love *be* with you all in Christ Jesus. Amen.

THE SECOND EPISTLE OF PAUL THE APOSTLE TO THE
CORINTHIANS

PAUL, an apostle of Jesus Christ by the will of God, and Timothy *our* brother,

To the church of God which is at Corinth, with all the saints who are in all Achaia:

2 Grace to you and peace from God our Father and the Lord Jesus Christ.

3 Blessed *be* the God and Father of our Lord Jesus Christ, the Father of mercies and God of all comfort,

4 who comforts us in all our tribulation, that we may be able to comfort those who are in any trouble, with the comfort with which we ourselves are comforted by God.

5 For as the sufferings of Christ abound in us, so our consolation also abounds through Christ.

6 Now if we are afflicted, *it is* for your consolation and salvation, which is effective for enduring the same sufferings which we also suffer. Or if we are comforted, *it is* for your consolation and salvation.

7 And our hope for you *is* steadfast, because we know that as you are partakers of the sufferings, so also *you will partake* of the consolation.

8 For we do not want you to be ignorant, brethren, of our trouble which came to us in Asia: that we were burdened beyond measure, above strength, so that we despaired even of life.

9 Yes, we had the sentence of death in ourselves, that we should not trust in ourselves but in God who raises the dead,

10 who delivered us from so great a death, and does deliver us; in

whom we trust that He will still deliver *us,*

11 you also helping together in prayer for us, that thanks may be given by many persons on our behalf for the gift *granted* to us through many.

12 For our boasting is this: the testimony of our conscience that we conducted ourselves in the world in simplicity and godly sincerity, not with fleshly wisdom but by the grace of God, and more abundantly toward you.

13 For we are not writing any other things to you than what you read or understand. Now I trust you will understand, even to the end

14 (as also you have understood us in part), that we are your boast as you also *are* ours, in the day of the Lord Jesus.

15 And in this confidence I intended to come to you before, that you might have a second benefit—

16 to pass by way of you to Macedonia, to come again from Macedonia to you, and be helped by you on my way to Judea.

17 Therefore, when I was planning this, did I do it lightly? Or the things I plan, do I plan according to the flesh, that with me there should be Yes, Yes, and No, No?

18 But *as* God *is* faithful, our word to you was not Yes and No.

19 For the Son of God, Jesus Christ, who was preached among you by us—by me, Silvanus, and Timothy—was not Yes and No, but in Him was Yes.

20 For all the promises of God in Him *are* Yes, and in Him Amen, to the glory of God through us.

21 Now He who establishes us with you in Christ and has anointed us *is* God,

22 who also has sealed us and given us the Spirit in our hearts as a deposit.

23 Moreover I call God as witness against my soul, that to spare you I came no more to Corinth.

24 Not that we have dominion over your faith, but are fellow workers for your joy; for by faith you stand.

2 But I determined this within myself, that I would not come again to you in sorrow.

2 For if I make you sorrowful, then who is he who makes me glad but the one who is made sorrowful by me?

3 And I wrote this very thing to you, lest, when I came, I should have sorrow over those from whom I ought to have joy, having confidence in you all that my joy is *the joy* of you all.

4 For out of much affliction and anguish of heart I wrote to you, with many tears, not that you should be grieved, but that you might know the love which I have so abundantly for you.

5 But if anyone has caused grief, he has not grieved me, but all of you to some extent—not to be too severe.

6 This punishment which *was inflicted* by the majority *is* sufficient for such a man,

7 so that, on the contrary, you *ought* rather to forgive and comfort *him,* lest perhaps such a one be swallowed up with too much sorrow.

8 Therefore I urge you to reaffirm *your* love to him.

9 For to this end I also wrote, that I might put you to the test, whether you are obedient in all things.

10 Now whom you forgive anything, I also *forgive.* For if indeed I have forgiven anything, I have forgiven that one for your sakes in the presence of Christ,

11 lest Satan should take advantage of us; for we are not ignorant of his devices.

12 Furthermore, when I came to Troas to *preach* Christ's gospel, and a door was opened to me by the Lord,

13 I had no rest in my spirit, because I did not find Titus my

brother; but taking my leave of them, I departed for Macedonia.

14 Now thanks *be* to God who always leads us in triumph in Christ, and through us diffuses the fragrance of His knowledge in every place.

15 For we are to God the fragrance of Christ among those who are being saved and among those who are perishing.

16 To the one *we are* the aroma of death to death, and to the other the aroma of life to life. And who *is* sufficient for these things?

17 For we are not, as so many, peddling the word of God; but as of sincerity, but as from God, we speak in the sight of God in Christ.

3 Do we begin again to commend ourselves? Or do we need, as some *others*, epistles of commendation to you or *letters* of commendation from you?

2 You are our epistle written in our hearts, known and read by all men;

3 *you are* manifestly an epistle of Christ, ministered by us, written not with ink but by the Spirit of the living God, not on tablets of stone but on tablets of flesh, *that is*, of the heart.

4 And we have such trust through Christ toward God.

5 Not that we are sufficient of ourselves to think of anything as *being* from ourselves, but our sufficiency *is* from God,

6 who also made us sufficient as ministers of the new covenant, not of the letter but of the Spirit; for the letter kills, but the Spirit gives life.

7 But if the ministry of death, written *and* engraved on stones, was glorious, so that the children of Israel could not look steadily at the face of Moses because of the glory of his countenance, which *glory* was passing away,

8 how will the ministry of the Spirit not be more glorious?

9 For if the ministry of condemnation *had* glory, the ministry of righteousness exceeds much more in glory.

10 For even what was made glorious had no glory in this respect, because of the glory that excels.

11 For if what is passing away *was* glorious, what remains *is* much more glorious.

12 Therefore, since we have such hope, we use great boldness of speech—

13 unlike Moses, *who* put a veil over his face so that the children of Israel could not look steadily at the end of what was passing away.

14 But their minds were hardened. For until this day the same veil remains unlifted in the reading of the Old Testament, because the *veil* is taken away in Christ.

15 But even to this day, when Moses is read, a veil lies on their heart.

16 Nevertheless when one turns to the Lord, the veil is taken away.

17 Now the Lord is the Spirit; and where the Spirit of the Lord *is*, there *is* liberty.

18 But we all, with unveiled face, beholding as in a mirror the glory of the Lord, are being transformed into the same image from glory to glory, just as by the Spirit of the Lord.

4 Therefore, since we have this ministry, as we have received mercy, we do not lose heart.

2 But we have renounced the hidden things of shame, not walking in craftiness nor handling the word of God deceitfully, but by manifestation of the truth commending ourselves to every man's conscience in the sight of God.

3 But even if our gospel is veiled, it is veiled to those who are perishing,

4 whose minds the god of this age has blinded, who do not believe, lest the light of the gospel of the glory of Christ, who is the image of God, should shine on them.

5 For we do not preach ourselves, but Christ Jesus the Lord, and ourselves your servants for Jesus' sake.

6 For it is the God who commanded light to shine out of darkness who has shone in our hearts to give the light of the knowledge of the glory of God in the face of Jesus Christ.

7 But we have this treasure in earthen vessels, that the excellence of the power may be of God and not of us.

8 *We are* hard pressed on every side, yet not crushed; *we are* perplexed, but not in despair;

9 persecuted, but not forsaken; struck down, but not destroyed—

10 always carrying about in the body the dying of the Lord Jesus, that the life of Jesus also may be manifested in our body.

11 For we who live are always delivered to death for Jesus' sake, that the life of Jesus also may be manifested in our mortal flesh.

12 So then death is working in us, but life in you.

13 But since we have the same spirit of faith, according to what is written, *"I believed and therefore I spoke,"* we also believe and therefore speak,

14 knowing that He who raised up the Lord Jesus will also raise us up with Jesus, and will present *us* with you.

15 For all things *are* for your sakes, that grace, having spread through the many, may cause thanksgiving to abound to the glory of God.

16 Therefore we do not lose heart. Even though our outward man is perishing, yet the inward *man* is being renewed day by day.

17 For our light affliction, which is but for a moment, is working for us a far more exceeding *and* eternal weight of glory,

18 while we do not look at the things which are seen, but at the things which are not seen. For the things which are seen *are* tem-

porary, but the things which are not seen *are* eternal.

5 For we know that if our earthly house, *this* tent, is destroyed, we have a building from God, a house not made with hands, eternal in the heavens.

2 For in this we groan, earnestly desiring to be clothed with our habitation which is from heaven,

3 if indeed, having been clothed, we shall not be found naked.

4 For we who are in *this* tent groan, being burdened, not because we want to be unclothed, but further clothed, that mortality may be swallowed up by life.

5 Now He who has prepared us for this very thing *is* God, who also has given us the Spirit as a guarantee.

6 Therefore *we are* always confident, knowing that while we are at home in the body we are absent from the Lord.

7 For we walk by faith, not by sight.

8 We are confident, yes, well pleased rather to be absent from the body and to be present with the Lord.

9 Therefore we make it our aim, whether present or absent, to be well pleasing to Him.

10 For we must all appear before the judgment seat of Christ, that each one may receive the things *done* in the body, according to what he has done, whether good or bad.

11 Knowing, therefore, the terror of the Lord, we persuade men; but we are well known to God, and I also trust are well known in your consciences.

12 For we do not commend ourselves again to you, but give you opportunity to glory on our behalf, that you may have *something to answer* those who glory in appearance and not in heart.

13 For if we are beside ourselves, *it is* for God; or if we are of sound mind, *it is* for you.

14 For the love of Christ constrains us, because we judge thus: that if One died for all, then all died;

15 and He died for all, that those who live should live no longer for themselves, but for Him who died for them and rose again.

16 Therefore, from now on, we regard no one according to the flesh. Even though we have known Christ according to the flesh, yet now we know Him thus no longer.

17 Therefore, if anyone is in Christ, he is a new creation; old things have passed away; behold, all things have become new.

18 Now all things are of God, who has reconciled us to Himself through Jesus Christ, and has given us the ministry of reconciliation,

19 that is, that God was in Christ reconciling the world to Himself, not imputing their trespasses to them, and has committed to us the word of reconciliation.

20 Therefore we are ambassadors for Christ, as though God were pleading through us: we implore you on Christ's behalf, be reconciled to God.

21 For He made Him who knew no sin to be sin for us, that we might become the righteousness of God in Him.

6 We then, as workers together with Him also plead with you not to receive the grace of God in vain.

2 For He says:

"In an acceptable time I have heard you,
And in the day of salvation I have helped you."

Behold, now is the accepted time; behold, now is the day of salvation.

3 We give no offense in anything, that our ministry may not be blamed.

4 But in all things we commend ourselves as ministers of God: in much patience, in tribulations, in needs, in distresses,

5 in stripes, in imprisonments, in tumults, in labors, in sleeplessness, in fastings;

6 by purity, by knowledge, by longsuffering, by kindness, by the Holy Spirit, by sincere love,

7 by the word of truth, by the power of God, by the armor of righteousness on the right hand and on the left,

8 by honor and dishonor, by evil report and good report; as deceivers, and yet true;

9 as unknown, and yet well known; as dying, and behold we live; as chastened, and yet not killed;

10 as sorrowful, yet always rejoicing; as poor, yet making many rich; as having nothing, and yet possessing all things.

11 O Corinthians! We have spoken openly to you, our heart is wide open.

12 You are not restricted by us, but you are restricted by your own affections.

13 Now in return for the same (I speak as to children), you also be open.

14 Do not be unequally yoked together with unbelievers. For what fellowship has righteousness with lawlessness? And what communion has light with darkness?

15 And what accord has Christ with Belial? Or what part has a believer with an unbeliever?

16 And what agreement has the temple of God with idols? For you are the temple of the living God. As God has said:

"I will dwell in them
And walk among them.
I will be their God,
And they shall be My people."

17 Therefore

"Come out from among them

See Proverbs 24:16, page 459

And be separate, says the Lord.
Do not touch what is unclean,
And I will receive you."
18 *"I will be a Father to you,*
   And you shall be My sons
      and daughters,
   Says the LORD *Almighty."*

7 Therefore, having these promises, beloved, let us cleanse ourselves from all filthiness of the flesh and spirit, perfecting holiness in the fear of God.

2 Open *your hearts* to us. We have wronged no one, we have corrupted no one, we have defrauded no one.

3 I do not say *this* to condemn; for I have said before that you are in our hearts, to die together and to live together.

4 Great *is* my boldness of speech toward you, great *is* my boasting on your behalf. I am filled with comfort. I am exceedingly joyful in all our tribulation.

5 For indeed, when we came to Macedonia, our flesh had no rest, but we were troubled on every side. Outside *were* conflicts, inside *were* fears.

6 Nevertheless God, who comforts the downcast, comforted us by the coming of Titus,

7 and not only by his coming, but also by the consolation with which he was comforted in you, when he told us of your earnest desire, your mourning, your zeal for me, so that I rejoiced even more.

8 For even if I made you sorry with my letter, I do not regret it; though I did regret it. For I perceive that the same epistle made you sorry, though only for a while.

9 Now I rejoice, not that you were made sorry, but that your sorrow led to repentance. For you were made sorry in a godly manner, that you might suffer loss from us in nothing.

10 For godly sorrow produces repentance to salvation, not to be regretted; but the sorrow of the world produces death.

11 For observe this very thing, that you sorrowed in a godly manner: What diligence it produced in you, *what* clearing *of yourselves, what* indignation, *what* fear, *what* vehement desire, *what* zeal, *what* vindication! In all *things* you proved yourselves to be clear in this matter.

12 Therefore, although I wrote to you, *I did* not *do it* for the sake of him who had done the wrong, nor for the sake of him who suffered wrong, but that our care for you in the sight of God might appear to you.

13 Therefore we have been comforted in your comfort. And we rejoiced exceedingly more for the joy of Titus, because his spirit has been refreshed by you all.

14 For if in anything I have boasted to him about you, I am not ashamed. But as we spoke all things to you in truth, even so our boasting to Titus was found true.

15 And his affections are greater for you as he remembers the obedience of you all, how with fear and trembling you received him.

16 Therefore I rejoice that I have confidence in you in everything.

8 Moreover, brethren, we make known to you the grace of God bestowed on the churches of Macedonia:

2 that in a great trial of affliction the abundance of their joy and their deep poverty abounded in the riches of their liberality.

3 For I bear witness that according to *their* ability, yes, and beyond *their* ability, *they were* freely willing,

4 imploring us with much urgency that we would receive the gift and the fellowship of the ministering to the saints.

5 And *this they did,* not as we had

hoped, but first gave themselves to the Lord, and *then* to us by the will of God.

6 So we urged Titus, that as he had begun, so he would also complete this grace in you as well.

7 But as you abound in everything—in faith, in speech, in knowledge, in all diligence, and in your love for us—*see* that you abound in this grace also.

8 I speak not by commandment, but I am testing the sincerity of your love by the diligence of others.

9 For you know the grace of our Lord Jesus Christ, that though He was rich, yet for your sakes He became poor, that you through His poverty might become rich.

10 And in this I give *my* advice: It is to your advantage not only to be doing what you began and were desiring to do a year ago;

11 but now you also must complete the doing *of it;* that as *there was* a readiness to desire *it,* so *there* also *may be* a completion out of what *you* have.

12 For if there is first a willing mind, *it is* accepted according to what one has, *and* not according to what he does not have.

13 For *I do* not *mean* that others should be eased and you burdened;

14 but by an equality, *that* now at this time your abundance may *supply* their lack, that their abundance also may *supply* your lack—that there may be equality.

15 As it is written, *"He who gathered much had nothing left over, and he who gathered little had no lack."*

16 But thanks *be* to God who puts the same earnest care for you into the heart of Titus.

17 For he not only accepted the exhortation, but being more diligent, he went to you of his own accord.

18 And we have sent with him the brother whose praise *is* in the gospel throughout all the churches,

19 and not only *that,* but who was also chosen by the churches to travel with us with this gift, which is administered by us to the glory of the Lord Himself and *to show* your ready mind,

20 avoiding this: that anyone should blame us in this lavish gift which is administered by us—

21 providing honorable things, not only in the sight of the Lord, but also in the sight of men.

22 And we have sent with them our brother whom we have often proved diligent in many things, but now much more diligent, because of the great confidence which *we have* in you.

23 If *anyone inquires* about Titus, *he is* my partner and fellow worker concerning you. Or if our brethren *are inquired about, they are* messengers of the churches, the glory of Christ.

24 Therefore show to them, and before the churches, the proof of your love and of our boasting on your behalf.

9 Now concerning the ministering to the saints, it is superfluous for me to write to you;

2 for I know your willingness, about which I boast of you to the Macedonians, that Achaia was ready a year ago; and your zeal has stirred up the majority.

3 Yet I have sent the brethren, lest our boasting of you should be in vain in this respect, that, as I said, you may be ready;

4 lest if *some* Macedonians come with me and find you unprepared, we (not to mention you!) should be ashamed of this confident boasting.

5 Therefore I thought it necessary to exhort the brethren to go to you ahead of time, and prepare your bountiful gift beforehand, which *you had* previously promised, that it may be ready as *a matter of* generosity and not as a grudging obligation.

6 But this *I say:* He who sows sparingly will also reap sparingly, and he who sows bountifully will also reap bountifully.

7 *So let* each one *give* as he purposes in his heart, not grudgingly or of necessity; for God loves a cheerful giver.

8 And God *is* able to make all grace abound toward you, that you, always having all sufficiency in all *things,* have an abundance for every good work.

9 As it is written:

> "He has dispersed abroad,
> He has given to the poor;
> *His righteousness remains
>   forever.*"

10 Now may He who supplies seed to the sower, and bread for food, supply and multiply the seed you have *sown* and increase the fruits of your righteousness,

11 while *you are* enriched in everything for all liberality, which causes thanksgiving through us to God.

12 For the administration of this service not only supplies the needs of the saints, but also is abounding through many thanksgivings to God,

13 while, through the proof of this ministry, they glorify God for the obedience of your confession to the gospel of Christ, and for *your* liberal sharing with them and all *men,*

14 and by their prayer for you, who long for you because of the exceeding grace of God in you.

15 Thanks *be* to God for His indescribable gift!

10 Now I, Paul, myself am pleading with you by the meekness and gentleness of Christ—who in presence *am* lowly among you, but being absent am bold toward you.

2 But I beg *you* that when I am present I may not be bold with that confidence by which I intend to be bold against some, who think of us as if we walked according to the flesh.

3 For though we walk in the flesh, we do not war according to the flesh.

4 For the weapons of our warfare *are* not carnal but mighty in God for pulling down strongholds,

5 casting down arguments and every high thing that exalts itself against the knowledge of God, bringing every thought into captivity to the obedience of Christ,

6 and being ready to punish all disobedience when your obedience is fulfilled.

7 Do you look at things according to the outward appearance? If anyone is convinced in himself that he is Christ's, let him again consider this in himself, that just as he *is* Christ's, even so we *are* Christ's.

8 For even if I should boast somewhat more about our authority, which the Lord gave us for edification and not for your destruction, I shall not be ashamed—

9 lest I seem to terrify you by letters.

10 "For *his* letters," they say, "*are* weighty and powerful, but *his* bodily presence *is* weak, and *his* speech contemptible."

11 Let such a person consider this, that what we are in word by letters when we are absent, such *we will* also *be* in deed when we are present.

12 For we dare not class ourselves or compare ourselves with those who commend themselves. But they, measuring themselves by themselves, and comparing themselves among themselves, are not wise.

13 We, however, will not boast beyond measure, but within the limits of the sphere which God appointed us—a sphere which especially includes you.

14 For we are not extending ourselves beyond *our sphere* (thus not reaching you), for it was to you that we came with the gospel of Christ;

15 not boasting of things beyond measure, *that is,* in other men's labors, but having hope, *that* as your faith is increased, we shall be greatly enlarged by you in our sphere,

16 to preach the gospel in the *regions* beyond you, *and* not to boast in another man's sphere of accomplishment.

17 But *"He who glories, let him glory in the* Lord."

18 For not he who commends himself is approved, but whom the Lord commends.

11 Oh, that you would bear with me in a little folly—and indeed you do bear with me.

2 For I am jealous for you with godly jealousy. For I have betrothed you to one husband, that I may present *you as* a chaste virgin to Christ.

3 But I fear, lest somehow, as the serpent deceived Eve by his craftiness, so your minds may be corrupted from the simplicity that is in Christ.

4 For if he who comes preaches another Jesus whom we have not preached, or *if* you receive a different spirit which you have not received, or a different gospel which you have not accepted, you may well put up with it.

5 For I consider that I am not at all inferior to the most eminent apostles.

6 Even though *I am* untrained in speech, yet *I am* not in knowledge. But we have been thoroughly made manifest among you in all things.

7 Did I commit sin in abasing myself that you might be exalted, because I preached the gospel of God to you free of charge?

8 I robbed other churches, taking wages *from them* to minister to you.

9 And when I was present with you, and in need, I was a burden to no one, for what was lacking to me the brethren who came from Macedonia supplied. And in everything I kept myself from being burdensome to you, and so I will keep *myself*.

10 As the truth of Christ is in me, no one shall stop me from this boasting in the regions of Achaia.

11 Why? Because I do not love you? God knows!

12 But what I do, I will also continue to do, that I may cut off the opportunity from those who desire an opportunity to be regarded just as we are in the things of which they boast.

13 For such *are* false apostles, deceitful workers, transforming themselves into apostles of Christ.

14 And no wonder! For Satan himself transforms himself into an angel of light.

15 Therefore *it is* no great thing if his ministers also transform themselves into ministers of righteousness, whose end will be according to their works.

16 I say again, let no one think me a fool. If otherwise, at least receive me as a fool, that I also may boast a little.

17 What I speak, I speak not according to the Lord, but as it were, foolishly, in this confidence of boasting.

18 Seeing that many boast according to the flesh, I also will boast.

19 For you put up with fools gladly, since you *yourselves* are wise!

20 For you put up with it if one brings you into bondage, if one devours *you*, if one takes *from you*, if one exalts himself, if one strikes you on the face.

21 To *our* shame, I say that we were too weak for that! But in whatever anyone is bold—I speak foolishly—I am bold also.

22 Are they Hebrews? So *am* I. Are

they Israelites? So *am* I. Are they the seed of Abraham? So *am* I.

23 Are they ministers of Christ?—I speak as a fool—I *am* more: in labors more abundant, in stripes above measure, in prisons more frequently, in deaths often.

24 From the Jews five times I received forty *stripes* minus one.

25 Three times I was beaten with rods; once I was stoned; three times I was shipwrecked; a night and a day I have been in the deep;

26 *in* journeys often, *in* perils of waters, *in* perils of robbers, *in* perils of *my own* countrymen, *in* perils of the Gentiles, *in* perils in the city, *in* perils in the wilderness, *in* perils in the sea, *in* perils among false brethren;

27 in weariness and toil, in sleeplessness often, in hunger and thirst, in fastings often, in cold and nakedness—

28 besides the other things, what comes upon me daily: my deep concern for all the churches.

29 Who is weak, and I am not weak? Who is made to stumble, and I do not burn with indignation?

30 If I must boast, I will boast in the things which concern my infirmity.

31 The God and Father of our Lord Jesus Christ, who is blessed forever, knows that I am not lying.

32 In Damascus the governor, under Aretas the king, was guarding the city of the Damascenes with a garrison, desiring to apprehend me;

33 but I was let down in a basket through a window in the wall, and escaped from his hands.

12 It is doubtless not profitable for me to boast. I will come to visions and revelations of the Lord:

2 I know a man in Christ who fourteen years ago—whether in the body I do not know, or whether out of the body I do not

know, God knows—such a one was caught up to the third heaven.

3 And I know such a man—whether in the body or out of the body I do not know, God knows—

4 how he was caught up into Paradise and heard inexpressible words, which it is not lawful for a man to utter.

5 Of such a one I will boast; yet of myself I will not boast, except in my infirmities.

6 For though I might desire to boast, I will not be a fool; for I will speak the truth. But I forbear, lest anyone should think of me above what he sees me *to be* or hears from me.

7 And lest I should be exalted above measure by the abundance of the revelations, a thorn in the flesh was given to me, a messenger of Satan to buffet me, lest I be exalted above measure.

8 Concerning this thing I pleaded with the Lord three times that it might depart from me.

9 And He said to me, "My grace is sufficient for you, for My strength is made perfect in weakness." Therefore most gladly I will rather boast in my infirmities, that the power of Christ may rest upon me.

10 Therefore I take pleasure in infirmities, in reproaches, in needs, in persecutions, in distresses, for Christ's sake. For when I am weak, then I am strong.

11 I have become a fool in boasting; you have compelled me. For I ought to have been commended by you; for in nothing was I behind the most eminent apostles, though I am nothing.

12 Truly the signs of an apostle were accomplished among you with all perseverance, in signs and wonders and mighty deeds.

13 For what is it in which you were inferior to other churches, except that I myself was not burdensome to you? Forgive me this wrong!

14 Now *for* the third time I am

ready to come to you. And I will not be burdensome to you; for I do not seek yours, but you. For the children ought not to lay up for the parents, but the parents for the children.

15 And I will very gladly spend and be spent for your souls; though the more abundantly I love you, the less I am loved.

16 But be that *as it may*, I did not burden you. Nevertheless, being crafty, I caught you with guile!

17 Did I take advantage of you by any of those whom I sent to you?

18 I urged Titus, and sent our brother with *him*. Did Titus take advantage of you? Did we not walk in the same spirit? Did *we* not *walk* in the same steps?

19 Again, do you think that we excuse ourselves to you? We speak before God in Christ. But *we do* all things, beloved, for your edification.

20 For I fear lest, when I come, I shall not find you such as I wish, and *that* I shall be found by you such as you do not wish; lest *there be* contentions, jealousies, outbursts of wrath, selfish ambitions, backbitings, whisperings, conceits, tumults;

21 *and* lest, when I come again, my God will humble me among you, and I shall mourn for many who have sinned before and have not repented of the uncleanness, fornication, and licentiousness which they have practiced.

13 This *will be* the third *time* I am coming to you. *"By the mouth of two or three witnesses every word shall be established."*

2 I have told you before, and foretell as if I were present the second time, and now being absent I write to those who have sinned before,

and to all the rest, that if I come again I will not spare—

3 since you seek a proof of Christ speaking in me, who is not weak toward you, but mighty in you.

4 For though He was crucified in weakness, yet He lives by the power of God. For we also are weak in Him, but we shall live with Him by the power of God toward you.

5 Examine yourselves *as to* whether you are in the faith. Prove yourselves. Do you not know yourselves, that Jesus Christ is in you?—unless indeed you are disqualified.

6 But I trust that you will know that we are not disqualified.

7 Now I pray to God that you do no evil, not that we should appear approved, but that you should do what is honorable, though we may seem disqualified.

8 For we can do nothing against the truth, but for the truth.

9 For we are glad when we are weak and you are strong. And this also we pray, that you may be made complete.

10 Therefore I write these things being absent, lest being present I should use sharpness, according to the authority which the Lord has given me for edification and not for destruction.

11 Finally, brethren, farewell. Become complete. Be of good comfort, be of one mind, live in peace; and the God of love and peace will be with you.

12 Greet one another with a holy kiss.

13 All the saints greet you.

14 The grace of the Lord Jesus Christ, and the love of God, and the communion of the Holy Spirit *be* with you all. Amen.

THE EPISTLE OF PAUL THE APOSTLE TO THE
GALATIANS

PAUL, an apostle (not from men nor through man, but through Jesus Christ and God the Father who raised Him from the dead),

2 and all the brethren who are with me,

To the churches of Galatia:

3 Grace to you and peace from God the Father and our Lord Jesus Christ,

4 who gave Himself for our sins, that He might deliver us from this present evil age, according to the will of our God and Father,

5 to whom be glory forever and ever. Amen.

6 I marvel that you are turning away so soon from Him who called you in the grace of Christ, to a different gospel,

7 which is not another; but there are some who trouble you and want to pervert the gospel of Christ.

8 But even if we, or an angel from heaven, preach any other gospel to you than what we have preached to you, let him be accursed.

9 As we have said before, so now I say again, if anyone preaches any other gospel to you than what you have received, let him be accursed.

10 For do I now persuade men, or God? Or do I seek to please men? For if I still pleased men, I would not be a servant of Christ.

11 But I make known to you, brethren, that the gospel which was preached by me is not according to man.

12 For I neither received it from man, nor was I taught it, but it came through the revelation of Jesus Christ.

13 For you have heard of my former conduct in Judaism, how I persecuted the church of God beyond measure and tried to destroy it.

14 And I advanced in Judaism beyond many of my contemporaries in my own nation, being more exceedingly zealous for the traditions of my fathers.

15 But when it pleased God, who separated me from my mother's womb and called me through His grace,

16 to reveal His Son in me, that I might preach Him among the Gentiles, I did not immediately confer with flesh and blood,

17 nor did I go up to Jerusalem to those who were apostles before me; but I went to Arabia, and returned again to Damascus.

18 Then after three years I went up to Jerusalem to see Peter, and remained with him fifteen days.

19 But I saw none of the other apostles except James, the Lord's brother.

20 (Now concerning the things which I write to you, indeed, before God, I do not lie.)

21 Afterward I went into the regions of Syria and Cilicia.

22 and I was unknown by face to the churches of Judea which were in Christ.

23 But they were hearing only, "He who formerly persecuted us now preaches the faith which he once tried to destroy."

24 And they glorified God in me.

2 Then after fourteen years I went up again to Jerusalem with Barnabas, and also took Titus with me.

2 And I went up by revelation, and communicated to them that gospel which I preach among the Gentiles, but privately to those who were of reputation, lest by any means I might run, or had run, in vain.

3 Yet not even Titus who was with me, being a Greek, was compelled to be circumcised.

4 But *this occurred* because of false brethren secretly brought in (who came in by stealth to spy out our liberty which we have in Christ Jesus, that they might bring us into bondage),

5 to whom we did not yield submission even for an hour, that the truth of the gospel might continue with you.

6 But from those who seemed to be something—whatever they were, it makes no difference to me; God shows personal favoritism to no man—for those who seemed *to be something* added nothing to me.

7 But on the contrary, when they saw that the gospel for the uncircumcised had been committed to me, as *the gospel* for the circumcised *was* to Peter

8 (for He who worked effectively in Peter for the apostleship to the circumcised also worked effectively in me toward the Gentiles),

9 and when James, Cephas, and John, who seemed to be pillars, perceived the grace that had been given to me, they gave me and Barnabas the right hand of fellowship, that we *should go* to the Gentiles and they to the circumcised.

10 *They desired* only that we should remember the poor, the very thing which I also was eager to do.

11 But when Peter had come to Antioch, I withstood him to his face, because he was to be blamed;

12 for before certain men came from James, he would eat with the Gentiles; but when they came, he withdrew and separated himself, fearing those who were of the circumcision.

13 And the rest of the Jews also played the hypocrite with him, so that even Barnabas was carried away with their hypocrisy.

14 But when I saw that they were not straightforward about the truth of the gospel, I said to Peter before *them* all, "If you, being a Jew, live in the manner of Gentiles and not as the Jews, why do you compel Gentiles to live as Jews?

15 "We *who are* Jews by nature, and not sinners of the Gentiles,

16 "knowing that a man is not justified by the works of the law but by faith in Jesus Christ, even we have believed in Christ Jesus, that we might be justified by faith in Christ and not by the works of the law; for by the works of the law no flesh shall be justified.

17 "But if, while we seek to be justified by Christ, we ourselves also are found sinners, *is* Christ therefore a minister of sin? Certainly not!

18 "For if I build again those things which I destroyed, I make myself a transgressor.

19 "For I through the law died to the law that I might live to God.

20 "I have been crucified with Christ; it is no longer I who live, but Christ lives in me; and the *life* which I now live in the flesh I live by faith in the Son of God, who loved me and gave Himself for me. ❤

21 "I do not set aside the grace of God; for if righteousness *comes* through the law, then Christ died in vain."

3 O foolish Galatians! Who has bewitched you that you should not obey the truth, before whose eyes Jesus Christ was clearly portrayed among you as crucified?

2 This only I want to learn from you: Did you receive the Spirit by the works of the law, or by the hearing of faith?

3 Are you so foolish? Having begun in the Spirit, are you now being made perfect by the flesh?

4 Have you suffered so many things in vain—if indeed *it was* in vain?

5 Therefore He who supplies the Spirit to you and works miracles among you, *does He do it* by the works of the law, or by the hearing of faith?—

231

6 just as Abraham *"believed God, and it was accounted to him for righteousness."*

7 Therefore know that *only* those who are of faith are sons of Abraham.

8 And the Scripture, foreseeing that God would justify the nations by faith, preached the gospel to Abraham beforehand, *saying, "In you all the nations shall be blessed."*

9 So then those who *are* of faith are blessed with believing Abraham.

10 For as many as are of the works of the law are under the curse; for it is written, *"Cursed is everyone who does not continue in all things which are written in the book of the law, to do them."*

11 But that no one is justified by the law in the sight of God *is* evident, for *"The just shall live by faith."*

12 Yet the law is not of faith, but *"The man who does them shall live by them."*

13 Christ has redeemed us from the curse of the law, having become a curse for us (for it is written, *"Cursed is everyone who hangs on a tree"*),

14 that the blessing of Abraham might come upon the Gentiles in Christ Jesus, that we might receive the promise of the Spirit through faith.

15 Brethren, I speak in the manner of men: Though *it is* only a man's covenant, yet *if it is* confirmed, no one annuls or adds to it.

16 Now to Abraham and his Seed were the promises made. He does not say, "And to seeds," as of many, but as of one, *"And to your Seed,"* who is Christ.

17 And this I say, *that* the law, which was four hundred and thirty years later, cannot annul the covenant that was confirmed before by God in Christ, that it should make the promise of no effect.

18 For if the inheritance *is* of the law, *it is* no longer of promise; but God gave *it* to Abraham by promise.

19 What purpose then *does* the law *serve?* It was added because of transgressions, till the Seed should come to whom the promise was made; *and it was* appointed through angels by the hand of a mediator.

20 Now a mediator does not *mediate* for one *only,* but God is one.

21 *Is* the law then against the promises of God? Certainly not! For if there had been a law given which could have given life, truly righteousness would have been by the law.

22 But the Scripture has confined all under sin, that the promise by faith in Jesus Christ might be given to those who believe.

23 But before faith came, we were kept under guard by the law, kept for the faith which would afterward be revealed.

24 Therefore the law was our tutor *to bring us* to Christ, that we might be justified by faith.

25 But after faith has come, we are no longer under a tutor.

26 For you are all sons of God through faith in Christ Jesus.

27 For as many of you as were baptized into Christ have put on Christ.

28 There is neither Jew nor Greek, there is neither slave nor free, there is neither male nor female; for you are all one in Christ Jesus.

29 And if you *are* Christ's, then you are Abraham's seed, and heirs according to the promise.

4 Now I say *that* the heir, as long as he is a child, does not differ at all from a slave, though he is master of all,

2 but is under guardians and stewards until the time appointed by the father.

3 Even so we, when we were children, were in bondage under the elements of the world.

4 But when the fullness of the time had come, God sent forth His Son, born of a woman, born under the law,

5 to redeem those who were under the law, that we might receive the adoption as sons.

6 And because you are sons, God has sent forth the Spirit of His Son into your hearts, crying out, "Abba, Father!"

7 Therefore you are no longer a slave but a son, and if a son, then an heir of God through Christ.

8 But then, indeed, when you did not know God, you served those which by nature are not gods.

9 But now after you have known God, or rather are known by God, how *is it that* you turn again to the weak and beggarly elements, to which you desire again to be in bondage?

10 You observe days and months and seasons and years.

11 I am afraid for you, lest I have labored for you in vain.

12 Brethren, I urge you to become as I *am,* for I *am* as you *are.* You have not injured me at all.

13 You know that because of physical infirmity I preached the gospel to you at the first.

14 And my trial which was in my flesh you did not despise or reject, but you received me as an angel of God, *even* as Christ Jesus.

15 What then was the blessing you *enjoyed?* For I bear you witness that, if possible, you would have plucked out your own eyes and given them to me.

16 Have I therefore become your enemy because I tell you the truth?

17 They zealously court you, *but* for no good; yes, they want to exclude you, that you may be zealous for them.

18 But it is good to be zealous in a good thing always, and not only when I am present with you.

19 My little children, for whom I labor in birth again until Christ is formed in you,

20 I would like to be present with you now and to change my tone; for I have doubts about you.

21 Tell me, you who desire to be under the law, do you not hear the law?

22 For it is written that Abraham had two sons: the one by a bondwoman, the other by a freewoman.

23 But he *who was* of the bondwoman was born according to the flesh, and he of the freewoman through promise,

24 which things are symbolic. For these are the two covenants: the one from Mount Sinai which gives birth to bondage, which is Hagar—

25 for this Hagar is Mount Sinai in Arabia, and corresponds to Jerusalem which now is, and is in bondage with her children—

26 but the Jerusalem above is free, which is the mother of us all.

27 For it is written:

> "Rejoice, O barren,
> You who do not bear!
> Break forth and shout,
> You who do not travail!
> For the desolate has
>   many more children
> Than she who has a husband."

28 Now we, brethren, as Isaac *was,* are children of promise.

29 But, as he who was born according to the flesh then persecuted him *who was born* according to the Spirit, even so *it is* now.

30 Nevertheless what does the Scripture say? *"Cast out the bondwoman and her son, for the son of the bondwoman shall not be heir with the son of the freewoman."*

31 So then, brethren, we are not children of the bondwoman but of the free.

5 Stand fast therefore in the liberty by which Christ has made us free, and do not be entangled again with a yoke of bondage.

2 Indeed I, Paul, say to you that if you become circumcised, Christ will profit you nothing.

3 And I testify again to every man who becomes circumcised that he is a debtor to keep the whole law.

4 You have become estranged from Christ, you who *attempt to* be justified by law; you have fallen from grace.

5 For we through the Spirit eagerly wait for the hope of righteousness by faith.

6 For in Christ Jesus neither circumcision nor uncircumcision avails anything, but faith working through love.

7 You ran well. Who hindered you from obeying the truth?

8 This persuasion does not *come* from Him who calls you.

9 A little leaven leavens the whole lump.

10 I have confidence in you, in the Lord, that you will have no other mind; but he who troubles you shall bear his judgment, whoever he is.

11 And I, brethren, if I still preach circumcision, why do I still suffer persecution? Then the offense of the cross has ceased.

12 I could wish that those who trouble you would even cut themselves off!

13 For you, brethren, have been called to liberty; only do not *use* liberty as an opportunity for the flesh, but through love serve one another.

14 For all the law is fulfilled in one word, *even* in this: *"You shall love your neighbor as yourself."*

15 But if you bite and devour one another, beware lest you be consumed by one another!

16 I say then: Walk in the Spirit, and you shall not fulfill the lust of the flesh.

17 For the flesh lusts against the Spirit, and the Spirit against the flesh; and these are contrary to one another, so that you do not do the things that you wish.

18 But if you are led by the Spirit, you are not under the law.

19 Now the works of the flesh are evident, which are: adultery, fornication, uncleanness, licentiousness,

20 idolatry, sorcery, hatred, contentions, jealousies, outbursts of wrath, selfish ambitions, dissensions, heresies,

21 envy, murders, drunkenness, revelries, and the like; of which I tell you beforehand, just as I also told *you* in time past, that those who practice such things will not inherit the kingdom of God.

22 But the fruit of the Spirit is love, joy, peace, longsuffering, kindness, goodness, faithfulness,

23 gentleness, self-control. Against such there is no law.

24 And those *who are* Christ's have crucified the flesh with its passions and desires.

25 If we live in the Spirit, let us also walk in the Spirit.

26 Let us not become conceited, provoking one another, envying one another.

6 Brethren, if a man is overtaken in any trespass, you who *are* spiritual restore such a one in a spirit of gentleness, considering yourself lest you also be tempted.

2 Bear one another's burdens, and so fulfill the law of Christ.

3 For if anyone thinks himself to be something, when he is nothing, he deceives himself.

4 But let each one examine his own work, and then he will have rejoicing in himself alone, and not in another.

5 For each one shall bear his own load.

6 Let him who is taught the word share in all good things with him who teaches.

7 Do not be deceived, God is not mocked; for whatever a man sows, that he will also reap.

8 For he who sows to his flesh will of the flesh reap corruption, but he

who sows to the Spirit will of the Spirit reap everlasting life.

9 And let us not grow weary while doing good, for in due season we shall reap if we do not lose heart.

10 Therefore, as we have opportunity, let us do good to all, especially to those who are of the household of faith.

11 See with what large letters I have written to you with my own hand!

12 As many as desire to make a good showing in the flesh, these *try to* compel you to be circumcised, only that they may not suffer persecution for the cross of Christ.

13 For not even those who are circumcised keep the law, but they desire to have you circumcised that they may glory in your flesh.

14 But God forbid that I should glory except in the cross of our Lord Jesus Christ, by whom the world has been crucified to me, and I to the world.

15 For in Christ Jesus neither circumcision nor uncircumcision avails anything, but a new creation.

16 And as many as walk according to this rule, peace and mercy *be* upon them, and upon the Israel of God.

17 From now on let no one trouble me, for I bear in my body the marks of the Lord Jesus.

18 Brethren, the grace of our Lord Jesus Christ *be* with your spirit. Amen.

THE EPISTLE OF PAUL THE APOSTLE TO THE
EPHESIANS

PAUL, an apostle of Jesus Christ by the will of God,

To the saints who are in Ephesus, and faithful in Christ Jesus:

2 Grace to you and peace from God our Father and the Lord Jesus Christ.

3 Blessed *be* the God and Father of our Lord Jesus Christ, who has blessed us with every spiritual blessing in the heavenly *places* in Christ,

4 just as He chose us in Him before the foundation of the world, that we should be holy and without blame before Him in love,

5 having predestined us to adoption as sons by Jesus Christ to Himself, according to the good pleasure of His will,

6 to the praise of the glory of His grace, by which He has made us accepted in the Beloved.

7 In Him we have redemption through His blood, the forgiveness of sins, according to the riches of His grace ❤

8 which He made to abound toward us in all wisdom and prudence,

9 having made known to us the mystery of His will, according to His good pleasure which He purposed in Himself,

10 that in the dispensation of the fullness of the times He might gather together in one all things in Christ, both which are in heaven and which are on earth—in Him,

11 in whom also we have obtained an inheritance, being predestined according to the purpose of Him who works all things according to the counsel of His will,

 See 1 John 1:9, page 288

12 that we who first trusted in Christ should be to the praise of His glory.

13 In Him you also *trusted*, after you heard the word of truth, the gospel of your salvation; in whom also, having believed, you were sealed with the Holy Spirit of promise,

14 who is the guarantee of our inheritance until the redemption of the purchased possession, to the praise of His glory.

15 Therefore I also, after I heard of your faith in the Lord Jesus and your love for all the saints,

16 do not cease to give thanks for you, making mention of you in my prayers:

17 that the God of our Lord Jesus Christ, the Father of glory, may give to you the spirit of wisdom and revelation in the knowledge of Him,

18 the eyes of your understanding being enlightened; that you may know what is the hope of His calling, what are the riches of the glory of His inheritance in the saints,

19 and what *is* the exceeding greatness of His power toward us who believe, according to the working of His mighty power

20 which He worked in Christ when He raised Him from the dead and seated *Him* at His right hand in the heavenly *places*,

21 far above all principality and power and might and dominion, and every name that is named, not only in this age but also in that which is to come.

22 And He put all *things* under His feet, and gave Him *to be* head over all *things* to the church,

23 which is His body, the fullness of Him who fills all in all.

2 And you He made alive, who were dead in trespasses and sins,

2 in which you once walked according to the course of this world,

according to the prince of the power of the air, the spirit who now works in the sons of disobedience,

3 among whom also we all once conducted ourselves in the lusts of our flesh, fulfilling the desires of the flesh and of the mind, and were by nature children of wrath, just as the others.

4 But God, who is rich in mercy, because of His great love with which He loved us,

5 even when we were dead in trespasses, made us alive together with Christ (by grace you have been saved),

6 and raised *us* up together, and made *us* sit together in the heavenly *places* in Christ Jesus,

7 that in the ages to come He might show the exceeding riches of His grace in *His* kindness toward us in Christ Jesus.

8 For by grace you have been saved through faith, and that not of yourselves; *it is* the gift of God,

9 not of works, lest anyone should boast.

10 For we are His workmanship, created in Christ Jesus for good works, which God prepared beforehand that we should walk in them.

11 Therefore remember that you, once Gentiles in the flesh—who are called Uncircumcision by what is called the Circumcision made in the flesh by hands—

12 that at that time you were without Christ, being aliens from the commonwealth of Israel and strangers from the covenants of promise, having no hope and without God in the world.

13 But now in Christ Jesus you who once were far off have been made near by the blood of Christ.

14 For He Himself is our peace, who has made both one, and has broken down the middle wall of division *between us*,

15 having abolished in His flesh the

enmity, *that is*, the law of commandments *contained* in ordinances, so as to create in Himself one new man *from* the two, *thus* making peace,

16 and that He might reconcile them both to God in one body through the cross, thereby putting to death the enmity.

17 And He came and preached peace to you who were afar off and to those who were near.

18 For through Him we both have access by one Spirit to the Father.

19 Now, therefore, you are no longer strangers and foreigners, but fellow citizens with the saints and members of the household of God,

20 having been built on the foundation of the apostles and prophets, Jesus Christ Himself being the chief corner*stone*,

21 in whom the whole building, being joined together, grows into a holy temple in the Lord,

22 in whom you also are being built together for a habitation of God in the Spirit.

3 For this reason I, Paul, the prisoner of Jesus Christ for you Gentiles—

2 if indeed you have heard of the dispensation of the grace of God which was given to me for you,

3 how that by revelation He made known to me the mystery (as I wrote before in a few words,

4 by which, when you read, you may understand my knowledge in the mystery of Christ),

5 which in other ages was not made known to the sons of men, as it has now been revealed by the Spirit to His holy apostles and prophets:

6 that the Gentiles should be fellow heirs, of the same body, and partakers of His promise in Christ through the gospel,

7 of which I became a minister according to the gift of the grace of God given to me by the effective working of His power.

8 To me, who am less than the least of all the saints, this grace was given, that I should preach among the Gentiles the unsearchable riches of Christ,

9 and to make all *people* see what *is* the fellowship of the mystery, which from the beginning of the ages has been hidden in God who created all things through Jesus Christ;

10 to the intent that now the manifold wisdom of God might be made known by the church to the principalities and powers in the heavenly *places*,

11 according to the eternal purpose which He accomplished in Christ Jesus our Lord,

12 in whom we have boldness and access with confidence through faith in Him.

13 Therefore I ask that you do not lose heart at my tribulations for you, which is your glory.

14 For this reason I bow my knees to the Father of our Lord Jesus Christ,

15 from whom the whole family in heaven and earth is named,

16 that He would grant you, according to the riches of His glory, to be strengthened with might through His Spirit in the inner man,

17 that Christ may dwell in your hearts through faith; that you, being rooted and grounded in love, ❤

18 may be able to comprehend with all the saints what *is* the width and length and depth and height—

19 to know the love of Christ which passes knowledge; that you may be filled with all the fullness of God.

20 Now to Him who is able to do exceedingly abundantly above all that we ask or think, according to the power that works in us,

21 to Him *be* glory in the church by Christ Jesus throughout all ages, world without end. Amen.

4 I, therefore, the prisoner of the Lord, beseech you to have a walk worthy of the calling with which you were called,

2 with all lowliness and gentleness, with longsuffering, bearing with one another in love,

3 endeavoring to keep the unity of the Spirit in the bond of peace.

4 *There is* one body and one Spirit, just as you were called in one hope of your calling;

5 one Lord, one faith, one baptism;

6 one God and Father of all, who *is* above all, and through all, and in you all.

7 But to each one of us grace was given according to the measure of Christ's gift.

8 Therefore He says:

"When He ascended on high,
    He led captivity captive,
    And gave gifts to men."

9 (Now this, *"He ascended"*— what does it mean but that He also first descended into the lower parts of the earth?

10 He who descended is also the One who ascended far above all the heavens, that He might fill all things.)

11 And He Himself gave some *to be* apostles, some prophets, some evangelists, and some pastors and teachers,

12 for the equipping of the saints for the work of ministry, for the edifying of the body of Christ,

13 till we all come to the unity of the faith and the knowledge of the Son of God, to a perfect man, to the measure of the stature of the fullness of Christ;

14 that we should no longer be children, tossed to and fro and carried about with every wind of doctrine, by the trickery of men, in the cunning craftiness by which they lie in wait to deceive,

15 but, speaking the truth in love,

may grow up in all things into Him who is the head—Christ—

16 from whom the whole body, joined and knit together by what every joint supplies, according to the effective working by which every part does its share, causes growth of the body for the edifying of itself in love.

17 This I say, therefore, and testify in the Lord, that you should no longer walk as the rest of the Gentiles walk, in the futility of their mind,

18 having their understanding darkened, being alienated from the life of God, because of the ignorance that is in them, because of the hardening of their heart;

19 who, being past feeling, have given themselves over to licentiousness, to work all uncleanness with greediness.

20 But you have not so learned Christ,

21 if indeed you have heard Him and have been taught by Him, as the truth is in Jesus:

22 that you put off, concerning your former conduct, the old man which grows corrupt according to the deceitful lusts,

23 and be renewed in the spirit of your mind,

24 and that you put on the new man which was created according to God, in righteousness and true holiness.

25 Therefore, putting away lying, each one speak truth with his neighbor, for we are members of one another.

26 *"Be angry, and do not sin":* do not let the sun go down on your wrath,

27 nor give place to the devil.

28 Let him who stole steal no longer, but rather let him labor, working with *his* hands what is good, that he may have something to give him who has need.

29 Let no corrupt communication proceed out of your mouth, but

See Colossians 3:12–13, page 247   **238**

what is good for necessary edification, that it may impart grace to the hearers.

30 And do not grieve the Holy Spirit of God, by whom you were sealed for the day of redemption.

31 Let all bitterness, wrath, anger, clamor, and evil speaking be put away from you, with all malice.

32 And be kind to one another, tenderhearted, forgiving one another, just as God in Christ also forgave you.

5 Therefore be followers of God as dear children.

2 And walk in love, as Christ also has loved us and given Himself for us, an offering and a sacrifice to God for a sweet-smelling aroma.

3 But fornication and all uncleanness or covetousness, let it not even be named among you, as is fitting for saints;

4 neither filthiness, nor foolish talking, nor coarse jesting, which are not fitting, but rather giving of thanks.

5 For this you know, that no fornicator, unclean person, nor covetous man, who is an idolater, has any inheritance in the kingdom of Christ and God.

6 Let no one deceive you with empty words, for because of these things the wrath of God comes upon the sons of disobedience.

7 Therefore do not be partakers with them.

8 For you were once darkness, but now you are light in the Lord. Walk as children of light

9 (for the fruit of the Spirit is in all goodness, righteousness, and truth),

10 proving what is acceptable to the Lord.

11 And have no fellowship with the unfruitful works of darkness, but rather expose them.

12 For it is shameful even to speak of those things which are done by them in secret.

13 But all things that are exposed are made manifest by the light, for whatever makes manifest is light.

14 Therefore He says:

"Awake, you who sleep,
  Arise from the dead,
  And Christ will give you light."

15 See then that you walk circumspectly, not as fools but as wise,

16 redeeming the time, because the days are evil.

17 Therefore do not be unwise, but understand what the will of the Lord is.

18 And do not be drunk with wine, in which is dissipation; but be filled with the Spirit,

19 speaking to one another in psalms and hymns and spiritual songs, singing and making melody in your heart to the Lord,

20 giving thanks always for all things to God the Father in the name of our Lord Jesus Christ,

21 submitting to one another in the fear of God.

22 Wives, submit to your own husbands, as to the Lord.

23 For the husband is head of the wife, as also Christ is head of the church; and He is the Savior of the body.

24 Therefore, just as the church is subject to Christ, so let the wives be to their own husbands in everything.

25 Husbands, love your wives, just as Christ also loved the church and gave Himself for it,

26 that He might sanctify and cleanse it with the washing of water by the word,

27 that He might present it to Himself a glorious church, not having spot or wrinkle or any such thing, but that it should be holy and without blemish.

28 So husbands ought to love their own wives as their own bodies; he who loves his wife loves himself.

29 For no one ever hated his own flesh, but nourishes and cherishes

it, just as the Lord *does* the church.

30 For we are members of His body, of His flesh and of His bones.

31 *"For this reason a man shall leave his father and mother and be joined to his wife, and the two shall become one flesh."*

32 This is a great mystery, but I speak concerning Christ and the church.

33 Nevertheless let each one of you in particular so love his own wife as himself, and let the wife *see* that she respects *her* husband.

6 Children, obey your parents in the Lord, for this is right.

2 *"Honor your father and mother,"* which is the first commandment with promise:

3 *"that it may be well with you and you may live long on the earth."*

4 And you, fathers, do not provoke your children to wrath, but bring them up in the training and admonition of the Lord.

5 Servants, be obedient to those who are your masters according to the flesh, with fear and trembling, in sincerity of heart, as to Christ;

6 not with eyeservice, as menpleasers, but as servants of Christ, doing the will of God from the heart,

7 with good will doing service, as to the Lord, and not to men,

8 knowing that whatever good anyone does, he will receive the same from the Lord, whether *he is* a slave or free.

9 And you, masters, do the same things to them, giving up threatening, knowing that your own Master also is in heaven, and there is no partiality with Him.

10 Finally, my brethren, be strong in the Lord and in the power of His might.

11 Put on the whole armor of God, that you may be able to stand against the wiles of the devil.

12 For we do not wrestle against flesh and blood, but against principalities, against powers, against the rulers of the darkness of this age, against spiritual *hosts* of wickedness in the heavenly *places*.

13 Therefore take up the whole armor of God, that you may be able to withstand in the evil day, and having done all, to stand.

14 Stand therefore, having girded your waist with truth, having put on the breastplate of righteousness,

15 and having shod your feet with the preparation of the gospel of peace;

16 above all, taking the shield of faith with which you will be able to quench all the fiery darts of the wicked one.

17 And take the helmet of salvation, and the sword of the Spirit, which is the word of God;

18 praying always with all prayer and supplication in the Spirit, being watchful to this end with all perseverance and supplication for all the saints—

19 and for me, that utterance may be given to me, that I may open my mouth boldly to make known the mystery of the gospel,

20 for which I am an ambassador in chains; that in it I may speak boldly, as I ought to speak.

21 But that you also may know my affairs *and* how I am doing, Tychicus, a beloved brother and faithful minister in the Lord, will make all things known to you;

22 whom I have sent to you for this very purpose, that you may know our affairs, and *that* he may comfort your hearts.

23 Peace to the brethren, and love with faith, from God the Father and the Lord Jesus Christ.

24 Grace *be* with all those who love our Lord Jesus Christ in sincerity. Amen.

THE EPISTLE OF PAUL THE APOSTLE TO THE

PHILIPPIANS

PAUL and Timothy, servants of Jesus Christ,

To all the saints in Christ Jesus who are in Philippi, with the bishops and deacons:

2 Grace to you and peace from God our Father and the Lord Jesus Christ.

3 I thank my God upon every remembrance of you,

4 always in every prayer of mine making request for you all with joy,

5 for your fellowship in the gospel from the first day until now,

6 being confident of this very thing, that He who has begun a good work in you will complete *it* until the day of Jesus Christ;

7 just as it is right for me to think this of you all, because I have you in my heart, inasmuch as both in my chains and in the defense and confirmation of the gospel, you all are partakers with me of grace.

8 For God is my witness, how greatly I long for you all with the affection of Jesus Christ.

9 And this I pray, that your love may abound still more and more in knowledge and all discernment,

10 that you may approve the things that are excellent, that you may be sincere and without offense till the day of Christ,

11 being filled with the fruits of righteousness which *are* by Jesus Christ, to the glory and praise of God.

12 But I want you to know, brethren, that the things *which happened* to me have actually turned out for the furtherance of the gospel,

13 so that it has become evident to the whole palace guard, and to all the rest, that my chains are in Christ;

14 and most of the brethren in the Lord, having become confident by my chains, are much more bold to speak the word without fear.

15 Some indeed preach Christ even from envy and strife, and some also from good will:

16 The former preach Christ from selfish ambition, not sincerely, supposing to add affliction to my chains;

17 but the latter out of love, knowing that I am appointed for the defense of the gospel.

18 What then? Only *that* in every way, whether in pretense or in truth, Christ is preached; and in this I rejoice, yes, and will rejoice.

19 For I know that this will turn out for my salvation through your prayer and the supply of the Spirit of Jesus Christ,

20 according to my earnest expectation and hope that in nothing I shall be ashamed, but *that* with all boldness, as always, so now also Christ will be magnified in my body, whether by life or by death.

21 For to me, to live *is* Christ, and to die *is* gain.

22 But if *I* live on in the flesh, this *will mean* fruit from *my* labor; yet what I shall choose I cannot tell.

23 For I am hard pressed between the two, having a desire to depart and be with Christ, *which is* far better.

24 Nevertheless to remain in the flesh *is* more needful for you.

25 And being confident of this, I know that I shall remain and continue with you all for your progress and joy of faith,

26 that your rejoicing for me may be more abundant in Jesus Christ by my coming to you again.

27 Only let your conduct be worthy of the gospel of Christ, so that whether I come and see you or am absent, I may hear of your affairs, that you stand fast in one spirit,

GOD FINISHES HIS WORK ❤

with one mind striving together for the faith of the gospel,

28 and not in any way terrified by your adversaries, which is to them a proof of perdition, but to you of salvation, and that from God.

29 For to you it has been granted on behalf of Christ, not only to believe in Him, but also to suffer for His sake,

30 having the same conflict which you saw in me and now hear is in me.

♥ 2 Therefore if *there is* any consolation in Christ, if any comfort of love, if any fellowship of the Spirit, if any affection and mercy,

2 fulfill my joy by being likeminded, having the same love, *being* of one accord, of one mind.

3 *Let* nothing *be done* through selfish ambition or conceit, but in lowliness of mind let each esteem others better than himself.

4 Let each of you look out not only for his own interests, but also for the interests of others.

5 Let this mind be in you which was also in Christ Jesus,

6 who, being in the form of God, did not consider it robbery to be equal with God,

7 but made Himself of no reputation, taking the form of a servant, *and* coming in the likeness of men.

8 And being found in appearance as a man, He humbled Himself and became obedient to *the point of* death, even the death of the cross.

9 Therefore God also has highly exalted Him and given Him the name which is above every name,

10 that at the name of Jesus every knee should bow, of those in heaven, and of those on earth, and of those under the earth,

11 and *that* every tongue should confess that Jesus Christ *is* Lord, to the glory of God the Father.

12 Therefore, my beloved, as you have always obeyed, not as in my presence only, but now much more in my absence, work out your own

salvation with fear and trembling;

13 for it is God who works in you both to will and to do for *His* good pleasure.

14 Do all things without murmuring and disputing,

15 that you may become blameless and harmless, children of God without fault in the midst of a crooked and perverse generation, among whom you shine as lights in the world,

16 holding fast the word of life, so that I may rejoice in the day of Christ that I have not run in vain or labored in vain.

17 Yes, and if I am being poured out *as a drink offering* on the sacrifice and service of your faith, I am glad and rejoice with you all.

18 For the same reason you also be glad and rejoice with me.

19 But I trust in the Lord Jesus to send Timothy to you shortly, that I also may be encouraged when I know your state.

20 For I have no one like-minded, who will sincerely care for your state.

21 For all seek their own, not the things which are of Christ Jesus.

22 But you know his proven character, that as a son with *his* father he served with me in the gospel.

23 Therefore I hope to send him at once, as soon as I see how it goes with me.

24 But I trust in the Lord that I myself shall also come shortly.

25 Yet I considered it necessary to send to you Epaphroditus, my brother, fellow worker, and fellow soldier, but your messenger and the one who ministered to my need;

26 since he was longing for you all, and was distressed because you had heard that he was sick.

27 For indeed he was sick almost unto death; but God had mercy on him, and not only on him but on me also, lest I should have sorrow upon sorrow.

See Matthew 28:18–20, page 41   **242**

28 Therefore I sent him the more eagerly, that when you see him again you may rejoice, and I may be less sorrowful.

29 Receive him therefore in the Lord with all gladness, and hold such men in esteem;

30 because for the work of Christ he came close to death, not regarding his life, to supply what was lacking in your service toward me.

3 Finally, my brethren, rejoice in the Lord. For me to write the same things to you *is* not tedious, but for you *it is* safe.

2 Beware of dogs, beware of evil workers, beware of the mutilation!

3 For we are the circumcision, who worship God in the Spirit, rejoice in Christ Jesus, and have no confidence in the flesh,

4 though I also might have confidence in the flesh. If anyone else thinks he may have confidence in the flesh, I more so:

5 circumcised the eighth day, of the stock of Israel, *of* the tribe of Benjamin, a Hebrew of the Hebrews; concerning the law, a Pharisee;

6 concerning zeal, persecuting the church; concerning the righteousness which is in the law, blameless.

7 But what things were gain to me, these I have counted loss for Christ.

8 But indeed I also count all things loss for the excellence of the knowledge of Christ Jesus my Lord, for whom I have suffered the loss of all things, and count them as rubbish, that I may gain Christ

9 and be found in Him, not having my own righteousness, which *is* from the law, but that which *is* through faith in Christ, the righteousness which is from God by faith;

10 that I may know Him and the power of His resurrection, and the fellowship of His sufferings, being conformed to His death,

11 if, by any means, I may attain to the resurrection from the dead.

12 Not that I have already attained, or am already perfected; but I press on, that I may lay hold of that for which Christ Jesus has also laid hold of me.

13 Brethren, I do not count myself to have apprehended; but one thing *I do*, forgetting those things which are behind and reaching forward to those things which are ahead,

14 I press toward the goal for the prize of the upward call of God in Christ Jesus.

15 Therefore let us, as many as are mature, have this mind; and if in anything you think otherwise, God will reveal even this to you.

16 Nevertheless, to *the degree* that we have already attained, let us walk by the same rule, let us be of the same mind.

17 Brethren, join in following my example, and note those who so walk, as you have us for a pattern.

18 For many walk, of whom I have told you often, and now tell you even weeping, *that they are* the enemies of the cross of Christ:

19 whose end *is* destruction, whose god *is their* belly, and *whose* glory *is* in their shame—who set their mind on earthly things.

20 For our citizenship is in heaven, from which we also eagerly wait for the Savior, the Lord Jesus Christ,

21 who will transform our lowly body that it may be conformed to His glorious body, according to the working by which He is able even to subdue all things to Himself.

4 Therefore, my beloved and longed-for brethren, my joy and crown, so stand fast in the Lord, beloved.

2 I implore Euodia and I implore Syntyche to be of the same mind in the Lord.

3 And I urge you also, true companion, help these women who la-

bored with me in the gospel, with Clement also, and the rest of my fellow workers, whose names *are* in the Book of Life.

4 Rejoice in the Lord always. Again I will say, rejoice!

5 Let your gentleness be known to all men. The Lord *is* at hand.

❤ 6 Be anxious for nothing, but in everything by prayer and supplication, with thanksgiving, let your requests be made known to God; 7 and the peace of God, which surpasses all understanding, will guard your hearts and minds through Christ Jesus.

❤ 8 Finally, brethren, whatever things are true, whatever things *are* noble, whatever things *are* just, whatever things *are* pure, whatever things *are* lovely, whatever things *are* of good report, if *there is* any virtue and if *there is* anything praiseworthy—meditate on these things.

9 The things which you learned and received and heard and saw in me, these do, and the God of peace will be with you.

10 But I rejoiced in the Lord greatly that now at last your care for me has flourished again; though you surely did care, but you lacked opportunity.

11 Not that I speak in regard to need, for I have learned in whatever state I am, to be content:

12 I know how to be abased, and I know how to abound. Everywhere and in all things I have learned both to be full and to be hungry, both to abound and to suffer need.

13 I can do all things through Christ who strengthens me.

14 Nevertheless you have done well that you shared in my distress.

15 Now you Philippians know also that in the beginning of the gospel, when I departed from Macedonia, no church shared with me concerning giving and receiving but you only.

16 For even in Thessalonica you sent *aid* once and again for my necessities.

17 Not that I seek the gift, but I seek the fruit that abounds to your account.

18 Indeed I have all and abound. I am full, having received from Epaphroditus the things *which were sent* from you, a sweet-smelling aroma, an acceptable sacrifice, well pleasing to God.

19 And my God shall supply all your need according to His riches in glory by Christ Jesus.

20 Now to our God and Father *be* glory forever and ever. Amen.

21 Greet every saint in Christ Jesus. The brethren who are with me greet you.

22 All the saints greet you, but especially those who are of Caesar's household.

23 The grace of our Lord Jesus Christ be with you all. Amen.

❤ REDIRECT YOUR THOUGHTS (4:8)

See Matthew 7:24-27, page 8

See Matthew 6:33-34, page 7   **244**

COLOSSIANS

PAUL, an apostle of Jesus Christ by the will of God, and Timothy our brother,

2 To the saints and faithful brethren in Christ *who are* in Colosse:

Grace to you and peace from God our Father and the Lord Jesus Christ.

3 We give thanks to the God and Father of our Lord Jesus Christ, praying always for you,

4 since we heard of your faith in Christ Jesus and of your love for all the saints;

5 because of the hope which is laid up for you in heaven, of which you heard before in the word of the truth of the gospel,

6 which has come to you, as *it has* also in all the world, and is bringing forth fruit, as *it is* also among you since the day you heard and knew the grace of God in truth;

7 as you also learned from Epaphras, our dear fellow servant, who is a faithful minister of Christ on your behalf,

8 who also declared to us your love in the Spirit.

9 For this reason we also, since the day we heard it, do not cease to pray for you, and to ask that you may be filled with the knowledge of His will in all wisdom and spiritual understanding;

10 that you may have a walk worthy of the Lord, fully pleasing *Him*, being fruitful in every good work and increasing in the knowledge of God;

11 strengthened with all might, according to His glorious power, for all patience and longsuffering with joy;

12 giving thanks to the Father who has qualified us to be partakers of the inheritance of the saints in the light.

13 He has delivered us from the power of darkness and translated *us* into the kingdom of the Son of His love,

14 in whom we have redemption through His blood, the forgiveness of sins.

15 He is the image of the invisible God, the firstborn over all creation.

16 For by Him all things were created that are in heaven and that are on earth, visible and invisible, whether thrones or dominions or principalities or powers. All things were created through Him and for Him.

17 And He is before all things, and in Him all things consist.

18 And He is the head of the body, the church, who is the beginning, the firstborn from the dead, that in all things He may have the preeminence.

19 For it pleased *the Father that* in Him all the fullness should dwell,

20 and by Him to reconcile all things to Himself, by Him, whether things on earth or things in heaven, having made peace through the blood of His cross.

21 And you, who once were alienated and enemies in your mind by wicked works, yet now He has reconciled

22 in the body of His flesh through death, to present you holy, and blameless, and irreproachable in His sight—

23 if indeed you continue in the faith, grounded and steadfast, and are not moved away from the hope of the gospel which you heard, which was preached to every creature under heaven, of which I, Paul, became a minister.

24 I now rejoice in my sufferings for you, and fill up in my flesh what is lacking in the afflictions of Christ, for the sake of His body, which is the church,

25 of which I became a minister

according to the stewardship from God which was given to me for you, to fulfill the word of God,

26 the mystery which has been hidden from ages and from generations, but now has been revealed to His saints.

27 To them God willed to make known what are the riches of the glory of this mystery among the Gentiles: which is Christ in you, the hope of glory.

28 Him we preach, warning every man and teaching every man in all wisdom, that we may present every man perfect in Christ Jesus.

29 To this *end* I also labor, striving according to His working which works in me mightily.

2 For I want you to know what a great conflict I have for you and those in Laodicea, and *for* as many as have not seen my face in the flesh,

2 that their hearts may be encouraged, being knit together in love, and *attaining* to all riches of the full assurance of understanding, to the knowledge of the mystery of God, both of the Father and of Christ,

3 in whom are hidden all the treasures of wisdom and knowledge.

4 Now this I say lest anyone should deceive you with persuasive words.

5 For though I am absent in the flesh, yet I am with you in spirit, rejoicing to see your *good* order and the steadfastness of your faith in Christ.

6 As you have therefore received Christ Jesus the Lord, so walk in Him,

7 rooted and built up in Him and established in the faith, as you have been taught, abounding in it with thanksgiving.

❤ 8 Beware lest anyone cheat you through philosophy and empty deceit, according to the tradition of men, according to the basic principles of the world, and not according to Christ.

9 For in Him dwells all the fullness of the Godhead bodily;

10 and you are complete in Him, who is the head of all principality and power.

11 In Him you were also circumcised with the circumcision made without hands, by putting off the body of the sins of the flesh, by the circumcision of Christ,

12 buried with Him in baptism, in which you also were raised with *Him* through faith in the working of God, who raised Him from the dead.

13 And you, being dead in your trespasses and the uncircumcision of your flesh, He has made alive together with Him, having forgiven you all trespasses,

14 having wiped out the handwriting of requirements that was against us, which was contrary to us. And He has taken it out of the way, having nailed it to the cross.

15 Having disarmed principalities and powers, He made a public spectacle of them, triumphing over them in it.

16 Therefore let no one judge you in food or in drink, or regarding a festival or a new moon or sabbaths,

17 which are a shadow of things to come, but the substance is of Christ.

18 Let no one defraud you of your reward, taking delight in *false* humility and worship of angels, intruding into those things which he has not seen, vainly puffed up by his fleshly mind,

19 and not holding fast to the Head, from whom all the body, nourished and knit together by joints and ligaments, grows with the increase *which is* from God.

20 Therefore, if you died with Christ from the basic principles of the world, why, as *though* living in the world, do you subject yourselves to regulations—

21 "Do not touch, do not taste, do not handle,"

See 2 Corinthians 5:21, page 223

22 which all concern things which perish with the using—according to the commandments and doctrines of men?

23 These things indeed have an appearance of wisdom in self-imposed religion, *false* humility, and neglect of the body, *but are* of no value against the indulgence of the flesh.

3 If then you were raised with Christ, seek those things which are above, where Christ is, sitting at the right hand of God.

2 Set your mind on things above, not on things on the earth.

3 For you died, and your life is hidden with Christ in God.

4 When Christ *who is* our life appears, then you also will appear with Him in glory.

5 Therefore put to death your members which are on the earth: fornication, uncleanness, passion, evil desire, and covetousness, which is idolatry.

6 Because of these things the wrath of God is coming upon the sons of disobedience,

7 in which you also once walked when you lived in them.

8 But now you must also put off all these: anger, wrath, malice, blasphemy, filthy language out of your mouth.

9 Do not lie to one another, since you have put off the old man with his deeds,

10 and have put on the new *man* who is renewed in knowledge according to the image of Him who created him,

11 where there is neither Greek nor Jew, circumcised nor uncircumcised, barbarian, Scythian, slave *nor* free, but Christ *is* all and in all.

12 Therefore, as *the* elect of God, holy and beloved, put on tender mercies, kindness, humbleness of mind, meekness, longsuffering;

13 bearing with one another, and forgiving one another, if anyone has a complaint against another; even as Christ forgave you, so you also *must do.*

14 But above all these things put on love, which is the bond of perfection.

15 And let the peace of God rule in your hearts, to which also you were called in one body; and be thankful.

16 Let the word of Christ dwell in you richly in all wisdom, teaching and admonishing one another in psalms and hymns and spiritual songs, singing with grace in your hearts to the Lord.

17 And *whatever* you do in word or deed, *do* all in the name of the Lord Jesus, giving thanks to God the Father through Him.

18 Wives, submit to your own husbands, as is fitting in the Lord.

19 Husbands, love your wives and do not be bitter toward them.

20 Children, obey your parents in all things, for this is well pleasing to the Lord.

21 Fathers, do not provoke your children, lest they become discouraged.

22 Servants, obey in all things your masters according to the flesh, not with eyeservice, as men-pleasers, but in sincerity of heart, fearing God.

23 And whatever you do, do it heartily, as to the Lord and not to men,

24 knowing that from the Lord you will receive the reward of the inheritance; for you serve the Lord Christ.

25 But he who does wrong will be repaid for *the wrong* which he has done, and there is no partiality.

4 Masters, give your servants what is just and fair, knowing that you also have a Master in heaven.

2 Continue earnestly in prayer, being vigilant in it with thanksgiving;

3 meanwhile praying also for us,

that God would open to us a door for the word, to speak the mystery of Christ, for which I am also in chains,

4 that I may make it manifest, as I ought to speak.

5 Walk in wisdom toward those *who are* outside, redeeming the time.

6 *Let* your speech always *be* with grace, seasoned with salt, that you may know how you ought to answer each one.

7 Tychicus, *who is* a beloved brother, a faithful minister, and a fellow servant in the Lord, will tell you all the news about me.

8 I am sending him to you for this very purpose, that he may know your circumstances and comfort your hearts,

9 with Onesimus, a faithful and beloved brother, who is *one* of you. They will make known to you all things which *are happening* here.

10 Aristarchus my fellow prisoner greets you, with Mark the cousin of Barnabas (about whom you received instructions: if he comes to you, welcome him),

11 and Jesus who is called Justus. These *are my* only fellow workers for the kingdom of God who are of the circumcision; they have proved to be a comfort to me.

12 Epaphras, who is *one* of you, a servant of Christ, greets you, always laboring fervently for you in prayers, that you may stand perfect and complete in all the will of God.

13 For I bear him witness that he has a great zeal for you, and those who are in Laodicea, and those in Hierapolis.

14 Luke the beloved physician and Demas greet you.

15 Greet the brethren who are in Laodicea, and Nymphas and the church that *is* in his house.

16 Now when this epistle is read among you, see that it is read also in the church of the Laodiceans, and that you likewise read the epistle from Laodicea.

17 And say to Archippus, "Take heed to the ministry which you have received in the Lord, that you may fulfill it."

18 This salutation by my own hand—Paul. Remember my chains. Grace *be* with you. Amen.

THE FIRST EPISTLE OF PAUL THE APOSTLE TO THE

THESSALONIANS

PAUL, Silvanus, and Timothy,

To the church of the Thessalonians in God the Father and the Lord Jesus Christ:

Grace to you and peace from God our Father and the Lord Jesus Christ.

2 We give thanks to God always for you all, making mention of you in our prayers,

3 remembering without ceasing your work of faith, labor of love, and patience of hope in our Lord Jesus Christ in the sight of our God and Father,

4 knowing, beloved brethren, your election by God.

5 For our gospel did not come to you in word only, but also in power, and in the Holy Spirit and in much assurance, as you know what kind of men we were among you for your sake.

6 And you became followers of us and of the Lord, having received the word in much affliction, with joy of the Holy Spirit,

7 so that you became examples to all in Macedonia and Achaia who believe.

8 For from you the word of the Lord has sounded forth, not only in Macedonia and Achaia, but also in every place. Your faith toward God has gone out, so that we do not need to say anything.

9 For they themselves declare concerning us what manner of entry we had to you, and how you turned to God from idols to serve the living and true God,

10 and to wait for His Son from heaven, whom He raised from the dead, *even* Jesus who delivers us from the wrath to come.

2 For you yourselves know, brethren, that our coming to you was not in vain.

2 But even after we had suffered before and were spitefully treated at Philippi, as you know, we were bold in our God to speak to you the gospel of God in much conflict.

3 For our exhortation *did* not *come* from deceit or uncleanness, nor *was it* in guile.

4 But as we have been approved by God to be entrusted with the gospel, even so we speak, not as pleasing men, but God who tests our hearts.

5 For neither at any time did we use flattering words, as you know, nor a cloak for covetousness—God *is* witness.

6 Nor did we seek glory from men, either from you or from others, when we might have made demands as apostles of Christ.

7 But we were gentle among you, just as a nursing *mother* cherishes her own children.

8 So, affectionately longing for you, we were well pleased to impart to you not only the gospel of God, but also our own lives, because you had become dear to us.

9 For you remember, brethren, our labor and toil; for laboring night and day, that we might not be a burden to any of you, we preached to you the gospel of God.

10 You *are* witnesses, and God *also*, how devoutly and justly and blamelessly we behaved ourselves among you who believe;

11 as you know how we exhorted, and comforted, and charged every one of you, as a father *does* his own children,

12 that you would have a walk worthy of God who calls you into His own kingdom and glory.

13 For this reason we also thank God without ceasing, because when you received the word of God which you heard from us, you welcomed *it* not *as* the word of men, but as it is in truth, the word of God, which also effectively works in you who believe.

14 For you, brethren, became imitators of the churches of God which are in Judea in Christ Jesus. For you also suffered the same things from your own countrymen, just as they *did* from the Jews,

15 who killed both the Lord Jesus and their own prophets, and have persecuted us; and they do not please God and are contrary to all men,

16 forbidding us to speak to the Gentiles that they may be saved, so as always to fill up *the measure of* their sins; but wrath has come upon them to the uttermost.

17 But we, brethren, having been taken away from you for a short time in presence, not in heart, endeavored more eagerly to see your face with great desire.

18 Therefore we wanted to come to you—even I, Paul, time and again—but Satan hindered us.

19 For what *is* our hope, or joy, or crown of rejoicing? *Is it* not even you in the presence of our Lord Jesus Christ at His coming?

20 For you are our glory and joy.

3 Therefore, when we could no longer endure it, we thought it good to be left in Athens alone,

2 and sent Timothy, our brother and minister of God, and our fellow laborer in the gospel of Christ, to establish you and encourage you concerning your faith,

3 that no one should be shaken by these afflictions; for you yourselves know that we are appointed to this.

4 For, in fact, we told you before when we were with you that we would suffer tribulation, just as it happened, and you know.

5 For this reason, when I could no longer endure it, I sent to know your faith, lest by some means the tempter had tempted you, and our labor might be in vain.

6 But now that Timothy has come to us from you, and brought us good news of your faith and love, and that you always have good remembrance of us, greatly desiring to see us, as we also *to see* you—

7 therefore, brethren, in all our affliction and distress we were comforted concerning you by your faith.

8 For now we live, if you stand fast in the Lord.

9 For what thanks can we render to God for you, for all the joy with which we rejoice for your sake before our God,

10 night and day praying exceedingly that we may see your face and perfect what is lacking in your faith?

11 Now may our God and Father Himself, and our Lord Jesus Christ, direct our way to you.

12 And may the Lord make you increase and abound in love to one another and to all, just as we *do* to you,

13 so that He may establish your hearts blameless in holiness before our God and Father at the coming of our Lord Jesus Christ with all His saints.

4 Finally then, brethren, we urge and exhort in the Lord Jesus that you should abound more and

more, just as you received from us how you ought to walk and to please God;

2 for you know what commandments we gave you through the Lord Jesus.

3 For this is the will of God, your sanctification: that you should abstain from sexual immorality;

4 that each of you should know how to possess his own vessel in sanctification and honor,

5 not in passion of lust, like the Gentiles who do not know God;

6 that no one should take advantage of and defraud his brother in this matter, because the Lord *is* the avenger of all such, as we also forewarned you and testified.

7 For God did not call us to uncleanness, but in holiness.

8 Therefore he who rejects *this* does not reject man, but God, who has also given us His Holy Spirit.

9 But concerning brotherly love you have no need that I should write to you, for you yourselves are taught by God to love one another;

10 and indeed you do so toward all the brethren who are in all Macedonia. But we urge you, brethren, that you increase more and more;

11 that you also aspire to lead a quiet life, to mind your own business, and to work with your own hands, as we commanded you,

12 that you may walk properly toward those who are outside, and *that* you may lack nothing.

13 But I do not want you to be ignorant, brethren, concerning those who have fallen asleep, lest you sorrow as others who have no hope.

14 For if we believe that Jesus died and rose again, even so God will bring with Him those who sleep in Jesus.

15 For this we say to you by the word of the Lord, that we who are alive *and* remain until the coming of the Lord will by no means precede those who are asleep.

16 For the Lord Himself will descend from heaven with a shout, with the voice of an archangel, and with the trumpet of God. And the dead in Christ will rise first.

17 Then we who are alive *and* remain shall be caught up together with them in the clouds to meet the Lord in the air. And thus we shall always be with the Lord.

18 Therefore comfort one another with these words.

5 But concerning the times and the seasons, brethren, you have no need that I should write to you.

2 For you yourselves know perfectly that the day of the Lord so comes as a thief in the night.

3 For when they say, "Peace and safety!" then sudden destruction comes upon them, as labor pains upon a pregnant woman. And they shall not escape.

4 But you, brethren, are not in darkness, so that this Day should overtake you as a thief.

5 You are all sons of light and sons of the day. We are not of the night nor of darkness.

6 Therefore let us not sleep, as others *do*, but let us watch and be sober.

7 For those who sleep, sleep at night, and those who get drunk are drunk at night.

8 But let us who are of the day be sober, putting on the breastplate of faith and love, and *as* a helmet the hope of salvation.

9 For God did not appoint us to wrath, but to obtain salvation through our Lord Jesus Christ,

10 who died for us, that whether we wake or sleep, we should live together with Him.

11 Therefore comfort each other and edify one another, just as you also are doing.

12 And we urge you, brethren, to recognize those who labor among you, and are over you in the Lord and admonish you,

13 and to esteem them very highly in love for their work's sake. Be at peace among yourselves.

14 Now we exhort you, brethren, warn those who are unruly, comfort the fainthearted, uphold the weak, be patient with all.

15 See that no one renders evil for evil to anyone, but always pursue what is good both for yourselves and for all.

16 Rejoice always,

17 pray without ceasing,

18 in everything give thanks; for this is the will of God in Christ Jesus for you.

19 Do not quench the Spirit.

20 Do not despise prophecies.

21 Test all things; hold fast what is good.

22 Abstain from every form of evil.

23 Now may the God of peace Himself sanctify you completely; and may your whole spirit, soul, and body be preserved blameless at the coming of our Lord Jesus Christ.

24 He who calls you *is* faithful, who also will do *it*.

25 Brethren, pray for us.

26 Greet all the brethren with a holy kiss.

27 I charge you by the Lord that this epistle be read to all the holy brethren.

28 The grace of our Lord Jesus Christ *be* with you. Amen.

THE SECOND EPISTLE OF PAUL THE APOSTLE TO THE

THESSALONIANS

PAUL, Silvanus, and Timothy,

To the church of the Thessalonians in God our Father and the Lord Jesus Christ:

2 Grace to you and peace from God our Father and the Lord Jesus Christ.

3 We are bound to thank God always for you, brethren, as it is fitting, because your faith grows exceedingly, and the love of every one of you all abounds toward each other,

4 so that we ourselves boast of you among the churches of God for your patience and faith in all your persecutions and tribulations that you endure,

5 *which is* manifest evidence of the righteous judgment of God, that you may be counted worthy of the kingdom of God, for which you also suffer;

6 since *it is* a righteous thing with God to repay with tribulation those who trouble you,

7 and to *give* you who are troubled rest with us when the Lord Jesus is revealed from heaven with His mighty angels,

8 in flaming fire taking vengeance on those who do not know God, and on those who do not obey the gospel of our Lord Jesus Christ.

9 These shall be punished with everlasting destruction from the presence of the Lord and from the glory of His power,

10 when He comes, in that Day, to be glorified in His saints and to be admired among all those who believe, because our testimony among you was believed.

11 Therefore we also pray always for you that our God would count you worthy of *this* calling, and fulfill all the good pleasure of His goodness and the work of faith with power,

12 that the name of our Lord Jesus Christ may be glorified in you, and you in Him, according to the grace of our God and the Lord Jesus Christ.

2 Now, brethren, concerning the coming of our Lord Jesus Christ and our gathering together to Him, we ask you,

2 not to be soon shaken in mind or troubled, either by spirit or by word or by letter, as if from us, as though the day of Christ had come.

3 Let no one deceive you by any means; for *that Day will not come* unless the falling away comes first, and the man of sin is revealed, the son of perdition,

4 who opposes and exalts himself above all that is called God or that is worshiped, so that he sits as God in the temple of God, showing himself that he is God.

5 Do you not remember that when I was still with you I told you these things?

6 And now you know what is restraining, that he may be revealed in his own time.

7 For the mystery of lawlessness is already at work; only He who now restrains *will do so* until He is taken out of the way.

8 And then the lawless one will be revealed, whom the Lord will consume with the breath of His mouth and destroy with the brightness of His coming.

9 The coming of the *lawless one* is according to the working of Satan, with all power, signs, and lying wonders,

10 and with all unrighteous deception among those who perish, because they did not receive the love of the truth, that they might be saved.

11 And for this reason God will send them strong delusion, that they should believe the lie,

12 that they all may be condemned who did not believe the truth but had pleasure in unrighteousness.

13 But we are bound to give thanks to God always for you, brethren beloved by the Lord, because God from the beginning chose you for salvation through sanctification by the Spirit and belief in the truth,

14 to which He called you by our gospel, for the obtaining of the glory of our Lord Jesus Christ.

15 Therefore, brethren, stand fast and hold the traditions which you were taught, whether by word or our epistle.

16 Now may our Lord Jesus Christ Himself, and our God and Father, who has loved us and given *us* everlasting consolation and good hope by grace,

17 comfort your hearts and establish you in every good word and work.

3 Finally, brethren, pray for us, that the word of the Lord may have *free* course and be glorified, just as *it is* with you,

2 and that we may be delivered from unreasonable and wicked men; for not all have faith.

3 But the Lord is faithful, who will establish you and guard *you* from the evil one.

4 And we have confidence in the Lord concerning you, both that you do and will do the things we command you.

5 Now may the Lord direct your hearts into the love of God and into the patience of Christ.

6 But we command you, brethren, in the name of our Lord Jesus Christ, that you withdraw from every brother who walks disorderly and not according to the tradition which he received from us.

7 For you yourselves know how you ought to follow us, for we were not disorderly among you;

8 nor did we eat anyone's bread free of charge, but worked with labor and toil night and day, that we might not be a burden to any of you,

9 not because we do not have authority, but to make ourselves an example of how you should follow us.

10 For even when we were with you, we commanded you this: If anyone will not work, neither shall he eat.

11 For we hear that there are some who walk among you in a disorderly manner, not working at all, but are busybodies.

12 Now those who are such we command and exhort through our Lord Jesus Christ that they work in quietness and eat their own bread.

13 But *as for* you, brethren, do not grow weary *in* doing good.

14 And if anyone does not obey our word in this epistle, note that person and do not keep company with him, that he may be ashamed.

15 Yet do not count *him* as an enemy, but admonish *him* as a brother.

16 Now may the Lord of peace Himself give you peace always in every way. The Lord *be* with you all.

17 The salutation of Paul with my own hand, which is a sign in every epistle; so I write.

18 The grace of our Lord Jesus Christ *be* with you all. Amen.

THE FIRST EPISTLE OF PAUL THE APOSTLE TO
TIMOTHY

PAUL, an apostle of Jesus Christ, by the commandment of God our Savior and the Lord Jesus Christ, our hope,

2 To Timothy, *my* true son in the faith:

Grace, mercy, *and* peace from God our Father and Jesus Christ our Lord.

3 As I urged you when I went into Macedonia—remain in Ephesus that you may charge some that they teach no other doctrine, 4 nor give heed to fables and endless genealogies, which cause disputes rather than godly edification which is in faith.

5 Now the purpose of the commandment is love from a pure heart, *from* a good conscience, and *from* sincere faith,

6 from which some, having strayed, have turned aside to idle talk,

7 desiring to be teachers of the law, understanding neither what they say nor the things which they affirm.

8 But we know that the law *is* good if one uses it lawfully,

9 knowing this: that the law is not made for a righteous person, but for *the* lawless and insubordinate, for *the* ungodly and for sinners, for *the* unholy and profane, for murderers of fathers and murderers of mothers, for manslayers, 10 for fornicators, for sodomites, for kidnappers, for liars, for perjurers, and if there is any other thing that is contrary to sound doctrine, 11 according to the glorious gospel of the blessed God which was committed to my trust.

12 And I thank Christ Jesus our Lord who has enabled me, because He counted me faithful, putting *me* into the ministry,

13 although I was formerly a blasphemer, a persecutor, and an insolent man; but I obtained mercy because I did *it* ignorantly in unbelief.

14 And the grace of our Lord was exceedingly abundant, with faith and love which are in Christ Jesus.

15 This *is* a faithful saying and worthy of all acceptance, that Christ Jesus came into the world to save sinners, of whom I am chief.

16 However, for this reason I obtained mercy, that in me first Jesus Christ might show all longsuffering, as a pattern to those who are going to believe on Him for everlasting life.

17 Now to the King eternal, immortal, invisible, to God who alone is wise, *be* honor and glory forever and ever. Amen.

18 This charge I commit to you, son Timothy, according to the prophecies previously made concerning you, that by them you may wage the good warfare,

19 having faith and a good conscience, which some having rejected, concerning the faith have suffered shipwreck,

20 of whom are Hymenaeus and Alexander, whom I delivered to Satan that they may learn not to blaspheme.

2 Therefore I exhort first of all that supplications, prayers, intercessions, *and* giving of thanks be made for all men,

2 for kings and all who are in authority, that we may lead a quiet and peaceable life in all godliness and reverence.

3 For this *is* good and acceptable in the sight of God our Savior,

4 who desires all men to be saved and to come to the knowledge of the truth.

5 For *there is* one God and one Mediator between God and men, *the* Man Christ Jesus,

6 who gave Himself a ransom for all, to be testified in due time,

7 for which I was appointed a preacher and an apostle—I am speaking the truth in Christ *and* not lying—a teacher of the Gentiles in faith and truth.

8 Therefore I desire that the men pray everywhere, lifting up holy hands, without wrath and doubting;

9 in like manner also, that the women adorn themselves in modest apparel, with propriety and moderation, not with braided hair or gold or pearls or costly clothing,

10 but, which is proper for women professing godliness, with good works.

11 Let a woman learn in silence with all submission.

12 And I do not permit a woman to teach or to have authority over a man, but to be in silence.

13 For Adam was formed first, then Eve.

14 And Adam was not deceived, but the woman being deceived, fell into transgression.

15 Nevertheless she will be saved in childbearing if they continue in faith, love, and holiness, with self-control.

3 This *is* a faithful saying: If a man desires the position of a bishop, he desires a good work.

2 A bishop then must be blameless, the husband of one wife, temperate, sober-minded, of good behavior, hospitable, able to teach;

3 not given to wine, not violent, not greedy for money, but gentle, not quarrelsome, not covetous;

4 one who rules his own house well, having *his* children in submission with all reverence

5 (for if a man does not know how to rule his own house, how will he take care of the church of God?);

6 not a novice, lest being puffed up with pride he fall into the *same* condemnation as the devil.

7 Moreover he must have a good testimony among those who are outside, lest he fall into reproach and the snare of the devil.

8 Likewise deacons *must be* reverent, not double-tongued, not given to much wine, not greedy for money,

9 holding the mystery of the faith with a pure conscience.

10 But let these also first be proved; then let them serve as deacons, being *found* blameless.

11 Likewise *their* wives *must be* reverent, not slanderers, temperate, faithful in all things.

12 Let deacons be the husbands of one wife, ruling *their* children and their own houses well.

13 For those who have served well as deacons obtain for themselves a good standing and great boldness in the faith which is in Christ Jesus.

14 These things I write to you, though I hope to come to you shortly;

15 but if I am delayed, *I write* so that you may know how you ought to conduct yourself in the house of God, which is the church of the living God, the pillar and ground of the truth.

16 And without controversy great is the mystery of godliness:

> God was manifested in the flesh,
> Justified in the Spirit,
> Seen by angels,
> Preached among the Gentiles,
> Believed on in the world,
> Received up in glory.

4 Now the Spirit expressly says that in latter times some will depart from the faith, giving heed to deceiving spirits and doctrines of demons,

2 speaking lies in hypocrisy, having their own conscience seared with a hot iron,

3 forbidding to marry, *and commanding* to abstain from foods

which God created to be received with thanksgiving by those who believe and know the truth.

4 For every creature of God *is* good, and nothing is to be refused if it is received with thanksgiving;

5 for it is sanctified by the word of God and prayer.

6 If you instruct the brethren in these things, you will be a good minister of Jesus Christ, nourished in the words of faith and of the good doctrine which you have carefully followed.

7 But reject profane and old wives' fables, and exercise yourself *rather* to godliness.

8 For bodily exercise profits a little, but godliness is profitable for all things, having promise of the life that now is and of that which is to come.

9 This *is* a faithful saying and worthy of all acceptance.

10 For to this *end* we both labor and suffer reproach, because we trust in the living God, who is *the* Savior of all men, especially of those who believe.

11 These things command and teach.

12 Let no one despise your youth, but be an example to the believers in word, in conduct, in love, in spirit, in faith, in purity.

13 Till I come, give attention to reading, to exhortation, to doctrine.

14 Do not neglect the gift that is in you, which was given to you by prophecy with the laying on of the hands of the presbytery.

15 Meditate on these things; give yourself entirely to them, that your progress may be evident to all.

16 Take heed to yourself and to the doctrine. Continue in them, for in doing this you will save both yourself and those who hear you.

5 Do not rebuke an older man, but exhort *him* as a father, *the* younger men as brothers,

2 *the* older women as mothers, *the* younger as sisters, with all purity.

3 Honor widows who are really widows.

4 But if any widow has children or grandchildren, let them first learn to show piety at home and to repay their parents; for this is good and acceptable before God.

5 Now she who is really a widow, and left alone, trusts in God and continues in supplications and prayers night and day.

6 But she who lives in pleasure is dead while she lives.

7 And these things command, that they may be blameless.

8 But if anyone does not provide for his own, and especially for those of his household, he has denied the faith and is worse than an unbeliever.

9 Do not let a widow under sixty years old be taken into the number, *and not unless* she has been the wife of one man,

10 well reported for good works: if she has brought up children, if she has lodged strangers, if she has washed the saints' feet, if she has relieved the afflicted, if she has diligently followed every good work.

11 But refuse *the* younger widows; for when they have begun to grow wanton against Christ, they desire to marry,

12 having condemnation because they have cast off their first faith.

13 And besides they learn *to be* idle, wandering about from house to house, and not only idle but also gossips and busybodies, saying things which they ought not.

14 Therefore I desire that *the* younger *widows* marry, bear children, manage the house, give no opportunity to the adversary to speak reproachfully.

15 For some have already turned aside after Satan.

16 If any believing man or woman has widows, let them relieve them,

and do not let the church be burdened, that it may relieve those who are really widows.

17 Let the elders who rule well be counted worthy of double honor, especially those who labor in the word and doctrine.

18 For the Scripture says, *"You shall not muzzle an ox while it treads out the grain,"* and, "The laborer *is* worthy of his wages."

19 Do not receive an accusation against an elder except from two or three witnesses.

20 Those who are sinning rebuke in the presence of all, that the rest also may fear.

21 I charge *you* before God and the Lord Jesus Christ and the elect angels that you observe these things without prejudice, doing nothing with partiality.

22 Do not lay hands on anyone hastily, nor share in other people's sins; keep yourself pure.

23 No longer drink only water, but use a little wine for your stomach's sake and your frequent infirmities.

24 Some men's sins are clearly evident, preceding *them* to judgment, but those of some *men* follow later.

25 Likewise, the good works *of some* are clearly evident, and those that are otherwise cannot be hidden.

6 Let as many servants as are under the yoke count their own masters worthy of all honor, so that the name of God and *His* doctrine may not be blasphemed.

2 And those who have believing masters, let them not despise *them* because they are brethren, but rather serve *them* because those who are benefited are believers and beloved. Teach and exhort these things.

3 If anyone teaches otherwise and does not consent to wholesome words, *even* the words of our Lord Jesus Christ, and to the doctrine which is according to godliness,

4 he is proud, knowing nothing, but is obsessed with disputes and arguments over words, from which come envy, strife, reviling, evil suspicions,

5 useless wranglings of men of corrupt minds and destitute of the truth, who suppose that godliness is a *means of* gain. From such withdraw yourself.

6 But godliness with contentment is great gain.

7 For we brought nothing into *this* world, *and it is* certain we can carry nothing out.

8 And having food and clothing, with these we shall be content.

9 But those who desire to be rich fall into temptation and a snare, and *into* many foolish and harmful lusts which drown men in destruction and perdition.

10 For the love of money is a root of all *kinds of* evil, for which some have strayed from the faith in their greediness, and pierced themselves through with many sorrows.

11 But you, O man of God, flee these things and pursue righteousness, godliness, faith, love, patience, gentleness.

12 Fight the good fight of faith, lay hold on eternal life, to which you were also called and have confessed the good confession in the presence of many witnesses.

13 I urge you in the sight of God who gives life to all things, and *before* Christ Jesus who witnessed the good confession before Pontius Pilate,

14 that you keep *this* commandment without spot, blameless until our Lord Jesus Christ's appearing,

15 which He will manifest in His own time, *He who is* the blessed and only Potentate, the King of kings and Lord of lords,

16 who alone has immortality, dwelling in unapproachable light, whom no man has seen or can see, to whom *be* honor and everlasting power. Amen.

17 Command those who are rich in this present age not to be haughty, nor to trust in uncertain riches but in the living God, who gives us richly all things to enjoy.

18 *Let them* do good, that they be rich in good works, ready to give, willing to share,

19 storing up for themselves a good foundation for the time to come, that they may lay hold on eternal life.

20 O Timothy! Guard what was committed to your trust, avoiding the profane *and* vain babblings and contradictions of what is falsely called knowledge—

21 by professing it, some have strayed concerning the faith. Grace *be* with you. Amen.

THE SECOND EPISTLE OF PAUL THE APOSTLE TO

TIMOTHY

PAUL, an apostle of Jesus Christ by the will of God, according to the promise of life which is in Christ Jesus,

2 To Timothy, *my* beloved son:

Grace, mercy, *and* peace from God the Father and Christ Jesus our Lord.

3 I thank God, whom I serve with a pure conscience, as *my* forefathers *did*, as without ceasing I remember you in my prayers night and day,

4 greatly desiring to see you, being mindful of your tears, that I may be filled with joy,

5 when I call to remembrance the genuine faith that is in you, which dwelt first in your grandmother Lois and your mother Eunice, and I am persuaded is in you also.

6 Therefore I remind you to stir up the gift of God which is in you through the laying on of my hands.

7 For God has not given us a spirit of fear, but of power and of love and of a sound mind.

8 Therefore do not be ashamed of the testimony of our Lord, nor of me His prisoner, but share with me in the sufferings for the gospel according to the power of God,

9 who has saved us and called *us* with a holy calling, not according to our works, but according to His own purpose and grace which was given to us in Christ Jesus before time began,

10 but has now been revealed by the appearing of our Savior Jesus Christ, *who* has abolished death and brought life and immortality to light through the gospel,

11 to which I was appointed a preacher, an apostle, and a teacher of the Gentiles.

12 For this reason I also suffer these things; nevertheless I am not ashamed, for I know whom I have believed and am persuaded that He is able to keep what I have committed to Him until that Day.

13 Hold fast the pattern of sound words which you have heard from me, in faith and love which are in Christ Jesus.

14 That good thing which was committed to you, keep by the Holy Spirit who dwells in us.

15 This you know, that all those in Asia have turned away from me, among whom are Phygellus and Hermogenes.

16 The Lord grant mercy to the household of Onesiphorus, for he often refreshed me, and was not ashamed of my chain;

17 but when he arrived in Rome, he sought me out very diligently and found *me.*

18 The Lord grant to him that he may find mercy from the Lord in that Day—and you know very well how many ways he ministered to me at Ephesus.

2 You therefore, my son, be strong in the grace that is in Christ Jesus.

2 And the things that you have heard from me among many witnesses, commit these to faithful men who will be able to teach others also.

3 You therefore must endure hardship as a good soldier of Jesus Christ.

4 No one engaged in warfare entangles himself with the affairs of *this* life, that he may please him who enlisted him as a soldier.

5 And also if anyone competes in athletics, he is not crowned unless he competes according to the rules.

6 The hard-working farmer must be first to partake of the crops.

7 Consider what I say, and may the Lord give you understanding in all things.

8 Remember that Jesus Christ, of the seed of David, was raised from the dead according to my gospel,

9 for which I suffer trouble as an evildoer, *even* to the point of chains; but the word of God is not chained.

10 Therefore I endure all things for the sake of the elect, that they also may obtain the salvation which is in Christ Jesus with eternal glory.

11 *This is* a faithful saying:

For if we died with *Him,*
  We shall also live with *Him.*
12 If we endure,
  We shall also reign with *Him.*
If we deny *Him,*
  He also will deny us.
13 If we are faithless,
  He remains faithful;
  He cannot deny Himself.

14 Remind *them* of these things, charging *them* before the Lord not to strive about words to no profit, to the ruin of the hearers.

15 Be diligent to present yourself approved to God, a worker who does not need to be ashamed, rightly dividing the word of truth.

16 But shun profane *and* vain babblings, for they will increase to more ungodliness.

17 And their message will spread like cancer. Hymenaeus and Philetus are of this sort,

18 who have strayed concerning the truth, saying that the resurrection is already past; and they overthrow the faith of some.

19 Nevertheless the solid foundation of God stands, having this seal: "The Lord knows those who are His," and, "Let everyone who names the name of Christ depart from iniquity."

20 But in a great house there are not only vessels of gold and silver, but also of wood and clay, some for honor and some for dishonor.

21 Therefore if anyone cleanses himself from the latter, he will be a vessel for honor, sanctified and useful for the Master, prepared for every good work.

22 Flee also youthful lusts; but pursue righteousness, faith, love, peace with those who call on the Lord out of a pure heart.

23 But avoid foolish and ignorant disputes, knowing that they generate strife.

24 And a servant of the Lord must not quarrel but be gentle to all, able to teach, patient,

25 in humility correcting those who are in opposition, if God perhaps will grant them repentance, so that they may know the truth,

26 and *that* they may come to their senses *and escape* the snare of the devil, having been taken captive by him to *do* his will.

3 But know this, that in the last days perilous times will come:

2 For men will be lovers of them-

selves, lovers of money, boasters, proud, blasphemers, disobedient to parents, unthankful, unholy,

3 unloving, unforgiving, slanderers, without self-control, brutal, despisers of good,

4 traitors, headstrong, haughty, lovers of pleasure rather than lovers of God,

5 having a form of godliness but denying its power. And from such people turn away!

6 For of this sort are those who creep into households and make captives of gullible women loaded down with sins, led away by various lusts,

7 always learning and never able to come to the knowledge of the truth.

8 Now as Jannes and Jambres resisted Moses, so do these also resist the truth: men of corrupt minds, disapproved concerning the faith;

9 but they will progress no further, for their folly will be manifest to all, as theirs also was.

10 But you have carefully followed my doctrine, manner of life, purpose, faith, longsuffering, love, perseverance,

11 persecutions, afflictions, which happened to me at Antioch, at Iconium, at Lystra—what persecutions I endured. And out of *them* all the Lord delivered me.

12 Yes, and all who desire to live godly in Christ Jesus will suffer persecution.

13 But evil men and impostors will grow worse and worse, deceiving and being deceived.

14 But *as for* you, continue in the things which you have learned and been assured of, knowing from whom you have learned *them*,

15 and that from childhood you have known the Holy Scriptures, which are able to make you wise for salvation through faith which is in Christ Jesus.

16 All Scripture *is* given by inspiration of God, and *is* profitable for doctrine, for reproof, for correc-

tion, for instruction in righteousness,

17 that the man of God may be complete, thoroughly equipped for every good work.

4 I charge *you* therefore before God and the Lord Jesus Christ, who will judge the living and the dead at His appearing and His kingdom:

2 Preach the word! Be ready in season *and* out of season. Convince, rebuke, exhort, with all longsuffering and teaching.

3 For the time will come when they will not endure sound doctrine, but according to their own desires, *because* they have itching ears, they will heap up for themselves teachers;

4 and they will turn *their* ears away from the truth, and be turned aside to fables.

5 But you be watchful in all things, endure afflictions, do the work of an evangelist, fulfill your ministry.

6 For I am already being poured out *as a drink offering*, and the time of my departure is at hand.

7 I have fought the good fight, I have finished the race, I have kept the faith.

8 Finally, there is laid up for me the crown of righteousness, which the Lord, the righteous Judge, will give to me on that Day, and not to me only but also to all who have loved His appearing.

9 Be diligent to come to me quickly;

10 for Demas has forsaken me, having loved this present world, and has departed for Thessalonica—Crescens for Galatia, Titus for Dalmatia.

11 Only Luke is with me. Get Mark and bring him with you, for he is useful to me for ministry.

12 And Tychicus I have sent to Ephesus.

13 Bring the cloak that I left with Carpus at Troas when you come—

and the books, especially the parchments.

14 Alexander the coppersmith did me much harm. May the Lord repay him according to his works.

15 You also must beware of him, for he has greatly resisted our words.

16 At my first defense no one stood with me, but all forsook me. May it not be charged against them.

17 But the Lord stood with me and strengthened me, so that the message might be preached fully through me, and *that* all the Gentiles might hear. And I was delivered out of the mouth of the lion.

18 And the Lord will deliver me from every evil work and preserve *me* for His heavenly kingdom. To Him *be* glory forever and ever. Amen!

19 Greet Prisca and Aquila, and the household of Onesiphorus.

20 Erastus stayed in Corinth, but Trophimus I have left in Miletus sick.

21 Do your utmost to come before winter. Eubulus greets you, as well as Pudens, Linus, Claudia, and all the brethren.

22 The Lord Jesus Christ be with your spirit. Grace be with you. Amen.

THE EPISTLE OF PAUL THE APOSTLE TO

TITUS

PAUL, a servant of God and an apostle of Jesus Christ, according to the faith of God's elect and the acknowledgment of the truth which is according to godliness,

2 in hope of eternal life which God, who cannot lie, promised before time began,

3 but has in due time manifested His word through preaching, which was committed to me according to the commandment of God our Savior;

4 To Titus, *my* true son in *our* common faith:

Grace, mercy, *and* peace from God the Father and the Lord Jesus Christ our Savior.

5 For this reason I left you in Crete, that you should set in order the things that are lacking, and appoint elders in every city as I commanded you—

6 if a man is blameless, the husband of one wife, having faithful children not accused of dissipation or insubordination.

7 For a bishop must be blameless, as a steward of God, not self-willed, not quick-tempered, not given to wine, not violent, not greedy for money,

8 but hospitable, a lover of what is good, sober-minded, just, holy, self-controlled,

9 holding fast the faithful word as he has been taught, that he may be able, by sound doctrine, both to exhort and convict those who contradict.

10 For there are many insubordinate, both idle talkers and deceivers, especially those of the circumcision,

11 whose mouths must be stopped, who subvert whole households, teaching things which they ought not, for the sake of dishonest gain.

12 One of them, a prophet of their own, said, "Cretans *are* always liars, evil beasts, lazy gluttons."

13 This testimony is true. There-

fore rebuke them sharply, that they may be sound in the faith,

14 not giving heed to Jewish fables and commandments of men who turn from the truth.

15 To the pure all things are pure, but to those who are defiled and unbelieving nothing is pure; but even their mind and conscience are defiled.

16 They profess to know God, but in works they deny Him, being abominable, disobedient, and disqualified for every good work.

2 But as for you, speak the things which are proper for sound doctrine:

2 that the older men be sober, reverent, temperate, sound in faith, in love, in patience;

3 the older women likewise, that they be reverent in behavior, not slanderers, not given to much wine, teachers of good things—

4 that they admonish the young women to love their husbands, to love their children,

5 to be discreet, chaste, homemakers, good, obedient to their own husbands, that the word of God may not be blasphemed.

6 Likewise exhort the young men to be sober-minded,

7 in all things showing yourself *to be* a pattern of good works; in doctrine *showing* integrity, reverence, incorruptibility,

8 sound speech that cannot be condemned, that one who is an opponent may be ashamed, having nothing evil to say of you.

9 *Exhort* servants to be obedient to their own masters, to be well pleasing in all *things*, not answering back,

10 not pilfering, but showing all good fidelity, that they may adorn the doctrine of God our Savior in all things.

11 For the grace of God that brings salvation has appeared to all men,

12 teaching us that, denying un-

godliness and worldly lusts, we should live soberly, righteously, and godly in the present age,

13 looking for the blessed hope and glorious appearing of our great God and Savior Jesus Christ,

14 who gave Himself for us, that He might redeem us from every lawless deed and purify for Himself *His* own special people, zealous for good works.

15 Speak these things, exhort, and rebuke with all authority. Let no one despise you.

3 Remind them to be subject to rulers and authorities, to obey, to be ready for every good work,

2 to speak evil of no one, to be peaceable, gentle, showing all humility to all men.

3 For we ourselves were also once foolish, disobedient, deceived, serving various lusts and pleasures, living in malice and envy, hateful and hating one another. ♥

4 But when the kindness and the love of God our Savior toward man appeared,

5 not by works of righteousness which we have done, but according to His mercy He saved us, through the washing of regeneration and renewing of the Holy Spirit,

6 whom He poured out on us abundantly through Jesus Christ our Savior,

7 that having been justified by His grace we should become heirs according to the hope of eternal life.

8 This is a faithful saying, and these things I want you to affirm constantly, that those who have believed in God should be careful to maintain good works. These things are good and profitable to men.

9 But avoid foolish disputes, genealogies, contentions, and strivings about the law; for they are unprofitable and useless.

See Romans 8:1, page 193   262

10 Reject a divisive man after the first and second admonition,

11 knowing that such a person is warped and sinning, being self-condemned.

12 When I send Artemas to you, or Tychicus, be diligent to come to me at Nicopolis, for I have decided to spend the winter there.

13 Send Zenas the lawyer and Apollos on their journey with haste, that they may lack nothing.

14 And let our *people* also learn to maintain good works, to *meet* urgent needs, that they may not be unfruitful.

15 All who *are* with me greet you. Greet those who love us in the faith. Grace *be* with you all. Amen.

THE EPISTLE OF PAUL THE APOSTLE TO
PHILEMON

PAUL, a prisoner of Christ Jesus, and Timothy *our* brother,

To Philemon our beloved *friend* and fellow laborer,

2 to the beloved Apphia, Archippus our fellow soldier, and to the church in your house:

3 Grace to you and peace from God our Father and the Lord Jesus Christ.

4 I thank my God, making mention of you always in my prayers,

5 hearing of your love and faith which you have toward the Lord Jesus and toward all the saints,

6 that the sharing of your faith may become effective by the acknowledgment of every good thing which is in you in Christ Jesus.

7 For we have great joy and consolation in your love, because the hearts of the saints have been refreshed by you, brother.

8 Therefore, though I might be very bold in Christ to command you what is fitting,

9 *yet* for love's sake I rather appeal *to you*—being such a one as Paul, the aged, and now also a prisoner of Jesus Christ—

10 I appeal to you for my son Onesimus, whom I have begotten *while* in my chains,

11 who once was unprofitable to you, but now is profitable to you and to me.

12 I am sending him back. You therefore receive him, that is, my own heart,

13 whom I wished to keep with me, that on your behalf he might minister to me in my chains for the gospel.

14 But without your consent I wanted to do nothing, that your good deed might not be by compulsion, as it were, but voluntary.

15 For perhaps he departed for a while for this *purpose*, that you might receive him forever,

16 no longer as a slave but more than a slave, *as* a beloved brother, especially to me but how much more to you, both in the flesh and in the Lord.

17 If then you count me as a partner, receive him as *you would* me.

18 But if he has wronged you or owes *you* anything, put that on my account.

19 I, Paul, am writing with my own hand. I will repay—not to mention to you that you owe me even your own self besides.

20 Yes, brother, let me have joy

from you in the Lord; refresh my heart in the Lord.

21 Having confidence in your obedience, I write to you, knowing that you will do even more than I say.

22 But, meanwhile, also prepare a guest room for me, for I trust that through your prayers I shall be granted to you.

23 Epaphras, my fellow prisoner in Christ Jesus, greets you,

24 *as do* Mark, Aristarchus, Demas, Luke, my fellow laborers.

25 The grace of our Lord Jesus Christ *be* with your spirit. Amen.

THE EPISTLE TO THE
HEBREWS

GOD, who at various times and in different ways spoke in time past to the fathers by the prophets, 2 has in these last days spoken to us by *His* Son, whom He has appointed heir of all things, through whom also He made the worlds; 3 who being the brightness of *His* glory and the express image of His person, and upholding all things by the word of His power, when He had by Himself purged our sins, sat down at the right hand of the Majesty on high, 4 having become so much better than the angels, as He has by inheritance obtained a more excellent name than they.

5 For to which of the angels did He ever say:

"You are My Son,
  Today I have begotten You"?

And again:

"I will be to Him a Father,
  And He shall be to Me a Son"?

6 But when He again brings the firstborn into the world, He says:

"Let all the angels of God
  worship Him."

7 And of the angels He says:

"Who makes His angels spirits
  And His ministers a flame of
    fire."

8 But to the Son He *says*:

"Your throne, O God,
  is forever and ever;
A scepter of righteousness is
  the scepter of Your Kingdom.
9 You have loved righteousness
    and hated lawlessness;
Therefore God, Your God,
    has anointed You
With the oil of gladness more
    than Your companions."

10 And:

"You, LORD, in the beginning
  laid the foundation of the
    earth,
And the heavens are the work
  of Your hands;
11 They will perish, but You
    remain;
And they will all grow old
    like a garment;
12 Like a cloak You will fold them
    up,
And they will be changed.
But You are the same,
And Your years will not fail."

264

13 But to which of the angels has He ever said:

> "Sit at My right hand,
> Till I make Your enemies
>   Your footstool"?

14 Are they not all ministering spirits sent forth to minister for those who will inherit salvation?

2 Therefore we must give the more earnest heed to the things we have heard, lest we drift away.
2 For if the word spoken through angels proved steadfast, and every transgression and disobedience received a just reward,
3 how shall we escape if we neglect so great a salvation, which at the first began to be spoken by the Lord, and was confirmed to us by those who heard *Him*,
4 God also bearing witness both with signs and wonders, with various miracles, and gifts of the Holy Spirit, according to His own will?
5 For He has not put the world to come, of which we speak, in subjection to angels.
6 But one testified in a certain place, saying:

> "What is man that You
>   are mindful of him,
> Or the son of man that You
>   take care of him?
> 7 You made him a little lower
>   than the angels;
> You crowned him with glory
>   and honor,
> And set him over the works
>   of Your hands.
> 8 You have put all things
>   in subjection under his feet."

For in that He put all in subjection under him, He left nothing *that is* not put under him. But now we do not yet see all things put under him.
9 But we see Jesus, who was made a little lower than the angels, for the suffering of death crowned with glory and honor, that He, by the grace of God, might taste death for everyone.
10 For it was fitting for Him, for whom *are* all things and by whom *are* all things, in bringing many sons to glory, to make the author of their salvation perfect through sufferings.
11 For both He who sanctifies and those who are being sanctified *are* all of one, for which reason He is not ashamed to call them brethren,
12 saying:

> "I will declare Your name to My
>   brethren;
> In the midst of the
>   congregation I will sing
>   praise to You."

13 And again:

> "I will put My trust in Him."

And again:

> "Here am I and the children
>   whom God has given Me."

14 Inasmuch then as the children have partaken of flesh and blood, He Himself likewise shared in the same, that through death He might destroy him who had the power of death, that is, the devil,
15 and release those who through fear of death were all their lifetime subject to bondage.
16 For indeed He does not give aid to angels, but He does give aid to the seed of Abraham.
17 Therefore, in all things He had to be made like *His* brethren, that He might be a merciful and faithful High Priest in things *pertaining* to God, to make propitiation for the sins of the people.
18 For in that He Himself has suffered, being tempted, He is able to aid those who are tempted.

3 Therefore, holy brethren, partakers of the heavenly calling, consider the Apostle and High

Priest of our confession, Christ Jesus,

2 who was faithful to Him who appointed Him, as Moses also *was faithful* in all His house.

3 For this One has been counted worthy of more glory than Moses, inasmuch as He who built the house has more honor than the house.

4 For every house is built by someone, but He who built all things *is* God.

5 And Moses indeed *was* faithful in all His house as a servant, for a testimony of those things which would be spoken *afterward,*

6 but Christ as a Son over His own house, whose house we are if we hold fast the confidence and the rejoicing of the hope firm to the end.

7 Therefore, as the Holy Spirit says:

"Today, if you will hear His voice,
8 *Do not harden your hearts as in the rebellion,*
In the day of trial in the wilderness,
9 *Where your fathers tested Me, proved Me,*
And saw My works forty years.
10 *Therefore I was angry with that generation,*
And said, 'They always go astray in their heart,
And they have not known My ways.'
11 *So I swore in My wrath,*
'They shall not enter My rest.'"

12 Beware, brethren, lest there be in any of you an evil heart of unbelief in departing from the living God;

13 but exhort one another daily, while it is called *"Today,"* lest any of you be hardened through the deceitfulness of sin.

14 For we have become partakers of Christ if we hold the beginning of our confidence steadfast to the end,

15 while it is said:

"Today, if you will hear His voice,
Do not harden your hearts as in the rebellion."

16 For who, having heard, rebelled? Indeed, *was it* not all who came out of Egypt, *led* by Moses?

17 Now with whom was He angry forty years? *Was it* not with those who sinned, whose corpses fell in the wilderness?

18 And to whom did He swear that they would not enter His rest, but to those who did not obey?

19 So we see that they could not enter in because of unbelief.

4 Therefore, since a promise remains of entering His rest, let us fear lest any of you seem to have come short of it.

2 For indeed the gospel was preached to us as well as to them; but the word which they heard did not profit them, not being mixed with faith in those who heard *it.*

3 For we who have believed do enter that rest, as He has said:

"So I swore in My wrath,
'They shall not enter My rest,'"

although the works were finished from the foundation of the world.

4 For He has spoken in a certain place of the seventh *day* in this way: *"And God rested on the seventh day from all His works";*

5 and again in this place: *"They shall not enter My rest."*

6 Since therefore it remains that some *must* enter it, and those to whom it was first preached did not enter because of disobedience,

7 again He designates a certain day, saying in David, *"Today,"* after such a long time, as it has been said:

266

*"Today, if you will hear His
    voice,
    Do not harden your hearts."*

8 For if Joshua had given them rest, then He would not afterward have spoken of another day.

9 There remains therefore a rest for the people of God.

10 For he who has entered His rest has himself also ceased from his works as God *did* from His.

11 Let us therefore be diligent to enter that rest, lest anyone fall after the same example of disobedience.

12 For the word of God *is* living and powerful, and sharper than any two-edged sword, piercing even to the division of soul and spirit, and of joints and marrow, and is a discerner of the thoughts and intents of the heart.

13 And there is no creature hidden from His sight, but all things *are* naked and open to the eyes of Him to whom we *must give* account.

14 Seeing then that we have a great High Priest who has passed through the heavens, Jesus the Son of God, let us hold fast *our* confession.

15 For we do not have a High Priest who cannot sympathize with our weaknesses, but was in all *points* tempted as *we are, yet* without sin.

16 Let us therefore come boldly to the throne of grace, that we may obtain mercy and find grace to help in time of need.

5 For every high priest taken from among men is appointed for men in things *pertaining* to God, that he may offer both gifts and sacrifices for sins.

2 He can have compassion on those who are ignorant and going astray, since he himself is also beset by weakness.

3 Because of this he is required as for the people, so also for himself, to offer for sins.

4 And no man takes this honor to himself, but he who is called by God, just as Aaron *was.*

5 So also Christ did not glorify Himself to become High Priest, *but it* was He who said to Him:

*"You are My Son,
    Today I have begotten You."*

6 As *He* also *says* in another *place:*

*"You are a priest forever
    According to the order of
    Melchizedek";*

7 who, in the days of His flesh, when He had offered up prayers and supplications, with vehement cries and tears to Him who was able to save Him from death, and was heard because of His godly fear,

8 though He was a Son, *yet* He learned obedience by the things which He suffered.

9 And having been perfected, He became the author of eternal salvation to all who obey Him,

10 called by God as High Priest *"according to the order of Melchizedek,"*

11 of whom we have much to say, and hard to explain, since you have become dull of hearing.

12 For though by this time you ought to be teachers, you need *someone* to teach you again the first principles of the oracles of God; and you have come to need milk and not solid food.

13 For everyone who partakes *only* of milk *is* unskilled in the word of righteousness, for he is a babe.

14 But solid food belongs to those who are of full age, *that is,* those who by reason of use have their senses exercised to discern both good and evil.

6 Therefore, leaving the discussion of the elementary *principles* of Christ, let us go on to per-

fection, not laying again the foundation of repentance from dead works and of faith toward God,

2 of the doctrine of baptisms, of laying on of hands, of resurrection of the dead, and of eternal judgment.

3 And this we will do if God permits.

4 For *it is* impossible for those who were once enlightened, and have tasted the heavenly gift, and have become partakers of the Holy Spirit,

5 and have tasted the good word of God and the powers of the age to come,

6 if they fall away, to renew them again to repentance, since they crucify again for themselves the Son of God, and put *Him* to an open shame.

7 For the earth which drinks in the rain that often comes upon it, and bears herbs useful for those by whom it is cultivated, receives blessing from God;

8 but if it bears thorns and briars, *it is* rejected and near to being cursed, whose end *is* to be burned.

9 But, beloved, we are confident of better things concerning you, yes, things that accompany salvation, though we speak in this manner.

10 For God *is* not unjust to forget your work and labor of love which you have shown toward His name, *in that* you have ministered to the saints, and do minister.

11 And we desire that each one of you show the same diligence to the full assurance of hope until the end,

12 that you do not become sluggish, but imitate those who through faith and patience inherit the promises.

13 For when God made a promise to Abraham, because He could swear by no one greater, He swore by Himself,

14 saying, *"Surely blessing I will bless you, and multiplying I will multiply you."*

15 And so, after he had patiently endured, he obtained the promise.

16 For men indeed swear by the greater, and an oath for confirmation *is* for them an end of all dispute.

17 Thus God, determining to show more abundantly to the heirs of promise the immutability of His counsel, confirmed *it* by an oath,

18 that by two immutable things, in which it *is* impossible for God to lie, we might have strong consolation, who have fled for refuge to lay hold of the hope set before *us*.

19 This *hope* we have as an anchor of the soul, both sure and steadfast, and which enters the Presence *behind* the veil,

20 where the forerunner has entered for us, *even* Jesus, having become High Priest forever according to the order of Melchizedek.

7 For this Melchizedek, king of Salem, priest of the Most High God, who met Abraham returning from the slaughter of the kings and blessed him,

2 to whom also Abraham gave a tenth part of all, first being translated "king of righteousness," and then also king of Salem, meaning "king of peace,"

3 without father, without mother, without genealogy, having neither beginning of days nor end of life, but made like the Son of God, remains a priest continually.

4 Now consider how great this man *was*, to whom even the patriarch Abraham gave a tenth of the spoils.

5 And indeed those who are of the sons of Levi, who receive the priesthood, have a commandment to receive tithes from the people according to the law, that is, from their brethren, though they have come from the loins of Abraham;

6 but he whose genealogy is not

derived from them received tithes from Abraham and blessed him who had the promises.

7 Now beyond all contradiction the lesser is blessed by the better.

8 Here mortal men receive tithes, but there he *receives them,* of whom it is witnessed that he lives.

9 Even Levi, who receives tithes, paid tithes through Abraham, so to speak,

10 for he was still in the loins of his father when Melchizedek met him.

11 Therefore, if perfection were through the Levitical priesthood (for under it the people received the law), what further need *was there* that another priest should rise according to the order of Melchizedek, and not be called according to the order of Aaron?

12 For the priesthood being changed, of necessity there is also a change of the law.

13 For He of whom these things are spoken belongs to another tribe, from which no man has officiated at the altar.

14 For *it is* evident that our Lord arose from Judah, of which tribe Moses spoke nothing concerning priesthood.

15 And it is yet far more evident if, in the likeness of Melchizedek, there arises another priest

16 who has come, not according to the law of a fleshly commandment, but according to the power of an endless life.

17 For He testifies:

> *"You are a priest forever*
> *According to the order of*
> *Melchizedek."*

18 For on the one hand there is an annulling of the former commandment because of its weakness and unprofitableness,

19 for the law made nothing perfect; on the other hand, *there is* a bringing in of a better hope, through which we draw near to God.

20 And inasmuch as *He was* not *made priest* without an oath

21 (for they have become priests without an oath, but He with an oath by Him who said to Him:

> *"The* Lord *has sworn*
> *And will not relent,*
> *'You are a priest forever*
> *According to the order of*
> *Melchizedek' "*),

22 by so much more Jesus has become a surety of a better covenant.

23 And there were many priests, because they were prevented by death from continuing.

24 But He, because He continues forever, has an unchangeable priesthood.

25 Therefore He is also able to save to the uttermost those who come to God through Him, since He ever lives to make intercession for them.

26 For such a High Priest was fitting for us, *who is* holy, harmless, undefiled, separate from sinners, and has become higher than the heavens;

27 who does not need daily, as those high priests, to offer up sacrifices, first for His own sins and then for the people's, for this He did once for all when He offered up Himself.

28 For the law appoints as high priests men who have weakness, but the word of the oath, which came after the law, *appoints* the Son who has been perfected forever.

8 Now *this is* the main point of the things we are saying: We have such a High Priest, who is seated at the right hand of the throne of the Majesty in the heavens,

2 a Minister of the sanctuary and of the true tabernacle which the Lord erected, and not man.

3 For every high priest is appointed to offer both gifts and sac-

rifices. Therefore *it is* necessary that this One also have something to offer.

4 For if He were on earth, He would not be a priest, since there are priests who offer the gifts according to the law;

5 who serve the copy and shadow of the heavenly things, as Moses was divinely instructed when he was about to make the tabernacle. For He said, *"See that you make all things according to the pattern shown you on the mountain."*

6 But now He has obtained a more excellent ministry, inasmuch as He is also Mediator of a better covenant, which was established on better promises.

7 For if that first *covenant* had been faultless, then no place would have been sought for a second.

8 Because finding fault with them, He says: *"Behold, the days are coming, says the LORD, when I will make a new covenant with the house of Israel and with the house of Judah—*

9 *"not according to the covenant that I made with their fathers in the day when I took them by the hand to lead them out of the land of Egypt; because they did not continue in My covenant, and I disregarded them, says the LORD.*

10 *"For this is the covenant that I will make with the house of Israel after those days, says the LORD: I will put My laws in their mind and write them on their hearts; and I will be their God, and they shall be My people.*

11 *"None of them shall teach his neighbor, and none his brother, saying, 'Know the LORD,' for all shall know Me, from the least of them to the greatest of them.*

12 *"For I will be merciful to their unrighteousness, and their sins and their lawless deeds I will remember no more."*

13 In that He says, *"A new covenant,"* He has made the first obsolete. Now what is becoming obsolete and growing old is ready to vanish away.

9 Then indeed, even the first *covenant* had ordinances of divine service and the earthly sanctuary.

2 For a tabernacle was prepared: the first *part*, in which *was* the lampstand, the table, and the showbread, which is called the sanctuary;

3 and behind the second veil, the part of the tabernacle which is called the Holiest of All,

4 which had the golden altar of incense and the ark of the covenant overlaid on all sides with gold, in which *were* the golden pot that had the manna, Aaron's rod that budded, and the tablets of the covenant;

5 and above it were the cherubim of glory overshadowing the mercy seat. Of these things we cannot now speak in detail.

6 Now when these things had been thus prepared, the priests always went into the first part of the tabernacle, performing *the services.*

7 But into the second part the high priest *went* alone once a year, not without blood, which he offered for himself and *for* the people's sins *committed* in ignorance;

8 the Holy Spirit indicating this, that the way into the Holiest of All was not yet made manifest while the first tabernacle was still standing.

9 It *was* symbolic for the present time in which both gifts and sacrifices are offered which cannot make him who performed the service perfect in regard to the conscience—

10 *concerned* only with foods and drinks, various washings, and fleshly ordinances imposed until the time of reformation.

11 But Christ came *as* High Priest of the good things to come, with the greater and more perfect tabernacle not made with hands, that is, not of this creation.

12 Not with the blood of goats and calves, but with His own blood He entered the Most Holy Place once for all, having obtained eternal redemption.

13 For if the blood of bulls and goats and the ashes of a heifer, sprinkling the unclean, sanctifies for the purifying of the flesh,

14 how much more shall the blood of Christ, who through the eternal Spirit offered Himself without spot to God, purge your conscience from dead works to serve the living God?

15 And for this reason He is the Mediator of the new covenant, by means of death, for the redemption of the transgressions under the first covenant, that those who are called may receive the promise of the eternal inheritance.

16 For where there *is* a testament, there must also of necessity be the death of the testator.

17 For a testament *is* in force after men are dead, since it has no power at all while the testator lives.

18 Therefore not even the first *covenant* was dedicated without blood.

19 For when Moses had spoken every precept to all the people according to the law, he took the blood of calves and goats, with water, scarlet wool, and hyssop, and sprinkled both the book itself and all the people,

20 saying, *"This is the blood of the covenant which God has commanded you."*

21 Then likewise he sprinkled with blood both the tabernacle and all the vessels of the ministry.

22 And according to the law almost all things are purged with blood, and without shedding of blood there is no remission.

23 Therefore *it was* necessary that the copies of the things in the heavens should be purified with these, but the heavenly things

themselves with better sacrifices than these.

24 For Christ has not entered the holy places made with hands, *which are* copies of the true, but into heaven itself, now to appear in the presence of God for us;

25 not that He should offer Himself often, as the high priest enters the Most Holy Place every year with blood of another—

26 He then would have had to suffer often since the foundation of the world; but now, once at the end of the ages, He has appeared to put away sin by the sacrifice of Himself.

27 And as it is appointed for men to die once, but after this the judgment,

28 so Christ was offered once to bear the sins of many. To those who eagerly wait for Him He will appear a second time, apart from sin, for salvation.

10 For the law, having a shadow of the good things to come, *and* not the very image of the things, can never with these same sacrifices, which they offer continually year by year, make those who approach perfect.

2 For then would they not have ceased to be offered? For the worshipers, once purged, would have had no more consciousness of sins.

3 But in those *sacrifices there is* a reminder of sins every year.

4 For *it is* not possible that the blood of bulls and goats could take away sins.

5 Therefore, when He came into the world, He said:

*"Sacrifice and offering You did
    not desire,
But a body You have prepared
    for Me.*
6 *In burnt offerings and
    sacrifices for sin
You had no pleasure.*
7 *Then I said, 'Behold, I have
    come—*

In the volume of the book
it is written of Me—
To do Your will, O God.' "

8 Previously saying, *"Sacrifice and offering, burnt offerings, and offerings for sin You did not desire, nor had pleasure in them"* (which are offered according to the law), 9 then He said, *"Behold, I have come to do Your will, O God."* He takes away the first that He may establish the second.

10 By that will we have been sanctified through the offering of the body of Jesus Christ once *for all.*

11 And every priest stands ministering daily and offering repeatedly the same sacrifices, which can never take away sins.

12 But this Man, after He had offered one sacrifice for sins forever, sat down at the right hand of God, 13 from that time waiting till His enemies are made His footstool.

14 For by one offering He has perfected forever those who are being sanctified.

15 And the Holy Spirit also witnesses to us; for after He had said before,

16 *"This is the covenant that I will make with them after those days, says the* Lord: *I will put My laws into their hearts, and in their minds I will write them,"*

17 then He adds, *"Their sins and their lawless deeds I will remember no more."*

18 Now where there is remission of these, *there is* no longer an offering for sin.

19 Therefore, brethren, having boldness to enter the Holiest by the blood of Jesus,

20 by a new and living way which He consecrated for us, through the veil, that is, His flesh,

21 and *having* a High Priest over the house of God,

22 let us draw near with a true heart in full assurance of faith, having our hearts sprinkled from an evil conscience and our bodies washed with pure water.

23 Let us hold fast the confession ❤ of *our* hope without wavering, for He who promised *is* faithful.

24 And let us consider one another in order to stir up love and good works,

25 not forsaking the assembling of ourselves together, as *is* the manner of some, but exhorting *one another,* and so much the more as you see the Day approaching.

26 For if we sin willfully after we have received the knowledge of the truth, there no longer remains a sacrifice for sins,

27 but a certain fearful expectation of judgment, and fiery indignation which will devour the adversaries.

28 Anyone who has rejected Moses' law dies without mercy on the testimony of two or three witnesses.

29 Of how much worse punishment, do you suppose, will he be thought worthy who has trampled the Son of God underfoot, counted the blood of the covenant by which he was sanctified a common thing, and insulted the Spirit of grace?

30 For we know Him who said, *"Vengeance is Mine, I will repay,"* says the Lord. And again, *"The* Lord *will judge His people."*

31 It is a fearful thing to fall into the hands of the living God.

32 But recall the former days in which, after you were illuminated, you endured a great struggle with sufferings:

33 partly while you were made a spectacle both by reproaches and tribulations, and partly while you became companions of those who were so treated;

34 for you had compassion on me in my chains, and joyfully accepted the plundering of your goods, knowing that you have a better and an enduring possession for yourselves in heaven.

35 Therefore do not cast away your confidence, which has great reward.

36 For you have need of endurance, so that after you have done the will of God, you may receive the promise:

37 *"For yet a little while,*
    And He who is coming will
        come and will not tarry.
38 *Now the just shall live by*
        faith;
    But if anyone draws back,
    My soul has no pleasure in
        him."

39 But we are not of those who draw back to perdition, but of those who believe to the saving of the soul.

11 Now faith is the substance of things hoped for, the evidence of things not seen.

2 For by it the elders obtained a *good* testimony.

3 By faith we understand that the worlds were framed by the word of God, so that the things which are seen were not made of things which are visible.

4 By faith Abel offered to God a more excellent sacrifice than Cain, through which he obtained witness that he was righteous, God testifying of his gifts; and through it he being dead still speaks.

5 By faith Enoch was translated so that he did not see death, *"and was not found because God had translated him"*; for before his translation he had this testimony, that he pleased God.

6 But without faith *it is* impossible to please *Him,* for he who comes to God must believe that He is, and *that* He is a rewarder of those who diligently seek Him.

7 By faith Noah, being divinely warned of things not yet seen, moved with godly fear, prepared an ark for the saving of his household, by which he condemned the world and became heir of the righteousness which is according to faith.

8 By faith Abraham obeyed when he was called to go out to the place which he would *afterward* receive as an inheritance. And he went out, not knowing where he was going.

9 By faith he sojourned in the land of promise as *in* a foreign country, dwelling in tents with Isaac and Jacob, the heirs with him of the same promise;

10 for he waited for the city which has foundations, whose builder and maker *is* God.

11 By faith Sarah herself also received strength to conceive seed, and she bore a child when she was past the age, because she judged Him faithful who had promised.

12 Therefore from one man, and him as good as dead, were born *as many* as the stars of the sky in multitude—innumerable as the sand which is by the seashore.

13 These all died in faith, not having received the promises, but having seen them afar off were assured of *them,* embraced *them,* and confessed that they were strangers and pilgrims on the earth.

14 For those who say such things declare plainly that they seek a homeland.

15 And truly if they had called to mind that *country* from which they had come out, they would have had opportunity to return.

16 But now they desire a better, that is, a heavenly *country.* Therefore God is not ashamed to be called their God, for He has prepared a city for them.

17 By faith Abraham, when he was tested, offered up Isaac, and he who had received the promises offered up his only begotten *son,*

18 of whom it was said, *"In Isaac your seed shall be called,"*

19 accounting that God *was* able to raise *him* up, even from the

dead, from which he also received him in a figurative sense.

20 By faith Isaac blessed Jacob and Esau concerning things to come.

21 By faith Jacob, when he was dying, blessed each of the sons of Joseph, and worshiped, *leaning* on the top of his staff.

22 By faith Joseph, when he was dying, made mention of the departure of the children of Israel, and gave instructions concerning his bones.

23 By faith Moses, when he was born, was hidden three months by his parents, because they saw *he was* a beautiful child; and they were not afraid of the king's command.

24 By faith Moses, when he became of age, refused to be called the son of Pharaoh's daughter,

25 choosing rather to suffer affliction with the people of God than to enjoy the passing pleasures of sin,

26 esteeming the reproach of Christ greater riches than the treasures in Egypt; for he looked to the reward.

27 By faith he forsook Egypt, not fearing the wrath of the king; for he endured as seeing Him who is invisible.

28 By faith he kept the Passover and the sprinkling of blood, lest he who destroyed the firstborn should touch them.

29 By faith they passed through the Red Sea as by dry *land*, *whereas* the Egyptians, attempting *to do* so, were drowned.

30 By faith the walls of Jericho fell down after they were encircled for seven days.

31 By faith the harlot Rahab did not perish with those who did not believe, when she had received the spies with peace.

32 And what more shall I say? For the time would fail me to tell of Gideon and Barak and Samson and Jephthah, also *of* David and Samuel and the prophets:

33 who through faith subdued kingdoms, worked righteousness, obtained promises, stopped the mouths of lions,

34 quenched the violence of fire, escaped the edge of the sword, out of weakness were made strong, became valiant in battle, turned to flight the armies of the aliens.

35 Women received their dead raised to life again. And others were tortured, not accepting deliverance, that they might obtain a better resurrection.

36 Still others had trial of mockings and scourgings, yes, and of chains and imprisonment.

37 They were stoned, they were sawn in two, were tempted, were slain with the sword. They wandered about in sheepskins and goatskins, being destitute, afflicted, tormented—

38 of whom the world was not worthy. They wandered in deserts and mountains, *in* dens and caves of the earth.

39 And all these, having obtained a good testimony through faith, did not receive the promise,

40 God having provided something better for us, that they should not be made perfect apart from us.

12 Therefore we also, since we are surrounded by so great a cloud of witnesses, let us lay aside every weight, and the sin which so easily ensnares *us*, and let us run with endurance the race that is set before us,

2 looking unto Jesus, the author and finisher of *our* faith, who for the joy that was set before Him endured the cross, despising the shame, and has sat down at the right hand of the throne of God.

3 For consider Him who endured such hostility from sinners against Himself, lest you become weary and discouraged in your souls.

4 You have not yet resisted to bloodshed, striving against sin.

5 And you have forgotten the ex-

hortation which speaks to you as to sons:

> *"My son, do not despise the chastening of the LORD,*
> *Nor be discouraged when you are rebuked by Him;*
> 6 *For whom the LORD loves He chastens,*
> *And scourges every son whom He receives."*

7 If you endure chastening, God deals with you as with sons; for what son is there whom a father does not chasten?

8 But if you are without chastening, of which all have become partakers, then you are illegitimate and not sons.

9 Furthermore, we have had human fathers who corrected *us*, and we paid *them* respect. Shall we not much more readily be in subjection to the Father of spirits and live?

10 For they indeed for a few days chastened *us* as seemed *best* to them, but He for *our* profit, that *we* may be partakers of His holiness.

11 Now no chastening seems to be joyful for the present, but grievous; nevertheless, afterward it yields the peaceable fruit of righteousness to those who have been trained by it.

12 Therefore strengthen the hands which hang down, and the feeble knees,

13 and make straight paths for your feet, so that what is lame may not be *dislocated*, but rather be healed.

14 Pursue peace with all *men*, and holiness, without which no one will see the Lord:

15 looking diligently lest anyone fall short of the grace of God; lest any root of bitterness springing up cause trouble, and by this many become defiled;

16 lest there *be* any fornicator or profane person like Esau, who for one morsel of food sold his birthright.

17 For you know that afterward, when he wanted to inherit the blessing, he was rejected, for he found no place for repentance, though he sought it diligently with tears.

18 For you have not come to the mountain that may be touched and that burned with fire, and to blackness and darkness and tempest,

19 and the sound of a trumpet and the voice of words, so that those who heard *it* begged that the word should not be spoken to them anymore.

20 (For they could not endure what was commanded: *"And if so much as a beast touches the mountain, it shall be stoned or thrust through with an arrow."*

21 And so terrifying was the sight *that* Moses said, *"I am exceedingly afraid* and trembling."

22 But you have come to Mount Zion and to the city of the living God, the heavenly Jerusalem, to an innumerable company of angels,

23 to the general assembly and church of the firstborn *who are* registered in heaven, to God the Judge of all, to the spirits of just men made perfect,

24 to Jesus the Mediator of the new covenant, and to the blood of sprinkling that speaks better things than *that of* Abel.

25 See that you do not refuse Him who speaks. For if they did not escape who refused Him who spoke on earth, much more *shall we not escape* if we turn away from Him who *speaks* from heaven,

26 whose voice then shook the earth; but now He has promised, saying, *"Yet once more I shake not only the earth, but also heaven."*

27 Now this, *"Yet once more,"* indicates the removal of those things

that are being shaken, as of things that are made, that the things which cannot be shaken may remain.

28 Therefore, since we are receiving a kingdom which cannot be shaken, let us have grace, by which we may serve God acceptably with reverence and godly fear. 29 For our God *is* a consuming fire.

13 Let brotherly love continue. 2 Do not forget to entertain strangers, for by so *doing* some have unwittingly entertained angels.

3 Remember the prisoners as if chained with them, *and* those who are mistreated, since you yourselves are in the body also.

4 Marriage *is* honorable among all, and the bed undefiled; but fornicators and adulterers God will judge.

5 *Let your* conduct *be* without covetousness, *and be* content with such things as you have. For He Himself has said, *"I will never leave you nor forsake you."*

6 So we may boldly say:

"The LORD is my helper;
I will not fear.
What can man do to me?"

7 Remember those who rule over you, who have spoken the word of God to you, whose faith follow, considering the outcome of *their* conduct.

8 Jesus Christ *is* the same yesterday, today, and forever.

9 Do not be carried about with various and strange doctrines. For *it is* good that the heart be established by grace, not with foods which have not profited those who have been occupied with them.

10 We have an altar from which those who serve the tabernacle have no right to eat.

11 For the bodies of those beasts, whose blood is brought into the sanctuary by the high priest for sin, are burned outside the camp.

12 Therefore Jesus also, that He might sanctify the people with His own blood, suffered outside the gate.

13 Therefore let us go forth to Him, outside the camp, bearing His reproach.

14 For here we have no continuing city, but we seek the one to come.

15 Therefore by Him let us continually offer the sacrifice of praise to God, that is, the fruit of *our* lips, giving thanks to His name.

16 But do not forget to do good and to share, for with such sacrifices God is well pleased.

17 Obey those who rule over you, and be submissive, for they watch out for your souls, as those who must give account. Let them do so with joy and not with grief, for that would be unprofitable for you.

18 Pray for us; for we are confident that we have a good conscience, in all things desiring to live honorably.

19 But I especially urge *you* to do this, that I may be restored to you the sooner.

20 Now may the God of peace who brought up our Lord Jesus from the dead, that great Shepherd of the sheep, through the blood of the everlasting covenant,

21 make you complete in every good work to do His will, working in you what is well pleasing in His sight, through Jesus Christ, to whom *be* glory forever and ever. Amen.

22 And I appeal to you, brethren, bear with the word of exhortation, for I have written to you in few words.

23 Know that *our* brother Timothy has been set free, with whom I shall see you if he comes shortly.

24 Greet all those who rule over you, and all the saints. Those from Italy greet you.

25 Grace *be* with you all. Amen.

THE EPISTLE OF

JAMES

JAMES, a servant of God and of the Lord Jesus Christ,

To the twelve tribes which are scattered abroad:

Greetings.

2 My brethren, count it all joy when you fall into various trials,

3 knowing that the testing of your faith produces patience.

4 But let patience have *its* perfect work, that you may be perfect and complete, lacking nothing.

5 If any of you lacks wisdom, let him ask of God, who gives to all liberally and without reproach, and it will be given to him.

6 But let him ask in faith, with no doubting, for he who doubts is like a wave of the sea driven and tossed by the wind.

7 For let not that man suppose that he will receive anything from the Lord;

8 *he is* a double-minded man, unstable in all his ways.

9 Let the lowly brother glory in his exaltation,

10 but the rich in his humiliation, because as a flower of the field he will pass away.

11 For no sooner has the sun risen with a burning heat than it withers the grass; its flower falls, and its beautiful appearance perishes. So the rich man also will fade away in his pursuits.

12 Blessed *is* the man who endures temptation; for when he has been proved, he will receive the crown of life which the Lord has promised to those who love Him.

13 Let no one say when he is tempted, "I am tempted by God"; for God cannot be tempted by evil, nor does He Himself tempt anyone.

14 But each one is tempted when he is drawn away by his own desires and enticed.

15 Then, when desire has con-ceived, it gives birth to sin; and sin, when it is full-grown, brings forth death.

16 Do not be deceived, my beloved brethren.

17 Every good gift and every perfect gift is from above, and comes down from the Father of lights, with whom there is no variation or shadow of turning.

18 Of His own will He brought us forth by the word of truth, that we might be a kind of firstfruits of His creatures.

19 Therefore, my beloved brethren, let every man be swift to hear, slow to speak, slow to wrath;

20 for the wrath of man does not produce the righteousness of God.

21 Therefore lay aside all filthiness and overflow of wickedness, and receive with meekness the implanted word, which is able to save your souls.

22 But be doers of the word, and not hearers only, deceiving yourselves.

23 For if anyone is a hearer of the word and not a doer, he is like a man observing his natural face in a mirror;

24 for he observes himself, goes away, and immediately forgets what kind of man he was.

25 But he who looks into the perfect law of liberty and continues *in it*, and is not a forgetful hearer but a doer of the work, this one will be blessed in what he does.

26 If anyone among you thinks he is religious, and does not bridle his tongue but deceives his own heart, this one's religion *is* useless.

27 Pure and undefiled religion before God and the Father is this: to visit orphans and widows in their trouble, *and* to keep oneself unspotted from the world.

2 My brethren, do not hold the faith of our Lord Jesus Christ,

the Lord of glory, with partiality.

2 For if there should come into your assembly a man with gold rings, in fine apparel, and there should also come in a poor man in filthy clothes,

3 and you pay attention to the one wearing the fine clothes and say to him, "You sit here in a good place," and say to the poor man, "You stand there," or, "Sit here at my footstool,"

4 have you not shown partiality among yourselves, and become judges with evil thoughts?

5 Listen, my beloved brethren: Has God not chosen the poor of this world *to be* rich in faith and heirs of the kingdom which He promised to those who love Him?

6 But you have dishonored the poor man. Do not the rich oppress you and drag you into the courts?

7 Do they not blaspheme that noble name by which you are called?

8 If you really fulfill *the* royal law according to the Scripture, *"You shall love your neighbor as yourself,"* you do well;

9 but if you show partiality, you commit sin, and are convicted by the law as transgressors.

10 For whoever shall keep the whole law, and yet stumble in one *point*, he is guilty of all.

11 For He who said, *"Do not commit adultery,"* also said, *"Do not murder."* Now if you do not commit adultery, but you do murder, you have become a transgressor of the law.

12 So speak and so do as those who will be judged by the law of liberty.

13 For judgment is without mercy to the one who has shown no mercy. Mercy triumphs over judgment.

14 What *does it* profit, my brethren, if someone says he has faith but does not have works? Can faith save him?

15 If a brother or sister is naked and destitute of daily food,

16 and one of you says to them, "Depart in peace, be warmed and filled," but you do not give them the things which are needed for the body, what *does it* profit?

17 Thus also faith by itself, if it does not have works, is dead.

18 But someone will say, "You have faith, and I have works." Show me your faith without your works, and I will show you my faith by my works.

19 You believe that there is one God. You do well. Even the demons believe—and tremble!

20 But do you want to know, O foolish man, that faith without works is dead?

21 Was not Abraham our father justified by works when he offered Isaac his son on the altar?

22 Do you see that faith was working together with his works, and by works faith was made perfect?

23 And the Scripture was fulfilled which says, *"Abraham believed God, and it was accounted to him for righteousness."* And he was called the friend of God.

24 You see then that a man is justified by works, and not by faith only.

25 Likewise, was not Rahab the harlot also justified by works when she received the messengers and sent *them* out another way?

26 For as the body without the spirit is dead, so faith without works is dead also.

3 My brethren, let not many of you become teachers, knowing that we shall receive a stricter judgment.

2 For we all stumble in many things. If anyone does not stumble in word, he *is* a perfect man, able also to bridle the whole body.

3 Indeed, we put bits in horses' mouths that they may obey us, and we turn their whole body.

4 Look also at ships: although

they are so large and are driven by fierce winds, they are turned by a very small rudder wherever the pilot desires.

5 Even so the tongue is a little member and boasts great things. See how great a forest a little fire kindles!

6 And the tongue *is* a fire, a world of iniquity. The tongue is so set among our members that it defiles the whole body, and sets on fire the course of nature; and it is set on fire by hell.

7 For every kind of beast and bird, of reptile and creature of the sea, is tamed and has been tamed by mankind.

8 But no man can tame the tongue. *It is* an unruly evil, full of deadly poison.

9 With it we bless our God and Father, and with it we curse men, who have been made in the similitude of God.

10 Out of the same mouth proceed blessing and cursing. My brethren, these things ought not to be so.

11 Does a spring send forth fresh *water* and bitter from the same opening?

12 Can a fig tree, my brethren, bear olives, or a grapevine bear figs? Thus no spring *can* yield both salt water and fresh.

13 Who *is* wise and understanding among you? Let him show by good conduct *that* his works *are done* in the meekness of wisdom.

14 But if you have bitter envy and self-seeking in your hearts, do not boast and lie against the truth.

15 This wisdom does not descend from above, but *is* earthly, sensual, demonic.

16 For where envy and self-seeking *exist,* confusion and every evil thing *will be* there.

17 But the wisdom that is from above is first pure, then peaceable, gentle, willing to yield, full of mercy and good fruits, without partiality and without hypocrisy.

18 Now the fruit of righteousness is sown in peace by those who make peace.

4 Where do wars and fights *come* from among you? Do *they* not *come* from your *desires for* pleasure that war in your members?

2 You lust and do not have. You murder and covet and cannot obtain. You fight and war. Yet you do not have because you do not ask.

3 You ask and do not receive, because you ask amiss, that you may spend *it* on your pleasures.

4 Adulterers and adulteresses! Do you not know that friendship with the world is enmity with God? Whoever therefore wants to be a friend of the world makes himself an enemy of God.

5 Or do you think that the Scripture says in vain, "The Spirit who dwells in us yearns jealously"?

6 But He gives more grace. Therefore He says:

"God resists the proud,
But gives grace to the
    humble."

7 Therefore submit to God. Resist the devil and he will flee from you.

8 Draw near to God and He will draw near to you. Cleanse *your* hands, *you* sinners; and purify *your* hearts, *you* double-minded.

9 Lament and mourn and weep! Let your laughter be turned to mourning and *your* joy to gloom.

10 Humble yourselves in the sight of the Lord, and He will lift you up.

11 Do not speak evil of one another, brethren. He who speaks evil of a brother and judges his brother, speaks evil of the law and judges the law. But if you judge the law, you are not a doer of the law but a judge.

12 There is one Lawgiver, who is able to save and to destroy. Who are you to judge another?

13 Come now, you who say, "Today or tomorrow we will go to such and such a city, spend a year there, buy and sell, and make a profit";

14 whereas you do not know what *will happen* tomorrow. For what is your life? It is even a vapor that appears for a little time and then vanishes away.

15 Instead you *ought* to say, "If the Lord wills, we shall live and do this or that."

16 But now you boast in your arrogance. All such boasting is evil.

17 Therefore, to him who knows to do good and does not do *it*, to him it is sin.

5 Come now, *you* rich, weep and howl for your miseries that are coming upon *you!*

2 Your riches are corrupted, and your garments are moth-eaten.

3 Your gold and silver are corroded, and their corrosion will be a witness against you and will eat your flesh like fire. You have heaped up treasure in the last days.

4 Indeed the wages of the laborers who mowed your fields, which you kept back by fraud, cry out; and the cries of the reapers have reached the ears of the Lord of Sabaoth.

5 You have lived on the earth in pleasure and luxury; you have fattened your hearts as in a day of slaughter.

6 You have condemned, you have murdered the just; he does not resist you.

7 Therefore be patient, brethren, until the coming of the Lord. See *how* the farmer waits for the precious fruit of the earth, waiting patiently for it until it receives the early and latter rain.

8 You also be patient. Establish your hearts, for the coming of the Lord is at hand.

9 Do not grumble against one another, brethren, lest you be condemned. Behold, the Judge is standing at the door!

10 My brethren, take the prophets, who spoke in the name of the Lord, as an example of suffering and patience.

11 Indeed we count them blessed who endure. You have heard of the perseverance of Job and seen the end *intended by* the Lord—that the Lord is very compassionate and merciful.

12 But above all, my brethren, do not swear, either by heaven or by earth or with any other oath. But let your "Yes" be "Yes," and *your* "No," "No," lest you fall into judgment.

13 Is anyone among you suffering? Let him pray. Is anyone cheerful? Let him sing psalms.

14 Is anyone among you sick? Let him call for the elders of the church, and let them pray over him, anointing him with oil in the name of the Lord.

15 And the prayer of faith will save the sick, and the Lord will raise him up. And if he has committed sins, he will be forgiven.

16 Confess *your* trespasses to one another, and pray for one another, that you may be healed. The effective, fervent prayer of a righteous man avails much.

17 Elijah was a man with a nature like ours, and he prayed earnestly that it would not rain; and it did not rain on the land for three years and six months.

18 And he prayed again, and the heaven gave rain, and the earth produced its fruit.

19 Brethren, if anyone among you wanders from the truth, and someone turns him back,

20 let him know that he who turns a sinner from the error of his way will save a soul from death and cover a multitude of sins.

THE FIRST EPISTLE OF
PETER

PETER, an apostle of Jesus Christ,

To the pilgrims of the Dispersion in Pontus, Galatia, Cappadocia, Asia, and Bithynia,
2 elect according to the foreknowledge of God the Father, in sanctification of the Spirit, for obedience and sprinkling of the blood of Jesus Christ:

Grace to you and peace be multiplied.
3 Blessed *be* the God and Father of our Lord Jesus Christ, who according to His abundant mercy has begotten us again to a living hope through the resurrection of Jesus Christ from the dead,
4 to an inheritance incorruptible and undefiled and that does not fade away, reserved in heaven for you,
5 who are kept by the power of God through faith for salvation ready to be revealed in the last time.
6 In this you greatly rejoice, though now for a little while, if need be, you have been grieved by various trials,
7 that the genuineness of your faith, *being* much more precious than gold that perishes, though it is tested by fire, may be found to praise, honor, and glory at the revelation of Jesus Christ,
8 whom having not seen you love. Though now you do not see *Him,* yet believing, you rejoice with joy inexpressible and full of glory,
9 receiving the end of your faith—the salvation of *your* souls.
10 Of this salvation the prophets have inquired and searched diligently, who prophesied of the grace *that would come* to you,
11 searching what, or what manner of time, the Spirit of Christ who was in them was indicating when He testified beforehand the sufferings of Christ and the glories that would follow.
12 To them it was revealed that, not to themselves, but to us they were ministering the things which now have been reported to you through those who have preached the gospel to you by the Holy Spirit sent from heaven—things which angels desire to look into.
13 Therefore gird up the loins of your mind, be sober, and rest *your* hope fully upon the grace that is to be brought to you at the revelation of Jesus Christ;
14 as obedient children, not conforming yourselves to the former lusts, *as* in your ignorance;
15 but as He who called you *is* holy, you also be holy in all *your* conduct,
16 because it is written, *"Be holy, for I am holy."*
17 And if you call on the Father, who without partiality judges according to each one's work, conduct yourselves throughout the time of your sojourning *here* in fear;
18 knowing that you were not redeemed with corruptible things, *like* silver or gold, from your aimless conduct *received* by tradition from your fathers,
19 but with the precious blood of Christ, as of a lamb without blemish and without spot,
20 He indeed was foreordained before the foundation of the world, but was manifest in these last times for you
21 who through Him believe in God, who raised Him from the dead and gave Him glory, so that your faith and hope are in God.
22 Since you have purified your souls in obeying the truth through the Spirit in sincere love of the brethren, love one another fervently with a pure heart,

281

23 having been born again, not of corruptible seed but incorruptible, through the word of God which lives and abides forever,
24 because

"All flesh is as grass,
    And all the glory of man
        as the flower of the grass.
    The grass withers,
    And its flower falls away,
25 But the word of the LORD
        endures forever."

Now this is the word which by the gospel was preached to you.

2 Therefore, laying aside all malice, all guile, hypocrisy, envy, and all evil speaking,
2 as newborn babes, desire the pure milk of the word, that you may grow thereby,
3 if indeed you have tasted that the Lord is gracious.
4 Coming to Him as to a living stone, rejected indeed by men, but chosen by God and precious,
5 you also, as living stones, are being built up a spiritual house, a holy priesthood, to offer up spiritual sacrifices acceptable to God through Jesus Christ.
6 Therefore it is also contained in the Scripture,

"Behold, I lay in Zion
    A chief cornerstone, elect,
        precious,
    And he who believes on Him
        will by no means be put to
        shame."

7 Therefore, to you who believe, He is precious; but to those who are disobedient,

"The stone which the builders
        rejected
    Has become the chief
        cornerstone,"

8 and

"A stone of stumbling
    And a rock of offense."

They stumble, being disobedient to the word, to which they also were appointed.
9 But you are a chosen generation, a royal priesthood, a holy nation, His own special people, that you may proclaim the praises of Him who called you out of darkness into His marvelous light;
10 who once were not a people but are now the people of God, who had not obtained mercy but now have obtained mercy.
11 Beloved, I beg you as sojourners and pilgrims, abstain from fleshly lusts which war against the soul,
12 having your conduct honorable among the Gentiles, that when they speak against you as evildoers, they may, by your good works which they observe, glorify God in the day of visitation.
13 Therefore submit yourselves to every ordinance of man for the Lord's sake, whether to the king as supreme,
14 or to governors, as to those who are sent by him for the punishment of evildoers and for the praise of those who do good.
15 For this is the will of God, that by doing good you may put to silence the ignorance of foolish men—
16 as free, yet not using your liberty as a cloak for vice, but as servants of God.
17 Honor all people. Love the brotherhood. Fear God. Honor the king.
18 Servants, be submissive to your masters with all fear, not only to the good and gentle, but also to the harsh.
19 For this is commendable, if because of conscience toward God one endures grief, suffering wrongfully.
20 For what credit is it if, when you are beaten for your faults, you take it patiently? But when you do

good and suffer *for it*, if you take it patiently, this *is* commendable before God.

21 For to this you were called, because Christ also suffered for us, leaving us an example, that you should follow His steps:

22 *"Who committed no sin,*
Nor was guile found in His
mouth";

23 who, when He was reviled, did not revile in return; when He suffered, He did not threaten, but committed *Himself* to Him who judges righteously;

24 who Himself bore our sins in His own body on the tree, that we, having died to sins, might live for righteousness—by whose stripes you were healed.

25 For you were like sheep going astray, but have now returned to the Shepherd and Overseer of your souls.

3 Likewise *you* wives, *be* submissive to your own husbands, that even if some do not obey the word, they, without a word, may be won by the conduct of their wives,

2 when they observe your chaste conduct *accompanied* by fear.

3 Do not let your beauty be that outward *adorning* of arranging the hair, of wearing gold, or of putting on *fine* apparel;

4 but *let it be* the hidden person of the heart, with the incorruptible *ornament* of a gentle and quiet spirit, which is very precious in the sight of God.

5 For in this manner, in former times, the holy women who trusted in God also adorned themselves, being submissive to their own husbands,

6 as Sarah obeyed Abraham, calling him lord, whose daughters you are if you do good and are not afraid with any terror.

7 Likewise *you* husbands, dwell with *them* with understanding,

giving honor to the wife, as to the weaker vessel, and as *being* heirs together of the grace of life, that your prayers may not be hindered.

8 Finally, all of *you be* of one mind, having compassion for one another; love as brothers, *be* tenderhearted, *be* courteous;

9 not returning evil for evil or reviling for reviling, but on the contrary blessing, knowing that you were called to this, that you may inherit a blessing.

10 For

"He who would love life
And see good days,
Let him refrain his tongue
from evil,
And his lips from speaking
guile;
11 *Let him turn away from evil*
and do good;
Let him seek peace and pursue
it.
12 *For the eyes of the LORD*
are on the righteous,
And his ears are open to their
prayers;
But the face of the LORD is
against those who do evil."

13 And who *is* he who will harm you if you become followers of what is good?

14 But even if you should suffer for righteousness' sake, *you are* blessed. *"And do not be afraid of their threats, nor be troubled."*

15 But sanctify the Lord God in your hearts, and always *be* ready to *give* a defense to everyone who asks you a reason for the hope that is in you, with meekness and fear;

16 having a good conscience, that when they defame you as evildoers, those who revile your good conduct in Christ may be ashamed.

17 For *it is* better, if it is the will of God, to suffer for doing good than for doing evil.

18 For Christ also suffered once for sins, the just for the unjust, that

He might bring us to God, being put to death in the flesh but made alive by the Spirit,

19 by whom also He went and preached to the spirits in prison,

20 who formerly were disobedient, when once the longsuffering of God waited in the days of Noah, while *the* ark was being prepared, in which a few, that is, eight souls, were saved through water.

21 There is also an antitype which now saves us, *namely* baptism (not the removal of the filth of the flesh, but the answer of a good conscience toward God), through the resurrection of Jesus Christ,

22 who has gone into heaven and is at the right hand of God, angels and authorities and powers having been made subject to Him.

4 Therefore, since Christ suffered for us in the flesh, arm yourselves also with the same mind, for he who has suffered in the flesh has ceased from sin,

2 that he no longer should live the rest of *his* time in the flesh for the lusts of men, but for the will of God.

3 For we *have spent* enough of our past lifetime in doing the will of the Gentiles—when we walked in licentiousness, lusts, drunkenness, revelries, drinking parties, and abominable idolatries.

4 In regard to these, they think it strange that you do not run with *them* in the same flood of dissipation, speaking evil of *you*.

5 They will give an account to Him who is ready to judge the living and the dead.

6 For this reason the gospel was preached also to those who are dead, that they might be judged according to men in the flesh, but live according to God in the spirit.

7 But the end of all things is at hand; therefore be serious and watchful in your prayers.

8 And above all things have fervent love for one another, for *"love will cover a multitude of sins."*

9 *Be* hospitable to one another without grumbling.

10 As each one has received a gift, minister it to one another, as good stewards of the manifold grace of God.

11 If anyone speaks, *let him speak* as the oracles of God. If anyone ministers, *let him do it* as with the ability which God supplies, that in all things God may be glorified through Jesus Christ, to whom belong the glory and the dominion forever and ever. Amen.

12 Beloved, do not think it strange concerning the fiery trial which is to try you, as though some strange thing happened to you;

13 but rejoice to the extent that you partake of Christ's sufferings, that when His glory is revealed, you may also be glad with exceeding joy.

14 If you are reproached for the name of Christ, blessed *are you*, for the Spirit of glory and of God rests upon you. On their part He is blasphemed, but on your part He is glorified.

15 But let none of you suffer as a murderer, a thief, an evildoer, or as a busybody in other people's matters.

16 Yet if *anyone suffers* as a Christian, let him not be ashamed, but let him glorify God in this matter.

17 For the time *has come* for judgment to begin at the house of God; and if *it begins* with us first, what will *be* the end of those who do not obey the gospel of God?

18 Now

> *"If the righteous one is scarcely saved,*
> *Where will the ungodly and the sinner appear?"*

19 Therefore let those who suffer according to the will of God commit their souls *to Him* in doing good, as to a faithful Creator.

5 The elders who are among you I exhort, I who am a fellow

elder and a witness of the sufferings of Christ, and also a partaker of the glory that will be revealed:

2 Shepherd the flock of God which is among you, serving as overseers, not by constraint but willingly, not for dishonest gain but eagerly;

3 nor as being lords over those entrusted to you, but being examples to the flock;

4 and when the Chief Shepherd appears, you will receive the crown of glory that does not fade away.

5 Likewise you younger people, submit yourselves to *your* elders. Yes, all of *you* be submissive to one another, and be clothed with humility, for

"God resists the proud,
   But gives grace to the
      humble."

6 Therefore humble yourselves under the mighty hand of God, that He may exalt you in due time,

7 casting all your care upon Him, for He cares for you.

8 Be sober, be vigilant; because your adversary the devil walks about like a roaring lion, seeking whom he may devour.

9 Resist him, steadfast in the faith, knowing that the same sufferings are experienced by your brotherhood in the world.

10 But may the God of all grace, who called us to His eternal glory by Christ Jesus, after you have suffered a while, perfect, establish, strengthen, and settle *you.*

11 To Him *be* the glory and the dominion forever and ever. Amen.

12 By Silvanus, our faithful brother as I consider him, I have written to you briefly, exhorting and testifying that this is the true grace of God in which you stand.

13 She who is in Babylon, elect together with *you,* greets you; and *so does* Mark my son.

14 Greet one another with a kiss of love. Peace to you all who are in Christ Jesus. Amen.

THE SECOND EPISTLE OF
PETER

SIMON PETER, a servant and apostle of Jesus Christ,

To those who have obtained like precious faith with us by the righteousness of our God and Savior Jesus Christ:

2 Grace and peace be multiplied to you in the knowledge of God and of Jesus our Lord,

3 as His divine power has given to us all things that *pertain* to life and godliness, through the knowledge of Him who called us by glory and virtue,

4 by which have been given to us

exceedingly great and precious promises, that through these you may be partakers of the divine nature, having escaped the corruption *that is* in the world through lust.

5 But also for this very reason, giving all diligence, add to your faith virtue, to virtue knowledge,

6 to knowledge self-control, to self-control perseverance, to perseverance godliness,

7 to godliness brotherly kindness, and to brotherly kindness love.

8 For if these things are yours and abound, *you will be* neither barren

nor unfruitful in the knowledge of our Lord Jesus Christ.

9 For he who lacks these things is shortsighted, even to blindness, and has forgotten that he was purged from his old sins.

10 Therefore, brethren, be even more diligent to make your calling and election sure, for if you do these things you will never stumble;

11 for so an entrance will be supplied to you abundantly into the everlasting kingdom of our Lord and Savior Jesus Christ.

12 Therefore I will not be negligent to remind you always of these things, though you know *them*, and *are* established in the present truth.

13 Yes, I think it is right, as long as I am in this tent, to stir you up by reminding *you*,

14 knowing that shortly I *must* put off my tent, just as our Lord Jesus Christ showed me.

15 Moreover I will be careful to ensure that you always have a reminder of these things after my decease.

16 For we did not follow cunningly devised fables when we made known to you the power and coming of our Lord Jesus Christ, but were eyewitnesses of His majesty.

17 For He received from God the Father honor and glory when such a voice came to Him from the Excellent Glory: "This is My beloved Son, in whom I am well pleased."

18 And we heard this voice which came from heaven when we were with Him on the holy mountain.

19 We also have the prophetic word made more sure, which you do well to heed as a light that shines in a dark place, until the day dawns and the morning star rises in your hearts;

20 knowing this first, that no prophecy of Scripture is of any private interpretation,

21 for prophecy never came by the will of man, but holy men of God spoke *as they were* moved by the Holy Spirit.

2 But there were also false prophets among the people, even as there will be false teachers among you, who will secretly bring in destructive heresies, even denying the Lord who bought them, *and* bring on themselves swift destruction.

2 And many will follow their destructive ways, because of whom the way of truth will be blasphemed.

3 By covetousness they will exploit you with deceptive words; for a long time their judgment has not been idle, and their destruction does not slumber.

4 For if God did not spare the angels who sinned, but cast *them* down to hell and delivered *them* into chains of darkness, to be reserved for judgment;

5 and did not spare the ancient world, but saved Noah, *one of* eight *people*, a preacher of righteousness, bringing in the flood on the world of the ungodly;

6 and turning the cities of Sodom and Gomorrah into ashes, condemned *them* to destruction, making *them* an example to those who afterward would live ungodly;

7 and delivered righteous Lot, *who was* oppressed with the filthy conduct of the wicked

8 (for that righteous man, dwelling among them, tormented *his* righteous soul from day to day by seeing and hearing *their* lawless deeds)—

9 *then* the Lord knows how to deliver the godly out of temptations and to reserve the unjust under punishment for the day of judgment,

10 and especially those who walk according to the flesh in the lust of uncleanness and despise authority. *They are* presumptuous, self-willed; they are not afraid to speak evil of dignitaries,

11 whereas angels, who are greater

in power and might, do not bring a reviling accusation against them before the Lord.

12 But these, like natural brute beasts made to be caught and destroyed, speak evil of the things they do not understand, and will utterly perish in their own corruption,

13 *and* will receive the wages of unrighteousness, *as* those who count it pleasure to carouse in the daytime. *They are* spots and blemishes, carousing in their own deceptions while they feast with you,

14 having eyes full of adultery and that cannot cease from sin, beguiling unstable souls. *They have* a heart trained in covetous practices, *and are* accursed children.

15 They have forsaken the right way and gone astray, following the way of Balaam the *son* of Beor, who loved the wages of unrighteousness;

16 but he was rebuked for his iniquity: a dumb donkey speaking with a man's voice restrained the madness of the prophet.

17 These are wells without water, clouds carried by a tempest, to whom the gloom of darkness is reserved forever.

18 For when they speak great swelling *words* of emptiness, they allure through the lusts of the flesh, through licentiousness, the ones who have actually escaped from those who live in error.

19 While they promise them liberty, they themselves are slaves of corruption; for by whom a person is overcome, by him also he is brought into bondage.

20 For if, after they have escaped the pollutions of the world through the knowledge of the Lord and Savior Jesus Christ, they are again entangled in them and overcome, the latter end is worse for them than the beginning.

21 For it would have been better for them not to have known the way of righteousness, than having known *it,* to turn from the holy commandment delivered to them.

22 But it has happened to them according to the true proverb: *"A dog returns to his own vomit,"* and, "a sow, having washed, to her wallowing in the mire."

3 Beloved, I now write to you this second epistle (in *both of* which I stir up your pure minds by way of reminder),

2 that you may be mindful of the words which were spoken before by the holy prophets, and of the commandment of us the apostles of the Lord and Savior,

3 knowing this first: that scoffers will come in the last days, walking according to their own lusts,

4 and saying, "Where is the promise of His coming? For since the fathers fell asleep, all things continue as *they were* from the beginning of creation."

5 For this they willfully forget: that by the word of God the heavens were of old, and the earth standing out of water and in the water,

6 by which the world *that* then existed perished, being flooded with water.

7 But the heavens and the earth *which* now *exist* are kept in store by the same word, reserved for fire until the day of judgment and perdition of ungodly men.

8 But, beloved, do not forget this one thing, that with the Lord one day *is* as a thousand years, and a thousand years as one day.

9 The Lord is not slack concerning *His* promise, as some count slackness, but is longsuffering toward us, not willing that any should perish but that all should come to repentance.

10 But the day of the Lord will come as a thief in the night, in which the heavens will pass away with a great noise, and the elements will melt with fervent heat;

287

both the earth and the works that are in it will be burned up.

11 Therefore, since all these things will be dissolved, what manner *of persons* ought you to be in holy conduct and godliness,

12 looking for and hastening the coming of the day of God, because of which the heavens will be dissolved being on fire, and the elements will melt with fervent heat?

13 Nevertheless we, according to His promise, look for new heavens and a new earth in which righteousness dwells.

14 Therefore, beloved, looking forward to these things, be diligent to be found by Him in peace, without spot and blameless;

15 and account *that* the longsuffering of our Lord *is* salvation—as also our beloved brother Paul, according to the wisdom given to him, has written to you,

16 as also in all his epistles, speaking in them of these things, in which are some things hard to understand, which those *who are* untaught and unstable twist to their own destruction, as *they do* also the rest of the Scriptures.

17 You therefore, beloved, since you know *these things* beforehand, beware lest you also fall from your own steadfastness, being led away with the error of the wicked;

18 but grow in the grace and knowledge of our Lord and Savior Jesus Christ. To Him *be* the glory both now and forever. Amen.

THE FIRST EPISTLE OF

JOHN

THAT which was from the beginning, which we have heard, which we have seen with our eyes, which we have looked upon, and our hands have handled, concerning the Word of life—

2 the life was manifested, and we have seen, and bear witness, and declare to you that eternal life which was with the Father and was manifested to us—

3 that which we have seen and heard we declare to you, that you also may have fellowship with us; and truly our fellowship *is* with the Father and with His Son Jesus Christ.

4 And these things we write to you that your joy may be full.

5 This is the message which we have heard from Him and declare to you, that God is light and in Him is no darkness at all.

6 If we say that we have fellowship with Him, and walk in darkness, we lie and do not practice the truth.

7 But if we walk in the light as He is in the light, we have fellowship with one another, and the blood of Jesus Christ His Son cleanses us from all sin.

8 If we say that we have no sin, we deceive ourselves, and the truth is not in us.

9 If we confess our sins, He is faithful and just to forgive us *our* sins and to cleanse us from all unrighteousness.

10 If we say that we have not sinned, we make Him a liar, and His word is not in us.

2 My little children, these things I write to you, that you may not sin. And if anyone sins, we have an Advocate with the Father, Jesus Christ the righteous.

288

2 And He Himself is the propitiation for our sins, and not for ours only but also for the whole world.
3 Now by this we know that we know Him, if we keep His commandments.
4 He who says, "I know Him," and does not keep His commandments, is a liar, and the truth is not in him.
5 But whoever keeps His word, truly the love of God is perfected in him. By this we know that we are in Him.
6 He who says he abides in Him ought himself also to walk just as He walked.
7 Brethren, I write no new commandment to you, but an old commandment which you have had from the beginning. The old commandment is the word which you heard from the beginning.
8 Again, a new commandment I write to you, which thing is true in Him and in you, because the darkness is passing away, and the true light is already shining.
9 He who says he is in the light, and hates his brother, is in darkness until now.
10 He who loves his brother abides in the light, and there is no cause for stumbling in him.
11 But he who hates his brother is in darkness and walks in darkness, and does not know where he is going, because the darkness has blinded his eyes.

12 I write to you, little children,
Because your sins are
forgiven you for His name's sake.
13 I write to you, fathers,
Because you have known
Him *who is* from the beginning.
I write to you, young men,
Because you have overcome the wicked one.
I write to you, little children,
Because you have known the Father.

14 I have written to you, fathers,
Because you have known
Him *who is* from the beginning.
I have written to you, young men,
Because you are strong, and the word of God abides in you,
And you have overcome the wicked one.

15 Do not love the world or the things in the world. If anyone loves the world, the love of the Father is not in him.
16 For all that *is* in the world—the lust of the flesh, the lust of the eyes, and the pride of life—is not of the Father but is of the world.
17 And the world is passing away, and the lust of it; but he who does the will of God abides forever.
18 Little children, it is the last hour; and as you have heard that the Antichrist is coming, even now many antichrists have come, by which we know that it is the last hour.
19 They went out from us, but they were not of us; for if they had been of us, they would have continued with us; but *they went out* that they might be made manifest, that none of them were of us.
20 But you have an anointing from the Holy One, and you know all things.
21 I have not written to you because you do not know the truth, but because you know it, and that no lie is of the truth.
22 Who is a liar but he who denies that Jesus is the Christ? He is antichrist who denies the Father and the Son.
23 Whoever denies the Son does not have the Father either; he who acknowledges the Son has the Father also.
24 Therefore let that abide in you which you heard from the beginning. If what you heard from the beginning abides in you, you also

will abide in the Son and in the Father.

25 And this is the promise that He has promised us—eternal life.

26 These *things* I have written to you concerning those who *try to* deceive you.

27 But the anointing which you have received from Him abides in you, and you do not need that anyone teach you; but as the same anointing teaches you concerning all things, and is true, and is not a lie, and just as it has taught you, you will abide in Him.

28 And now, little children, abide in Him, that when He appears, we may have confidence and not be ashamed before Him at His coming.

29 If you know that He is righteous, you know that everyone who practices righteousness is born of Him.

3 Behold what manner of love the Father has bestowed on us, that we should be called children of God! Therefore the world does not know us, because it did not know Him.

2 Beloved, now we are children of God; and it has not yet been revealed what we shall be, but we know that when He is revealed, we shall be like Him, for we shall see Him as He is.

3 And everyone who has this hope in Him purifies himself, just as He is pure.

4 Whoever commits sin also commits lawlessness, and sin is lawlessness.

5 And you know that He was manifested to take away our sins, and in Him there is no sin.

6 Whoever abides in Him does not sin. Whoever sins has neither seen Him nor known Him.

7 Little children, let no one deceive you. He who practices righteousness is righteous, just as He is righteous.

8 He who sins is of the devil, for the devil has sinned from the beginning. For this purpose the Son of God was manifested, that He might destroy the works of the devil.

9 Whoever has been born of God does not sin, for His seed remains in him; and he cannot sin, because he has been born of God.

10 In this the children of God and the children of the devil are manifest: Whoever does not practice righteousness is not of God, nor *is* he who does not love his brother.

11 For this is the message that you heard from the beginning, that we should love one another,

12 not as Cain *who* was of the wicked one and murdered his brother. And why did he murder him? Because his works were evil and his brother's righteous.

13 Do not marvel, my brethren, if the world hates you.

14 We know that we have passed from death to life, because we love the brethren. He who does not love *his* brother abides in death.

15 Whoever hates his brother is a murderer, and you know that no murderer has eternal life abiding in him.

16 By this we know love, because He laid down His life for us. And we also ought to lay down *our* lives for the brethren.

17 But whoever has this world's goods, and sees his brother in need, and shuts up his heart from him, how does the love of God abide in him?

18 My little children, let us not love in word or in tongue, but in deed and in truth.

19 And by this we know that we are of the truth, and shall assure our hearts before Him.

20 For if our heart condemns us, God is greater than our heart, and knows all things.

21 Beloved, if our heart does not condemn us, we have confidence toward God.

22 And whatever we ask we receive from Him, because we keep

His commandments and do those things that are pleasing in His sight.

23 And this is His commandment: that we should believe on the name of His Son Jesus Christ and love one another, as He gave us commandment.

24 Now he who keeps His commandments abides in Him, and He in him. And by this we know that He abides in us, by the Spirit whom He has given us.

4 Beloved, do not believe every spirit, but test the spirits, whether they are of God; because many false prophets have gone out into the world.

2 By this you know the Spirit of God: Every spirit that confesses that Jesus Christ has come in the flesh is of God,

3 and every spirit that does not confess that Jesus Christ has come in the flesh is not of God. And this is the *spirit* of the Antichrist, which you have heard was coming, and is now already in the world.

4 You are of God, little children, and have overcome them, because He who is in you is greater than he who is in the world.

5 They are of the world. Therefore they speak *as* of the world, and the world hears them.

6 We are of God. He who knows God hears us; he who is not of God does not hear us. By this we know the spirit of truth and the spirit of error.

7 Beloved, let us love one another, for love is of God; and everyone who loves is born of God and knows God.

8 He who does not love does not know God, for God is love.

♥ 9 In this the love of God was manifested toward us, that God has sent His only begotten Son into the world, that we might live through Him.

10 In this is love, not that we loved God, but that He loved us and sent His Son *to be* the propitiation for our sins.

11 Beloved, if God so loved us, we also ought to love one another.

12 No one has seen God at any time. If we love one another, God abides in us, and His love has been perfected in us.

13 By this we know that we abide in Him, and He in us, because He has given us of His Spirit.

14 And we have seen and testify that the Father has sent the Son *as* Savior of the world.

15 Whoever confesses that Jesus is the Son of God, God abides in him, and he in God.

16 And we have known and believed the love that God has for us. God is love, and he who abides in love abides in God, and God in him.

17 Love has been perfected among us in this: that we may have boldness in the day of judgment; because as He is, so are we in this world.

18 There is no fear in love; but perfect love casts out fear, because fear involves torment. But he who fears has not been made perfect in love.

19 We love Him because He first loved us.

20 If someone says, "I love God," and hates his brother, he is a liar; for he who does not love his brother whom he has seen, how can he love God whom he has not seen?

21 And this commandment we have from Him: that he who loves God *must* love his brother also.

5 Whoever believes that Jesus is the Christ is born of God, and everyone who loves Him who begot also loves him who is begotten of Him.

2 By this we know that we love the children of God, when we love God and keep His commandments.

3 For this is the love of God, that we keep His commandments. And

291   *See John 13:34, 35, page 133*

His commandments are not burdensome.

4 For whatever is born of God overcomes the world. And this is the victory that has overcome the world—our faith.

5 Who is he who overcomes the world, but he who believes that Jesus is the Son of God?

6 This is He who came by water and blood—Jesus Christ; not only by water, but by water and blood. And it is the Spirit who bears witness, because the Spirit is truth.

7 For there are three who bear witness in heaven: the Father, the Word, and the Holy Spirit; and these three are one.

8 And there are three that bear witness on earth: the Spirit, the water, and the blood; and these three agree as one.

9 If we receive the witness of men, the witness of God is greater; for this is the witness of God which He has testified of His Son.

10 He who believes in the Son of God has the witness in himself; he who does not believe God has made Him a liar, because he has not believed the testimony that God has given of His Son.

11 And this is the testimony: that God has given us eternal life, and this life is in His Son.

12 He who has the Son has life; he who does not have the Son of God does not have life.

13 These things I have written to you who believe in the name of the Son of God, that you may know that you have eternal life, and that you may *continue to* believe in the name of the Son of God.

14 Now this is the confidence that we have in Him, that if we ask anything according to His will, He hears us.

15 And if we know that He hears us, whatever we ask, we know that we have the petitions that we have asked of Him.

16 If anyone sees his brother sinning a sin *which does* not *lead* to death, he will ask, and He will give him life for those who commit sin not *leading* to death. There is sin *leading* to death. I do not say that he should pray about that.

17 All unrighteousness is sin, and there is sin not *leading* to death.

18 We know that whoever is born of God does not sin; but he who has been born of God keeps himself, and the wicked one does not touch him.

19 We know that we are of God, and the whole world lies *under the sway of* the wicked one.

20 And we know that the Son of God has come and has given us an understanding, that we may know Him who is true; and we are in Him who is true, in His Son Jesus Christ. This is the true God and eternal life.

21 Little children, keep yourselves from idols. Amen.

THE SECOND EPISTLE OF
JOHN

THE ELDER,

To the elect lady and her children, whom I love in truth, and not only I, but also all those who have known the truth,

2 because of the truth which abides in us and will be with us forever:

3 Grace, mercy, *and* peace will be with you from God the Father and from the Lord Jesus Christ, the Son of the Father, in truth and love.

4 I rejoiced greatly that I have found *some* of your children walking in truth, as we received commandment from the Father.

5 And now I plead with you, lady, not as though I wrote a new commandment to you, but that which we have had from the beginning: that we love one another.

6 This is love, that we walk according to His commandments. This is the commandment, that as you have heard from the beginning, you should walk in it.

7 For many deceivers have gone out into the world who do not confess Jesus Christ *as* coming in the flesh. This is a deceiver and an antichrist.

8 Look to yourselves, that we do not lose those things we worked for, but *that* we may receive a full reward.

9 Whoever transgresses and does not abide in the doctrine of Christ does not have God. He who abides in the doctrine of Christ has both the Father and the Son.

10 If anyone comes to you and does not bring this doctrine, do not receive him into your house nor greet him;

11 for he who greets him shares in his evil deeds.

12 Having many things to write to you, I did not wish *to do so* with paper and ink; but I hope to come to you and speak face to face, that our joy may be full.

13 The children of your elect sister greet you. Amen.

THE THIRD EPISTLE OF
JOHN

THE ELDER,

To the beloved Gaius, whom I love in truth:

2 Beloved, I pray that you may prosper in all things and be in health, just as your soul prospers.

3 For I rejoiced greatly when brethren came and testified of the truth *that is* in you, just as you walk in the truth.

4 I have no greater joy than to hear that my children walk in truth.

5 Beloved, you do faithfully whatever you do for the brethren and for strangers,

6 who have borne witness of your love before the church. *If* you send them forward on their journey in a manner worthy of God, you will do well,

7 because they went forth for His name's sake, taking nothing from the Gentiles.

8 We therefore ought to receive such, that we may become fellow workers for the truth.

9 I wrote to the church, but Diotrephes, who loves to have the preeminence among them, does not receive us.

10 Therefore, if I come, I will call to mind his deeds which he does, prating against us with malicious words. And not content with that, he himself does not receive the brethren, and forbids those who wish to, putting *them* out of the church.

11 Beloved, do not imitate what is evil, but what is good. He who does good is of God, but he who does evil has not seen God.

12 Demetrius has a good testimony from all, and from the truth itself. And we also bear witness, and you know that our testimony is true.

13 I had many things to write, but I do not wish to write to you with pen and ink;

14 but I hope to see you shortly, and we shall speak face to face. Peace to you. Our friends greet you. Greet the friends by name.

THE EPISTLE OF
JUDE

JUDE, a servant of Jesus Christ, and brother of James,

To those who are called, sanctified by God the Father, and preserved in Jesus Christ:

2 Mercy, peace, and love be multiplied to you.

3 Beloved, while I was very diligent to write to you concerning our common salvation, I found it necessary to write to you exhorting you to contend earnestly for the faith which was once for all delivered to the saints.

4 For certain men have crept in unnoticed, who long ago were marked out for this condemnation, ungodly men, who turn the grace of our God into licentiousness and deny the only Lord God and our Lord Jesus Christ.

5 But I want to remind you, though you once knew this, that the Lord, having saved the people out of the land of Egypt, afterward destroyed those who did not believe.

6 And the angels who did not keep their proper domain, but left their own habitation, He has reserved in everlasting chains under darkness for the judgment of the great day;

7 as Sodom and Gomorrah, and the cities around them in a similar manner to these, having given themselves over to sexual immorality and gone after strange flesh, are set forth as an example, suffering the vengeance of eternal fire.

8 Likewise also these dreamers defile the flesh, reject authority, and speak evil of dignitaries.

9 Yet Michael the archangel, in contending with the devil, when he disputed about the body of Moses, dared not bring against him a reviling accusation, but said, "The Lord rebuke you!"

10 But these speak evil of whatever they do not know; and whatever they know naturally, like brute beasts, in these things they corrupt themselves.

11 Woe to them! For they have gone in the way of Cain, have run

greedily in the error of Balaam for profit, and perished in the rebellion of Korah.

12 These are spots in your love feasts, while they feast with you without fear, serving *only* themselves; *they are* clouds without water, carried about by the winds; late autumn trees without fruit, twice dead, pulled up by the roots; 13 raging waves of the sea, foaming up their own shame; wandering stars for whom is reserved the blackness of darkness forever.

14 Now Enoch, the seventh from Adam, prophesied about these men also, saying, "Behold, the Lord comes with ten thousands of His saints, 15 "to execute judgment on all, to convict all who are ungodly among them of all their ungodly deeds which they have committed in an ungodly way, and of all the harsh things which ungodly sinners have spoken against Him."

16 These are murmurers, complainers, walking according to their own lusts; and they mouth great swelling *words*, flattering people to gain advantage.

17 But you, beloved, remember the words which were spoken before by the apostles of our Lord Jesus Christ:

18 how they told you that there would be mockers in the last time who would walk according to their own ungodly lusts.

19 These are sensual persons, who cause divisions, not having the Spirit.

20 But you, beloved, building yourselves up on your most holy faith, praying in the Holy Spirit,

21 keep yourselves in the love of God, looking for the mercy of our Lord Jesus Christ unto eternal life.

22 And on some have compassion, making a distinction;

23 but others save with fear, pulling *them* out of the fire, hating even the garment defiled by the flesh.

24 Now to Him who is able
　　to keep you from stumbling,
And to present *you* faultless
Before the presence of His
　　glory with exceeding joy,
25 To God our Savior,
Who alone is wise,
Be glory and majesty,
Dominion and power,
Both now and forever.
Amen.

THE REVELATION

OF JESUS CHRIST

THE Revelation of Jesus Christ, which God gave Him to show His servants—things which must shortly take place. And He sent and signified *it* by His angel to His servant John,

2 who bore witness to the word of God, and to the testimony of Jesus Christ, and to all things that he saw.

3 Blessed *is* he who reads and those who hear the words of this prophecy, and keep those things which are written in it; for the time *is* near.

4 John, to the seven churches which are in Asia:

Grace to you and peace from Him who is and who was and who is to come, and from the seven Spirits who are before His throne, 5 and from Jesus Christ, the faithful witness, the firstborn from the dead, and the ruler over the kings of the earth. To Him who loved us and washed us from our sins in His own blood,

6 and has made us kings and priests to His God and Father, to Him be glory and dominion forever and ever. Amen.

7 Behold, He is coming with clouds, and every eye will see Him, and they *also* who pierced Him. And all the tribes of the earth will mourn because of Him. Even so, Amen.

8 "I am the Alpha and the Omega, *the* Beginning and *the* End," says the Lord, "who is and who was and who is to come, the Almighty."

9 I, John, both your brother and companion in tribulation, and in the kingdom and patience of Jesus Christ, was on the island that is called Patmos for the word of God and for the testimony of Jesus Christ.

10 I was in the Spirit on the Lord's Day, and I heard behind me a loud voice, as of a trumpet,

11 saying, "I am the Alpha and the Omega, the First and the Last," and, "What you see, write in a book and send *it* to the seven churches which are in Asia: to Ephesus, to Smyrna, to Pergamos, to Thyatira, to Sardis, to Philadelphia, and to Laodicea."

12 Then I turned to see the voice that spoke with me. And having turned I saw seven golden lampstands,

13 and in the midst of the seven lampstands *One* like the Son of Man, clothed with a garment down to the feet and girded about the chest with a golden band.

14 His head and *His* hair *were* white like wool, as white as snow, and His eyes like a flame of fire;

15 His feet *were* like fine brass, as if refined in a furnace, and His voice as the sound of many waters;

16 He had in His right hand seven stars, out of His mouth went a

sharp two-edged sword, and His countenance *was* like the sun shining in its strength.

17 And when I saw Him, I fell at His feet as dead. But He laid His right hand on me, saying to me, "Do not be afraid; I am the First and the Last.

18 "I *am* He who lives, and was dead, and behold, I am alive forevermore. Amen. And I have the keys of Hades and of Death.

19 "Write the things which you have seen, and the things which are, and the things which will take place after this.

20 "The mystery of the seven stars which you saw in My right hand, and the seven golden lampstands: The seven stars are the angels of the seven churches, and the seven lampstands which you saw are the seven churches.

2 "To the angel of the church of Ephesus write,

'These things says He who holds the seven stars in His right hand, who walks in the midst of the seven golden lampstands:

2 "I know your works, your labor, your patience, and that you cannot bear those who are evil. And you have tested those who say they are apostles and are not, and have found them liars;

3 "and you have persevered and have patience, and have labored for My name's sake and have not become weary.

4 "Nevertheless I have *this* against you, that you have left your first love.

5 "Remember therefore from where you have fallen; repent and do the first works, or else I will come to you quickly and remove your lampstand from its place—unless you repent.

6 "But this you have, that you hate the deeds of the Nicolaitans, which I also hate.

7 "He who has an ear, let him hear what the Spirit says to the churches. To him who overcomes I

will give to eat from the tree of life, which is in the midst of the Paradise of God." '

8 "And to the angel of the church in Smyrna write,

'These things says the First and the Last, who was dead, and came to life:

9 "I know your works, tribulation, and poverty (but you are rich); and *I know* the blasphemy of those who say they are Jews and are not, but *are* a synagogue of Satan.

10 "Do not fear any of those things which you are about to suffer. Indeed, the devil is about to throw *some* of you into prison, that you may be tested, and you will have tribulation ten days. Be faithful until death, and I will give you the crown of life.

11 "He who has an ear, let him hear what the Spirit says to the churches. He who overcomes shall not be hurt by the second death." '

12 "And to the angel of the church in Pergamos write,

'These things says He who has the sharp two-edged sword:

13 "I know your works, and where you dwell, where Satan's throne *is*. And you hold fast to My name, and did not deny My faith even in the days in which Antipas *was* My faithful martyr, who was killed among you, where Satan dwells.

14 "But I have a few things against you, because you have there those who hold the doctrine of Balaam, who taught Balak to put a stumbling block before the children of Israel, to eat things sacrificed to idols, and to commit sexual immorality.

15 "Thus you also have those who hold the doctrine of the Nicolaitans, which thing I hate.

16 "Repent, or else I will come to you quickly and will fight against them with the sword of My mouth.

17 "He who has an ear, let him hear what the Spirit says to the churches. To him who overcomes I will give some of the hidden manna to eat. And I will give him a white stone, and on the stone a new name written which no one knows except him who receives *it*." '

18 "And to the angel of the church in Thyatira write,

'These things says the Son of God, who has eyes like a flame of fire, and His feet like fine brass:

19 "I know your works, love, service, faith, and your patience; and *as* for your works, the last *are* more than the first.

20 "Nevertheless I have a few things against you, because you allow that woman Jezebel, who calls herself a prophetess, to teach and beguile My servants to commit sexual immorality and to eat things sacrificed to idols.

21 "And I gave her time to repent of her sexual immorality, and she did not repent.

22 "Indeed I will cast her into a sickbed, and those who commit adultery with her into great tribulation, unless they repent of their deeds.

23 "And I will kill her children with death. And all the churches shall know that I am He who searches the minds and hearts. And I will give to each one of you according to your works.

24 "But to you I say, and to the rest in Thyatira, as many as do not have this doctrine, and who have not known the depths of Satan, as they call *them*, I will put on you no other burden.

25 "But hold fast what you have till I come.

26 "And he who overcomes, and keeps My works until the end, to him I will give power over the nations—

27 'He shall rule them with a rod of iron;
   As the potter's vessels
      shall be broken to pieces'—

297

as I also have received from My Father;

28 "and I will give him the morning star.

29 "He who has an ear, let him hear what the Spirit says to the churches." '

3 "And to the angel of the church in Sardis write,

'These things says He who has the seven Spirits of God and the seven stars: "I know your works, that you have a name that you are alive, but you are dead.

2 "Be watchful, and strengthen the things which remain, that are ready to die, for I have not found your works perfect before God.

3 "Remember therefore how you have received and heard; hold fast and repent. Therefore if you will not watch, I will come upon you as a thief, and you will not know what hour I will come upon you.

4 "You have a few names even in Sardis who have not defiled their garments; and they shall walk with Me in white, for they are worthy.

5 "He who overcomes shall be clothed in white garments, and I will not blot out his name from the Book of Life; but I will confess his name before My Father and before His angels.

6 "He who has an ear, let him hear what the Spirit says to the churches." '

7 "And to the angel of the church in Philadelphia write,

'These things says He who is holy, He who is true, "*He who has the key of David, He who opens and no one shuts, and shuts and no one opens*":

8 "I know your works. See, I have set before you an open door, and no one can shut it; for you have a little strength, have kept My word, and have not denied My name.

9 "Indeed I will make *those* of the synagogue of Satan, who say they are Jews and are not, but lie— indeed I will make them come and

worship before your feet, and to know that I have loved you.

10 "Because you have kept My command to persevere, I also will keep you from the hour of trial which shall come upon the whole world, to test those who dwell on the earth.

11 "Behold, I come quickly! Hold fast what you have, that no one may take your crown.

12 "He who overcomes, I will make him a pillar in the temple of My God, and he shall go out no more. And I will write on him the name of My God and the name of the city of My God, the New Jerusalem, which comes down out of heaven from My God. And *I will write on him* My new name.

13 "He who has an ear, let him hear what the Spirit says to the churches." '

14 "And to the angel of the church of the Laodiceans write,

'These things says the Amen, the Faithful and True Witness, the Beginning of the creation of God:

15 "I know your works, that you are neither cold nor hot. I could wish you were cold or hot.

16 "So then, because you are lukewarm, and neither cold nor hot, I will spew you out of My mouth.

17 "Because you say, 'I am rich, have become wealthy, and have need of nothing'—and do not know that you are wretched, miserable, poor, blind, and naked—

18 "I counsel you to buy from Me gold refined in the fire, that you may be rich; and white garments, that you may be clothed, *that* the shame of your nakedness may not be revealed; and anoint your eyes with eye salve, that you may see.

19 "As many as I love, I rebuke and chasten. Therefore be zealous and repent.

20 "Behold, I stand at the door and knock. If anyone hears My voice and opens the door, I will come in to him and dine with him, and he with Me.

21 "To him who overcomes I will grant to sit with Me on My throne, as I also overcame and sat down with My Father on His throne.

22 "He who has an ear, let him hear what the Spirit says to the churches." ' "

4 After these things I looked, and behold, a door *standing* open in heaven. And the first voice which I heard *was* like a trumpet speaking with me, saying, "Come up here, and I will show you things which must take place after this."

2 Immediately I was in the Spirit; and behold, a throne set in heaven, and *One* sat on the throne.

3 And He who sat there was like a jasper and a sardius stone in appearance; and *there was* a rainbow around the throne, in appearance like an emerald.

4 Around the throne *were* twenty-four thrones, and on the thrones I saw twenty-four elders sitting, clothed in white robes; and they had crowns of gold on their heads.

5 And from the throne proceeded lightnings, thunderings, and voices. And *there were* seven lamps of fire burning before the throne, which are the seven Spirits of God.

6 Before the throne *there was* a sea of glass, like crystal. And in the midst of the throne, and around the throne, *were* four living creatures full of eyes in front and in back.

7 The first living creature *was* like a lion, the second living creature like a calf, the third living creature had a face like a man, and the fourth living creature *was* like a flying eagle.

8 And *the* four living creatures, each having six wings, were full of eyes around and within. And they do not rest day or night, saying:

"Holy, holy, holy,
    Lord God Almighty,

Who was and is and is to
    come!"

9 Whenever the living creatures give glory and honor and thanks to Him who sits on the throne, who lives forever and ever,

10 the twenty-four elders fall down before Him who sits on the throne and worship Him who lives forever and ever, and cast their crowns before the throne, saying:

11 "You are worthy, O Lord,
    To receive glory and honor and
        power;
    For You created all things,
    And by Your will they exist
        and were created."

5 And I saw in the right *hand* of Him who sat on the throne a scroll written inside and on the back, sealed with seven seals.

2 Then I saw a strong angel proclaiming with a loud voice, "Who is worthy to open the scroll and to loose its seals?"

3 And no one in heaven or on the earth or under the earth was able to open the scroll, or to look at it.

4 So I wept much, because no one was found worthy to open and read the scroll, or to look at it.

5 But one of the elders said to me, "Do not weep. Behold, the Lion of the tribe of Judah, the Root of David, has prevailed to open the scroll and to loose its seven seals."

6 And I looked, and behold, in the midst of the throne and of the four living creatures, and in the midst of the elders, stood a Lamb as though it had been slain, having seven horns and seven eyes, which are the seven Spirits of God sent out into all the earth.

7 Then He came and took the scroll out of the right hand of Him who sat on the throne.

8 Now when He had taken the scroll, the four living creatures and the twenty-four elders fell down

before the Lamb, each having a harp, and golden bowls full of incense, which are the prayers of the saints.

9 And they sang a new song, saying:

> "You are worthy to take the scroll,
> And to open its seals;
> For You were slain,
> And have redeemed us to God by Your blood
> Out of every tribe and tongue and people and nation,
> 10 And have made us kings and priests to our God;
> And we shall reign on the earth."

11 Then I looked, and I heard the voice of many angels around the throne, the living creatures, and the elders; and the number of them was ten thousand times ten thousand, and thousands of thousands, 12 saying with a loud voice:

> "Worthy is the Lamb who was slain
> To receive power and riches and wisdom,
> And strength and honor and glory and blessing!"

13 And every creature which is in heaven and on the earth and under the earth and such as are in the sea, and all that are in them, I heard saying:

> "Blessing and honor and glory and power
> *Be* to Him who sits on the throne,
> And to the Lamb, forever and ever!"

14 Then the four living creatures said, "Amen!" And the twenty-four elders fell down and worshiped Him who lives forever and ever.

6 Now I saw when the Lamb opened one of the seals; and I heard one of the four living creatures saying with a voice like thunder, "Come and see."

2 And I looked, and behold, a white horse. And he who sat on it had a bow; and a crown was given to him, and he went out conquering and to conquer.

3 When He opened the second seal, I heard the second living creature saying, "Come and see." 4 And another horse, fiery red, went out. And it was granted to the one who sat on it to take peace from the earth, and that *people* should kill one another; and there was given to him a great sword.

5 When He opened the third seal, I heard the third living creature say, "Come and see." And I looked, and behold, a black horse, and he who sat on it had a pair of scales in his hand. 6 And I heard a voice in the midst of the four living creatures saying, "A quart of wheat for a denarius, and three quarts of barley for a denarius; and do not harm the oil and the wine."

7 When He opened the fourth seal, I heard the voice of the fourth living creature saying, "Come and see." 8 And I looked, and behold, a pale horse. And the name of him who sat on it was Death, and Hades followed with him. And power was given to them over a fourth of the earth, to kill with sword, with hunger, with death, and by the beasts of the earth.

9 When He opened the fifth seal, I saw under the altar the souls of those who had been slain for the word of God and for the testimony which they held. 10 And they cried with a loud voice, saying, "How long, O Lord, holy and true, until You judge and avenge our blood on those who dwell on the earth?"

11 And a white robe was given to each of them; and it was said to

them that they should rest a little while longer, until both *the number of* their fellow servants and their brethren, who would be killed as they *were*, was completed.

12 I looked when He opened the sixth seal, and behold, there was a great earthquake; and the sun became black as sackcloth of hair, and the moon became like blood.

13 And the stars of heaven fell to the earth, as a fig tree drops its late figs when it is shaken by a mighty wind.

14 Then the sky receded as a scroll when it is rolled up, and every mountain and island was moved out of its place.

15 And the kings of the earth, the great men, the rich men, the commanders, the mighty men, every slave and every free man, hid themselves in the caves and in the rocks of the mountains,

16 and said to the mountains and rocks, "Fall on us and hide us from the face of Him who sits on the throne and from the wrath of the Lamb!

17 "For the great day of His wrath has come, and who is able to stand?"

7 After these things I saw four angels standing at the four corners of the earth, holding the four winds of the earth, that the wind should not blow on the earth, on the sea, or on any tree.

2 Then I saw another angel ascending from the east, having the seal of the living God. And he cried with a loud voice to the four angels to whom it was granted to harm the earth and the sea,

3 saying, "Do not harm the earth, the sea, or the trees till we have sealed the servants of our God on their foreheads."

4 And I heard the number of those who were sealed. One hundred *and* forty-four thousand of all the tribes of the children of Israel *were* sealed:

5 of the tribe of Judah
   twelve thousand *were* sealed;
of the tribe of Reuben
   twelve thousand *were* sealed;
of the tribe of Gad
   twelve thousand *were* sealed;

6 of the tribe of Asher
   twelve thousand *were* sealed;
of the tribe of Naphtali
   twelve thousand *were* sealed;
of the tribe of Manasseh
   twelve thousand *were* sealed;

7 of the tribe of Simeon
   twelve thousand *were* sealed;
of the tribe of Levi
   twelve thousand *were* sealed;
of the tribe of Issachar
   twelve thousand *were* sealed;

8 of the tribe of Zebulun
   twelve thousand *were* sealed;
of the tribe of Joseph
   twelve thousand *were* sealed;
of the tribe of Benjamin
   twelve thousand *were* sealed.

9 After these things I looked, and behold, a great multitude which no one could number, of all nations, tribes, peoples, and tongues, standing before the throne and before the Lamb, clothed with white robes, with palm branches in their hands,

10 and crying out with a loud voice, saying, "Salvation *belongs* to our God who sits on the throne, and to the Lamb!"

11 And all the angels stood around the throne and the elders and the four living creatures, and fell on their faces before the throne and worshiped God,

12 saying:

   "Amen! Blessing and glory
      and wisdom,
   Thanksgiving and honor and
      power and might,
   Be to our God forever and
      ever.
   Amen."

13 Then one of the elders answered, saying to me, "Who are

these arrayed in white robes, and where did they come from?"

14 And I said to him, "Sir, you know." So he said to me, "These are the ones who come out of the great tribulation, and washed their robes and made them white in the blood of the Lamb.

15 "Therefore they are before the throne of God, and serve Him day and night in His temple. And He who sits on the throne will dwell among them.

16 "They shall neither hunger anymore nor thirst anymore; the sun shall not strike them, nor any heat;

17 "for the Lamb who is in the midst of the throne will shepherd them and lead them to living fountains of waters. And God will wipe away every tear from their eyes."

8 When He opened the seventh seal, there was silence in heaven for about half an hour.

2 And I saw the seven angels who stand before God, and to them were given seven trumpets.

3 Then another angel, having a golden censer, came and stood at the altar. And he was given much incense, that he should offer *it* with the prayers of all the saints upon the golden altar which was before the throne.

4 And the smoke of the incense, with the prayers of the saints, ascended before God from the angel's hand.

5 Then the angel took the censer, filled it with fire from the altar, and threw *it* to the earth. And there were noises, thunderings, lightnings, and an earthquake.

6 So the seven angels who had the seven trumpets prepared themselves to sound.

7 The first angel sounded: And hail and fire followed, mingled with blood, and they were thrown to the earth; and a third of the trees were burned up, and all green grass was burned up.

8 Then the second angel sounded:

And *something* like a great mountain burning with fire was thrown into the sea, and a third of the sea became blood;

9 and a third of the living creatures in the sea died, and a third of the ships were destroyed.

10 Then the third angel sounded: And a great star fell from heaven, burning like a torch, and it fell on a third of the rivers and on the springs of water;

11 and the name of the star is Wormwood; and a third of the waters became wormwood; and many men died from the water, because it was made bitter.

12 Then the fourth angel sounded: And a third of the sun was struck, a third of the moon, and a third of the stars, so that a third of them were darkened; and a third of the day did not shine, and likewise the night.

13 And I looked, and I heard an angel flying through the midst of heaven, saying with a loud voice, "Woe, woe, woe to the inhabitants of the earth, because of the remaining blasts of the trumpet of the three angels who are about to sound!"

9 Then the fifth angel sounded: And I saw a star fallen from heaven to the earth. And to him was given the key to the bottomless pit.

2 And he opened the bottomless pit, and smoke arose out of the pit like the smoke of a great furnace. And the sun and the air were darkened because of the smoke of the pit.

3 Then out of the smoke locusts came upon the earth. And to them was given power, as the scorpions of the earth have power.

4 They were commanded not to harm the grass of the earth, or any green thing, or any tree, but only those men who do not have the seal of God on their foreheads.

5 And they were not given *authority* to kill them, but to torment

them *for* five months. And their torment *was* like the torment of a scorpion when it strikes a man.

6 In those days men will seek death and will not find it; they will desire to die, and death will flee from them.

7 And the shape of the locusts was like horses prepared for battle; and on their heads were crowns of something like gold, and their faces *were* like the faces of men.

8 They had hair like women's hair, and their teeth were like lions' *teeth.*

9 And they had breastplates like breastplates of iron, and the sound of their wings *was* like the sound of chariots with many horses running into battle.

10 They had tails like scorpions, and there were stings in their tails. And their power *was* to hurt men five months.

11 And they had as king over them the angel of the bottomless pit, whose name in Hebrew *is* Abaddon, but in Greek he has the name Apollyon.

12 One woe is past. Behold, still two more woes are coming after these things.

13 Then the sixth angel sounded: And I heard a voice from the four horns of the golden altar which is before God,

14 saying to the sixth angel who had the trumpet, "Release the four angels who are bound at the great river Euphrates."

15 So the four angels, who had been prepared for the hour and day and month and year, were released to kill a third of mankind.

16 Now the number of the army of the horsemen *was* two hundred million, and I heard the number of them.

17 And thus I saw the horses in the vision: those who sat on them had breastplates of fiery red, hyacinth blue, and sulfur yellow; and the heads of the horses *were* like the heads of lions; and out of their mouths came fire, smoke, and brimstone.

18 By these three *plagues* a third of mankind was killed—by the fire and the smoke and the brimstone which came out of their mouths.

19 For their power is in their mouth and in their tails; for their tails *are* like serpents, having heads; and with them they do harm.

20 But the rest of mankind, who were not killed by these plagues, did not repent of the works of their hands, that they should not worship demons, and idols of gold, silver, brass, stone, and wood, which can neither see nor hear nor walk;

21 and they did not repent of their murders or their sorceries or their sexual immorality or their thefts.

10 And I saw still another mighty angel coming down from heaven, clothed with a cloud. And a rainbow *was* on his head, his face *was* like the sun, and his feet like pillars of fire.

2 And he had a little book open in his hand. And he set his right foot on the sea and *his* left *foot* on the land,

3 and cried with a loud voice, as *when* a lion roars. And when he cried out, seven thunders uttered their voices.

4 Now when the seven thunders uttered their voices, I was about to write; but I heard a voice from heaven saying to me, "Seal up the things which the seven thunders uttered, and do not write them."

5 And the angel whom I saw standing on the sea and on the land lifted up his hand to heaven

6 and swore by Him who lives forever and ever, who created heaven and the things that are in it, the earth and the things that are in it, and the sea and the things that are in it, that there should be delay no longer,

7 but in the days of the sounding

of the seventh angel, when he is about to sound, the mystery of God would be finished, as He declared to His servants the prophets.

8 Then the voice which I heard from heaven spoke to me again and said, "Go, take the little book which is open in the hand of the angel who stands on the sea and on the earth."

9 And I went to the angel and said to him, "Give me the little book." And he said to me, "Take and eat it; and it will make your stomach bitter, but it will be as sweet as honey in your mouth."

10 And I took the little book out of the angel's hand and ate it, and it was as sweet as honey in my mouth. But when I had eaten it, my stomach became bitter.

11 And he said to me, "You must prophesy again about many peoples, nations, tongues, and kings."

11 Then I was given a reed like a measuring rod. And the angel stood, saying, "Rise and measure the temple of God, the altar, and those who worship there.

2 "But leave out the court which is outside the temple, and do not measure it, for it has been given to the Gentiles. And they will tread the holy city under foot *for* forty-two months.

3 "And I will give *power* to my two witnesses, and they will prophesy one thousand two hundred and sixty days, clothed in sackcloth."

4 These are the two olive trees and the two lampstands standing before the God of the earth.

5 And if anyone wants to harm them, fire proceeds from their mouth and devours their enemies. And if anyone wants to harm them, he must be killed in this manner.

6 These have power to shut heaven, so that no rain falls in the days of their prophecy; and they have power over waters to turn them to blood, and to strike the earth with all plagues, as often as they desire.

7 Now when they finish their testimony, the beast that ascends out of the bottomless pit will make war against them, overcome them, and kill them.

8 And their dead bodies *will lie* in the street of the great city which spiritually is called Sodom and Egypt, where also our Lord was crucified.

9 Then *those* from the peoples, tribes, tongues, and nations will see their dead bodies three and a half days, and not allow their dead bodies to be put into graves.

10 And those who dwell on the earth will rejoice over them, make merry, and send gifts to one another, because these two prophets tormented those who dwell on the earth.

11 Now after the three and a half days the breath of life from God entered them, and they stood on their feet, and great fear fell on those who saw them.

12 And they heard a loud voice from heaven saying to them, "Come up here." And they ascended to heaven in a cloud, and their enemies saw them.

13 In the same hour there was a great earthquake, and a tenth of the city fell. In the earthquake seven thousand men were killed, and the rest were afraid and gave glory to the God of heaven.

14 The second woe is past. Behold, the third woe is coming quickly.

15 Then the seventh angel sounded: And there were loud voices in heaven, saying, "The kingdoms of this world have become *the kingdoms* of our Lord and of His Christ, and He shall reign forever and ever!"

16 And the twenty-four elders who sat before God on their thrones fell on their faces and worshiped God, 17 saying:

"We give You thanks,
O Lord God Almighty,
The One who is and who was
and who is to come,
Because You have taken Your
great power and reigned.
18 The nations were angry,
and Your wrath has come,
And the time of the dead,
that they should be judged,
And that You should reward
Your servants the prophets
and the saints,
And those who fear Your
name, small and great,
And should destroy those
who destroy the earth."

19 Then the temple of God was opened in heaven, and the ark of His covenant was seen in His temple. And there were lightnings, noises, thunderings, an earthquake, and great hail.

12 Now a great sign appeared in heaven: a woman clothed with the sun, with the moon under her feet, and on her head a garland of twelve stars.
2 Then being with child, she cried out in labor and in pain to give birth.
3 And another sign appeared in heaven: behold, a great, fiery red dragon having seven heads and ten horns, and seven diadems on his heads.
4 His tail drew a third of the stars of heaven and threw them to the earth. And the dragon stood before the woman who was ready to give birth, to devour her Child as soon as it was born.
5 And she bore a male Child who was to rule all nations with a rod of iron. And her Child was caught up to God and *to* His throne.
6 Then the woman fled into the wilderness, where she has a place prepared by God, that they should feed her there one thousand two hundred and sixty days.
7 And war broke out in heaven:

Michael and his angels fought against the dragon; and the dragon and his angels fought,
8 but they did not prevail, nor was a place found for them in heaven any longer.
9 So the great dragon was cast out, that serpent of old, called the Devil and Satan, who deceives the whole world; he was cast to the earth, and his angels were cast out with him.
10 Then I heard a loud voice saying in heaven, "Now salvation, and strength, and the kingdom of our God, and the power of His Christ have come, for the accuser of our brethren, who accused them before our God day and night, has been cast down.
11 "And they overcame him by the blood of the Lamb and by the word of their testimony, and they did not love their lives to the death.
12 "Therefore rejoice, O heavens, and you who dwell in them! Woe to the inhabitants of the earth and the sea! For the devil has come down to you, having great wrath, because he knows that he has a short time."
13 Now when the dragon saw that he had been cast to the earth, he persecuted the woman who gave birth to the male *Child.*
14 But the woman was given two wings of a great eagle, that she might fly into the wilderness to her place, where she is nourished for a time and times and half a time, from the presence of the serpent.
15 So the serpent spewed water out of his mouth like a flood after the woman, that he might cause her to be carried away by the flood.
16 But the earth helped the woman, and the earth opened its mouth and swallowed up the flood which the dragon had spewed out of his mouth.
17 And the dragon was enraged with the woman, and he went to make war with the rest of her off-

spring, who keep the commandments of God and have the testimony of Jesus Christ.

13 Then I stood on the sand of the sea. And I saw a beast rising up out of the sea, having seven heads and ten horns, and on his horns ten crowns, and on his heads a blasphemous name.

2 Now the beast which I saw was like a leopard, his feet were like *the feet of* a bear, and his mouth like the mouth of a lion. And the dragon gave him his power, his throne, and great authority.

3 I saw one of his heads as if it had been mortally wounded, and his deadly wound was healed. And all the world marveled and followed the beast.

4 So they worshiped the dragon who gave authority to the beast; and they worshiped the beast, saying, "Who *is* like the beast? Who is able to make war with him?"

5 And he was given a mouth speaking great things and blasphemies, and he was given authority to continue for forty-two months.

6 Then he opened his mouth in blasphemy against God, to blaspheme His name, His tabernacle, and those who dwell in heaven.

7 And it was granted to him to make war with the saints and to overcome them. And authority was given him over every tribe, tongue, and nation.

8 And all who dwell on the earth will worship him, whose names have not been written in the Book of Life of the Lamb slain from the foundation of the world.

9 If anyone has an ear, let him hear.

10 He who leads into captivity shall go into captivity; he who kills with the sword must be killed with the sword. Here is the patience and the faith of the saints.

11 Then I saw another beast coming up out of the earth, and he had two horns like a lamb and spoke like a dragon.

12 And he exercises all the authority of the first beast in his presence, and causes the earth and those who dwell in it to worship the first beast, whose deadly wound was healed.

13 He performs great signs, so that he even makes fire come down from heaven on the earth in the sight of men.

14 And he deceives those who dwell on the earth by those signs which he was granted to do in the sight of the beast, telling those who dwell on the earth to make an image to the beast who was wounded by the sword and lived.

15 He was granted *power* to give breath to the image of the beast, that the image of the beast should both speak and cause as many as would not worship the image of the beast to be killed.

16 And he causes all, both small and great, rich and poor, free and slave, to receive a mark on their right hand or on their foreheads,

17 and that no one may buy or sell except one who has the mark or the name of the beast, or the number of his name.

18 Here is wisdom. Let him who has understanding calculate the number of the beast, for it is the number of a man: His number *is* 666.

14 Then I looked, and behold, a Lamb standing on Mount Zion, and with Him one hundred *and* forty-four thousand, having His Father's name written on their foreheads.

2 And I heard a voice from heaven, like the voice of many waters, and like the voice of loud thunder. And I heard the sound of harpists playing their harps.

3 And they sang as it were a new song before the throne, before the four living creatures, and the elders; and no one could learn that song except the hundred *and* forty-four thousand who were redeemed from the earth.

4 These are the ones who were not defiled with women, for they are virgins. These are the ones who follow the Lamb wherever He goes. These were redeemed from *among* men, *being* firstfruits to God and to the Lamb.

5 And in their mouth was found no guile, for they are without fault before the throne of God.

6 Then I saw another angel flying in the midst of heaven, having the everlasting gospel to preach to those who dwell on the earth—to every nation, tribe, tongue, and people—

7 saying with a loud voice, "Fear God and give glory to Him, for the hour of His judgment has come; and worship Him who made heaven and earth, the sea and springs of water."

8 And another angel followed, saying, "Babylon is fallen, is fallen, that great city, because she has made all nations drink of the wine of the wrath of her fornication."

9 Then a third angel followed them, saying with a loud voice, "If anyone worships the beast and his image, and receives *his* mark on his forehead or on his hand,

10 "he himself shall also drink of the wine of the wrath of God, which is poured out full strength into the cup of His indignation. And he shall be tormented with fire and brimstone in the presence of the holy angels and in the presence of the Lamb.

11 "And the smoke of their torment ascends forever and ever; and they have no rest day or night, who worship the beast and his image, and whoever receives the mark of his name."

12 Here is the patience of the saints; here *are* those who keep the commandments of God and the faith of Jesus.

13 Then I heard a voice from heaven saying to me, "Write: 'Blessed *are* the dead who die in the Lord from now on.'" "Yes,"

says the Spirit, "that they may rest from their labors, and their works follow them."

14 And I looked, and behold, a white cloud, and on the cloud sat *One* like the Son of Man, having on His head a golden crown, and in His hand a sharp sickle.

15 And another angel came out of the temple, crying with a loud voice to Him who sat on the cloud, "Thrust in Your sickle and reap, for the time has come for You to reap, for the harvest of the earth is ripe."

16 So He who sat on the cloud thrust in His sickle on the earth, and the earth was reaped.

17 Then another angel came out of the temple which is in heaven, he also having a sharp sickle.

18 And another angel came out from the altar, who had power over fire, and he cried with a loud cry to him who had the sharp sickle, saying, "Thrust in your sharp sickle and gather the clusters of the vine of the earth, for her grapes are fully ripe."

19 So the angel thrust his sickle into the earth and gathered the vine of the earth, and threw *it* into the great winepress of the wrath of God.

20 And the winepress was trampled outside the city, and blood came out of the winepress, up to the horses' bridles, for one thousand six hundred furlongs.

15 Then I saw another sign in heaven, great and marvelous: seven angels having the seven last plagues, for in them the wrath of God is complete.

2 And I saw *something* like a sea of glass mingled with fire, and those who have the victory over the beast, over his image and over his mark *and* over the number of his name, standing on the sea of glass, having harps of God.

3 And they sing the song of Moses, the servant of God, and the song of the Lamb, saying:

"Great and marvelous *are* Your
   works,
Lord God Almighty!
Just and true *are* Your ways,
O King of the saints!
4 Who shall not fear You, O
   Lord, and glorify Your name?
For *You* alone *are* holy.
For all nations shall come and
   worship before You,
For Your judgments have been
   manifested."

5 After these things I looked, and
behold, the temple of the tabernacle of the testimony in heaven was
opened.
6 And out of the temple came the
seven angels having the seven
plagues, clothed in pure bright
linen, and having their chests
girded with golden bands.
7 Then one of the four living creatures gave to the seven angels
seven golden bowls full of the
wrath of God who lives forever
and ever.
8 The temple was filled with
smoke from the glory of God and
from His power, and no one was
able to enter the temple till the
seven plagues of the seven angels
were completed.

16 Then I heard a loud voice
from the temple saying to the
seven angels, "Go and pour out
the bowls of the wrath of God on
the earth."
2 So the first went and poured out
his bowl upon the earth, and a foul
and loathsome sore came upon the
men who had the mark of the
beast and those who worshiped his
image.
3 Then the second angel poured
out his bowl on the sea, and it
became blood as of a dead *man;*
and every living creature in the sea
died.
4 Then the third angel poured out
his bowl on the rivers and springs
of water, and they became blood.
5 And I heard the angel of the
waters saying:

"You are righteous, O Lord,
The One who is and who was
   and who is to be,
Because You have judged
   these things.
6 For they have shed the blood
   of saints and prophets,
And You have given them
   blood to drink.
For it is their just due."

7 And I heard another from the
altar saying, "Even so, Lord God
Almighty, true and righteous *are*
Your judgments."
8 Then the fourth angel poured
out his bowl on the sun, and power
was given to him to scorch men
with fire.
9 And men were scorched with
great heat, and they blasphemed
the name of God who has power
over these plagues; and they did
not repent and give Him glory.
10 Then the fifth angel poured out
his bowl on the throne of the
beast, and his kingdom became full
of darkness; and they gnawed their
tongues because of the pain.
11 And they blasphemed the God
of heaven because of their pains
and their sores, and did not repent
of their deeds.
12 Then the sixth angel poured out
his bowl on the great river Euphrates, and its water was dried up, so
that the way of the kings from the
east might be prepared.
13 And I saw three unclean spirits
like frogs *coming* out of the mouth
of the dragon, out of the mouth of
the beast, and out of the mouth of
the false prophet.
14 For they are spirits of demons,
performing signs, *which* go out to
the kings of the earth and of the
whole world, to gather them to the
battle of that great day of God
Almighty.
15 "Behold, I am coming as a thief.
Blessed *is* he who watches, and
keeps his garments, lest he walk
naked and they see his shame."

16 And they gathered them together to the place called in Hebrew, Armageddon.

17 Then the seventh angel poured out his bowl into the air, and a loud voice came out of the temple of heaven, from the throne, saying, "It is done!"

18 And there were noises and thunderings and lightnings; and there was a great earthquake, such a mighty and great earthquake as had not occurred since men were on the earth.

19 Now the great city was divided into three parts, and the cities of the nations fell. And great Babylon was remembered before God, to give her the cup of the wine of the fierceness of His wrath.

20 Then every island fled away, and the mountains were not found.

21 And great hail from heaven fell upon men, *every hailstone* about the weight of a talent. And men blasphemed God because of the plague of the hail, since that plague was exceedingly great.

17 Then one of the seven angels who had the seven bowls came to me, and talked with me, saying to me, "Come, I will show you the judgment of the great harlot who sits on many waters,

2 "with whom the kings of the earth committed fornication, and the inhabitants of the earth were made drunk with the wine of her fornication."

3 So he carried me away in the Spirit into the wilderness. And I saw a woman sitting on a scarlet beast *which was* full of names of blasphemy, having seven heads and ten horns.

4 The woman was arrayed in purple and scarlet, and adorned with gold and precious stones and pearls, having in her hand a golden cup full of abominations and the filthiness of her fornication.

5 And on her forehead a name *was* written:

MYSTERY,
BABYLON THE GREAT,
THE MOTHER OF HARLOTS
AND OF THE ABOMINATIONS
OF THE EARTH.

6 And I saw the woman, drunk with the blood of the saints and with the blood of the martyrs of Jesus. And when I saw her, I marveled with great amazement.

7 But the angel said to me, "Why did you marvel? I will tell you the mystery of the woman and of the beast that carries her, which has the seven heads and the ten horns.

8 "The beast that you saw was, and is not, and will ascend out of the bottomless pit and go to perdition. And those who dwell on the earth will marvel, whose names are not written in the Book of Life from the foundation of the world, when they see the beast that was, and is not, and yet is.

9 "Here *is* the mind which has wisdom: The seven heads are seven mountains on which the woman sits.

10 There are also seven kings. Five have fallen, one is, *and* the other has not yet come. And when he comes, he must continue a short time.

11 "And the beast that was, and is not, is himself also the eighth, and is of the seven, and is going to perdition.

12 "And the ten horns which you saw are ten kings who have received no kingdom as yet, but they receive authority for one hour as kings with the beast.

13 "These are of one mind, and they will give their power and authority to the beast.

14 "These will make war with the Lamb, and the Lamb will overcome them, for He is Lord of lords and King of kings; and those *who are* with Him *are* called, chosen, and faithful."

15 And he said to me, "The waters

309

which you saw, where the harlot sits, are peoples, multitudes, nations, and tongues.

16 "And the ten horns which you saw on the beast, these will hate the harlot, make her desolate and naked, eat her flesh and burn her with fire.

17 "For God has put it into their hearts to fulfill His purpose, to be of one mind, and to give their kingdom to the beast, until the words of God are fulfilled.

18 "And the woman whom you saw is that great city which reigns over the kings of the earth."

18 After these things I saw another angel coming down from heaven, having great authority, and the earth was illuminated with his glory.

2 And he cried mightily with a loud voice, saying, "Babylon the great is fallen, is fallen, and has become a habitation of demons, a prison for every foul spirit, and a cage for every unclean and hated bird!

3 "For all the nations have drunk of the wine of the wrath of her fornication, the kings of the earth have committed fornication with her, and the merchants of the earth have become rich through the abundance of her luxury."

4 And I heard another voice from heaven saying, "Come out of her, my people, lest you share in her sins, and lest you receive of her plagues.

5 "For her sins have reached to heaven, and God has remembered her iniquities.

6 "Render to her just as she rendered to you, and repay her double according to her works; in the cup which she has mixed, mix for her double.

7 "In the measure that she glorified herself and lived luxuriously, in the same measure give her torment and sorrow; for she says in her heart, 'I sit *as* queen, and am

no widow, and will not see sorrow.'

8 "Therefore her plagues will come in one day—death and mourning and famine. And she will be utterly burned with fire, for strong *is* the Lord God who judges her.

9 "And the kings of the earth who committed fornication and lived luxuriously with her will weep and lament for her, when they see the smoke of her burning,

10 "standing at a distance for fear of her torment, saying, 'Alas, alas, that great city Babylon, that mighty city! For in one hour your judgment has come.'

11 "And the merchants of the earth will weep and mourn over her, for no one buys their merchandise anymore:

12 "merchandise of gold and silver, precious stones and pearls, fine linen and purple, silk and scarlet, every kind of citron wood, every kind of object of ivory, every kind of object of most precious wood, bronze, iron, and marble;

13 "and cinnamon and incense, fragrant oil and frankincense, wine and oil, fine flour and wheat, cattle and sheep, horses and chariots, and bodies and souls of men.

14 "And the fruit that your soul longed for has gone from you, and all the things which are rich and splendid have gone from you, and you shall find them no more at all.

15 "The merchants of these things, who became rich by her, will stand at a distance for fear of her torment, weeping and wailing,

16 "and saying, 'Alas, alas, that great city that was clothed in fine linen, purple, and scarlet, and adorned with gold and precious stones and pearls!

17 'For in one hour such great riches came to nothing.' And every shipmaster, all who travel by ship, sailors, and as many as trade on the sea, stood at a distance

18 "and cried out when they saw

the smoke of her burning, saying, 'What *is* like this great city?'

19 "And they threw dust on their heads and cried out, weeping and wailing, and saying, 'Alas, alas, that great city, in which all who had ships on the sea became rich by her wealth! For in one hour she is made desolate.'

20 "Rejoice over her, O heaven, and *you* holy apostles and prophets, for God has avenged you on her!"

21 Then a mighty angel took up a stone like a great millstone and threw *it* into the sea, saying, "Thus with violence the great city Babylon shall be thrown down, and shall not be found anymore.

22 "The sound of harpists, musicians, flutists, and trumpeters shall not be heard in you anymore. And no craftsman of any craft shall be found in you anymore. And the sound of a millstone shall not be heard in you anymore.

23 "And the light of a lamp shall not shine in you anymore. And the voice of bridegroom and bride shall not be heard in you anymore. For your merchants were the great men of the earth, for by your sorcery all the nations were deceived.

24 "And in her was found the blood of prophets and saints, and of all who were slain on the earth."

19 After these things I heard a loud voice of a great multitude in heaven, saying, "Alleluia! Salvation and glory and honor and power to the Lord our God!

2 "For true and righteous *are* His judgments, because He has judged the great harlot who corrupted the earth with her fornication; and He has avenged on her the blood of His servants *shed* by her."

3 Again they said, "Alleluia! And her smoke rises up forever and ever!"

4 And the twenty-four elders and the four living creatures fell down and worshiped God who sat on the throne, saying, "Amen! Alleluia!"

5 Then a voice came from the throne, saying, "Praise our God, all you His servants and those who fear Him, both small and great!"

6 And I heard, as it were, the voice of a great multitude, as the sound of many waters and as the sound of mighty thunderings, saying, "Alleluia! For the Lord God Omnipotent reigns!

7 "Let us be glad and rejoice and give Him glory, for the marriage of the Lamb has come, and His wife has made herself ready."

8 And to her it was granted to be arrayed in fine linen, clean and bright, for the fine linen is the righteous acts of the saints.

9 Then he said to me, "Write: 'Blessed *are* those who are called to the marriage supper of the Lamb!' " And he said to me, "These are the true sayings of God."

10 And I fell at his feet to worship him. But he said to me, "See that *you* do not *do that!* I am your fellow servant, and of your brethren who have the testimony of Jesus. Worship God! For the testimony of Jesus is the spirit of prophecy."

11 Then I saw heaven opened, and behold, a white horse. And He who sat on him *was* called Faithful and True, and in righteousness He judges and makes war.

12 His eyes *were* like a flame of fire, and on His head *were* many crowns. He had a name written that no one knew except Himself.

13 He *was* clothed with a robe dipped in blood, and His name is called The Word of God.

14 And the armies in heaven, clothed in fine linen, white and clean, followed Him on white horses.

15 Now out of His mouth goes a sharp sword, that with it He should strike the nations. And He Himself will rule them with a rod of iron. He Himself treads the winepress of the fierceness and wrath of Almighty God.

16 And He has on *His* robe and on His thigh a name written:

KING OF KINGS
AND LORD OF LORDS.

17 Then I saw an angel standing in the sun; and he cried with a loud voice, saying to all the birds that fly in the midst of heaven, "Come and gather together for the supper of the great God,

18 "that you may eat the flesh of kings, the flesh of captains, the flesh of mighty men, the flesh of horses and of those who sit on them, and the flesh of all *people,* free and slave, both small and great."

19 And I saw the beast, the kings of the earth, and their armies, gathered together to make war against Him who sat on the horse and against His army.

20 Then the beast was captured, and with him the false prophet who worked signs in his presence, by which he deceived those who received the mark of the beast and those who worshiped his image. These two were cast alive into the lake of fire burning with brimstone.

21 And the rest were killed with the sword which proceeded from the mouth of Him who sat on the horse. And all the birds were filled with their flesh.

20 Then I saw an angel coming down from heaven, having the key to the bottomless pit and a great chain in his hand.

2 He laid hold of the dragon, that serpent of old, who is *the* Devil and Satan, and bound him for a thousand years;

3 and he cast him into the bottomless pit, and shut him up, and set a seal on him, so that he should deceive the nations no more till the thousand years were finished. But after these things he must be released for a little while.

4 And I saw thrones, and they sat on them, and judgment was committed to them. And *I saw* the souls of those who had been beheaded for their witness to Jesus and for the word of God, who had not worshiped the beast or his image, and had not received *his* mark on their foreheads or on their hands. And they lived and reigned with Christ for a thousand years.

5 But the rest of the dead did not live again until the thousand years were finished. This *is* the first resurrection.

6 Blessed and holy *is* he who has part in the first resurrection. Over such the second death has no power, but they shall be priests of God and of Christ, and shall reign with Him a thousand years.

7 Now when the thousand years have expired, Satan will be released from his prison

8 and will go out to deceive the nations which are in the four corners of the earth, Gog and Magog, to gather them together to battle, whose number *is* as the sand of the sea.

9 They went up on the breadth of the earth and surrounded the camp of the saints and the beloved city. And fire came down from God out of heaven and devoured them.

10 And the devil, who deceived them, was cast into the lake of fire and brimstone where the beast and the false prophet *are.* And they will be tormented day and night forever and ever.

11 Then I saw a great white throne and Him who sat on it, from whose face the earth and the heaven fled away. And there was found no place for them.

12 And I saw the dead, small and great, standing before God, and books were opened. And another book was opened, which is *the Book* of Life. And the dead were judged according to their works, by the things which were written in the books.

13 The sea gave up the dead who were in it, and Death and Hades delivered up the dead who were in them. And they were judged, each one according to his works.

14 Then Death and Hades were cast into the lake of fire. This is the second death.

15 And anyone not found written in the Book of Life was cast into the lake of fire.

21 And I saw a new heaven and a new earth, for the first heaven and the first earth had passed away. Also there was no more sea.

2 Then I, John, saw the holy city, New Jerusalem, coming down out of heaven from God, prepared as a bride adorned for her husband.

3 And I heard a loud voice from heaven saying, "Behold, the tabernacle of God *is* with men, and He will dwell with them, and they shall be His people, and God Himself will be with them *and be* their God.

4 "And God will wipe away every tear from their eyes; there shall be no more death, nor sorrow, nor crying; and there shall be no more pain, for the former things have passed away."

5 Then He who sat on the throne said, "Behold, I make all things new." And He said to me, "Write, for these words are true and faithful."

6 And He said to me, "It is done! I am the Alpha and the Omega, the Beginning and the End. I will give of the fountain of the water of life freely to him who thirsts.

7 "He who overcomes shall inherit all things, and I will be his God and he shall be My son.

8 "But the cowardly, unbelieving, abominable, murderers, sexually immoral, sorcerers, idolaters, and all liars shall have their part in the lake which burns with fire and brimstone, which is the second death."

9 Then one of the seven angels who had the seven bowls filled with the seven last plagues came to me and talked with me, saying, "Come, I will show you the bride, the Lamb's wife."

10 And he carried me away in the Spirit to a great and high mountain, and showed me the great city, the holy Jerusalem, descending out of heaven from God,

11 having the glory of God. And her light *was* like a most precious stone, like a jasper stone, clear as crystal.

12 Also she had a great and high wall with twelve gates, and twelve angels at the gates, and names written on them, which are *the names* of the twelve tribes of the children of Israel:

13 three gates on the east, three gates on the north, three gates on the south, and three gates on the west.

14 Now the wall of the city had twelve foundations, and on them were the names of the twelve apostles of the Lamb.

15 And he who talked with me had a gold reed to measure the city, its gates, and its wall.

16 And the city is laid out as a square, and its length is as great as its breadth. And he measured the city with the reed: twelve thousand furlongs. Its length, breadth, and height are equal.

17 Then he measured its wall: one hundred *and* forty-four cubits, *according* to the measure of a man, that is, of an angel.

18 And the construction of its wall was *of* jasper; and the city *was* pure gold, like clear glass.

19 And the foundations of the wall of the city *were* adorned with all kinds of precious stones: the first foundation *was* jasper, the second sapphire, the third chalcedony, the fourth emerald,

20 the fifth sardonyx, the sixth sardius, the seventh chrysolite, the eighth beryl, the ninth topaz, the

tenth chrysoprase, the eleventh jacinth, and the twelfth amethyst.

21 And the twelve gates *were* twelve pearls: each individual gate was of one pearl. And the street of the city *was* pure gold, like transparent glass.

22 But I saw no temple in it, for the Lord God Almighty and the Lamb are its temple.

23 And the city had no need of the sun or of the moon to shine in it, for the glory of God illuminated it, and the Lamb *is* its light.

24 And the nations of those who are saved shall walk in its light, and the kings of the earth bring their glory and honor into it.

25 Its gates shall not be shut at all by day (there shall be no night there).

26 And they shall bring the glory and the honor of the nations into it.

27 But there shall by no means enter it anything that defiles, or causes an abomination or a lie, but only those who are written in the Lamb's Book of Life.

22 And he showed me a pure river of water of life, clear as crystal, proceeding from the throne of God and of the Lamb.

2 In the middle of its street, and on either side of the river, *was* the tree of life, which bore twelve fruits, each *tree* yielding its fruit every month. And the leaves of the tree *were* for the healing of the nations.

3 And there shall be no more curse, but the throne of God and of the Lamb shall be in it, and His servants shall serve Him.

4 They shall see His face, and His name *shall be* on their foreheads.

5 And there shall be no night there: They need no lamp nor light of the sun, for the Lord God gives them light. And they shall reign forever and ever.

6 Then he said to me, "These words *are* faithful and true." And the Lord God of the holy prophets sent His angel to show His servants the things which must shortly take place.

7 "Behold, I am coming quickly! Blessed *is* he who keeps the words of the prophecy of this book."

8 Now I, John, saw and heard these things. And when I heard and saw, I fell down to worship before the feet of the angel who showed me these things.

9 Then he said to me, "See *that you do* not *do that*. For I am your fellow servant, and of your brethren the prophets, and of those who keep the words of this book. Worship God."

10 And he said to me, "Do not seal the words of the prophecy of this book, for the time is at hand.

11 "He who is unjust, let him be unjust still; he who is filthy, let him be filthy still; he who is righteous, let him be righteous still; he who is holy, let him be holy still."

12 "And behold, I am coming quickly, and My reward *is* with Me, to give to every one according to his work.

13 "I am the Alpha and the Omega, *the* Beginning and *the* End, the First and the Last."

14 Blessed *are* those who do His commandments, that they may have the right to the tree of life, and may enter through the gates into the city.

15 But outside *are* dogs and sorcerers and sexually immoral and murderers and idolaters, and whoever loves and practices a lie.

16 "I, Jesus, have sent My angel to testify to you these things in the churches. I am the Root and the Offspring of David, the Bright and Morning Star."

17 And the Spirit and the bride say, "Come!" And let him who hears say, "Come!" And let him who thirsts come. And whoever desires, let him take the water of life freely.

18 For I testify to everyone who hears the words of the prophecy of

this book: If anyone adds to these things, God will add to him the plagues that are written in this book;

19 and if anyone takes away from the words of the book of this prophecy, God shall take away his part from the Book of Life, from the holy city, and *from* the things which are written in this book.

20 He who testifies to these things says, "Surely I am coming quickly." Amen. Even so, come, Lord Jesus!

21 The grace of our Lord Jesus Christ *be* with you all. Amen.

The Books

of

PSALMS

and

PROVERBS

THE BOOK OF
PSALMS

BOOK ONE
Psalms 1–41

PSALM 1

BLESSED *is* the man
    Who walks not in the
      counsel of the ungodly,
  Nor stands in the path of
    sinners,
  Nor sits in the seat of the
    scornful;
2 But his delight *is* in the law of
    the LORD,
  And in His law he meditates
    day and night.
3 He shall be like a tree
    Planted by the rivers of
      water,
  That brings forth its fruit in
    its season,
  Whose leaf also shall not
    wither;
  And whatever he does shall
    prosper.

4 The ungodly *are* not so,
  But *are* like the chaff which
    the wind drives away.
5 Therefore the ungodly shall
    not stand in the
    judgment,
  Nor sinners in the
    congregation of the
    righteous.

6 For the LORD knows the way
    of the righteous,
  But the way of the ungodly
    shall perish.

PSALM 2

WHY do the nations rage,
    And the people plot a vain
    thing?
2 The kings of the earth set
    themselves,
  And the rulers take counsel
    together,

Against the LORD and against
  His Anointed, *saying,*
3 "Let us break Their bonds in
    pieces
  And cast away Their cords
    from us."

4 He who sits in the heavens
    shall laugh;
  The LORD shall hold them in
    derision.
5 Then He shall speak to them
    in His wrath,
  And distress them in His deep
    displeasure:
6 "Yet I have set My King
  On My holy hill of Zion."

7 "I will declare the decree:
  The LORD has said to Me,
  You *are* My Son,
  Today I have begotten You.
8 Ask of Me, and I will give *You*
  The nations *for* Your
    inheritance,
  And the ends of the earth *for*
    Your possession.
9 You shall break them with a
    rod of iron;
  You shall dash them in pieces
    like a potter's vessel.' "

10 Now therefore, be wise, O
    kings;
  Be instructed, you judges of
    the earth.
11 Serve the LORD with fear,
  And rejoice with trembling.
12 Kiss the Son, lest He be angry,
  And you perish *in* the way,
  When His wrath is kindled but
    a little.
  Blessed *are* all those who put
    their trust in Him.

PSALM 3

A Psalm of David when he fled from Absalom
his son.

LORD, how they have increased
  who trouble me!

Many *are* they who rise up
    against me.

2 Many *are* they who say of me,
    "*There is* no help for him in
    God."   Selah

3 But You, O LORD, *are* a shield
    for me,
My glory and the One who
    lifts up my head.

4 I cried to the LORD with my
    voice,
And He heard me from His
    holy hill.   Selah

5 I lay down and slept;
I awoke, for the LORD
    sustained me.

6 I will not be afraid of ten
    thousands of people
Who have set *themselves*
    against me all around.

7 Arise, O LORD;
Save me, O my God!
For You have struck all my
    enemies on the cheekbone;
You have broken the teeth of
    the ungodly.

8 Salvation *belongs* to the LORD.
Your blessing *is* upon Your
    people.   Selah

PSALM 4

To the Chief Musician. With stringed
instruments. A Psalm of David.

HEAR me when I call,
    O God of my righteousness!
You have relieved me *when I
    was* in distress;
Have mercy on me,
    and hear my prayer.

2 How long, O you sons of men,
Will you turn my glory to
    shame?
How long will you love
    worthlessness
And seek falsehood?   Selah

3 But know that the LORD has
    set apart for Himself him
    who is godly;

The LORD will hear when I
    call to Him.

4 Be angry, and do not sin.
Meditate within your heart on
    your bed, and be still. Selah

5 Offer the sacrifices of
    righteousness,
And put your trust in the
    LORD.

6 *There are* many who say,
"Who will show us *any* good?"
LORD, lift up the light of Your
    countenance upon us.

7 You have put gladness in my
    heart,
More than in the season that
    their grain and wine
    increased.

8 I will both lie down in peace,
    and sleep;
For You alone, O LORD, make
    me dwell in safety.

PSALM 5

To the Chief Musician. With flutes. A Psalm of
David.

GIVE ear to my words, O LORD,
    Consider my meditation.

2 Give heed to the voice of my
    cry,
My King and my God,
For to You I will pray.

3 My voice You shall hear in
    the morning, O LORD;
In the morning I will direct *it*
    to You,
And I will look up.

4 For You *are* not a God who
    takes pleasure in
    wickedness,
Nor shall evil dwell with You.

5 The boastful shall not stand in
    Your sight;
You hate all workers of
    iniquity.

6 You shall destroy those who
    speak falsehood;
The LORD abhors the
    bloodthirsty and deceitful
    man.

7 But as for me, I will come into
  Your house in the multitude
  of Your mercy;
  In fear of You I will worship
  toward Your holy temple.
8 Lead me, O Lord, in Your
  righteousness because of
  my enemies;
  Make Your way straight
  before my face.

9 For *there is* no faithfulness in
  their mouth;
  Their inward part *is*
  destruction;
  Their throat *is* an open tomb;
  They flatter with their tongue.
10 Pronounce them guilty, O
  God!
  Let them fall by their own
  counsels;
  Cast them out in the
  multitude of their
  transgressions,
  For they have rebelled against
  You.

11 But let all those rejoice who
  put their trust in You;
  Let them ever shout for joy,
  because You defend them;
  Let those also who love Your
  name
  Be joyful in You.
12 For You, O Lord, will bless
  the righteous;
  With favor You will surround
  him as *with* a shield.

PSALM 6

To the Chief Musician. With stringed
instruments. On an eight-stringed harp. A
Psalm of David.

O LORD, do not rebuke me in
  Your anger,
  Nor chasten me in Your hot
  displeasure.
2 Have mercy on me, O Lord,
  for I *am* weak;
  O Lord, heal me,
  for my bones are troubled.

3 My soul also is greatly
  troubled;
  But You, O Lord—how long?

4 Return, O Lord, deliver me!
  Oh, save me for Your mercies'
  sake!
5 For in death *there is* no
  remembrance of You;
  In the grave who will give
  You thanks?

6 I am weary with my groaning;
  All night I make my bed
  swim;
  I drench my couch with my
  tears.
7 My eye wastes away because
  of grief;
  It grows old because of all my
  enemies.

8 Depart from me,
  all you workers of iniquity;
  For the Lord has heard the
  voice of my weeping.
9 The Lord has heard my
  supplication;
  The Lord will receive my
  prayer.
10 Let all my enemies be
  ashamed and greatly
  troubled;
  Let them turn back
  and be ashamed suddenly.

PSALM 7

A Meditation of David, which he sang to the
Lord concerning the words of Cush, a
Benjamite.

O LORD my God,
  in You I put my trust;
  Save me from all those who
  persecute me;
  And deliver me,
2 Lest they tear me like a lion,
  Rending *me* in pieces,
  while *there is* none to
  deliver.

3 O Lord my God, if I have
  done this:

Prayer for Deliverance

If there is iniquity in my
hands,
4 If I have repaid evil to him
who was at peace with me,
Or have plundered my enemy
without cause,
5 Let the enemy pursue me
and overtake *me;*
Yes, let him trample my life to
the earth,
And lay my honor in the dust.
Selah

6 Arise, O LORD, in Your anger;
Lift Yourself up because of
the rage of my enemies,
And awake for me *to* the
judgment You have
commanded!
7 So the congregation of the
peoples shall surround You;
For their sakes, therefore,
return on high.
8 The LORD shall judge the
peoples;
Judge me, O LORD, according
to my righteousness,
And according to my integrity
within me.

9 Oh, let the wickedness of the
wicked come to an end,
But establish the just;
For the righteous God tests
the hearts and minds.
10 My defense *is* of God,
Who saves the upright in
heart.

11 God *is* a just judge,
And God is angry *with the
wicked* every day.
12 If he does not turn back,
He will sharpen His sword;
He bends His bow and makes
it ready.
13 He also prepares for Himself
instruments of death;
He makes His arrows into
fiery shafts.

14 Behold, *the wicked* travails
with iniquity,

Conceives trouble and brings
forth falsehood.
15 He made a pit and dug it out,
And has fallen into the ditch
which he made.
16 His trouble shall return upon
his own head,
And his violent dealing shall
come down on his own
crown.

17 I will praise the LORD
according to His
righteousness,
And will sing praise to the
name of the LORD Most
High.

PSALM 8

To the Chief Musician. On the instrument of
Gath. A Psalm of David.

O LORD, our Lord,
How excellent *is* Your name
in all the earth,
You who set Your glory above
the heavens!

2 Out of the mouth of babes
and infants
You have ordained strength,
Because of Your enemies,
That You may silence the
enemy and the avenger.

3 When I consider Your
heavens, the work of
Your fingers,
The moon and the stars,
which You have ordained,
4 What is man that You are
mindful of him,
And the son of man that You
visit him?
5 For You have made him a
little lower than the angels,
And You have crowned him
with glory and honor.

6 You have made him to have
dominion over the works of
Your hands;
You have put all *things* under
his feet,

7 All sheep and oxen—
  Even the beasts of the field,
8 The birds of the air,
  And the fish of the sea
  That pass through the paths
    of the seas.

9 O LORD, our Lord,
  How excellent *is* Your name
    in all the earth!

PSALM 9

To the Chief Musician. To *the tune of* "Death
of the Son." A Psalm of David.

I WILL praise *You,* O LORD,
  with my whole heart;
  I will tell of all Your
    marvelous works.
2 I will be glad and rejoice in
    You;
  I will sing praise to Your
    name, O Most High.

3 When my enemies turn back,
  They shall fall and perish at
    Your presence.
4 For You have maintained my
    right and my cause;
  You sat on the throne judging
    in righteousness.
5 You have rebuked the nations,
  You have destroyed the
    wicked;
  You have blotted out their
    name forever and ever.

6 O enemy, destructions are
    finished forever!
  And you have destroyed cities;
  Even their memory has
    perished.
7 But the LORD shall endure
    forever;
  He has prepared His throne
    for judgment.
8 He shall judge the world in
    righteousness,
  And He shall administer
    judgment for the peoples in
    uprightness.

9 The LORD also will be a refuge
    for the oppressed,

A refuge in times of trouble.
10 And those who know Your
    name will put their trust in
    You;
  For You, LORD, have not
    forsaken those who seek
    You.

11 Sing praises to the LORD,
    who dwells in Zion!
  Declare His deeds among the
    people.
12 When He avenges blood,
    He remembers them;
  He does not forget the cry of
    the humble.

13 Have mercy on me, O LORD!
  Consider my trouble from
    those who hate me,
  You who lift me up from the
    gates of death,
14 That I may tell of all Your
    praise
  In the gates of the daughter
    of Zion.
  I will rejoice in Your
    salvation.

15 The nations have sunk down
    in the pit *which* they made;
  In the net which they hid,
    their own foot is caught.
16 The LORD is known *by* the
    judgment He executes;
  The wicked is snared in the
    work of his own hands.
  Meditation.   Selah

17 The wicked shall be turned
    into hell,
  And all the nations that forget
    God.
18 For the needy shall not always
    be forgotten;
  The expectation of the poor
    shall *not* perish forever.

19 Arise, O LORD,
  Do not let man prevail;
  Let the nations be judged in
    Your sight.

20 Put them in fear, O LORD,
   That the nations may know
      themselves *to be but* men.
                                    Selah

PSALM 10

WHY do You stand afar off, O
      LORD?
   Why do You hide *Yourself* in
      times of trouble?
2 The wicked in *his* pride
      persecutes the poor;
   Let them be caught in the
      plots which they have
      devised.

3 For the wicked boasts of his
      heart's desire;
   He blesses the greedy
      and renounces the LORD.
4 The wicked in his proud
      countenance does not seek
      God;
   God *is* in none of his
      thoughts.

5 His ways are always
      prospering;
   Your judgments *are* far above,
      out of his sight;
   As for all his enemies,
      he sneers at them.
6 He has said in his heart,
   "I shall not be moved;
   I shall never be in adversity."
7 His mouth is full of cursing
      and deceit and oppression;
   Under his tongue *is* trouble
      and iniquity.

8 He sits in the lurking places of
      the villages;
   In the secret places he
      murders the innocent;
   His eyes are secretly fixed on
      the helpless.
9 He lies in wait secretly,
      as a lion in his den;
   He lies in wait to catch the
      poor;
   He catches the poor when he
      draws him into his net.

10 So he crouches, he lies low,
   That the helpless may fall by
      his strength.
11 He has said in his heart,
   "God has forgotten;
   He hides His face;
   He will never see *it."*

12 Arise, O LORD!
   O God, lift up Your hand!
   Do not forget the humble.
13 Why do the wicked renounce
      God?
   He has said in his heart,
   "You will not require *an
      account."*

14 But You have seen *it,*
      for You observe trouble and
      grief,
   To repay *it* by Your hand.
   The helpless commits himself
      to You;
   You are the helper of the
      fatherless.
15 Break the arm of the wicked
      and the evil *man;*
   Seek out his wickedness *until*
      You find none.

16 The LORD *is* King forever and
      ever;
   The nations have perished out
      of His land.
17 LORD, You have heard the
      desire of the humble;
   You will prepare their heart;
   You will cause Your ear to
      hear,
18 To do justice to the fatherless
      and the oppressed,
   That the man of the earth
      may oppress no more.

PSALM 11

To the Chief Musician. A Psalm of David.

IN the LORD I put my trust;
   How can you say to my soul,
   "Flee *as* a bird to your
      mountain"?
2 For look! The wicked bend
      their bow,

They make ready their arrow
on the string,
That they may shoot secretly
at the upright in heart.
3 If the foundations are
destroyed,
What can the righteous do?

4 The LORD *is* in His holy
temple,
The LORD's throne *is* in
heaven;
His eyes behold,
His eyelids test the sons of
men.
5 The LORD tests the righteous,
But the wicked and the one
who loves violence His soul
hates.
6 Upon the wicked He will rain
coals,
Fire and brimstone and a
burning wind;
This shall be the portion of
their cup.

7 For the LORD *is* righteous,
He loves righteousness;
His countenance beholds the
upright.

PSALM 12

To the Chief Musician. On an eight-stringed
harp. A Psalm of David.

HELP, LORD, for the godly man
ceases!
For the faithful disappear
from among the sons of
men.
2 They speak idly everyone with
his neighbor;
With flattering lips *and* a
double heart they speak.

3 May the LORD cut off all
flattering lips,
And the tongue that speaks
proud things,
4 Who have said,
"With our tongue we will
prevail;
Our lips *are* our own;
Who *is* lord over us?"

5 "For the oppression of the
poor, for the sighing of the
needy,
Now I will arise," says the
LORD;
"I will set *him* in the safety for
which he yearns."

6 The words of the LORD *are*
pure words,
Like silver tried in a furnace
of earth,
Purified seven times.
7 You shall keep them, O LORD,
You shall preserve them from
this generation forever.

8 The wicked prowl on every
side,
When vileness is exalted
among the sons of men.

PSALM 13

To the Chief Musician. A Psalm of David.

HOW long, O LORD?
Will You forget me forever?
How long will You hide Your
face from me?
2 How long shall I take counsel
in my soul,
Having sorrow in my heart
daily?
How long will my enemy be
exalted over me?

3 Consider *and* hear me,
O LORD my God;
Enlighten my eyes,
Lest I sleep the *sleep of* death;
4 Lest my enemy say,
"I have prevailed against him";
Lest those who trouble me
rejoice when I am moved.

5 But I have trusted in Your
mercy;
My heart shall rejoice in Your
salvation.
6 I will sing to the LORD,
Because He has dealt
bountifully with me.

PSALM 14

To the Chief Musician. A Psalm of David.

THE fool has said in his heart,
  "*There is* no God."
They are corrupt,
They have done abominable
  works,
There is none who does good.

2 The LORD looks down from
  heaven upon the children of
  men,
To see if there are any who
  understand, who seek God.
3 They have all turned aside,
They have together become
  corrupt;
There is none who does good,
No, not one.

4 Have all the workers of
  iniquity no knowledge,
Who eat up my people *as* they
  eat bread,
And do not call on the LORD?
5 There they are in great fear,
For God *is* with the
  generation of the righteous.
6 You shame the counsel of the
  poor,
But the LORD *is* his refuge.

7 Oh, that the salvation of Israel
  would come out of Zion!
When the LORD brings back
  the captivity of His people,
Let Jacob rejoice *and* Israel be
  glad.

PSALM 15

A Psalm of David.

LORD, who may abide in Your
  tabernacle?
Who may dwell in Your holy
  hill?

2 He who walks uprightly,
  And works righteousness,
  And speaks the truth in his
    heart;
3 He *who* does not backbite
  with his tongue,

Nor does evil to his
  neighbor,
Nor does he take up a
  reproach against his
  friend;
4 In whose eyes a vile person is
  despised,
  But he honors those who
    fear the LORD;
He *who* swears to his own
  hurt and does not change;
5 He *who* does not put out his
  money at usury,
  Nor does he take a bribe
    against the innocent.

He who does these *things*
  shall never be moved.

PSALM 16

A Michtam of David.

PRESERVE me, O God,
  for in You I put my trust.

2 *O my soul,* you have said to
  the LORD,
  "You *are* my Lord,
  My goodness is nothing apart
    from You"—
3 *And* to the saints who *are* on
  the earth,
  "They are the excellent ones,
    in whom is all my delight."

4 Their sorrows shall be
  multiplied who hasten *after*
  another *god;*
Their drink offerings of blood
  I will not offer,
Nor take up their names on
  my lips.

5 *You,* O LORD, *are* the portion
  of my inheritance and my
  cup;
You maintain my lot.
6 The lines have fallen to me in
  pleasant *places;*
  Yes, I have a good
    inheritance.

7 I will bless the LORD who has
 given me counsel;
 My heart also instructs me in
 the night seasons.
8 I have set the LORD always
 before me;
 Because *He is* at my right
 hand I shall not be moved.

9 Therefore my heart is glad,
 and my glory rejoices;
 My flesh also will rest in hope.
10 For You will not leave my
 soul in Sheol,
 Nor will You allow Your Holy
 One to see corruption.
11 You will show me the path of
 life;
 In Your presence *is* fullness of
 joy;
 At Your right hand *are*
 pleasures forevermore.

PSALM 17

A Prayer of David.

HEAR a just cause, O LORD,
 Attend to my cry;
 Give ear to my prayer *that is*
 not from deceitful lips.
2 Let my vindication come from
 Your presence;
 Let Your eyes look on the
 things that are upright.

3 You have tested my heart;
 You have visited *me* in the
 night;
 You have tried me
 and have found nothing;
 I have purposed that my
 mouth shall not transgress.
4 Concerning the works of men,
 By the word of Your lips,
 I have kept *myself* from the
 paths of the destroyer.
5 Uphold my steps in Your
 paths,
 That my footsteps may not
 slip.

6 I have called upon You,
 for You will hear me, O
 God;

Incline Your ear to me, *and*
 hear my speech.
7 Show Your marvelous
 lovingkindness by Your
 right hand,
 O You who save those who
 trust *in You*
 From those who rise up
 against them.
8 Keep me as the apple of Your
 eye;
 Hide me under the shadow of
 Your wings,
9 From the wicked who oppress
 me,
 From my deadly enemies who
 surround me.

10 They have closed up their fat
 hearts;
 With their mouths they speak
 proudly.
11 They have now surrounded us
 in our steps;
 They have set their eyes,
 crouching down to the
 earth,
12 Like a lion *that* is eager to
 tear his prey,
 And as a young lion lurking in
 secret places.

13 Arise, O LORD,
 Confront him, cast him down;
 Deliver my life from the
 wicked with Your sword,
14 With Your hand from men, O
 LORD,
 From men of the world *who
 have* their portion in *this*
 life,
 And whose belly You fill with
 Your hidden treasure.
 They are satisfied with
 children,
 And leave the rest of their
 substance for their babes.

15 As for me, I will see Your face
 in righteousness;
 I shall be satisfied when I
 awake in Your likeness.

PSALM 18

To the Chief Musician. A Psalm of David the servant of the LORD, who spoke to the LORD the words of this song on the day that the LORD delivered him from the hand of all his enemies and from the hand of Saul. And he said:

I WILL love You, O LORD, my strength.
2 The LORD is my rock and my fortress and my deliverer;
My God, my strength,
in whom I will trust;
My shield and the horn of my salvation, my stronghold.
3 I will call upon the LORD,
who is worthy to be praised;
So shall I be saved from my enemies.

4 The pangs of death encompassed me,
And the floods of ungodliness made me afraid.
5 The sorrows of Sheol surrounded me;
The snares of death confronted me.
6 In my distress I called upon the LORD,
And cried out to my God;
He heard my voice from His temple,
And my cry came before Him,
even to His ears.

7 Then the earth shook and trembled;
The foundations of the hills also quaked and were shaken,
Because He was angry.
8 Smoke went up from His nostrils,
And devouring fire from His mouth;
Coals were kindled by it.
9 He bowed the heavens also, and came down
With darkness under His feet.
10 And He rode upon a cherub, and flew;
He flew upon the wings of the wind.

11 He made darkness His secret place;
His canopy around Him *was* dark waters
And thick clouds of the skies.
12 From the brightness before Him,
His thick clouds passed with hailstones and coals of fire.

13 The LORD also thundered in the heavens,
And the Most High uttered His voice,
Hailstones and coals of fire.
14 He sent out His arrows and scattered the foe,
Lightnings in abundance, and He vanquished them.
15 Then the channels of waters were seen,
And the foundations of the world were uncovered
At Your rebuke, O LORD,
At the blast of the breath of Your nostrils.

16 He sent from above, He took me;
He drew me out of many waters.
17 He delivered me from my strong enemy,
From those who hated me,
For they were too strong for me.
18 They confronted me in the day of my calamity,
But the LORD was my support.
19 He also brought me out into a broad place;
He delivered me because He delighted in me.

20 The LORD rewarded me according to my righteousness;
According to the cleanness of my hands He has recompensed me.
21 For I have kept the ways of the LORD,
And have not wickedly departed from my God.

22 For all His judgments *were*
   before me,
   And I did not put away His
   statutes from me.
23 I was also blameless before
   Him,
   And I kept myself from my
   iniquity.
24 Therefore the LORD has
   recompensed me according
   to my righteousness,
   According to the cleanness
   of my hands in His sight.

25 With the merciful
   You will show Yourself
   merciful;
   With a blameless man
   You will show Yourself
   blameless;
26 With the pure You will show
   Yourself pure;
   And with the devious
   You will show Yourself
   shrewd.
27 For You will save the humble
   people,
   But will bring down haughty
   looks.

28 For You will light my lamp;
   The LORD my God will
   enlighten my darkness.
29 For by You I can run against
   a troop,
   And by my God I can leap
   over a wall.
30 *As for* God, His way *is* perfect;
   The word of the LORD *is*
   proven;
   He *is* a shield to all who trust
   in Him.

31 For who *is* God, except the
   LORD?
   And who *is* a rock, except our
   God?
32 *It is* God who arms me with
   strength,
   And makes my way perfect.
33 He makes my feet like the
   feet of deer,
   And sets me on my high
   places.

34 He teaches my hands to make
   war,
   So that my arms can bend a
   bow of bronze.

35 You have also given me the
   shield of Your salvation;
   Your right hand has held me
   up,
   Your gentleness has made me
   great.
36 You enlarged my path under
   me,
   So that my feet did not slip.

37 I have pursued my enemies
   and overtaken them;
   Neither did I turn back again
   till they were destroyed.
38 I have wounded them,
   So that they were not able to
   rise;
   They have fallen under my
   feet.
39 For You have armed me with
   strength for the battle;
   You have subdued under me
   those who rose up against
   me.
40 You have also given me
   the necks of my enemies,
   So that I destroyed those who
   hated me.
41 They cried out, but *there was*
   none to save *them,*
   Even to the LORD,
   but He did not answer them.
42 Then I beat them as fine as
   the dust before the wind;
   I cast them out like dirt in the
   streets.

43 You have delivered me from
   the strivings of the people,
   You have made me the head
   of the nations;
   A people I have not known
   shall serve me.
44 As soon as they hear of me
   they obey me;
   The foreigners submit to me.
45 The foreigners fade away,
   And come frightened from
   their hideouts.

His Perfect Revelation

46 The LORD lives!
Blessed *be* my Rock!
Let the God of my salvation
be exalted.
47 *It is* God who avenges me,
And subdues the peoples
under me;
48 He delivers me from my
enemies.
You also lift me up above
those who rise against me;
You have delivered me from
the violent man.
49 Therefore I will give thanks to
You, O LORD, among the
Gentiles,
And sing praises to Your
name.

50 Great deliverance He gives to
His king,
And shows mercy to His
anointed,
To David and his descendants
forevermore.

PSALM 19

To the Chief Musician. A Psalm of David.

THE heavens declare the glory
of God;
And the firmament shows His
handiwork.
2 Day unto day utters speech,
And night unto night reveals
knowledge.
3 *There is* no speech nor
language
Where their voice is not
heard.
4 Their line has gone out
through all the earth,
And their words to the end of
the world.

In them He has set a
tabernacle for the sun,
5 Which *is* like a bridegroom
coming out of his chamber,
And rejoices like a strong man
to run its race.
6 Its rising *is* from one end of
heaven,

And its circuit to the other
end;
And there is nothing hidden
from its heat.

7 The law of the LORD *is*
perfect, converting the soul;
The testimony of the LORD *is*
sure, making wise the
simple;
8 The statutes of the LORD *are*
right, rejoicing the heart;
The commandment of the
LORD *is* pure, enlightening
the eyes;
9 The fear of the LORD *is* clean,
enduring forever;
The judgments of the LORD
are true *and* righteous
altogether.
10 More to be desired *are they*
than gold,
Yea, than much fine gold;
Sweeter also than honey and
the honeycomb.
11 Moreover by them Your
servant is warned,
And in keeping them *there is*
great reward.

12 Who can understand *his*
errors?
Cleanse me from secret *faults.*
13 Keep back Your servant also
from presumptuous *sins;*
Let them not have dominion
over me.
Then I shall be blameless,
And I shall be innocent of
great transgression.

14 Let the words of my mouth
and the meditation of my
heart
Be acceptable in Your sight,
O LORD, my strength and my
redeemer.

PSALM 20

To the Chief Musician. A Psalm of David.

MAY the LORD answer you in
the day of trouble;

May the name of the God of
Jacob defend you;
2 May He send you help from
the sanctuary,
And strengthen you out of
Zion;
3 May He remember all your
offerings,
And accept your burnt
sacrifice. Selah

4 May He grant you according
to your heart's *desire*,
And fulfill all your purpose.
5 We will rejoice in your
salvation,
And in the name of our God
we will set up *our* banners!
May the LORD fulfill all your
petitions.

6 Now I know that the LORD
saves His anointed;
He will answer him from His
holy heaven
With the saving strength of
His right hand.

7 Some *trust* in chariots,
and some in horses;
But we will remember the
name of the LORD our God.
8 They have bowed down and
fallen;
But we have risen and stand
upright.

9 Save, LORD!
May the King answer us when
we call.

PSALM 21

To the Chief Musician. A Psalm of David.

THE king shall have joy in Your
strength, O LORD;
And in Your salvation how
greatly shall he rejoice!
2 You have given him his
heart's desire,
And have not withheld the
request of his lips. Selah

3 For You meet him with the
blessings of goodness;
You set a crown of pure gold
upon his head.
4 He asked life from You,
and You gave *it* to him—
Length of days forever and
ever.
5 His glory *is* great in Your
salvation;
Honor and majesty You have
placed upon him.
6 For You have made him most
blessed forever;
You have made him
exceedingly glad with Your
presence.
7 For the king trusts in the
LORD,
And through the mercy of the
Most High he shall not be
moved.

8 Your hand will find all Your
enemies;
Your right hand will find
those who hate You.
9 You shall make them as a
fiery oven in the time of
Your anger;
The LORD shall swallow them
up in His wrath,
And the fire shall devour
them.
10 Their offspring You shall
destroy from the earth,
And their descendants from
among the sons of men.
11 For they intended evil against
You;
They devised a plot *which*
they are not able *to
perform.*
12 Therefore You will make them
turn their back;
You will make ready *Your
arrows* on Your string
toward their faces.

13 Be exalted, O LORD, in Your
own strength!
We will sing and praise Your
power.

PSALM 22

To the Chief Musician. Set to "The Deer of the
Dawn." A Psalm of David.

M Y God, My God, why have
You forsaken Me?
Why are You so far from
helping Me,
And from the words of My
groaning?
2 O My God, I cry in the
daytime, but You do not
hear;
And in the night season,
and am not silent.

3 But You *are* holy,
Who inhabit the praises of
Israel.
4 Our fathers trusted in You;
They trusted, and You
delivered them.
5 They cried to You, and were
delivered;
They trusted in You, and were
not ashamed.

6 But I *am* a worm, and no
man;
A reproach of men, and
despised of the people.
7 All those who see Me laugh
Me to scorn;
They shoot out the lip,
they shake the head, *saying,*
8 "He trusted in the LORD,
let Him rescue Him;
Let Him deliver Him,
since He delights in Him!"

9 But You *are* He who took Me
out of the womb;
You made Me trust *when I
was* on My mother's breasts.
10 I was cast upon You from
birth.
From My mother's womb
You *have been* My God.
11 Be not far from Me,
For trouble *is* near;
For *there is* none to help.

12 Many bulls have surrounded
Me;

Strong *bulls* of Bashan have
encircled Me.
13 They gape at Me *with* their
mouths,
As a raging and roaring lion.

14 I am poured out like water,
And all My bones are out of
joint;
My heart is like wax;
It has melted within Me.
15 My strength is dried up like a
potsherd,
And My tongue clings to My
jaws;
You have brought Me to the
dust of death.

16 For dogs have surrounded Me;
The assembly of the wicked
has enclosed Me.
They pierced My hands and
My feet;
17 I can count all My bones.
They look *and* stare at Me.
18 They divide My garments
among them,
And for My clothing they cast
lots.

19 But You, O LORD, do not be
far from Me;
O My Strength, hasten to help
Me!
20 Deliver Me from the sword,
My precious *life* from the
power of the dog.
21 Save Me from the lion's
mouth
And from the horns of the
wild oxen!

You have answered Me.

22 I will declare Your name to
My brethren;
In the midst of the congre-
gation I will praise You.
23 You who fear the LORD, praise
Him!
All you descendants of Jacob,
glorify Him,

And fear Him, all you
offspring of Israel!
24 For He has not despised nor
abhorred the affliction of
the afflicted;
Nor has He hidden His face
from Him;
But when He cried to Him, He
heard.

25 My praise *shall be* of You in
the great congregation;
I will pay My vows before
those who fear Him.
26 The poor shall eat and be
satisfied;
Those who seek Him will
praise the LORD.
Let your heart live forever!

27 All the ends of the world
Shall remember and turn to
the LORD,
And all the families of the
nations
Shall worship before You.
28 For the kingdom *is* the
LORD'S,
And He rules over the nations.

29 All the prosperous of the earth
Shall eat and worship;
All those who go down to the
dust
Shall bow before Him,
Even he who cannot keep
himself alive.

30 A posterity shall serve Him.
It will be recounted of the
Lord to the *next* generation,
31 They will come and declare
His righteousness to a
people who will be born,
That He has done *this*.

PSALM 23

A Psalm of David.

THE LORD *is* my shepherd;
I shall not want.
2 He makes me to lie down in
green pastures;
He leads me beside the still
waters.
3 He restores my soul;
He leads me in the paths of
righteousness
For His name's sake.

4 Yea, though I walk through
the valley of the shadow of
death,
I will fear no evil;
For You *are* with me;
Your rod and Your staff,
they comfort me.

5 You prepare a table before me
in the presence of my
enemies;
You anoint my head with oil;
My cup runs over.
6 Surely goodness and mercy
shall follow me
All the days of my life;
And I will dwell in the house
of the LORD
Forever.

PSALM 24

A Psalm of David.

THE earth *is* the LORD'S,
and all its fullness,
The world and those who
dwell therein.
2 For He has founded it upon
the seas,
And established it upon the
waters.

3 Who may ascend into the hill
of the LORD?
Or who may stand in His holy
place?
4 He who has clean hands and a
pure heart,
Who has not lifted up his soul
to an idol,
Nor sworn deceitfully.
5 He shall receive blessing from
the LORD,
And righteousness from the
God of his salvation.

See Psalm 139:7–10, page 423

6 This *is* Jacob, the generation
   of those who seek Him,
   Who seek Your face.   Selah

7 Lift up your heads, O you
   gates!
   And be lifted up, you
   everlasting doors!
   And the King of glory shall
   come in.
8 Who *is* this King of glory?
   The LORD strong and mighty,
   The LORD mighty in battle.
9 Lift up your heads, O you
   gates!
   And lift *them* up, you
   everlasting doors!
   And the King of glory shall
   come in.
10 Who is this King of glory?
   The LORD of hosts,
   He *is* the King of glory.   Selah

PSALM 25

A Psalm of David.

TO You, O LORD, I lift up my
   soul.
2 O my God, I trust in You;
   Let me not be ashamed;
   Let not my enemies triumph
   over me.
3 Indeed, let no one who waits
   on You be ashamed;
   Let those be ashamed who
   deal treacherously without
   cause.

4 Show me Your ways, O LORD;
   Teach me Your paths.
5 Lead me in Your truth and
   teach me,
   For You *are* the God of my
   salvation;
   On You I wait all the day.

6 Remember, O LORD, Your
   tender mercies and Your
   lovingkindnesses,
   For they *have been* from of
   old.
7 Do not remember the sins of
   my youth, nor my
   transgressions;

According to Your mercy
   remember me,
   For Your goodness' sake, O
   LORD.

8 Good and upright *is* the LORD;
   Therefore He teaches sinners
   in the way.
9 The humble He guides in
   justice,
   And the humble He teaches
   His way.
10 All the paths of the LORD *are*
   mercy and truth,
   To such as keep His covenant
   and His testimonies.
11 For Your name's sake, O
   LORD,
   Pardon my iniquity, for it *is*
   great.

12 Who *is* the man that fears the
   LORD?
   Him shall He teach in the way
   He chooses.
13 He himself shall dwell in
   prosperity,
   And his descendants shall
   inherit the earth.
14 The secret of the LORD *is* with
   those who fear Him,
   And He will show them His
   covenant.
15 My eyes *are* ever toward the
   LORD,
   For He shall pluck my feet out
   of the net.

16 Turn Yourself to me,
   and have mercy on me,
   For I *am* desolate and
   afflicted.
17 The troubles of my heart have
   enlarged;
   Oh, bring me out of my
   distresses!
18 Look on my affliction and my
   pain,
   And forgive all my sins.
19 Consider my enemies,
   for they are many;
   And they hate me with cruel
   hatred.

20 Oh, keep my soul, and deliver
   me;
   Let me not be ashamed,
   for I put my trust in You.
21 Let integrity and uprightness
   preserve me,
   For I wait for You.

22 Redeem Israel, O God,
   Out of all their troubles!

PSALM 26
A Psalm of David.

VINDICATE me, O LORD,
For I have walked in my
   integrity.
   I have also trusted in the
   LORD;
   I shall not slip.
2 Examine me, O LORD, and
   prove me;
   Try my mind and my heart.
3 For Your lovingkindness *is*
   before my eyes,
   And I have walked in Your
   truth.
4 I have not sat with idolatrous
   mortals,
   Nor will I go in with
   hypocrites.
5 I have hated the congregation
   of evildoers,
   And will not sit with the
   wicked.

6 I will wash my hands in
   innocence;
   So I will go about Your altar,
   O LORD,
7 That I may proclaim with the
   voice of thanksgiving,
   And tell of all Your wondrous
   works.
8 LORD, I have loved the
   habitation of Your house,
   And the place where Your
   glory dwells.

9 Do not gather my soul
   together with sinners,
   Nor my life with bloodthirsty
   men,

10 In whose hands *is* a sinister
   scheme,
   And whose right hand is full
   of bribes.

11 But as for me,
   I will walk in my integrity;
   Redeem me and be merciful to
   me.
12 My foot stands in an even
   place;
   In the congregations I will
   bless the LORD.

PSALM 27
A Psalm of David.

THE LORD *is* my light and my
   salvation;
   Whom shall I fear?
   The LORD *is* the strength of
   my life;
   Of whom shall I be afraid?
2 When the wicked came
   against me
   To eat up my flesh,
   My enemies and foes,
   They stumbled and fell.
3 Though an army should
   encamp against me,
   My heart shall not fear;
   Though war should rise
   against me,
   In this I *will be* confident.

4 One *thing* I have desired of
   the LORD,
   That will I seek:
   That I may dwell in the house
   of the LORD
   All the days of my life,
   To behold the beauty of the
   LORD,
   And to inquire in His temple.
5 For in the time of trouble
   He shall hide me in His
   pavilion;
   In the secret place of His
   tabernacle
   He shall hide me;
   He shall set me high upon a
   rock.

6 And now my head shall be
    lifted up above my enemies
    all around me;
  Therefore I will offer sacrifices
    of joy in His tabernacle;
  I will sing, yes, I will sing
    praises to the LORD.

7 Hear, O LORD, *when* I cry
    with my voice!
  Have mercy also upon me,
    and answer me.

8 *When You said,* "Seek My
    face,"
  My heart said to You,
  "Your face, LORD, I will
    seek."

9 Do not hide Your face from
    me;
  Do not turn Your servant
    away in anger;
  You have been my help;
  Do not leave me nor forsake
    me,
  O God of my salvation.

10 When my father and my
    mother forsake me,
  Then the LORD will take care
    of me.

11 Teach me Your way, O LORD,
  And lead me in a smooth
    path, because of my
    enemies.

12 Do not deliver me to the will
    of my adversaries;
  For false witnesses have risen
    against me,
  And such as breathe out
    violence.

13 *I would have lost heart,* unless
    I had believed
  That I would see the goodness
    of the LORD
  In the land of the living.

14 Wait on the LORD;
  Be of good courage,
  And He shall strengthen your
    heart;
  Wait, I say, on the LORD!

PSALM 28

A Psalm of David.

To You I will cry, O LORD my
    Rock:
  Do not be silent to me,
  Lest, if You *are* silent to me,
  I become like those who go
    down to the pit.

2 Hear the voice of my
    supplications
  When I cry to You,
  When I lift up my hands
    toward Your holy
    sanctuary.

3 Do not take me away with the
    wicked
  And with the workers of
    iniquity,
  Who speak peace to their
    neighbors,
  But evil *is* in their hearts.

4 Give to them according to
    their deeds,
  And according to the
    wickedness of their
    endeavors;
  Give to them according to the
    work of their hands;
  Render to them what they
    deserve.

5 Because they do not regard
    the works of the LORD,
  Nor the operation of His
    hands,
  He shall destroy them
  And not build them up.

6 Blessed *be* the LORD,
  Because He has heard the
    voice of my supplications!

7 The LORD *is* my strength
    and my shield;
  My heart trusted in Him,
    and I am helped;
  Therefore my heart greatly
    rejoices,
  And with my song I will
    praise Him.

8 The LORD *is* their strength,
  And He *is* the saving refuge of
    His anointed.

9 Save Your people,
And bless Your inheritance;
Shepherd them also,
And bear them up forever.

PSALM 29

A Psalm of David.

GIVE unto the LORD,
O you mighty ones,
Give unto the LORD
glory and strength.
2 Give unto the LORD
the glory due to His name;
Worship the LORD
in the beauty of holiness.

3 The voice of the LORD *is* over
the waters;
The God of glory thunders;
The LORD *is* over many
waters.
4 The voice of the LORD *is*
powerful;
The voice of the LORD *is* full
of majesty.

5 The voice of the LORD breaks
the cedars,
Yes, the LORD splinters the
cedars of Lebanon.
6 He makes them also skip like
a calf,
Lebanon and Sirion like a
young wild ox.
7 The voice of the LORD divides
the flames of fire.

8 The voice of the LORD shakes
the wilderness;
The LORD shakes the
Wilderness of Kadesh.
9 The voice of the LORD makes
the deer give birth,
And strips the forests bare;
And in His temple everyone
says, "Glory!"

10 The LORD sat *enthroned* at the
Flood,
And the LORD sits as King
forever.
11 The LORD will give strength to
His people;

The LORD will bless His people
with peace.

PSALM 30

A Psalm. A Song at the dedication of the house of David.

I WILL extol You, O LORD,
for You have lifted me up,
And have not let my foes
rejoice over me.
2 O LORD my God, I cried out to
You,
And You have healed me.
3 O LORD, You have brought my
soul up from the grave;
You have kept me alive, that I
should not go down to the
pit.

4 Sing praise to the LORD,
you saints of His,
And give thanks at the
remembrance of His holy
name.
5 For His anger *is but for* a
moment,
His favor *is for* life;
Weeping may endure for a
night,
But joy *comes* in the morning.

6 Now in my prosperity I said,
"I shall never be moved."
7 LORD, by Your favor You have
made my mountain stand
strong;
You hid Your face, *and* I was
troubled.

8 I cried out to You, O LORD;
And to the LORD I made
supplication:
9 "What profit *is there* in my
blood,
When I go down to the pit?
Will the dust praise You?
Will it declare Your truth?
10 Hear, O LORD, and have mercy
on me;
LORD, be my helper!"

11 You have turned for me my
mourning into dancing;

337

You have put off my
sackcloth and clothed me
with gladness,
12 To the end that *my* glory may
sing praise to You and not
be silent.
O LORD my God,
I will give thanks to You
forever.

PSALM 31

To the Chief Musician. A Psalm of David.

IN You, O LORD, I put my trust;
Let me never be ashamed;
Deliver me in Your
righteousness.
2 Bow down Your ear to me,
Deliver me speedily;
Be my rock of refuge,
A fortress of defense to save
me.

3 For You *are* my rock and my
fortress;
Therefore, for Your name's
sake,
Lead me and guide me.
4 Pull me out of the net which
they have secretly laid for
me,
For You *are* my strength.
5 Into Your hand I commit my
spirit;
You have redeemed me,
O LORD God of truth.

6 I have hated those who regard
vain idols;
But I trust in the LORD.
7 I will be glad
and rejoice in Your mercy,
For You have considered my
trouble;
You have known my soul in
adversities;
8 And have not shut me up into
the hand of the enemy;
You have set my feet in a
wide place.

9 Have mercy on me, O LORD,
for I am in trouble;

My eye wastes away with
grief,
Yes, my soul and my body!
10 For my life is spent with grief,
And my years with sighing;
My strength fails because of
my iniquity,
And my bones waste away.

11 I am a reproach among all my
enemies,
But especially among my
neighbors,
And *am* repulsive to my
acquaintances;
Those who see me outside flee
from me.
12 I am forgotten like a dead
man, out of mind;
I am like a broken vessel.
13 For I hear the slander of
many;
Fear *is* on every side;
While they take counsel
together against me,
They scheme to take away my
life.

14 But as for me, I trust in You,
O LORD;
I say, "You *are* my God."
15 My times *are* in Your hand;
Deliver me from the hand of
my enemies,
And from those who persecute
me.
16 Make Your face shine upon
Your servant;
Save me for Your mercies'
sake.
17 Do not let me be ashamed, O
LORD, for I have called upon
You;
Let the wicked be ashamed;
Let them be silent in the
grave.
18 Let the lying lips be put to
silence,
Which speak insolent things
proudly and contemptuously
against the righteous.

19 Oh, how great *is* Your
goodness,

Which You have laid up for
those who fear You,
Which You have prepared for
those who trust in You
In the presence of the sons of
men!
20 You shall hide them in the
secret place of Your
presence
From the plots of man;
You shall keep them secretly
in a pavilion
From the strife of tongues.

21 Blessed *be* the LORD,
For He has shown me His
marvelous kindness in a
strong city!
22 For I said in my haste,
"I am cut off from before Your
eyes";
Nevertheless You heard the
voice of my supplications
When I cried out to You.

23 Oh, love the LORD, all you His
saints!
For the LORD preserves the
faithful,
And fully repays the proud
person.
24 Be of good courage,
And He shall strengthen your
heart,
All you who hope in the LORD.

PSALM 32

A Psalm of David. A Contemplation.

BLESSED *is he whose*
transgression *is* forgiven,
Whose sin *is* covered.
2 Blessed *is* the man to whom
the LORD does not impute
iniquity,
And in whose spirit *there is*
no guile.

♥ 3 When I kept silent, my bones
grew old
Through my groaning all the
day long.
4 For day and night Your hand
was heavy upon me;

My vitality was turned into
the drought of summer.
Selah
5 I acknowledged my sin to
You,
And my iniquity I have not
hidden.
I said, "I will confess my
transgressions to the LORD,"
And You forgave the iniquity
of my sin.   Selah

6 For this cause everyone who
is godly shall pray to You
In a time when You may be
found;
Surely in a flood of great
waters
They shall not come near him.
7 You *are* my hiding place;
You shall preserve me from
trouble;
You shall surround me with
songs of deliverance.   Selah

8 I will instruct you and teach
you in the way you should
go;
I will guide you with My eye.
9 Do not be like the horse
or like the mule,
Which have no understanding,
Which must be harnessed
with bit and bridle,
Else they will not come near
you.

10 Many sorrows *shall be* to the
wicked;
But he who trusts in the
LORD, mercy shall surround
him.
11 Be glad in the LORD and
rejoice, you righteous;
And shout for joy,
all *you* upright in heart!

PSALM 33

REJOICE in the LORD, O you
righteous!
For praise from the upright is
beautiful.

339   *See Acts 13:38, page 163*

2 Praise the LORD with the harp;
  Make melody to Him with an
    instrument of ten strings.
3 Sing to Him a new song;
  Play skillfully with a shout of
    joy.

4 For the word of the LORD *is*
    right,
  And all His work *is done* in
    truth.
5 He loves righteousness and
    justice;
  The earth is full of the
    goodness of the LORD.

6 By the word of the LORD
    the heavens were made,
  And all the host of them
    by the breath of His mouth.
7 He gathers the waters of the
    sea together as a heap;
  He lays up the deep in
    storehouses.

8 Let all the earth fear the
    LORD;
  Let all the inhabitants of the
    world stand in awe of Him.
9 For He spoke, and it was
    done;
  He commanded, and it stood
    fast.

10 The LORD brings the counsel
     of the nations to nothing;
   He makes the plans of the
     peoples of no effect.
11 The counsel of the LORD
     stands forever,
   The plans of His heart to all
     generations.
12 Blessed *is* the nation whose
     God *is* the LORD,
   And the people *whom* He has
     chosen as His own
     inheritance.

13 The LORD looks from heaven;
   He sees all the sons of men.
14 From the place of His
     habitation He looks
   On all the inhabitants of the
     earth;

15 He fashions their hearts
     individually;
   He considers all their works.

16 No king *is* saved by the
     multitude of an army;
   A mighty man is not delivered
     by great strength.
17 A horse *is* a vain hope for
     safety;
   Neither shall it deliver *any*
     by its great strength.

18 Behold, the eye of the LORD *is*
     on those who fear Him,
   On those who hope in His
     mercy,
19 To deliver their soul from
     death,
   And to keep them alive in
     famine.

20 Our soul waits for the LORD;
   He *is* our help and our shield.
21 For our heart shall rejoice in
     Him,
   Because we have trusted in
     His holy name.
22 Let Your mercy, O LORD, be
     upon us,
   Just as we hope in You.

PSALM 34

A Psalm of David when he pretended madness
before Abimelech, who drove him away, and he
departed.

I WILL bless the LORD at all
    times;
  His praise *shall* continually *be*
    in my mouth.
2 My soul shall make its boast
    in the LORD;
  The humble shall hear *of it*
    and be glad.
3 Oh, magnify the LORD with
    me,
  And let us exalt His name
    together.

4 I sought the LORD, and He
    heard me,

And delivered me from all my fears.

5 They looked to Him and were radiant,
And their faces were not ashamed.

6 This poor man cried out,
and the LORD heard *him,*
And saved him out of all his troubles.

7 The angel of the LORD encamps all around those who fear Him,
And delivers them.

8 Oh, taste and see that the LORD *is* good;
Blessed *is* the man *who* trusts in Him!

9 Oh, fear the LORD, you His saints!
There is no want to those who fear Him.

10 The young lions lack and suffer hunger;
But those who seek the LORD shall not lack any good *thing.*

11 Come, you children, listen to me;
I will teach you the fear of the LORD.

12 Who *is* the man *who* desires life,
And loves *many* days, that he may see good?

13 Keep your tongue from evil,
And your lips from speaking guile.

14 Depart from evil, and do good;
Seek peace, and pursue it.

15 The eyes of the LORD *are* on the righteous,
And His ears *are open* to their cry.

16 The face of the LORD *is* against those who do evil,
To cut off the remembrance of them from the earth.

17 *The righteous* cry out,
and the LORD hears,

And delivers them out of all their troubles.

18 The LORD *is* near to those who have a broken heart,
And saves such as have a contrite spirit.

19 Many *are* the afflictions of the righteous,
But the LORD delivers him out of them all.

20 He guards all his bones;
Not one of them is broken.

21 Evil shall slay the wicked,
And those who hate the righteous shall be condemned.

22 The LORD redeems the soul of His servants,
And none of those who trust in Him shall be condemned.

PSALM 35

A Psalm of David.

PLEAD *my cause,* O LORD, with those who strive with me;
Fight against those who fight against me.

2 Take hold of shield and buckler,
And stand up for my help.

3 Also draw out the spear,
And stop those who pursue me.
Say to my soul,
"I *am* your salvation."

4 Let those be put to shame and brought to dishonor
Who seek after my life;
Let those be turned back and brought to confusion
Who plot my hurt.

5 Let them be like chaff before the wind,
And let the angel of the LORD chase *them.*

6 Let their way be dark and slippery,
And let the angel of the LORD pursue them.

7 For without cause they have
hidden their net for me *in* a
pit,
Which they have dug without
cause for my life.
8 Let destruction come upon
him unexpectedly,
And let his net that he has
hidden catch himself;
Into that very destruction let
him fall.

9 And my soul shall be joyful in
the LORD;
It shall rejoice in His
salvation.
10 All my bones shall say,
"LORD, who *is* like You,
Delivering the poor from him
who is too strong for him,
Yes, the poor and the needy
from him who plunders
him?"

11 Fierce witnesses rise up;
They ask me *things* that I do
not know.
12 They reward me evil for good,
To the sorrow of my soul.
13 But as for me, when they
were sick,
My clothing *was* sackcloth;
I humbled myself with fasting;
And my prayer would return
to my own heart.
14 I paced about as though *he*
were my friend or brother;
I bowed down heavily, as one
who mourns *for his* mother.

15 But in my adversity they
rejoiced
And gathered together;
Attackers gathered against
me,
And I did not know *it*;
They tore *at me* and did not
cease;
16 With ungodly mockers at
feasts
They gnashed at me with
their teeth.

17 Lord, how long will You look
on?
Rescue me from their
destructions,
My precious *life* from the
lions.
18 I will give You thanks in the
great congregation;
I will praise You among many
people.

19 Let them not rejoice over me
who are wrongfully my
enemies;
Nor let them wink with the
eye who hate me without a
cause.
20 For they do not speak peace,
But they devise deceitful
matters
Against *those who are* quiet in
the land.
21 They also opened their mouth
wide against me,
And said, "Aha, aha!
Our eyes have seen *it.*"

22 *This* You have seen, O LORD;
Do not keep silence.
O Lord, do not be far from
me.
23 Stir up Yourself,
and awake to my
vindication,
To my cause, my God and my
Lord.
24 Vindicate me, O LORD my
God, according to Your
righteousness;
And let them not rejoice over
me.
25 Let them not say in their
hearts, "Ah, so we would
have it!"
Let them not say,
"We have swallowed him
up."

26 Let them be ashamed
and brought to mutual
confusion
Who rejoice at my hurt;

Let them be clothed with
shame and dishonor
Who magnify themselves
against me.

27 Let them shout for joy and be
glad,
Who favor my righteous
cause;
And let them say continually,
"Let the LORD be magnified,
Who has pleasure in the
prosperity of His servant."
28 And my tongue shall speak of
Your righteousness
And of Your praise all the day
long.

PSALM 36

To the Chief Musician. A Psalm of David the
servant of the LORD.

AN oracle within my heart
concerning the
transgression of the wicked:
There is no fear of God before
his eyes.
2 For he flatters himself in his
own eyes,
When he finds out his iniquity
and when he hates.
3 The words of his mouth *are*
wickedness and deceit;
He has ceased to be wise *and*
to do good.
4 He devises wickedness on his
bed;
He sets himself in a way *that
is* not good;
He does not abhor evil.

5 Your mercy, O LORD, *is* in the
heavens,
And Your faithfulness *reaches*
to the clouds.
6 Your righteousness *is* like the
great mountains;
Your judgments *are* a great
deep;
O LORD, You preserve man
and beast.

7 How precious *is* Your
lovingkindness, O God!
Therefore the children of men
put their trust under the
shadow of Your wings.
8 They are abundantly satisfied
with the fullness of Your
house,
And You give them drink
from the river of Your
pleasures.
9 For with You *is* the fountain
of life;
In Your light we see light.

10 Oh, continue Your
lovingkindness to those who
know You,
And Your righteousness
to the upright in heart.
11 Let not the foot of pride come
against me,
And let not the hand of the
wicked drive me away.
12 There the workers of iniquity
have fallen;
They have been cast down
and are not able to rise.

PSALM 37

A Psalm of David.

DO not fret because of
evildoers,
Nor be envious of the workers
of iniquity.
2 For they shall soon be cut
down like the grass,
And wither as the green herb.

3 Trust in the LORD, and do
good;
Dwell in the land, and feed on
His faithfulness.
4 Delight yourself also in the
LORD,
And He shall give you the
desires of your heart.

5 Commit your way to the
LORD,
Trust also in Him,
And He shall bring *it* to pass.

6 He shall bring forth your
    righteousness as the light,
And your justice as the
    noonday.

7 Rest in the LORD,
    and wait patiently for Him;
Do not fret because of him
    who prospers in his way,
Because of the man who
    brings wicked schemes to
    pass.

8 Cease from anger, and forsake
    wrath;
Do not fret—*it* only *causes*
    harm.

9 For evildoers shall be cut off;
But those who wait on the
    LORD,
They shall inherit the earth.

10 For yet a little while and the
    wicked *shall be* no *more;*
Indeed, you will look
    diligently for his place,
But it *shall be* no *more.*

11 But the meek shall inherit the
    earth,
And shall delight themselves
    in the abundance of peace.

12 The wicked plots against the
    just,
And gnashes at him with his
    teeth.

13 The Lord laughs at him,
For He sees that his day is
    coming.

14 The wicked have drawn the
    sword
And have bent their bow,
To cast down the poor and
    needy,
To slay those who are of
    upright conduct.

15 Their sword shall enter their
    own heart,
And their bows shall be
    broken.

16 A little that a righteous man
    has

Is better than the riches of
    many wicked.

17 For the arms of the wicked
    shall be broken,
But the LORD upholds the
    righteous.

18 The LORD knows the days of
    the upright,
And their inheritance shall be
    forever.

19 They shall not be ashamed in
    the evil time,
And in the days of famine
    they shall be satisfied.

20 But the wicked shall perish;
And the enemies of the LORD,
Like the splendor of the
    meadows, shall vanish.
Into smoke they shall vanish
    away.

21 The wicked borrows
    and does not repay,
But the righteous shows
    mercy and gives.

22 For *those who are* blessed by
    Him shall inherit the earth,
But *those who are* cursed by
    Him shall be cut off.

23 The steps of a *good* man are
    ordered by the LORD,
And He delights in his way.

24 Though he fall, he shall not be
    utterly cast down;
For the LORD upholds *him*
    with His hand.

25 I have been young, and *now*
    am old;
Yet I have not seen the
    righteous forsaken,
Nor his descendants begging
    bread.

26 *He is* ever merciful, and lends;
And his descendants *are*
    blessed.

27 Depart from evil, and do good;
And dwell forevermore.

28 For the LORD loves justice,

And does not forsake His
   saints;
They are preserved forever,
But the descendants of the
   wicked shall be cut off.
29 The righteous shall inherit the
   land,
   And dwell in it forever.

30 The mouth of the righteous
   speaks wisdom,
   And his tongue talks of
   justice.
31 The law of his God *is* in his
   heart;
   None of his steps shall slide.

32 The wicked watches the
   righteous,
   And seeks to slay him.
33 The LORD will not leave him
   in his hand,
   Nor condemn him when he is
   judged.

34 Wait on the LORD,
   And keep His way,
   And He shall exalt you to
   inherit the land;
   When the wicked are cut off,
   you shall see *it.*
35 I have seen the wicked in
   great power,
   And spreading himself like a
   native green tree.
36 Yet he passed away, and
   behold, he *was* no *more;*
   Indeed I sought him,
   but he could not be found.

37 Mark the blameless *man,*
   and observe the upright;
   For the future of *that* man *is*
   peace.
38 But the transgressors shall be
   destroyed together;
   The future of the wicked shall
   be cut off.

39 But the salvation of the
   righteous *is* from the LORD;
   He is their strength in the
   time of trouble.

40 And the LORD shall help them
   and deliver them;
   He shall deliver them from the
   wicked,
   And save them,
   Because they trust in Him.

PSALM 38

A Psalm of David. To bring to remembrance.

O LORD, do not rebuke me in
   Your wrath,
   Nor chasten me in Your hot
   displeasure!
2 For Your arrows pierce me
   deeply,
   And Your hand presses me
   down.

3 *There is* no soundness in my
   flesh
   Because of Your anger,
   Nor *is there any* health in my
   bones
   Because of my sin.
4 For my iniquities have gone
   over my head;
   Like a heavy burden they are
   too heavy for me.
5 My wounds are foul *and*
   festering
   Because of my foolishness.

6 I am troubled,
   I am bowed down greatly;
   I go mourning all the day
   long.
7 For my loins are full of
   inflammation,
   And *there is* no soundness in
   my flesh.
8 I am feeble and severely
   broken;
   I groan because of the turmoil
   of my heart.

9 Lord, all my desire *is* before
   You;
   And my sighing is not hidden
   from You.
10 My heart pants, my strength
   fails me;

As for the light of my eyes,
it also has gone from me.

11 My loved ones and my friends
stand aloof from my plague,
And my kinsmen stand afar
off.

12 Those also who seek my life
lay snares *for me;*
Those who seek my hurt
speak of destruction,
And plan deception all the day
long.

13 But I, like a deaf *man,* do not
hear;
And I *am* like a mute *who*
does not open his mouth.

14 Thus I am like a man who
does not hear,
And in whose mouth *is* no
response.

15 For in You, O LORD, I hope;
You will hear, O Lord my
God.

16 For I said, *"Hear me,*
lest they rejoice over me,
Lest, when my foot slips,
they magnify *themselves*
against me."

17 For I *am* ready to fall,
And my sorrow *is* continually
before me.

18 For I will declare my iniquity;
I will be in anguish over my
sin.

19 But my enemies *are* vigorous,
and they are strong;
And those who hate me
wrongfully have multiplied.

20 Those also who render evil for
good,
They are my adversaries,
because I follow *what is*
good.

21 Do not forsake me, O LORD;
O my God, be not far from
me!

22 Make haste to help me,
O Lord, my salvation!

PSALM 39

To the Chief Musician. To Jeduthun. A Psalm
of David.

I SAID, "I will guard my ways,
Lest I sin with my tongue;
I will restrain my mouth with
a muzzle,
While the wicked are before
me."

2 I was mute with silence,
I held my peace *even* from
good;
And my sorrow was stirred
up.

3 My heart was hot within me;
While I was musing, the fire
burned.
Then I spoke with my tongue:

4 "LORD, make me to know my
end,
And what *is* the measure of
my days,
That I may know how frail I
am.

5 Indeed, You have made my
days *as* handbreadths,
And my age *is* as nothing
before You;
Certainly every man at his
best state *is* but vapor.
Selah

6 Surely every man walks about
like a shadow;
Surely they busy themselves
in vain;
He heaps up *riches,*
And does not know who will
gather them.

7 "And now, Lord, what do I
wait for?
My hope *is* in You.

8 Deliver me from all my
transgressions;
Do not make me the reproach
of the foolish.

9 I was mute, I did not open my
mouth,
Because it was You who did
it.

10 Remove Your plague from me;

I am consumed by the blow of
Your hand.
11 When with rebukes You
correct man for iniquity,
You make his beauty melt
away like a moth;
Surely every man *is* vapor.
                                      Selah

12 "Hear my prayer, O LORD,
And give ear to my cry;
Do not be silent at my tears;
For I *am* a stranger with You,
A sojourner, as all my fathers
were.
13 Remove Your gaze from me,
that I may regain strength,
Before I go away and am no
more."

PSALM 40

To the Chief Musician. A Psalm of David.

I WAITED patiently for the
LORD;
And He inclined to me,
And heard my cry.
2 He also brought me up out of
a horrible pit,
Out of the miry clay,
And set my feet upon a rock,
And established my steps.
3 He has put a new song in my
mouth—
Praise to our God;
Many will see *it* and fear,
And will trust in the LORD.

4 Blessed *is* that man who
makes the LORD his trust,
And does not respect the
proud, nor such as turn
aside to lies.
5 Many, O LORD my God,
are Your wonderful works
Which You have done;
And Your thoughts *which are*
toward us
Cannot be recounted to You
in order;
If I would declare and speak
of them,

They are more than can be
numbered.

6 Sacrifice and offering
You did not desire;
My ears You have opened;
Burnt offering and sin offering
You did not require.
7 Then I said, "Behold, I come;
In the scroll of the Book *it is*
written of me.
8 I delight to do Your will, O
my God,
And Your law *is* within my
heart."

9 I have proclaimed the good
news of righteousness
In the great congregation;
Indeed, I do not restrain my
lips,
O LORD, You Yourself know.
10 I have not hidden Your
righteousness within my
heart;
I have declared Your
faithfulness and Your
salvation;
I have not concealed Your
lovingkindness and Your
truth
From the great congregation.

11 Do not withhold Your tender
mercies from me, O LORD;
Let Your lovingkindness and
Your truth continually
preserve me.
12 For innumerable evils have
surrounded me;
My iniquities have overtaken
me, so that I am not able to
look up;
They are more than the hairs
of my head;
Therefore my heart fails me.

13 Be pleased, O LORD, to deliver
me;
O LORD, make haste to help
me!

14 Let them be ashamed
        and brought to mutual
        confusion
    Who seek to destroy my life;
    Let them be driven backward
        and brought to dishonor
    Who wish me evil.
15 Let them be appalled because
        of their shame,
    Who say to me, "Aha, aha!"

16 Let all those who seek You
        rejoice and be glad in You;
    Let such as love Your
        salvation say continually,
    "The LORD be magnified!"
17 But I *am* poor and needy;
    Yet the LORD thinks upon me.
    You *are* my help and my
        deliverer;
    Do not delay, O my God.

PSALM 41

To the Chief Musician. A Psalm of David.

BLESSED *is* he who considers
        the poor;
    The LORD will deliver him in
        time of trouble.
2 The LORD will preserve him
        and keep him alive,
    And he will be blessed on the
        earth;
    You will not deliver him to
        the will of his enemies.
3 The LORD will strengthen him
        on his bed of illness;
    You will sustain him on his
        sickbed.

4 I said, "LORD, be merciful to
        me;
    Heal my soul, for I have
        sinned against You."
5 My enemies speak evil of me:
    "When will he die,
        and his name perish?"
6 And if he comes to see *me*,
    he speaks vain *words*;
    His heart gathers iniquity to
        itself;
    When he goes out, he tells *it*.

7 All who hate me whisper
        together against me;
    Against me they devise my
        hurt.
8 "An evil disease," *they say*,
    "clings to him.
    And *now* that he lies down,
        he will rise up no more."
9 Even my own familiar friend
        in whom I trusted,
    Who ate my bread,
    Has lifted up *his* heel against
        me.

10 But You, O LORD, be merciful
        to me, and raise me up,
    That I may repay them.
11 By this I know that You are
        well pleased with me,
    Because my enemy does not
        triumph over me.
12 As for me, You uphold me in
        my integrity,
    And set me before Your face
        forever.

13 Blessed *be* the LORD God of
        Israel
    From everlasting to
        everlasting!
    Amen and Amen.

BOOK TWO

Psalms 42–72

PSALM 42

To the Chief Musician. A Contemplation of the
sons of Korah.

AS the deer pants for the water
        brooks,
    So pants my soul for You, O
        God.
2 My soul thirsts for God,
        for the living God.
    When shall I come and appear
        before God?
3 My tears have been my food
        day and night,
    While they continually say to
        me,
    Where *is* your God?"

4 When I remember these
      things,
   I pour out my soul within me.
   For I used to go with the
      multitude;
   I went with them to the house
      of God,
   With the voice of joy and
      praise,
   With a multitude that kept a
      pilgrim feast.

5 Why are you cast down, O my
      soul?
   And *why* are you disquieted
      within me?
   Hope in God,
      for I shall yet praise Him
   For the help of His
      countenance.

6 O my God, my soul is cast
      down within me;
   Therefore I will remember
      You from the land of the
      Jordan,
   And from the heights of
      Hermon,
   From the Hill Mizar.
7 Deep calls unto deep at the
      noise of Your waterfalls;
   All Your waves and billows
      have gone over me.
8 The LORD will command His
      lovingkindness in the
      daytime,
   And in the night His song
      shall be with me—
   A prayer to the God of my
      life.

9 I will say to God my Rock,
   Why have You forgotten me?
   Why do I go mourning
      because of the oppression of
      the enemy?"
10 *As* with a breaking of my
      bones,
   My enemies reproach me,
   While they say to me all day
      long,
   "Where *is* your God?"

11 Why are you cast down, O my
      soul?
   And why are you disquieted
      within me?
   Hope in God;
   For I shall yet praise Him,
   The help of my countenance
      and my God.

PSALM 43

VINDICATE me, O God,
   And plead my cause against
      an ungodly nation;
   Oh, deliver me from the
      deceitful and unjust man!
2 For You *are* the God of my
      strength;
   Why do You cast me off?
   Why do I go mourning
      because of the oppression of
      the enemy?

3 Oh, send out Your light and
      Your truth!
   Let them lead me;
   Let them bring me to Your
      holy hill
   And to Your tabernacle.
4 Then I will go to the altar of
      God,
   To God my exceeding joy;
   And on the harp I will praise
      You,
   O God, my God.

5 Why are you cast down, O my
      soul?
   And why are you disquieted
      within me?
   Hope in God;
   For I shall yet praise Him,
   The help of my countenance
      and my God.

PSALM 44

To the Chief Musician. A Contemplation of the
sons of Korah.

WE have heard with our ears,
      O God,
   Our fathers have told us,

What deeds You did in their
days,
In days of old:

2 *How* You drove out the
nations with Your hand,
But them You planted;
How You afflicted the peoples,
and cast them out.

3 For they did not gain
possession of the land by
their own sword,
Nor did their own arm save
them;
But it was Your right hand,
Your arm, and the light of
Your countenance,
Because You favored them.

4 You are my King, O God;
Command victories for Jacob.

5 Through You we will push
down our enemies;
Through Your name we will
trample those who rise up
against us.

6 For I will not trust in my bow,
Nor shall my sword save me.

7 But You have saved us from
our enemies,
And have put to shame those
who hated us.

8 In God we boast all day long,
And praise Your name
forever.   Selah

9 But You have cast *us* off and
put us to shame,
And You do not go out with
our armies.

10 You make us turn back from
the enemy,
And those who hate us have
taken spoil for themselves.

11 You have given us up like
sheep *intended* for food,
And have scattered us among
the nations.

12 You sell Your people for
naught,
And are not enriched by their
price.

13 You make us a reproach
to our neighbors,

A scorn and a derision
to those all around us.

14 You make us a byword
among the nations,
A shaking of the head
among the peoples.

15 My dishonor *is* continually
before me,
And the shame of my face
has covered me,

16 Because of the voice of him
who reproaches and reviles,
Because of the enemy and the
avenger.

17 All this has come upon us;
But we have not forgotten
You,
Nor have we dealt falsely with
Your covenant.

18 Our heart has not turned
back,
Nor have our steps departed
from Your way;

19 But You have severely broken
us in the place of jackals,
And covered us with the
shadow of death.

20 If we had forgotten the name
of our God,
Or stretched out our hands to
a foreign god,

21 Would not God search this
out?
For He knows the secrets of
the heart.

22 Yet for Your sake we are
killed all day long;
We are accounted as sheep for
the slaughter.

23 Awake! Why do You sleep, O
Lord?
Arise! Do not cast *us* off
forever.

24 Why do You hide Your face,
And forget our affliction and
our oppression?

25 For our soul is bowed down to
the dust;
Our body clings to the ground.

26 Arise for our help,

And redeem us for Your
mercies' sake.

PSALM 45

To the Chief Musician. Set to "The Lilies." A
Contemplation of the sons of Korah. A Song of
Love.

MY heart is overflowing with a
good theme;
I recite my composition
concerning the King;
My tongue *is* the pen of a
ready writer.

2 You are fairer than the sons
of men;
Grace is poured upon Your
lips;
Therefore God has blessed
You forever.

3 Gird Your sword upon *Your*
thigh, O Mighty One,
With Your glory and Your
majesty.

4 And in Your majesty ride
prosperously because of
truth, humility, *and*
righteousness;
And Your right hand shall
teach You awesome things.

5 Your arrows *are* sharp in the
heart of the King's enemies;
The peoples fall under You.

6 Your throne, O God, *is* forever
and ever;
A scepter of righteousness *is*
the scepter of Your
kingdom.

7 You love righteousness
and hate wickedness;
Therefore God, Your God, has
anointed You
With the oil of gladness more
than Your companions.

8 All Your garments are scented
with myrrh and aloes *and*
cassia,
Out of the ivory palaces,
by which they have made
You glad.

9 Kings' daughters *are* among
Your honorable women;

At Your right hand stands the
queen in gold from Ophir.

10 Listen, O daughter,
Consider and incline your ear;
Forget your own people also,
and your father's house;

11 So the King will greatly desire
your beauty;
Because He *is* your Lord,
worship Him.

12 And the daughter of Tyre *will
be there* with a gift;
The rich among the people
will seek your favor.

13 The royal daughter *is* all
glorious within *the palace;*
Her clothing *is* woven with
gold.

14 She shall be brought to the
King in robes of many
colors;
The virgins, her companions
who follow her, shall be
brought to You.

15 With gladness and rejoicing
they shall be brought;
They shall enter the King's
palace.

16 Instead of Your fathers shall
be Your sons,
Whom You shall make princes
in all the earth.

17 I will make Your name to be
remembered in all
generations;
Therefore the people shall
praise You forever and ever.

PSALM 46

To the Chief Musician. A Psalm of the sons of
Korah. A Song for Alamoth.

GOD *is* our refuge and
strength,
A very present help in trouble.

2 Therefore we will not fear,
Though the earth be removed,
And though the mountains be
carried into the midst of the
sea;

351

3   *Though* its waters roar *and* be
    troubled,
    Though the mountains shake
    with its swelling.   Selah

4   *There is* a river whose streams
    shall make glad the city of
    God,
    The holy *place* of the
    tabernacle of the Most High.

5   God *is* in the midst of her,
    she shall not be moved;
    God shall help her,
    just at the break of dawn.

6   The nations raged, the
    kingdoms were moved;
    He uttered His voice, the
    earth melted.

7   The LORD of hosts *is* with us;
    The God of Jacob *is* our
    refuge.   Selah

8   Come, behold the works of
    the LORD,
    Who has made desolations in
    the earth.

9   He makes wars cease to the
    end of the earth;
    He breaks the bow
    and cuts the spear in two;
    He burns the chariot in the
    fire.

10 Be still, and know that I *am*
    God;
    I will be exalted among the
    nations,
    I will be exalted in the earth!

11 The LORD of hosts *is* with us;
    The God of Jacob *is* our
    refuge.   Selah

PSALM 47

To the Chief Musician. A Psalm of the sons of
Korah.

OH, clap your hands, all you
   peoples!
   Shout to God with the voice
   of triumph!
2 For the LORD Most High *is*
   awesome;

He is a great King over all the
earth.

3   He will subdue the peoples
    under us,
    And the nations under our
    feet.

4   He will choose our inheritance
    for us,
    The excellence of Jacob whom
    He loves.   Selah

5   God has gone up with a shout,
    The LORD with the sound of a
    trumpet.

6   Sing praises to God, sing
    praises!
    Sing praises to our King, sing
    praises!

7   For God *is* the King of all the
    earth;
    Sing praises with
    understanding.

8   God reigns over the nations;
    God sits on His holy throne.

9   The princes of the people have
    gathered together,
    The people of the God of
    Abraham.
    For the shields of the earth
    belong to God;
    He is greatly exalted.

PSALM 48

A Song. A Psalm of the sons of Korah.

GREAT *is* the LORD,
    and greatly to be praised
In the city of our God,
In His holy mountain.
2 Beautiful in elevation,
   The joy of the whole earth,
   Is Mount Zion *on* the sides of
   the north,
   The city of the great King.
3 God *is* in her palaces;
   He is known as her refuge.

4 For behold, the kings
   assembled,
   They passed by together.
5 They saw *it, and* so they
   marveled;

They were troubled, they
hastened away.
6 Fear took hold of them there,
And pain, as of a woman in
travail,
7 *As when* You break the ships
of Tarshish
With an east wind.

8 As we have heard,
So we have seen
In the city of the Lord of
hosts,
In the city of our God:
God will establish it forever.
Selah

9 We have thought, O God, on
Your lovingkindness,
In the midst of Your temple.
10 According to Your name, O
God,
So *is* Your praise to the ends
of the earth;
Your right hand is full of
righteousness.
11 Let Mount Zion rejoice,
Let the daughters of Judah be
glad,
Because of Your judgments.

12 Walk about Zion,
And go all around her.
Count her towers;
13 Mark well her bulwarks;
Consider her palaces;
That you may tell *it*
to the generation following.
14 For this *is* God,
Our God forever and ever;
He will be our guide
Even to death.

PSALM 49

To the Chief Musician. A Psalm of the sons of
Korah.

H EAR this, all *you* peoples;
Give ear, all *you* inhabitants
of the world,
2 Both low and high,
Rich and poor together.
3 My mouth shall speak
wisdom,

And the meditation of my
heart *shall bring*
understanding.
4 I will incline my ear to a
proverb;
I will disclose my dark saying
on the harp.

5 Why should I fear in the days
of evil,
When the iniquity at my heels
surrounds me?
6 Those who trust in their
wealth
And boast in the multitude of
their riches,
7 None *of them* can by any
means redeem *his* brother,
Nor give to God a ransom for
him—
8 For the redemption of their
souls *is* costly,
And it shall cease forever—
9 That he should continue to
live eternally,
And not see the Pit.

10 For he sees *that* wise men die;
Likewise the fool and the
senseless person perish,
And leave their wealth to
others.
11 Their inner thought *is that*
their houses *will continue*
forever,
And their dwelling places to
all generations;
They call *their* lands after
their own names.
12 Nevertheless man, *though* in
honor, does not remain;
He is like the beasts *that*
perish.

13 This is the way of those who
are foolish,
And of their posterity who
approve their sayings. Selah
14 Like sheep they are laid in the
grave;
Death shall feed on them;
The upright shall have
dominion over them in the
morning;

And their beauty shall be
    consumed in the grave, far
    from their dwelling.
15 But God will redeem my soul
    from the power of the
    grave,
    For He shall receive me. Selah

16 Do not be afraid when one
    becomes rich,
    When the glory of his house is
    increased;
17 For when he dies he shall
    carry nothing away;
    His glory shall not descend
    after him.
18 Though while he lives he
    blesses himself
    (For *men* will praise you when
    you do well for yourself),
19 He shall go to the generation
    of his fathers;
    They shall never see light.
20 Man *who is* in honor,
    yet does not understand,
    Is like the beasts *that* perish.

PSALM 50

A Psalm of Asaph.

THE Mighty One, God the
    LORD,
    Has spoken and called the
    earth
    From the rising of the sun to
    its going down.
2 Out of Zion, the perfection of
    beauty,
    God will shine forth.
3 Our God shall come,
    and shall not keep silent;
    A fire shall devour before
    Him,
    And it shall be very
    tempestuous all around
    Him.

4 He shall call to the heavens
    from above,
    And to the earth,
    that He may judge His
    people:

5 "Gather My saints together to
    Me,
    Those who have made a
    covenant with Me by
    sacrifice."
6 Let the heavens declare His
    righteousness,
    For God Himself *is* Judge.
                                    Selah

7 "Hear, O My people, and I will
    speak,
    O Israel, and I will testify
    against you;
    I *am* God, your God!
8 I will not reprove you for your
    sacrifices
    Or your burnt offerings,
    Which are continually before
    Me.
9 I will not take a bull from
    your house,
    Nor goats out of your folds.
10 For every beast of the forest *is*
    Mine,
    And the cattle on a thousand
    hills.
11 I know all the birds of the
    mountains,
    And the wild beasts of the
    field *are* Mine.

12 "If I were hungry, I would not
    tell you;
    For the world *is* Mine,
    and all its fullness.
13 Will I eat the flesh of bulls,
    Or drink the blood of goats?
14 Offer to God thanksgiving,
    And pay your vows to the
    Most High.
15 Call upon Me in the day of
    trouble;
    I will deliver you,
    and you shall glorify Me."

16 But to the wicked God says:
    "What *right* have you to
    declare My statutes,
    Or take My covenant in your
    mouth,
17 Seeing you hate instruction

354

And cast My words behind
you?

18 When you saw a thief,
you consented with him,
And have been a partaker
with adulterers.

19 You give your mouth to evil,
And your tongue frames
deceit.

20 You sit *and* speak against
your brother;
You slander your own
mother's son.

21 These *things* you have done,
and I kept silent;
You thought that I was
altogether like you;
But I will reprove you,
And set *them* in order before
your eyes.

22 "Now consider this, you who
forget God,
Lest I tear *you* in pieces,
And *there be* none to deliver:

23 Whoever offers praise glorifies
Me;
And to him who orders *his*
conduct *aright*
I will show the salvation of
God."

PSALM 51

To the Chief Musician. A Psalm of David when
Nathan the prophet went to him, after he had
gone in to Bathsheba.

HAVE mercy upon me, O God,
According to Your
lovingkindness;
According to the multitude of
Your tender mercies,
Blot out my transgressions.

2 Wash me thoroughly from my
iniquity,
And cleanse me from my sin.

3 For I acknowledge my
transgressions,
And my sin *is* ever before me.

4 Against You, You only, have I
sinned,
And done *this* evil in Your
sight—

That You may be found just
when You speak,
And blameless when You
judge.

5 Behold, I was brought forth in
iniquity,
And in sin my mother
conceived me.

6 Behold, You desire truth in
the inward parts,
And in the hidden *part* You
will make me to know
wisdom.

7 Purge me with hyssop,
and I shall be clean;
Wash me, and I shall be
whiter than snow.

8 Make me to hear joy and
gladness,
That the bones *which* You
have broken may rejoice.

9 Hide Your face from my sins,
And blot out all my iniquities.

10 Create in me a clean heart, O
God,
And renew a steadfast spirit
within me.

11 Do not cast me away from
Your presence,
And do not take Your Holy
Spirit from me.

12 Restore to me the joy of Your
salvation,
And uphold me *with Your*
generous Spirit.

13 *Then* I will teach
transgressors Your ways,
And sinners shall be converted
to You.

14 Deliver me from
bloodguiltiness, O God,
The God of my salvation,
And my tongue shall sing
aloud of Your righteousness.

15 O Lord, open my lips,
And my mouth shall show
forth Your praise.

16 For You do not desire sacrifice, or else I would give *it;*
You do not delight in burnt
offering.
17 The sacrifices of God *are* a
broken spirit,
A broken and a contrite
heart—
These, O God, You will not
despise.

18 Do good in Your good
pleasure to Zion;
Build the walls of Jerusalem.
19 Then You shall be pleased
with the sacrifices of
righteousness,
With burnt offering and whole
burnt offering;
Then they shall offer bulls on
Your altar.

PSALM 52

To the Chief Musician. A Contemplation of
David when Doeg the Edomite went and told
Saul, and said to him, "David has gone to the
house of Ahimelech."

WHY do you boast in evil,
O mighty man?
The goodness of God *endures*
continually.
2 Your tongue devises
destruction,
Like a sharp razor, working
deceitfully.
3 You love evil more than good,
And lying rather than
speaking righteousness.
                              Selah
4 You love all devouring words,
You deceitful tongue.

5 God shall likewise destroy you
forever;
He shall take you away, and
pluck you out of *your*
dwelling place,
And uproot you from the land
of the living.   Selah
6 The righteous also shall see
and fear,

And shall laugh at him,
saying,
7 "Here is the man *who* did not
make God his strength,
But trusted in the abundance
of his riches,
And strengthened himself
in his wickedness."

8 But I *am* like a green olive
tree in the house of God;
I trust in the mercy of God
forever and ever.
9 I will praise You forever,
Because You have done *it;*
And in the presence of Your
saints
I will wait on Your name,
for *it is* good.

PSALM 53

To the Chief Musician. Set to "Mahalath." A
Contemplation of David.

THE fool has said in his heart,
"*There is* no God."
They are corrupt,
and have done abominable
iniquity;
There is none who does good.

2 God looks down from heaven
upon the children of men,
To see if there are *any* who
understand, who seek God.
3 Every one of them has turned
aside;
They have together become
corrupt;
There is none who does good,
No, not one.

4 Have the workers of iniquity
no knowledge,
Who eat up my people *as* they
eat bread,
And do not call upon God?
5 There they are in great fear
Where no fear was,
For God has scattered the
bones of him who encamps
against you;
You have put *them* to shame,
Because God has despised
them.

6 Oh, that the salvation of Israel
   would come out of Zion!
   When God brings back the
   captivity of His people,
   Let Jacob rejoice *and* Israel be
   glad.

PSALM 54

To the Chief Musician. With stringed
instruments. A Contemplation of David when
the Ziphites went and said to Saul, "Is David
not hiding with us?"

SAVE me, O God, by Your
   name,
   And vindicate me by Your
   strength.
2 Hear my prayer, O God;
   Give ear to the words of my
   mouth.
3 For strangers have risen up
   against me,
   And oppressors have sought
   after my life;
   They have not set God before
   them.   Selah

4 Behold, God *is* my helper;
   The Lord *is* with those who
   uphold my life.
5 He will repay my enemies for
   their evil.
   Cut them off in Your truth.

6 I will freely sacrifice to You;
   I will praise Your name, O
   Lord, for *it is* good.
7 For He has delivered me out
   of all trouble;
   And my eye has seen *its
   desire* upon my enemies.

PSALM 55

To the Chief Musician. With stringed
instruments. A Contemplation of David.

GIVE ear to my prayer, O God,
   And do not hide Yourself
   from my supplication.
2 Attend to me, and hear me;
   I am restless in my complaint,
   and moan noisily,

3 Because of the voice of the
   enemy,
   Because of the oppression of
   the wicked;
   For they bring down trouble
   upon me,
   And in wrath they hate me.

4 My heart is severely pained
   within me,
   And the terrors of death have
   fallen upon me.
5 Fearfulness and trembling
   have come upon me,
   And horror has overwhelmed
   me.
6 And I said, "Oh, that I had
   wings like a dove!
   For then I would fly away
   and be at rest.
7 Indeed, I would wander far
   off,
   And remain in the wilderness.
                           Selah
8 I would hasten my escape
   From the windy storm *and*
   tempest."

9 Destroy, O Lord, *and* divide
   their tongues,
   For I have seen violence and
   strife in the city.
10 Day and night they go around
   it on its walls;
   Iniquity and trouble *are* also
   in the midst of it.
11 Destruction *is* in its midst;
   Deceit and guile do not depart
   from its streets.

12 For *it is* not an enemy *who*
   reproaches me;
   Then I could bear *it*.
   Nor *is it* one *who* hates me
   who has magnified *himself*
   against me;
   Then I could hide from him.
13 But *it was* you, a man my
   equal,
   My companion and my
   acquaintance.
14 We took sweet counsel
   together,

357

And walked to the house of God in the throng.

15 Let death seize them;
Let them go down alive into hell,
For wickedness *is* in their dwellings *and* among them.

16 As for me, I will call upon God,
And the LORD shall save me.

17 Evening and morning and at noon
I will pray, and cry aloud,
And He shall hear my voice.

18 He has redeemed my soul in peace from the battle *which was* against me,
For there were many against me.

19 God will hear, and afflict them,
Even He who abides from of old.   Selah
Because they do not change,
Therefore they do not fear God.

20 He has put forth his hands against those who were at peace with him;
He has broken his covenant.

21 *The words* of his mouth were smoother than butter,
But war *was* in his heart;
His words were softer than oil,
Yet they *were* drawn swords.

❤ 22 Cast your burden on the LORD,
And He shall sustain you;
He shall never permit the righteous to be moved.

23 But You, O God, shall bring them down to the pit of destruction;
Bloodthirsty and deceitful men shall not live out half their days;
But I will trust in You.

See Psalm 139:13–18, page 423

PSALM 56

To the Chief Musician. Set to "The Silent Dove in Distant Lands." A Michtam of David when the Philistines captured him in Gath.

BE merciful to me, O God,
for man would swallow me up;
Fighting all day he oppresses me.

2 My enemies would hound *me* all day,
For *there are* many who fight against me, O Most High.

3 Whenever I am afraid,
I will trust in You.

4 In God (I will praise His word),
In God I have put my trust;
I will not fear.
What can flesh do to me?

5 All day they twist my words;
All their thoughts *are* against me for evil.

6 They gather together,
They hide, they mark my steps,
When they lie in wait for my life.

7 Shall they escape by iniquity?
In anger cast down the peoples, O God!

8 You number my wanderings;
Put my tears into Your bottle;
Are they not in Your book?

9 When I cry out *to You,*
Then my enemies will turn back;
This I know, because God *is* for me.

10 In God (I will praise *His* word),
In the LORD (I will praise *His* word),

11 In God I have put my trust;
I will not be afraid.
What can man do to me?

12 Vows *made* to You *are* binding upon me, O God;
I will render praises to You,

13 For You have delivered my
soul from death.
Have You not *delivered my*
feet from falling,
That I may walk before God
In the light of the living?

PSALM 57

To the Chief Musician. Set to "Do Not
Destroy." A Michtam of David when he fled
from Saul into the cave.

BE merciful to me, O God,
be merciful to me!
For my soul trusts in You;
And in the shadow of Your
wings I will make my
refuge,
Until *these* calamities have
passed by.

2 I will cry out to God Most
High,
To God who performs *all
things* for me.
3 He shall send from heaven
and save me;
He reproaches the one who
would swallow me up. Selah
God shall send forth His
mercy and His truth.

4 My soul *is* among lions;
I lie *among* the sons of men
Who are set on fire,
Whose teeth *are* spears and
arrows,
And their tongue a sharp
sword.
5 Be exalted, O God, above the
heavens;
Let Your glory *be* above all
the earth.

6 They have prepared a net for
my steps;
My soul is bowed down;
They have dug a pit before
me;
Into the midst of it they
themselves have fallen.
Selah
359

7 My heart is steadfast, O God,
my heart is steadfast;
I will sing and give praise.
8 Awake, my glory!
Awake, lute and harp!
I will awaken the dawn.

9 I will praise You, O Lord,
among the peoples;
I will sing to You among the
nations.
10 For Your mercy reaches unto
the heavens,
And Your truth unto the
clouds.

11 Be exalted, O God, above the
heavens;
Let Your glory *be* above all
the earth.

PSALM 58

To the Chief Musician. Set to "Do Not
Destroy." A Michtam of David.

DO you indeed speak
righteousness,
you silent ones?
Do you judge uprightly,
you sons of men?
2 No, in heart you work
wickedness;
You weigh out the violence of
your hands in the earth.

3 The wicked are estranged
from the womb;
They go astray as soon as
they are born, speaking lies.
4 Their poison *is* like the poison
of a serpent;
They are like the deaf cobra
that stops its ear,
5 Which will not heed the voice
of charmers,
Charming ever so skillfully.

6 Break their teeth in their
mouth, O God!
Break out the fangs of the
young lions, O LORD!
7 Let them flow away as waters
which run continually;

When he bends *his bow,*
Let his arrows be as if cut in
    pieces.
8   *Let them be* like a snail which
    melts away as it goes,
    Like a stillborn child of a
    woman, that they may not
    see the sun.

9   Before your pots can feel *the
    burning* thorns,
    He shall take them away as
    with a whirlwind,
    As in His living and burning
    wrath.
10 The righteous shall rejoice
    when he sees the
    vengeance;
    He shall wash his feet in the
    blood of the wicked,
11 So that men will say,
    "Surely *there is* a reward for
    the righteous;
    Surely He is God who judges
    in the earth."

PSALM 59

To the Chief Musician. Set to "Do Not
Destroy." A Michtam of David when Saul sent
men, and they watched the house in order to
kill him.

DELIVER me from my enemies,
    O my God;
    Defend me from those who
    rise up against me.
2   Deliver me from the workers
    of iniquity,
    And save me from
    bloodthirsty men.

3   For look, they lie in wait for
    my life;
    The mighty gather against me,
    Not *for* my transgression nor
    for my sin, O LORD.
4   They run and prepare
    themselves through no fault
    of *mine.*

    Awake to help me, and
    behold!

5   You therefore, O LORD God of
    hosts, the God of Israel,
    Awake to punish all the
    nations;
    Do not be merciful to any
    wicked transgressors.   Selah

6   At evening they return,
    They growl like a dog,
    And go all around the city.
7   Indeed, they belch out with
    their mouth;
    Swords *are* in their lips;
    For *they* say, "Who hears?"

8   But You, O LORD, shall laugh
    at them;
    You shall have all the nations
    in derision.
9   *O You* his Strength,
    I will wait for You.

    For God *is* my defense;
10 My merciful God shall come
    to meet me;
    God shall let me see *my desire*
    on my enemies.

11 Do not slay them,
    lest my people forget;
    Scatter them by Your power,
    And bring them down,
    O Lord our shield.
12 *For* the sin of their mouth *and*
    the words of their lips,
    Let them even be taken in
    their pride,
    And for the cursing and lying
    which they speak.
13 Consume *them* in wrath,
    consume *them,*
    That they *may* not *be;*
    And let them know that God
    rules in Jacob
    To the ends of the earth.
                              Selah

14 And at evening they return,
    They growl like a dog,
    And go all around the city.
15 They wander up and down for
    food,
    And howl if they are not
    satisfied.

16 But I will sing of Your power;
　Yes, I will sing aloud of Your
　　mercy in the morning;
　For You have been my
　　defense
　And refuge in the day of my
　　trouble.
17 To You, O my Strength,
　I will sing praises;
　For God *is* my defense,
　The God of my mercy.

PSALM 60

To the Chief Musician. Set to "Lily of the
Testimony." A Michtam of David. For
teaching. When he fought against
Mesopotamia and Syria of Zobah, and Joab
returned and killed twelve thousand Edomites
in the Valley of Salt.

O GOD, You have cast us off;
　You have broken us down;
　You have been displeased;
　Oh, restore us again!
2 You have made the earth
　　tremble;
　You have broken it;
　Heal its breaches, for it is
　　shaking.
3 You have shown Your people
　　hard things;
　You have made us drink the
　　wine of confusion.

4 You have given a banner to
　　those who fear You,
　That it may be displayed
　　because of the truth.　Selah
5 That Your beloved may be
　　delivered,
　Save *with* Your right hand,
　　and hear me.

6 God has spoken in His
　　holiness:
　"I will rejoice;
　I will divide Shechem
　And measure out the Valley of
　　Succoth.
7 Gilead *is* Mine, and Manasseh
　　is Mine;
　Ephraim also *is* the helmet for
　　My head;
　Judah *is* My lawgiver.

8 Moab *is* My washpot;
　Over Edom I will cast My
　　shoe;
　Philistia, shout in triumph
　　because of Me."

9 Who will bring me *into* the
　　strong city?
　Who will lead me to Edom?
10 *Is it* not You, O God, *who* cast
　　us off?
　And *You*, O God, *who* did not
　　go out with our armies?
11 Give us help from trouble,
　For vain *is* the help of man.
12 Through God we will do
　　valiantly,
　For *it is* He *who* shall tread
　　down our enemies.

PSALM 61

To the Chief Musician. On a stringed
instrument. A Psalm of David.

H EAR my cry, O God;
　Attend to my prayer.
2 From the end of the earth I
　　will cry to You,
　When my heart is
　　overwhelmed;
　Lead me to the rock that is
　　higher than I.

3 For You have been a shelter
　　for me,
　And a strong tower from the
　　enemy.
4 I will abide in Your tabernacle
　　forever;
　I will trust in the shelter of
　　Your wings.　　　　Selah

5 For You, O God, have heard
　　my vows;
　You have given *me* the
　　heritage of those who fear
　　Your name.
6 You will prolong the king's
　　life,
　His years as many
　　generations.
7 He shall abide before God
　　forever.

Oh, prepare mercy and truth,
which may preserve him!

8 So I will sing praise to Your
name forever,
That I may daily perform my
vows.

PSALM 62

*To the Chief Musician. To Jeduthun. A Psalm
of David.*

TRULY my soul silently *waits*
for God;
From Him *comes* my
salvation.
2 He only *is* my rock and my
salvation;
He is my defense;
I shall not be greatly moved.

3 How long will you attack a
man?
You shall be slain, all of you,
Like a leaning wall and a
tottering fence.
4 They only consult to cast *him*
down from his high
position;
They delight in lies;
They bless with their mouth,
But they curse inwardly.
Selah

5 My soul, wait silently for God
alone,
For my expectation *is* from
Him.
6 He only *is* my rock and my
salvation;
He is my defense;
I shall not be moved.
7 In God *is* my salvation and
my glory;
The rock of my strength,
And my refuge, *is* in God.

8 Trust in Him at all times, you
people;
Pour out your heart before
Him;
God *is* a refuge for us.   Selah

9 Surely men of low degree *are*
a vapor,

Men of high degree *are* a lie;
If they are weighed in the
balances,
They *are* altogether *lighter*
than vapor.
10 Do not trust in oppression,
Nor vainly hope in robbery;
If riches increase,
Do not set *your* heart on
them.

11 God has spoken once,
Twice I have heard this:
That power *belongs* to God.
12 Also to You, O Lord, *belongs*
mercy;
For You render to each one
according to his work.

PSALM 63

*A Psalm of David when he was in the
wilderness of Judah.*

O GOD, You *are* my God;
Early will I seek You;
My soul thirsts for You;
My flesh longs for You
In a dry and thirsty land
Where there is no water.
2 So I have looked for You
in the sanctuary,
To see Your power and
Your glory.

3 Because Your lovingkindness
is better than life,
My lips shall praise You.
4 Thus I will bless You while I
live;
I will lift up my hands in Your
name.
5 My soul shall be satisfied as
with marrow and fatness,
And my mouth shall praise
You with joyful lips.

6 When I remember You on my
bed,
I meditate on You in the *night*
watches.
7 Because You have been my
help,
Therefore in the shadow of
Your wings I will rejoice.

8 My soul follows close behind
      You;
   Your right hand upholds me.

9 But those *who* seek my life,
      to destroy *it,*
   Shall go into the lower parts
      of the earth.
10 They shall fall by the sword;
   They shall be a portion for
      jackals.

11 But the king shall rejoice in
      God;
   Everyone who swears by Him
      shall glory;
   But the mouth of those who
      speak lies shall be stopped.

PSALM 64

To the Chief Musician. A Psalm of David.

HEAR my voice, O God, in my
      meditation;
   Preserve my life from fear of
      the enemy.
2 Hide me from the secret
      counsel of the wicked,
   From the insurrection of the
      workers of iniquity,
3 Who sharpen their tongue like
      a sword,
   And bend *their bows to shoot*
      their arrows—bitter words,
4 That they may shoot in secret
      at the blameless;
   Suddenly they shoot at him
      and do not fear.

5 They encourage themselves *in*
      an evil matter;
   They talk of laying snares
      secretly;
   They say, "Who will see
      them?"
6 They devise iniquities:
   "We have perfected a shrewd
      scheme."
   Both the inward thought and
      the heart of man are deep.

7 But God shall shoot at them
      with an arrow;

Suddenly they shall be
      wounded.
8 So He will make them stumble
      over their own tongue;
   All who see them shall flee
      away.
9 All men shall fear,
   And shall declare the work of
      God;
   For they shall wisely consider
      His doing.

10 The righteous shall be glad in
      the LORD, and trust in Him.
   And all the upright in heart
      shall glory.

PSALM 65

To the Chief Musician. A Psalm of David. A
Song.

PRAISE is awaiting You, O
      God, in Zion;
   And to You the vow shall be
      performed.
2 O You who hear prayer,
   To You all flesh will come.
3 Iniquities prevail against me;
   As for our transgressions,
   You will provide atonement
      for them.

4 Blessed *is the man whom* You
      choose,
   And cause to approach *You,*
   That he may dwell in Your
      courts.
   We shall be satisfied with the
      goodness of Your house,
   Of Your holy temple.

5 *By* awesome deeds in
      righteousness You will
      answer us,
   O God of our salvation,
   You who are the confidence of
      all the ends of the earth,
   And of the far-off seas;
6 Who established the
      mountains by His strength,
   Being clothed with power;
7 You who still the noise of the
      seas,

The noise of their waves,
And the tumult of the peoples.
8 They also who dwell in the
farthest parts are afraid of
Your signs;
You make the outgoings of
the morning and evening
rejoice.

9 You visit the earth and water
it,
You greatly enrich it;
The river of God is full of
water;
You provide their grain,
For so You have prepared it.
10 You water its ridges
abundantly,
You settle its furrows;
You make it soft with
showers,
You bless its growth.

11 You crown the year with
Your goodness,
And Your paths drip *with*
abundance.
12 They drop *on* the pastures of
the wilderness,
And the little hills rejoice on
every side.
13 The pastures are clothed with
flocks;
The valleys also are covered
with grain;
They shout for joy, they also
sing.

PSALM 66

To the Chief Musician. A Song. A Psalm.

MAKE a joyful shout to God,
all the earth!
2 Sing out the honor of His
name;
Make His praise glorious.
3 Say to God,
"How awesome are Your
works!
Through the greatness of
Your power
Your enemies shall submit
themselves to You.

4 All the earth shall worship
You
And sing praises to You;
They shall sing praises *to*
Your name." Selah

5 Come and see the works of
God;
He is awesome *in His* doing
toward the sons of men.
6 He turned the sea into dry
land;
They went through the river
on foot.
There we will rejoice in Him.
7 He rules by His power forever;
His eyes observe the nations;
Do not let the rebellious exalt
themselves. Selah

8 Oh, bless our God, you
peoples!
And make the voice of His
praise to be heard,
9 Who keeps our soul among
the living,
And does not allow our feet to
be moved.
10 For You, O God, have proved
us;
You have refined us as silver
is refined.
11 You brought us into the net;
You laid affliction on our
backs.
12 You have caused men to ride
over our heads;
We went through fire
and through water;
But You brought us out to
rich *fulfillment.*

13 I will go into Your house with
burnt offerings;
I will pay You my vows,
14 Which my lips have uttered
And my mouth has spoken
when I was in trouble.
15 I will offer You burnt
sacrifices of fat animals,
With the sweet aroma of
rams;
I will offer bulls with goats.
Selah

16 Come *and* hear, all you who
    fear God,
  And I will declare what He
    has done for my soul.
17 I cried to Him with my
    mouth,
  And He was extolled with my
    tongue.
18 If I regard iniquity in my
    heart,
  The Lord will not hear.
19 *But* certainly God has heard
    me;
  He has attended to the voice
    of my prayer.

20 Blessed *be* God,
  Who has not turned away my
    prayer,
  Nor His mercy from me!

PSALM 67

To the Chief Musician. On stringed
instruments. A Psalm. A Song.

GOD be merciful to us and
  bless us,
  And cause His face to shine
    upon us,   Selah
2 That Your way may be known
    on earth,
  Your salvation among all
    nations.

3 Let the peoples praise You, O
    God;
  Let all the peoples praise You.
4 Oh, let the nations be glad
    and sing for joy!
  For You shall judge the
    people righteously,
  And govern the nations on
    earth.   Selah

5 Let the peoples praise You, O
    God;
  Let all the peoples praise You.
6 *Then* the earth shall yield her
    increase;
  God, our own God, shall bless
    us.
7 God shall bless us,
  And all the ends of the earth
    shall fear Him.

PSALM 68

To the Chief Musician. A Psalm of David. A
Song.

LET God arise,
  Let His enemies be scattered;
  Let those also who hate Him
    flee before Him.
2 As smoke is driven away,
  So drive *them* away;
  As wax melts before the fire,
  So let the wicked perish at the
    presence of God.
3 But let the righteous be glad;
  Let them rejoice before God;
  Yes, let them rejoice
    exceedingly.

4 Sing to God, sing praises to
    His name;
  Extol Him who rides on the
    clouds,
  By His name YAH,
  And rejoice before Him.

5 A father of the fatherless,
    a defender of widows,
  Is God in His holy habitation.
6 God sets the solitary in
    families;
  He brings out those who are
    bound into prosperity;
  But the rebellious dwell in a
    dry *land.*

7 O God, when You went out
    before Your people,
  When You marched through
    the wilderness,   Selah
8 The earth shook;
  The heavens also dropped *rain*
    at the presence of God;
  Sinai itself *was moved* at the
    presence of God, the God of
    Israel.
9 You, O God, sent a plentiful
    rain,
  Whereby You confirmed Your
    inheritance,
  When it was weary.
10 Your congregation dwelt in it;
  You, O God, provided from
    Your goodness for the poor.

11 The Lord gave the word;
   Great *was* the company of
      those who proclaimed *it:*
12 "Kings of armies flee, they flee,
   And she who remains at home
      divides the spoil.
13 Though you lie down among
      the sheepfolds,
   Yet you will be like the wings
      of a dove covered with
      silver,
   And her feathers with yellow
      gold."
14 When the Almighty scattered
      kings in it,
   It was *white* as snow in
      Zalmon.

15 A mountain of God *is* the
      mountain of Bashan;
   A mountain *of many* peaks
      is the mountain of Bashan.
16 Why do you fume with envy,
      you mountains of *many*
      peaks?
   This is the mountain *which*
      God desires to dwell in;
   Yes, the LORD will dwell *in it*
      forever.

17 The chariots of God *are*
      twenty thousand,
   Even thousands of thousands;
   The Lord is among them *as in*
      Sinai, in the Holy *Place.*
18 You have ascended on high,
   You have led captivity
      captive;
   You have received gifts
      among men,
   Even *among* the rebellious,
   That the LORD God might
      dwell *there.*

19 Blessed *be* the Lord,
   Who daily loads us *with*
      benefits,
   The God of our salvation!
                              Selah
20 Our God *is* the God of
      salvation;
   And to GOD the Lord *belong*
      escapes from death.

21 But God will wound the head
      of His enemies,
   The hairy scalp of the one
      who still goes on in His
      trespasses.
22 The Lord said, "I will bring
      back from Bashan,
   I will bring *them* back from
      the depths of the sea,
23 That your foot may crush
      them in blood,
   And the tongues of your dogs
      may have their portion from
      your enemies."

24 They have seen Your
      procession, O God,
   The procession of my God, my
      King, into the sanctuary.
25 The singers went before, the
      players on instruments
      followed after;
   Among *them were* the
      maidens playing timbrels.
26 Bless God in the
      congregations,
   The Lord, from the fountain
      of Israel.
27 There *is* little Benjamin, their
      leader,
   The princes of Judah *and* their
      company,
   The princes of Zebulun *and*
      the princes of Naphtali.

28 Your God has commanded
      your strength;
   Strengthen, O God, what You
      have done for us.
29 Because of Your temple at
      Jerusalem,
   Kings will bring presents to
      You.
30 Rebuke the beasts of the
      reeds,
   The herd of bulls with the
      calves of the peoples,
   Till everyone submits himself
      with pieces of silver.
   Scatter the peoples *who*
      delight in war.
31 Envoys will come out of
      Egypt;

Ethiopia will quickly stretch
out her hands to God.

32 Sing to God, you kingdoms of
the earth;
Oh, sing praises to the Lord,
Selah

33 To Him who rides on the
heaven of heavens, *which
were* of old!
Indeed, He sends out His
voice, a mighty voice.

34 Ascribe strength to God;
His excellence *is* over Israel,
And His strength *is* in the
clouds.

35 O God, *You are* more
awesome than Your holy
places.
The God of Israel *is* He who
gives strength and power to
His people.

Blessed *be* God!

PSALM 69

To the Chief Musician. Set to "The Lilies." A
Psalm of David.

SAVE me, O God!
For the waters have come up
to *my* neck.

2 I sink in deep mire,
Where *there is* no standing;
I have come into deep waters,
Where the floods overflow me.

3 I am weary with my crying;
My throat is dry;
My eyes fail while I wait for
my God.

4 Those who hate me without a
cause
Are more than the hairs of my
head;
They are mighty who would
destroy me,
Being my enemies wrongfully;
Though I have stolen nothing,
I *still* must restore *it.*

5 O God, You know my
foolishness;

And my sins are not hidden
from You.

6 Let not those who wait for
You, O Lord GOD of hosts,
be ashamed because of me;
Let not those who seek You
be confounded because of
me, O God of Israel.

7 Because for Your sake I have
borne reproach;
Shame has covered my face.

8 I have become a stranger to
my brothers,
And an alien to my mother's
children;

9 Because zeal for Your house
has eaten me up,
And the reproaches of those
who reproach You have
fallen on me.

10 When I wept *and chastened*
my soul with fasting,
That became my reproach.

11 I also made sackcloth my
garment;
I became a byword to them.

12 Those who sit in the gate
speak against me,
And I *am* the song of the
drunkards.

13 But as for me, my prayer *is* to
You,
O LORD, *in* the acceptable
time;
O God, in the multitude of
Your mercy,
Hear me in the truth of Your
salvation.

14 Deliver me out of the mire,
And let me not sink;
Let me be delivered from
those who hate me,
And out of the deep waters.

15 Let not the floodwater
overflow me,
Nor let the deep swallow me
up;
And let not the pit shut its
mouth on me.

16 Hear me, O LORD,
    for Your lovingkindness *is*
    good;
  Turn to me according to the
    multitude of Your tender
    mercies.
17 And do not hide Your face
    from Your servant,
  For I am in trouble;
  Hear me speedily.
18 Draw near to my soul, *and*
    redeem it;
  Deliver me because of my
    enemies.

19 You know my reproach, my
    shame, and my dishonor;
  My adversaries *are* all before
    You.
20 Reproach has broken my
    heart,
  And I am full of heaviness;
  I looked *for someone* to take
    pity, but *there was* none;
  And for comforters, but I
    found none.
21 They also gave me gall for my
    food,
  And for my thirst they gave
    me vinegar to drink.

22 Let their table become a snare
    before them,
  And their well-being a trap.
23 Let their eyes be darkened,
    so that they do not see;
  And make their loins shake
    continually.
24 Pour out Your indignation
    upon them,
  And let Your wrathful anger
    take hold of them.
25 Let their habitation be
    desolate;
  Let no one dwell in their
    tents.
26 For they persecute *him* whom
    You have struck,
  And talk of the grief of those
    You have wounded.
27 Add iniquity to their iniquity,
  And let them not come into
    Your righteousness.

28 Let them be blotted out of the
    book of the living,
  And not be written with the
    righteous.

29 But I *am* poor and sorrowful;
  Let Your salvation, O God, set
    me up on high.
30 I will praise the name of God
    with a song,
  And will magnify Him with
    thanksgiving.
31 *This* also shall please the LORD
    better than an ox *or* bull,
  Which has horns and hooves.
32 The humble shall see *this and*
    be glad;
  And you who seek God,
    your hearts shall live.
33 For the LORD hears the poor,
  And does not despise His
    prisoners.

34 Let heaven and earth praise
    Him,
  The seas and everything that
    moves in them.
35 For God will save Zion
  And build the cities of Judah,
  That they may dwell there
    and possess it.
36 Also, the descendants of His
    servants shall inherit it,
  And those who love His name
    shall dwell in it.

PSALM 70

To the Chief Musician. *A Psalm* of David. To
bring to remembrance.

MAKE *haste,* O God, to deliver
  me!
  Make haste to help me, O
    LORD!

2 Let them be ashamed and
    confounded
  Who seek my life;
  Let them be turned back and
    confused
  Who desire my hurt.
3 Let them be turned back
    because of their shame,
  Who say, "Aha, aha!"

4 Let all those who seek You
    rejoice and be glad in You;
And let those who love Your
    salvation say continually,
"Let God be magnified!"

5 But I *am* poor and needy;
    Make haste to me, O God!
You *are* my help and my
    deliverer;
O Lord, do not delay.

PSALM 71

I N You, O Lord, I put my trust;
    Let me never be put to shame.
2 Deliver me in Your
    righteousness,
    and cause me to escape;
Incline Your ear to me, and
    save me.
3 Be my strong habitation,
To which I may resort
    continually;
You have given the
    commandment to save me,
For You *are* my rock and my
    fortress.

4 Deliver me, O my God, out of
    the hand of the wicked,
Out of the hand of the
    unrighteous and cruel man.
5 For You are my hope, O Lord
    God;
You are my trust from my
    youth.
6 By You I have been upheld
    from *my* birth;
You are He who took me out
    of my mother's womb.
My praise *shall be* continually
    of You.

7 I have become as a wonder to
    many,
But You *are* my strong refuge.
8 Let my mouth be filled *with*
    Your praise
And with Your glory all the
    day.

9 Do not cast me off in the time
    of old age;
Do not forsake me when my
    strength fails.
10 For my enemies speak against
    me;
And those who lie in wait for
    my life take counsel
    together,
11 Saying, "God has forsaken
    him;
Pursue and take him,
    for *there is* none to deliver
    him."

12 O God, do not be far from me;
O my God, make haste to help
    me!
13 Let them be confounded *and*
    consumed
Who are adversaries of my
    life;
Let them be covered *with*
    reproach and dishonor
Who seek my hurt.

14 But I will hope continually,
And will praise You yet more
    and more.
15 My mouth shall tell of Your
    righteousness
And Your salvation all the
    day,
For I do not know *their* limits.
16 I will go in the strength of the
    Lord God;
I will make mention of Your
    righteousness, of Yours
    only.

17 O God, You have taught me
    from my youth;
And to this *day* I declare Your
    wondrous works.
18 Now also when *I am* old and
    grayheaded,
O God, do not forsake me,
Until I declare Your strength
    to *this* generation,
Your power to everyone *who*
    is to come.

19 Also Your righteousness, O
God, *is* very high,
You who have done great
things;
O God, who *is* like You?

20 *You,* who have shown me
great and severe troubles,
Shall revive me again,
And bring me up again from
the depths of the earth.

21 You shall increase my
greatness,
And comfort me on every
side.

22 Also with the lute I will praise
You—
And Your faithfulness, O my
God!
To You I will sing with the
harp,
O Holy One of Israel.

23 My lips shall greatly rejoice
when I sing to You,
And my soul, which You have
redeemed.

24 My tongue also shall talk of
Your righteousness all the
day long;
For they are confounded,
For they are brought to shame
Who seek my hurt.

PSALM 72

A Psalm of Solomon.

GIVE the king Your judgments,
O God,
And Your righteousness to the
king's Son.

2 He will judge Your people
with righteousness,
And Your poor with justice.

3 The mountains will bring
peace to the people,
And the little hills, by
righteousness.

4 He will bring justice to the
poor of the people;
He will save the children of
the needy,
And will break in pieces the
oppressor.

5 They shall fear You
As long as the sun and moon
endure,
Throughout all generations.

6 He shall come down like rain
upon the mown grass,
Like showers *that* water the
earth.

7 In His days the righteous shall
flourish,
And abundance of peace,
Until the moon is no more.

8 He shall have dominion also
from sea to sea,
And from the River to the
ends of the earth.

9 Those who dwell in the
wilderness will bow before
Him,
And His enemies will lick the
dust.

10 The kings of Tarshish and of
the isles
Will bring presents;
The kings of Sheba and Seba
Will offer gifts.

11 Yes, all kings shall fall down
before Him;
All nations shall serve Him.

12 For He will deliver the needy
when he cries,
The poor also, and *him* who
has no helper.

13 He will spare the poor and
needy,
And will save the souls of the
needy.

14 He will redeem their life from
oppression and violence;
And precious shall be their
blood in His sight.

15 And He shall live;
And the gold of Sheba will be
given to Him;
Prayer also will be made for
Him continually,
And daily He shall be praised.

16 There will be an abundance of
grain in the earth,

On the top of the mountains;
Its fruit shall wave like
Lebanon;
And *those* of the city shall
flourish like grass of the
earth.

17 His name shall endure forever;
His name shall continue as
long as the sun.
And *men* shall be blessed in
Him;
All nations shall call Him
blessed.

18 Blessed *be* the LORD God,
the God of Israel,
Who only does wondrous
things!

19 And blessed *be* His glorious
name forever!
And let the whole earth be
filled *with* His glory.
Amen and Amen.

20 The prayers of David the son
of Jesse are ended.

BOOK THREE
Psalms 73–89

PSALM 73
A Psalm of Asaph.

TRULY God *is* good to Israel,
To such as are pure in heart.

2 But as for me, my feet had
almost stumbled;
My steps had nearly slipped.

3 For I *was* envious of the
boastful,
When I saw the prosperity of
the wicked.

4 For *there are* no pangs in
their death,
But their strength *is* firm.

5 They *are* not in trouble *as
other* men,
Nor are they plagued like
other men.

6 Therefore pride serves as their
necklace;
Violence covers them *like* a
garment.

7 Their eyes bulge with
abundance;
They have more than heart
could wish.

8 They scoff and speak wickedly
concerning oppression;
They speak loftily.

9 They set their mouth
against the heavens,
And their tongue walks
through the earth.

10 Therefore his people return
here,
And waters of a full *cup* are
drained by them.

11 And they say, "How does God
know?
And is there knowledge in the
Most High?"

12 Behold, these *are* the ungodly,
Who are always at ease;
They increase *in* riches.

13 Surely I have cleansed my
heart *in* vain,
And washed my hands in
innocence.

14 For all day long I have been
plagued,
And chastened every morning.

15 If I had said, "I will speak
thus,"
Behold, I would have been
untrue to the generation of
Your children.

16 When I thought *how* to
understand this,
It *was* too painful for me—

17 Until I went into the
sanctuary of God;
Then I understood their end.

18 Surely You set them in
slippery places;
You cast them down to
destruction.

19 Oh, how they are *brought* to
desolation, as in a moment!

371

They are utterly consumed
with terrors.
20 As a dream when *one* awakes,
So, Lord, when You awake,
You shall despise their image.

21 Thus my heart was grieved,
And I was vexed in my mind.
22 I *was* so foolish and ignorant;
I was *like* a beast before You.
23 Nevertheless I *am* continually
with You;
You hold *me* by my right
hand.
24 You will guide me with Your
counsel,
And afterward receive me *to*
glory.

25 Whom have I in heaven *but*
You?
And *there is* none upon earth
that I desire besides You.
26 My flesh and my heart fail;
But God *is* the strength of my
heart and my portion
forever.

27 For indeed, those who are far
from You shall perish;
You have destroyed all those
who desert You for harlotry.
28 But *it is* good for me to draw
near to God;
I have put my trust in the
Lord GOD,
That I may declare all Your
works.

PSALM 74

A Contemplation of Asaph.

O GOD, why have You cast *us*
off forever?
Why does Your anger smoke
against the sheep of Your
pasture?
2 Remember Your congregation,
which You have purchased
of old,
The tribe of Your inheritance,
which You have
redeemed—

This Mount Zion where You
have dwelt.
3 Lift up Your feet to the
perpetual desolations.
The enemy has damaged
everything in the sanctuary.
4 Your enemies roar in the
midst of Your meeting
place;
They set up their banners *for*
signs.
5 They seem like men who lift
up
Axes among the thick trees.
6 And now they break down its
carved work, all at once,
With axes and hammers.
7 They have set fire to Your
sanctuary;
They have defiled the dwelling
place of Your name to the
ground.
8 They said in their hearts,
"Let us destroy them
altogether."
They have burned up all the
meeting places of God in
the land.

9 We do not see our signs;
There is no longer any
prophet;
Nor *is there* any among us
who knows how long.
10 O God, how long will the
adversary reproach?
Will the enemy blaspheme
Your name forever?
11 Why do You withdraw Your
hand, even Your right hand?
Take it out of Your bosom
and destroy *them*.
12 For God *is* my King from of
old,
Working salvation in the
midst of the earth.
13 You divided the sea by Your
strength;
You broke the heads of the
sea serpents in the waters.
14 You broke the heads of
Leviathan in pieces,

And gave him *as* food to the
   people inhabiting the
   wilderness.
15 You broke open the fountain
   and the flood;
   You dried up mighty rivers.
16 The day *is* Yours,
   the night also *is* Yours;
   You have prepared the light
   and the sun.
17 You have set all the borders
   of the earth;
   You have made summer and
   winter.

18 Remember this, *that* the
   enemy has reproached, O
   Lord,
   And *that* a foolish people has
   blasphemed Your name.
19 Oh, do not deliver the life of
   Your turtledove to the wild
   beast!
   Do not forget the life of Your
   poor forever.
20 Have respect to the covenant;
   For the dark places of the
   earth are full of the
   habitations of cruelty.
21 Oh, do not let the oppressed
   return ashamed!
   Let the poor and needy praise
   Your name.

22 Arise, O God, plead Your own
   cause;
   Remember how the foolish
   man reproaches You daily.
23 Do not forget the voice of
   Your enemies;
   The tumult of those who rise
   up against You increases
   continually.

PSALM 75

To the Chief Musician. Set to "Do Not
Destroy." A Psalm of Asaph. A Song.

WE give thanks to You, O
   God, we give thanks!
For Your wondrous works
   declare *that* Your name is
   near.

2 "When I choose the proper
   time,
   I will judge uprightly.
3 The earth and all its
   inhabitants are dissolved;
   I set up its pillars firmly.
                 Selah

4 "I said to the boastful,
   'Do not deal boastfully,'
   And to the wicked,
   'Do not lift up the horn.
5 Do not lift up your horn on
   high;
   Do *not* speak with a stiff
   neck.' "

6 For exaltation *comes* neither
   from the east
   Nor from the west nor from
   the south.
7 But God *is* the Judge:
   He puts down one,
   And exalts another.
8 For in the hand of the Lord
   there is a cup,
   And the wine is red;
   It is fully mixed, and He pours
   it out;
   Surely its dregs shall all the
   wicked of the earth
   Drain *and* drink down.

9 But I will declare forever,
   I will sing praises to the God
   of Jacob.

10 "All the horns of the wicked
   I will also cut off,
   But the horns of the righteous
   shall be exalted."

PSALM 76

To the Chief Musician. On stringed
instruments. A Psalm of Asaph. A Song.

IN Judah God *is* known;
   His name *is* great in Israel.
2 In Salem also is His
   tabernacle,
   And His dwelling place in
   Zion.
3 There He broke the arrows of
   the bow,

The shield and sword of
    battle.   Selah

4 You *are* more glorious and
    excellent
    Than the mountains of prey.
5 The stouthearted were
    plundered;
    They have sunk into their
    sleep;
    And none of the mighty men
    have found the use of their
    hands.
6 At Your rebuke, O God of
    Jacob,
    Both the chariot and horse
    were cast into a dead sleep.

7 You, Yourself, *are* to be
    feared;
    And who may stand in Your
    presence
    When once You are angry?
8 You caused judgment to be
    heard from heaven;
    The earth feared and was still,
9 When God arose to judgment,
    To deliver all the oppressed of
    the earth.   Selah

10 Surely the wrath of man shall
    praise You;
    With the remainder of wrath
    You shall gird Yourself.

11 Make vows to the LORD your
    God, and pay *them;*
    Let all who are around Him
    bring presents to Him who
    ought to be feared.
12 He shall cut off the spirit of
    princes;
    He is awesome to the kings of
    the earth.

PSALM 77

To the Chief Musician. To Jeduthun. A Psalm
of Asaph.

I CRIED out to God with my
    voice—
    To God with my voice;
    And He gave ear to me.

2 In the day of my trouble I
    sought the Lord;
    My hand was stretched out in
    the night without ceasing;
    My soul refused to be
    comforted.
3 I remembered God, and was
    troubled;
    I complained, and my spirit
    was overwhelmed.   Selah

4 You hold my eyelids *open;*
    I am so troubled that I cannot
    speak.
5 I have considered the days of
    old,
    The years of ancient times.
6 I call to remembrance my
    song in the night;
    I meditate within my heart,
    And my spirit makes diligent
    search.

7 Will the Lord cast off forever?
    And will He be favorable no
    more?
8 Has His mercy ceased forever?
    Has *His* promise failed
    forevermore?
9 Has God forgotten to be
    gracious?
    Has He in anger shut up His
    tender mercies?   Selah

10 And I said, "This *is* my
    anguish;
    But I will remember the years
    of the right hand of the
    Most High."
11 I will remember the works of
    the LORD;
    Surely I will remember Your
    wonders of old.
12 I will also meditate on all
    Your work,
    And talk of Your deeds.
13 Your way, O God, *is* in the
    sanctuary;
    Who *is* so great a God as *our*
    God?
14 You *are* the God who does
    wonders;
    You have declared Your
    strength among the peoples.

15 You have with *Your* arm
   redeemed Your people,
   The sons of Jacob and Joseph.
                               Selah

16 The waters saw You, O God;
   The waters saw You, they
   were afraid;
   The depths also trembled.
17 The clouds poured out water;
   The skies sent out a sound;
   Your arrows also flashed
   about.
18 The voice of Your thunder
   was in the whirlwind;
   The lightnings lit up the
   world;
   The earth trembled and shook.
19 Your way *was* in the sea,
   Your path in the great waters,
   And Your footsteps were not
   known.
20 You led Your people like a
   flock
   By the hand of Moses and
   Aaron.

PSALM 78

A Contemplation of Asaph.

G IVE ear, O my people, *to* my
   law;
   Incline your ears to the words
   of my mouth.
2 I will open my mouth in a
   parable;
   I will utter dark sayings of
   old,
3 Which we have heard and
   known,
   And our fathers have told us.
4 We will not hide *them* from
   their children,
   Telling to the generation to
   come the praises of the
   LORD,
   And His strength and His
   wonderful works that He
   has done.

5 For He established a
   testimony in Jacob,
   And appointed a law in Israel,

Which He commanded our
   fathers,
   That they should make them
   known to their children;
6 That the generation to come
   might know *them,*
   The children *who* would be
   born,
   That they may arise and
   declare *them* to their
   children,
7 That they may set their hope
   in God,
   And not forget the works of
   God,
   But keep His commandments;
8 And may not be like their
   fathers,
   A stubborn and rebellious
   generation,
   A generation *that* did not set
   its heart aright,
   And whose spirit was not
   faithful to God.

9 The children of Ephraim,
   being armed *and* carrying
   bows,
   Turned back in the day of
   battle.
10 They did not keep the
   covenant of God;
   They refused to walk in His
   law,
11 And forgot His works
   And His wonders that He had
   shown them.

12 Marvelous things He did
   in the sight of their fathers,
   In the land of Egypt,
   in the field of Zoan.
13 He divided the sea
   and caused them to pass
   through;
   And He made the waters
   stand up like a heap.
14 In the daytime also He led
   them with the cloud,
   And all the night with a light
   of fire.
15 He split the rocks in the
   wilderness,

And gave *them* drink in
abundance like the depths.

16 He also brought streams out
of the rock,
And caused waters to run
down like rivers.

17 But they sinned even more
against Him
By rebelling against the Most
High in the wilderness.
18 And they tested God in their
heart
By asking for the food of their
fancy.
19 Yes, they spoke against God:
They said, "Can God prepare
a table in the wilderness?
20 Behold, He struck the rock,
So that the waters gushed
out,
And the streams overflowed.
Can He give bread also?
Can He provide meat for His
people?"

21 Therefore the LORD heard *this*
and was furious;
So a fire was kindled against
Jacob,
And anger also came up
against Israel,
22 Because they did not believe
in God,
And did not trust in His
salvation.
23 Yet He had commanded the
clouds above,
And opened the doors of
heaven,
24 Had rained down manna on
them to eat,
And given them of the bread
of heaven.
25 Men ate angels' food;
He sent them food to the full.

26 He caused an east wind to
blow in the heavens;
And by His power He brought
in the south wind.
27 He also rained meat on them
like the dust,

Feathered fowl like the sand
of the seas;
28 And He let *them* fall in the
midst of their camp,
All around their habitations.
29 So they ate and were well
filled,
For He gave them their own
desire.
30 They were not deprived of
their craving;
But while their food *was* still
in their mouths,
31 The wrath of God came
against them,
And slew the stoutest of them,
And struck down the choice
men of Israel.

32 In spite of this they still
sinned,
And did not believe in His
wondrous works.
33 Therefore their days He
consumed in futility,
And their years in fear.

34 When He slew them,
then they sought Him;
And they returned and sought
diligently for God.
35 Then they remembered that
God *was* their rock,
And the Most High God their
redeemer.
36 Nevertheless they flattered
Him with their mouth,
And they lied to Him with
their tongue;
37 For their heart was not
steadfast with Him,
Nor were they faithful in His
covenant.
38 But He, *being* full of
compassion, forgave *their*
iniquity,
And did not destroy *them*.
Yes, many a time He turned
His anger away,
And did not stir up all His
wrath;
39 For He remembered that they
were but flesh,

A breath that passes away
and does not come again.

40 How often they provoked Him
in the wilderness,
And grieved Him in the
desert!
41 Yes, again and again they
tempted God,
And limited the Holy One of
Israel.
42 They did not remember His
power:
The day when He redeemed
them from the enemy,
43 When He worked His signs in
Egypt,
And His wonders in the field
of Zoan;
44 Turned their rivers into blood,
And their streams,
that they could not drink.
45 He sent swarms of flies among
them, which devoured them,
And frogs, which destroyed
them.
46 He also gave their crops to the
caterpillar,
And their labor to the locust.
47 He destroyed their vines with
hail,
And their sycamore trees with
frost.
48 He also gave up their cattle to
the hail,
And their flocks to fiery
lightning.
49 He cast on them the fierceness
of His anger,
Wrath, indignation, and
trouble,
By sending angels of
destruction *among them.*
50 He made a path for His anger;
He did not spare their soul
from death,
But gave their life over to the
plague,
51 And destroyed all the firstborn
in Egypt,
The first of *their* strength in
the tents of Ham.
52 But He made His own people
go forth like sheep,

And guided them in the
wilderness like a flock;
53 And He led them on safely,
so that they did not fear;
But the sea overwhelmed their
enemies.
54 And He brought them to His
holy border,
This mountain *which* His right
hand had acquired.
55 He also drove out the nations
before them,
Allotted them an inheritance
by survey,
And made the tribes of Israel
dwell in their tents.

56 Yet they tested and provoked
the Most High God,
And did not keep His
testimonies,
57 But turned back and acted
unfaithfully like their
fathers;
They were turned aside like a
deceitful bow.
58 For they provoked Him to
anger with their high places,
And moved Him to jealousy
with their carved images.
59 When God heard *this,* He was
furious,
And greatly abhorred Israel,
60 So that He forsook the
tabernacle of Shiloh,
The tent *which* He had placed
among men,
61 And delivered His strength
into captivity,
And His glory into the
enemy's hand.
62 He also gave His people over
to the sword,
And was furious with His
inheritance.
63 The fire consumed their young
men,
And their maidens were not
given in marriage.
64 Their priests fell by the sword,
And their widows made no
lamentation.

65 Then the Lord awoke as *one
      out of* sleep,
    And like a mighty man who
      shouts because of wine.
66 And He beat back His
      enemies;
    He put them to a perpetual
      reproach.

67 Moreover He rejected the tent
      of Joseph,
    And did not choose the tribe
      of Ephraim,
68 But chose the tribe of Judah,
    Mount Zion which He loved.
69 And He built His sanctuary
      like the heights,
    Like the earth which He has
      established forever.
70 He also chose David His
      servant,
    And took him from the
      sheepfolds;
71 From following the ewes that
      had young He brought him,
    To shepherd Jacob His people,
    And Israel His inheritance.
72 So he shepherded them
      according to the integrity of
      his heart,
    And guided them by the
      skillfulness of his hands.

PSALM 79

A Psalm of Asaph.

O GOD, the nations have come
    into Your inheritance;
  Your holy temple they have
    defiled;
  They have laid Jerusalem in
    heaps.
2 The dead bodies of Your
    servants
  They have given *as* food
    for the birds of the heavens,
  The flesh of Your saints
    to the beasts of the earth.
3 Their blood they have shed
    like water all around
    Jerusalem,
  And *there was* no one to bury
    them.

4 We have become a reproach
    to our neighbors,
  A scorn and derision to those
    who are around us.

5 How long, Lord?
  Will You be angry forever?
  Will Your jealousy burn like
    fire?
6 Pour out Your wrath on the
    nations that do not know
    You,
  And on the kingdoms that do
    not call on Your name.
7 For they have devoured Jacob,
  And laid waste his dwelling
    place.

8 Oh, do not remember former
    iniquities against us!
  Let Your tender mercies come
    speedily to meet us,
  For we have been brought
    very low.
9 Help us, O God of our
    salvation,
  For the glory of Your name;
  And deliver us, and provide
    atonement for our sins,
  For Your name's sake!
10 Why should the nations say,
    "Where *is* their God?"
  Let there be known among
    the nations in our sight
  The avenging of the blood of
    Your servants *which has
    been* shed.

11 Let the groaning of the
    prisoner come before You;
  According to the greatness of
    Your power
  Preserve those who are
    appointed to die;
12 And return to our neighbors
    sevenfold into their bosom
  Their reproach with which
    they have reproached You,
    O Lord.

13 So we, Your people and sheep
    of Your pasture,

Will give You thanks forever;
We will show forth Your
    praise to all generations.

PSALM 80

To the Chief Musician. Set to "The Lilies." A
Testimony of Asaph. A Psalm.

GIVE ear, O Shepherd of Israel,
    You who lead Joseph like a
    flock;
You who dwell *between* the
    cherubim, shine forth!
2 Before Ephraim, Benjamin,
    and Manasseh,
Stir up Your strength,
And come *and* save us!

3 Restore us, O God;
Cause Your face to shine,
And we shall be saved!

4 O Lord God of hosts,
How long will You be angry
Against the prayer of Your
    people?
5 You have fed them with the
    bread of tears,
And given them tears to drink
    in great measure.
6 You have made us a strife to
    our neighbors,
And our enemies laugh among
    themselves.

7 Restore us, O God of hosts;
Cause Your face to shine,
And we shall be saved!

8 You have brought a vine out
    of Egypt;
You have cast out the nations,
    and planted it.
9 You prepared *room* for it,
And caused it to take deep
    root,
And it filled the land.
10 The hills were covered with its
    shadow,
And the mighty cedars with
    its boughs.
11 She sent out her boughs to
    the Sea,
And her branches to the
    River.

12 Why have You broken down
    her hedges,
So that all who pass by the
    way pluck her *fruit?*
13 The boar out of the woods
    uproots it,
And the wild beast of the field
    devours it.

14 Return, we beseech You,
    O God of hosts;
Look down from heaven and
    see,
And visit this vine
15 And the vineyard which Your
    right hand has planted,
And the branch *that* You
    made strong for Yourself.
16 *It is* burned with fire, *it is* cut
    down;
They perish at the rebuke of
    Your countenance.
17 Let Your hand be upon the
    man of Your right hand,
Upon the son of man *whom*
    You made strong for
    Yourself.
18 Then we will not turn back
    from You;
Revive us, and we will call
    upon Your name.

19 Restore us, O Lord God of
    hosts;
Cause Your face to shine,
And we shall be saved!

PSALM 81

To the Chief Musician. On an instrument of
Gath. A Psalm of Asaph.

SING aloud to God our
    strength;
Make a joyful shout to the
    God of Jacob.
2 Raise a song and strike the
    timbrel,
The pleasant harp with the
    lute.

3 Blow the trumpet at the time
    of the New Moon,
At the full moon,
    on our solemn feast day.

4 For this *is* a statute for Israel,
  And a law of the God of
    Jacob.
5 This He established in Joseph
    for a testimony,
  When He went throughout
    the land of Egypt,
  Where I heard a language
    that I did not understand.

6 "I removed his shoulder from
    the burden;
  His hands were freed from the
    baskets.
7 You called in trouble,
    and I delivered you;
  I answered you in the secret
    place of thunder;
  I proved you at the waters of
    Meribah.   Selah

8 "Hear, O My people,
    and I will admonish you!
  O Israel, if you will listen to
    Me!
9 There shall be no foreign god
    among you;
  Nor shall you worship any
    foreign god.
10 I *am* the Lord your God,
  Who brought you out of the
    land of Egypt;
  Open your mouth wide,
    and I will fill it.

11 "But My people would not heed
    My voice,
  And Israel would *have* none
    of Me.
12 So I gave them over to their
    own stubborn heart,
  To walk in their own counsels.

13 "Oh, that My people would
    listen to Me,
  That Israel would walk in My
    ways!
14 I would soon subdue their
    enemies,
  And turn My hand against
    their adversaries.
15 The haters of the Lord would
    pretend submission to Him,

But their fate would endure
    forever.
16 He would have fed them also
    with the finest of wheat;
  And with honey from the rock
    I would have satisfied you."

PSALM 82

A Psalm of Asaph.

GOD stands in the
    congregation of the mighty;
  He judges among the gods.
2 How long will you judge
    unjustly,
  And show partiality to the
    wicked?   Selah
3 Defend the poor and
    fatherless;
  Do justice to the afflicted and
    needy.
4 Deliver the poor and needy;
  Free *them* from the hand of
    the wicked.

5 They do not know,
    nor do they understand;
  They walk about in darkness;
  All the foundations of the
    earth are unstable.

6 I said, "You *are* gods,
  And all of you *are* children of
    the Most High.
7 But you shall die like men,
  And fall like one of the
    princes."

8 Arise, O God, judge the earth;
  For You shall inherit all
    nations.

PSALM 83

A Song. A Psalm of Asaph.

DO not keep silent, O God!
  Do not hold Your peace,
  And do not be still, O God!
2 For behold, Your enemies
    make a tumult;
  And those who hate You have
    lifted up their head.
3 They have taken crafty
    counsel against Your people,

And consulted together
  against Your sheltered ones.
4 They have said, "Come, and
  let us cut them off from
  being a nation,
That the name of Israel may
  be remembered no more."

5 For they have consulted
  together with one *consent;*
They form a confederacy
  against You:
6 The tents of Edom and the
  Ishmaelites;
Moab and the Hagarites;
7 Gebal, Ammon, and Amalek;
Philistia with the inhabitants
  of Tyre;
8 Assyria also has joined with
  them;
They have helped the children
  of Lot.　　　　　　Selah

9 Deal with them as *with*
  Midian,
As *with* Sisera,
As *with* Jabin at the Brook
  Kishon,
10 Who perished at En Dor,
Who became *as* refuse on the
  earth.
11 Make their nobles like Oreb
  and like Zeeb,
Yes, all their princes like
  Zebah and Zalmunna,
12 Who said, "Let us take for
  ourselves
The pastures of God for a
  possession."

13 O my God, make them like
  the whirling dust,
Like the chaff before the
  wind!
14 As the fire burns the woods,
And as the flame sets the
  mountains on fire,
15 So pursue them with Your
  tempest,
And frighten them with Your
  storm.
16 Fill their faces with shame,
That they may seek Your
  name, O LORD.

17 Let them be confounded
  and dismayed forever;
Yes, let them be put to shame
  and perish,
18 That *men* may know that
  You, whose name alone *is*
  the LORD,
Are the Most High over all the
  earth.

PSALM 84

To the Chief Musician. On an instrument of
Gath. A Psalm of the sons of Korah.

HOW lovely *is* Your tabernacle,
  O LORD of hosts!
2 My soul longs, yes, even faints
For the courts of the LORD;
My heart and my flesh cry out
  for the living God.

3 Even the sparrow has found a
  home,
And the swallow a nest for
  herself,
Where she may lay her
  young—
Even Your altars, O LORD of
  hosts,
My King and my God.
4 Blessed *are* those who dwell in
  Your house;
They will still be praising You.
　　　　　　　　　　Selah

5 Blessed *is* the man whose
  strength *is* in You,
Whose heart *is* set on
  pilgrimage.
6 *As they* pass through the
  Valley of Baca,
They make it a spring;
The rain also covers it with
  pools.
7 They go from strength to
  strength;
Every one of them appears
  before God in Zion.

8 O LORD God of hosts, hear my
  prayer;
Give ear, O God of Jacob!
　　　　　　　　　　Selah

Prayer for Restoration

9 O God, behold our shield,
  And look upon the face of
    Your anointed.

10 For a day in Your courts *is*
    better than a thousand.
  I would rather be a
    doorkeeper in the house of
    my God
  Than dwell in the tents of
    wickedness.
11 For the LORD God *is* a sun and
    shield;
  The LORD will give grace and
    glory;
  No good *thing* will He
    withhold
  From those who walk
    uprightly.

12 O LORD of hosts,
  Blessed *is* the man who trusts
    in You!

PSALM 85

To the Chief Musician. A Psalm of the sons of
Korah.

LORD, You have been favorable
    to Your land;
  You have brought back the
    captivity of Jacob.
2 You have forgiven the iniquity
    of Your people;
  You have covered all their sin.
                                Selah
3 You have taken away all Your
    wrath;
  You have turned from the
    fierceness of Your anger.

4 Restore us, O God of our
    salvation,
  And cause Your anger toward
    us to cease.
5 Will You be angry with us
    forever?
  Will You prolong Your anger
    to all generations?
6 Will You not revive us again,
  That Your people may rejoice
    in You?
7 Show us Your mercy, O LORD,

And grant us Your salvation.

8 I will hear what God the LORD
    will speak,
  For He will speak peace
  To His people and to His
    saints;
  But let them not turn back to
    folly.
9 Surely His salvation *is* near to
    those who fear Him,
  That glory may dwell in our
    land.

10 Mercy and truth have met
    together;
  Righteousness and peace have
    kissed *each other.*
11 Truth shall spring out of the
    earth,
  And righteousness shall look
    down from heaven.
12 Yes, the LORD will give *what
    is* good;
  And our land will yield its
    increase.
13 Righteousness will go before
    Him,
  And shall make His footsteps
    our pathway.

PSALM 86

A Prayer of David.

BOW down Your ear, O LORD,
    hear me;
  For I *am* poor and needy.
2 Preserve my life, for I *am*
    holy;
  You are my God;
  Save Your servant who trusts
    in You!
3 Be merciful to me, O Lord,
  For I cry to You all day long.
4 Rejoice the soul of Your
    servant,
  For to You, O Lord, I lift up
    my soul.
5 For You, Lord, *are* good,
    and ready to forgive,
  And abundant in mercy to all
    those who call upon You.

6 Give ear, O LORD, to my
   prayer;
And attend to the voice of my
   supplications.
7 In the day of my trouble I will
   call upon You,
For You will answer me.

8 Among the gods *there is* none
   like You, O Lord;
Nor *are there any works* like
   Your works.
9 All nations whom You have
   made
Shall come and worship before
   You, O Lord,
And shall glorify Your name.
10 For You *are* great,
   and do wondrous things;
You alone *are* God.

11 Teach me Your way, O LORD;
I will walk in Your truth;
Unite my heart to fear Your
   name.
12 I will praise You, O Lord my
   God, with all my heart,
And I will glorify Your name
   forevermore.
13 For great *is* Your mercy
   toward me,
And You have delivered my
   soul from the depths of
   Sheol.

14 O God, the proud have risen
   against me,
And a mob of violent *men*
   have sought my life,
And have not set You before
   them.
15 But You, O Lord, *are* a God
   full of compassion, and
   gracious,
Longsuffering and abundant
   in mercy and truth.

16 Oh, turn to me,
   and have mercy on me!
Give Your strength to Your
   servant,
And save the son of Your
   maidservant.

17 Show me a sign for good,
That those who hate me may
   see *it* and be ashamed,
Because You, LORD, have
   helped me and comforted
   me.

PSALM 87

A Psalm of the sons of Korah. A Song.

HIS foundation *is* in the holy
   mountains.
2 The LORD loves the gates of
   Zion
More than all the dwellings of
   Jacob.
3 Glorious things are spoken of
   you,
O city of God!   Selah

4 "I will make mention of Rahab
   and Babylon to those who
   know Me;
Behold, O Philistia and Tyre,
   with Ethiopia:
'This *one* was born there.' "

5 And of Zion it will be said,
"This *one* and that *one* were
   born in her;
And the Most High Himself
   shall establish her."
6 The LORD will record,
When He registers the
   peoples:
"This *one* was born there."
     Selah

7 Both the singers and the
   players on instruments *say*,
"All my springs *are* in you."

PSALM 88

A Song. A Psalm of the sons of Korah. To the
Chief Musician. Set to "Mahalath Leannoth." A
Contemplation of Heman the Ezrahite.

O LORD, God of my salvation,
   I have cried out day and
   night before You.
2 Let my prayer come before
   You;
Incline Your ear to my cry.

3 For my soul is full of troubles,
   And my life draws near to the
     grave.
4 I am counted with those who
     go down to the pit;
   I am like a man *who has* no
     strength,
5 Adrift among the dead,
   Like the slain who lie in the
     grave,
   Whom You remember no
     more,
   And who are cut off from
     Your hand.

6 You have laid me in the
     lowest pit,
   In darkness, in the depths.
7 Your wrath lies heavy upon
     me,
   And You have afflicted *me*
     with all Your waves.   Selah
8 You have put away my
     acquaintances far from me;
   You have made me an
     abomination to them;
   I am shut up, and I cannot get
     out;
9 My eye wastes away because
     of affliction.

   LORD, I have called daily upon
     You;
   I have stretched out my hands
     to You.
10 Will You work wonders for
     the dead?
   Shall the dead arise *and* praise
     You?   Selah
11 Shall Your lovingkindness be
     declared in the grave?
   Or Your faithfulness
     in the place of destruction?
12 Shall Your wonders be known
     in the dark?
   And Your righteousness
     in the land of forgetfulness?

13 But to You I have cried out, O
     LORD,
   And in the morning my prayer
     comes before You.
14 LORD, why do You cast off my
     soul?

Why do You hide Your face
     from me?
15 I *have been* afflicted and
     ready to die from *my* youth
     up;
   I suffer Your terrors;
   I am distraught.
16 Your fierce wrath has gone
     over me;
   Your terrors have cut me off.
17 They came around me all day
     long like water;
   They engulfed me altogether.
18 Loved one and friend You
     have put far from me,
   And my acquaintances into
     darkness.

PSALM 89

A Contemplation of Ethan the Ezrahite.

I WILL sing of the mercies of
   the LORD forever;
   With my mouth will I make
     known Your faithfulness to
     all generations.
2 For I have said, "Mercy shall
     be built up forever;
   Your faithfulness You shall
     establish in the very
     heavens."

3 "I have made a covenant with
     My chosen,
   I have sworn to My servant
     David:
4 'Your seed I will establish
     forever,
   And build up your throne to
     all generations.'"   Selah

5 And the heavens will praise
     Your wonders, O LORD;
   Your faithfulness also in the
     congregation of the saints.
6 For who in the heavens can
     be compared to the LORD?
   Who among the sons of the
     mighty can be likened to
     the LORD?
7 God is greatly to be feared in
     the assembly of the saints,

And to be held in reverence
by all *those who are* around
Him.

8 O LORD God of hosts,
Who *is* mighty like You, O
LORD?
Your faithfulness also
surrounds You.

9 You rule the raging of the sea;
When its waves rise, You still
them.

10 You have broken Rahab in
pieces, as one who is slain;
You have scattered Your
enemies with Your mighty
arm.

11 The heavens *are* Yours,
the earth also *is* Yours;
The world and all its fullness,
You have founded them.

12 The north and the south,
You have created them;
Tabor and Hermon rejoice in
Your name.

13 You have a mighty arm;
Strong is Your hand,
and high is Your right hand.

14 Righteousness and justice *are*
the foundation of Your
throne;
Mercy and truth go before
Your face.

15 Blessed *are* the people who
know the joyful sound!
They walk, O LORD, in the
light of Your countenance.

16 In Your name they rejoice all
day long,
And in Your righteousness
they are exalted.

17 For You *are* the glory of their
strength,
And in Your favor our horn is
exalted.

18 For our shield *belongs* to the
LORD,
And our king to the Holy One
of Israel.

19 Then You spoke in a vision
to Your holy one,
And said: "I have given help
to *one who is* mighty;

I have exalted one chosen
from the people.

20 I have found My servant
David;
With My holy oil I have
anointed him,

21 With whom My hand shall be
established;
Also My arm shall strengthen
him.

22 The enemy shall not outwit
him,
Nor the son of wickedness
afflict him.

23 I will beat down his foes
before his face,
And plague those who hate
him.

24 "But My faithfulness and My
mercy *shall be* with him,
And in My name his horn
shall be exalted.

25 Also I will set his hand over
the sea,
And his right hand over the
rivers.

26 He shall cry to Me,
'You *are* my Father,
My God, and the rock of my
salvation.'

27 Also I will make him My
firstborn,
The highest of the kings of
the earth.

28 My mercy I will keep for him
forever,
And My covenant shall stand
firm with him.

29 His seed also I will make *to
endure* forever,
And his throne as the days of
heaven.

30 "If his sons forsake My law
And do not walk in My
judgments,

31 If they break My statutes
And do not keep My
commandments,

32 Then I will visit their
transgression with the rod,
And their iniquity with stripes.

385

33 Nevertheless My lovingkindness I will not utterly
   take from him,
   Nor allow My faithfulness to
   fail.
34 My covenant I will not break,
   Nor alter the word that has
   gone out of My lips.
35 Once I have sworn by My
   holiness;
   I will not lie to David:
36 His seed shall endure forever,
   And his throne as the sun
   before Me;
37 It shall be established forever
   like the moon,
   Even *like* the faithful witness
   in the sky."   Selah

38 But You have cast off and
   abhorred,
   You have been furious with
   Your anointed.
39 You have renounced the
   covenant of Your servant;
   You have profaned his crown
   by casting it to the ground.
40 You have broken down all his
   hedges;
   You have brought his
   strongholds to ruin.
41 All who pass by the way
   plunder him;
   He is a reproach to his
   neighbors.
42 You have exalted the right
   hand of his adversaries;
   You have made all his
   enemies rejoice.
43 You have also turned back
   the edge of his sword,
   And have not sustained him in
   the battle.
44 You have made his glory
   cease,
   And cast his throne down to
   the ground.
45 The days of his youth You
   have shortened;
   You have covered him with
   shame.   Selah

46 How long, Lord?

Will You hide Yourself
   forever?
Will Your wrath burn like
   fire?
47 Remember how short my time
   is;
   For what futility have You
   created all the children of
   men?
48 What man can live and not
   see death?
   Can he deliver his life from
   the power of the grave?
        Selah

49 Lord, where *are* Your former
   lovingkindnesses,
   Which You swore to David in
   Your truth?
50 Remember, Lord, the reproach
   of Your servants—
   How I bear in my bosom *the
   reproach of* all the many
   peoples,
51 With which Your enemies
   have reproached, O Lord,
   With which they have
   reproached the footsteps of
   Your anointed.

52 Blessed *be* the Lord
   forevermore!
   Amen and Amen.

BOOK FOUR
Psalms 90–106

PSALM 90
A Prayer of Moses the man of God.

LORD, You have been our
   dwelling place in all
   generations.
2 Before the mountains were
   brought forth,
   Or ever You had formed the
   earth and the world,
   Even from everlasting to
   everlasting, You *are* God.

3 You turn man to destruction,
   And say, "Return, O children
   of men."

4 For a thousand years in Your
    sight
  Are like yesterday when it is
    past,
  And *like* a watch in the night.
5 You carry them away *like* a
    flood;
  They are like a sleep.
  In the morning they are like
    grass *which* grows up:
6 In the morning it flourishes
    and grows up;
  In the evening it is cut down
    and withers.

7 For we have been consumed
    by Your anger,
  And by Your wrath we are
    terrified.
8 You have set our iniquities
    before You,
  Our secret *sins* in the light of
    Your countenance.
9 For all our days have passed
    away in Your wrath;
  We finish our years like a
    sigh.
10 The days of our lives *are*
    seventy years;
  And if by reason of strength
    they are eighty years,
  Yet their boast *is* only labor
    and sorrow;
  For it is soon cut off, and we
    fly away.
11 Who knows the power of
    Your anger?
  For as the fear of You,
    so is Your wrath.
12 So teach *us* to number our
    days,
  That we may gain a heart of
    wisdom.

13 Return, O Lord!
  How long?
  And have compassion on Your
    servants.
14 Oh, satisfy us early with Your
    mercy,
  That we may rejoice and be
    glad all our days!

15 Make us glad according to the
    days *in which* You have
    afflicted us,
  And the years *in which* we
    have seen evil.
16 Let Your work appear to Your
    servants,
  And Your glory to their
    children.
17 And let the beauty of the
    Lord our God be upon us,
  And establish the work of our
    hands for us;
  Yes, establish the work of our
    hands.

PSALM 91

HE who dwells in the secret
  place of the Most High
  Shall abide under the shadow
    of the Almighty.
2 I will say of the Lord, "*He is*
    my refuge and my fortress;
  My God, in Him I will trust."

3 Surely He shall deliver you
    from the snare of the fowler
  And from the perilous
    pestilence.
4 He shall cover you with His
    feathers,
  And under His wings you shall
    take refuge;
  His truth *shall be your* shield
    and buckler.
5 You shall not be afraid of the
    terror by night,
  Nor of the arrow *that* flies by
    day,
6 *Nor* of the pestilence *that*
    walks in darkness,
  Nor of the destruction *that*
    lays waste at noonday.

7 A thousand may fall at your
    side,
  And ten thousand at your
    right hand;
  But it shall not come near
    you.
8 Only with your eyes shall you
    look,

And see the reward of the
wicked.

9 Because you have made the
LORD, *who is* my refuge,
Even the Most High, your
habitation,
10 No evil shall befall you,
Nor shall any plague come
near your dwelling;
11 For He shall give His angels
charge over you,
To keep you in all your ways.
12 They shall bear you up in
their hands,
Lest you dash your foot
against a stone.
13 You shall tread upon
the lion and the cobra,
The young lion and the
serpent you shall trample
underfoot.

14 "Because he has set his love
upon Me, therefore I will
deliver him;
I will set him on high,
because he has known My
name.
15 He shall call upon Me,
and I will answer him;
I *will be* with him in trouble;
I will deliver him and honor
him.
16 With long life I will satisfy
him,
And show him My salvation."

PSALM 92

A Psalm. A Song for the Sabbath day.

*I*T *is* good to give thanks to the
LORD,
And to sing praises to Your
name, O Most High;
2 To declare Your loving-
kindness in the morning,
And Your faithfulness every
night,
3 On an instrument of ten
strings,
On the lute,

And on the harp,
With harmonious sound.
4 For You, LORD, have made me
glad through Your work;
I will triumph in the works of
Your hands.

5 O LORD, how great are Your
works!
Your thoughts are very deep.
6 A senseless man does not
know,
Nor does a fool understand
this.
7 When the wicked spring up
like grass,
And when all the workers of
iniquity flourish,
It is that they may be
destroyed forever.

8 But You, LORD, *are* on high
forevermore.
9 For behold, Your enemies, O
LORD,
For behold, Your enemies
shall perish;
All the workers of iniquity
shall be scattered.

10 But my horn You have
exalted like a wild ox;
I have been anointed with
fresh oil.
11 My eye also has seen *my
desire* on my enemies;
My ears hear *my desire* on the
wicked
Who rise up against me.

12 The righteous shall flourish
like a palm tree,
He shall grow like a cedar in
Lebanon.
13 Those who are planted in the
house of the LORD
Shall flourish in the courts of
our God.
14 They shall still bear fruit in
old age;
They shall be fresh and
flourishing,
15 To declare that the LORD is
upright;

He is my rock, and *there is* no
unrighteousness in Him.

PSALM 93

THE LORD reigns,
He is clothed with majesty;
The LORD is clothed,
He has girded Himself with
strength.
Surely the world is
established, so that it
cannot be moved.
2 Your throne *is* established
from of old;
You *are* from everlasting.

3 The floods have lifted up, O
LORD,
The floods have lifted up their
voice;
The floods lift up their waves.
4 The LORD on high *is* mightier
Than the noise of many
waters,
Than the mighty waves of the
sea.

5 Your testimonies are very
sure;
Holiness adorns Your house,
O LORD, forever.

PSALM 94

O LORD God, to whom
vengeance belongs—
O God, to whom vengeance
belongs, shine forth!
2 Rise up, O Judge of the earth;
Render punishment to the
proud.
3 LORD, how long will the
wicked,
How long will the wicked
triumph?

4 They utter speech,
and speak insolent things;
All the workers of iniquity
boast in themselves.
5 They break in pieces Your
people, O LORD,
And afflict Your heritage.

6 They slay the widow and the
stranger,
And murder the fatherless.
7 Yet they say, "The LORD does
not see,
Nor does the God of Jacob
understand."

8 Understand, you senseless
among the people;
And *you* fools, when will you
be wise?
9 He who planted the ear,
shall He not hear?
He who formed the eye,
shall He not see?
10 He who instructs the nations,
shall He not correct,
He who teaches man
knowledge?
11 The LORD knows the thoughts
of man,
That they *are* futile.

12 Blessed *is* the man whom You
instruct, O LORD,
And teach out of Your law,
13 That You may give him rest
from the days of adversity,
Until the pit is dug for the
wicked.
14 For the LORD will not cast off
His people,
Nor will He forsake His
inheritance.
15 But judgment will return to
righteousness,
And all the upright in heart
will follow it.

16 Who will rise up for me
against the evildoers?
Who will stand up for me
against the workers of
iniquity?
17 Unless the LORD *had been* my
help,
My soul would soon have
settled in silence.
18 If I say, "My foot slips,"
Your mercy, O LORD, will hold
me up.
19 In the multitude of my
anxieties within me,

Your comforts delight my
    soul.

20 Shall the throne of iniquity,
    which devises evil by law,
    Have fellowship with You?
21 They gather together against
    the life of the righteous,
    And condemn innocent blood.
22 But the LORD has been my
    defense,
    And my God the rock of my
    refuge.
23 He has brought on them their
    own iniquity,
    And shall cut them off in their
    own wickedness;
    The LORD our God shall cut
    them off.

PSALM 95

OH come, let us sing to the
    LORD!
    Let us shout joyfully to the
    Rock of our salvation.
2 Let us come before His
    presence with thanksgiving;
    Let us shout joyfully to Him
    with psalms.
3 For the LORD *is* the great God,
    And the great King above all
    gods.
4 In His hand *are* the deep
    places of the earth;
    The heights of the hills *are*
    His also.
5 The sea *is* His, for He made it;
    And His hands formed the dry
    land.

6 Oh come, let us worship
    and bow down;
    Let us kneel before the LORD
    our Maker.
7 For He *is* our God,
    And we *are* the people of His
    pasture,
    And the sheep of His hand.

Today, if you will hear His
    voice:
8 "Do not harden your hearts,
    as in the rebellion,

And as *in* the day of trial in
    the wilderness,
9 When your fathers tested Me;
    They proved Me,
    though they saw My work.
10 For forty years I was grieved
    with *that* generation,
    And said, 'It *is* a people who
    go astray in their hearts,
    And they do not know My
    ways.'
11 So I swore in My wrath,
    'They shall not enter My
    rest.' "

PSALM 96

OH, sing to the LORD a new
    song!
    Sing to the LORD, all the
    earth.
2 Sing to the LORD, bless His
    name;
    Proclaim the good news of His
    salvation from day to day.
3 Declare His glory among the
    nations,
    His wonders among all
    peoples.

4 For the LORD *is* great
    and greatly to be praised;
    He *is* to be feared above all
    gods.
5 For *all* the gods of the peoples
    are idols,
    But the LORD made the
    heavens.
6 Honor and majesty *are* before
    Him;
    Strength and beauty *are* in
    His sanctuary.

7 Give to the LORD,
    O kindreds of the peoples,
    Give to the LORD glory and
    strength.
8 Give to the LORD the glory
    due His name;
    Bring an offering,
    and come into His courts.
9 Oh, worship the LORD in the
    beauty of holiness!

Tremble before Him, all the
earth.

10 Say among the nations,
"The LORD reigns;
The world also is firmly
established,
It shall not be moved;
He shall judge the peoples
righteously."

11 Let the heavens rejoice,
and let the earth be glad;
Let the sea roar, and all its
fullness;
12 Let the field be joyful, and all
that *is* in it.
Then all the trees of the
woods will rejoice before
the LORD.
13 For He is coming, for He is
coming to judge the earth.
He shall judge the world with
righteousness,
And the peoples with His
truth.

PSALM 97

THE LORD reigns;
Let the earth rejoice;
Let the multitude of isles be
glad!

2 Clouds and darkness surround
Him;
Righteousness and justice *are*
the foundation of His
throne.
3 A fire goes before Him,
And burns up His enemies
round about.
4 His lightnings light the world;
The earth sees and trembles.
5 The mountains melt like wax
at the presence of the LORD,
At the presence of the Lord of
the whole earth.
6 The heavens declare His
righteousness,
And all the peoples see His
glory.

7 Let all be put to shame who
serve carved images,
Who boast of idols.
Worship Him, all *you* gods.
8 Zion hears and is glad,
And the daughters of Judah
rejoice
Because of Your judgments, O
LORD.
9 For You, LORD, *are* most high
above all the earth;
You are exalted far above all
gods.

10 You who love the LORD, hate
evil!
He preserves the souls of His
saints;
He delivers them out of the
hand of the wicked.
11 Light is sown for the
righteous,
And gladness for the upright
in heart.
12 Rejoice in the LORD, you
righteous,
And give thanks at the
remembrance of His holy
name.

PSALM 98

A Psalm.

OH, sing to the LORD a new
song!
For He has done marvelous
things;
His right hand and His holy
arm have gained Him the
victory.
2 The LORD has made known
His salvation;
His righteousness He has
openly shown in the sight of
the nations.
3 He has remembered His mercy
and His faithfulness to the
house of Israel;
All the ends of the earth have
seen the salvation of our
God.

4 Shout joyfully to the LORD,
all the earth;

Break forth in song, rejoice,
and sing praises.
5 Sing to the LORD with the
harp,
With the harp and the sound
of a psalm,
6 With trumpets and the sound
of a horn;
Shout joyfully before the
LORD, the King.

7 Let the sea roar, and all its
fullness,
The world and those who
dwell in it;
8 Let the rivers clap *their* hands;
Let the hills be joyful together
before the LORD,
9 For He is coming to judge the
earth.
With righteousness He shall
judge the world,
And the peoples with equity.

PSALM 99

THE LORD reigns;
Let the peoples tremble!
He dwells *between* the
cherubim;
Let the earth be moved!
2 The LORD *is* great in Zion,
And He *is* high above all the
peoples.
3 Let them praise Your great
and awesome name—
He *is* holy.

4 The King's strength also loves
justice;
You have established equity;
You have executed justice and
righteousness in Jacob.
5 Exalt the LORD our God,
And worship at His footstool;
For He *is* holy.

6 Moses and Aaron were among
His priests,
And Samuel was among those
who called upon His name;
They called upon the LORD,
and He answered them.

7 He spoke to them in the
cloudy pillar;
They kept His testimonies and
the ordinance *that* He gave
them.

8 You answered them, O LORD
our God;
You were to them God-Who-
Forgives,
Though You took vengeance
on their deeds.
9 Exalt the LORD our God,
And worship at His holy hill;
For the LORD our God *is* holy.

PSALM 100

A Psalm of Thanksgiving.

MAKE a joyful shout to the
LORD, all you lands!
2 Serve the LORD with gladness;
Come before His presence
with singing.
3 Know that the LORD, He *is*
God;
It is He *who* has made us,
and not we ourselves;
We are His people
and the sheep of His
pasture.

4 Enter into His gates with
thanksgiving,
And into His courts with
praise.
Be thankful to Him,
and bless His name.
5 For the LORD *is* good;
His mercy *is* everlasting,
And His truth *endures* to all
generations.

PSALM 101

A Psalm of David.

I WILL sing of mercy and
justice;
To You, O LORD, I will sing
praises.

2 I will behave wisely in a
perfect way.

Oh, when will You come to
me?
I will walk within my house
with a perfect heart.

3 I will set nothing wicked
before my eyes;
I hate the work of those who
fall away;
It shall not cling to me.

4 A perverse heart shall depart
from me;
I will not know wickedness.

5 Whoever secretly slanders his
neighbor,
Him I will destroy;
The one who has a haughty
look and a proud heart,
Him I will not endure.

6 My eyes *shall be* on the
faithful of the land,
That they may dwell with me;
He who walks in a perfect
way,
He shall serve me.

7 He who works deceit shall not
dwell within my house;
He who tells lies shall not
continue in my presence.

8 Early I will destroy all the
wicked of the land,
That I may cut off all the
evildoers from the city of
the LORD.

PSALM 102

A Prayer of the afflicted, when he is
overwhelmed and pours out his complaint
before the LORD.

HEAR my prayer, O LORD,
And let my cry come to You.

2 Do not hide Your face from
me in the day of my trouble;
Incline Your ear to me;
In the day that I call,
answer me speedily.

3 For my days are consumed
like smoke,

And my bones are burned like
a hearth.

4 My heart is stricken and
withered like grass,
So that I forget to eat my
bread.

5 Because of the sound of my
groaning
My bones cling to my skin.

6 I am like a pelican of the
wilderness;
I am like an owl of the desert.

7 I lie awake,
And am like a sparrow alone
on the housetop.

8 My enemies reproach me all
day long,
And those who deride me
swear an oath against me.

9 For I have eaten ashes like
bread,
And mingled my drink with
weeping,

10 Because of Your indignation
and Your wrath;
For You have lifted me up
and cast me away.

11 My days *are* like a shadow
that lengthens,
And I wither away like grass.

12 But You, O LORD, shall endure
forever,
And the remembrance of Your
name to all generations.

13 You will arise *and* have mercy
on Zion;
For the time to favor her,
Yes, the set time, has come.

14 For Your servants take
pleasure in her stones,
And show favor to her dust.

15 So the nations shall fear
the name of the LORD,
And all the kings of the earth
Your glory.

16 For the LORD shall build up
Zion;
He shall appear in His glory.

17 He shall regard the prayer of
the destitute,
And shall not despise their
prayer.

18 This will be written for the
generation to come,
That a people yet to be
created may praise the
Lord.

19 For He looked down from the
height of His sanctuary;
From heaven the Lord viewed
the earth,

20 To hear the groaning of the
prisoner,
To loose those appointed to
death,

21 To declare the name of the
Lord in Zion,
And His praise in Jerusalem,

22 When the peoples are
gathered together,
And the kingdoms, to serve
the Lord.

23 He weakened my strength in
the way;
He shortened my days.

24 I said, "O my God,
Do not take me away in the
midst of my days;
Your years *are* throughout all
generations.

25 Of old You laid the foundation
of the earth,
And the heavens *are* the work
of Your hands.

26 They will perish, but You will
endure;
Yes, all of them will grow old
like a garment;
Like a cloak You will change
them,
And they will be changed.

27 But You *are* the same,
And Your years will have no
end.

28 The children of Your servants
will continue,
And their descendants will be
established before You."

PSALM 103

A Psalm of David.

B LESS the Lord, O my soul;
And all that is within me,
bless His holy name!

2 Bless the Lord, O my soul,
And forget not all His
benefits:

3 Who forgives all your
iniquities,
Who heals all your diseases,

4 Who redeems your life from
destruction,
Who crowns you with
lovingkindness and tender
mercies,

5 Who satisfies your mouth
with good *things,*
So that your youth is renewed
like the eagle's.

6 The Lord executes
righteousness
And justice for all who are
oppressed.

7 He made known His ways to
Moses,
His acts to the children of
Israel.

8 The Lord *is* merciful and
gracious,
Slow to anger,
and abounding in mercy.

9 He will not always strive *with
us,*
Nor will He keep *His anger*
forever.

10 He has not dealt with us
according to our sins,
Nor punished us according to
our iniquities.

11 For as the heavens are high
above the earth,
So great is His mercy toward
those who fear Him;

12 As far as the east is from the
west,
So far has He removed our
transgressions from us.

13 As a father pities *his* children,
So the Lord pities those who
fear Him.

14 For He knows our frame;
He remembers that we *are*
dust.

15 *As for* man, his days *are* like
grass;

As a flower of the field,
so he flourishes.
16 For the wind passes over it,
and it is gone,
And its place remembers it no
more.
17 But the mercy of the LORD *is*
from everlasting to
everlasting
On those who fear Him,
And His righteousness to
children's children,
18 To such as keep His covenant,
And to those who remember
His commandments to do
them.

19 The LORD has established His
throne in heaven,
And His kingdom rules over
all.

20 Bless the LORD, you His
angels,
Who excel in strength,
who do His word,
Heeding the voice of His
word.
21 Bless the LORD, all *you* His
hosts,
You ministers of His,
who do His pleasure.
22 Bless the LORD, all His works,
In all places of His dominion.

Bless the LORD, O my soul!

PSALM 104

BLESS the LORD, O my soul!

O LORD my God, You are very
great:
You are clothed with honor
and majesty,
2 Who cover *Yourself* with light
as *with* a garment,
Who stretch out the heavens
like a curtain.

3 He lays the beams of His
upper chambers in the
waters,

Who makes the clouds His
chariot,
Who walks on the wings of
the wind,
4 Who makes His angels spirits,
His ministers a flame of fire.

5 *You who* laid the foundations
of the earth,
So *that* it should not be
moved forever,
6 You covered it with the deep
as *with* a garment;
The waters stood above the
mountains.
7 At Your rebuke they fled;
At the voice of Your thunder
they hastened away.
8 They went up over the
mountains;
They went down into the
valleys,
To the place which You
founded for them.
9 You have set a boundary that
they may not pass over,
That they may not return to
cover the earth.

10 He sends the springs into the
valleys,
Which flow among the hills.
11 They give drink to every beast
of the field;
The wild donkeys quench
their thirst.
12 By them the birds of the
heavens have their
habitation;
They sing among the
branches.
13 He waters the hills from His
upper chambers;
The earth is satisfied with the
fruit of Your works.

14 He causes the grass to grow
for the cattle,
And vegetation for the service
of man,
That he may bring forth food
from the earth,
15 And wine *that* makes glad the
heart of man,

Oil to make *his* face shine,
And bread *which* strengthens
man's heart.

16 The trees of the LORD are full
of sap,
The cedars of Lebanon which
He planted;

17 Where the birds make their
nests;
The stork has her home in the
fir trees.

18 The high hills *are* for the wild
goats;
The cliffs are a refuge for the
rock badgers.

19 He appointed the moon for
seasons;
The sun knows its going
down.

20 You make darkness, and it is
night,
In which all the beasts of the
forest creep about.

21 The young lions roar after
their prey,
And seek their food from God.

22 *When* the sun arises, they
gather together
And lie down in their dens.

23 Man goes out to his work
And to his labor until the
evening.

24 O LORD, how manifold are
Your works!
In wisdom You have made
them all.
The earth is full of Your
possessions—

25 This great and wide sea,
In which *are* innumerable
teeming things,
Living things both small and
great.

26 There the ships sail about;
And there is that Leviathan
Which You have made to play
there.

27 These all wait for You,
That You may give *them* their
food in due season.

28 *What* You give them they
gather in;
You open Your hand,
they are filled with good.

29 You hide Your face, they are
troubled;
You take away their breath,
they die and return to their
dust.

30 You send forth Your Spirit,
they are created;
And You renew the face of
the earth.

31 May the glory of the LORD
endure forever;
May the LORD rejoice in His
works.

32 He looks on the earth, and it
trembles;
He touches the hills, and they
smoke.

33 I will sing to the LORD as long
as I live;
I will sing praise to my God
while I have my being.

34 May my meditation be sweet
to Him;
I will be glad in the LORD.

35 May sinners be consumed
from the earth,
And the wicked be no more.

Bless the LORD, O my soul!
Praise the LORD!

PSALM 105

OH, give thanks to the LORD!
Call upon His name;
Make known His deeds among
the peoples.

2 Sing to Him, sing psalms to
Him;
Talk of all His wondrous
works.

3 Glory in His holy name;
Let the hearts of those rejoice
who seek the LORD.

4 Seek the LORD and His
strength;
Seek His face evermore.

5 Remember His marvelous
  works which He has done,
  His wonders, and the
  judgments of His mouth,
6 O seed of Abraham His
  servant,
  You children of Jacob,
  His chosen ones!

7 He *is* the Lord our God;
  His judgments *are* in all the
  earth.
8 He has remembered His
  covenant forever,
  The word *which* He
  commanded, for a thousand
  generations,
9 *The covenant* which He made
  with Abraham,
  And His oath to Isaac,
10 And confirmed it to Jacob for
  a statute,
  To Israel *for* an everlasting
  covenant,
11 Saying, "To you I will give the
  land of Canaan
  As the allotment of your
  inheritance,"
12 When they were *but* few in
  number,
  Indeed very few, and
  strangers in it.

13 When they went from one
  nation to another,
  From *one* kingdom to another
  people,
14 He permitted no one to do
  them wrong;
  Yes, He reproved kings for
  their sakes,
15 *Saying,* "Do not touch My
  anointed ones,
  And do My prophets no
  harm."

16 Moreover He called for a
  famine in the land;
  He destroyed all the provision
  of bread.
17 He sent a man before them—
  Joseph—*who* was sold as a
  slave.

18 They hurt his feet with fetters,
  He was laid in irons.
19 Until the time that his word
  came to pass,
  The word of the Lord tested
  him.
20 The king sent and released
  him,
  The ruler of the people let him
  go free.
21 He made him lord of his
  house,
  And ruler of all his
  possessions,
22 To bind his princes at his
  pleasure,
  And teach his elders wisdom.

23 Israel also came into Egypt,
  And Jacob sojourned in the
  land of Ham.
24 And He increased His people
  greatly,
  And made them stronger than
  their enemies.
25 He turned their heart to hate
  His people,
  To deal craftily with His
  servants.

26 He sent Moses His servant,
  And Aaron whom He had
  chosen.
27 They performed His signs
  among them,
  And wonders in the land of
  Ham.
28 He sent darkness, and made *it*
  dark;
  And they did not rebel against
  His word.
29 He turned their waters into
  blood,
  And killed their fish.
30 Their land abounded with
  frogs,
  Even in the chambers of their
  kings.
31 He spoke, and there came
  swarms of flies,
  And lice in all their territory.
32 He gave them hail for rain,
  And flaming fire in their land.

Joy in Forgiveness

33 He struck their vines also,
    and their fig trees,
    And splintered the trees of
    their territory.
34 He spoke, and locusts came,
    Young locusts without
    number,
35 And ate up all the vegetation
    in their land,
    And devoured the fruit of
    their ground.
36 He also destroyed all the
    firstborn in their land,
    The first of all their strength.

37 He also brought them out
    with silver and gold,
    And *there was* none feeble
    among His tribes.
38 Egypt was glad when they
    departed,
    For the fear of them had
    fallen upon them.
39 He spread a cloud for a
    covering,
    And fire to give light in the
    night.
40 *The people* asked, and He
    brought quail,
    And satisfied them with the
    bread of heaven.
41 He opened the rock,
    and water gushed out;
    It ran in the dry places *like* a
    river.

42 For He remembered His holy
    promise,
    And Abraham His servant.
43 He brought out His people
    with joy,
    His chosen ones with
    gladness.
44 He gave them the lands of the
    Gentiles,
    And they inherited the labor
    of the nations,
45 That they might observe His
    statutes
    And keep His laws.

Praise the LORD!

PSALM 106

PRAISE the LORD!

Oh, give thanks to the LORD,
    for *He is* good!
For His mercy *endures*
    forever.

2 Who can utter the mighty
    acts of the LORD?
    Or can declare all His praise?
3 Blessed *are* those who keep
    justice,
    And he who does
    righteousness at all times!

4 Remember me, O LORD, with
    the favor *You have toward*
    Your people;
    Oh, visit me with Your
    salvation,
5 That I may see the benefit of
    Your chosen ones,
    That I may rejoice in the
    gladness of Your nation,
    That I may glory with Your
    inheritance.

6 We have sinned with our
    fathers,
    We have committed iniquity,
    We have done wickedly.
7 Our fathers in Egypt did not
    understand Your wonders;
    They did not remember the
    multitude of Your mercies,
    But rebelled by the sea—the
    Red Sea.

8 Nevertheless He saved them
    for His name's sake,
    That He might make His
    mighty power known.
9 He rebuked the Red Sea also,
    and it dried up;
    So He led them through the
    depths,
    As through the wilderness.
10 He saved them from the hand
    of him who hated *them*,
    And redeemed them from the
    hand of the enemy.

11 The waters covered their
enemies;
There was not one of them
left.

12 Then they believed His words;
They sang His praise.

13 They soon forgot His works;
They did not wait for His
counsel,

14 But lusted exceedingly in the
wilderness,
And tested God in the desert.

15 And He gave them their
request,
But sent leanness into their
soul.

16 When they envied Moses in
the camp,
And Aaron the saint of the
LORD,

17 The earth opened up and
swallowed Dathan,
And covered the faction of
Abiram.

18 A fire was kindled in their
company;
The flame burned up the
wicked.

19 They made a calf in Horeb,
And worshiped the molded
image.

20 Thus they changed their glory
Into the image of an ox that
eats grass.

21 They forgot God their Savior,
Who had done great things in
Egypt,

22 Wondrous works in the land
of Ham,
Awesome things by the Red
Sea.

23 Therefore He said that He
would destroy them,
Had not Moses His chosen
one stood before Him in the
breach,
To turn away His wrath,
lest He destroy *them.*

24 Then they despised the
pleasant land;

25 They did not believe His word,
But murmured in their tents,
And did not heed the voice of
the LORD.

26 Therefore He lifted up His
hand *in an oath* against
them,
To overthrow them in the
wilderness,

27 To overthrow their
descendants among the
nations,
And to scatter them in the
lands.

28 They joined themselves also
to Baal of Peor,
And ate sacrifices made to the
dead.

29 Thus they provoked *Him* to
anger with their deeds,
And the plague broke out
among them.

30 Then Phinehas stood up and
intervened,
And *so* the plague was
stopped.

31 And that was accounted to
him for righteousness
To all generations
forevermore.

32 They angered *Him* also at the
waters of strife,
So that it went ill with Moses
on account of them;

33 Because they rebelled against
His Spirit,
So that he spoke rashly with
his lips.

34 They did not destroy the
peoples,
Concerning whom the LORD
had commanded them,

35 But they mingled with the
Gentiles
And learned their works;

36 They served their idols,
Which became a snare to
them.

37 They even sacrificed their
sons

Praise of the Redeemed

And their daughters to
demons,

38 And shed innocent blood,
Even the blood of their sons
and daughters,
Whom they sacrificed to the
idols of Canaan;
And the land was polluted
with blood.

39 Thus they were defiled by
their own works,
And played the harlot by their
own deeds.

40 Therefore the wrath of the
LORD was kindled against
His people,
So that He abhorred His own
inheritance.

41 And He gave them into the
hand of the Gentiles,
And those who hated them
ruled over them.

42 Their enemies also oppressed
them,
And they were brought into
subjection under their hand.

43 Many times He delivered
them;
But they rebelled *against Him*
by their counsel,
And were brought low for
their iniquity.

44 Nevertheless He regarded
their affliction,
When He heard their cry;

45 And for their sake He
remembered His covenant,
And relented according to the
multitude of His mercies.

46 He also made them to be
pitied
By all those who carried them
away captive.

47 Save us, O LORD our God,
And gather us from among
the Gentiles,
To give thanks to Your holy
name,
And to triumph in Your
praise.

48 Blessed *be* the LORD God of
Israel
From everlasting to
everlasting!
And let all the people say,
"Amen!"

Praise the LORD!

BOOK FIVE
Psalms 107–150

PSALM 107

OH, give thanks to the LORD,
for *He is* good!
For His mercy *endures*
forever.

2 Let the redeemed of the LORD
say *so,*
Whom He has redeemed from
the hand of the enemy,

3 And gathered out of the lands,
From the east and from the
west,
From the north and from the
south.

4 They wandered in the
wilderness in a desolate
way;
They found no city to dwell
in.

5 Hungry and thirsty,
Their soul fainted in them.

6 Then they cried out to the
LORD in their trouble,
And He delivered them out of
their distresses.

7 And He led them forth by the
right way,
That they might go to a city
for habitation.

8 Oh, that *men* would give
thanks to the LORD *for* His
goodness,
And *for* His wonderful works
to the children of men!

9 For He satisfies the longing
soul,
And fills the hungry soul with
goodness.

10 Those who sat in darkness
and in the shadow of death,
Bound in affliction and irons—
11 Because they rebelled against
the words of God,
And despised the counsel of
the Most High,
12 Therefore He brought down
their heart with labor;
They fell down,
and *there was* none to help.
13 Then they cried out to the
LORD in their trouble,
And He saved them out of
their distresses.
14 He brought them out of
darkness and the shadow of
death,
And broke their chains in
pieces.
15 Oh, that *men* would give
thanks to the LORD *for* His
goodness,
And *for* His wonderful works
to the children of men!
16 For He has broken the gates
of bronze,
And cut the bars of iron in
two.

17 Fools, because of their
transgression,
And because of their
iniquities, were afflicted.
18 Their soul abhorred all
manner of food,
And they drew near to the
gates of death.
19 Then they cried out to the
LORD in their trouble,
And He saved them out of
their distresses.
20 He sent His word and healed
them,
And delivered *them* from their
destructions.
21 Oh, that *men* would give
thanks to the LORD *for* His
goodness,
And *for* His wonderful works
to the children of men!
22 Let them sacrifice the
sacrifices of thanksgiving,

And declare His works with
rejoicing.

23 Those who go down to the sea
in ships,
Who do business on great
waters,
24 They see the works of the
LORD,
And His wonders in the deep.
25 For He commands and raises
the stormy wind,
Which lifts up the waves of
the sea.
26 They mount up to the
heavens,
They go down again to the
depths;
Their soul melts because of
trouble.
27 They reel to and fro, and
stagger like a drunken man,
And are at their wits' end.
28 Then they cry out to the LORD
in their trouble,
And He brings them out of
their distresses.
29 He calms the storm,
So that its waves are still.
30 Then they are glad because
they are quiet;
So He guides them to their
desired haven.
31 Oh, that *men* would give
thanks to the LORD *for* His
goodness,
And *for* His wonderful works
to the children of men!
32 Let them exalt Him also in the
congregation of the people,
And praise Him in the
assembly of the elders.

33 He turns rivers into a
wilderness,
And the watersprings into dry
ground;
34 A fruitful land into
barrenness,
For the wickedness of those
who dwell in it.
35 He turns a wilderness into
pools of water,

And dry land into
watersprings.
36 There He makes the hungry
dwell,
That they may establish a city
for habitation,
37 And sow fields and plant
vineyards,
That they may yield a fruitful
harvest.
38 He also blesses them,
and they multiply greatly;
And He does not let their
cattle decrease.

39 When they are diminished
and brought low
Through oppression, affliction
and sorrow,
40 He pours contempt on princes,
And causes them to wander in
the wilderness *where there
is* no way;
41 Yet He sets the poor on high,
far from affliction,
And makes *their* families like
a flock.
42 The righteous see *it* and
rejoice,
And all iniquity stops its
mouth.

43 Whoever *is* wise will observe
these *things,*
And they will understand the
lovingkindness of the LORD.

PSALM 108

A Song. A Psalm of David.

O GOD, my heart is steadfast;
I will sing and give praise,
even with my glory.
2 Awake, lute and harp!
I will awaken the dawn.
3 I will praise You, O LORD,
among the peoples,
And I will sing praises to You
among the nations.
4 For Your mercy *is* great above
the heavens,
And Your truth *reaches* to the
clouds.

5 Be exalted, O God, above the
heavens,
And Your glory above all the
earth;
6 That Your beloved may be
delivered,
Save *with* Your right hand,
and hear me.

7 God has spoken in His
holiness:
"I will rejoice;
I will divide Shechem
And measure out the Valley of
Succoth.
8 Gilead *is* Mine;
Manasseh *is* Mine;
Ephraim also *is* the helmet for
My head;
Judah *is* My lawgiver.
9 Moab *is* My washpot;
Over Edom I will cast My
shoe;
Over Philistia I will triumph."

10 Who will bring me into the
strong city?
Who will lead me to Edom?
11 *Is it* not You, O God, *who* cast
us off?
And You, O God, *who* did not
go out with our armies?
12 Give us help from trouble,
For vain *is* the help of man.
13 Through God we will do
valiantly,
For *it is* He *who* shall tread
down our enemies.

PSALM 109

To the Chief Musician. A Psalm of David.

DO not keep silent,
O God of my praise!
2 For the mouth of the wicked
and the mouth of the
deceitful
Have opened against me;
They have spoken against me
with a lying tongue.
3 They have also surrounded me
with words of hatred,
And fought against me
without a cause.

4 In return for my love they are my accusers,
But I *give myself to* prayer.

5 Thus they have rewarded me evil for good,
And hatred for my love.

6 Set a wicked man over him,
And let an accuser stand at his right hand.

7 When he is judged,
let him be found guilty,
And let his prayer become sin.

8 Let his days be few,
And let another take his office.

9 Let his children be fatherless,
And his wife a widow.

10 Let his children continually be vagabonds, and beg;
Let them seek *their bread* also from their desolate places.

11 Let the creditor seize all that he has,
And let strangers plunder his labor.

12 Let there be none to extend mercy to him,
Nor let there be any to favor his fatherless children.

13 Let his posterity be cut off,
And in the generation following let their name be blotted out.

14 Let the iniquity of his fathers be remembered before the LORD,
And let not the sin of his mother be blotted out.

15 Let them be continually before the LORD,
That He may cut off the memory of them from the earth;

16 Because he did not remember to show mercy,
But persecuted the poor and needy man,
That he might even slay the broken in heart.

17 As he loved cursing,
so let it come to him;

As he did not delight in blessing, so let it be far from him.

18 As he clothed himself with cursing as with his garment,
So let it enter his body like water,
And like oil into his bones.

19 Let it be to him like the garment which covers him,
And for a belt with which he girds himself continually.

20 *Let* this *be* the LORD's reward to my accusers,
And to those who speak evil against my person.

21 But You, O GOD the Lord,
Deal with me for Your name's sake;
Because Your mercy *is* good, deliver me.

22 For I *am* poor and needy,
And my heart is wounded within me.

23 I am gone like a shadow when it lengthens;
I am shaken off like a locust.

24 My knees are weak through fasting,
And my flesh is feeble from lack of fatness.

25 I also have become a reproach to them;
When they look at me,
they shake their heads.

26 Help me, O LORD my God!
Oh, save me according to Your mercy,

27 That they may know that this *is* Your hand—
That You, LORD, have done it!

28 Let them curse, but You bless;
When they arise, let them be ashamed,
But let Your servant rejoice.

29 Let my accusers be clothed with shame,
And let them cover themselves with their own disgrace as with a mantle.

30 I will greatly praise the LORD with my mouth;

403

Yes, I will praise Him among
the multitude.
31 For He shall stand at the right
hand of the poor,
To save *him* from those who
condemn him.

PSALM 110

A Psalm of David.

THE LORD said to my Lord,
"Sit at My right hand,
Till I make Your enemies
Your footstool."
2 The LORD shall send the rod of
Your strength out of Zion.
Rule in the midst of Your
enemies!

3 Your people *shall be*
volunteers
In the day of Your power;
In the beauties of holiness,
from the womb of the
morning,
You have the dew of Your
youth.
4 The LORD has sworn
And will not relent,
"You *are* a priest forever
According to the order of
Melchizedek."

5 The Lord *is* at Your right
hand;
He shall execute kings in the
day of His wrath.
6 He shall judge among the
nations,
He shall fill *the places* with
dead bodies,
He shall execute the heads of
many countries.
7 He shall drink of the brook by
the wayside;
Therefore He shall lift up the
head.

PSALM 111

PRAISE the LORD!

I will praise the LORD with *my*
whole heart,

Messiah's Reign Announced

In the assembly of the upright
and *in* the congregation.

2 The works of the LORD *are*
great,
Studied by all who have
pleasure in them.
3 His work *is* honorable and
glorious,
And His righteousness
endures forever.
4 He has made His wonderful
works to be remembered;
The LORD *is* gracious
and full of compassion.
5 He has given food to those
who fear Him;
He will ever be mindful of His
covenant.
6 He has declared to His people
the power of His works,
In giving them the heritage of
the nations.

7 The works of His hands
are verity and justice;
All His precepts *are* sure.
8 They stand fast forever and
ever,
And are done in truth and
uprightness.
9 He has sent redemption to His
people;
He has commanded His
covenant forever:
Holy and awesome *is* His
name.

10 The fear of the LORD
is the beginning of wisdom;
A good understanding have all
those who do *His
commandments*.
His praise endures forever.

PSALM 112

PRAISE the LORD!

Blessed *is* the man *who* fears
the LORD,
Who delights greatly in His
commandments.

404

2 His descendants will be
    mighty on earth;
  The generation of the upright
    will be blessed.
3 Wealth and riches *will be* in
    his house,
  And his righteousness endures
    forever.
4 Unto the upright there arises
    light in the darkness;
  He is gracious, and full of
    compassion, and righteous.
5 A good man deals graciously
    and lends;
  He will guide his affairs with
    discretion.
6 Surely he will never be
    shaken;
  The righteous will be in
    everlasting remembrance.
7 He will not be afraid of evil
    tidings;
  His heart is steadfast,
    trusting in the LORD.
8 His heart *is* established;
  He will not be afraid,
  Until he sees *his desire* upon
    his enemies.

9 He has dispersed abroad,
  He has given to the poor;
  His righteousness endures
    forever;
  His horn will be exalted with
    honor.
10 The wicked will see *it* and be
    grieved;
  He will gnash his teeth and
    melt away;
  The desire of the wicked shall
    perish.

PSALM 113

PRAISE the LORD!

Praise, O servants of the
    LORD,
Praise the name of the LORD!
2 Blessed be the name of the
    LORD
  From this time forth and
    forevermore!

3 From the rising of the sun to
    its going down
  The LORD's name *is* to be
    praised.

4 The LORD *is* high above all
    nations,
  And His glory above the
    heavens.
5 Who *is* like the LORD our God,
  Who dwells on high,
6 Who humbles Himself to
    behold
  The things that are in the
    heavens and in the earth?

7 He raises the poor out of the
    dust,
  And lifts the needy out of the
    ash heap,
8 That He may seat *him* with
    princes—
  With the princes of His
    people.
9 He grants the barren woman a
    home,
  Like a joyful mother of
    children.

Praise the LORD!

PSALM 114

WHEN Israel went out of
    Egypt,
  The house of Jacob from a
    people of strange language,
2 Judah became His sanctuary,
  And Israel His dominion.

3 The sea saw *it* and fled;
  Jordan turned back.
4 The mountains skipped like
    rams,
  The little hills like lambs.
5 What ails you, O sea, that you
    fled?
  O Jordan, *that* you turned
    back?
6 O mountains, *that* you
    skipped like rams?
  O little hills, like lambs?

7 Tremble, O earth, at the
    presence of the Lord,
   At the presence of the God of
    Jacob,
8 Who turned the rock *into* a
    pool of water,
   The flint into a fountain of
    waters.

PSALM 115

NOT unto us, O LORD, not unto
    us,
   But to Your name give glory,
   Because of Your mercy,
   And because of Your truth.
2 Why should the Gentiles say,
   Where now *is* their God?"

3 But our God *is* in heaven;
   He does whatever He pleases.
4 Their idols *are* silver and gold,
   The work of men's hands.
5 They have mouths,
    but they do not speak;
   Eyes they have, but they do
    not see;
6 They have ears, but they do
    not hear;
   Noses they have,
    but they do not smell;
7 They have hands,
    but they do not handle;
   Feet they have, but they do
    not walk;
   Nor do they mutter through
    their throat.
8 Those who make them are
    like them;
   So is everyone who trusts in
    them.

9 O Israel, trust in the LORD;
   He *is* their help and their
    shield.
10 O house of Aaron, trust in the
    LORD;
   He *is* their help and their
    shield.
11 You who fear the LORD,
    trust in the LORD;
   He *is* their help and their
    shield.

12 The LORD has been mindful of
    us;
   He will bless us;
   He will bless the house of
    Israel;
   He will bless the house of
    Aaron.
13 He will bless those who fear
    the LORD,
   Both small and great.

14 May the LORD give you
    increase more and more,
   You and your children.
15 *May* you *be* blessed by the
    LORD,
   Who made heaven and earth.

16 The heaven, *even* the heavens,
    are the LORD's;
   But the earth He has given to
    the children of men.
17 The dead do not praise the
    LORD,
   Nor any who go down into
    silence.
18 But we will bless the LORD
   From this time forth and
    forevermore.

   Praise the LORD!

PSALM 116

I LOVE the LORD, because He
    has heard
   My voice *and* my
    supplications.
2 Because He has inclined His
    ear to me,
   Therefore I will call *upon Him*
    as long as I live.

3 The pains of death
    encompassed me,
   And the pangs of Sheol laid
    hold of me;
   I found trouble and sorrow.
4 Then I called upon the name
    of the LORD:
   "O LORD, I implore You,
    deliver my soul!"

5 Gracious *is* the LORD, and
righteous;
Yes, our God *is* merciful.
6 The LORD preserves the
simple;
I was brought low, and He
saved me.
7 Return to your rest, O my
soul,
For the LORD has dealt
bountifully with you.

8 For You have delivered my
soul from death,
My eyes from tears,
And my feet from falling.
9 I will walk before the LORD
In the land of the living.
10 I believed, therefore I spoke,
"I am greatly afflicted."
11 I said in my haste,
"All men *are* liars."

12 What shall I render to the
LORD
For all His benefits toward
me?
13 I will take up the cup of
salvation,
And call upon the name of the
LORD.
14 I will pay my vows to the
LORD
Now in the presence of all His
people.

15 Precious in the sight of the
LORD
Is the death of His saints.

16 O LORD, truly I *am* Your
servant;
I *am* Your servant, the son of
Your maidservant;
You have loosed my bonds.
17 I will offer to You the sacrifice
of thanksgiving,
And will call upon the name
of the LORD.

18 I will pay my vows to the
LORD

Now in the presence of all His
people,
19 In the courts of the LORD's
house,
In the midst of you, O
Jerusalem.

Praise the LORD!

PSALM 117

OH, praise the LORD, all you
Gentiles!
Laud Him, all you peoples!
2 For His merciful kindness is
great toward us,
And the truth of the LORD
endures forever.

Praise the LORD!

PSALM 118

OH, give thanks to the LORD,
for *He is* good!
Because His mercy *endures*
forever.

2 Let Israel now say,
"His mercy *endures* forever."
3 Let the house of Aaron now
say,
"His mercy *endures* forever."
4 Let those who fear the LORD
now say,
"His mercy *endures* forever."

5 I called on the LORD in
distress;
The LORD answered me
and set me in a broad place.
6 The LORD *is* on my side;
I will not fear.
What can man do to me?
7 The LORD is for me among
those who help me;
Therefore I shall see *my desire*
on those who hate me.
8 *It is* better to trust in the
LORD
Than to put confidence in
man.
9 *It is* better to trust in the
LORD

407

God's Everlasting Mercy

Than to put confidence in princes.

10 All nations surrounded me,
But in the name of the LORD I will destroy them.
11 They surrounded me,
Yes, they surrounded me;
But in the name of the LORD I will destroy them.
12 They surrounded me like bees;
They were quenched like a fire of thorns;
For in the name of the LORD I will destroy them.
13 You pushed me violently, that I might fall,
But the LORD helped me.
14 The LORD *is* my strength and song,
And He has become my salvation.

15 The voice of rejoicing and salvation
Is in the tents of the righteous;
The right hand of the LORD does valiantly.
16 The right hand of the LORD is exalted;
The right hand of the LORD does valiantly.
17 I shall not die, but live,
And declare the works of the LORD.
18 The LORD has chastened me severely,
But He has not given me over to death.

19 Open to me the gates of righteousness;
I will go through them,
And I will praise the LORD.
20 This is the gate of the LORD,
Through which the righteous shall enter.

21 I will praise You,
For You have answered me,
And have become my salvation.

22 The stone *which* the builders rejected
Has become the chief cornerstone.
23 This was the LORD'S doing;
It *is* marvelous in our eyes.
24 This *is* the day *which* the LORD has made;
We will rejoice and be glad in it.

25 Save now, I pray, O LORD;
O LORD, I pray, send now prosperity.
26 Blessed *is* he who comes in the name of the LORD!
We have blessed you from the house of the LORD.
27 God *is* the LORD,
And He has given us light;
Bind the sacrifice with cords to the horns of the altar.
28 You *are* my God, and I will praise You;
You are my God, I will exalt You.

29 Oh, give thanks to the LORD, for *He is* good!
For His mercy *endures* forever.

PSALM 119

א ALEPH

BLESSED *are* the undefiled in the way,
Who walk in the law of the LORD!
2 Blessed *are* those who keep His testimonies,
Who seek Him with the whole heart!
3 They also do no iniquity;
They walk in His ways.
4 You have commanded *us*
To keep Your precepts diligently.
5 Oh, that my ways were directed
To keep Your statutes!

6 Then I would not be ashamed,
   When I look into all Your
   commandments.
7 I will praise You with
   uprightness of heart,
   When I learn Your righteous
   judgments.
8 I will keep Your statutes;
   Oh, do not forsake me utterly!

‫ב‬ BETH

9 How can a young man cleanse
   his way?
   By taking heed according to
   Your word.
10 With my whole heart I have
   sought You;
   Oh, let me not wander from
   Your commandments!
11 Your word I have hidden in
   my heart,
   That I might not sin against
   You.
12 Blessed *are* You, O LORD!
   Teach me Your statutes.
13 With my lips I have declared
   All the judgments of Your
   mouth.
14 I have rejoiced in the way of
   Your testimonies,
   As *much as* in all riches.
15 I will meditate on Your
   precepts,
   And contemplate Your ways.
16 I will delight myself in Your
   statutes;
   I will not forget Your word.

‫ג‬ GIMEL

17 Deal bountifully with Your
   servant,
   That I may live and keep
   Your word.
18 Open my eyes, that I may see
   Wondrous things from Your
   law.
19 I *am* a stranger in the earth;
   Do not hide Your
   commandments from me.
20 My soul breaks with longing

For Your judgments at all
   times.
21 You rebuke the proud—the
   cursed,
   Who stray from Your
   commandments.
22 Remove from me reproach
   and contempt,
   For I have kept Your
   testimonies.
23 Princes also sit *and* speak
   against me,
   But Your servant meditates
   on Your statutes.
24 Your testimonies also *are* my
   delight
   And my counselors.

‫ד‬ DALETH

25 My soul clings to the dust;
   Revive me according to Your
   word.
26 I have declared my ways,
   and You answered me;
   Teach me Your statutes.
27 Make me understand the way
   of Your precepts;
   So shall I meditate on Your
   wondrous works.
28 My soul melts from heaviness;
   Strengthen me according to
   Your word.
29 Remove from me the way of
   lying,
   And grant me Your law
   graciously.
30 I have chosen the way of
   truth;
   Your judgments I have laid
   before me.
31 I cling to Your testimonies;
   O LORD, do not put me to
   shame!
32 I will run in the way of Your
   commandments,
   For You shall enlarge my
   heart.

‫ה‬ HE

33 Teach me, O LORD, the way of
   Your statutes,

And I shall keep it *to* the end.

34 Give me understanding,
   and I shall keep Your law;
   Indeed, I shall observe it with
   my whole heart.

35 Make me walk in the path of
   Your commandments,
   For I delight in it.

36 Incline my heart to Your
   testimonies,
   And not to covetousness.

37 Turn away my eyes from
   looking at worthless things,
   And revive me in Your way.

38 Establish Your word to Your
   servant,
   Who *is devoted* to fearing
   You.

39 Turn away my reproach
   which I dread,
   For Your judgments *are* good.

40 Behold, I long for Your
   precepts;
   Revive me in Your
   righteousness.

ו WAW

41 Let Your mercies come also to
   me, O LORD—
   Your salvation according to
   Your word.

42 So shall I have an answer for
   him who reproaches me,
   For I trust in Your word.

43 And take not the word of
   truth utterly out of my
   mouth,
   For I have hoped in Your
   ordinances.

44 So shall I keep Your law
   continually,
   Forever and ever.

45 And I will walk at liberty,
   For I seek Your precepts.

46 I will speak of Your
   testimonies also before
   kings,
   And will not be ashamed.

47 And I will delight myself in
   Your commandments,
   Which I love.

48 My hands also I will lift up to
   Your commandments,
   Which I love,
   And I will meditate on Your
   statutes.

ז ZAYIN

49 Remember the word to Your
   servant,
   Upon which You have caused
   me to hope.

50 This *is* my comfort in my
   affliction,
   For Your word has given me
   life.

51 The proud have me in great
   derision,
   Yet I do not turn aside from
   Your law.

52 I remembered Your
   judgments of old, O LORD,
   And have comforted myself.

53 Indignation has taken hold of
   me
   Because of the wicked,
   who forsake Your law.

54 Your statutes have been my
   songs
   In the house of my
   pilgrimage.

55 I remember Your name in the
   night, O LORD,
   And I keep Your law.

56 This has become mine,
   Because I kept Your precepts.

ח HETH

57 *You are* my portion, O LORD;
   I have said that I would keep
   Your words.

58 I entreated Your favor with
   my whole heart;
   Be merciful to me according
   to Your word.

59 I thought about my ways,
   And turned my feet to Your
   testimonies.

60 I made haste, and did not
   delay
   To keep Your commandments.

61 The cords of the wicked have
bound me,
But I have not forgotten Your
law.
62 At midnight I will rise to give
thanks to You,
Because of Your righteous
judgments.
63 I *am* a companion of all *those*
who fear You,
And of those who keep Your
precepts.
64 The earth, O Lord, is full of
Your mercy;
Teach me Your statutes.

ט TETH

65 You have dealt well with Your
servant,
O Lord, according to Your
word.
66 Teach me good judgment and
knowledge,
For I believe Your
commandments.
67 Before I was afflicted I went
astray,
But now I keep Your word.
68 You *are* good, and do good;
Teach me Your statutes.
69 The proud have forged a lie
against me,
But I will keep Your precepts
with *my* whole heart.
70 Their heart is as fat as grease,
But I delight in Your law.
71 *It is* good for me that I have
been afflicted,
That I may learn Your
statutes.
72 The law of Your mouth *is*
better to me
Than thousands of *shekels of*
gold and silver.

י YOD

73 Your hands have made me
and fashioned me;
Give me understanding, that I
may learn Your
commandments.

74 Those who fear You will be
glad when they see me,
Because I have hoped in Your
word.
75 I know, O Lord, that Your
judgments *are* right,
And *that* in faithfulness You
have afflicted me.
76 Let, I pray, Your merciful
kindness be for my comfort,
According to Your word to
Your servant.
77 Let Your tender mercies come
to me, that I may live;
For Your law *is* my delight.
78 Let the proud be ashamed,
For they treated me
wrongfully with falsehood;
But I will meditate on Your
precepts.
79 Let those who fear You turn
to me,
Those who know Your
testimonies.
80 Let my heart be blameless
regarding Your statutes,
That I may not be ashamed.

כ KAPH

81 My soul faints for Your
salvation,
But I hope in Your word.
82 My eyes fail *from seeking*
Your word,
Saying, "When will You
comfort me?"
83 For I have become like a
wineskin in smoke,
Yet I do not forget Your
statutes.
84 How many *are* the days of
Your servant?
When will You execute
judgment on those who
persecute me?
85 The proud have dug pits for
me,
Which *is* not according to
Your law.
86 All Your commandments *are*
faithful;

They persecute me
   wrongfully;
Help me!
87 They almost made an end of
   me on earth,
But I did not forsake Your
   precepts.
88 Revive me according to Your
   lovingkindness,
So that I may keep the
   testimony of Your mouth.

ל LAMED

89 Forever, O Lord,
Your word is settled in
   heaven.
90 Your faithfulness *endures* to
   all generations;
You established the earth,
   and it abides.
91 They continue this day
   according to Your
   ordinances,
For all *are* Your servants.
92 Unless Your law *had been* my
   delight,
I would then have perished in
   my affliction.
93 I will never forget Your
   precepts,
For by them You have given
   me life.
94 I *am* Yours, save me;
For I have sought Your
   precepts.
95 The wicked wait for me to
   destroy me,
But I will consider Your
   testimonies.
96 I have seen the consummation
   of all perfection,
But Your commandment *is*
   exceedingly broad.

מ MEM

97 Oh, how I love Your law!
It *is* my meditation all the
   day.

98 You, through Your
   commandments, make me
   wiser than my enemies;
For they *are* ever with me.
99 I have more understanding
   than all my teachers,
For Your testimonies *are* my
   meditation.
100 I understand more than the
   ancients,
Because I keep Your precepts.
101 I have restrained my feet from
   every evil way,
That I may keep Your word.
102 I have not departed from
   Your judgments,
For You Yourself have taught
   me.
103 How sweet are Your words to
   my taste,
Sweeter than honey to my
   mouth!
104 Through Your precepts I get
   understanding;
Therefore I hate every false
   way.

נ NUN

105 Your word *is* a lamp to my
   feet
And a light to my path.
106 I have sworn and confirmed
That I will keep Your
   righteous judgments.
107 I am afflicted very much;
Revive me, O Lord, according
   to Your word.
108 Accept, I pray, the freewill
   offerings of my mouth, O
   Lord,
And teach me Your
   judgments.
109 My life *is* continually in my
   hand,
Yet I do not forget Your law.
110 The wicked have laid a snare
   for me,
Yet I have not strayed from
   Your precepts.

111 Your testimonies I have taken
      as a heritage forever,
    For they *are* the rejoicing of
      my heart.
112 I have inclined my heart to
      perform Your statutes
    Forever, to the very end.

ﬠ SAMEK

113 I hate the double-minded,
    But I love Your law.
114 You *are* my hiding place and
      my shield;
    I hope in Your word.
115 Depart from me, you
      evildoers,
    For I will keep the
      commandments of my God!
116 Uphold me according to Your
      word, that I may live;
    And do not let me be ashamed
      of my hope.
117 Hold me up, and I shall be
      safe,
    And I shall observe Your
      statutes continually.
118 You reject all those who stray
      from Your statutes,
    For their deceit *is* falsehood.
119 You put away all the wicked
      of the earth *like* dross;
    Therefore I love Your
      testimonies.
120 My flesh trembles for fear of
      You,
    And I am afraid of Your
      judgments.

ﬠ AYIN

121 I have done justice and
      righteousness;
    Do not leave me to my
      oppressors.
122 Be surety for Your servant for
      good;
    Do not let the proud oppress
      me.
123 My eyes fail *from seeking*
      Your salvation
    And Your righteous word.

124 Deal with Your servant
      according to Your mercy,
    And teach me Your statutes.
125 I *am* Your servant;
    Give me understanding,
    That I may know Your
      testimonies.
126 *It is* time for *You* to act, O
      LORD,
    For they have regarded Your
      law as void.
127 Therefore I love Your
      commandments
    More than gold, yes, than fine
      gold!
128 Therefore all *Your* precepts
      concerning all *things*
    I consider *to be* right;
    I hate every false way.

ﬡ PE

129 Your testimonies are
      wonderful;
    Therefore my soul keeps
      them.
130 The entrance of Your words
      gives light;
    It gives understanding to the
      simple.
131 I opened my mouth and
      panted,
    For I longed for Your
      commandments.
132 Look upon me and be merciful
      to me,
    As Your custom *is* toward
      those who love Your name.
133 Direct my steps by Your word,
    And let no iniquity have
      dominion over me.
134 Redeem me from the
      oppression of man,
    That I may keep Your
      precepts.
135 Make Your face shine upon
      Your servant,
    And teach me Your statutes.
136 Rivers of water run down
      from my eyes,
    Because *men* do not keep
      Your law.

 צ **TSADDE**

137 Righteous *are* You, O Lord,
And upright *are* Your
    judgments.
138 Your testimonies, *which* You
    have commanded,
Are righteous and very
    faithful.
139 My zeal has consumed me,
Because my enemies have
    forgotten Your words.
140 Your word *is* very pure;
Therefore Your servant loves
    it.
141 I *am* small and despised,
Yet I do not forget Your
    precepts.
142 Your righteousness *is* an
    everlasting righteousness,
And Your law *is* truth.
143 Trouble and anguish have
    overtaken me,
Yet Your commandments *are*
    my delights.
144 The righteousness of Your
    testimonies *is* everlasting;
Give me understanding,
    and I shall live.

ק **QOPH**

145 I cry out with *my* whole
    heart;
Hear me, O Lord!
I will keep Your statutes.
146 I cry out to You;
Save me, and I will keep Your
    testimonies.
147 I rise before the dawning of
    the morning,
And cry for help;
I hope in Your word.
148 My eyes are awake through
    the *night* watches,
That I may meditate on Your
    word.
149 Hear my voice according to
    Your lovingkindness;
O Lord, revive me according
    to Your justice.
150 They draw near who follow
    after wickedness;
They are far from Your law.

151 You *are* near, O Lord,
And all Your commandments
    are truth.
152 Concerning Your testimonies,
I have known of old that You
    have founded them forever.

ר **RESH**

153 Consider my affliction and
    deliver me,
For I do not forget Your law.
154 Plead my cause and redeem
    me;
Revive me according to Your
    word.
155 Salvation *is* far from the
    wicked,
For they do not seek Your
    statutes.
156 Great *are* Your tender
    mercies, O Lord;
Revive me according to Your
    judgments.
157 Many *are* my persecutors and
    my enemies,
Yet I do not turn from Your
    testimonies.
158 I see the treacherous,
    and am disgusted,
Because they do not keep
    Your word.
159 Consider how I love Your
    precepts;
Revive me, O Lord, according
    to Your lovingkindness.
160 The entirety of Your word *is*
    truth,
And every one of Your
    righteous judgments
endures forever.

ש **SHIN**

161 Princes persecute me without
    a cause,
But my heart stands in awe of
    Your word.
162 I rejoice at Your word
As one who finds great
    treasure.

414

163 I hate and abhor lying,
But I love Your law.
164 Seven times a day I praise
You,
Because of Your righteous
judgments.
165 Great peace have those who
love Your law,
And nothing causes them to
stumble.
166 Lord, I hope for Your
salvation,
And I do Your
commandments.
167 My soul keeps Your
testimonies,
And I love them exceedingly.
168 I keep Your precepts and
Your testimonies,
For all my ways *are* before
You.

ת TAU

169 Let my cry come before You,
O Lord;
Give me understanding
according to Your word.
170 Let my supplication come
before You;
Deliver me according to Your
word.
171 My lips shall utter praise,
For You teach me Your
statutes.
172 My tongue shall speak of
Your word,
For all Your commandments
are righteousness.
173 Let Your hand become my
help,
For I have chosen Your
precepts.
174 I long for Your salvation, O
Lord,
And Your law *is* my delight.
175 Let my soul live,
and it shall praise You;
And let Your judgments help
me.
176 I have gone astray like a lost
sheep;
Seek Your servant,

For I do not forget Your
commandments.

PSALM 120

A Song of Ascents.

I N my distress I cried to the
Lord,
And He heard me.
2 Deliver my soul, O Lord, from
lying lips
And from a deceitful tongue.

3 What shall be given to you,
Or what shall be done to you,
You false tongue?
4 Sharp arrows of the warrior,
With coals of the broom tree!

5 Woe is me, that I sojourn in
Meshech,
That I dwell among the tents
of Kedar!
6 My soul has dwelt too long
With one who hates peace.
7 I *am* for peace;
But when I speak, they *are* for
war.

PSALM 121

A Song of Ascents.

I WILL lift up my eyes to the
hills—
From whence comes my help?
2 My help *comes* from the Lord,
Who made heaven and earth.

3 He will not allow your foot to
be moved;
He who keeps you will not
slumber.
4 Behold, He who keeps Israel
Shall neither slumber nor
sleep.

5 The Lord *is* your keeper;
The Lord *is* your shade at
your right hand.
6 The sun shall not strike you
by day,
Nor the moon by night.

7 The LORD shall preserve you
    from all evil;
    He shall preserve your soul.
8 The LORD shall preserve your
    going out and your coming
    in
    From this time forth,
    and even forevermore.

PSALM 122

A Song of Ascents. Of David.

I WAS glad when they said to
    me,
    Let us go into the house of
    the LORD."
2 Our feet have been standing
    Within your gates, O
    Jerusalem!

3 Jerusalem is built
    As a city that is compact
    together,
4 Where the tribes go up,
    The tribes of the LORD,
    To the Testimony of Israel,
    To give thanks to the name of
    the LORD.
5 For thrones are set there for
    judgment,
    The thrones of the house of
    David.

6 Pray for the peace of
    Jerusalem:
    "May they prosper who love
    you.
7 Peace be within your walls,
    Prosperity within your
    palaces."
8 For the sake of my brethren
    and companions,
    I will now say, "Peace *be*
    within you."
9 Because of the house of the
    LORD our God
    I will seek your good.

PSALM 123

A Song of Ascents.

UNTO You I lift up my eyes,
    O You who dwell in the
    heavens.

2 Behold, as the eyes of servants
    look to the hand of their
    masters,
    As the eyes of a maid to the
    hand of her mistress,
    So our eyes *look* to the LORD
    our God,
    Until He has mercy on us.

3 Have mercy on us, O LORD,
    have mercy on us!
    For we are exceedingly filled
    with contempt.
4 Our soul is exceedingly filled
    With the scorn of those who
    are at ease,
    With the contempt of the
    proud.

PSALM 124

A Song of Ascents. Of David.

"IF it had not been the LORD
    who was on our side,"
    Let Israel now say—
2 "If it had not been the LORD
    who was on our side,
    When men rose up against us,
3 Then they would have
    swallowed us alive,
    When their wrath was kindled
    against us;
4 Then the waters would have
    overwhelmed us,
    The stream would have gone
    over our soul;
5 Then the swollen waters
    Would have gone over our
    soul."

6 Blessed *be* the LORD,
    Who has not given us *as* prey
    to their teeth.
7 Our soul has escaped as a bird
    from the snare of the
    fowlers;
    The snare is broken,
    and we have escaped.
8 Our help *is* in the name of the
    LORD,
    Who made heaven and earth.

PSALM 125

A Song of Ascents.

THOSE who trust in the LORD
Are like Mount Zion,
Which cannot be moved,
but abides forever.
2 As the mountains surround
Jerusalem,
So the LORD surrounds His
people
From this time forth and
forever.

3 For the scepter of wickedness
shall not rest
On the land allotted to the
righteous,
Lest the righteous reach out
their hands to iniquity.

4 Do good, O LORD, to *those
who are* good,
And to *those who are* upright
in their hearts.

5 As for such as turn aside to
their crooked ways,
The LORD shall lead them
away
With the workers of iniquity.

Peace *be* upon Israel!

PSALM 126

A Song of Ascents.

WHEN the LORD brought back
the captivity of Zion,
We were like those who
dream.
2 Then our mouth was filled
with laughter,
And our tongue with singing.
Then they said among the
nations,
"The LORD has done great
things for them."
3 The LORD has done great
things for us,
Whereof we are glad.

4 Bring back our captivity, O
LORD,

As the streams in the South.

5 Those who sow in tears
Shall reap in joy.
6 He who continually goes forth
weeping,
Bearing seed for sowing,
Shall doubtless come again
with rejoicing,
Bringing his sheaves *with him.*

PSALM 127

A Song of Ascents. Of Solomon.

UNLESS the LORD builds the
house,
They labor in vain who build
it;
Unless the LORD guards the
city,
The watchman stays awake in
vain.
2 *It is* vain for you to rise up
early,
To sit up late,
To eat the bread of sorrows;
For so He gives His beloved
sleep.

3 Behold, children *are* a heritage
from the LORD,
The fruit of the womb *is His*
reward.
4 Like arrows in the hand of a
warrior,
So *are* the children of one's
youth.
5 Happy *is* the man who has his
quiver full of them;
They shall not be ashamed,
But shall speak with their
enemies in the gate.

PSALM 128

A Song of Ascents.

BLESSED *is* every one who
fears the LORD,
Who walks in His ways.

2 When you eat the labor of
your hands,

417

You *shall be* happy,
  and *it shall be* well with
    you.
3 Your wife *shall be* like a
    fruitful vine
  In the very heart of your
    house,
  Your children like olive plants
    All around your table.
4 Behold, thus shall the man be
    blessed
  Who fears the Lord.

5 The Lord bless you out of
    Zion,
  And may you see the good of
    Jerusalem
  All the days of your life.
6 Yes, may you see your
    children's children.

  Peace *be* upon Israel!

PSALM 129

A Song of Ascents.

"MANY a time they have
    afflicted me from my
    youth,"
  Let Israel now say—
2 "Many a time they have
    afflicted me from my youth;
  Yet they have not prevailed
    against me.
3 The plowers plowed on my
    back;
  They made their furrows
    long."
4 The Lord *is* righteous;
  He has cut in pieces the cords
    of the wicked.

5 Let all those who hate Zion
  Be put to shame and turned
    back.
6 Let them be as the grass *on*
    the housetops,
  Which withers before it grows
    up,
7 With which the reaper does
    not fill his hand,
  Nor he who binds sheaves, his
    arms.

8 Neither let those who pass by
    them say,
  The blessing of the Lord *be*
    upon you;
  We bless you in the name of
    the Lord!"

PSALM 130

A Song of Ascents.

OUT of the depths I have cried
    to You, O Lord;
2 Lord, hear my voice!
  Let Your ears be attentive
  To the voice of my
    supplications.

3 If You, Lord, should mark
    iniquities,
  O Lord, who could stand?
4 But *there is* forgiveness with
    You,
  That You may be feared.

5 I wait for the Lord, my soul
    waits,
  And in His word I do hope.
6 My soul *waits* for the Lord
  More than those who watch
    for the morning—
  I say, more than those who
    watch for the morning.

7 O Israel, hope in the Lord;
  For with the Lord *there is*
    mercy,
  And with Him *is* abundant
    redemption.
8 And He shall redeem Israel
  From all his iniquities.

PSALM 131

A Song of Ascents. Of David.

LORD, my heart is not haughty,
    Nor my eyes lofty.
  Neither do I concern myself
    with great matters,
  Nor with things too profound
    for me.

2 Surely I have calmed and
    quieted my soul,

Like a weaned child with his
    mother;
Like a weaned child *is* my
    soul within me.

3 O Israel, hope in the LORD
From this time forth and
    forever.

PSALM 132

A Song of Ascents.

LORD, remember David
    And all his afflictions;
2 How he swore to the LORD,
    And vowed to the Mighty *God*
    of Jacob:
3 "Surely I will not go into the
    chamber of my house,
Or go up to the comfort of my
    bed;
4 I will not give sleep to my
    eyes
Or slumber to my eyelids,
5 Until I find a place for the
    LORD,
A dwelling place for the
    Mighty *God* of Jacob."

6 Behold, we heard of it in
    Ephrathah;
We found it in the fields of
    the woods.
7 Let us go into His tabernacle;
Let us worship at His
    footstool.
8 Arise, O LORD, to Your resting
    place,
You and the ark of Your
    strength.
9 Let Your priests be clothed
    with righteousness,
And let Your saints shout for
    joy.

10 For Your servant David's
    sake,
Do not turn away the face of
    Your Anointed.

11 The LORD has sworn *in* truth
    to David;
He will not turn from it:

"I will set upon your throne
    the fruit of your body.
12 If your sons will keep My
    covenant
And My testimony which I
    shall teach them,
Their sons also shall sit upon
    your throne forevermore."

13 For the LORD has chosen
    Zion;
He has desired *it* for His
    habitation:
14 "This *is* My resting place
    forever;
Here I will dwell, for I have
    desired it.
15 I will abundantly bless her
    provision;
I will satisfy her poor with
    bread.
16 I will also clothe her priests
    with salvation,
And her saints shall shout
    aloud for joy.
17 There I will make the horn of
    David grow;
I will prepare a lamp for My
    Anointed.
18 His enemies I will clothe with
    shame,
But upon Himself His crown
    shall flourish."

PSALM 133

A Song of Ascents. Of David.

BEHOLD, how good and how
    pleasant *it is*
For brethren to dwell together
    in unity!

2 *It is* like the precious oil upon
    the head,
Running down on the beard,
The beard of Aaron,
Running down on the edge of
    his garments.
3 *It is* like the dew of Hermon,
Descending upon the
    mountains of Zion;
For there the LORD
    commanded the blessing—
Life forevermore.

PSALM 134

A Song of Ascents.

BEHOLD, bless the LORD,
　All *you* servants of the LORD,
　Who by night stand in the
　　house of the LORD!
2 Lift up your hands *in* the
　　sanctuary,
　And bless the LORD.

3 The LORD who made heaven
　　and earth
　Bless you from Zion!

PSALM 135

PRAISE the LORD!

　Praise the name of the LORD;
　Praise *Him*,
　　O you servants of the LORD!
2 You who stand in the house
　　of the LORD,
　In the courts of the house of
　　our God,
3 Praise the LORD, for the LORD
　　is good;
　Sing praises to His name,
　　for *it is* pleasant.
4 For the LORD has chosen
　　Jacob for Himself,
　Israel for His special treasure.

5 For I know that the LORD *is*
　　great,
　And our Lord *is* above all
　　gods.
6 Whatever the LORD pleases He
　　does,
　In heaven and in earth,
　In the seas and in all deep
　　places.
7 He causes the vapors to
　　ascend from the ends of the
　　earth;
　He makes lightning for the
　　rain;
　He brings the wind out of His
　　treasuries.

8 He destroyed the firstborn of
　　Egypt,
　Both of man and beast.

9 He sent signs and wonders
　　into the midst of you, O
　　Egypt,
　Upon Pharaoh and all his
　　servants.
10 He defeated many nations
　And slew mighty kings—
11 Sihon king of the Amorites,
　Og king of Bashan,
　And all the kingdoms of
　　Canaan—
12 And gave their land *as* a
　　heritage,
　A heritage to Israel His
　　people.

13 Your name, O LORD, *endures*
　　forever,
　Your fame, O LORD,
　　throughout all generations.
14 For the LORD will judge His
　　people,
　And He will have compassion
　　on His servants.

15 The idols of the nations *are*
　　silver and gold,
　The work of men's hands.
16 They have mouths,
　　but they do not speak;
　Eyes they have, but they do
　　not see;
17 They have ears, but they do
　　not hear;
　Nor is there *any* breath in
　　their mouths.
18 Those who make them are
　　like them;
　So is everyone who trusts in
　　them.

19 Bless the LORD, O house of
　　Israel!
　Bless the LORD, O house of
　　Aaron!
20 Bless the LORD, O house of
　　Levi!
　You who fear the LORD,
　　bless the LORD!
21 Blessed be the LORD out of
　　Zion,
　Who dwells in Jerusalem!

Praise the LORD!

PSALM 136

Oh, give thanks to the LORD,
for *He is* good!
For His mercy *endures*
forever.

2 Oh, give thanks to the God of
gods!
For His mercy *endures*
forever.

3 Oh, give thanks to the Lord of
lords!
For His mercy *endures*
forever:

4 To Him who alone does great
wonders,
For His mercy *endures*
forever;

5 To Him who by wisdom made
the heavens,
For His mercy *endures*
forever;

6 To Him who laid out the earth
above the waters,
For His mercy *endures*
forever;

7 To Him who made great
lights,
For His mercy *endures*
forever—

8 The sun to rule by day,
For His mercy *endures*
forever;

9 The moon and stars to rule by
night,
For His mercy *endures*
forever.

10 To Him who struck Egypt in
their firstborn,
For His mercy *endures*
forever;

11 And brought out Israel from
among them,
For His mercy *endures*
forever;

12 With a strong hand,
and with an
outstretched arm,
For His mercy *endures*
forever;

13 To Him who divided the Red
Sea in two,

14 And made Israel pass through
the midst of it,
For His mercy *endures*
forever;

15 But overthrew Pharaoh and
his army in the Red
Sea,
For His mercy *endures*
forever;

16 To Him who led His people
through the wilderness,
For His mercy *endures*
forever;

17 To Him who struck down
great kings,
For His mercy *endures*
forever;

18 And slew famous kings,
For His mercy *endures*
forever—

19 Sihon king of the Amorites,
For His mercy *endures*
forever;

20 And Og king of Bashan,
For His mercy *endures*
forever—

21 And gave their land as a
heritage,
For His mercy *endures*
forever;

22 A heritage to Israel His
servant,
For His mercy *endures*
forever.

23 Who remembered us in our
lowly state,
For His mercy *endures*
forever;

24 And rescued us from our
enemies,
For His mercy *endures*
forever;

25 Who gives food to all flesh,
For His mercy *endures*
forever.

26 Oh, give thanks to the God of
heaven!
For His mercy *endures*
forever.

PSALM 137

B Y the rivers of Babylon,
　　There we sat down, yea, we
　　wept
　　When we remembered Zion.
2　We hung our harps
　　Upon the willows in the midst
　　　of it.
3　For there those who carried
　　　us away captive required of
　　　us a song,
　　And those who plundered us
　　　required of us mirth,
　　Saying, "Sing us *one* of the
　　　songs of Zion!"

4　How shall we sing the LORD's
　　　song
　　In a foreign land?
5　If I forget you, O Jerusalem,
　　Let my right hand forget *her
　　　skill!*
6　If I do not remember you,
　　Let my tongue cling to the
　　　roof of my mouth—
　　If I do not exalt Jerusalem
　　Above my chief joy.

7　Remember, O LORD, against
　　　the sons of Edom
　　The day of Jerusalem,
　　Who said, "Raze *it,* raze *it,*
　　To its very foundation!"

8　O daughter of Babylon,
　　　who are to be destroyed,
　　Happy *shall he be* who repays
　　　you as you have served us!
9　Happy *shall he be* who takes
　　　and dashes
　　Your little ones against the
　　　rock.

PSALM 138

A Psalm of David.

I WILL praise You with my
　　whole heart;
　　Before the gods I will sing
　　　praises to You.
2　I will worship toward Your
　　　holy temple,
　　And praise Your name

See Romans 8:38–39, page 195

For Your lovingkindness and
　　Your truth;
　　For You have magnified Your
　　　word above all Your name.
3　In the day when I cried out,
　　　You answered me,
　　And made me bold *with*
　　　strength in my soul.

4　All the kings of the earth shall
　　　praise You, O LORD,
　　When they hear the words of
　　　Your mouth.
5　Yes, they shall sing of the
　　　ways of the LORD,
　　For great *is* the glory of the
　　　LORD.
6　Though the LORD *is* on high,
　　Yet He regards the lowly;
　　But the proud He knows from
　　　afar.

7　Though I walk in the midst of
　　　trouble, You will revive me;
　　You will stretch out Your
　　　hand
　　Against the wrath of my
　　　enemies,
　　And Your right hand will save
　　　me.
8　The LORD will perfect *that
　　　which* concerns me;
　　Your mercy, O LORD, *endures*
　　　forever;
　　Do not forsake the works of
　　　Your hands.

PSALM 139

For the Chief Musician. A Psalm of David.

O LORD, You have searched
　　me and known *me.*
2　You know my sitting down
　　　and my rising up;
　　You understand my thought
　　　afar off.
3　You comprehend my path
　　　and my lying down,
　　And are acquainted with all
　　　my ways.
4　For *there is* not a word on my
　　　tongue,

But behold, O LORD,
  You know it altogether.
5 You have hedged me behind
    and before,
  And laid Your hand upon me.
6 *Such* knowledge *is* too
    wonderful for me;
  It is high, I cannot *attain* it.

❤ 7 Where can I go from Your
      Spirit?
  Or where can I flee from Your
    presence?
8 If I ascend into heaven, You
    are there;
  If I make my bed in hell,
    behold, You *are there*.
9 *If* I take the wings of the
    morning,
  And dwell in the uttermost
    parts of the sea,
10 Even there Your hand shall
     lead me,
  And Your right hand shall
    hold me.
11 If I say, "Surely the darkness
     shall fall on me,"
  Even the night shall be light
    about me;
12 Indeed, the darkness shall not
     hide from You,
  But the night shines as the
    day;
  The darkness and the light *are*
    both alike *to* You.

❤ 13 For You have formed my
      inward parts;
  You have covered me in my
    mother's womb.
14 I will praise You, for I am
     fearfully *and* wonderfully
     made;
  Marvelous are Your works,
  And *that* my soul knows very
    well.
15 My frame was not hidden
     from You,
  When I was made in secret,
  And skillfully wrought in the
    lowest parts of the earth.
16 Your eyes saw my substance,
     being yet unformed.

And in Your book they all
    were written,
  The days fashioned for me,
  When *as yet there were* none
    of them.

17 How precious also are Your
     thoughts to me, O God!
  How great is the sum of them!
18 *If* I should count them, they
     would be more in number
     than the sand;
  When I awake, I am still with
    You.

19 Oh, that You would slay the
     wicked, O God!
  Depart from me, therefore,
    you bloodthirsty men.
20 For they speak against You
     wickedly;
  Your enemies take *Your name*
    in vain.
21 Do I not hate them, O LORD,
     who hate You?
  And do I not loathe those who
    rise up against You?
22 I hate them with perfect
     hatred;
  I count them my enemies.

23 Search me, O God,
     and know my heart;
  Try me, and know my
    anxieties;
24 And see if *there is any* wicked
     way in me,
  And lead me in the way
    everlasting.

PSALM 140

To the Chief Musician. A Psalm of David.

DELIVER me, O LORD, from
     evil men;
  Preserve me from violent men,
2 Who plan evil things in *their*
    hearts;
  They continually gather
    together *for* war.
3 They sharpen their tongues
    like a serpent;

See Acts 2:42, page 147

The poison of asps *is* under
their lips.   Selah

4 Keep me, O LORD, from the
   hands of the wicked;
   Preserve me from violent men,
   Who have purposed to make
   my steps stumble.
5 The proud have hidden a
   snare for me, and cords;
   They have spread a net by the
   wayside;
   They have set traps for me.
                      Selah

6 I said to the LORD: "You *are*
   my God;
   Hear the voice of my
   supplications, O LORD.
7 O GOD the Lord, the strength
   of my salvation,
   You have covered my head in
   the day of battle.
8 Do not grant, O LORD, the
   desires of the wicked;
   Do not further his *wicked*
   scheme,
   Lest they be exalted.   Selah

9 "*As for* the head of those who
   surround me,
   Let the evil of their lips cover
   them;
10 Let burning coals fall upon
   them;
   Let them be cast into the fire,
   Into deep pits, that they rise
   not up again.
11 Let not a slanderer be
   established in the earth;
   Let evil hunt the violent man
   to overthrow *him*."

12 I know that the LORD will
   maintain
   The cause of the afflicted,
   And justice for the poor.
13 Surely the righteous shall give
   thanks to Your name;
   The upright shall dwell in
   Your presence.

PSALM 141

A Psalm of David.

LORD, I cry out to You;
   Make haste to me!
   Give ear to my voice when I
   cry out to You.
2 Let my prayer be set before
   You *as* incense,
   The lifting up of my hands *as*
   the evening sacrifice.

3 Set a guard, O LORD, over my
   mouth;
   Keep watch over the door of
   my lips.
4 Do not incline my heart
   to any evil thing,
   To practice wicked works
   With men who work iniquity;
   And do not let me eat of their
   delicacies.

5 Let the righteous strike me;
   It shall be a kindness.
   And let him reprove me;
   It shall be as excellent oil;
   Let my head not refuse it.

   For still my prayer *is* against
   the deeds of the wicked.
6 Their judges are overthrown
   by the sides of the cliff,
   And they hear my words,
   for they are sweet.
7 Our bones are scattered at the
   mouth of the grave,
   As when one plows and
   breaks up the earth.

8 But my eyes *are* upon You,
   O GOD the Lord;
   In You I take refuge;
   Do not leave my soul
   destitute.
9 Keep me from the snares
   which they have laid for me,
   And from the traps of the
   workers of iniquity.
10 Let the wicked fall into their
   own nets,
   While I escape safely.

PSALM 142

A Contemplation of David. A Prayer when he
was in the cave.

I CRY out to the LORD with my
voice;
With my voice to the LORD I
make my supplication.
2 I pour out my complaint
before Him;
I declare before Him my
trouble.

3 When my spirit was
overwhelmed within me,
Then You knew my path.
In the way in which I walk
They have secretly set a snare
for me.
4 Look on *my* right hand and
see,
For *there is* no one who
acknowledges me;
Refuge has failed me;
No one cares for my soul.

5 I cried out to You, O LORD:
I said, "You *are* my refuge,
My portion in the land
of the living.
6 Attend to my cry,
For I am brought very low;
Deliver me from my
persecutors,
For they are stronger than I.
7 Bring my soul out of prison,
That I may praise Your name;
The righteous shall surround
me,
For You shall deal bountifully
with me."

PSALM 143

A Psalm of David.

H EAR my prayer, O LORD,
Give ear to my
supplications!
In Your faithfulness answer
me,
And in Your righteousness.
2 Do not enter into judgment
with Your servant,

For in Your sight no one
living is righteous.

3 For the enemy has persecuted
my soul;
He has crushed my life to the
ground;
He has made me dwell in
darkness,
Like those who have long
been dead.
4 Therefore my spirit is
overwhelmed within me;
My heart within me is
distressed.

5 I remember the days of old;
I meditate on all Your works;
I muse on the work of Your
hands.
6 I spread out my hands to You;
My soul *longs* for You like a
thirsty land.   Selah

7 Answer me speedily, O LORD;
My spirit fails!
Do not hide Your face from
me,
Lest I be like those who go
down into the pit.
8 Cause me to hear Your
lovingkindness in the
morning,
For in You do I trust;
Cause me to know the way in
which I should walk,
For I lift up my soul to You.

9 Deliver me, O LORD, from my
enemies;
In You I take shelter.
10 Teach me to do Your will,
For You *are* my God;
Your Spirit *is* good.
Lead me in the land of
uprightness.

11 Revive me, O LORD, for Your
name's sake!
For Your righteousness' sake
bring my soul out of
trouble.

12 In Your mercy cut off my
      enemies,
   And destroy all those who
      afflict my soul;
   For I *am* Your servant.

PSALM 144

A Psalm of David.

BLESSED *be* the LORD my
      Rock,
   Who trains my hands for war,
   And my fingers for battle—
2 My lovingkindness and my
      fortress,
   My high tower and my
      deliverer,
   My shield and *the One* in
      whom I take refuge,
   Who subdues my people under
      me.

3 LORD, what *is* man,
      that You take knowledge of
      him?
   Or the son of man, that You
      are mindful of him?
4 Man is like a breath;
   His days *are* like a passing
      shadow.

5 Bow down Your heavens, O
      LORD, and come down;
   Touch the mountains,
      and they shall smoke.
6 Flash forth lightning and
      scatter them;
   Shoot out Your arrows
      and destroy them.
7 Stretch out Your hand from
      above;
   Rescue me and deliver me out
      of great waters,
   From the hand of foreigners,
8 Whose mouth speaks vain
      words,
   And whose right hand *is* a
      right hand of falsehood.

9 I will sing a new song to You,
      O God;
   On a harp of ten strings I will
      sing praises to You,

10 *The One* who gives salvation
      to kings,
   Who delivers David His
      servant
   From the deadly sword.

11 Rescue me and deliver me
      from the hand of foreigners,
   Whose mouth speaks vain
      words,
   And whose right hand *is* a
      right hand of falsehood—
12 That our sons *may be* as
      plants grown up in their
      youth;
   That our daughters *may be* as
      pillars,
   Sculptured in palace style;
13 *That* our barns *may be* full,
   Supplying all kinds of
      produce;
   That our sheep may bring
      forth thousands
   And ten thousands in our
      fields;
14 *That* our oxen *may be* well-
      laden;
   That there be no breaking in
      or going out;
   That there be no outcry in our
      streets.
15 Happy *are* the people
      who are in such a state;
   Happy *are* the people
      whose God *is* the LORD!

PSALM 145

A Praise of David.

I WILL extol You, my God, O
      King;
   And I will bless Your name
      forever and ever.
2 Every day I will bless You,
   And I will praise Your name
      forever and ever.
3 Great *is* the LORD,
      and greatly to be praised;
   And His greatness *is*
      unsearchable.

4 One generation shall praise
      Your works to another,

426

And shall declare Your mighty acts.

5 I will meditate on the glorious splendor of Your majesty,
And on Your wondrous works.

6 *Men* shall speak of the might of Your awesome acts,
And I will declare Your greatness.

7 They shall utter the memory of Your great goodness,
And shall sing of Your righteousness.

8 The LORD *is* gracious and full of compassion,
Slow to anger and great in mercy.

9 The LORD *is* good to all,
And His tender mercies *are* over all His works.

10 All Your works shall praise You, O LORD,
And Your saints shall bless You.

11 They shall speak of the glory of Your kingdom,
And talk of Your power,

12 To make known to the sons of men His mighty acts,
And the glorious majesty of His kingdom.

13 Your kingdom *is* an everlasting kingdom,
And Your dominion *endures* throughout all generations.

14 The LORD upholds all who fall,
And raises up all *those who are* bowed down.

15 The eyes of all look expectantly to You,
And You give them their food in due season.

16 You open Your hand
And satisfy the desire of every living thing.

17 The LORD *is* righteous in all His ways,
Gracious in all His works.

18 The LORD *is* near to all who call upon Him,
To all who call upon Him in truth.

19 He will fulfill the desire of those who fear Him;
He also will hear their cry and save them.

20 The LORD preserves all who love Him,
But all the wicked He will destroy.

21 My mouth shall speak the praise of the LORD,
And all flesh shall bless His holy name
Forever and ever.

PSALM 146

PRAISE the LORD!

Praise the LORD, O my soul!
2 While I live I will praise the LORD;
I will sing praises to my God while I have my being.

3 Do not put your trust in princes,
Nor in a son of man,
in whom *there is* no help.

4 His spirit departs,
he returns to his earth;
In that very day his plans perish.

5 Happy *is* he who *has* the God of Jacob for his help,
Whose hope *is* in the LORD his God,

6 Who made heaven and earth,
The sea, and all that *is* in them;
Who keeps truth forever,

7 Who executes justice for the oppressed,
Who gives food to the hungry.
The LORD gives freedom to the prisoners.

8 The LORD opens *the eyes of* the blind;

The LORD raises those who are
    bowed down;
The LORD loves the righteous.
9 The LORD watches over the
    strangers;
He relieves the fatherless and
    widow;
But the way of the wicked He
    turns upside down.

10 The LORD shall reign forever—
    Your God, O Zion, to all
    generations.

Praise the LORD!

PSALM 147

PRAISE the LORD!
For *it is* good to sing praises
    to our God;
For *it is* pleasant, *and* praise is
    beautiful.

2 The LORD builds up Jerusalem;
He gathers together the
    outcasts of Israel.
3 He heals the brokenhearted
And binds up their wounds.
4 He counts the number of the
    stars;
He calls them all by name.
5 Great *is* our Lord,
    and mighty in power;
His understanding *is* infinite.
6 The LORD lifts up the humble;
He casts the wicked down to
    the ground.

7 Sing to the LORD with
    thanksgiving;
Sing praises on the harp to
    our God,
8 Who covers the heavens with
    clouds,
Who prepares rain for the
    earth,
Who makes grass to grow on
    the mountains.
9 He gives to the beast its food,
And to the young ravens that
    cry.

10 He does not delight
    in the strength of the horse;
He takes no pleasure
    in the legs of a man.
11 The LORD takes pleasure
    in those who fear Him,
In those who hope in His
    mercy.

12 Praise the LORD, O Jerusalem!
Praise your God, O Zion!
13 For He has strengthened the
    bars of your gates;
He has blessed your children
    within you.
14 He makes peace *in* your
    borders,
And fills you with the finest
    wheat.

15 He sends out His command *to*
    the earth;
His word runs very swiftly.
16 He gives snow like wool;
He scatters the frost like
    ashes;
17 He casts out His hail like
    morsels;
Who can stand before His
    cold?
18 He sends out His word
    and melts them;
He causes His wind to blow,
    and the waters flow.

19 He declares His word to
    Jacob,
His statutes and His
    judgments to Israel.
20 He has not dealt thus with
    any nation;
And *as for His* judgments,
    they have not known them.

Praise the LORD!

PSALM 148

PRAISE the LORD!

Praise the LORD from the
    heavens;
Praise Him in the heights!

2 Praise Him, all His angels;
Praise Him, all His hosts!
3 Praise Him, sun and moon;
Praise Him, all you stars of
light!
4 Praise Him, you heavens of
heavens,
And you waters above the
heavens!

5 Let them praise the name of
the LORD,
For He commanded
and they were created.
6 He has also established them
forever and ever;
He has made a decree which
shall not pass away.

7 Praise the LORD from the
earth,
You great sea creatures and
all the depths;
8 Fire and hail, snow and
clouds;
Stormy wind, fulfilling His
word;
9 Mountains and all hills;
Fruitful trees and all cedars;
10 Beasts and all cattle;
Creeping things and flying
fowl;
11 Kings of the earth and all
peoples;
Princes and all judges of the
earth;
12 Both young men and maidens;
Old men and children.

13 Let them praise the name of
the LORD,
For His name alone is exalted;
His glory *is* above the earth
and heaven.
14 And He has exalted the horn
of His people,
The praise of all His saints—
Of the children of Israel,
A people near to Him.

Praise the LORD!

PSALM 149

PRAISE the LORD!

Sing to the LORD a new song,
And His praise in the
congregation of saints.

2 Let Israel rejoice in their
Maker;
Let the children of Zion be
joyful in their King.
3 Let them praise His name
with the dance;
Let them sing praises to Him
with the timbrel and harp.
4 For the LORD takes pleasure in
His people;
He will beautify the humble
with salvation.

5 Let the saints be joyful in
glory;
Let them sing aloud on their
beds.
6 *Let* the high praises of God *be*
in their mouth,
And a two-edged sword in
their hand,
7 To execute vengeance on the
nations,
And punishments on the
peoples;
8 To bind their kings with
chains,
And their nobles with fetters
of iron;
9 To execute on them the
written judgment—
This honor have all His saints.

Praise the LORD!

PSALM 150

PRAISE the LORD!

Praise God in His sanctuary;
Praise Him in His mighty
firmament!

2 Praise Him for His mighty
acts;
Praise Him according to His
excellent greatness!

Let All Things Praise God

3 Praise Him with the sound of
  the trumpet;
  Praise Him with the lute and
  harp!
4 Praise Him with the timbrel
  and dance;
  Praise Him with stringed
  instruments and flutes!

5 Praise Him with loud cymbals;
  Praise Him with high
  sounding cymbals!

6 Let everything that has breath
  praise the LORD.

Praise the LORD!

THE BOOK OF
PROVERBS

THE proverbs of Solomon the son of David, king of Israel:

2 To know wisdom and
  instruction,
  To perceive the words of
  understanding,
3 To receive the instruction of
  wisdom,
  Justice, judgment, and equity;
4 To give prudence to the simple,
  To the young man knowledge
  and discretion—
5 A wise *man* will hear
  and increase learning,
  And a man of understanding
  will attain wise counsel,
6 To understand a proverb
  and an enigma,
  The words of the wise
  and their riddles.

7 The fear of the LORD *is* the
  beginning of knowledge,
  But fools despise wisdom and
  instruction.

8 My son, hear the instruction
  of your father,
  And do not forsake the law
  of your mother;
9 For they *will be* graceful
  ornaments on your head,
  And chains about your neck.

10 My son, if sinners entice you,
  Do not consent.
11 If they say, "Come with us,
  Let us lie in wait to *shed* blood;
  Let us lurk secretly for the
  innocent without cause;
12 Let us swallow them alive like
  Sheol,
  And whole, like those who go
  down to the Pit;
13 We shall find all *kinds* of
  precious possessions,
  We shall fill our houses with
  spoil;

14 Cast in your lot among us,
  Let us all have one purse"—
15 My son, do not walk in the
  way with them,
  Keep your foot from their path;
16 For their feet run to evil,
  And they make haste to shed
  blood.
17 Surely, in vain the net is
  spread
  In the sight of any bird;
18 But they lie in wait for their
  own blood,
  They lurk secretly for their
  own lives.
19 So *are* the ways of everyone
  who is greedy for gain;
  It takes away the life of its
  owners.

20 Wisdom calls aloud outside;
  She raises her voice in the
  open squares.
21 She cries out in the chief
  concourses,
  At the openings of the gates in
  the city
  She speaks her words:
22 "How long, you simple ones,
  will you love simplicity?
  For scorners delight in their
  scorning,
  And fools hate knowledge.
23 Turn at my reproof;
  Surely I will pour out my spirit
  on you;
  I will make my words known
  to you.
24 Because I have called and you
  refused,
  I have stretched out my hand
  and no one regarded,
25 Because you disdained all my
  counsel,
  And would have none of my
  reproof,
26 I also will laugh at your
  calamity;
  I will mock when your terror
  comes,

27 When your terror comes like a
   storm,
   And your destruction comes
   like a whirlwind,
   When distress and anguish
   come upon you.

28 "Then they will call on me,
   but I will not answer;
   They will seek me diligently,
   but they will not find me.
29 Because they hated knowledge
   And did not choose the fear of
   the LORD,
30 They would have none of my
   counsel
   And despised all my reproof,
31 Therefore they shall eat the
   fruit of their own way,
   And be filled to the full with
   their own fancies.
32 For the turning away of the
   simple will slay them,
   And the complacency of fools
   will destroy them;
33 But whoever listens to me
   will dwell safely,
   And will be secure,
   without fear of evil."

2 My son, if you receive my
   words,
   And treasure my commands
   within you,
2 So that you incline your ear to
   wisdom,
   And apply your heart to
   understanding;
3 Yes, if you cry out for
   discernment,
   And lift up your voice for
   understanding,
4 If you seek her as silver,
   And search for her as *for*
   hidden treasures;
5 Then you will understand the
   fear of the LORD,
   And find the knowledge of
   God.
6 For the LORD gives wisdom;
   From His mouth *come*
   knowledge and under-
   standing;

7 He stores up sound wisdom for
   the upright;
   He is a shield to those who
   walk uprightly;
8 He guards the paths of justice,
   And preserves the way of His
   saints.
9 Then you will understand
   righteousness and justice,
   Equity *and* every good path.

10 When wisdom enters your
   heart,
   And knowledge is pleasant to
   your soul,
11 Discretion will preserve you;
   Understanding will keep you,
12 To deliver you from the way of
   evil,
   From the man who speaks
   perverse things,
13 From those who leave the
   paths of uprightness
   To walk in the ways of
   darkness;
14 Who rejoice in doing evil,
   And delight in the perversity
   of the wicked;
15 Whose ways *are* crooked,
   And *who are* devious in their
   paths;
16 To deliver you from the
   immoral woman,
   From the seductress *who*
   flatters with her words,
17 Who forsakes the companion
   of her youth,
   And forgets the covenant of
   her God.
18 For her house leads down to
   death,
   And her paths to the dead;
19 None who go to her return,
   Nor do they regain the paths of
   life—
20 So you may walk in the way of
   goodness,
   And keep *to* the paths of
   righteousness.
21 For the upright will dwell in
   the land,
   And the blameless will remain
   in it;

432

22 But the wicked will be cut off
    from the earth,
    And the unfaithful will be
    uprooted from it.

3 My son, do not forget my law,
    But let your heart keep my
    commands;
2 For length of days and long life
    And peace they will add to
    you.

3 Let not mercy and truth
    forsake you;
    Bind them around your neck,
    Write them on the tablet of
    your heart,
4 *And* so find favor and high
    esteem
    In the sight of God and man.

5 Trust in the LORD with all your
    heart,
    And lean not on your own
    understanding;
6 In all your ways acknowledge
    Him,
    And He shall direct your paths.

7 Do not be wise in your own
    eyes;
    Fear the LORD and depart from
    evil.
8 It will be health to your flesh,
    And strength to your bones.

9 Honor the LORD with your
    possessions,
    And with the firstfruits of all
    your increase;
10 So your barns will be filled
    with plenty,
    And your vats will overflow
    with new wine.

11 My son, do not despise the
    chastening of the LORD,
    Nor detest His correction;
12 For whom the LORD loves He
    corrects,
    Just as a father the son *in
    whom* he delights.

13 Happy *is* the man *who* finds
    wisdom,
    And the man *who* gains
    understanding;
14 For her proceeds *are* better
    than the profits of silver,
    And her gain than fine gold.
15 She *is* more precious than
    rubies,
    And all the things you may
    desire cannot compare with
    her.
16 Length of days *is* in her right
    hand,
    In her left hand riches and
    honor.
17 Her ways *are* ways of
    pleasantness,
    And all her paths *are* peace.
18 She *is* a tree of life to those
    who take hold of her,
    And happy *are all* who retain
    her.

19 The LORD by wisdom
    founded the earth;
    By understanding
    He established the heavens;
20 By His knowledge
    the depths were broken up,
    And clouds drop down the
    dew.

21 My son, let them not depart
    from your eyes—
    Keep sound wisdom and
    discretion;
22 So they will be life to your soul
    And grace to your neck.
23 Then you will walk safely in
    your way,
    And your foot will not stumble.
24 When you lie down,
    you will not be afraid;
    Yes, you will lie down
    and your sleep will be sweet.
25 Do not be afraid of sudden
    terror,
    Nor of trouble from the wicked
    when it comes;
26 For the LORD will be your
    confidence,
    And will keep your foot from
    being caught.

433

Security in Wisdom

27 Do not withhold good from
those to whom it is due,
When it is in the power of your
hand to do *so.*

28 Do not say to your neighbor,
"Go, and come back,
And tomorrow I will give *it,*"
When *you have* it with you.

29 Do not devise evil against your
neighbor,
For he dwells by you for
safety's sake.

30 Do not strive with a man
without cause,
If he has done you no harm.

31 Do not envy the oppressor,
And choose none of his ways;

32 For the perverse *person is* an
abomination to the LORD,
But His secret *counsel
is* with the upright.

33 The curse of the LORD *is* on the
house of the wicked,
But He blesses the habitation
of the just.

34 Surely He scorns the scornful,
But gives grace to the humble.

35 The wise shall inherit glory,
But shame shall be the legacy
of fools.

4 Hear, *my* children,
the instruction of a father,
And give attention to know
understanding;

2 For I give you good doctrine:
Do not forsake my law.

3 When I was my father's son,
Tender and the only one in the
sight of my mother,

4 He also taught me, and said to
me:
"Let your heart retain my
words;
Keep my commands, and live.

5 Get wisdom! Get understanding!
Do not forget, nor turn away
from the words of my mouth.

6 Do not forsake her,
and she will preserve you;
Love her, and she will keep
you.

7 Wisdom *is* the principal thing;
Therefore get wisdom.
And in all your getting,
get understanding.

8 Exalt her, and she will promote
you;
She will bring you honor,
when you embrace her.

9 She will place on your head an
ornament of grace;
A crown of glory she will
deliver to you."

10 Hear, my son, and receive my
sayings,
And the years of your life will
be many.

11 I have taught you in the way
of wisdom;
I have led you in right paths.

12 When you walk, your steps will
not be hindered,
And when you run,
you will not stumble.

13 Take firm hold of instruction,
do not let go;
Keep her, for she *is* your life.

14 Do not enter the path of the
wicked,
And do not walk in the way of
evil.

15 Avoid it, do not travel on it;
Turn away from it and pass on.

16 For they do not sleep
unless they have done evil;
And their sleep is taken away
unless they make *someone*
fall.

17 For they eat the bread of
wickedness,
And drink the wine of violence.

18 But the path of the just *is* like
the shining sun,
That shines ever brighter unto
the perfect day.

19 The way of the wicked *is* like
darkness;
They do not know what makes
them stumble.

20 My son, give attention to my
words;

Incline your ear to my sayings.

21 Do not let them depart from
your eyes;
Keep them in the midst of your
heart;

22 For they *are* life to those who
find them,
And health to all their flesh.

23 Keep your heart with all
diligence,
For out of it *spring* the issues
of life.

24 Put away from you a deceitful
mouth,
And put perverse lips far from
you.

25 Let your eyes look straight
ahead,
And your eyelids look right
before you.

26 Ponder the path of your feet,
And let all your ways be
established.

27 Do not turn to the right or the
left;
Remove your foot from evil.

5 My son, pay attention to my
wisdom;
Lend your ear to my
understanding,

2 That you may preserve
discretion,
And *that* your lips may keep
knowledge.

3 For the lips of an immoral
woman drip honey,
And her mouth *is* smoother
than oil;

4 But in the end she is bitter as
wormwood,
Sharp as a two-edged sword.

5 Her feet go down to death,
Her steps lay hold of hell.

6 Lest you ponder *her* path of
life—
Her ways are unstable;
You do not know *them.*

7 Therefore hear me now, *my*
children,
And do not depart from the
words of my mouth.

8 Remove your way far from her,

And do not go near the door of
her house,

9 Lest you give your honor to
others,
And your years to the cruel
one;

10 Lest aliens be filled with your
wealth,
And your labors *go* to the
house of a foreigner;

11 And you mourn at last,
When your flesh and your
body are consumed,

12 And say:
"How I have hated instruction,
And my heart despised reproof!

13 I have not obeyed the voice of
my teachers,
Nor inclined my ear to those
who instructed me!

14 I was on the verge of total
ruin,
In the midst of the
congregation and assembly."

15 Drink water from your own
cistern,
And running water from your
own well.

16 Should your fountains be
dispersed abroad,
Streams of water in the
streets?

17 Let them be only your own,
And not for strangers with
you.

18 Let your fountain be blessed,
And rejoice with the wife of
your youth.

19 *As a* loving deer and a graceful
doe,
Let her breasts satisfy you at
all times;
And always be enraptured with
her love.

20 For why should you, my son,
be enraptured by an immoral
woman,
And be embraced in the arms
of a seductress?

21 For the ways of man *are* before
the eyes of the Lord,

And He ponders all his paths.

22 His own iniquities entrap the
wicked man,
And he is caught in the cords
of his sin.

23 He shall die for lack of
instruction,
And in the greatness of his
folly he shall go astray.

6 My son, if you become surety
for your friend,
If you have shaken hands in
pledge for a stranger,

2 You are snared by the words of
your *own* mouth;
You are taken by the words of
your mouth.

3 So do this, my son,
and deliver yourself;
For you have come into the
hand of your friend:
Go and humble yourself;
Plead with your friend.

4 Give no sleep to your eyes,
Nor slumber to your eyelids.

5 Deliver yourself like a gazelle
from the hand *of the hunter*,
And like a bird from the hand
of the fowler.

6 Go to the ant, you sluggard!
Consider her ways and be wise,

7 Which, having no captain,
Overseer or ruler,

8 Provides her supplies in the
summer,
And gathers her food in the
harvest.

9 How long will you slumber,
O sluggard?
When will you rise from your
sleep?

10 A little sleep, a little slumber,
A little folding of the hands to
sleep—

11 So shall your poverty come on
you like a robber,
And your need like an armed
man.

12 A worthless person, a wicked
man,

Walks with a perverse mouth;

13 He winks with his eyes,
He shuffles his feet,
He points with his fingers;

14 Perversity *is* in his heart,
He devises evil continually,
He sows discord.

15 Therefore his calamity shall
come suddenly;
Suddenly he shall be broken
without remedy.

16 These six *things* the LORD
hates,
Yes, seven *are* an abomination
to Him:

17 A proud look,
A lying tongue,
Hands that shed innocent
blood,

18 A heart that devises wicked
plans,
Feet that are swift in running
to evil,

19 A false witness *who* speaks
lies,
And one who sows discord
among brethren.

20 My son, keep your father's
command,
And do not forsake the law of
your mother.

21 Bind them continually upon
your heart;
Tie them around your neck.

22 When you roam, they will lead
you;
When you sleep, they will keep
you;
And *when* you awake, they
will speak with you.

23 For the commandment *is* a
lamp,
And the law *is* light;
Reproofs of instruction *are* the
way of life,

24 To keep you from the evil
woman,
From the flattering tongue of a
seductress.

25 Do not lust after her beauty in
your heart,

Nor let her allure you with her
    eyelids.
26 For by means of a harlot
    A man is reduced to a crust of
    bread;
    And an adulteress will prey
    upon his precious life.
27 Can a man take fire to his
    bosom,
    And his clothes not be burned?
28 Can one walk on hot coals,
    And his feet not be seared?
29 So *is* he who goes in to his
    neighbor's wife;
    Whoever touches her shall not
    be innocent.

30 *People* do not despise a thief
    If he steals to satisfy himself
    when he is starving.
31 Yet *when* he is found,
    he must restore sevenfold;
    He may have to give up all the
    substance of his house.
32 Whoever commits adultery
    with a woman lacks
    understanding;
    He *who* does so destroys his
    own soul.
33 Wounds and dishonor he will
    get,
    And his reproach will not be
    wiped away.
34 For jealousy *is* a husband's
    fury;
    Therefore he will not spare in
    the day of vengeance.
35 He will accept no recompense,
    Nor will he be appeased
    though you give many gifts.

7 My son, keep my words,
    And treasure my commands
    within you.
2 Keep my commands and live,
    And my law as the apple of
    your eye.
3 Bind them on your fingers;
    Write them on the tablet of
    your heart.
4 Say to wisdom, "You *are* my
    sister,"
    And call understanding *your*
    nearest kin,

5 That they may keep you from
    the immoral woman,
    From the seductress
    who flatters with her words.

6 For at the window of my house
    I looked through my lattice,
7 And saw among the simple,
    I perceived among the youths,
    A young man devoid of
    understanding,
8 Passing along the street near
    her corner;
    And he took the path to her
    house
9 In the twilight, in the evening,
    In the black and dark night.

10 And there a woman met him,
    With the attire of a harlot,
    and a crafty heart.
11 She *was* loud and rebellious,
    Her feet would not stay at
    home.
12 At times *she was* outside,
    at times in the open square,
    Lurking at every corner.
13 So she caught him and kissed
    him;
    With an impudent face
    she said to him:
14 "*I have* peace offerings with me;
    Today I have paid my vows.
15 So I came out to meet you,
    Diligently to seek your face,
    And I have found you.
16 I have spread my bed with
    tapestry,
    Colored coverings of Egyptian
    linen.
17 I have perfumed my bed
    With myrrh, aloes, and
    cinnamon.
18 Come, let us take our fill of
    love until morning;
    Let us delight ourselves with
    love.
19 For my husband *is* not at
    home;
    He has gone on a long journey;
20 He has taken a bag of money
    with him,

And will come home on the
  appointed day."

21 With her enticing speech
     she caused him to yield,
   With her flattering lips
     she seduced him.
22 Immediately he went after her,
     as an ox goes to the
     slaughter,
   Or as a fool to the correction
     of the stocks,
23 Till an arrow struck his liver.
   As a bird hastens to the snare,
   He did not know it *would take*
     his life.

24 Now therefore, listen to me,
     my children;
   Pay attention to the words of
     my mouth:
25 Do not let your heart turn
     aside to her ways,
   Do not stray into her paths;
26 For she has cast down many
     wounded,
   And all who were slain by her
     were strong *men.*
27 Her house *is* the way to hell,
   Descending to the chambers of
     death.

8 Does not wisdom cry out,
  And understanding lift up her
    voice?
2 She takes her stand on the top
    of the high hill,
  Beside the way, where the
    paths meet.
3 She cries out by the gates,
    at the entry of the city,
  At the entrance of the doors:
4 "To you, O men, I call,
  And my voice *is* to the sons of
    men.
5 O you simple ones,
    understand prudence,
  And you fools,
    be of an understanding heart.
6 Listen, for I will speak of
    excellent things,
  And from the opening of my
    lips *will come* right things;
7 For my mouth will speak truth;

Wickedness *is* an abomination
  to my lips.
8 All the words of my mouth *are*
    with righteousness;
  Nothing crooked or perverse *is*
    in them.
9 They *are* all plain to him
    who understands,
  And right to those
    who find knowledge.
10 Receive my instruction, and
     not silver,
   And knowledge rather than
     choice gold;
11 For wisdom *is* better than
     rubies,
   And all the things one may
     desire cannot be compared
     with her.

12 "I, wisdom, dwell with
     prudence,
   And find out knowledge *and*
     discretion.
13 The fear of the LORD *is* to hate
     evil;
   Pride and arrogance and the
     evil way
   And the perverse mouth I hate.
14 Counsel *is* mine, and sound
     wisdom;
   I *am* understanding, I have
     strength.
15 By me kings reign,
   And rulers decree justice.
16 By me princes rule, and nobles,
   All the judges of the earth.
17 I love those who love me,
   And those who seek me
     diligently will find me.
18 Riches and honor *are* with me,
   Enduring riches and
     righteousness.
19 My fruit *is* better than gold,
     yes, than fine gold,
   And my revenue than choice
     silver.
20 I traverse the way of
     righteousness,
   In the midst of the paths of
     justice,
21 That I may cause those who
     love me to inherit wealth,
   That I may fill their treasuries.

22 "The LORD possessed me at the
   beginning of His way,
   Before His works of old.
23 I have been established from
   everlasting,
   From the beginning, before
   there was ever an earth.
24 When *there were* no depths
   I was brought forth,
   When *there were* no fountains
   abounding with water.
25 Before the mountains were
   settled,
   Before the hills, I was brought
   forth;
26 While as yet He had not made
   the earth or the fields,
   Or the primeval dust of the
   world.
27 When He prepared the
   heavens, I *was* there,
   When He drew a circle on the
   face of the deep,
28 When He established the
   clouds above,
   When He strengthened the
   fountains of the deep,
29 When He assigned to the sea
   its limit,
   So that the waters would not
   transgress His command,
   When He marked out the
   foundations of the earth,
30 Then I was beside Him,
   as a master craftsman;
   And I was daily *His* delight,
   Rejoicing always before Him,
31 Rejoicing in His inhabited
   world,
   And my delight *was* with the
   sons of men.

32 "Now therefore, listen to me,
   my children,
   For blessed *are those who* keep
   my ways.
33 Hear instruction and be wise,
   And do not disdain *it*.
34 Blessed is the man who listens
   to me,
   Watching daily at my gates,

Waiting at the posts of my
   doors.
35 For whoever finds me finds life,
   And obtains favor from the
   LORD;
36 But he who sins against me
   wrongs his own soul;
   All those who hate me love
   death."

9 Wisdom has built her house,
   She has hewn out her seven
   pillars;
2 She has slaughtered her meat,
   She has mixed her wine,
   She has also furnished her
   table.
3 She has sent out her maidens,
   She cries out from the highest
   places of the city,
4 "Whoever *is* simple,
   let him turn in here!"
   As for him who lacks
   understanding, she says to
   him,
5 "Come, eat of my bread
   And drink of the wine *which* I
   have mixed.
6 Forsake foolishness and live,
   And go in the way of
   understanding.

7 "He who reproves a scoffer
   gets shame for himself,
   And he who rebukes a wicked
   man gets himself a blemish.
8 Do not reprove a scoffer,
   lest he hate you;
   Rebuke a wise man,
   and he will love you.
9 Give *instruction* to a wise *man*,
   and he will be still wiser;
   Teach a just *man*,
   and he will increase in
   learning.

10 "The fear of the LORD
   is the beginning of wisdom,
   And the knowledge of the Holy
   One *is* understanding.
11 For by me your days will be
   multiplied,
   And years of life will be added
   to you.

12 If you are wise,
   you are wise for yourself,
   And *if* you scoff,
   you alone will bear *it*."

13 A foolish woman is clamorous;
   She is simple, and knows
   nothing.
14 For she sits at the door of her
   house,
   On a seat *by* the highest places
   of the city,
15 To call to those who pass by,
   Who go straight on their way:
16 "Whoever *is* simple,
   let him turn in here";
   And *as for* him who lacks
   understanding, she says to
   him,
17 "Stolen water is sweet,
   And bread *eaten* in secret is
   pleasant."
18 But he does not know that the
   dead *are* there,
   That her guests *are* in the
   depths of hell.

10 The proverbs of Solomon:

A wise son makes a glad father,
But a foolish son *is* the grief of
his mother.

2 Treasures of wickedness profit
   nothing,
   But righteousness delivers from
   death.
3 The LORD will not allow the
   righteous soul to famish,
   But He casts away the desire of
   the wicked.

4 He who deals *with* a slack
   hand becomes poor,
   But the hand of the diligent
   makes *one* rich.
5 He who gathers in summer
   is a wise son,
   But he who sleeps in harvest
   is a son who causes shame.

6 Blessings *are* on the head of
   the righteous,

But violence covers the mouth
of the wicked.
7 The memory of the righteous *is*
   blessed,
   But the name of the wicked
   will rot.

8 The wise in heart will receive
   commands,
   But a prating fool will fall.

9 He who walks with integrity
   walks securely,
   But he who perverts his ways
   will become known.

10 He who winks with the eye
   causes trouble,
   But a prating fool will fall.

11 The mouth of the righteous *is*
   a well of life,
   But violence covers the mouth
   of the wicked.

12 Hatred stirs up strife,
   But love covers all sins.

13 Wisdom is found on the lips of
   him who has understanding,
   But a rod *is* for the back of
   him who is devoid of
   understanding.

14 Wise *people* store up
   knowledge,
   But the mouth of the foolish *is*
   near destruction.

15 The rich man's wealth
   is his strong city;
   The destruction of the poor
   is their poverty.

16 The labor of the righteous
   leads to life,
   The wages of the wicked to
   sin.

17 He who keeps instruction *is in*
   the way of life,

But he who refuses reproof
goes astray.

18 Whoever hides hatred *has*
lying lips,
And whoever spreads slander *is*
a fool.

19 In the multitude of words
sin is not lacking,
But he who restrains his lips *is*
wise.
20 The tongue of the righteous
is choice silver;
The heart of the wicked *is*
worth little.
21 The lips of the righteous feed
many,
But fools die for lack of
wisdom.

22 The blessing of the LORD
makes *one* rich,
And He adds no sorrow with it.

23 To do evil *is* like sport to a
fool,
But a man of understanding
has wisdom.
24 The fear of the wicked
will come upon him,
And the desire of the righteous
will be granted.
25 When the whirlwind passes by,
the wicked *is* no *more,*
But the righteous *has* an
everlasting foundation.

26 As vinegar to the teeth
and smoke to the eyes,
So *is* the sluggard to those
who send him.

27 The fear of the LORD prolongs
days,
But the years of the wicked
will be shortened.
28 The hope of the righteous
will be gladness,
But the expectation of the
wicked will perish.
29 The way of the LORD *is*
strength for the upright,

But destruction *will come*
to the workers of iniquity.

30 The righteous will never be
removed,
But the wicked will not inhabit
the earth.
31 The mouth of the righteous
brings forth wisdom,
But the perverse tongue will be
cut out.
32 The lips of the righteous know
what is acceptable,
But the mouth of the wicked
what is perverse.

11 A false balance *is* an
abomination to the LORD,
But a just weight *is* His delight.

2 When pride comes, then comes
shame;
But with the humble *is*
wisdom.

3 The integrity of the upright
will guide them,
But the perversity of the
unfaithful will destroy them.
4 Riches do not profit in the day
of wrath,
But righteousness delivers from
death.
5 The righteousness of the
blameless will direct his way
aright,
But the wicked will fall
by his own wickedness.
6 The righteousness of the
upright will deliver them,
But the unfaithful will be taken
by *their own* lust.

7 When a wicked man dies,
his expectation will perish,
And the hope of the unjust
perishes.
8 The righteous is delivered from
trouble,
And it comes to the wicked
instead.
9 The hypocrite with *his* mouth
destroys his neighbor,

But through knowledge the
   righteous will be delivered.
10 When it goes well with the
   righteous, the city rejoices;
   And when the wicked perish,
   there is shouting.
11 By the blessing of the upright
   the city is exalted,
   But it is overthrown
   by the mouth of the wicked.

12 He who is devoid of wisdom
   despises his neighbor,
   But a man of understanding
   holds his peace.

13 A talebearer reveals secrets,
   But he who is of a faithful
   spirit conceals a matter.

14 Where *there is* no counsel,
   the people fall;
   But in the multitude of
   counselors *there is* safety.

15 He who is surety for a stranger
   will suffer *for it*,
   But one who hates being
   surety is secure.

16 A gracious woman retains
   honor,
   But ruthless *men* retain riches.
17 The merciful man
   does good for his own soul,
   But *he who is* cruel
   troubles his own flesh.
18 The wicked man does
   deceptive work,
   But to him who sows
   righteousness *will be* a sure
   reward.
19 As righteousness *leads* to life,
   So he who pursues evil *pursues
   it* to his own death.
20 Those who are of a perverse
   heart *are* an abomination to
   the LORD,
   But *such as are* blameless in
   their ways *are* His delight.
21 *Though they join* forces,
   the wicked will not go
   unpunished;

But the posterity of the
   righteous will be delivered.

22 *As* a ring of gold in a swine's
   snout,
   So is a lovely woman who
   lacks discretion.

23 The desire of the righteous
   is only good,
   But the expectation of the
   wicked *is* wrath.

24 There is *one* who scatters,
   yet increases more;
   And there is *one* who
   withholds more than is right,
   But it *leads* to poverty.
25 The generous soul will be made
   rich,
   And he who waters will also be
   watered himself.
26 The people will curse him who
   withholds grain,
   But blessing *will be* on the
   head of him who sells *it*.

27 He who diligently seeks good
   finds favor,
   But trouble will come to him
   who seeks *evil*.

28 He who trusts in his riches will
   fall,
   But the righteous will flourish
   like foliage.

29 He who troubles his own house
   will inherit the wind,
   And the fool *will be* servant to
   the wise of heart.

30 The fruit of the righteous *is a*
   tree of life,
   And he who wins souls *is* wise.

31 If the righteous will be
   recompensed on the earth,
   How much more the wicked
   and the sinner.

12 Whoever loves instruction
         loves knowledge,

But he who hates reproof *is*
  stupid.

2 A good *man* obtains favor from
  the Lord,
  But a man of wicked devices
  He will condemn.

3 A man is not established
  by wickedness,
  But the root of the righteous
  cannot be moved.

4 An excellent wife *is* the crown
  of her husband,
  But she who causes shame *is*
  like rottenness in his bones.

5 The thoughts of the righteous
  are right,
  But the counsels of the wicked
  are deceitful.

6 The words of the wicked *are,*
  "Lie in wait for blood,"
  But the mouth of the upright
  will deliver them.

7 The wicked are overthrown
  and *are* no more,
  But the house of the righteous
  will stand.

8 A man will be commended
  according to his wisdom,
  But he who is of a perverse
  heart will be despised.

9 Better *is the one* who is
  slighted but has a servant,
  Than he who honors himself
  but lacks bread.

10 A righteous *man* regards the
  life of his animal,
  But the tender mercies of the
  wicked *are* cruel.

11 He who tills his land will be
  satisfied with bread,
  But he who follows frivolity *is*
  devoid of understanding.

12 The wicked covet the catch of
  evil *men,*

But the root of the righteous
  yields *fruit.*

13 The wicked is ensnared by the
  transgression of *his* lips,
  But the righteous will come
  through trouble.

14 A man will be satisfied with
  good by the fruit of *his*
  mouth,
  And the recompense of a man's
  hands will be rendered to
  him.

15 The way of a fool *is* right in his
  own eyes,
  But he who heeds counsel *is*
  wise.

16 A fool's wrath is known at
  once,
  But a prudent *man* covers
  shame.

17 He *who* speaks truth declares
  righteousness,
  But a false witness, deceit.

18 There is one who speaks like
  the piercings of a sword,
  But the tongue of the wise
  promotes health.

19 The truthful lip shall be
  established forever,
  But a lying tongue *is* but for a
  moment.

20 Deceit is in the heart of those
  who devise evil,
  But counselors of peace have
  joy.

21 No grave trouble will overtake
  the righteous,
  But the wicked shall be filled
  with evil.

22 Lying lips *are* an abomination
  to the Lord,
  But those who deal truthfully
  are His delight.

23 A prudent man conceals
  knowledge,
  But the heart of fools
  proclaims foolishness.

24 The hand of the diligent will
  rule,
  But the slothful will be put to
  forced labor.

25 Anxiety in the heart of man
causes depression,
But a good word makes it glad.

26 The righteous should choose
his friends carefully,
For the way of the wicked
leads them astray.

27 The slothful *man* does not
roast what he took in
hunting,
But diligence *is* man's precious
possession.

28 In the way of righteousness *is*
life,
And in *its* pathway *there is* no
death.

13 A wise son *heeds* his father's
instruction,
But a scoffer does not listen to
rebuke.

2 A man shall eat well
by the fruit of *his* mouth,
But the soul of the unfaithful
feeds on violence.

3 He who guards his mouth
preserves his life,
But he who opens wide his lips
shall have destruction.

4 The soul of a sluggard desires,
and *has* nothing;
But the soul of the diligent
shall be made rich.

5 A righteous *man* hates lying,
But a wicked *man* is loathsome
and comes to shame.

6 Righteousness keeps *him*
whose way is blameless,
But wickedness overthrows the
sinner.

7 There is one who makes
himself rich, yet *has* nothing;
And one who makes himself
poor, yet *has* great riches.

8 The ransom of a man's life *is*
his riches,
But the poor does not hear
rebuke.

9 The light of the righteous
rejoices,
But the lamp of the wicked will
be put out.

10 By pride comes only
contention,
But with the well-advised *is*
wisdom.

11 Wealth *gained by* dishonesty
will be diminished,
But he who gathers by labor
will increase.

12 Hope deferred makes the heart
sick,
But *when* the desire comes,
it is a tree of life.

13 He who despises the word
will be destroyed,
But he who fears the
commandment will be
rewarded.

14 The law of the wise *is* a
fountain of life,
To turn *one* away from the
snares of death.

15 Good understanding gains
favor,
But the way of the unfaithful *is*
hard.

16 Every prudent *man* acts with
knowledge,
But a fool lays open *his* folly.

17 A wicked messenger falls into
trouble,
But a faithful ambassador
brings health.

18 Poverty and shame *will come*
to him who disdains
correction,
But he who regards reproof
will be honored.

19 A desire accomplished is sweet
to the soul,

But *it is* an abomination to
fools to depart from evil.

20 He who walks with wise *men*
will be wise,
But the companion of fools
will be destroyed.

21 Evil pursues sinners,
But to the righteous,
good shall be repaid.

22 A good *man* leaves an
inheritance to his children's
children,
But the wealth of the sinner is
stored up for the righteous.

23 Much food *is in* the fallow
ground of the poor,
And for lack of justice there is
waste.

24 He who spares his rod hates
his son,
But he who loves him
disciplines him promptly.

25 The righteous eats to the
satisfying of his soul,
But the stomach of the wicked
shall be in want.

14 Every wise woman builds
her house,
But the foolish pulls it down
with her hands.

2 He who walks in his
uprightness fears the LORD,
But *he who is* perverse in his
ways despises Him.

3 In the mouth of a fool *is* a rod
of pride,
But the lips of the wise will
preserve them.

4 Where no oxen *are*, the trough
is clean;
But much increase *comes* by
the strength of an ox.

5 A faithful witness does not lie,

But a false witness will utter
lies.

6 A scoffer seeks wisdom
and does not *find it*,
But knowledge *is* easy to him
who understands.

7 Go from the presence of a
foolish man,
When you do not perceive *in
him* the lips of knowledge.

8 The wisdom of the prudent
is to understand his way,
But the folly of fools *is* deceit.

9 Fools mock at sin,
But among the upright *there is*
favor.

10 The heart knows its own
bitterness,
And a stranger does not share
its joy.

11 The house of the wicked will
be overthrown,
But the tent of the upright will
flourish.

12 There is a way *that seems*
right to a man,
But its end *is* the way of death.

13 Even in laughter the heart may
sorrow,
And the end of mirth *may be*
grief.

14 The backslider in heart will be
filled with his own ways,
But a good man *will be
satisfied* from above.

15 The simple believes every
word,
But the prudent *man* considers
well his steps.

16 A wise *man* fears
and departs from evil,
But a fool rages and is self-
confident.

17 *He who is* quick-tempered
acts foolishly,

445

And a man of wicked
    intentions is hated.
18 The simple inherit folly,
    But the prudent are crowned
    with knowledge.
19 The evil will bow before the
    good,
    And the wicked at the gates of
    the righteous.

20 The poor *man* is hated
    even by his own neighbor,
    But the rich *has* many friends.
21 He who despises his neighbor
    sins;
    But he who has mercy on the
    poor, happy *is* he.

22 Do they not go astray who
    devise evil?
    But mercy and truth *belong* to
    those who devise good.

23 In all labor there is profit,
    But idle chatter *leads* only to
    poverty.

24 The crown of the wise is their
    riches,
    But the foolishness of fools *is*
    folly.

25 A true witness delivers souls,
    But a deceitful *witness* speaks
    lies.

26 In the fear of the LORD
    there is strong confidence,
    And His children will have a
    place of refuge.
27 The fear of the LORD
    is a fountain of life,
    To avoid the snares of death.

28 In a multitude of people
    is a king's honor,
    But in the lack of people
    is the downfall of a prince.

29 *He who is* slow to wrath
    has great understanding,
    But *he who is* impulsive exalts
    folly.

30 A sound heart *is* life to the
    body,
    But envy *is* rottenness to the
    bones.

31 He who oppresses the poor
    reproaches his Maker,
    But he who honors Him
    has mercy on the needy.

32 The wicked is banished
    in his wickedness,
    But the righteous has a refuge
    in his death.

33 Wisdom rests *quietly* in the
    heart of him who has
    understanding,
    But *what is* in the heart of
    fools is made known.

34 Righteousness exalts a nation,
    But sin *is* a reproach to *any*
    people.

35 The king's favor *is* toward a
    wise servant,
    But his wrath *is against* him
    who causes shame.

15 A soft answer turns away
    wrath,
    But a harsh word stirs up
    anger.
2 The tongue of the wise uses
    knowledge rightly,
    But the mouth of fools pours
    forth foolishness.

3 The eyes of the LORD *are* in
    every place,
    Keeping watch on the evil and
    the good.

4 A wholesome tongue *is* a tree
    of life,
    But perverseness in it breaks
    the spirit.

5 A fool despises his father's
    instruction,
    But he who receives reproof is
    prudent.

6   *In* the house of the righteous
     there is much treasure,
     But in the revenue of the
     wicked is trouble.

7   The lips of the wise disperse
     knowledge,
     But the heart of the fool *does*
     not *do* so.

8   The sacrifice of the wicked
     is an abomination to the
     LORD,
     But the prayer of the upright
     is His delight.

9   The way of the wicked *is* an
     abomination to the LORD,
     But He loves him
     who follows righteousness.

10 Harsh correction *is* for him
     who forsakes the way,
     And he who hates reproof will
     die.

11 Hell and Destruction *are* before
     the LORD;
     So how much more the hearts
     of the sons of men.

12 A scoffer does not love one
     who reproves him,
     Nor will he go to the wise.

13 A merry heart makes a
     cheerful countenance,
     But by sorrow of the heart
     the spirit is broken.

14 The heart of him who has
     understanding seeks
     knowledge,
     But the mouth of fools feeds
     on foolishness.

15 All the days of the afflicted *are*
     evil,
     But he who is of a merry heart
     has a continual feast.

16 Better *is* a little with the fear
     of the LORD,

Than great treasure with
     trouble.

17 Better *is* a dinner of herbs
     where love is,
     Than a fatted calf with hatred.

18 A wrathful man stirs up strife,
     But *he who is* slow to anger
     allays contention.

19 The way of the slothful *man*
     is like a hedge of thorns,
     But the way of the upright
     is a highway.

20 A wise son makes a father
     glad,
     But a foolish man despises his
     mother.

21 Folly *is* joy *to him who is*
     destitute of discernment,
     But a man of understanding
     walks uprightly.

22 Without counsel, plans go
     awry,
     But in the multitude of
     counselors they are
     established.

23 A man has joy by the answer
     of his mouth,
     And a word *spoken* in due
     season, how good *it is!*

24 The way of life *winds* upward
     for the wise,
     That he may turn away from
     hell below.

25 The LORD will destroy the
     house of the proud,
     But He will establish the
     boundary of the widow.

26 The thoughts of the wicked
     are an abomination to the
     LORD,
     But *the words* of the pure *are*
     pleasant.

27 He who is greedy for gain
     troubles his own house,

447

But he who hates bribes will
    live.

28 The heart of the righteous
    studies how to answer,
But the mouth of the wicked
    pours forth evil.

29 The LORD *is* far from the
    wicked,
But He hears the prayer of the
    righteous.

30 The light of the eyes rejoices
    the heart,
And a good report makes the
    bones healthy.

31 The ear that hears the reproof
    of life
Will abide among the wise.
32 He who disdains instruction
    despises his own soul,
But he who heeds reproof
    gets understanding.
33 The fear of the LORD *is* the
    instruction of wisdom,
And before honor *is* humility.

16 The preparations of the
    heart *belong* to man,
But the answer of the tongue
    is from the LORD.

2 All the ways of a man *are* pure
    in his own eyes,
But the LORD weighs the
    spirits.

3 Commit your works to the
    LORD,
And your thoughts will be
    established.

4 The LORD has made all *things*
    for Himself,
Yes, even the wicked for the
    day of doom.

5 Everyone *who is* proud in heart
    is an abomination to the
    LORD;

Though they join forces,
    none will go unpunished.

6 In mercy and truth
Atonement is provided for
    iniquity;
And by the fear of the LORD
    one departs from evil.

7 When a man's ways please the
    LORD,
He makes even his enemies to
    be at peace with him.

8 Better *is* a little with
    righteousness,
Than vast revenues without
    justice.

9 A man's heart plans his way,
But the LORD directs his steps.

10 *Even though* divination *is* on
    the lips of the king,
His mouth must not transgress
    in judgment.
11 A just weight and balance
    are the LORD's;
All the weights in the bag
    are His work.
12 *It is* an abomination for kings
    to commit wickedness,
For a throne is established by
    righteousness.
13 Righteous lips *are* the delight
    of kings,
And they love him who speaks
    what is right.
14 As messengers of death *is* the
    king's wrath,
But a wise man will appease it.
15 In the light of the king's face *is*
    life,
And his favor *is* like a cloud of
    the latter rain.

16 How much better *it is* to get
    wisdom than gold!
And to get understanding is to
    be chosen rather than silver.

17 The highway of the upright *is*
    to depart from evil;

He who keeps his way
preserves his soul.

18 Pride *goes* before destruction,
And a haughty spirit before a
fall.

19 Better *to be* of a humble spirit
with the lowly,
Than to divide the spoil
with the proud.

20 He who heeds the word wisely
will find good,
And whoever trusts in the
LORD, happy *is* he.

21 The wise in heart will be called
prudent,
And sweetness of the lips
increases learning.

22 Understanding *is* a wellspring
of life to him who has it.
But the correction of fools *is*
folly.

23 The heart of the wise teaches
his mouth,
And adds learning to his lips.

24 Pleasant words *are like* a
honeycomb,
Sweetness to the soul
and health to the bones.

25 There is a way *that seems*
right to a man,
But its end *is* the way of death.

26 The person who labors,
labors for himself,
For his *hungry* mouth drives
him *on*.

27 An ungodly man digs up evil,
And *it is* on his lips like a
burning fire.

28 A perverse man sows strife,
And a whisperer separates the
best of friends.

29 A violent man entices his
neighbor,
And leads him in a way *that is*
not good.

30 He winks his eye to devise
perverse things;
He purses his lips
and brings about evil.

31 The silver-haired head *is* a
crown of glory,
If it is found in the way of
righteousness.

32 *He who is* slow to anger *is*   ♥
better than the mighty,
And he who rules his spirit
than he who takes a city.

33 The lot is cast into the lap,
But its every decision *is* from
the LORD.

17 Better *is* a dry morsel
with quietness,
Than a house full of feasting
with strife.

2 A wise servant will rule over a
son who causes shame,
And will share an inheritance
among the brothers.

3 The refining pot *is* for silver
and the furnace for gold,
But the LORD tests the hearts.

4 An evildoer gives heed to false
lips;
A liar listens eagerly to a
spiteful tongue.

5 He who mocks the poor
reproaches his Maker;
He who is glad at calamity
will not go unpunished.

6 Children's children *are* the
crown of old men,
And the glory of children *is*
their father.

7 Excellent speech is not
becoming to a fool,
Much less lying lips to a prince.

449

See Proverbs 19:11, page 452

8 A present *is* a precious stone in
the eyes of its possessor;
Wherever he turns, he
prospers.

9 He who covers a transgression
seeks love,
But he who repeats a matter
separates *the best of* friends.

10 Reproof is more effective for a
wise man
Than a hundred blows on a
fool.

11 An evil *man* seeks only
rebellion;
Therefore a cruel messenger
will be sent against him.

12 Let a man meet a bear robbed
of her cubs,
Rather than a fool in his folly.

13 Whoever rewards evil for good,
Evil will not depart from his
house.

14 The beginning of strife *is like*
releasing water;
Therefore stop contention
before a quarrel starts.

15 He who justifies the wicked,
and he who condemns the
just,
Both of them alike *are* an
abomination to the LORD.

16 Why *is there* in the hand of a
fool the purchase price of
wisdom,
Since *he has* no heart *for it?*

17 A friend loves at all times,
And a brother is born for
adversity.

18 A man devoid of understanding
shakes hands in a pledge,
And becomes surety for his
friend.

19 He who loves transgression
loves strife,
And he who exalts his gate
seeks destruction.

20 He who has a deceitful heart
finds no good,
And he who has a perverse
tongue falls into evil.

21 He who begets a scoffer *does
so* to his sorrow,
And the father of a fool has no
joy.

22 A merry heart does good,
like medicine,
But a broken spirit dries the
bones.

23 A wicked *man* accepts a bribe
behind the back
To pervert the ways of justice.

24 Wisdom *is* in the sight of him
who has understanding,
But the eyes of a fool *are* on
the ends of the earth.

25 A foolish son *is* a grief to his
father,
And bitterness to her who bore
him.

26 Also, to punish the righteous *is*
not good,
Nor to strike princes for *their*
uprightness.

27 He who has knowledge
spares his words,
And a man of understanding
is of a calm spirit.

28 Even a fool is counted wise
when he holds his peace;
When he shuts his lips,
he is considered perceptive.

18 A man who isolates himself
seeks his own desire;
He rages against all wise
judgment.

2 A fool has no delight in
   understanding,
   But in expressing his own
   heart.

3 When the wicked comes,
   contempt comes also;
   And with dishonor *comes*
   reproach.

4 The words of a man's mouth
   are deep waters;
   The wellspring of wisdom
   is a flowing brook.

5 *It is* not good to show
   partiality to the wicked,
   Or to overthrow the righteous
   in judgment.

6 A fool's lips enter into
   contention,
   And his mouth calls for blows.
7 A fool's mouth *is* his
   destruction,
   And his lips *are* the snare of
   his soul.
8 The words of a talebearer *are*
   like tasty trifles,
   And they go down into the
   inmost body.

9 He who is slothful in his work
   Is a brother to him who is a
   great destroyer.

10 The name of the LORD
   is a strong tower;
   The righteous run to it and are
   safe.
11 The rich man's wealth
   is his strong city,
   And like a high wall in his own
   esteem.

12 Before destruction the heart of
   a man is haughty,
   And before honor *is* humility.

13 He who answers a matter
   before he hears *it,*
   It *is* folly and shame to him.

14 The spirit of a man will sustain
   him in sickness,
   But who can bear a broken
   spirit?

15 The heart of the prudent
   acquires knowledge,
   And the ear of the wise
   seeks knowledge.

16 A man's gift makes room for
   him,
   And brings him before great
   men.

17 The first *one* to plead his cause
   seems right,
   Until his neighbor comes and
   examines him.

18 Casting lots causes contentions
   to cease,
   And keeps the mighty apart.

19 A brother offended *is harder to
   win* than a strong city,
   And contentions *are* like the
   bars of a castle.

20 A man's stomach shall be
   satisfied from the fruit of his
   mouth,
   And from the produce of his
   lips he shall be filled.

21 Death and life *are* in the power
   of the tongue,
   And those who love it will eat
   its fruit.

22 *He who* finds a wife finds a
   good *thing,*
   And obtains favor from the
   LORD.

23 The poor *man* uses entreaties,
   But the rich answers roughly.

24 A man *who has* friends must
   himself be friendly,
   But there is a friend *who* sticks
   closer than a brother.

19 Better *is* the poor
who walks in his integrity
Than *one who is* perverse in
his lips, and is a fool.

2 Also it is not good *for* a soul *to*
be without knowledge,
And he sins who hastens with
his feet.

3 The foolishness of a man twists
his way,
And his heart frets against the
LORD.

4 Wealth makes many friends,
But the poor is separated from
his friend.

5 A false witness will not go
unpunished,
And *he* who speaks lies will
not escape.

6 Many entreat the favor of the
nobility,
And every man *is* a friend to
one who gives gifts.

7 All the brothers of the poor
hate him;
How much more do his friends
go far from him!
He may pursue *them with*
words, *yet* they abandon *him.*

8 He who gets wisdom
loves his own soul;
He who keeps understanding
will find good.

9 A false witness will not go
unpunished,
And *he* who speaks lies shall
perish.

10 Luxury is not fitting for a fool,
Much less for a servant to rule
over princes.

♥ 11 The discretion of a man makes
him slow to anger,
And *it is to* his glory to
overlook a transgression.

See James 1:19–20, page 277   452

12 The king's wrath *is* like the
roaring of a lion,
But his favor *is* like dew on the
grass.

13 A foolish son *is* the ruin of his
father,
And the contentions of a wife
are a continual dripping.

14 Houses and riches *are* an
inheritance from fathers,
But a prudent wife *is* from the
LORD.

15 Slothfulness casts *one* into a
deep sleep,
And an idle person will suffer
hunger.

16 He who keeps the commandment keeps his soul,
But he who is careless of his
ways will die.

17 He who has pity on the poor
lends to the LORD,
And He will pay back what he
has given.

18 Chasten your son while there
is hope,
And do not set your heart on
his destruction.

19 *A man of* great wrath will
suffer punishment;
For if you deliver *him,*
you will have to do it again.

20 Listen to counsel
and receive instruction,
That you may be wise in your
latter days.

21 There are many plans in a
man's heart,
Nevertheless the LORD's
counsel—that will stand.

22 What is desired in a man is
kindness,
And a poor man is better than
a liar.

23 The fear of the LORD *leads* to
   life,
   And *he who has it* will abide in
   satisfaction;
   He will not be visited with evil.

24 A slothful *man* buries his hand
   in the bowl,
   And will not so much as bring
   it to his mouth again.

25 Strike a scoffer, and the simple
   will become wary;
   Reprove one who has
   understanding, *and* he will
   discern knowledge.

26 He who mistreats *his* father
   and chases away *his* mother
   Is a son who causes shame
   and brings reproach.

27 Cease listening to instruction,
   my son,
   And you will stray from the
   words of knowledge.

28 A disreputable witness scorns
   justice,
   And the mouth of the wicked
   devours iniquity.

29 Judgments are prepared for
   scoffers,
   And beatings for the backs of
   fools.

20 Wine is a mocker,
   Intoxicating drink arouses
   brawling,
   And whoever is led astray by it
   is not wise.

2 The wrath of a king *is* like the
   roaring of a lion;
   Whoever provokes him to
   anger sins *against* his own
   life.

3 *It is* honorable for a man to
   stop striving,

Since any fool can start a
   quarrel.

4 The sluggard will not plow
   because of winter;
   Therefore he will beg during
   the harvest
   And *have* nothing.

5 Counsel in the heart of man *is
   like* deep water,
   But a man of understanding
   will draw it out.

6 Most men will proclaim each
   his own goodness,
   But who can find a faithful
   man?

7 The righteous *man* walks in his
   integrity;
   His children *are* blessed after
   him.

8 A king who sits on the throne
   of judgment
   Scatters all evil with his eyes.

9 Who can say, "I have made my
   heart clean,
   I am pure from my sin"?

10 Diverse weights *and* diverse
   measures,
   They *are* both alike,
   an abomination to the LORD.

11 Even a child is known by his
   deeds,
   By whether what he does *is*
   pure and right.

12 The hearing ear and the seeing
   eye,
   The LORD has made both of
   them.

13 Do not love sleep,
   lest you come to poverty;
   Open your eyes, *and* you will
   be satisfied with bread.

14 "*It is* good for nothing,"
   cries the buyer;

453

But when he has gone his way,
  then he boasts.

15 There is gold and a multitude
     of rubies,
   But the lips of knowledge *are* a
     precious jewel.

16 Take the garment of one who
     is surety *for* a stranger,
   And hold it as a pledge *when it*
     is for a seductress.

17 Bread gained by deceit *is* sweet
     to a man,
   But afterward his mouth will
     be filled with gravel.

18 *Every* purpose is established by
     counsel;
   By wise counsel wage war.

19 He who goes about *as* a
     talebearer reveals secrets;
   Therefore do not associate with
     one who flatters with his lips.

20 Whoever curses his father or
     his mother,
   His lamp will be put out in
     deep darkness.

21 An inheritance gained hastily
     at the beginning
   Will not be blessed at the end.

22 Do not say, "I will recompense
     evil";
   Wait for the LORD,
     and He will save you.

23 Diverse weights *are* an
     abomination to the LORD,
   And a false balance *is* not
     good.

24 A man's steps *are* of the LORD;
   How then can a man
     understand his own way?

25 *It is* a snare for a man to
     devote rashly *something as*
     holy,

And afterward to reconsider
  his vows.

26 A wise king sifts out the
     wicked,
   And brings the threshing wheel
     over them.

27 The spirit of a man *is* the lamp
     of the LORD,
   Searching all the inner depths
     of his heart.

28 Mercy and truth preserve the
     king,
   And by lovingkindness he
     upholds his throne.

29 The glory of young men
     is their strength,
   And the splendor of old men
     is their gray head.

30 Blows that hurt cleanse away
     evil,
   As *do* stripes the inner depths
     of the heart.

21 The king's heart *is* in the
     hand of the LORD,
   Like the rivers of water;
   He turns it wherever He
     wishes.

2 Every way of a man *is* right
     in his own eyes,
   But the LORD weighs the
     hearts.

3 To do righteousness and justice
   Is more acceptable to the LORD
     than sacrifice.

4 A haughty look, a proud heart,
   And the plowing of the wicked
     are sin.

5 The plans of the diligent *lead*
     surely to plenty,
   But *those of* everyone *who is*
     hasty, surely to poverty.

6 Getting treasures by a lying
     tongue

Is the fleeting fantasy of those
who seek death.

7 The violence of the wicked will
destroy them,
Because they refuse to do
justice.

8 The way of a guilty man *is*
perverse;
But *as for* the pure, his work *is*
right.

9 *It is* better to dwell in a corner
of a housetop,
Than in a house shared with a
contentious woman.

10 The soul of the wicked desires
evil;
His neighbor finds no favor in
his eyes.

11 When the scoffer is punished,
the simple is made wise;
But when the wise is
instructed, he receives
knowledge.

12 The righteous *God* wisely
considers the house of the
wicked,
Overthrowing the wicked for
their wickedness.

13 Whoever shuts his ears to the
cry of the poor
Will also cry himself and not
be heard.

14 A gift in secret pacifies anger,
And a bribe behind the back,
strong wrath.

15 *It is* a joy for the just to do
justice,
But destruction *will come* to
the workers of iniquity.

16 A man who wanders from the
way of understanding
Will rest in the congregation of
the dead.

17 He who loves pleasure
will be a poor man;
He who loves wine and oil
will not be rich.

18 The wicked *shall be* a ransom
for the righteous,
And the unfaithful for the
upright.

19 *It is* better to dwell in the
wilderness,
Than with a contentious and
angry woman.

20 *There is* desirable treasure,
And oil in the dwelling of the
wise,
But a foolish man squanders it.

21 He who follows righteousness
and mercy
Finds life, righteousness and
honor.

22 A wise *man* scales the city of
the mighty,
And brings down the trusted
stronghold.

23 Whoever guards his mouth and
tongue
Keeps his soul from troubles.

24 A proud *and* haughty *man*—
"Scoffer" *is* his name;
He acts with arrogant pride.

25 The desire of the slothful kills
him,
For his hands refuse to labor.

26 He covets greedily all day long,
But the righteous gives
and does not spare.

27 The sacrifice of the wicked *is*
an abomination;
How much more *when* he
brings it with wicked intent!

28 A false witness shall perish,
But the man who hears *him*
will speak endlessly.

29 A wicked man hardens his
   face,
   But *as for* the upright,
   he establishes his way.

30 *There is* no wisdom or
   understanding
   Or counsel against the LORD.

31 The horse *is* prepared for the
   day of battle,
   But deliverance *is* of the LORD.

22 A *good* name is to be chosen
   rather than great riches,
   Loving favor rather than silver
   and gold.

2 The rich and the poor have this
   in common,
   The LORD *is* the maker of them
   all.

3 A prudent *man* foresees evil
   and hides himself,
   But the simple pass on
   and are punished.

4 By humility *and* the fear of the
   LORD
   Are riches and honor and life.

5 Thorns *and* snares *are* in the
   way of the perverse;
   He who guards his soul will be
   far from them.

6 Train up a child
   in the way he should go,
   And when he is old
   he will not depart from it.

7 The rich rules over the poor,
   And the borrower *is* servant to
   the lender.

8 He who sows iniquity will reap
   sorrow,
   And the rod of his anger will
   fail.

9 He who has a bountiful eye
   will be blessed,

For he gives of his bread to the
   poor.

10 Cast out the scoffer,
   and contention will leave;
   Yes, strife and reproach will
   cease.

11 He who loves purity of heart
   And has grace on his lips,
   The king *will be* his friend.

12 The eyes of the LORD preserve
   knowledge,
   But He overthrows the words
   of the faithless.

13 The slothful *man* says,
   "*There is* a lion outside!
   I shall be slain in the streets!"

14 The mouth of an immoral
   woman *is* a deep pit;
   He who is abhorred of the
   LORD will fall there.

15 Foolishness *is* bound up in the
   heart of a child,
   But the rod of correction will
   drive it far from him.

16 He who oppresses the poor to
   increase his *riches*,
   And he who gives to the rich,
   will surely *come* to poverty.

17 Incline your ear and hear the
   words of the wise,
   And apply your heart to my
   knowledge;

18 For *it is* a pleasant thing if you
   keep them within you;
   Let them all be fixed upon your
   lips,

19 So that your trust may be in
   the LORD;
   I have instructed you today,
   even you.

20 Have I not written to you
   excellent things
   Of counsels and knowledge,

21 That I may make you know
the certainty of the words of
truth,
That you may answer
words of truth
To those who send to you?

22 Do not rob the poor because he
is poor,
Nor oppress the afflicted at the
gate;
23 For the LORD will plead their
cause,
And plunder the soul of those
who plunder them.

24 Make no friendship with an
angry man,
And with a furious man do not
go,
25 Lest you learn his ways
And set a snare for your soul.

26 Do not be one of those
who shakes hands in a
pledge,
One of those who is surety for
debts;
27 If you have nothing *with
which* to pay,
Why should he take away your
bed from under you?

28 Do not remove the ancient
landmark
Which your fathers have set.

29 Do you see a man *who* excels
in his work?
He will stand before kings;
He will not stand before
unknown *men*.

23 When you sit down to eat
with a ruler,
Consider carefully what *is*
before you;
2 And put a knife to your throat
If you *are* a man given to
appetite.
3 Do not desire his delicacies,
For they *are* deceptive food.

4 Do not overwork to be rich;   ❤
Because of your own
understanding, cease!
5 Will you set your eyes on that
which is not?
For *riches* certainly make
themselves wings;
They fly away like an eagle
toward heaven.

6 Do not eat the bread of a
miser,
Nor desire his delicacies;
7 For as he thinks in his heart,
so *is* he.
"Eat and drink!" he says to you,
But his heart is not with you.
8 The morsel you have eaten,
you will vomit up,
And waste your pleasant
words.

9 Do not speak in the hearing of
a fool,
For he will despise the wisdom
of your words.

10 Do not remove the ancient
landmark,
Nor enter the fields of the
fatherless;
11 For their Redeemer *is* mighty;
He will plead their cause
against you.

12 Apply your heart to
instruction,
And your ears to words of
knowledge.

13 Do not withhold correction
from a child,
For *if* you beat him with a rod,
he will not die.
14 You shall beat him with a rod,
And deliver his soul from hell.

15 My son, if your heart is wise,
My heart will rejoice—indeed, I
myself;
16 Yes, my inmost being will
rejoice
When your lips speak right
things.

457   *See Ephesians 2:10, page 236*

17 Do not let your heart envy
    sinners,
  But in the fear of the Lord
    continue all day *long;*
18 For surely there is a hereafter,
    And your hope will not be cut
    off.

19 Hear, my son, and be wise;
    And guide your heart in the
    way.
20 Do not mix with winebibbers,
    Or with gluttonous eaters of
    meat;
21 For the drunkard and the
    glutton will come to poverty,
    And drowsiness will clothe *a
    man* with rags.

22 Listen to your father who
    begot you,
    And do not despise your
    mother when she is old.

23 Buy the truth, and do not sell
    it,
    Also wisdom and instruction
    and understanding.

24 The father of the righteous
    will greatly rejoice,
    And he who begets a wise *child*
    will delight in him.
25 Let your father and your
    mother be glad,
    And let her who bore you
    rejoice.

26 My son, give me your heart,
    And let your eyes observe my
    ways.
27 For a harlot *is* a deep pit,
    And a seductress *is* a narrow
    well.
28 She also lies in wait as *for* a
    victim,
    And increases the unfaithful
    among men.

29 Who has woe?
    Who has sorrow?
    Who has contentions?
    Who has complaints?

Who has wounds without
    cause?
  Who has redness of eyes?
30 Those who linger long at the
    wine,
    Those who go in search of
    mixed wine.
31 Do not look on the wine when
    it is red,
    When it sparkles in the cup,
    When it swirls around
    smoothly;
32 At the last it bites like a
    serpent,
    And stings like a viper.
33 Your eyes will see strange
    things,
    And your heart will utter
    perverse things.
34 Yes, you will be like one who
    lies down in the midst of the
    sea,
    Or like one who lies at the top
    of the mast, *saying:*
35 "They have struck me,
    but I was not hurt;
    They have beaten me,
    but I did not feel *it.*
    When shall I awake, that I
    may seek another *drink?*"

24

Do not be envious of evil
    men,
    Nor desire to be with them;
2 For their heart devises
    violence,
    And their lips talk of
    troublemaking.

3 Through wisdom a house is
    built,
    And by understanding it is
    established;
4 By knowledge the rooms are
    filled
    With all precious and pleasant
    riches.

5 A wise man *is* strong,
    Yes, a man of knowledge
    increases strength;

6 For by wise counsel
you will wage your own war,
And in a multitude of
counselors *there is* safety.

7 Wisdom *is* too lofty for a fool;
He does not open his mouth in
the gate.

8 He who plots to do evil
Will be called a schemer.
9 The devising of foolishness *is*
sin,
And the scoffer *is* an
abomination to men.

10 *If* you faint in the day of
adversity,
Your strength *is* small.

11 Deliver *those who* are drawn
toward death,
And hold back *those* stumbling
to the slaughter.
12 If you say, "Surely we did not
know this,"
Does not He who weighs the
hearts consider *it*?
He who keeps your soul,
does He *not* know *it*?
And will He *not* render to *each*
man according to his deeds?

13 My son, eat honey because *it is*
good,
And the honeycomb *which is*
sweet to your taste;
14 So *shall* the knowledge of
wisdom *be* to your soul;
If you have found *it*,
there is a prospect,
And your hope will not be cut
off.

15 Do not lie in wait, O wicked
man, against the dwelling of
the righteous;
Do not plunder his resting
place;
❤ 16 For a righteous *man* may fall
seven times
And rise again,

But the wicked shall fall by
calamity.

17 Do not rejoice when your
enemy falls,
And do not let your heart be
glad when he stumbles;
18 Lest the LORD see *it*,
and it displease Him,
And He turn away His wrath
from him.

19 Do not fret because of
evildoers,
Nor be envious of the wicked;
20 For there will be no prospect
for the evil *man;*
The lamp of the wicked
will be put out.

21 My son, fear the LORD and the
king;
Do not associate with those
given to change;
22 For their calamity will rise
suddenly,
And who knows the ruin those
two can bring?

23 These *things* also *belong* to the
wise:

It is not good to show
partiality in judgment.
24 He who says to the wicked,
"You *are* righteous,"
Him the people will curse;
Nations will abhor him.
25 But those who rebuke *the
wicked* will have delight,
And a good blessing will come
upon them.

26 He who gives a right answer
kisses the lips.

27 Prepare your outside work,
Make it fit for yourself in the
field;
And afterward build your
house.

28 Do not be a witness against
your neighbor without cause,

See Galatians 2:20, page 231

For would you deceive with
your lips?
29 Do not say, "I will do to him
just as he has done to me;
I will render to the man
according to his work."

30 I went by the field of the
slothful,
And by the vineyard of the
man devoid of understanding;
31 And there it was,
all overgrown with thorns;
Its surface was covered with
nettles;
Its stone wall was broken
down.
32 When I saw *it*, I considered *it*
well;
I looked on *it and* received
instruction:
33 A little sleep, a little slumber,
A little folding of the hands to
rest;
34 So your poverty will come *like*
a prowler,
And your want like an armed
man.

25 These also *are* proverbs of
Solomon which the men of
Hezekiah king of Judah copied:

2 *It is* the glory of God
to conceal a matter,
But the glory of kings
is to search out a matter.

3 *As* the heavens for height
and the earth for depth,
So the heart of kings *is*
unsearchable.

4 Take away the dross from
silver,
And it will go to the
silversmith *for* jewelry.
5 Take away the wicked from
before the king,
And his throne will be
established in righteousness.

6 Do not exalt yourself in the
presence of the king,

And do not stand in the place
of great *men;*
7 For *it is* better that he say to
you,
"Come up here,"
Than that you should be put
lower in the presence of the
prince,
Whom your eyes have seen.

8 Do not go hastily to court;
For what will you do in the
end,
When your neighbor has put
you to shame?
9 Debate your case with your
neighbor *himself,*
And do not disclose the secret
to another;
10 Lest he who hears *it* expose
your shame,
And your reputation be ruined.

11 A word fitly spoken
is like apples of gold
In settings of silver.
12 *Like* an earring of gold
and an ornament of fine gold
Is a wise reprover to an
obedient ear.

13 Like the cold of snow in time
of harvest
Is a faithful messenger to those
who send him,
For he refreshes the soul of his
masters.

14 Whoever falsely boasts of
giving
Is like clouds and wind without
rain.

15 By long forbearance a ruler is
persuaded,
And a gentle tongue breaks a
bone.

16 Have you found honey?
Eat only as much as you need,
Lest you be filled with it and
vomit.

460

17 Seldom set foot in your
    neighbor's house,
Lest he become weary of you
    and hate you.

18 A man who bears false witness
    against his neighbor
Is like a club, a sword,
    and a sharp arrow.

19 Confidence in an unfaithful
    man in time of trouble
Is like a bad tooth
    and a foot out of joint.

20 *Like* one who takes away a
    garment in cold weather,
And like vinegar on soda,
Is one who sings songs to a
    heavy heart.

21 If your enemy is hungry,
    give him bread to eat;
And if he is thirsty,
    give him water to drink;
22 For *so* you will heap coals of
    fire on his head,
And the LORD will reward you.

23 The north wind brings forth
    rain,
And a backbiting tongue an
    angry countenance.

24 *It is* better to dwell in a corner
    of a housetop,
Than in a house shared with a
    contentious woman.

25 *As* cold water to a weary soul,
So *is* good news from a far
    country.

26 A righteous man who falters
    before the wicked
Is like a murky spring
    and a polluted well.

27 *It is* not good to eat much
    honey;
So to seek one's own glory *is*
    not glory.

28 Whoever *has* no rule over his
    own spirit
Is like a city broken down,
    without walls.

26 As snow in summer
    and rain in harvest,
So honor is not fitting for a
    fool.

2 Like a flitting sparrow,
    like a flying swallow,
So a curse without cause shall
    not alight.

3 A whip for the horse,
A bridle for the donkey,
And a rod for the fool's back.
4 Do not answer a fool according
    to his folly,
Lest you also be like him.
5 Answer a fool according to his
    folly,
Lest he be wise in his own
    eyes.
6 He who sends a message by
    the hand of a fool
Cuts off *his own* feet
    and drinks violence.
7 *Like* the legs of the lame that
    hang limp
Is a proverb in the mouth of
    fools.
8 Like one who binds a stone in
    a sling
Is he who gives honor to a
    fool.
9 *Like* a thorn *that* goes into the
    hand of a drunkard
Is a proverb in the mouth of
    fools.
10 The great *God* who formed all
    things
Gives the fool *his* hire and the
    transgressor *his* wages.
11 As a dog returns to his own
    vomit,
    So a fool repeats his folly.
12 Do you see a man wise in his
    own eyes?
    There is more hope for a fool
    than for him.

13 The slothful *man* says,
  "*There is* a lion in the road!
  A fierce lion *is* in the streets!"
14 *As* a door turns on its hinges,
  So *does* the slothful *turn* on his
  bed.
15 The slothful *man* buries his
  hand in the bowl;
  It wearies him to bring it back
  to his mouth.
16 The sluggard *is* wiser in his
  own eyes
  Than seven men who can
  answer sensibly.

17 He who passes by *and* meddles
  in a quarrel not his own
  Is like one who takes a dog by
  the ears.

18 Like a madman who throws
  firebrands, arrows, and death,
19 *Is* the man *who* deceives his
  neighbor,
  And says, "I was only joking!"

20 Where *there is* no wood,
  the fire goes out;
  And where *there is* no
  talebearer, strife ceases.
21 *As* charcoal *is* to burning coals,
  and wood to fire,
  So *is* a contentious man
  to kindle strife.
22 The words of a talebearer *are*
  like tasty trifles,
  And they go down into the
  inmost body.

23 Fervent lips with a wicked
  heart
  Are like earthenware covered
  with silver dross.

24 He who hates, disguises *it* with
  his lips,
  And lays up deceit within
  himself;
25 When he speaks kindly,
  do not believe him,
  For *there are* seven
  abominations in his heart;

Wickedness Will Be Revealed

26 *Though his* hatred is covered
  by deceit,
  His wickedness will be revealed
  before the *whole* congregation.

27 Whoever digs a pit will fall into
  it,
  And he who rolls a stone
  will have it roll back on him.

28 A lying tongue hates *those
  who are* crushed by it,
  And a flattering mouth works
  ruin.

27 Do not boast about
  tomorrow,
  For you do not know what a
  day may bring forth.

2 Let another man praise you,
  and not your own mouth;
  A stranger, and not your own
  lips.

3 A stone *is* heavy and sand *is*
  weighty,
  But a fool's wrath *is* heavier
  than both of them.

4 Wrath *is* cruel and anger a
  torrent,
  But who *is* able to stand before
  jealousy?

5 Open rebuke *is* better
  Than love carefully concealed.

6 Faithful *are* the wounds of a
  friend,
  But the kisses of an enemy *are*
  deceitful.

7 A satisfied soul loathes the
  honeycomb,
  But to a hungry soul every
  bitter thing *is* sweet.

8 Like a bird that wanders from
  its nest
  Is a man who wanders from his
  place.

9 Ointment and perfume
   delight the heart,
   And the sweetness of a man's
   friend *does so* by hearty
   counsel.

10 Do not forsake your own
   friend or your father's friend,
   Nor go to your brother's house
   in the day of your calamity;
   For better *is* a neighbor nearby
   than a brother far away.

11 My son, be wise,
   and make my heart glad,
   That I may answer him who
   reproaches me.

12 A prudent *man* foresees evil
   and hides himself;
   The simple pass on *and* are
   punished.

13 Take the garment of him who
   is surety for a stranger,
   And hold it in pledge *when* he
   is surety for a seductress.

14 He who blesses his friend with
   a loud voice, rising early in
   the morning,
   It will be counted a curse to
   him.

15 A continual dripping on a very
   rainy day
   And a contentious woman are
   alike;
16 Whoever restrains her
   restrains the wind,
   And grasps oil with his right
   hand.

♥ 17 As iron sharpens iron,
   So a man sharpens the
   countenance of his friend.

18 Whoever keeps the fig tree
   will eat its fruit;
   So he who waits on his master
   will be honored.

19 As in water face *reveals* face,

So a man's heart *reveals* the
man.

20 Hell and Destruction are never
   full;
   So the eyes of man are never
   satisfied.

21 The refining pot *is* for silver
   and the furnace for gold,
   And a man *is valued* by what
   others say of him.

22 Though you grind a fool in a
   mortar with a pestle along
   with crushed grain,
   Yet his foolishness will not
   depart from him.

23 Be diligent to know the state
   of your flocks,
   And attend to your herds;
24 For riches *are* not forever,
   Nor does a crown *endure* to all
   generations.
25 *When* the hay is removed,
   and the tender grass shows
   itself,
   And the herbs of the
   mountains are gathered in,
26 The lambs *will provide* your
   clothing,
   And the goats the price of a
   field;
27 *You shall have* enough goats'
   milk for your food,
   For the food of your
   household,
   And the nourishment of your
   maidservants.

28 The wicked flee when no
   one pursues,
   But the righteous are bold as a
   lion.

2 Because of the transgression of
   a land, many *are* its princes;
   But by a man of understanding
   and knowledge
   Right will be prolonged.

3 A poor man who oppresses the
   poor

463   *See Ephesians 4:26, page 238*

Is like a driving rain which
   leaves no food.

4 Those who forsake the law
   praise the wicked,
But such as keep the law
   contend with them.

5 Evil men do not understand
   justice,
But those who seek the Lord
   understand all.

6 Better *is* the poor who walks
   in his integrity
Than one perverse *in his* ways,
   though he *be* rich.

7 Whoever keeps the law
   is a discerning son,
But a companion of gluttons
   shames his father.

8 One who increases his
   possessions by usury and
   extortion
Gathers it for him who will
   pity the poor.

9 One who turns away his ear
   from hearing the law,
Even his prayer *shall be* an
   abomination.

10 Whoever causes the upright to
   go astray in an evil way,
He himself will fall into his
   own pit;
But the blameless will inherit
   good *things*.

11 The rich man *is* wise in his
   own eyes,
But the poor who has
   understanding searches him
   out.

12 When the righteous rejoice,
   there is great glory;
But when the wicked arise,
   men hide themselves.

13 He who covers his sins will not
   prosper,

But whoever confesses and
   forsakes *them* will have
   mercy.

14 Happy *is* the man
   who is always reverent,
But he who hardens his heart
   will fall into calamity.

15 *Like* a roaring lion and a
   charging bear
Is a wicked ruler over poor
   people.

16 A ruler who lacks understanding *is* a great oppressor,
But he who hates covetousness
   will prolong *his* days.

17 A man burdened with
   bloodshed will flee into a pit;
Let no one help him.

18 Whoever walks blamelessly
   will be saved,
But *he who is* perverse *in his*
   ways will fall at once.

19 He who tills his land
   will have plenty of bread,
But he who follows frivolity
   will have poverty enough!

20 A faithful man
   will abound with blessings,
But he who hastens to be rich
   will not go unpunished.

21 To show partiality *is* not good,
Because for a piece of bread a
   man will transgress.

22 A man with an evil eye hastens
   after riches,
And does not consider that
   poverty will come upon him.

23 He who rebukes a man will
   find more favor afterward
Than he who flatters with the
   tongue.

24 Whoever robs his father or his
  mother,
  And says, "*It is* no
  transgression,"
  The same *is* companion to a
  destroyer.

25 He who is of a proud heart
  stirs up strife,
  But he who trusts in the LORD
  will be prospered.

26 He who trusts in his own heart
  is a fool,
  But whoever walks wisely
  will be delivered.

27 He who gives to the poor will
  not lack,
  But he who hides his eyes will
  have many curses.

28 When the wicked arise,
  men hide themselves;
  But when they perish,
  the righteous increase.

29 He who is often reproved,
  and hardens *his* neck,
  Will suddenly be destroyed,
  and that without remedy.

2 When the righteous are in
  authority, the people rejoice;
  But when a wicked *man* rules,
  the people groan.

3 Whoever loves wisdom makes
  his father rejoice,
  But a companion of harlots
  wastes *his* wealth.

4 The king establishes the land
  by justice,
  But he who receives bribes
  overthrows it.

5 A man who flatters his
  neighbor
  Spreads a net for his feet.

6 By transgression an evil man is
  snared,

But the righteous sings and
  rejoices.

7 The righteous considers the
  cause of the poor,
  But the wicked does not
  understand *such* knowledge.

8 Scoffers ensnare a city,
  But wise *men* turn away wrath.

9 *If* a wise man contends with a
  foolish man,
  Whether the fool rages or
  laughs, *there is* no peace.

10 The bloodthirsty hate the
  blameless,
  But the just seek his well-
  being.

11 A fool vents all his feelings,
  But a wise *man* holds them
  back.

12 If a ruler pays attention to lies,
  All his servants *become*
  wicked.

13 The poor *man* and the
  oppressor have this in
  common:
  The LORD gives light to the
  eyes of both.

14 The king who judges the poor
  with truth,
  His throne will be established
  forever.

15 The rod and reproof give
  wisdom,
  But a child left *to himself*
  brings shame to his mother.

16 When the wicked are
  multiplied, transgression
  increases;
  But the righteous will see their
  fall.

17 Correct your son,
  and he will give you rest;

465

Yes, he will give delight to
your soul.

18 Where *there is* no revelation,
the people cast off restraint;
But happy *is* he who keeps the
law.

19 A servant will not be corrected
by mere words;
For though he understands,
he will not respond.

20 Do you see a man hasty in his
words?
There is more hope for a fool
than for him.

21 He who pampers his servant
from childhood
Will have him as a son in the
end.

22 An angry man stirs up strife,
And a furious man abounds in
transgression.

23 A man's pride will bring him
low,
But the humble in spirit will
retain honor.

24 Whoever is a partner with a
thief hates his own life;
He swears to tell the truth,
but reveals nothing.

25 The fear of man brings a snare,
But whoever trusts in the LORD
shall be safe.

26 Many seek the ruler's favor,
But justice for man *comes*
from the LORD.

27 An unjust man *is* an
abomination to the righteous,
And *he who is* upright in the
way *is* an abomination to the
wicked.

30 The words of Agur the son of
Jakeh, *his* utterance. This

man declared to Ithiel—to Ithiel
and Ucal:

2 Surely I *am* more stupid than
any man,
And do not have the
understanding of a man.
3 I neither learned wisdom
Nor have knowledge of the
Holy One.
4 Who has ascended into heaven,
or descended?
Who has gathered the wind in
His fists?
Who has bound the waters in a
garment?
Who has established all the
ends of the earth?
What *is* His name,
and what *is* His Son's name,
If you know?

5 Every word of God *is* pure;
He *is* a shield to those who put
their trust in Him.
6 Do not add to His words,
Lest He reprove you,
and you be found a liar.

7 Two *things* I request of You
(Deprive me not before I die):
8 Remove falsehood and lies far
from me;
Give me neither poverty nor
riches—
Feed me with the food You
prescribe for me;
9 Lest I be full and deny *You*,
And say, "Who *is* the LORD?"
Or lest I be poor and steal,
And profane the name of my
God.

10 Do not malign a servant to his
master,
Lest he curse you,
and you be found guilty.

11 *There is* a generation
that curses its father,
And does not bless its mother.
12 *There is* a generation
that is pure in its own eyes,

Yet is not washed from its
   filthiness.
13 *There is* a generation—
   oh, how lofty are their eyes!
   And their eyelids are lifted up.
14 *There is* a generation whose
   teeth *are like* swords,
   And whose fangs *are like*
   knives,
   To devour the poor from off
   the earth,
   And the needy from *among*
   men.

15 The leech has two daughters,
   Crying, "Give! Give!"

   There are three *things that* are
   never satisfied,
   Four *things* never say, "*It is*
   enough":
16 The grave,
   The barren womb,
   The earth *that* is not satisfied
   with water,
   And the fire *that* never says,
   "*It is* enough."

17 The eye *that* mocks *his* father,
   And scorns obedience to *his*
   mother,
   The ravens of the valley will
   pick it out,
   And the young eagles will eat
   it.

18 There are three *things which*
   are too wonderful for me,
   Yes, four *which* I do not
   understand:
19 The way of an eagle in the air,
   The way of a serpent on a
   rock,
   The way of a ship in the midst
   of the sea,
   And the way of a man with a
   virgin.

20 This *is* the way of an
   adulterous woman:
   She eats and wipes her mouth,
   And says, "I have done no
   wickedness."

21 For three *things* the earth is
   perturbed,
   Yes, for it cannot bear up:
22 For a servant when he reigns,
   A fool when he is filled with
   food,
23 A hateful *woman* when she is
   married,
   And a maidservant who
   succeeds her mistress.

24 There are four *things which*
   are little on the earth,
   But they *are* exceedingly wise:
25 The ants *are* a people not
   strong,
   Yet they prepare their food in
   the summer;
26 The rock badgers are a feeble
   folk,
   Yet they make their homes in
   the crags;
27 The locusts have no king,
   Yet they all advance in ranks;
28 The spider skillfully grasps
   with its hands,
   And it is in kings' palaces.

29 There are three *things which*
   are majestic in pace,
   Yes, four *which* are stately in
   walk:
30 A lion, *which is* mighty among
   beasts
   And does not turn away from
   any;
31 A greyhound,
   A male goat also,
   And a king *whose* troops *are*
   with him.

32 If you have been foolish in
   exalting yourself,
   Or if you have devised evil,
   put your hand on *your*
   mouth.
33 For *as* the churning of milk
   produces butter,
   And *as* wringing the nose
   produces blood,
   So the forcing of wrath
   produces strife.

31 The words of King Lemuel, the utterance which his mother taught him:

2 What, my son?
And what, son of my womb?
And what, son of my vows?

3 Do not give your strength to women,
Nor your ways to that which destroys kings.

4 *It is* not for kings, O Lemuel,
It is not for kings to drink wine,
Nor for princes intoxicating drink;

5 Lest they drink and forget the law,
And pervert the justice of all the afflicted.

6 Give strong drink to him who is perishing,
And wine to those who are bitter of heart.

7 Let him drink and forget his poverty,
And remember his misery no more.

8 Open your mouth for the speechless,
In the cause of all *who are* appointed to die.

9 Open your mouth, judge righteously,
And plead the cause of the poor and needy.

10 Who can find a virtuous woman?
For her worth *is* far above rubies.

11 The heart of her husband safely trusts her;
So he will have no lack of gain.

12 She does him good and not evil All the days of her life.

13 She seeks wool and flax,
And willingly works with her hands.

14 She is like the merchant ships,
She brings her food from afar.

15 She also rises while it is yet night,

And provides food for her household,
And a portion for her maidservants.

16 She considers a field and buys it;
From her profits she plants a vineyard.

17 She girds herself with strength,
And strengthens her arms.

18 She perceives that her merchandise *is* good,
And her lamp does not go out by night.

19 She stretches out her hands to the distaff,
And her hand holds the spindle.

20 She extends her hand to the poor,
Yes, she reaches out her hands to the needy.

21 She is not afraid of snow for her household,
For all her household *is* clothed with scarlet.

22 She makes tapestry for herself;
Her clothing *is* fine linen and purple.

23 Her husband is known in the gates,
When he sits among the elders of the land.

24 She makes linen garments and sells *them*,
And supplies sashes for the merchants.

25 Strength and honor *are* her clothing;
She shall rejoice in time to come.

26 She opens her mouth with wisdom,
And on her tongue *is* the law of kindness.

27 She watches over the ways of her household,
And does not eat the bread of idleness.

28 Her children rise up and call her blessed;

Her husband *also*, and he
   praises her:
29 "Many daughters have done
   well,
   But you excel them all."
30 Charm *is* deceitful and beauty
   is vain,

But a woman *who* fears the
   Lord, she shall be praised.
31 Give her of the fruit of her
   hands,
   And let her own works praise
   her in the gates.

Are You Ready to Receive
God's Offer of Eternal Life and Hope?

If so, please pray the following prayer. Remember, it is not the words that you use, but the attitude of your heart that is important. If you pray this prayer sincerely, Jesus will come into your life, and in Him you will have eternal life and hope.

"Dear God, I know that Jesus is Your Son and that He died on the cross and was raised from the dead. Because I have sinned and need forgiveness, I ask Jesus to come into my heart. I am willing to change the direction of my life by acknowledging Jesus as my Lord and Savior, and by turning away from my sins. Thank you for giving me forgiveness, eternal life, and hope. In Jesus' name, amen."

You Are Assured of Eternal Life and Hope Because:
• You can trust God's promise.

"Whoever calls upon the name of the Lord will be saved" (Rom. 10:13).

Did you sincerely ask Jesus into your heart as Lord and Savior? Where is He right now? What does God's Word promise?

• You are a member of God's family.

"The Spirit Himself bears witness with our spirit that we are children of God" (Rom. 8:16).

• Your life is eternally secure in God.

"For I am persuaded that neither death nor life, nor angels nor principalities nor powers, nor things present nor things to come, nor height nor depth, nor any other created thing, shall be able to separate us from the love of God which is in Christ Jesus our Lord" (Rom. 8:38,39).

What Happens After You Receive Hope from God?
• You will begin to live for God (Romans 12:1–2, 9–18).
• You will publicly profess your faith by being baptized (Matthew 28:19–20; Luke 3:21; Romans 6:4).
• You will share with others what Jesus has done for you (Romans 10:14).
• You will get to know God better through prayer, Bible study, and fellowship with other Christians as a member of a local church (Romans 15:4–6).